D0572410

FileMaker Pro 11

THE MISSING MANUAL

*The book that
should have been
in the box®*

FileMaker Pro 11

Susan Prosser and Stuart Gripman

POGUE PRESS™
O'REILLY®

Beijing · Cambridge · Farnham · Köln · Sebastopol · Taipei · Tokyo

FileMaker Pro 11: The Missing Manual

by Susan Prosser and Stuart Gripman

Copyright © 2010 Susan Prosser and Stuart Gripman. All rights reserved.

Printed in the United States of America.

Published by O'Reilly Media, Inc., 1005 Gravenstein Highway North, Sebastopol, CA 95472.

O'Reilly Media books may be purchased for educational, business, or sales promotional use. Online editions are also available for most titles: *safari.oreilly.com*. For more information, contact our corporate/institutional sales department: 800-998-9938 or *corporate@oreilly.com*.

Printing History:

June 2010:   First Edition.

Nutshell Handbook, the Nutshell Handbook logo, the O'Reilly logo, and "The book that should have been in the box" are registered trademarks of O'Reilly Media, Inc. *FileMaker Pro 11: The Missing Manual*, The Missing Manual logo, Pogue Press, and the Pogue Press logo are trademarks of O'Reilly Media, Inc.

Many of the designations used by manufacturers and sellers to distinguish their products are claimed as trademarks. Where those designations appear in this book, and O'Reilly Media, Inc. was aware of a trademark claim, the designations have been printed in caps or initial caps.

While every precaution has been taken in the preparation of this book, the publisher and authors assume no responsibility for errors or omissions, or for damages resulting from the use of the information contained herein.

ISBN: 978-1-449-38259-9

[M]

Table of Contents

Part Three: Thinking Like a Developer

Part Five: Integration and Security

The Missing Credits

About the Authors

Susan Prosser (coauthor) saw FileMaker for the first time as a reporter, where the database ran the paper's classified ads. That first glimpse tempted her to a new career helping people organize and manage their data. Susan's first professional database is still used at the US Fish & Wildlife Service nearly twenty years on. Since then, Susan formed DBHQ (*www.dbhq.net*), which has used FileMaker to help a semiconductor company manage legal documents, a financial advisor analyze retirement programs, an NGO track providers of autism services to school districts, a dart manufacturer track inventory/sales and a major bank track projections. One of the first FileMaker Certified Developers, Susan has presented at FileMaker DevCon and develops FileMaker training curricula. Susan tends her organic garden, quilts, bakes sourdough bread, and tries to log 110+ miles per week on her bike. Susan and husband Paul share their home with one semi-feral cat, one Vespa, and eight bicycles. Send suggestions for achieving a balanced lifestyle or new names for graph organization schemes to *susanprosser@gmail.com*. Follow prosserDBHQ on twitter.

Stuart Gripman (coauthor) is a native of Akron, Ohio, who grew up in suburban Orange County before migrating to San Francisco to get out of the sun. After a two-year stint at FileMaker Inc. (née Claris Corporation), he became Webmaster at StarNine Technologies. In 2000, Stuart founded Crooked Arm Consulting to provide custom FileMaker databases for a wide variety of clientele. Crooked Arm's databases have since benefitted the U.S. space program, fine art patrons, system administrators, digital projection cinemas, vintners, oenophiles, data recovery practitioners, architects, commercial artists, and a Grammy-winning ensemble. Stuart enjoys spending time with his wife and son hiking, camping, cycling, playing Legos, and baking snickerdoodles. Email: *stuart@crookedarm.com*. Blog: *http://whosthebarber.blogspot.com*.

About the Creative Team

Nan Barber (editor) is associate editor for the Missing Manual series. She lives in Massachusetts with her husband and iMac. Email: *nanbarber@gmail.com*.

Adam Zaremba (production editor) recently received his M.A. from the Editorial Institute at Boston University. He lives in Chestnut Hill, Mass., and would gladly pay you Tuesday for a hamburger today.

Alison O'Byrne (copy editor) is a full-time freelance editor with over eight years experience specializing in corporate and government projects for international clients. She lives with her family in Dublin, Ireland. Email: *alison@alhaus.com*. Web: *www.alhaus.com*.

Christian Smith (technical reviewer) is a FileMaker 7/8/9/10 Certified Developer and a member of FileMaker Business Alliance, FileMaker Technical Network, and FMPug. Web: *www.m3web.com*.

Angela Howard (indexer) has been indexing for over 10 years, mostly for computer books, but occasionally for books on other topics such as travel, alternative medicine, and leopard geckos. She lives in California with her husband, daughter, and two cats.

Acknowledgments

As usual, everyone at O'Reilly has been wonderful—special thanks to Angela Howard, Karen Shaner, and Alison O'Byrne. If there is any sanity in this book, it's due to Nan Barber, who excels at checking reality when things get tough. Tech reviewers often do thankless work under incredible deadlines. I can't change the deadline part, but want to thank Christian Smith. Your thoughtful comments helped us make the book better. Stuart, our collaboration was everything I hoped it would be. We must agree to partake in adult beverages at DevCon and speak about the glamorous lives of famous authors. Do we know any? Jamie, Joe, Krys, Erich, Chanelle and Paul: Without my weekly meetings with you amazing, creative people I would be a puddle of dripping goo by now. Paul: You put up with much, my good man. Thank you, dear. Marlowe: I miss you every day, darling parrot.

—Susan Prosser

I wish to express most sincere thanks to my coauthor Susan Prosser. I appreciate your leap of faith in inviting me into this project, your guidance and patience as I learned the process and most of all, the good humor that sustained me through the challenges along the way. Many thanks also to editor Nan Barber for giving me the latitude to write with my own voice and diplomatically applying her wisdom when that voice needed some modulation. My thanks also to our technical reviewer Christian Smith, and all the kind, hard-working folks at O'Reilly—Alison O'Byrne, Angela Howard, and Karen Shaner in particular. Thank you David Pogue, not only for the Missing Manual series, but also for being so nice to me the last time we spoke (in 1997 when you called for FileMaker tech support and I was the agent who assisted you). I'm also deeply grateful to my parents Floyd and Sally, my sisters, and my entire extended family for your support and enthusiasm. And most of all my beloved wife, Jen, and our boy, Benjamin. Thank you for your sustaining support, love, and patience. Benny, I love the robot you made for me. Thanks, Buddy.

—Stuart Gripman

The Missing Manual Series

Missing Manuals are witty, superbly written guides to computer products that don't come with printed manuals (which is just about all of them). Each book features a handcrafted index; cross-references to specific pages (not just chapters); and Rep-Kover, a detached-spine binding that lets the book lie perfectly flat without the assistance of weights or cinder blocks.

Recent and upcoming titles include:

Access 2007: The Missing Manual by Matthew MacDonald

Access 2010: The Missing Manual by Matthew MacDonald

Buying a Home: The Missing Manual by Nancy Conner

CSS: The Missing Manual, Second Edition, by David Sawyer McFarland

Creating a Web Site: The Missing Manual, Second Edition, by Matthew MacDonald

David Pogue's Digital Photography: The Missing Manual by David Pogue

Dreamweaver CS4: The Missing Manual by David Sawyer McFarland

Dreamweaver CS5: The Missing Manual by David Sawyer McFarland

Excel 2007: The Missing Manual by Matthew MacDonald

Excel 2010: The Missing Manual by Matthew MacDonald

Facebook: The Missing Manual, Second Edition by E.A. Vander Veer

FileMaker Pro 10: The Missing Manual by Susan Prosser and Geoff Coffey

Flash CS4: The Missing Manual by Chris Grover with E.A. Vander Veer

Flash CS5: The Missing Manual by Chris Grover

Google Apps: The Missing Manual by Nancy Conner

The Internet: The Missing Manual by David Pogue and J.D. Biersdorfer *iMovie '08 & iDVD: The Missing Manual* by David Pogue

iMovie '09 & iDVD: The Missing Manual by David Pogue and Aaron Miller

iPad: The Missing Manual by J.D. Biersdorfer and David Pogue

iPhone: The Missing Manual, Second Edition by David Pogue

iPhone App Development: The Missing Manual by Craig Hockenberry

iPhoto '08: The Missing Manual by David Pogue

iPhoto '09: The Missing Manual by David Pogue and J.D. Biersdorfer

iPod: The Missing Manual, Eigth Edition by J.D. Biersdorfer and David Pogue

JavaScript: The Missing Manual by David Sawyer McFarland

Living Green: The Missing Manual by Nancy Conner

Mac OS X: The Missing Manual, Leopard Edition by David Pogue

Mac OS X Snow Leopard: The Missing Manual by David Pogue

Microsoft Project 2007: The Missing Manual by Bonnie Biafore

Microsoft Project 2010: The Missing Manual by Bonnie Biafore

Netbooks: The Missing Manual by J.D. Biersdorfer

Office 2007: The Missing Manual by Chris Grover, Matthew MacDonald, and E.A. Vander Veer

Office 2010: The Missing Manual by Nancy Connor, Chris Grover, and Matthew MacDonald

Office 2008 for Macintosh: The Missing Manual by Jim Elferdink

Palm Pre: The Missing Manual by Ed Baig

PCs: The Missing Manual by Andy Rathbone

Personal Investing: The Missing Manual by Bonnie Biafore

Photoshop CS4: The Missing Manual by Lesa Snider

Photoshop CS5: The Missing Manual by Lesa Snider

Photoshop Elements 7: The Missing Manual by Barbara Brundage

Photoshop Elements 8 for Mac: The Missing Manual by Barbara Brundage

Photoshop Elements 8 for Windows: The Missing Manual by Barbara Brundage

PowerPoint 2007: The Missing Manual by E.A. Vander Veer

Premiere Elements 8: The Missing Manual by Chris Grover

QuickBase: The Missing Manual by Nancy Conner

QuickBooks 2010: The Missing Manual by Bonnie Biafore

QuickBooks 2011: The Missing Manual by Bonnie Biafore

Quicken 2009: The Missing Manual by Bonnie Biafore

Switching to the Mac: The Missing Manual, Leopard Edition by David Pogue

Switching to the Mac: The Missing Manual, Snow Leopard Edition by David Pogue

Wikipedia: The Missing Manual by John Broughton

Windows XP Home Edition: The Missing Manual, Second Edition by David Pogue

Windows XP Pro: The Missing Manual, Second Edition by David Pogue, Craig Zacker, and Linda Zacker

Windows Vista: The Missing Manual by David Pogue

Windows 7: The Missing Manual by David Pogue

Word 2007: The Missing Manual by Chris Grover

Your Body: The Missing Manual by Matthew MacDonald

Your Brain: The Missing Manual by Matthew MacDonald

Your Money: The Missing Manual by J.D. Roth

Introduction

For many people, the word "database" conjures up the idea of a vast collection of information that requires a computer and a technical degree to access. But databases are all around you—a phone book, a cookbook, and an encyclopedia are each databases. So is the stock page in your newspaper. In fact, if you look up the word "database" in a dictionary (which is a database, too), you'll probably read that a database is just a collection of information, or data.

Ideally, the information in a database is organized so you can find what you're looking for quickly and easily. For example, a Rolodex has information about people organized alphabetically by name. You can find any person's card because you know approximately where it is, even though there may be *thousands* of cards to look through. But physical databases have major limitations compared to those stored on a computer. What if you want to get a list of all your associates in California? A Rolodex isn't organized by state, so you have to flip through every card one by one to get a list. The first database programs were created to help you avoid that kind of tedium. And FileMaker Pro is an easy-to-use, but powerful, database program.

The term *database program* means a computer program designed to help you build a database so you can store information you need. A database stored on a computer isn't much different in theory from one collected on Rolodex cards or other forms of paper. It contains lots of information, like addresses, Zip codes, and phone numbers, and organizes that info in useful ways (see Figure I-1 for an example). But since it's stored on a computer, you can organize the *same* information in numerous ways with ease—say, by name *or* by state. Computers make searching databases a whole lot faster. That list of associates in California you took hours to generate from a Rolodex? A computer can do it in less than a second.

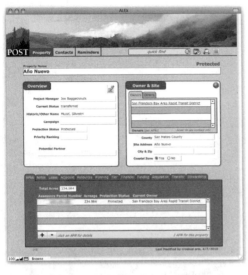

Figure I-1:
FileMaker Pro lets you do just about anything with the information you give it. You can use it like a Rolodex to simply store and retrieve information, or run your entire business with this one program. FileMaker's built-in number crunching and word processing tools let you track people, processes, and things, creating all your reports, correspondence, and collateral documents along the way. Here are two examples of real-world FileMaker databases created for very different kinds of businesses.

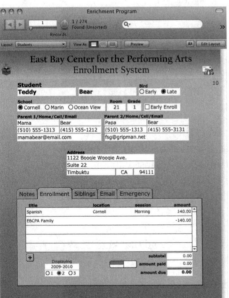

This book will teach you how FileMaker Pro stores your information, and how you can rearrange that information to get the answers to meaningful questions, like which employees are due for performance reviews, who's coming to the company picnic, and which amusement park has the best deal on Laser Tag so you can throw a party for your top 50 performers. You won't have to learn to think like a programmer (or know the arcane terms they use), but you will learn how to bend FileMaker Pro's hidden power to your will, and make it tell you everything it knows about your company, your stock portfolio, or how much you've spent on the replacement parts for the '58 Bonneville Sport Coupe you're rebuilding.

Why FileMaker Pro?

If you're reading this book, you've already decided to use a computer database instead of the mulched-up tree variety. *Choosing* a database program from the many options on the market is overwhelming. Some are enormously powerful but take years to learn how to use. Others let you easily get started, but don't offer much help when you're ready to incorporate some more advanced features. Here are a few reasons why FileMaker Pro is a great choice for most folks:

- FileMaker Pro is the ease-of-use champion. While other programs use jargon words like *query, join*, and *alias*, FileMaker Pro uses simple concepts like *find, sort*, and *connect*. FileMaker Pro is designed from the ground up for nontechnical people who have a *real* job to do. It's designed to let you get in, build your database, and get back to work.

- FileMaker Pro can do almost anything. Some other database programs are simple to use, but they're just plain simple, too—they can't do the kinds of things most businesses need to do. FileMaker Pro, despite its focus on ease of use, is very powerful. It can handle large amounts of data. It lets lots of people on different computers share data (even at different locations around the world). It even meets the needs of bigger companies, like integrating with high-end systems. And it's adaptable enough to solve most problems. If your home-based crafting business is taking off, and you need to figure out how much it costs you to create your top-selling items, FileMaker can do that. But if you're a large school district tracking dozens of test scores for more than 50,000 students in grades K-12, and you have to make sure those scores are tied to federal standards, then FileMaker can handle that, too.

- FileMaker Pro works on Macs or PCs. If you use both types of computers, FileMaker Pro makes the connection seamless. You can use the exact same databases on any computer, and even share them over the network simultaneously without a hitch (Chapter 17).

- FileMaker Pro is fun! It may sound corny, but it's exciting (and a little addictive) to have such a powerful tool at your fingertips. If you get the bug, you'll find yourself solving all kinds of problems you never knew you had. You might not think that getting married is an occasion for breaking out a new database, but you'll be amazed at how helpful it is. You can make a mailing list for your invitations, track RSVPs, note which favorite aunt sent you a whole set of bone china (and which cousin cheaped out by signing his name on his brother's gift card), and you can even record what date you mailed the thank-you notes.

- Everybody uses it. Perhaps best of all, FileMaker Pro is very popular—more people buy FileMaker Pro than any other database program. And the program's fans love it so much they're actually willing to help you if *you* get stuck. You can find user groups, Websites, discussion boards, chat rooms, mailing lists, and professional consultants all devoted to FileMaker Pro. This is one case where there's good reason to follow the crowd.

What's New in FileMaker Pro 11

FileMaker Pro 11 is a single software package that serves two fundamentally different types of people: users and designers. Users are the folks who need a database to help them organize and manage the data they work with in order to do their jobs. Developers create the databases that users use. No matter which category you're in (and lots of people fall into both categories, sometimes popping back and forth dozens of times a day), you'll find that FileMaker doesn't play favorites. The features you need for both roles are equally accessible.

FileMaker Pro 11 includes many features that make day-to-day work in FileMaker easier than ever:

- FileMaker Pro 11 gives you one more reason not to fire up Excel—**charts**! Bar charts, line charts, pie charts and more are built right in and easy to create.

- Speaking of spreadsheets, the **updated table view** adds spreadsheet-style conveniences. Adding a new column no longer requires a trip to the database manager window and a visit to layout mode. You can do it all without leaving the familiar data entry view.

- FileMaker has taken (and improved upon) an old developer technique called **Quick Find**. With no programming necessary, you can place a Quick Find box in your toolbar, and then use it to search every field on the current layout in one shot.

- Long a stalwart of word processors, **text highlighting** offers a way to emphasize text beyond bold and italic.

- **Instant Web Publishing** now has an improved status toolbar so your online databases look and work more like FileMaker Pro. Using a database via a web browser just got simpler.

- If you regularly import information from the same source, say an Excel spreadsheet, the **Recurring Import** feature can simplify the process. Once you point FileMaker to the data source, it sets up a special script and layout. To update your database with the most current information, simply switch to that layout.

Hello Bento

What's this Bento program I keep hearing about? Should I be using it along with FileMaker Pro? Or maybe instead?

Well, if you use Windows, you don't even have the option of using Bento, so quit worrying. It's Mac OS X only. But if you're a Mac fan, read on.

You can think of Bento as FileMaker Pro's much, much younger sister. FileMaker's been around since 1985. And even before that, it had a previous life under the name Nutshell in DOS (an ancient operating system that didn't even have pictures). So FileMaker has a lot of mileage under its belt and is a mature, stable player in the professional database world.

FileMaker, Inc. introduced Bento in January 2008. It's an inexpensive ($49) program whose goal is to get you up and running in minutes without any previous database experience. Its greatest asset is how effortlessly you can create databases with information you already have in your Mac OS X programs like iCal, Address Book, and Apple Mail.

As with FileMaker, though, you can customize Bento for special applications like cataloging your home inventory, your Mom's antique saltshaker collection, or even what you discussed with your clients on their weekly appointments. The name Bento refers to a Japanese lunchbox, with tidy little compartments to hold various kinds of food. And in fact, using Bento is as easy as dragging and dropping to arrange and fill onscreen compartments.

But if your needs change, or your business grows (say you hire another person who has to share your database), you might need to step up to FileMaker, which permits multiple users and has a powerful scripting engine to automate processes and create brand new features. In that case, you might have to play with the big kids and move your Bento data into FileMaker. So if you already have FileMaker, you don't need to rush out and buy Bento. But you may have occasion to import data from Bento into FileMaker—see page 843 to learn how.

Database developers will appreciate these new features that help create databases (or improve those you already have):

- Developers spend a whole lot of time in Layout mode and until now there was no single place where all the most commonly used tools were grouped. Rejoice click-weary developers, now you have the **Inspector**. A three-tabbed floating palette, the Inspector consolidates all the position, appearance, and data formatting options of Layout mode.

- **Portal Filtering** vastly simplifies the work required to build dynamic changing lists of related data. It also reduces the number of single use table occurrences and relationships necessary to display your information.

- **Snapshot Links** are tiny files that record the layout, found set of records, and sort order of your database at the time you create the snapshot link. Now, rather than asking someone to open a particular database, switch to a particular layout, find a given set of records and sort them by fields A, B, and C, you can just email a snapshot link and say "double click this."

- If your layouts have prodigiously proliferated, use **Layout Folders** to tame them. Much like the script folders introduced in FileMaker Pro 10, Layout Folders give you a way to organize layouts into logical groupings instead of one very long list.

- **External File Protection** is a new way to prevent unauthorized access between FileMaker files. It works like a "white list" permitting connections only from preapproved files.

- **New and Revised Script Triggers.**

  — *OnObjectValidate* triggers just before field validation to give you the ability to intercept invalid data and deal with it as you wish.

  — *OnLayoutExit* runs when a user attempts to leave a layout, or close the window while viewing that layout. The script runs before leaving the layout.

  — *OnViewChange* activates when changing between Form, List, or Table views and executes after arriving at the new view.

- Similar to Merge Fields, new **Merge Variables** lets you display the value of a global variable dynamically, as layout text. "Live" text on a layout no longer needs to be in a field.

- A huge limitation of scripted finds has been lifted with the arrival of **Scripted Find Variables**. Previously, the search terms of a scripted find request had to be static. FileMaker now permits the use of variables, simplifying dynamic scripted finds.

- **Layout Badges**, those little icons that appear on layout objects, have a few additions:

- Objects with **Conditional Formatting** get a new diamond shaped badge.

  — **Quick Find** fields (page 35) will either a green or yellow magnifying glass badge depending on the estimated speed that a find can be performed. Local, indexed fields get the green badge while related and unindexed fields get the yellow version.

  — All **badges now come in two sizes** that FileMaker Pro automatically sets based on the size of the object they're attached to.

If you use FileMaker Pro Advanced for its developers' tools (and if you aren't using it, you should), your professional life just got a whole lot easier. Here's a partial list of its new features:

- Moving custom functions from one file to another used to be a multistep, error prone process. Now you can **copy and paste custom functions** or import them from another file.

- The **Custom Menu** interface has been extensively revamped with simplified controls and clearer language.

- The absolutely invaluable **Script Debugger** has some new powers. It can now debug buttons and menu items even if they don't trigger scripts. If you assign object names to your buttons, those names appear in the Script Debuggers call stack.

If you share databases over the network, then you'll be glad to know about FileMaker Server's new features. Here are the highlights:

- **Administrator Groups** let FileMaker Server Advanced administrators define groups of related databases and delegate limited administration duties to others. These "junior administrators" can perform administrative tasks in their group and only in their group.

- Reinstalling FileMaker Server or migrating a server to new hardware typically means recreating your backup schedules. FileMaker Server Advanced is now able to **backup your schedules and administrator groups,** and then reload them after a fresh install of the server software.

- The **Client Statistics** view assists in troubleshooting connection problems. It offers a real-time view of a particular FileMaker Server client's vital connection statistics.

- Server administration relies on an Admin Server process that can fail even when the database server process continues to operate. FileMaker Server now monitors and repeatedly attempts to **automatically restart the Admin Server** if it fails.

- Under the hood, FileMaker Server's unified **ODBC/JDBC** (Open- and Java- Database Connectivity) module has been extensively revised to improve performance and compatibility.

UP TO SPEED

What About the Big Guys?

The word *database* is a little abused in the computer world. Both FileMaker Pro and MySQL—an open-source database that you can use free, if you have the skills, manpower, hardware, and know-how—are considered database programs, but they're about as similar as chocolate cake and dry flour. In reality, two kinds of database programs are available. One kind is very powerful (as in run-the-federal-government powerful) and very complicated. This type of database program just holds data, and computer programmers use sophisticated, and expensive, tools to structure and put a user interface on that data.

The other kind of database program—sometimes called a *desktop database*—is less powerful and a lot easier, but it actually has more features. In addition to holding lots of data, these programs provide an interface to access, organize, and search the data. This interface includes the menus, graphics, and text that let you work with the data, much like any other computer program. In other words, you don't need a computer science degree to create a powerful database with a desktop program like FileMaker Pro.

And with FileMaker Pro 11's powerful ESS connection feature, you can have the best of both worlds. You (or even better, an IT person who's a database nerd) can create and administer an SQL database, and then use FileMaker to create a snazzy display for the SQL data. Your nerd colleague would say you're using FileMaker as a "front end" to the SQL database. You can just call it common sense.

The Very Basics

You'll find very little jargon or nerd terminology in this book. You will, however, encounter a few terms and concepts that you'll see frequently in your computer life. They include:

- **Clicking.** This book offers three kinds of instructions that require you to use the mouse or trackpad attached to your computer. To *click* means to point the arrow cursor at something onscreen, and then—without moving the cursor at all—press and release the clicker button on the mouse (or laptop trackpad). Right-clicking works the same as clicking, but you use the right mouse button instead. (If you use a Mac and don't have a right mouse button, press the Control key as you click.) To *double-click*, of course, means to click twice in rapid succession, again without moving the cursor at all. And to *drag* means to move the cursor while keeping the clicker button continuously pressed.

  When you're told to *Ctrl-click* something, you click while pressing the Ctrl key (the *Control* key on the Mac) on the bottom row of your keyboard. Related procedures like *Shift-clicking* and *Alt-clicking* work the same way—just click while pressing the corresponding key.

Tip: On the Mac, the key that does most of the Alt key functions is the Option key. Macs also have an extra key called the Command key, which has a cloverleaf (⌘) on it. When the Mac keystroke is different from the one in Windows, this book gives it in parentheses.

- **Menus** are the lists of commands you pull down from the words at the top of the FileMaker window. (On the Mac, they're always in the bar across the top of the screen.) You have two equally valid ways to choose from these pull-down menus with your mouse: Click once to open the menu, and then click again to choose a command; or click and *hold* the button as you drag down the menu, and then release when you get to the desired command. Use whichever method you find easier.

- **Keyboard shortcuts.** Every time you take your hand off the keyboard to move the mouse, you lose time and potentially disrupt your creative flow. That's why many experienced computer jockeys use keystroke combinations instead of menu commands wherever possible. Ctrl+P (⌘-P) opens the Print dialog box, for example.

- When you see a shortcut like Ctrl+Q (⌘-Q), which closes the current program, it's telling you to hold down the Ctrl (⌘) key, and, while it's down, type the letter Q, and then release both keys.

If you've mastered this much information, you have all the technical background you need to enjoy *FileMaker Pro 11: The Missing Manual*.

About This Book

FileMaker Pro comes with a PDF manual and an impressive online help system. These resources are actually pretty helpful—if you're a programmer, that is, or if you've been working with FileMaker for a while. Between the manual and the help system, you can figure out how FileMaker works. But you have to jump back and forth between page and screen to get the complete picture. And neither source does a great job of letting you know which features apply to the problem you're trying to solve.

This book is designed to serve as the FileMaker Pro manual, the book that should have been in the box. It explores each feature in depth, offers shortcuts and work-arounds, and explains the ramifications of options that the manual doesn't even mention. Plus, it lets you know which features are really useful and which ones you should worry about only in very limited circumstances. Try putting sticky tabs in your help file or marking the good parts with a highlighter!

FileMaker comes in several flavors, and this book addresses them all. FileMaker Pro, the base program, takes up most of the book's focus. FileMaker Pro Advanced is an enhanced version of the program. Like the name promises, it contains advanced tools and utilities aimed at making development and maintenance of your databases easier. Its features are covered in Chapter 12. FileMaker Server lets you share your databases more safely and quickly than FileMaker Pro's peer-to-peer sharing. Learn about FileMaker Server in Chapter 17.

About the Outline

FileMaker Pro 11: The Missing Manual is divided into six parts:

- **Part 1: Getting Started with FileMaker.** Here, you'll learn about FileMaker Pro's interface and how you perform basic tasks, like entering data and then sorting through it again. You'll also find out how FileMaker Pro stores your data inside fields, and then organizes those fields into units called *records*. You'll see how to *define* fields, and make them do some of the data entry work for you. Just as your actual data is organized into fields and records, the appearance of your database is organized into layouts. FileMaker Pro provides a whole raft of tools that make creating layouts fast and powerful. You'll find out how to use layouts to make data entry easier, and how to create layouts that list and summarize your data.

- **Part 2: Building Your First Database.** It's time to put theory into practice and build a new database from scratch. You'll learn the ingredients that go into a functional database, and then spice it up with calculations that do some thinking for you and scripts that do some grunt work for you. You'll take your flat database and make it *relational*, putting a very powerful spin on data organization.

- **Part 3: Thinking Like a Developer.** You've kicked the tires and driven around town with FileMaker. Now, do you want to see what this baby can really do? You'll learn some theory behind relational database design and how to create a variety of relationship types. The world of fields will open up with *auto-enter data* and *validation* to keep your information consistent and accurate. You'll dig into the vast capabilities offered in Layouts—like using colors and images for an attractive look, making clickable *buttons* and building *reports*. And you'll get a handle on the remarkable power of *calculations* and *scripts*.

- **Part 4: Becoming a Power Developer.** Now you're a living, breathing database machine. It's time to trade up to FileMaker Pro Advanced, the FileMaker version expressly for power developers. You'll learn how to reuse database components, step through a running script with the Script Debugger, and even bend FileMaker's menus to your will. You'll literally tunnel deeply into relationships, make layouts pop with conditional formatting and charts, and even put a real live web browser *inside* your database. You'll learn enough about calculations to derive the answer to life, the universe, everything!

- **Part 5: Security and Integration.** FileMaker knows your data's important enough to keep it safe from prying eyes. In this section, you'll learn how to protect your database with passwords, and how to use privileges to determine what folks can do once they get into your database. This part also teaches you how to move data into and out of your database, and how to share that data with other people, and even with other databases.

- **Part 6: Appendixes.** No book can include all the information you'll need for the rest of your FileMaker Pro career. Well, it could, but you wouldn't be able to lift it. Eventually, you'll need to seek extra troubleshooting help or consult the program's online documentation. So, at the end of the book, Appendix A explains how to find your way around FileMaker's built-in help files and website. It also covers the vast online community of fans and experts: People are the best resource for fresh ideas and creative solutions. Appendix B lists FileMaker error codes.

Living Examples

Each chapter contains *living examples*—step by step tutorials that help you learn how to build a database by actually doing it. If you take the time to work through these examples at the computer, you'll discover that these tutorials give you invaluable insight into the way professional developers create databases. To help you along, online database files provide sample data, and completed examples against which to check your work.

You can get these files any time from the Missing CD page (see "About Missing-Manuals.com" on page 12). To download, simply click this book's title, and then click the link for the relevant chapter.

Macintosh and Windows

FileMaker Pro works almost precisely the same in its Macintosh and Windows versions. Every button in every dialog box is exactly the same; the software response to every command is identical. In this book, the illustrations get even-handed treatment, rotating between Windows Vista and Mac OS X by chapter.

One of the biggest differences between the Mac and Windows versions is the keystrokes, because the Ctrl key in Windows is the equivalent of the Macintosh ⌘ key.

Whenever this book refers to a key combination, you'll see the Windows keystroke listed first (with + symbols, as is customary in Windows documentation); the Macintosh keystroke follows in parentheses (with - symbols, in time-honored Mac fashion). In other words, you may read, "The keyboard shortcut for saving a file is Ctrl+S (⌘-S)."

About→These→Arrows

Throughout this book, and throughout the Missing Manual series, you'll find sentences like this one: "Open your Home→Library→Preferences folder." That's shorthand for a much longer instruction that directs you to open three nested folders in sequence, like this: "In the Finder, choose Go→Home. In your Home folder, you'll find a folder called Library. Open that. Inside the Library window is a folder called Preferences. Double-click to open it, too."

Similarly, this kind of arrow shorthand helps to simplify the business of choosing commands in menus, as shown in Figure I-2.

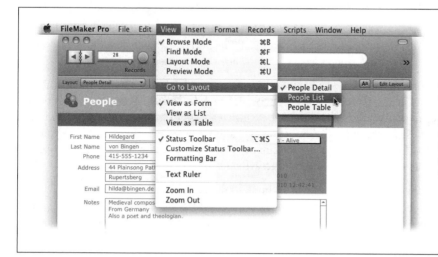

Figure I-2:
When you read in a Missing Manual, "Choose View→Go to Layout→People List," that means: "Click the View menu to open it, in that menu, click Go to Layout, and then, in the resulting submenu, choose People List."

About MissingManuals.com

At *www.missingmanuals.com*, you'll find articles, tips, and updates to *FileMaker Pro 11: The Missing Manual*. In fact, we invite and encourage you to submit such corrections and updates yourself. In an effort to keep the book as up to date and accurate as possible, each time we print more copies of this book, we'll make any confirmed corrections you've suggested. We'll also note such changes on the website, so that you can mark important corrections into your own copy of the book, if you like. (Go to *www.missingmanuals.com/feedback*, choose the book's name from the pop-up menu, and then click Go to see the changes.)

Also on our Feedback page, you can get expert answers to questions that come to you while reading this book, write a book review, and find groups for folks who share your interest in FileMaker Pro.

While you're there, sign up for our free monthly email newsletter. Click the "Sign Up for Our Newsletter" link in the left-hand column. You'll find out what's happening in Missing Manual land, meet the authors and editors, see bonus video and book excerpts, and so on.

We'd love to hear your suggestions for new books in the Missing Manual line. There's a place for that on missingmanuals.com, too. And while you're online, you can also register this book at *www.oreilly.com* (you can jump directly to the registration page by going here: *http://tinyurl.com/yo82k3*). Registering means we can send you updates about this book, and you'll be eligible for special offers like discounts on future editions of *FileMaker Pro 11: The Missing Manual*.

Safari® Books Online

 Safari® Books Online is an on-demand digital library that lets you easily search over 7,500 technology and creative reference books and videos to find the answers you need quickly.

With a subscription, you can read any page and watch any video from our library online. Read books on your cellphone and mobile devices. Access new titles before they're available for print, and get exclusive access to manuscripts in development and post feedback for the authors. Copy and paste code samples, organize your favorites, download chapters, bookmark key sections, create notes, print out pages, and benefit from tons of other timesaving features.

O'Reilly Media has uploaded this book to the Safari Books Online service. To have full digital access to this book and others on similar topics from O'Reilly and other publishers, sign up for free at *http://my.safaribooksonline.com*.

Part One: Getting Started with FileMaker

I

Working with a Database

FileMaker Pro databases can be as simple as a list of your antique saltshaker collection or as complex as a company-wide system for purchasing, sales, inventory, invoicing, shipping, and customer tracking. But all of them essentially *work* the same way. This chapter gives you a tour of FileMaker's major features and gets you up and running on your very first database.

FileMaker's vast assortment of tools and options can make the program's window as intimidating as a jumbo-jet cockpit. But the program's menu commands, dialog boxes, keyboard shortcuts, and other options stay largely consistent across all databases, so everything you learn in the next few pages applies to almost every database you'll ever use.

Tip: Because a database usually solves a *problem* of some kind, some FileMaker experts call a database a *solution*, as in, "I can create an inventory solution for your bakery, but it's going to cost you some dough." Usually, *database* and *solution* mean the same thing, although the term *solution* sometimes implies a system of several connected databases (more on that in Part 3).

A Very Quick Database Tour

Every FileMaker Pro database has two major working parts. First, the data you're storing. And second, the tools that help you view and manage your data. Since data can change radically from file to file, you'll start this tour focusing on the elements you find in nearly every FileMaker database—the tools. And since the first database you create won't have any data in it yet, the tools take center stage at first.

Those tools—buttons, controls, and pop-up menus—help you fill your database with data. And once you have data in the file, your tools help you find the specific data you need.

Every database window has the same basic structure—the *content area* in the middle is where the data goes, and as you can see in Figure 1-1, a handful of special items at the top and bottom of the window.

Note: You can download a sample database from this book's Missing CD page at *www.missingmanuals. com/cds*.

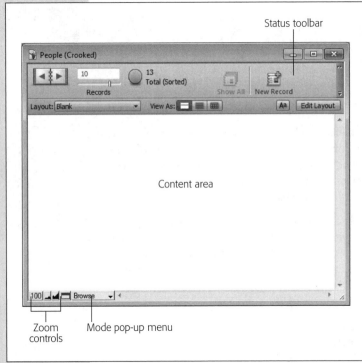

Status toolbar

Content area

Zoom
controls

Mode pop-up menu

Figure 1-1:
Every database window has the same apparatus around the edges— what's inside the window is up to you. Compare this window with the one shown in Figure 1-2. Both windows have a Status toolbar, zoom controls, and a Mode pop-up menu. The content area is the only difference.

Content Area

The content area is where you put the information (data) that makes your database work for you.

When you create a new FileMaker database, the standard view looks a little like Figure 1-2: It's plain, with just a few boxes for storing data. That's because you haven't added any content yet, and you haven't started arranging your data in a way that mirrors your needs. In Figure 1-3, you can see that data's been entered, and the fields are arranged so that they look more like information you'd expect to see outside your database. For example, address fields look like addresses on envelopes. (In Chapter 4, you'll learn more about changing the way your data looks.)

Figure 1-2:
Unlike the stark emptiness shown in Figure 1-1, this database has fields for entering information, and some fields even have something in them before you start to type (see page 240 for more information on auto-enter fields). These fields are arranged in a column, just the way FileMaker throws them on the screen when you first create them. Compare this screen to Figure 1-3 where the fields are resized and rearranged to create a more pleasing interface to showcase your data.

Scroll Bars

Just as with most windows on your computer, you can resize FileMaker's windows. And if you make your window too small to display all the data in the content area, scroll bars appear so you can see the stuff outside the current window size.

FileMaker's scroll bars work just like the ones in any other program—drag them to see any areas of the screen that aren't visible. Press Page Up on your keyboard to scroll up one screenful, and Page Down to scroll the other direction.

If your mouse has a scroll wheel, then notice that it scrolls differently based on where you put your mouse cursor. That's FileMaker's *contextual* scrolling. The wheel scrolls through the window when the cursor is inside the window's content area. It scrolls through the records in your database if you run the cursor over the book icon in the Status toolbar (see page 30). And if you put your cursor over a field that has a scroll bar (see page 27), then the scroll wheel scrolls through the text in the field.

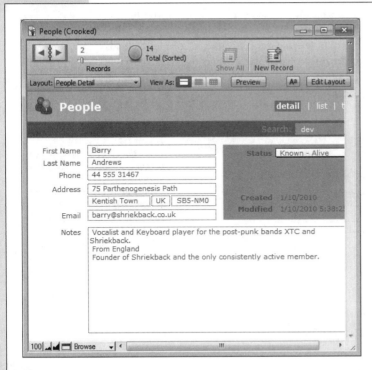

Figure 1-3:
The zoom level in this window is set to 100 percent, but you still can't see everything in the window, as evidenced by the scroll bar along the bottom edge. You've got three options for viewing more information. You can reduce the zoom level so everything fits in the window, or make the window larger (if you have the monitor real estate), or you can drag the scroll bar to scan across the screen.

Zoom Controls

One of FileMaker's neatest features is the *zoom control*. No matter what you're doing, you can always zoom in for a closer look or zoom out for the big picture. This feature works no matter what mode you're in—even when you're previewing a printout.

To use FileMaker's zoom control, click the Zoom In button for a closer look (each click zooms in a little more). You can zoom in up to 400 percent, so that everything is four times bigger than normal. If you click Zoom Out, everything shrinks, to as small as one quarter of its normal size. The Zoom Level shows your current level, and clicking it takes you back to 100 percent. Clicking the Zoom Level a second time returns you to the *last zoom* level you were viewing.

Note: Since you probably don't need to examine the words and numbers in your database on a microscopic level, you'll probably use the zoom control mostly in Preview mode to fit the whole page on the screen, or to adjust the contents of your FileMaker window to the most easily readable size (depending on the resolution of your monitor). You might notice, though, that some fonts don't enlarge well, so they're actually most legible at 100 percent.

Understanding Modes

Each of FileMaker's four *modes* is a work environment unto itself, specially designed to help you view, edit, organize, or present your information in a specific way. Switch modes depending on what you need to do.

- Browse mode is the one you see when you first open a database, since it's the one you use most often. In this mode, you can add, change, and view data in your database. Browse mode is the view shown in Figure 1-3, and it's where you'll spend most of this chapter.

- When you have a lot of data, looking through it all for a particular bit of information can be tedious. Use Find mode to let FileMaker do the looking for you. You tell FileMaker what you're looking for in Find mode; when it's done looking, FileMaker returns you to Browse mode, and shows what it found. For more details on finding specific records, see page 32.

- In addition to using databases (viewing, finding, sorting, adding, and changing data), you can use FileMaker to *build* databases. Layout mode is where you design the screens (called *layouts* in FileMaker parlance) that present your database information to best advantage. Part 2 is all about Layout mode.

- Although computers make maintaining and manipulating mountains of information a breeze, you still can't avoid paper. Eventually you'll want to print something out, like a set of mailing labels or a paper backup of all your records. If you're ever curious about how something will look when printed, then switch to Preview mode. It shows a one-page-at-a-time view of your data exactly as it'll appear when printed.

The Mode pop-up menu is the easiest way to change modes (Figure 1-1). To use the Mode pop-up menu, just click it, and then choose one of the four modes. Your FileMaker window instantly switches to the new mode. You can also glance at the Mode pop-up menu to see which mode you're currently in. (The Mode pop-up menu is the most popular way to mode-hop, but you have plenty more options; see the box on page 20.)

Status toolbar

Changing modes may be confusing when you're getting started, but the Status toolbar gives you constant feedback about the features available in your current mode. So as you switch modes, you see the tools in the Status toolbar changing, too. In fact, the Status toolbar changes so much, you'll soon find that you barely have to glance at the Mode pop-up menu any more, because you can see the tools you need for the job at hand. Figure 1-4 shows the Status toolbar in each of its four modes. When you're familiar with these tools, you can do all the major tasks necessary for any FileMaker database.

UP TO SPEED

Changing Modes

Switching between FileMaker's four modes is so common that you have many ways to do it. The Mode pop-up menu (see Figure 1-1) is just one way. The Status toolbar, along the top of your screen, typically has Find, Preview, and Edit Layout buttons (as shown in Figure 1-4). Or, from FileMaker's View menu, you can pick a mode.

The keyboard shortcuts are speediest of all:

- Press Ctrl+B (⌘-B) to switch to Browse mode.
- Press Ctrl+F (⌘-F) to switch to Find mode.
- Press Ctrl+L (⌘-L) to switch to Layout mode.
- Press Ctrl+U (⌘-U) to switch to Preview mode.

If you ever forget these shortcuts, check the View menu to refresh your memory.

Note: Don't be alarmed when the menus across the top of your screen change a bit when you switch modes. That's just FileMaker being smart. Some commands aren't useful in some modes, so the program doesn't clutter up your screen—or your brain space—with menus when you don't need them. For example, the Insert and Format menus change from black to gray (meaning *unavailable*) when you enter Find mode and the Records menu you saw in Browse mode has changed to Requests.

FileMaker also gives you a couple ways to find out which mode you're in. The Mode pop-up menu at the bottom of the window displays the current mode, and the View menu indicates the current mode with a checkmark.

Tip: Get in the habit of glancing at the Mode pop-up menu before you type. If you enter information in Find mode, thinking you're in Browse mode, FileMaker doesn't save that information, and you have to start over.

Opening and Closing Database Files

Each database you create with FileMaker Pro is stored in a *file* on your hard drive—just like your Microsoft Word documents, Excel spreadsheets, and all the Power-Point presentations you've ever created. This file contains all the information about how the database is structured, plus all the information stored inside it, which means you can open, close, copy, or back up a database as you would any other file. But if you need a bit more explanation, then this section explains how to do those tasks, and some quirks that are particular to FileMaker files.

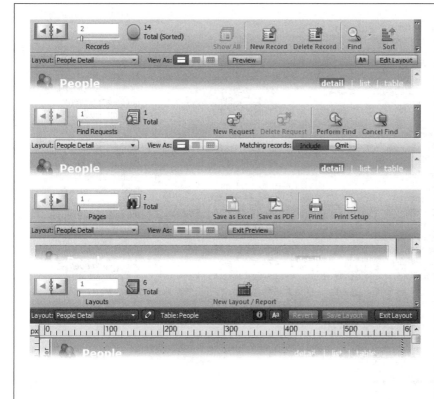

Figure 1-4:
*Use this illustration as
a cheat sheet for lo-
cating all FileMaker's
most commonly used
features. In Browse
mode (top), you
can click the "New
record" button, and
then start entering
data. Find mode
(second from top) lets
you look for records—
say all your clients
who live in Iowa—with
all the tools you need
to create brand new
Find requests or to
select a recent or a
Saved Find. And if
you inspect a report
before you print it
using Preview mode
(third from top),
then you get handy
tools for saving the
report as a PDF,
exporting the data to
Excel, and plain old
printing. When you're
in Browse mode the
Edit Layout button
lets you change the
appearance of your
database with access
to text, field, and
object formatting
features of Layout
mode (bottom).*

Opening a Database

To open a database, open FileMaker Pro, and then choose File→Open. FileMaker's
Open File dialog box appears. Select the file with which you want to work (see Fig-
ure 1-5), and then click Open. If you prefer, you can find the file using Windows
Explorer (Windows) or the Finder (Mac OS X), and then double-click its icon.

When you open a database, you see one or more windows on your screen. If you open the People database that you downloaded at the beginning of this chapter, then you see one database window.

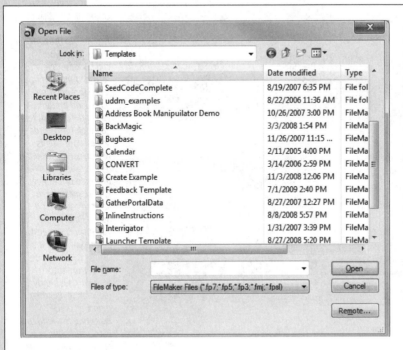

Figure 1-5:
FileMaker's Open File dialog box is pretty standard stuff, but notice the pop-up menu near the bottom left that helps you find specific kinds of files on your hard drive. If you choose "FileMaker Pro files" as shown here, then all non-FileMaker files in the window are grayed out, so you can easily ignore them as you're looking for the database you want to open.

Closing a Database

To close a database, choose File→Close or press Ctrl+W (⌘-W). This command actually closes a window, and if your database has only one window, you've closed the whole database. But you can open more than one window into a single database (see page 42), and if you do, then you need to close each window individually before the file is closed. When you have more than one database open, you can't always easily tell which windows go with each database.

If you're not sure what to close, you have an easy way to close all the windows in all the databases you currently have open. Press Alt (Windows) or Option (Mac), and then click the trusty File menu. In Windows, the menu command doesn't look any different, but as long as you're holding down Alt when selecting Close, all FileMaker windows will be closed. In Mac OS X, the Close command is gone, replaced by a more powerful Close All. Choose it, and FileMaker closes all its windows, which also saves and closes all your open databases.

Adding Data to Your Database

Now that you understand the basic components of a FileMaker database, it's time to start adding your own information. Whether your database contains information about individual persons, eBay auctions, products you sell, student grades, or whatever, FileMaker always thinks of that information in individual chunks called *records*. Each record contains everything the database knows about that person, auction, product, or student.

Since you need to store many smaller pieces of information in each record (like a person's phone number, address, birthday, and so on), FileMaker can give each record an almost infinite number of *fields*—the specific bits of data that define each record and make it unique.

For example, each person in a database of magazine subscribers gets her own record. First name, last name, phone number, street address, city, state, Zip code, and her subscription's expiration date are all examples of fields each record can include.

The techniques in this section work the same way whether you're creating a new database for the first time, or adding to an existing one.

Note: All records in a database have to have the same fields, but that doesn't mean you have to fill them all in. For instance, in your saltshaker collection database, you might not know the year a particular shaker was manufactured, so you can leave that field blank.

Creating a Record

Adding a new record is simple: Choose Records→New Record or press Ctrl+N (⌘-N). (Since you'll be creating lots of records in your FileMaker career, memorize this keyboard shortcut.)

Note: When you're adding new records, you have to be in Browse mode (see page 19). If you're in Find mode, you'll make new requests instead of records, and if you're in Layout mode, you'll create new layouts.

Entering Data

Once you create a new record, you can enter information about the person you want to keep track of—that's where those fields come in handy. To enter information in any field in a record, just click it, and then type. What to type? As Figure 1-6 shows, most fields in this database have a label at left indicating the type of information the field contains. Field borders have turned to dotted lines—a confirmation that you're doing data entry.

Figure 1-6:
Fields can look like just about anything, but in the People database, they're pretty simple. When you click in the content area, dotted borders indicate the fields you can edit. The field you're currently editing gets a solid border. With the miracle of conditional formatting (page 618), the fields in the People database are shaded yellow as you type in them, which helps keep you oriented when you're entering information in a screen full of fields.

Note: A label is just a bit of text that appears near a field. It's meant to help you figure out what kind of data belongs in the field. See the box below for more on recognizing fields and labels.

UP TO SPEED

The Many Faces of a Field

Fields always appear inside the content area, but other than that, they can have amazing variety. FileMaker Pro's content area is one place you can let your creative urges go wild. You can design your database to make fields look almost any way you want. A field can have a label to the right of—or below or above—where you enter text, or no label at all.

A field can be white, blue, green, or any other color. The same goes for the border around a field. In fact, if mystery is your thing, then you can make your field invisible—no label, no border, and no color. (But here's a tip: If you want

happy database users, then make sure they can tell where the fields are and what goes in them.) One thing you *can't* vary about a field is its shape. Fields are always right-angle parallelograms.

When you're editing a record, the fields *usually* appear with the dotted outline shown in Figure 1-6, but you can't count on this (you can turn this feature off, as described on page 284). So don't expect every field to look the same.

See Chapter 3 for more detail on customizing and beautifying the fields in your database.

Moving between fields

Efficient data entry is all about typing something in a field, and then moving right along to the next field. Lather, rinse, repeat. You can use the mouse to click the next field, but unless you're eager to burn that extra half a calorie, you may want to try a quicker, less exercise-intensive way, like the following:

- Press the Tab key to move to the next field. If you're not in any field, then the Tab key puts you in the first field.

- Press Shift-Tab to move to the previous field. This time, if you're not in any field, then FileMaker puts you in the *last* field.

Note: If you're wondering who decides which field is *next* or *previous*, dig this: *You* do. When you design a database, you get to set the *Tab order*. That's the order FileMaker follows when you press Tab or Shift-Tab to move among fields. See page 158 for details.

Editing a record

You're not stuck with the data you enter in a record if something changes. For example, when people move, you can change their address data. Just click in the field to be updated, select the data, and then start typing the new information. (If you try this on the sample People.fp7 file provided on the Missing CD page, then you'll notice that a field called Modified changes when you commit the record's changes. You'll learn what that field is used for later.)

Tip: To edit a record, you may need to find it first. See page 32 for details on the Find feature.

Reverting a record

After you edit a record, you may decide you've made a mistake and wish you could put things back the way they were before. That's no problem for the Revert Record command. Its purpose is simple: When you choose Records→Revert Record, File-Maker throws away any changes you made since you first entered the record. This trick comes in handy when you accidentally modify a field by bumping into the keyboard, or realize you accidentally entered Steve Jobs' address in Bill Gates' record. Just revert the record, and you can be confident that whatever you did has been forgotten.

The Revert Record command is available only when you're in a record (see the box on page 26) *and* you've made changes. If you don't have the record open, or you haven't made any changes since you last committed the record, then the Revert Record command is grayed out.

Note: One of the easiest ways to commit a record is to simply click some empty space (not in a field) in the content area. FileMaker dutifully saves the record for you. Once you've committed a record, you can no longer choose the Revert Record command. (How's that for commitment?) If you want a little more control, then you can tell FileMaker to ask you for confirmation before committing a record. You'll learn how to do that on page 284.

UP TO SPEED

Commitment, or On the Record

To get *out* of all fields—so you're not in any field at all—click a blank spot in the content area. Pressing Enter on your numeric keypad also has the same effect, though that behavior can be changed. This process is called *committing* the record. No, you're not sending the record away for a little quiet time; rather, you're telling FileMaker you're ready to commit to the changes you've made. (If you don't want to commit to the changes you've made, then you can choose Records→Revert Record to get out of all fields and discard those changes.)

When you first click a field, you've *opened* the record. Imagine an old-fashioned file cabinet, where you have to open someone's file before you can change something in it.

As long as you have a record open, you're *in* the record. You can be in only one record at any given moment, and that record is said to be *active*. Rounding out this technobabble, when you've committed the record, you're *on* the record but you're not *in* the record. Believe it or not, getting this terminology straight will make things easier later on.

Duplicating a record

While no two people are alike, it may not always seem that way from their contact information. For instance, if you want to include three people from the same city in your database, the data in the City field is the same for each person.

The Email and Phone fields won't be the same, but they may be close. It's time for a little organized laziness: Instead of making new blank records and retyping all that stuff, just choose Records→Duplicate Record (see Figure 1-7) or press Ctrl+D (⌘-D). FileMaker displays a new record containing all the same information as the record you chose to duplicate. (FileMaker copies everything from the first record into a new one for you.) Now you can edit just the information that needs to be changed.

Tip: Be sure you don't accidentally leave in the first person's email address or phone number, lest a message or phone call get misdirected later.

Figure 1-7:
If you go looking for your duplicated record later, you may be surprised where you find it. If your records aren't sorted when you duplicate a record, that new record is added at the end of your database, no matter where the original started out. So if you have seven unsorted records in your database and you duplicate record #3, then the duplicated record is #8. Notice the thin black line just to the left of the last record in this list. That's File-Maker's way of telling you which record is active..

Fields for Lots of Text

FileMaker fields can hold *a lot* of text. Technically, each field is limited to 2 GB of data *per record*, which is a fancy way of saying, "Way more than you'll ever need."

To see for yourself, in the People database, click in the Notes field. When you do, a scroll bar appears at the right side of the field. If you type lots of notes, then you can scroll through them. (When you design a database, you get to decide which fields have scroll bars, as discussed on page 289.)

You can enter text into a field in all the usual ways, like typing on your keyboard or pasting text you copied from another field or another program.

Note: Even if a field doesn't have scroll bars, you can still add lots of text. As you type, FileMaker just makes the field grow to hold whatever you type. When you leave the field, it shrinks back to its normal size, hiding anything that goes outside the edges. Don't worry, though, the text reappears when you click back into the field.

Deleting Records

Getting rid of a record you don't need is a breeze. FileMaker Pro gives you three commands that let you delete one record, a group of records, or even *all* the records in your database.

Warning: You can't undo deleting a record, because FileMaker saves changes automatically. So when you delete a record (or all the records in a database), make sure you're ready to part with the information. Consider saving a backup copy of your file first (see page 47).

- **One record.** Choose Records→Delete Record or press Ctrl+E (⌘-E) to delete the record you're currently on. FileMaker asks if you're sure you want to delete the record, lest you accidentally send, say, your best client's address to the trash bin. If you've indeed written her—or anyone else—out of your life, then, in the message box, simply click Delete to complete the purge.

- **Multiple records.** FileMaker has a helpful command that trashes any group of records of your choosing. Before you use this command, you have to tell File-Maker which records to delete. You do that with the Find command (page 32). Then once you have the set of records to be deleted, choose Records→Delete Found Records. Again, FileMaker gives you a chance to change your mind with a message box that tells you how many records you have in your found set, and asks you to click either the Delete All or the Cancel button.

- **All records.** In some cases, you may want to delete all the records in a database. Maybe a colleague wants an empty copy of your database for his own use. Or perhaps your database holds data you just don't need anymore, like test results you're about to reproduce. You can easily accomplish complete record elimination with two menu commands: Just choose Records→Show All Records, and then choose Records→Delete All Records. (Of course, if you just want an empty copy of your database, cloning is easier; see page 47.)

Note: In reality, the Delete Found Records and Delete All Records commands are one and the same. But FileMaker knows whether you're in a subset of your database or looking at all the records, and changes the wording of the menu command accordingly. It's just another bit of feedback that helps you get the results you need.

Once you get used to deleting records, you may get tired of FileMaker nagging you about being sure you want to delete. You can bypass the dialog box by holding down the Shift (Windows) or Option (Mac) key when you choose Records→Delete Record. Or, if you're a fan of keyboard shortcuts, you can type Ctrl+Shift+E (⌘-Option-E) to get the same results.

UP TO SPEED

Lost in the Wilderness

The sample file you're using in this chapter has an assortment of *buttons* in its content area (like the Details buttons in Figure 1-7). These buttons can look like tabs, text links, or just about anything else (a few even look like buttons). Clicking one of these may show you things you're not familiar with—maybe even make you feel like you've lost your place.

To avoid an accidental left turn when you try to commit the record, try not to click a button. Instead click somewhere in the empty white area around the fields.

If you've already clicked a button, and now you're lost in the wilderness, finding your way back doesn't require a trail of breadcrumbs.

Just follow these steps, in order:

- If you see a button in the Status Toolbar called Continue, click it. (If you don't see that button, don't worry—just skip to the next step.)
- If the Mode pop-up menu doesn't say Browse, click it, and then, from the menu that appears, choose Browse.
- In the Status toolbar, beside Layout, you should see a pop-up menu. Choose People Detail to get back to the main layout.

You should now be back in your comfort zone. Phew!

Understanding Browse Mode Error Messages

As you just learned in the section on deleting records, FileMaker gives you frequent feedback about what you're doing. The program's not being a control freak (although after the umpteenth dialog box it's understandable if you feel that way). FileMaker's just trying to keep you informed so you can make good choices. So you sometimes see dialog boxes that FileMaker calls *error messages*. Unlike the Delete warning, when you get an error message, all you can do is click OK. There's no real choice to make, but you usually have to take some kind of action after you've dismissed the error message.

Typing in vain

If you try typing something *before* you've clicked in a field, then FileMaker warns you with the box shown in Figure 1-8. You'll see this same missive in the event you try to type into a database with no records in the found set, or indeed no records at all. It may seem overly protective to warn you that you're not actually entering anything anywhere, but in this day of multitasking and distractions, it's helpful to know that FileMaker doesn't let your information disappear into space as you type it.

So, annoyingly, you have to dismiss an error message every time you accidentally bump a key, but you can't get rid of the error message for good. Just remember that you have to have at least one found record in your database (Choose File→New Record) and have your cursor *in* a field before you can start typing. (And take that book off your laptop's keyboard, eh?)

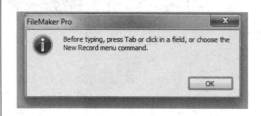

Figure 1-8:
In this communiqué, FileMaker asks you to tell it where to put all that data your 110 wpm typing power is delivering. Until you click in a field, your information has nowhere to go.

Navigating Your Database

Once you've entered a few dozen—or a few hundred—records into your database, the next challenge is to get back to a specific record. But first, you need to learn how to *navigate* through the records in the database. Hint: It's not called Browse mode for nothing, you know. The Status toolbar gives you several tools that help you get where you need to go.

Note: As you go through this section on navigating, it helps to have a database open in front of you so you can follow along and try some of these techniques. You can download a sample on this book's Missing CD page at *www.missingmanuals.com/cds*.

Navigating Record by Record

In the People database, you can add as many records as you want. To tell FileMaker which record you want to look at, you have three options:

- The book icon lets you flip from record to record one at a time. Pretend your database is a book, with each record on its own page. To get to the next record, click the right-hand page. To go back, click the left-hand page. If you can't go any further in one direction, then the appearance of the icon's "page" changes, as shown in Figure 1-9.

Figure 1-9:
In addition to displaying the controls for switching records, the Status toolbar indicates where you are in the database. You're looking at the 13th record in the found set of records. And the pie chart tool tells you that your current found set is showing 13 of the 14 total records in the database. If you click the pie chart, then the found set switches to show you the one record that isn't in the current found set.

- The slider is kind of a turbo-charged version of the book icon. Instead of clicking once for each record, you can advance through a bunch of records by dragging. If you know approximately where you want to go (like "around halfway" or "about one-third from the end"), then the slider is the quickest way to get there. The slider is most handy when you want to get to the beginning or the end of the database. In that case, just drag the slider as far as it goes in either direction.

- The Current Record indicator serves two purposes. First, it shows you which record you're on. Second, if you know which record you *want* to be on, then you can simply type the record number to jump to it. Beside the Current Record, the Found Set display also shows you how many records you have in your database.

Note: All navigation methods let you move within what FileMaker calls a *found set*, which lets you look at a specific set of records at one time. Learn more about finds and found sets on page 55.

UP TO SPEED

Numbers Sometimes Lie

As you create the records in your database, FileMaker numbers each new record as you add it—with a record number that appears next to the book icon (see Figure 1-9). You may think that this number is a great way to locate a particular record later: "I need to give Jim over at Dunder-Mifflin a call to reorder supplies. I put his contact information in record #79. I'll just go to that number." Alas, record numbers are ephemeral and change when you perform a find (page 32), add records, delete records, or sort them (page 38).

For instance, if you delete the first record in a database, every record below it moves up one slot. Now, what used to be record #2 becomes record #1, what used to be #3 is now #2, and so on. Jim could've transferred out of the Scranton branch before you find his record that way. If you want to assign every record its own number, and have that number stay with the record forever, then you want *serial numbers*. Serial numbers are discussed on page 137.

Keyboard Shortcuts

FileMaker also has a few keyboard shortcuts to make record navigation painless. If you haven't used a database program before, then you'll notice that some keys act in ways you may not expect—like the Enter key, as described below. Still, spending a little time getting used to using these keystrokes saves you hours of time down the road:

- To go to the next record, press Ctrl+Down arrow.

- To move to the previous record, press Ctrl+Up arrow.

- To activate the Current Record indicator without using the mouse, press Esc. Now type a record number, and then press Enter to go to that record. (This shortcut works only when you're not in the record; see the box on page 26.)

- Pressing Enter on your keyboard's numeric keypad automatically *commits* the record, rather than inserting a new line in a field, as you may expect based on what the Enter key does in other programs. To insert a new line in FileMaker, press Return.

Note: Some keyboards don't have a Return key—instead, two keys are labeled Enter. In this case, the Enter key that's near the number keypad commits the record, while the other (normal) Enter key enters a blank line in the field.

- Pressing Tab moves you from one field to another. (To indent a line, you have to *type* a tab character into a field, by pressing Ctrl+Tab [Option-Tab].)

Finally, bear in mind that you can change which key moves the cursor on a field-by-field basis as you'll learn in Chapter 7. For instance, FileMaker lets you decide if Enter—not Tab—should move you from field to field. If you make that choice, then Tab types a *tab* into a field, and Enter doesn't commit the record. Unfortunately, you can't tell which key does what by looking at a field; you just have to try some of these keys to find out.

Finding Records

When your database really gains some size, you realize that even keyboard shortcuts aren't the fastest way to get to the record you want. You need to *tell* FileMaker to pull up the record for you. For example, you have a season ticket holder whose last name is Andrews, who just renewed her subscription for a year. You need to find her record and make the update, and you don't have all day.

If you have hundreds of records in your People database, it could take ages to find the one you want by clicking the book icon. Instead, switch to Find mode, and then tell FileMaker what you're looking for, and the program finds it for you. This section explains how to use Find mode to search for a record or group of records, and how to edit your search if you don't get the results you anticipated. (If you downloaded the example file discussed on page 16, you can open it, and try out Find mode now.)

You can get to Find mode in four ways:

- From the Mode pop-up menu, select Find.
- Choose View→Find Mode.
- In the Status toolbar, click the Find tool.
- Press Ctrl+F (⌘-F).

The Mode pop-up menu, and View menu indicate which mode you're currently in. Once you're in Find mode, your window should look like Figure 1-10.

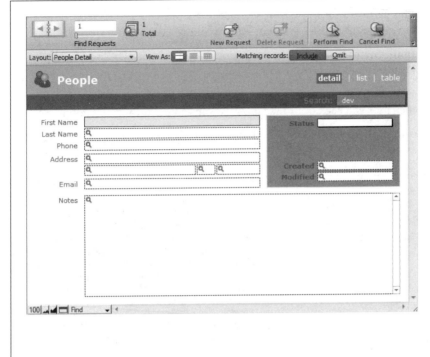

Figure 1-10:
Because Find mode
looks so much like
Browse mode, File-
Maker gives you lots
of feedback about the
mode change. Instead
of data, the fields
now show magnifying
glass icons to remind
you that you're typing
search criteria, not
new information. The
borders around the
fields have a dashed
line instead of Browse
mode's dotted line.
Notice that the Status
toolbar has changed.
Now you have a Per-
form Find button, and
even better, a Saved
Finds tool that lets
you store frequently
used find criteria.
That way, you don't
have to remember
and recreate compli-
cated finds. (See page
66 for details.)

Even though it may look like you're editing records in Find mode, you're actually not—you're editing *requests* instead. Requests are just descriptions of data you're looking for, so FileMaker can find them for you.

To make a request, enter enough information to tell FileMaker what you want. It then looks for records that have the same information you entered, much like searches you conduct using other programs, like a Google or Dogpile search.

Performing a Find

To find every person in your People database whose last name is Andrews, do the following:

1. **Choose View→Find Mode (or use any of the other methods described above to get to Find mode).**

   Magnifying glass icons show up in all the fields you can use for searching, indicating that you're in Find mode.

2. **In the Last Name field, type Andrews.**

   This part works just like Browse mode: Click the field, and then type. (Remember, you aren't editing a record—you're editing a *request*.)

3. **In the Status toolbar, click the Perform Find button. (Or choose Requests→ Perform Find, or press the Enter key.)**

   FileMaker finds all records that have "Andrews" in the Last Name field, and then puts you back in Browse mode so you can flip through the found set.

You can see how many records you found by looking at the count in the Status toolbar, as shown in Figure 1-11.

Figure 1-11:
After a find, the Status toolbar shows how many records match your request. Here, FileMaker found two records with the last name of Andrews. You can flip between these two records to your heart's content, but you can't see any records not in your found set. To see the other records, click the pie chart or choose Records→Show Omitted Only. FileMaker swaps your found set, and shows you the other records in your database. Then, when you're ready to look at all your records again, click the Show All button. If you can't see the Show All button, stretch your window. The Status toolbar drops some tools in smaller windows, but they reappear when the window's wide enough.

Tip: If your find didn't come out exactly the way you wanted, don't just return to Find mode. If you do, then you have an empty request, and you have to start all over again. Instead, choose Records→Modify Last Find, which takes you to Find mode, and then displays the request you used last. Now you can make any necessary modifications, and perform the find again.

FastMatch

In the previous find examples, you had FileMaker search for records by telling it what to look for. But sometimes you're already looking at a record that has the right information in it—you just want to find more records that match.

Say you need a list of everybody in the People file who composes. Flip to any record with the word "composer" in the Notes field. Drag to select the word "composer". Right-click (Control-click) the highlighted text.

From the shortcut menu that pops up, select Find Matching Records (see Figure 1-12). Shazaam! Faster than you can say "bass clef," FileMaker shows you a found set of all your composer contacts.

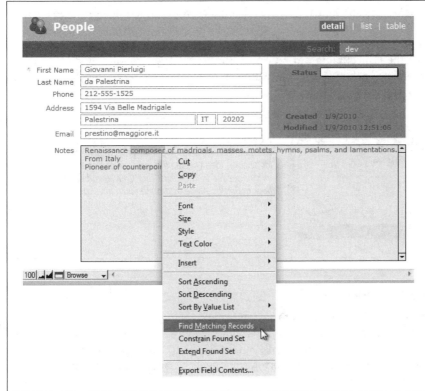

Figure 1-12:
FastMatch lets you select a piece of information from the record you're viewing (in this case, it's "composer" from the Notes field) and find all other records that match it without the rigmarole of switching to Find mode. Right-click the selection, and then, from the shortcut menu, choose Find Matching Records.

QuickFind

If FastMatch isn't flexible enough for you, try Quick Find. Quick Find is a text box residing in the toolbar that automatically searches every field on the layout you're currently browsing. If you don't see it on the right-hand side of your toolbar, you may need to make the window a bit wider. Using Quick Find couldn't be easier—click in the box, type a word or phrase, and then press Enter (Return). FileMaker displays a found set of records that contain your search term in any visible field. Click the magnifying glass in the Quick Find box for a list of recent finds. Choose one to perform that find again.

Understanding Find Mode Error Messages

Just as it does in Browse mode, FileMaker warns you if something goes wrong when you're trying to find specific records. There are three main types of errors. Read on to see why each one occurs, and what you need to do to correct the error.

No records match

If FileMaker can't find any records that match your request, then you see the message pictured in Figure 1-13. You might see this error if you're looking for a record that doesn't exist in your database, or maybe you've misspelled the search criteria. Click the Cancel button to return to Browse mode, or Modify Find to try again. You end up back in Find mode, with your original search terms showing so you can check your typing or enter new search terms.

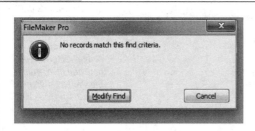

Figure 1-13:
If FileMaker can't find any records that match what you're looking for, then you see the message pictured here. If that's all you needed to know, just click Cancel, and you wind up back in Browse mode as though you'd never performed a find.

No valid criteria

If you don't type anything into any of the fields before you click Perform Find, then FileMaker doesn't try to find records with all empty fields. Instead, it warns you that you didn't enter any search terms. But it uses the terms you see in Figure 1-14. Just as with the No Records Match error, you can click Cancel to return to Browse mode, or you can click Modify Find to try again.

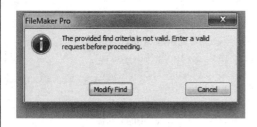

Figure 1-14:
You see this message if you don't enter search terms in at least one field before you click the Perform Find button. Sometimes, though, you might really want to find records that don't have data in them. In that case, you can enter "==" in a field. FileMaker finds blank fields, and now you can start entering the missing data in those records. Chapter 2 gives you lots more detail on special search symbols and other tricky finds.

Accidental data entry in Find mode

Even with the magnifying glasses (Figure 1-10), Find mode looks so much like Browse mode that you can easily forget which mode you're in. It's a real drag if you *think* you're in Browse mode, and you start entering data. You can make quite a bit of progress entering records and never realize your mistake. When you finally do figure it out, it's a rude awakening: None of the requests you've just entered can be turned into real records; you have to re-enter them all in Browse mode.

FileMaker gives you a warning if it thinks you're entering data in Find mode. See Figure 1-15 to see what you're in for. If you create more than 10 find requests while in Find mode, then FileMaker shows this message. If you've been entering data in Find mode by mistake (at least you're finding out now, not after you've typed for 3 hours), just click No, switch to Browse mode, and then start over with your data entry. If you know you're in Find mode, and you really want to add all these requests, then just click Yes. FileMaker doesn't bother you again.

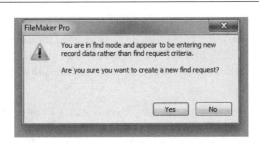

Figure 1-15:
If you create more than 10 requests in Find Mode, then FileMaker wonders if you're actually trying to enter data. If you're setting up a magnificently complex find, then you may be annoyed. Just click Yes and keep up the good work. But if you just forgot to switch back to Browse mode, then this warning can save you lots of lost keystrokes.

UP TO SPEED

Refining Your Finds

When FileMaker looks for records, it expects them to match your find request *exactly*. For example, if you put "Barry" in the First Name field, and "Andrews" in the Last Name field, FileMaker finds only Barry Andrews. Barry Manilow doesn't cut it, and neither does Julie Andrews. FileMaker ignores any fields that are empty in your request, so it doesn't matter what Barry's title is, because you didn't type anything into the Title field when setting up your find request.

Finding the right records can be a real balancing act. Be too specific and you may not find anything at all; be too vague and you find more than you can handle. When determining whether or not a given record matches your Find request, FileMaker may be more liberal than you'd expect. The next chapter explains how FileMaker decides when a match is good enough, and how you can change its decision-making process.

Here are some rules of thumb for creating find requests:

- Since FileMaker matches field values flexibly, you can often save typing and improve accuracy by being brief. For example, if you're looking for someone named "Rufus Xavier Sarsaparilla," just type *ruf* in the First Name field and *sar* in the Last Name field. Chances are you'll find the right guy, and you don't have to worry about spelling out the whole name.

- Enter data only in fields you're sure you need. For example, even if you know Rufus lives in Montana, you don't have to put Montana in the State field in your find request.

- If you find more records than you wanted, just go back to Find mode and enter more specific data in more fields to narrow the search. Better yet, read Chapter 2, where you'll learn about the many powers of Find mode.

Sorting Records

Your old paper Rolodex is limited to an alphabetical arrangement, but a FileMaker database has no such limitation. You can sort the records in any order you want, as often as you want. You can even do a sort within a sort, as you'll see later in this section.

Understanding Sorting

Don't confuse sorting with finding. When you sort, FileMaker doesn't change the records in your found set. Instead, it rearranges the records you're viewing into a new order. For example, if you need a short-term loan, you might sort your contacts by annual income. FileMaker still shows the same found set of contacts, but with Uncle Moneybags at the very top of the list.

The process always begins the same way: First, choose Records→Sort Records or click the Sort button in the Status toolbar. You see the Sort Records dialog box shown in Figure 1-16, with all available fields listed on the left. You tell FileMaker how to sort by moving a field to the list on the right.

Note: By "available," FileMaker means only the fields showing on the Current Layout. If the field you want to sort by isn't in the list, then, from the pop-up menu above the list, choose the second option. Instead of Current Layout, that option starts with Current Table. (Learn more about tables in Chapter 5.)

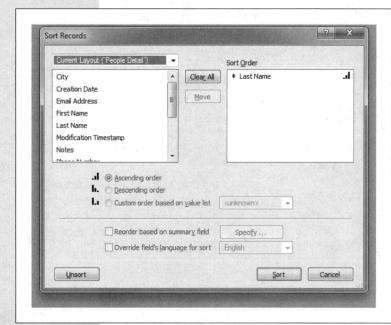

Figure 1-16:
The Sort Records dialog box has a lot of options, but the two lists on top and the first two radio buttons are critical to every sort you'll ever do in FileMaker. You pick the fields you want to sort by and the order in which they should be sorted, and then click Sort. That's the essence of any sort, from the simple to the most complex.

Here's how to sort your found set of records by Last Name:

1. **In the Status toolbar, click the Sort button. Or choose Records→Sort Records, or press Ctrl+S (⌘-S).**

   The Sort Records dialog box (Figure 1-16) appears.

2. **From the list on the left, select the Last Name field, and then click Move. (Or double-click the field name.)**

   The field name appears in the Sort Order list on the right.

3. **Click Sort.**

   FileMaker sorts the records in the traditional alphabetical-by-last-name order.

You can browse the sorted found set using any of your favorite navigation methods.

Beyond the Simple Sort

FileMaker figures that if you've sorted your data once, you'll probably want to sort it the same way again, so once you've done a sort, the dialog box retains the last sort order you set up. That's a nice shortcut if you want to repeat the last sort, but if you want something new, just click Clear All, and then start with a clean slate.

Each sort field has an *order* associated with it. The most frequently used are "Ascending order" (Alphabetical from A to Z) and "Descending order" (Alphabetical from Z to A). Once you've selected a field on the left, you can click one of these radio buttons *before* you click Move, and the field has the setting by the time it makes it to the Sort Order list. It's OK, though, if you move the field over before you think about the order. In this case, from the Sort Order list, just click to select the field, and then pick the order. Each field in the Sort Order list shows a bar chart icon representing the order assigned to it, which matches the icons next to each radio button.

If you change your mind and don't want to sort after all, click Cancel, and FileMaker forgets everything you've done while in this window.

The Status toolbar lets you know if your records are sorted (no surprise there). Below the Record Count, it says Sorted if you've done a sort, and Unsorted otherwise. (See the box on page 40 to learn more about sorting.)

Multiple Sort Fields

FileMaker lets you pick more than one field to sort by, which comes in handy when you have lots of records with the same data in some fields. For example, you might often have several people in your database with the same last name. If you just sort by last name, there's no telling in which order the like-named people fall. In this case, it would be ideal to sort by last name first and then, when the last names are the same, break the tie using the first name.

FREQUENTLY ASKED QUESTION

Feeling Out of Sorts?

When I haven't sorted my records, the Status toolbar says "Unsorted". What order is that, exactly? Is it completely random?

Remain calm. When the records are unsorted, they're in creation order. The first record you ever created (and haven't deleted yet) shows first, followed by the next one you created, and so on. Creation order is FileMaker's natural order for the records. Once you sort the records, they stay in that order until you sort again or explicitly unsort them. (In the Sort dialog box, use the Unsort button.)

Whew, that's a relief. But if I create a new record while I'm viewing a list that's sorted, I can't always tell where the new record will appear.

Yes, that can be disorienting. The record lands in a different place in the list depending on how your data is sorted. If it's sorted by Last Name only, and then you duplicate a record with "Andrews" in the Last Name field, the new record appears at the end of all the Andrews records. But if you have a multisort by Last Name and then by First Name, then the duplicate record appears right after the original. In other words, FileMaker creates the new record *within* the sort order you've chosen.

That's not all, though. If you edit the data in the first name or last name field, then FileMaker re-sorts the list as soon as you commit the record. The record you've just edited stays active, but you may have to scroll your list to see where its landed. Test this out by duplicating the John Dunstable record while the data is sorted by Last Name and then First Name. Then change "Dunstable" to "Runstable" and watch what happens.

To set this up, simply open the Sort dialog box using Records→Sort Records or Ctrl+S (⌘-S), and then add the First Name field to the Sort Order List after the Last Name field. The sort field order is important: The first field you want to sort by (called the *primary* sort field) has to be at the top of the list, followed by each subsort field in order. In this example, the Last Name field is the primary sort field, followed by First Name. You can see the results of this multiple sort in Figure 1-17. If your sort fields don't appear in the desired order in the Sort dialog box, fret not. FileMaker provides a convenient way to shuffle them around. Drag the double arrow immediately to the left of any field in the sort list to rearrange it as needed.

Note: If you change your mind about one of the fields in the Sort Order list, click it. The Move button changes to Clear, and a click removes the selected field from the list.

Multifield sorts can get as complicated as you like. Sometimes, they're a little tricky to get right, particularly if you're sorting by more than two or three fields (Figure 1-17 shows a report that uses multiple sorts).

If you do a Multifield sort, and then discover you didn't get quite what you expected (because you had the fields in the wrong order), just choose Records→Sort Records again, move the fields in the Sort Order list to the right places, and then click Sort

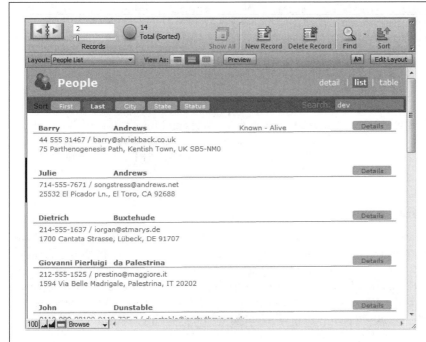

Figure 1-17:
The records in this window are sorted by Last Name and First Name. The last names are in alphabetical order, and when several people have the same last name, they appear together alphabetized by First Name. The Status toolbar shows you're viewing Sorted (as opposed to Unsorted) records. Once you've done a sort, the Sort dialog box remembers the sort order, so if you forget how the records are sorted, just press Ctrl+S (⌘-S) to check.

Note: Sorting records when you're creating a report can change the way FileMaker tallies data. See page 269 for info on creating layout parts that use sorted data to make sophisticated reports.

Same Database, Different Views

So far, you've spent all your time in one People window, where you can see either a single record or a list, but not both at the same time. With only one window, you can't compare two records or found sets side-by-side. This section will show you how to open and manage multiple windows.

Viewing a List

In the People file, you've probably noticed the "detail" text near the content area's upper right. Turns out, that's giving you feedback about the data you're currently viewing. If you click the word "list" (it's written in lowercase letters just because the database developers like it that way), then the scene switches to a list of all the records you're currently viewing. List views are particularly apt for examining the results of a Find or Sort.

Note: The word you're clicking is called a "button," which is just a tool that you can configure yourself. See page 317 to learn how you can create custom buttons for your database. You can also see the View menu for the menu commands that switch views of your data.

Viewing a Table

Since it's a database, FileMaker has lots of power that spreadsheets don't have. But lots of people prefer to see their data in columns and rows that look like a spreadsheet. That's what the "table" button does for you here. Click the button to view your found set in FileMaker's Table view, and then see page 51 for more information on how you can customize this view of your data.

Creating a New Window

At any time, you can get yourself another window by choosing Window→New Window. You get an exact copy of the window you were just looking at. It's the same size and shape, just offset a little down and to the right of the original. And it has the exact same set of records you were browsing, along with the same current record. What's the big deal, you ask? The big deal is that you can switch to another record or do something completely different in the new window, without affecting what's displayed in the first one.

When you have multiple windows open, you can change most of the settings you've seen so far for each window. For example, if you want to compare two contacts side by side, then you can show one contact in each window.

Note: If your original window is maximized, the new window lands right on top of it, not to the lower right.

Multiple windows are useful when you're working with one set of found records but suppose you need to do another search. You can perform a find in a new window without disrupting your work in the original window. Say you've been fiddling with the Find command to come up with a list of all your contacts who are composers, and then suddenly get the paperwork you need to edit the detail on another record. Although you can enter data on the list layout, all the fields you need may not be present on that layout. Just create a new window, switch to the detail layout, and then look up the record you want to edit (see Figure 1-18). Your composer group is safe and sound in the first window. (See the box on page 44 to see what problems can happen when you edit the same record in multiple windows.)

Note: If you have two windows open, both of them *are* connected in one way. If you edit the data in one window, the changes show up in the other window (and every window you have open, if you're working with three or more windows). Since FileMaker's windows display only the records in your database, a second window doesn't mean you have a second database—instead, both windows share the same data.

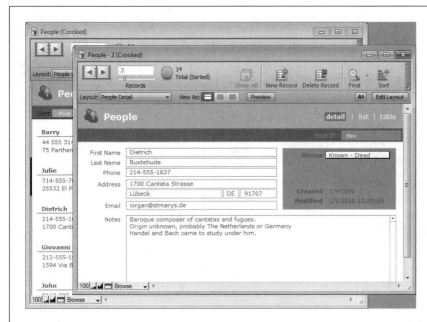

Figure 1-18:
The back window shows several records in the People database's List View layout. But the window in the front shows one record in Detail view. You can also tell that the front window was spawned from the back window because its name has a "–2" added to it. You can flip through records in the front window in their detailed glory and leave your list intact in the background.

Hiding Windows

If you have a window just the way you want it (for example, showing a list of customers Assistant Manager Dwight Schrute left behind when he went to work for Staples), but it's in your way onscreen, then you can *hide* it instead of closing it. When you *close* a window after using the Find command, your results disappear. Hiding a window makes it disappear from your screen, but FileMaker remembers everything about the window and can pop it back into view instantly. It's a great timesaver when your screen is crowded—or when you want to keep prying eyes away from your information.

To hide the current window (that's the one displayed at the front of your screen), choose Window→Hide Window. To bring it back again, choose Window→Show Window, and then, from the list, pick the window you want. In order for this to work, you have to remember the *name* of the window you hid (its name appears in the title bar, across the top of the window).

Record Locking

If you try editing a record in one window while it's showing in another window, then your changes don't appear in the second window as you type. In order for the changes to appear, you have to first commit the record (see the box on page 26). Once you do, the changes appear everywhere else.

Here's a hypothetical example. Suppose you start making changes to Jim Halpert's contact information in one window, but you're interrupted by a phone call before you finish. To help the caller, you need to look something up in the database. Since you're a savvy FileMaker guru, you make a new window, and look it up there so you don't have to lose track of the changes you're making to Jim. (He's getting all Dwight's former customers.)

Unfortunately, by the time you finish the phone call, you've forgotten that you already started editing Jim's record. Now you go to Jim's record *in the new window* to make the changes.

Bear in mind the record is already half-changed but uncommitted in the first window.

What happens if you start making changes now? Which set of changes wins?

To avoid the problem of which changes "win," FileMaker automatically performs *record locking* for you. If you try to edit a record that's already being edited in another window, you see an error message that reads, "This record cannot be modified in this window because it is already being modified in a different window." Yes, it's frustrating to get this message, but just remember that automatic record locking really is your protection against major problems. (This is especially true when you have multiple users accessing your database at the same time—see Chapter 17.) This message is your friend.

Warning: You may be in the habit of using your operating system's built-in features for dealing with windows, like minimizing them to the Mac OS X Dock. These techniques work just fine in FileMaker, but they can play havoc when a FileMaker *script* needs to control the same window. If you're using FileMaker Scripts to automate tasks, as you'll learn in Chapter 10, it's best to stick to FileMaker's own window commands.

Closing hidden windows

On page 22, you learned to close a database by closing all its windows. As with most rules, there's an exception: Even if you close all visible windows, the database itself may still be open—in a hidden window.

The easiest way to close all FileMaker's open windows, hidden ones included, is to press Alt (Option), and then choose File→Close (File→Close All on Mac OS X). The ordinary Close command closes every window, hidden or not, when you press this key.

Automatically Arranging Windows

If you have a lot of windows on your screen and don't feel like rearranging them yourself, you can use one of several commands that arrange the windows for you. Using FileMaker's Window menu, you can choose one of three commands: Tile Vertically, Tile Horizontally, or Cascade. Each command rearranges the windows in a different manner, as shown in Figure 1-19.

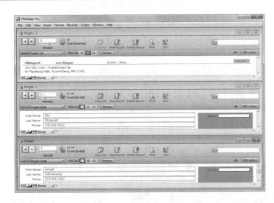

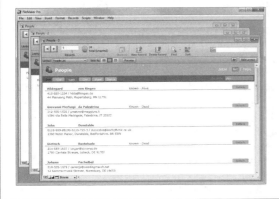

Figure 1-19:
FileMaker offers three automatic window arrangements: Tile Horizontally, Tile Vertically, and Cascade Windows. Choose Tile Horizontally or Tile Vertically to shrink every window enough that they all fit onscreen with no overlapping. If you choose Cascade, then FileMaker makes every window the same size, and puts each a little below and to the right of the one above. The window that was active when you chose Cascade lands in front.

The Window menu commands are a great place to start when you have so many windows open, you don't even know which one you're looking for! Auto-arranging is a blunt tool, however, and will move and resize your windows without any regard for a window's content. So use these commands with the understanding that you may *still* have to do some rearranging yourself.

Saving Your Database

Everybody knows it's important to save files early and often. So you're working along in FileMaker entering information about your office birthday roster, and as good habit dictates, you type the keyboard shortcut that saves in practically every program in the known universe (Ctrl+S on Windows and ⌘-S on the Mac). Up pops the wrong dialog box. This one's asking you how you want to sort your data! What gives?

Don't worry, FileMaker has you covered. The program automatically saves all your work in a *cache*, which is part of your computer's RAM (Random Access Memory). Then, periodically, FileMaker transfers the information from the cache to your hard drive, where it's less likely to be lost in case of a crash.

You can control how much work is held in cache before it's saved to your hard drive, as described in Figure 1-20. In Windows, choose Edit→Preferences, and then click the Memory tab. On the Mac, choose FileMaker Pro→Preferences, and then click the Memory tab.

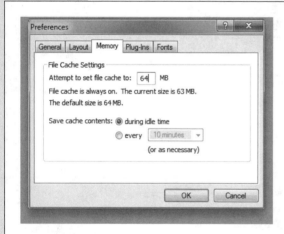

Figure 1-20:
Specify the size of FileMaker's cache and how often your work is moved from the cache to your hard drive. (Nerds call that flushing the cache.) A larger cache yields better performance but leaves more data in RAM. If you're working on a laptop, you can conserve battery power by saving cache contents less frequently. But infrequent cache saving comes with some risk: In case of a power outage or other catastrophe, the work that's in cache is lost for good.

Saving a Copy of Your Database

Chances are the data in your database is important. (Would you really go to all this trouble if it weren't?) Although FileMaker automatically saves your work as you go, what if the database file itself gets lost or suffers some digital harm? It's in your best interest to *back up* your database periodically. You can perform a backup by closing all your database's windows, and then simply copying the database file. For example, you can copy it to a CD, email it to a friend, or duplicate it and tuck the copy away in another folder. The easiest way to make a backup is to choose File→Save a Copy As. In the dialog box that appears, make sure that "copy of current file" is selected as the Type option. When you click Save, FileMaker makes your copy in the background, and you can continue working in the original file.

But if you want to start working in the copy you've just made, then select the "Automatically open file" option before you click OK. FileMaker makes the copy of your file, and then opens it for you. FileMaker *doesn't* close the original file for you, so if you're finished with the original, choose it from the Window menu, and then close it to avoid confusion. Now only your new copy of the file is open.

If you want to make a copy of your database to send to an associate in another office, choose the "Create email with file as attachment" option. FileMaker copies your file, and then launches your email program, creates a new email, and attaches your newly minted file copy to it. All you have to do is provide an email address, type your message, and then click Send. See page 800 to see how you can use similar options if you want to send data to your associate in another format, like Excel or a PDF file.

Warning: You should always make sure a database is *closed* before you copy its file using any of the desktop methods (like Edit→Copy in Windows Explorer or the Mac's Finder). If you copy a database file while it's open in FileMaker, both the original and the copy may be damaged, missing information, or in the most serious cases, rendered totally unusable!

Saving a Clone of Your Database

There's no ban on cloning in FileMaker. Clones are clean copies of your database, but without the data. Clones are really useful, like when you've designed a killer database for running sales in your Dart and Billiards Supply Shop, and you want to send the files to all your franchisees without giving away your store's sales data. Just make clones of your files, and then give them to your proud new owners. To make a clone, choose File→Save a Copy As, and then make sure "clone (no records)" is selected as the Type option.

Using FileMaker's Help Menu

As helpful as this introduction to databases has been, you may want to use FileMaker's onboard help to get more information (Figure 1-21). There you find commands for FileMaker's Help application and for online help at FileMaker's website. See Appendix A: Getting Help for more information on getting help from those sources, plus help from third parties.

The quickest way to get help, outside of sitting beside a willing guru, is to use the handy search field at the top of the Help menu. To get help, just start typing the subject you need help with. As you type each letter, the Help application changes its menu items to display topics it thinks you might need. When you see the item you need, select it from the menu, and Help appears, showing the page for the term or topic you chose.

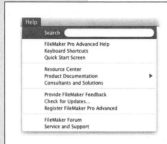

Figure 1-21:
Here's the Help menu on a Mac in its pristine state, and showing its initial menu items. As you type a search term, FileMaker searches its Help application to create a list of choices that may relate to your search terms.

Tip: If you bought FileMaker in a box, you'll find there's no printed manual. Instead there's a lengthy PDF document included on the CD. To check out FileMaker's own documentation, choose Help→Product Documentation→User's Guide.

Organizing and Editing Records

In the first chapter, you learned how to use FileMaker's basic tools and get around your database. But you've just begun to scratch the surface of FileMaker's power. Now it's time to learn how to see, sort, move, and shape your information in myriad ways. For example, you may want to print a list of names and addresses for all the folks in your database who live in the western U.S. In an invoicing database, you may want to find everybody who's ordered 16-pound offset widgets in the last month so you can email them a special offer for widget accessories. In a student database, you may need to print a report of all third-grade students who were involved in lunchroom disciplinary actions during the first semester.

Whatever your needs, you can build on basic techniques to view your data in ever more sophisticated ways. After all, slicing, dicing, and analyzing your data is the whole point of storing the information in a database.

Views

The most common way to view and edit records is called *Form view*. In Form view, you work with just one record at a time. In *List view*, you see the same arrangement of your records in, well, a list. If they don't all fit in the window, then you can use the vertical scroll bar to scroll through them. If you've used a spreadsheet program like Microsoft Excel, then *Table view* looks familiar—it looks a lot like a spreadsheet, with one row for each record, and one column for each field.

To switch among views in any FileMaker database, use the View menu. Choose View→As Form, View→As List, or View→As Table. You'll see what each view looks like as you learn about them on the following pages.

Note: The Chapter 1 version of the People database had custom buttons that let you switch views of your data, but that's not the only way to customize the views of your database. You can even turn *off* certain views if you want. If your database holds mostly digital photographs, it wouldn't make sense to look at in Table view, so you can make sure no one ever sees it that way. (You'll learn how in Chapter 7.) If you can't choose View→As List in the People file you have open, then download the Chapter 2 version of the file from this book's Missing CD page at *www.missingmanuals.com/cds*.

Form View

In Form view, you see only one record at a time. If you want to see the next record, click the pages of the book icon, press Ctrl+down arrow, or use some other method of switching records (see page 30). Most of the database work you did in the first chapter was in Form view, so it should be very familiar by now. You can use Form view when you have a lot of information to see about one record, or when you want to focus on just one record without being distracted by all the others.

Tip: The Status toolbar has handy buttons for switching between views of your data. The tools are well designed so you can easily guess which is which, but if you're not sure, just point your mouse to any button to see a handy tooltip that explains what the tool is for.

List View

List view works *almost* the same as Form view. All the fields are arranged exactly as on a form, but if you stretch or scroll your window, then you see that your records appear one on top of the other, like a long list of forms. You can sort or find data in List view, but since you have more than one record onscreen at once, you need to know which record you're in. You can tell by the thin black line along the left edge of the window (see Figure 2-1) at the edge of the active record.

When you're working with a *group* of records—updating one field in several records or browsing through all your records in search of something—List view comes in handy.

Table View

If List view doesn't provide enough of a change for you, try Table view (Figure 2-2). It appeals to spreadsheet fans since it offers a consistent rows-and-columns design, the ability to sort with the click of a button, and the freedom to rearrange columns by dragging them around. Of course you can add, edit, delete, and find records in Table view, just like the other two views.

When you put your layout into Table view, any graphical embellishments disappear from the content area. Instead, FileMaker displays the fields of your layout in a no-nonsense, spreadsheet arrangement (Figure 2-2).

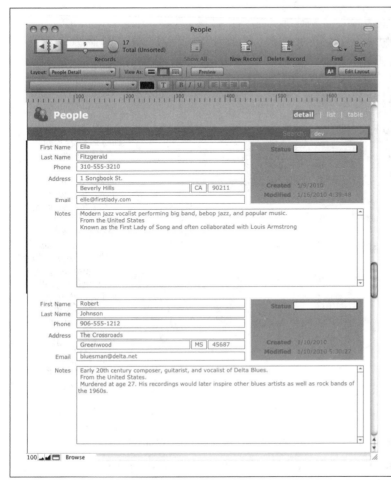

Figure 2-1:
When you switch to List view, your records look just like Form view, but you can scroll down through them with the scroll bar. A thin black line shows you which record is active, so you can edit it. And just like in Form view, you can click a record's fields to edit information if you need to. The feedback is just like Form view, too. Fields get a dotted line around them to show the record is active, and the active field has a solid border and a blinking cursor.

Each column represents one of your fields, and the order of the columns matches the order you go through the fields when tabbing (see page 323 to learn how to change the tab order). For example, the first column is the field you wind up in when you press Tab for the first time. Another Tab takes you to the second column.

In Table view, you can move columns around by dragging them. To switch the First Name and Last Name columns, for example, do the following:

1. **Point to the words Last Name, and then hold down the mouse button.**

    FileMaker darkens the column header to show you it's selected.

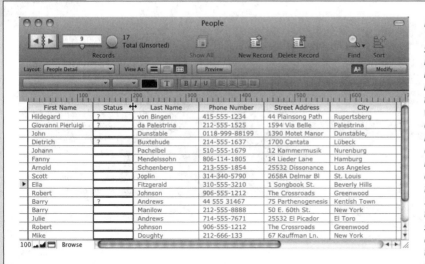

Figure 2-2:
This database is the same one shown in Figure 2-1, showing the same active record, but this time the layout is in Table view. The field labels are now column headers that act as clickable buttons, letting you sort the data by a specific field. The data in the Status field is too big to fit, so all you can see is a column of question marks, and the mouse is hovering over the dividing line at the right edge of that column. If you drag this line to the right, then the column expands. You can also gain a little room in the window by shrinking the State and Zip Code fields.

2. **Drag the column to the left of the First Name column.**

   You see a black line extending from the top of the window to the bottom. This line shows you where the column lands when you let go. All the other columns shift around to make room. In this case, you want the black line to appear to the left of the First Name column.

3. **Let go of the mouse button.**

   FileMaker moves the Last Name column to its new home, shifting other columns to the right to make room.

The column headings also make it easy to *sort* your data, if sorting by a single field is all you need. However, if you use the column headings to sort by Last Name, that doesn't automatically sort the First Name field, too. So if you need to do a multifield sort, then you need the Sort Records dialog box (page 38).

Modifying Table view

Table view is handy for scanning through a lot of data quickly. It's the only view where the Status toolbar shows a Modify button that lets you customize the view. Out of the box, Table view shows every field you see in Form view, but you may prefer to see less information when you're scanning tables, and you can do that with the Modify button. For example, the Created and Modified fields may not be useful to you in Table view, so you can remove them; they still show up in Form View. Here's how to change the fields you see in Table view:

1. **In the Status toolbar, click the Modify button.**

   The Modify Table View dialog box appears with all the fields from your Form view listed and checked.

2. **Click the checkbox to the left of the fields you don't want to see, like Creation Date, Modification Timestamp, and Notes, as shown in Figure 2-3, for comparison.**

   In the background, you can see the fields disappear from Table view as you click each one.

3. **Drag the double arrow just to the left of a field name to rearrange the columns.**

   The columns behind the dialog box move as you rearrange the list.

4. **Click OK when you're done.**

   The dialog box disappears, and you're back to an unobstructed Table view.

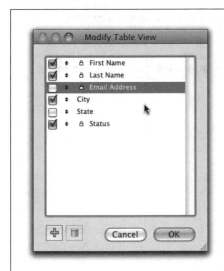

Figure 2-3:
Modify Table View lets you move columns and even keep them from appearing. There's a Plus button on the lower left that lets you add fields that aren't available in your current table. If that thought intrigues you, read Chapter 5 to learn about using more than one table in a single database.

As powerful as the Modify Table View dialog box is, FileMaker gives you even more ways to exert control over this view. Here's how to find those hidden gems:

1. **Choose View→Layout Mode, or press Ctrl+L (⌘-L).**

   FileMaker switches to Layout mode, showing you the structure of your Form view. Although this window is where you usually go to change the way Form view looks, you can also change Table view in this mode.

2. **Choose Layout→Layout Setup.**

   The Layout Setup dialog box appears. You can ignore all these settings for now, but see page 283 if you want to know what these options do.

3. **Click the Views tab.**

   The Views options appear. If you want to, you can turn off the options for Form and List view so this layout is available only in Table view. But that's not what you're after right now.

4. **Beside the Table view option, click the Properties button.**

   The Table View Properties dialog box appears (Figure 2-4). Options in this dialog box let you turn off the ability to move or resize columns and the clickable sorting of the column headers.

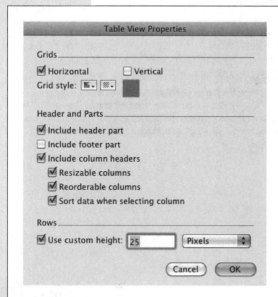

Figure 2-4:
The Table View Properties dialog box gives you control over how the view looks while you're in Browse mode. Of course, those changes also affect how the screen prints. Switch to Preview Mode to see how the layout will print. You probably need to make changes to the layout to make it print-worthy, so check out the section beginning on page 337 to see how to design a layout for printing.

5. **Click the Vertical option to remove the checkmark.**

   This removes the lines between each column.

6. Turn on the "Use custom height" option, and then, in the measurement field, type *25*. If necessary, from the increment pop-up menu, choose pixels.

    This setting makes each table row a little taller.

7. Click OK to close each dialog box until you're back in Layout mode, and then switch to Browse mode.

    If your layout isn't set to save changes automatically FileMaker will ask if you want to save the changes you've just made. Confirm that you want to save the changes and you'll see all the changes you made to the table. See the box on page 92 to learn more details about Table view properties.

By controlling the appearance of your different views, you can start to see how much customization power FileMaker gives you over your data in Browse mode. And now that you've gotten your feet wet in Layout mode, be sure to read Chapter 7 to learn how to control the look and behavior of the Form layout itself. Now, though, it's time to learn some sophisticated ways to find specific records.

Advanced Find Techniques

In Chapter 1, you learned about using Find mode for simple searches. But the more records you have in your database, the more you need advanced finding techniques to avoid wasting precious minutes clicking the book icon 1,057 times in a row just to find the record or records you want to display, edit, or print. FileMaker's Find tools give you the power to track down the 1 record in 100,000 you need *right this minute*, or the 5 records with missing phone numbers that you created a week ago Tuesday.

Modify Last Find

FileMaker always keeps track of your most recent find criteria, even if it's been a while since you did the search. So if you have to run another copy of your last report, or you just need to see if any new records match since the last time you did the find, all you have to do is choose Records→Modify Last Find. FileMaker does the equivalent of entering Find mode and typing in your find criteria. You can edit the criteria if you want, or just click Find, and you're done.

Modify Last Find (Ctrl+R or ⌘-R) isn't just a speedy way to recreate a find, though. You might have a found set of records, but you can't remember the search criteria. Choose Modify Last Find and you'll be looking at them. Then you can click the Cancel Find or the Perform Find button. Either way, you're right back in your found set.

Multiple Requests

You can tell FileMaker to search for more than one item at the time. But depending on how you enter your search terms, you can get very different results.

Searching with AND conditions

If you want to find every vocalist in the People database who lives in New York, a computer geek would say that you need to do an *AND search*. This odd term means you're asking for records where the city is New York *and* the Notes field contains the word "vocalist". Just New York alone, or vocalist alone, doesn't get the job done. An AND search is more restrictive than a single-field search because more of your search terms have to match before FileMaker puts a record into your found set. Though it's complex to think about, you can easily set up a multiple request search. Here's how:

1. **Choose View→Find Mode or, in the Status toolbar, click the Find tool.**

   FileMaker opens a new find request.

2. **In the State field, type *NY*.**

   You're telling FileMaker to find all records for people who live in the state of New York. That's your first search term.

3. **In the Notes field, type *vocalist*.**

   This second search term narrows the range of matching records. FileMaker knows that it has to show only those records that match *both* search terms you've entered.

4. **In the Status toolbar, click the Perform Find button.**

   FileMaker shows you the two records that match both your search terms.

Searching with OR conditions

If an AND search is more restrictive than a single criteria search, an OR search is less restrictive. That is, you almost always find more records with an OR search, since a record has to match only *one* of the many search terms you set up in order to get into the found set. To convert the previous example to an OR condition, think of it like this: "I need to find everybody who *either* lives in New York *or* is a vocalist." So sirens who live in Nebraska (or anywhere, for that matter) show up in your found set, as do regular-Joe New Yorkers.

To create an OR condition, you add one small step to the process you just learned. Before you type the second search term, create a new request by choosing Requests→Add New Request. Notice that the New Request command is the same one that creates a new record when you're in Browse mode. Different modes, different menus, same keyboard shortcut—Ctrl+N (⌘-N). Once you've typed your second request, you can use the book icon to flip back and review or edit the first one.

Tip: You can make your search criteria as complicated as you like, with dozens of requests, even mixing AND and OR terms within the same search. Just remember that you put a new term in the same request for an AND condition, and you create a new request for an OR condition.

FREQUENTLY ASKED QUESTION

Finding Special Characters

How do I find mrbill@microsoft.com *when "@" means something special?*

The @ symbol is one of 17 special "operators" in File-Maker. The operators change the character of a search term to make your find more or less precise. If what you're actually looking for includes one of these special operators, you need to take extra precautions. When searching for *mrbill@microsoft.com*, the "@" operator matches

any letter, number, or punctuation mark. But the @ in the email address is none of these, so the search doesn't work.

To prevent FileMaker from interpreting the @ as a special character, use the Match Phrase operators described on page 61. In other words, putting the search text in quotes ("*mrbill@microsoft.com*") does the trick. You could also search for *mrbill Microsoft*, since FileMaker sees these as two separate words.

Finding by Omitting

FileMaker's normal search behavior is to *include* in the found set everything you type in search fields. You can confirm this fact in Find mode by looking at the Include and Omit buttons in the Status toolbar (Figure 2-5). Every time you start a search, the Include button is automatically selected.

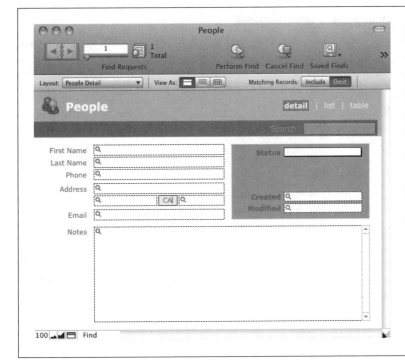

Figure 2-5:
The Omit button tells FileMaker to do an "unfind." You can see the Omit button near the right edge of the Status toolbar. And of course, it appears only when you're in Find mode. In this example, the Omit button tells FileMaker to show you all the records for people who don't live in California. Once you get used to this inverted logic, you see that it's often easier to create an Omit search than the complicated Include search you may have to come up with if you use FileMaker's normal Include behavior.

The Omit button comes in handy when the records you're looking for can best be described by what they aren't. For example, "Every person who isn't from California" is a lot easier to say (and to search for) than "Everyone from Alabama, Alaska, Arizona, Arkansas, Colorado…." In this case, you can get what you want by creating one find request, with California in the State field. Then, before you perform the find, just click the Omit button, which you can see in Figure 2-5. That's all there is to it. When you click Perform Find, FileMaker starts with every record in the table, and then omits all the records with "California" in the State field, so you're left with everything else.

Omit also works with multiple find requests. If *all* your requests have the Omit option turned on, then all the records that match *any* of your requests are excluded from the found set. Whatever's left over goes in your found set. If you have a mix of requests with and without Omit turned on, then FileMaker goes through them in order. If the first request isn't an omit request, then FileMaker finds all the matching records. If your first request is an omit, then FileMaker finds every record that doesn't match, and then moves on to the next request. That request may add new records to the found set, or remove records that are already there. In fact, a record can be found by one request, omitted by the next, and then found again by the third, so the record is ultimately included in the found set since the last request added it. In the end, you're left with a found set in which every record matches at least one of your requests.

Refining a found set with Omit commands

FileMaker gives you a few menu commands to help you fine-tune your found set. Sometimes, after you've done the best find request you can, you still end up with a couple of records in the found set that you don't really want to see. FileMaker offers three commands that make tossing out misfit records as easy as pie:

- **Omit Record.** Go to the record you don't want (using the book icon, for example), and then choose Records→Omit Record. This one-off command tosses the record out of the found set, reducing your found count by one. Don't confuse it with the Omit button that shows up in the Status toolbar when you're in Find mode (see page 57), which tells FileMaker to omit all the records that match your find request. The Records→Omit Record command omits just the single record you're sitting on.

- **Omit Multiple.** If you have a whole stretch of records you don't want, then use Records→Omit Multiple. It omits a contiguous group of records from the found set, starting with the current record. For instance, if you want to omit 10 records in a row, then navigate to the *first* record of the 10. Choose Records→Omit Multiple, and then, in the dialog box that appears, type *10*. Click Omit, and the job is done.

- **Show Omitted Only.** You can use this option when you're printing two separate lists—one of the California customers, and one of everyone else, for example. Once you've printed the California records, your found set happens to be exactly what you *don't* need. Choose Records→Show Omitted Only. This command effectively puts every record that's *not* in the found set into the new found set, and takes every currently found record out.

Tip: You can also use Show Omitted Only if you forgot to use the Omit option in your find request. Instead of going back to Find mode to fix your request, just choose Records→Show Omitted Only, and you get the same effect.

POWER USERS' CLINIC

Over-Omitted

If you try to omit more records than possible (for example, you're on the third-to-last record, and you ask FileMaker to omit 12 records), then FileMaker complains. But don't take offense: It's also nice enough to fix the problem for you. When you click OK, FileMaker returns you to the Omit dialog box, and changes the number you entered to the maximum number possible. You need only to click Omit again to get what you probably wanted in the first place.

Use this feature to your advantage. If you know you're looking at the last record that should be in your found set, you could try to do the math the dialog box needs. But that's

more trouble than it's worth. Just choose Records→Omit Multiple, and then enter something really big, like "999," or "9999999." When you click Omit, FileMaker complains, does the math for you, and enters the right value.

This routine may sound contrived, but it's fairly common among FileMaker pros. Imagine you're doing a direct-mail campaign and you can afford to send only 1,200 postcards. Your find request, however, produces 1,931 potential recipients. Rather than do the math, just go to record 1201, and then use this Omit Multiple trick.

Constraining and Extending the Found Set

When you perform a regular find, it forgets any found set you had before, searches through all the records in the database, and then produces a *new* found set. But you can also tell FileMaker to *constrain* the found set (that is, search within your last find results) or *extend* it (add matching records to the current found set).

Constraining the found set

Suppose you've just created a great product, and you want to send out some free samples to see how people like it. You can't afford the postage to send everyone in your database a sample, so you decide to start with a smaller sampling—just people who live in New York.

Problem is, a simple find reveals that your database has too many New Yorkers listed. Some quick math in your head reveals that it's still too expensive. How about sending samples to just the New Yorkers who are vocalists? You *could* go back to Find

---

mode and construct a request to find based on both criteria (by putting *New York* in the City field and *vocalist* in the Notes field), but FileMaker gives you an easier way. After all, you've already got all the New Yorkers in your found set. You really want to search *inside* this found set for all the records with *vocalist* in the Notes field.

Here's how the whole procedure goes:

1. **First, you find all the New Yorkers. Switch to Find mode and, in the City field, type *New York*, and then click the Perform Find button.**

   FileMaker shows you a found set of all your New York residents.

2. **Switch to Find mode again using your favorite method.**

   Be careful *not* to choose Records→Show All Records, and don't do anything to tamper with the current found set, or else the Constrain search won't work. You're now in Find mode again, ready to enter a request.

Note: In Find mode, you can't see your current found set. You just have to remember that you last searched for "New York" in the City field. If you need to see the found set, just switch back to Browse mode, and then flip through the records.

---

3. **In the Notes field, type *vocalist*.**

   Since the found set already has only New Yorkers in it, you don't need to repeat that information.

4. **Choose Requests→Constrain Found Set.**

   FileMaker searches out the singers, but this time it looks only in the current found set of New York residents. In the end, you get what you want with less typing.

At this point, you're probably thinking that Constrain Found Set is just like doing an AND search. In fact, an AND search is usually easier. But sometimes, you don't know all the conditions you need until you do a search and scan through the list of found records. And if you've just done a complex search with seven conditions, or tricky spellings, you don't want to have to retype all that stuff, so Constrain Found Set saves the day.

Note: Once you're in Find mode, FileMaker is just itching for you to perform a find. If you press Enter, it assumes you want to abandon your last found set and make a new one. If you pressed Enter when you intended to constrain, Modify Last Find isn't going to help. Fortunately, FileMaker remembers more than just your last find request. Click and hold the Find button in the status toolbar to see a list of your saved and recent finds, and then choose the second item listed under Recent Finds. Faster than you can say flux capacitor, your old found set is restored and you can try again. See page 65 for a complete description of the Find pop-up menu.

Extending the found set

Extending the found set works a lot like constraining it. This time, though, you're asking FileMaker to perform a new find (through all records in the database), and then *add* the records it finds into your found set. You end up with all the records you already had, plus any new ones found. Suppose you've already found your *New York* folks, and you want all the *Texans* as well:

1. **In Find mode, in the State field, type** *TX.*

   So far, you're doing exactly what you'd do in every other find.

2. **Choose Requests→Extend Found Set.**

   This time, FileMaker looks through every record in the database for any Texas natives. Each time it finds one, it adds it to your existing found set. When it's done, you have all the New Yorkers *and* Texans in one found set.

Refining Searches with Find Operators

Normally, FileMaker uses a pretty simple rule to decide whether a field's value matches the search term you entered (the *criteria*): If every search term you entered in the criteria appears at the *beginning* (within the first few characters) of any word in the field, then FileMaker considers it a match.

For example, if you put *for* in the Note field in a find request, any of these notes match:

- All for one and one for all.

- We will forever remember.

- Back and forth it went.

On the other hand, neither of these match:

- Wherefore art thou, Romeo?

- Before there was art, there was an artist.

Note: This match-the-beginning mode of operation may seem odd, but it's surprisingly useful. Imagine you're looking for someone named Giovanni Pierluigi de Palestrina in your database. Of course, you could find the record by typing the full name, but chances are you'll get the same results if you search for *Gio Pal* instead. Since Giovanni starts with Gio and Palestrina starts with Pal, FileMaker finds him with this abbreviated request, saving you from all that typing—and remembering how to spell the full name.

How do you tell FileMaker that you're seeking the term "for" *wherever* it appears in a word, not just at the beginning? You can use a special *operator*—a character that has special meaning in a Find request—to stand for part of a word.

The Insert Operators pop-up menu, which appears in the Status toolbar when you're in Find mode, lets you add these special characters to your searches, thus gaining more control over FileMaker's decision-making process when it's looking for records. Read on to find about more special operators.

Zero or More Characters, a.k.a. "Wildcard" (*)

In the "Wherefore art thou Romeo" example, use the * wildcard operator, which stands for "anything." It tells FileMaker that you don't mind if there's something *right before or right after* the "for." If you type **for** as your find criteria, then FileMaker displays records that contain "therefore," "before," "George Foreman," and so on. (Of course, if you want things that only start with "for" [forthwith, forsaken or forced], then you can type *for** in the find request.)

Less Than (<), Less Than or Equal (≤), Greater Than (>), and Greater Than or Equal (≥)

These operators tell FileMaker to use your criteria as a maximum or minimum rather than a direct match. For example, the criteria *<David* finds every person whose name comes before David alphabetically. ≤David is just about the same, but it includes any Davids as well.

People use these operators more frequently to find numeric or date information rather than text. For example, *<10* in a field that expects numbers finds real numbers less than 10 (like 9). FileMaker performs the correct function with dates and times as well, in which case Less Than means *before* and Greater Than means *after*. You'll learn more about field types in the next chapter.

Match Whole Word (=), Match Phrase (" "), and Match Entire Field (= =)

The rule FileMaker uses automatically for determining a match is pretty loose. But sometimes you want exactly what you say: "Smith," not "Smithers" or "Smithey" or "Smithsonian." In this case, use the Match Whole Word operator (=). In this example, type *=Smith* in the Last Name field, and then perform your find.

If you want to exactly match *more* than one word, put the words in quotes. This Match Phrase capability is also good for criteria that contain punctuation, like "Mr. Smith."

Note: Like French fries, quote marks come in two varieties: curly and straight. If you're someone who notices this kind of thing, then you may wonder if it matters which kind you use. It doesn't. Usually FileMaker turns your quotes curly for you, but you can turn off smart quotes for a database in the File→File Options dialog box.

For the ultimate in specificity, use the Match Entire Field operator (==) instead. Match Whole Word requires that each *word* in your criteria match one or more words in the field. Match Phrase seeks to match only what's in the quotes *anywhere* in the field. Match Entire Field insists that the entire field matches the criteria text exactly. For example, =*Smith* matches "Smith," "Mr. Smith," and "Smith-Johnson." However, ==*Smith* matches only "Smith" in the field and nothing else.

Note: Match Phrase doesn't actually match text *anywhere* in the field. The criteria text has to match starting at the beginning of a word. For instance, a search for "Mr. Smith" matches "Mr. Smith" and "Mr. Smithers," but if you search for *"r. Smith"* (no M) instead, then you get the "no matches found" error.

Range (…)

The Range operator is like the "Greater Than or Equal To" and "Less Than or Equal To" operators combined. The criteria "1/1/2011…6/15/2011" matches those two dates and everything in between. Just like the other operators, the Range operator is smart enough to understand numbers, dates, and times, as long as the field contains that kind of data.

Find Duplicate Values (!)

You might find it hard to get the hang of the Find Duplicate Values operator (!). When you put ! in a field in Find mode, FileMaker finds records with *duplicate data* in that field. In other words, it looks for records with the *same* value in that particular field. The same as *what*, you ask? The same as *any other record*. Think of it this way: If you have only *one* person in your database from Idaho, and you perform a find with *!* in the State field, then the person from Idaho doesn't appear. That's because—when considering the State field alone—the person from Idaho has no duplicates. On the other hand, if you have 11 people from Oklahoma and six people from Georgia, they'll *all* be found because they all have duplicates (each one has 10 others [or five others] just like it, statewide). In order to figure out what's up, sort the new found set of 16 records by the State field to make sure all the Georgians are grouped together, followed by all the Oklahomans. Then you can more easily compare them to the proper duplicates.

Unlike most other operators, the ! operator is always used alone in a field in Find mode. You never put *! Smith* in the last name field. Instead, you just put *!* all by itself.

Today's Date (//) and Invalid Date or Time (?)

Like the ! operator, these operators can go in a field in Find mode all by themselves. The double slash is convenient shorthand for the current date. If you're looking for all the payments due today, you can type // in the Due field more quickly than "February 22, 2010".

The Invalid Date or Time operator (?) is another helper when it comes time to clean house. It's possible to end up with the wrong kind of data in fields that are supposed to hold dates or times (like "N/A", "Never", or "Next Week"). Put ? in the Due field, and FileMaker finds every payment whose due date isn't valid, giving you an opportunity to fix them.

Finding Duplicate Records

Every database user eventually makes the mistake of entering the same data twice. Maybe you assume a person isn't in your database and add him, only to discover months later that he was there all along. The ! operator can help you hunt down this sort of thing.

If you want to find *whole records* that are exact duplicates, then you have to put *!* in every field when you're in Find mode. But it isn't at all uncommon for "duplicate" records to be slightly different. Maybe you updated the phone number in one but not the other, for instance.

Or perhaps you misspelled the street name the first time you entered this person, and spelled it right the second time. Finding exact duplicate records doesn't catch these kinds of duplicate records.

If you're looking for duplicate records, you're usually best off putting the ! operator in as few fields as possible. Try to pick fields that tend to be entered the same every time, and stand a good chance of identifying an individual person. You can use just First Name and Last Name, for instance.

Note: You can mix and match these operators in any combinations that make sense. For example, to find everything after today's date, just search for *>//* instead of *>4/1/2011*.

Any One Character (@), Any One Digit (#), and Zero or More Characters (*)

These operators are like the wildcard characters you sometimes see in other programs. You already saw the Zero or More Characters operator (*) at the beginning of this section. It simply tells FileMaker you're willing to accept some text—*any text*—in place of the * operator. If you're not ready to go that far, you can instead permit just one character (letter, number, or punctuation) with the Any One Character (@) operator. When matching numbers, you can be even more specific, permitting just one numerical digit with the Any One Digit (#) operator. Here are a few examples:

- **smith** matches "Smith," "blacksmith," "Smithsonian," and "blacksmiths"

- **smith* matches "Smith" and "blacksmith," but not "blacksmiths" or "Smithsonian"

- *smith@* matches "smithy" but not "Smith" or "smithers"

- *@*smith* matches "blacksmith" but not "Smith" or "blacksmiths"

- *smith#* matches "smith1" and "smith42" but not "smithy"

Note: As discussed at the start of this section, when you do a Find, FileMaker matches the *beginning* of a word in the field. But as soon as you add these wildcard operators to your search, it becomes a little less lenient: FileMaker insists on a complete word match. You can see this in the second example above. You might expect **smith* to match "blacksmiths" but it doesn't because FileMaker now wants the whole word to match.

Relaxed Search (~)

The last operator, called Relaxed Search (~) applies only to searching Japanese language text. It instructs FileMaker to consider characters to match if they make the same sound, even if they aren't exactly the same character. Alas, in English, spelling always counts (you can't expect "~phat" to match "fat").

Using the Find Pop-up Menu

Once you've figured out how to create the complex find to get that end-of-month report showing, say, all females in a 10–Zip code range who've emailed you, but who haven't made a purchase in the last quarter, you can use the Find pop-up menu (Figure 2-6) to recreate that find if you need it again. If you've done the find recently (within your last 10 finds), then it appears in this menu. Plus, you see another way to access the Modify Last Find command (page 56). Best of all, Save Current Find lets you save as many frequently used finds as you need.

Figure 2-6:
The Find pop-up menu appears when you hold down the mouse button on the Find icon instead of clicking it. The menu gives you an easy way to manage finds that you have to perform repeatedly. Although you can't see the name of the field (or fields) you've searched in the Recent Finds section of the menu, each item gives you as much data as it can. The highlighted search found all Zip codes that start with either "10" OR "79". There's no indication of that in the menu, so you have to rely on your memory for that bit of the puzzle. If it's all too confusing, the "Clear All Recent Finds" command lets you start from scratch.

Saving finds

You can most easily save a find when you perform it first. When you perform a find, FileMaker remembers the criteria you set. (For a challenge, see page 66 to see how to save a find you *haven't* performed yet.) To get started, search for all Zip codes that start with either "10" or "79" (see page 55 for help creating an OR condition search). Then follow these steps:

1. **In the Status toolbar, click the Find icon, and keep the mouse button pressed.**

   The pop-up menu appears, with the Find you just performed at the top of the menu's Recent Finds section.

2. **Choose Save Current Find.**

   The Specify Options for the Saved Find dialog box appears. FileMaker suggests a name for your saved find.

3. **In the Name field, type *End of the Month Report*.**

   Type a name to help you remember what the find does. Consider putting the field you're searching somewhere in the name. You have 100 characters to work with, but a lengthy name can make the menu unwieldy.

4. **Click Save.**

   Press the Find pop-up menu again, and you see the saved find.

Now you can test the new find by choosing it from the pop-up menu. FileMaker does all the work: It enters Find mode, enters the search criteria, and then performs the find. You can also enter Find mode, and then, from the Saved Finds pop-up menu, choose a saved find. In that case, though, FileMaker enters your criteria, but you have to click Perform Find. Using this method, you can create a find that's slightly different from the saved request—just edit the request any way you like before clicking Perform Find.

Note: Saved Finds are specific to a single account in your file. To see your saved finds, log in with the account under which you created the finds. Chapter 18 tells you about accounts and privileges.

Editing saved finds

If you have a saved find that needs tweaking—maybe the end of the month report needs to include a new set of Zip codes from now on or maybe you just made a mistake when you set it up—use Edit Saved Finds. You can choose the command from the Find pop-up menu, or by choosing Records→Saved Finds→Edit Saved Finds (Figure 2-7). Either way, you see a dialog box that shows you all your saved finds, and lets you create a new find without performing it first. You can also delete or edit finds.

To edit a saved find:

1. **From the Saved Finds pop-up menu, choose Edit Saved Finds.**

   The Edit Saved Finds dialog box appears (Figure 2-7).

2. **Click the "Vocalist (notes field)" find.**

   The selected find appears highlighted, and the Edit button becomes active.

Figure 2-7:
The Edit Saved Finds dialog box shows all your saved finds. You can sort the list with the "View by" pop-up menu. You can sort alphabetically by name, by creation order or in a custom order, by dragging the arrow to the left of each find's name. Use the Duplicate button as a starting point for creating a new find that's similar to one you've already saved. The Delete button cleans up finds you won't be using any more.

3. **Click Edit, double-click the Vocalist find, or simply press Enter.**

   The Specify Options for the Saved Finds dialog box appears. If you're changing the action of the find, it makes sense to change its name. In this case, though, you're repairing a find that wasn't set up correctly, so leave the name the same.

4. **Click the Advanced button.**

   The Specify Find Requests dialog box appears. The actions that create the find requests are in a list. In this case, there's only one action, which is equivalent to a request in a manual find.

5. **Click the Find Records action, and then click the Edit button (or double-click the action).**

   The Edit Find Request dialog box appears. Here you can change the way this specific request does its work. Currently, it's set to search in the Address field for the word "central".

6. **Click the action in the top list, then scroll the list of fields near the bottom left of the window until you see the Notes field. Click it.**

   You're telling FileMaker to search the Notes field instead of the Street Address field. The Change button becomes active as soon as you select the field. The change doesn't take place until you click the button or press Enter, though.

7. **Click into the box on the right marked "Criteria", and then type *vocalist*.**

   You've entered the second part of the changed request, which is to search the field for the word "vocalist". See Figure 2-8 for the settings.

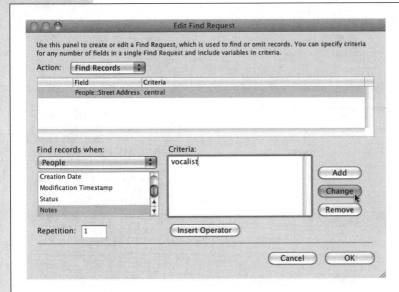

Figure 2-8:
This dialog box changes a find request from searching the Street Address field for the word "central" to searching the Notes field for the word "vocalist." The Action pop-up menu lets you choose between "Find Records" and "Omit Records". In a single request, you can search more than one field, which is like setting up an AND condition in Find mode. Multiple requests within a single find are the same as an OR condition in Find mode.

8. **Click Change, and then click OK or Save in all the dialog boxes until you're back on your People Detail layout.**

    If you click Cancel on the last dialog box, then FileMaker warns you that all your changes will be discarded. Use this technique when you're not sure if your settings are correct. Since the Delete button doesn't warn you before it deletes a find request or a saved find, you can use this technique instead as a fail-safe. When you click Cancel, FileMaker discards all the changes you made while the dialog box was open.

Try out the edited search, by choosing it from the Find pop-up menu or by choosing Records→Saved Finds→"Vocalist (notes field)". This process involves a lot of steps, but once you understand the Edit Find Request dialog box, the process is easy. You can use a slight variation to create a new saved find without performing it first. Just choose Edit Saved Finds, and then click New instead of selecting an existing find and editing it.

Tip: Practice creating finds from scratch comes in handy when you start scripting static finds (page 488). Several find script steps use the Specify Find Requests and Edit Find Request dialog boxes you've just seen.

Editing What's in Your Fields

Once you've found the records you want to work on, it's time to learn timesaving and creative ways to revise and format your record text. Each field is actually like a mini–word processor, with features that you're familiar with if you've ever written a letter on a computer. You can do basic things like select text, and cut, copy, and paste. You even have a Find and Replace feature, and flexible text formatting powers.

Drag-and-drop Editing

In addition to copying and pasting, you can drag text from one place to another. But first, you have to turn it on in FileMaker's preferences, like so:

1. **In Windows, choose Edit→Preferences. In Mac OS X, choose FileMaker Pro→Preferences.**

    The Preferences dialog box appears.

2. **Select "Allow drag and drop text selection".**

    If you don't like using drag and drop, just come back here and turn it off.

3. **Click OK.**

    The dialog box disappears.

Now that dragging is turned on, here's how it works:

4. **Make a new record (Records→New Record).**

    Now you've got a nice clean work surface.

5. **In the Notes field, type *FileMaker has editing super power*.**

    Next you'll drag to fix it.

6. **Double-click the word "super".**

    The word is highlighted to let you know it's selected.

7. **Drag the selected word between "has" and "editing".**

    Figuring out where dragged text is going to land can be tricky. If you look closely, you see that in addition to the text you're dragging, a little vertical line moves along under your arrow. You can see this in action in Figure 2-9. (Unless you have excruciatingly precise mouse movements, you probably have to fix the spaces between words. Unlike most word processors, FileMaker isn't smart enough to figure out where they go for you.)

Notes | FileMaker has editing super power.

Figure 2-9:
When you turn on "Allow drag and drop text selection" in Preferences, FileMaker lets you drag selected text around with the mouse. Here, the word "super" is being moved after "has" by dragging. The little vertical line under the arrow shows you exactly where the text will go when you drop it.

Tip: You can also drag text from one *field* to another. Instead of *moving* the text, FileMaker *copies* it. In other words, once you let go of the mouse button, the text is both where it started *and* where you drop it. If you want this behavior when dragging *within* a field, then hold down the Ctrl (Option) key while you drag.

Using the Replace Command

Sometimes the whole reason you performed a find is to change something in several records. Maybe you just noticed that your data entry person put "New Yorq" on all the records she entered. The first step to fixing them is to *find* them. Once your found set includes the proper records, you could change the City field one record at a time (especially if you're billing by the hour). But you use your time better if you use the Replace Field Contents command. Here's how it works:

1. **Click the City field (it doesn't matter which record), and then correct the spelling to "New York".**

   You've just fixed one of the records. All the others in the found set need the same fix. (Make sure your cursor is still in the City field or the next step won't work.)

2. **Choose Records→Replace Field Contents.**

   The Replace Field Contents dialog box appears (Figure 2-10). It has a handful of options that may not make sense to you yet. That's OK; just choose the first one: "Replace with". The new data you just typed is listed beside this option.

3. **Click Replace.**

   FileMaker now updates the City field in *every record in the found set*. When it's done, you're still sitting on the same record, but if you use the book icon to click through the records, then you see that they've all been changed.

Find and Find Again

Unlike the Find/Replace window in most other programs, FileMaker's doesn't politely step aside. If you try to click in your database window to switch back to it, then FileMaker just beeps at you. In fact, you can't do *anything else* but find and replace unless you close the Find/Replace window first. You can always move the Find/Replace window around the screen by dragging it, but if your database window is big, or your screen is small, the Find/Replace window can really get in the way, keeping the very results it's finding hidden behind it. Here are a few pointers to help you cope:

Make sure the Find/Replace window is as small as possible by dragging the resize handle in the lower-right corner. Like most windows, it's resizable, but its smallest size is almost always big enough.

If you close the Find/Replace window (click Close or press Esc), then FileMaker keeps the last-found item highlighted. Since FileMaker remembers all your settings, you can always open the Find/Replace window again, and then continue searching where you left off.

Wouldn't it be great if you could click the buttons in the Find/Replace window without having it open onscreen? Fact is, you can. In the Edit→Find/Replace menu, you see two handy commands: Find Again and Replace & Find Again. (They're grayed out unless you've done a Find/Replace operation, though.)

Choosing these menu commands is just like clicking the Find Next and Replace & Find buttons in the Find/Replace dialog box.

FileMaker also offers one more convenient shortcut. If you have some text already in a field, and you want to find *the next* occurrence of the same text, then you can choose Edit→Find/Replace→Find Selected. This one command does the same thing as copying the text, opening the Find/Replace window, pasting into the "Find what" box, clicking Find Next, and then clicking Close. All the other options in the Find/Replace window stay just as when you last used them.

These handy commands all have keyboard shortcuts that, somewhat confusingly, only work when the Find/Replace dialog box is *closed*:

- To find the next occurrence (Find Again), just press Ctrl+G (⌘-G).
- To replace the currently selected text, and find the next occurrence (Replace & Find Again), press Ctrl+Shift+G (Option-⌘-G).
- To find other occurrences of the selected text, press Ctrl+Shift+H (Option-⌘-H).

Note: The Replace Field Contents command can be very dangerous. It really does change every record in the found set, even if that wasn't your intent. Make sure you're absolutely certain you have the right found set before clicking Replace, because you can't use the Undo command afterwards. Saving a backup copy of your database just *before* using Replace Field Contents is advisable.

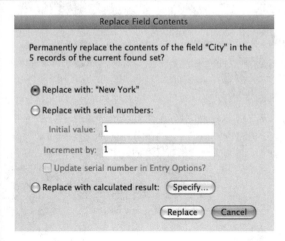

Figure 2-10:
The Replace Field Contents dialog box has three options: "Replace with", "Replace with serial numbers", and "Replace with calculated result". You're concerned only with the first option right now. It replaces the contents of the current field in every record in the found set with whatever's in the current record when you click Replace. So, in the current record, type what you want to be in every record before you call up this dialog box. (You'll learn about serial numbers in Chapter 3 and calculations in Chapter 8.)

Find and Replace

Like your word processor, FileMaker has a Find and Replace feature. Also as in your word processor, you can (and should) use Find and Replace tools as often as possible to automate your editing process and eliminate retyping.

Suppose one of your clients is called MegaBank. For one reason or another, they decide to change their name to Bay Lout Bank. Unfortunately, you have 27 folks in your database with the old name, and the name is sprinkled in Company Name fields, Notes fields, and so on. You could look through your records one by one and fix them yourself, but you're never going to become a database maestro that way. Instead, do a Find/Replace operation.

FileMaker fields can hold a lot of information, and people often put things like letters, emails, product descriptions, and other potentially long documents into a field. In cases like this, the Find/Replace command is just as useful as it is in your word processing program.

Since FileMaker has fields and records to worry about, though, its Find/Replace dialog box is a little more complicated than what you may be familiar with. Luckily, the concepts are simple, as shown in Figure 2-11. The Find/Replace dialog box lets you search for a snippet of text in one field or all fields of one record or all found records. It can also replace every occurrence of that text with something new—either one at a time, or all at once.

Note: Don't confuse Find/Replace with Find mode. Find/Replace is for finding *text* in one or more fields and one or more records. Find mode is for finding *records*. You'll probably use Find mode much more often than Find/Replace. For the full story, see the box on page 76.

Figure 2-11:
In FileMaker, you use the same dialog box both to find text and to find and replace text. If you aren't replacing anything, don't click any of the Replace buttons. The text you're looking for goes in the "Find what" text box. If you're replacing it with something new, type that text in the "Replace with" text box. (If you want to replace some text with nothing, making it go away, then leave the "Replace with" box empty.)

Here's FileMaker's version of Find and Replace:

1. **Choose Edit→Find/Replace→Find/Replace.**

   The Find/Replace dialog box opens, as shown in Figure 2-11.

Tip: Turning on "Match case" ensures that FileMaker looks for an exact uppercase and lowercase match. For example, when "Match case" is turned on, "Kite" and "kite" don't come up as a match. If you turn on "Match whole words only", FileMaker eliminates partial word matches. For example, "Drag" matches "Drag" and not "Dragon."

---

2. **Under "Search across", select "All records."**

   You've just told FileMaker you want it to look through all the records in the found set.

3. **Under "Search within", select "Current field."**

   "Current field" refers to the field you were editing when you opened the Find/Replace dialog box. If you weren't clicked into a field when you opened the dialog box, FileMaker still lets you select the "Current field" option, but it complains when you start the find, so if you want to search a specific field, close the dialog box, click in your intended field, and then reopen the dialog box. You can select any combination of Search across and Search within. Here's how that shakes out:

   - **All records and All fields.** FileMaker looks through every field on the layout for a match, and repeats the process for each record in the found set.

   - **Current record and All fields.** FileMaker looks through every field on the layout in the current record only.

   - **Current record and Current field.** FileMaker looks only in the current field. When it reaches the end of the text in that field, it stops.

- **All records and Current field.** FileMaker looks through the current field, and then moves to the next record. It keeps looking through records for more matches, but it pays attention only to the current field.

4. **From the Direction pop-up menu, choose All.**

    The Direction pop-up menu controls which way FileMaker goes when it starts its search. To figure out what that means, imagine a long string running through your database. One end is tied to the first letter of the first field of the first record in the found set. The other end is tied to the last letter of the last field of the last found record. This concept is pictured in Figure 2-12.

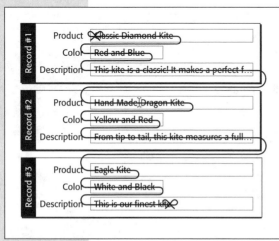

Figure 2-12:
The Find/Replace command expects you to give it a direction. To decipher what that means, you have to do a little visualization. Here's a picture of the imaginary string, starting at the beginning of the first record, and stopping at the end of the last. When you click into a field, and the insertion point sits there blinking in front of a letter, it's marking a spot on the imaginary string. If you're not clicked into a field, then FileMaker decides to mark the string right before the first letter of the first field of the current record. In this example, your cursor is sitting right there between "Made" and "Dragon".

- **Forward.** FileMaker starts looking at your current spot on the string, and moves *forward* (towards the end of the string). When it gets to the end, it beeps.

- **Backward.** FileMaker starts looking at your current spot on the string, and moves *backward* (towards the beginning of the string). When it gets to the beginning, it beeps.

- **All.** FileMaker starts off just like a Forward search. When it reaches the end of the string, instead of beeping, it loops back to the start of the string, and keeps looking. It finally beeps and stops when it gets back where it started.

Now that you're through setting all your Find/Replace options, it's time to decide which button to click:

5. **Click Find Next.**

- **Find Next** starts FileMaker looking. When it finds a match, it highlights the match right in the field. The Find/Replace window stays put, so you can click Find Next as many times as necessary to find what you're looking for, and then click Replace to change it to your replacement text. Click Find Next again to go to the next match.

- If you feel the need to work more quickly—say you've done Find Next and Replace a couple times, and everything looks in order—click **Replace & Find** instead. It replaces the current match, and then finds the next one all in one step. Repeat as many times as necessary.

- If you're sure you want *every* match replaced, then click **Replace All**, and FileMaker does the entire find-replace-find-replace dance for you. File-Maker always asks you if you're sure about Replace All first, just in case. For instance, if you have some clients whose last name is Anderson and others whose company name is Anderson, you may *not* want to use the Replace All option. You need to check each occurrence individually to make sure you don't accidentally change someone's last name.

6. **When you're done with the Find/Replace window, click Close.**

Note: Find/Replace has no undo, and since you can replace across all records and fields, it can be dangerous. Be careful with this command. Also, it can take a long time because it looks through the individual words in each field. If you're searching across all records, and you have lots of records, be prepared to wait a while as FileMaker does its magic.

Changing Text Appearance

Much like a word processor, FileMaker has commands to set the font, size, style, and alignment of the text in a field. When a field is active, or you've selected some text in a field, you can choose from any command in the Format menu. Also like a word processor, you can apply formats to paragraphs of text and you can even create tab stops within a field.

Text Formatting

You can use all the usual commands (font, size, style, alignment, line spacing, and text color) individually, or use the handy Formatting bar.

Find with Replace vs. Find/Replace

You may be wondering how Find mode combined with Replace Field Contents is different from Find/Replace (discussed earlier in this chapter). In fact, they're very different, but deciding which to use can be confusing. Here are some guidelines:

- Find mode is significantly faster at finding things than Find/Replace. In Find mode, FileMaker uses something called an *index*, which lets it find 10 matching records out of 293,000 in an instant. Find/Replace, on the other hand, looks through the fields the same way you would: one by one. It's faster than you, but it still takes time.

- Replace Field Contents always operates on one field across the entire found set. Find/Replace, on the other hand, also lets you replace across all fields in just the current record, as well as all fields in all records of the found set.

- Replace Field Contents always replaces the *entire* contents of the field. You can't replace every occurrence of "teh" with "the" for example. You can only give a new value that replaces everything in the field.

- Most important, Replace Field Contents assumes you've already found the records you want, and always modifies every record in the found set. Find/Replace adds a second layer of searching, as it scours the record or the found set looking for matches.

So why would you ever use Replace Field Contents? Sometimes you really do want to replace everything in the field every time, just like in the Company Name example on page 72. Also, Replace Field Contents is *significantly* faster at changing lots of records than Find/Replace. It takes just a few seconds to accomplish what Find/Replace would spend several minutes doing.

In general, if you want to find records, use Find mode, but if you want to find certain bits of text, use Find/Replace. Likewise, if you want to replace everything in a field in *every* record, use Replace Field Contents, but if you want to replace little bits of text, use Find/Replace. (If you want to replace little bits of text across thousands of records, study first, or be prepared to take a vacation while your computer thinks about it.)

Finally, you have no reason not to mix Find/Replace with Find mode. Since Find/Replace searches records only in the found set, you can establish a good found set *first* to make your Find/Replace go faster. (For example, if you're replacing "teh" with "the" in the Notes field, then you may as well find all the records that have "teh" in their Notes fields first, since Find mode is so much faster than Find/Replace.)

Each of these text formatting commands lets you override the original formatting for a field on a record-by-record basis. That is, changing a word to bold on one record doesn't affect any words in any other record in the database. So while it can be handy to make the occasional note stand out (as you see in Figure 2-13), professional database designers rarely use these commands to format individual chunks of text. Instead, they change the formatting of a given field in Layout mode. Formatting performed in Layout mode will apply to every record in the database. You'll learn how to do that in Part 2.

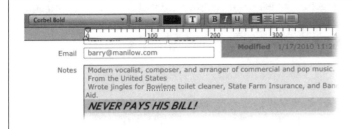

Figure 2-13:
The results of a session using the Formatting bar. The Notes field shows the formatted text, and the toolbar shows the font, size, style, and colors chosen. You can access the toolbar by choosing View→Formatting Bar.

Tip: If you change your mind about formatting, and want to put the text back to its normal state, here's a trick that lets you do it with four quick keystrokes: Select all the text (Ctrl+A or ⌘-A), cut the selection (Ctrl+X or ⌘-X), paste it right back in the field (Ctrl+V or ⌘-V), and finally Undo (Ctrl+Z or ⌘-Z). The pasted text comes back with its ugly formatting at first, but the undo doesn't remove the *text*, it removes the *formatting*. The same trick works if you paste data in from another source, like Word or an email message. If the text comes with formatting you want to lose, just do that undo voodoo that you do right after you paste.

Paragraph Formatting

FileMaker doesn't stop with text (or *character*) formatting. It also has some paragraph formatting tools that come in handy. Well, they're handy if you can find them. You have to go through the Line Spacing dialog box to get there. To see the dialog box in Figure 2-14, choose Format→Line Spacing→Other.

There you see all the stuff you'd expect to be able to do to a paragraph in a field. You can align the paragraph, indent it from the left or the right, and give it a first-line indent. You can change line spacing and add space above and below a paragraph. There's even a handy Apply button so you can examine how it's going to look before you close the dialog box. Finally, a Tabs button gives you access to another dialog box, this time for setting tab stops.

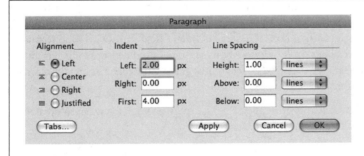

Figure 2-14:
This hidden dialog box can make text in a field more legible. In your sample database, you may have noticed how the text stands a little away from the left edge of the field border (see Figure 2-13). That was done on the layout, but you can add this effect to a field in one record with the settings shown above.

Remember, just like text formatting commands, any paragraph formatting you apply in Browse mode changes only the record and the field that's active when you choose the command. This ability comes in handy sometimes, but people use the Layout cousins of these commands far more often.

The Text Ruler

The Text Ruler (View→Text Ruler) is a visual version of the Paragraph formatting dialog box. Use it to set indents and tab stops. The ruler has an arrow icon for the Left, Right, and First Line indent settings (Figure 2-15), which you just drag to the spot on the ruler where you want the indent set. You'll learn how to set tab stops on the next page.

When you turn on the Text Ruler, FileMaker adds a space along the top of the window to hold the ruler. When you're in a field, the ruler itself appears in the portion of this space directly above the field, with the zero point on the ruler lined up with the left edge of the field. (When you're not in a field, the ruler just measures the width of the content area.)

Figure 2-15:
Like most word processors, FileMaker has a text ruler that lets you position margin markers right where you want them. When you drag the Left indent arrow (the one on the bottom), it moves the First Line arrow (the one on the top) with it, so first drag the Left indent arrow where you want it, and then move the First Line arrow. If you want to move the Left indent arrow without moving the First Line arrow, then hold down the Alt (Option) key while you drag.

Formatting Tabs

Since a field can hold just about any kind of text, you might eventually need to use tab stops *within* a field. For example, you could have a nice large field into which you paste rows of text from a spreadsheet. To make things line up properly, you can set tab stops for each column of text. To type a tab into a field, press Ctrl+Tab (Option-Tab). This is a special keystroke, obviously, because in FileMaker pressing Tab jumps you to the next *field*. See page 302 to learn how Field Controls make plain old tabs work the way you're used to.

Like most word processing programs, FileMaker gives you two ways to create tab stops: the Text Ruler and the Tabs dialog box.

Setting tabs in the Text Ruler

With your cursor in a field, you can insert a new tab stop simply by clicking anywhere in the ruler. A small right-pointing arrow appears where you clicked, representing a *left* tab stop. (The arrow shows you what direction text goes when you start typing.) FileMaker also supports other kinds of tab stops, but to get them, you have to visit the Tabs dialog box, described next.

Setting tabs in the Tabs dialog box

The Tabs dialog box is a laborious way of setting tabs, but it gives you more options because you can control all aspects of each tab stop manually. Here's the drill:

1. **With your cursor in a field choose Format→Line Spacing→Other.**

   The Paragraph dialog box makes its entrance.

2. **Click Tabs.**

   Ta-da! You found the Tabs dialog box (Figure 2-16).

Tip: If the Text Ruler is showing (Figure 2-15), then you can get to the Tabs dialog box quickly. Just double-click any tab stop in the ruler. The Tabs dialog box opens with the clicked tab preselected.

To make a new tab stop, simply select the appropriate options, and then click New. A new entry appears in the list named after the Position you specified. The Apply button lets you see the results of your settings without closing the dialog box. You can create up to 20 tab stops, after which the New button is turned off. If you try to add a tab stop at a ruler position where one already exists, then the new stop simply replaces the old one.

Once you've created a tab stop, you can edit or delete it at will. Drag a tab around on the Text ruler to move it, or drag it off the bottom to delete it. Use the dialog box's Clear button to delete a tab, if you prefer that method.

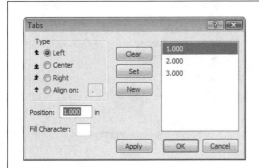

Figure 2-16:
The Tabs dialog box lists all the tab stops set for a field in the list on the right. You can also adjust a tab stop, delete it, or add a new one. Each stop has a Type, Position, and Fill Character. To change the settings for any existing stop, first select the stop, edit the settings, and then click Set.

Checking Spelling

Before printing out your database or otherwise sharing it with the greater public, you want to make sure your spelling is correct. Nothing screams "amateur" louder than a City field that reads "Chciago." All the spell checking commands are found under the Edit→Spelling menu.

Spell Checking with Menu Commands

Sometimes you want to fly through data entry, and then do your spell checking later. If this is your preference, you have three choices:

- Choose Edit→Spelling→Check Selection to spell check selected text only. This method comes in handy when you're pretty sure a short passage, or even a single word, is wrong. Highlight the text you want to check, and then choose the menu command.

- To check an entire record, choose Edit→Spelling→Check Record.

- Finally, you might want to check spelling on many records at once. In this case, choose Edit→Spelling→Check All. When you choose this option, you're telling the spell checker to look at every field of every record in the current found set (choose Records→Show All first if you want to check *every* record in the database).

No matter how many records you're checking, FileMaker opens the same Spelling dialog box shown in Figure 2-17.

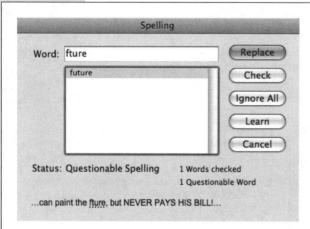

Figure 2-17:
The spell checker found a typo—"fture". You can see the misspelled word in the Word box, and underlined in red in the box at the bottom of the window. If FileMaker figures out the correct spelling, then, in the list under the Word box, it selects the spelling. And if you're the type who calculates your gas mileage every time you fuel up, you'll be delighted to discover that FileMaker keeps track of how many words you've spelled wrong so far, and tells you at the bottom of the window.

TROUBLESHOOTING MOMENT

Units

In the figures in this chapter, the Indent options are specified in inches (you see "in" next to each text box). FileMaker actually has a setting for the unit used here and other places. FileMaker comes factory-set to inches, but it's nothing if not flexible. You can use inches, centimeters, or pixels—the choice is yours. If you're used to the metric system, by all means tell FileMaker to use centimeters. Or choose pixels for *really* precise control over text positioning. Here's how to change how FileMaker displays measurements:

If the Paragraph dialog box is open, click Cancel. The remainder of these steps work only if your database's main window is in front.

1. Choose View→Layout Mode. In this mode, the content area of the window changes somewhat. Don't be alarmed…and don't click anything in the window. (If you accidentally change something, that's OK. FileMaker soon asks if you want to save.)

2. Choose Layouts→Set Rulers to open the Set Rulers dialog box.

3. In the Units pop-up menu, choose Pixels. (If you'd rather use different units, you can select anything you like. You can always repeat these steps later to get things back.)

4. Click OK, and then choose View→Browse Mode.

You should be back where you started now. If you get a message asking if you want to save your changes, click Don't Save; this question refers to any accidental changes you made to the layout itself, not to the change of ruler units.

Note: Even if, by the magic of planetary alignment, you have no misspellings, FileMaker still opens the Spelling dialog box. In this case, though, it says "Status: Finished Spelling" in small print in the middle of the busy window. You're supposed to spot this right away and know the program's done. Of course, if you're like most people, you stare blankly at the screen for 30 seconds trying to figure out what went wrong first. Save yourself the confusion: Check the Status line when the window first appears. If FileMaker is finished, click Done.

Near the bottom, the Spelling window says Status: Questionable Spelling. The Word text box displays the word in question. Things can proceed from here few different ways:

- Usually the correctly spelled word appears in the list of suggested spellings. If it does, click the correct spelling, and then click Replace. (Or just double-click the correct word.)

- If you don't see the right spelling, correct it yourself. Type the correct spelling into the Word box. To confirm that your new spelling is correct, click Check; the status line changes to say Correct Spelling if you got it right. Otherwise, you're back where you started, with a misspelled word and a few suggestions below it.

- If you spelled it right originally, but FileMaker doesn't agree, click Ignore All to tell FileMaker to skip this so-called misspelling. Better yet, click Learn to teach FileMaker the word so it doesn't bother you in the future. (Clicking Learn adds the word to your current user dictionary, which is explained below. Ignore All only ignores the word temporarily; if you quit FileMaker and come back later, then it thinks the word is misspelled again.)

- If you change your mind and want to stop the spell checker, just click Cancel. This doesn't undo your changes; it just closes the dialog box.

- When the spell checker has finished, the status line changes to say Finished Spelling, and the Replace button says Done. Click the Done button to close the dialog box.

Spell Checking As You Type

FileMaker's spell checker also works automatically as you type. This *visual* spell check is a per-database setting, so you control it from the File Options dialog box. Choose File→File Options, and then click the Spelling tab. You find two options that you can mix and match to help you spell better, run faster, and jump higher. Well, you'll spell better, anyway.

The first option is "Indicate questionable words with special underline." If you miss your word processor, this one makes you feel right at home. You see that familiar red line underneath any word FileMaker doesn't like the looks of. Plus, if you right-click (Control-click on the Mac) the underlined word, and then, from the shortcut menu, choose Suggested Spellings, then FileMaker offers suggestions for spelling the word properly. If you see the correct spelling among the suggestions, just click it and File-Maker will replace the misspelled version. From the same menu, you can also tell FileMaker to learn the word or ignore it.

If red lines don't get your attention, then you can turn on "Beep on questionable spellings", and FileMaker makes your computer beep when you type a space after a misspelled word. Unfortunately, it's just the same old alert beep that your computer makes in all kinds of other situations—so you can easily miss it. But in combination with the red line, this pair can be a formidable reminder to spell better.

Tip: Visual spell checking can be handy. But often in a database your data entry includes things that don't need to be spell checked (inventory codes, abbreviations, email addresses and the like). Luckily, when you design your own databases, you can turn off the as-you-type version of spell checking for any particular field. See page 304 for details.

Managing Spelling Dictionaries

FileMaker comes with spelling dictionaries for various languages, and you can easily choose among them. Just choose Edit→Spelling→Select Dictionaries. The Select Dictionaries window lets you choose the language to use for all spell checking operations. You can see it in Figure 2-18.

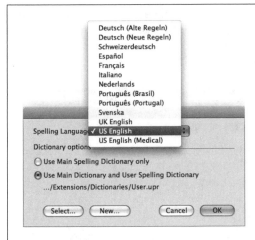

Figure 2-18:
Out of the box, FileMaker uses a Spelling Language that matches the language of your operating system. But you can use a different language if you prefer. Just select it from this pop-up menu. As you can see, FileMaker even has a medical language dictionary that keeps it from balking at all your ER terms. Use the New button to create as many user dictionaries as you want, and then select the one you want to use for a particular database.

User dictionaries

Remember from "Spell Checking as You Type" when you clicked the Learn button to teach FileMaker a new word? When you did so, behind the scenes, FileMaker actually added that word to the *user dictionary*, which is separate from the normal dictionary that comes with FileMaker.

You can even have multiple user dictionaries for different purposes. For example, if you have two databases, one that tracks your apparel products and one that stores information about tools, it might make sense to keep two user dictionaries. The tools version might include words like "mm" and "pcs" while the apparel version would have "XXL" and "CottonPoly".

Tip: In reality, it's nine times easier to just use one user dictionary, so you don't have to worry about which one is selected. It doesn't hurt to have thousands of words in your user dictionary, but not having enough makes spell checking more time consuming. Nothing's more boring than wading through the same dozen correctly spelled words over and over. But, if you want more than one dictionary, you can have it.

Preview Mode and Printing

It's a cruel fact of life that eventually you need to put your data on paper. You might want mailing labels for all your customers in Canada, or a special printed form prefilled with patient information for insurance filing. Sometimes you just need your data with you when you're away from your computer. As you'll learn in Part 2, you can arrange the data any way you want in FileMaker, and make certain *layouts* that are particularly suitable for printing. But for now, remember that FileMaker lets you print *anything* you see onscreen (just choose File→Print). Its Print dialog box has a few special options. Figure 2-19 shows the Windows version. You can see the Mac OS X version (which requires a little more digging) in Figure 2-20.

POWER USERS' CLINIC

Rewriting the Dictionary

You've already learned how to add to your dictionary using the Learn button in the spell checker. Well, if you've ever wanted to just *tell* it what words you want it to skip, you can. Just choose Edit→Spelling→Edit User Dictionary to open the User Dictionary dialog box. Here you can add new entries to the dictionary (type the word, and then click Add), or remove existing entries (select the word, and then click Remove).

You can also export all the entries to a text file where you can edit them to your heart's content. When you click Export, FileMaker asks where it should save the export file. The file is a plain text file with one word on each line, which you can edit in a text-editing program.

If you already have a file that has words you want, then you can import those words into your user dictionary in one shot. For instance, if you use a lot of technical terms, then you might be able to download a list of terms from your industry and load them into a dictionary. The file has to have each word on its own line, so if it's in some other format, then you need to clean it up first. (For example, use your word processor's Find/Replace function to turn a comma-separated list into one with a carriage return between each word.)

Also, make sure the file is plain text. A Microsoft Word file (.doc) or other special format won't work. (Making a plain-text file on Windows is a breeze: Just use Notepad, the simple text-editor program in the Accessories folder in your Start menu. On Mac OS X, however, you need a little more care. You can use Text Edit—it's in your Applications folder—but you have to tell it you want plain text. Just choose Format→Make Plain Text before you save the file.)

Using the Import and Export features together can be particularly useful. You can export your user dictionary, edit it manually in the text-editing program (where making lots of edits might be easier), and then import it back in.

Figure 2-19:
FileMaker's Print dialog box gives you all the standard options, plus a little more. The Print pop-up menu (at the top in the dialog box in Windows) lets you tell FileMaker which records to print.

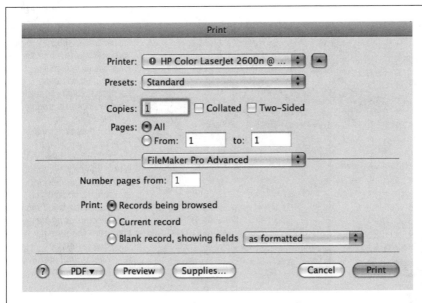

Figure 2-20:
On Mac OS X, FileMaker's special print options are tucked away in a secret place. You have to choose FileMaker Pro or FileMaker Pro Advanced from this unnamed but very important pop-up menu. In this example, you can see the field styles you can pick from if you elect to print a "Blank record, showing fields".

- "Records being browsed" tells FileMaker to print every record in the found set. To print all your Canadian customers, find them first, and then choose this option.

- Current record prints just the current record, which comes in handy when you just want to print *one* thing: your doctor's contact information to keep in the car, perhaps, or maybe Aunt Edna's candied yams recipe.

- Blank record, showing fields tells FileMaker to print what's onscreen with no data at all. You can change the look of each field to a box or an underline if you want (from the pop-up menu shown in Figures 2-19 and 2-20, just pick your choice). Choose this option if you want to hand out pages for people to fill out with a pen (it's a kind of antique writing device), and later type their responses into the real database.

To see how the printout is going to look without committing trees to it, you can use *Preview mode* (Figure 2-21). You access Preview mode via the View menu, the Mode pop-up menu, or Ctrl+U (⌘-U) (see page 19).

Note: When you first go to Preview mode, the page count says "?" instead of the number of pages. FileMaker doesn't know how many pages it'll print until you force it to count them. If you drag the Page Slider all the way to the right, then FileMaker shows the last page. On its way there, FileMaker counts the pages, too. The process may take some time in a large document, but FileMaker catches up eventually.

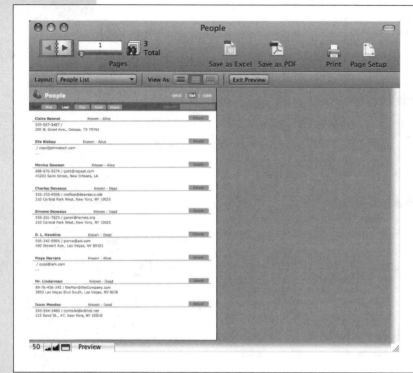

Figure 2-21:
Preview mode shows you what your database looks like as though it were printed on paper. For instance, you can see whether FileMaker's going to chop off any information that doesn't fit on the page (anything beyond the width of the page simply isn't printed). Preview mode also indicates the margins, and lets you flip through the found set page by page using the book icon. The current page number appears where the current record number was displayed in Browse mode.

On some computers and printers, you can reduce the printout by a percentage using File→Print Setup (Page Setup on Mac). When you do, Preview mode shows the page proportionately larger or smaller so you can see how the content area fits on the page. The scaling options you get vary by computer, operating system, and printer.

Note: Preview mode also has some green, tree-saving tools: Instead of printing, you can use one of the buttons in the Status toolbar to save the records you're viewing as an Excel file or a PDF. But if you do have to print, the Page Setup and Print dialog boxes are just a click away. Those standard page setup options affect Preview mode. If you change the paper orientation, then your print preview changes right away.

Part Two: Building Your First Database

II

Creating a Custom Database

In Part 1, you learned that you can work organically, flowing smoothly from finding, to sorting, and then to editing data as your needs dictate. In Part 2, you'll learn that FileMaker lets you create databases in a natural order, too. For starters, you'll create some fields for storing data about your property leasing business, and then you'll learn how to control layouts so they display data the way you want to see it.

Note: The tutorials in Part 2 serve as a general introduction to database creation. You'll go through the basics of all the major tasks associated with creating most databases. Later sections go into more detail on the bigger topics, but you'll get a solid foundation by reading Chapters 3 and 4 straight through.

Creating a New Database

When you create a database from scratch, you see both familiar territory and some brand new concepts right away. For example, when you launch a word processing program, and then open a new document, you can type a lot of text before you remember to save your document. But when you create a database, you need to give your document a name and some basic structure before you can enter any data. That's partly because of the automatic saving feature you learned about on page 46. Another reason is that you have to tell FileMaker about the fields you'll be using to store your data. Here's how to get started creating a new database file:

1. **Double-click the FileMaker Pro icon to launch the program.**

   The Quick Start screen appears (Figure 3-1).

Tip: If you see a standard Open File dialog box instead of the Quick Start screen, just go to the Help menu, and then choose Quick Start screen. Select "Show this screen when FileMaker Pro opens" at the bottom of the Quick Start screen to make that your preferred open screen.

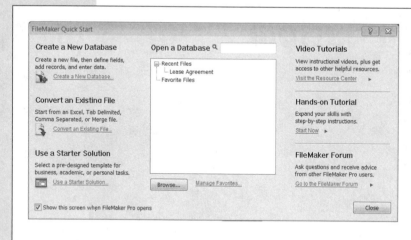

Figure 3-1:
From the Quick Start screen, you can create new files or click shortcut links to existing ones. Get help from a hands-on tutorial, watch instructional videos, or hang out with other FileMaker Pro fans in a forum sponsored by FileMaker, Inc. Tell the Quick Start screen not to show up by turning off "Show this screen when FileMaker opens". That way, the next time you launch FileMaker, you'll see a standard Open File dialog box.

2. **Click the "Create a New Database" option. In the Save As field, type** *Lease Agreement,* **and then choose a location to save your file.**

   The "Create a new file named" dialog box is very similar to a Save dialog box. You can name your new file and navigate through your folders to find your favorite storage spot.

3. **Click Save when you're done.**

   A new database window appears in Table view (page 50) ready for you to start creating fields.

Note: It might seem odd to name the file "Lease Agreement" (singular) and not "Lease Agreements" (plural). After all, the file is meant to store many agreements. True enough, and for that reason many developers always use the plural case for their file and table names. But at the record level, you'd never put two peoples' first names in one field, so it doesn't make sense to name the field "First Names." It's easier to remember never to use plural case than it is to remember a set of rules for naming database structural items, so in this chapter you'll stick to singular case.

UP TO SPEED

Jumpstart the Quick Start Screen

There's a lot of power packed into the Quick Start screen. On page 90, you learned how to use the "Create a New Database" link to get started on a custom database. The "Use a Starter Solution" link gives you access to FileMaker's handy templates, including business, academic and personal templates.

Click the "Convert an Existing File" link to convert older files (those with a pre-fp7 file extension) to the fp7 format. If you select a file that's already got an fp7 file extension, FileMaker creates a new copy of the file you select. This command also converts databases from other sources, like Excel, dBase, or Bento (Mac only).

In the middle section, you see a list of shortcuts to File-Maker files:

- **Recent Files.** FileMaker remembers which files you've opened recently. Set the number displayed in

the list (it's automatically set at 10) by choosing File-Maker Pro→Preferences (Mac) or Edit→Preferences (Windows), and then type the number you want in the "Show recently opened files" field.

- **Favorite Files.** You determine which files appear in this list. Click Manage Favorites in the Quick Start screen or choose File→Open Favorites→Manage Favorites to customize your favorites list. Or add the file you're working on to the list with File→Open Favorites→Add Current File to Favorites.

- **FileMaker Server.** FileMaker Server lets lots of people share the same database (Chapter 17). You can add your favorites to this list with the tools listed above.

- **The Browse Button.** Click to show the standard Open File dialog box, from which you can navigate your computer or network to the file(s) you need.

Creating and Managing Fields in Table View

When you create a new database in FileMaker Pro 11, the file starts out in Table view. There isn't much else to look at though. Figure 3-2 shows the familiar tools of your Status toolbar. But since the file has no fields and no records, these tools aren't very useful yet. First you need to think about the fields the database needs for storing data in a logical manner.

Figure 3-2:
This database window looks like a brand-new spreadsheet with only one cell. Unlike a spreadsheet, you determine how many "columns" of data you need before you store data in the file. The Create Field button lets you give that first field a name. Once your first field is named, a "+" symbol lets you create and name more fields. The "+" symbol to the left of the "row" creates new records.

UP TO SPEED

Think Table

You need to understand the concept of a *table* when you're creating a database. So in addition to having some tools that aren't available in other views, Table view can also help you visualize how FileMaker stores your data.

In any particular table, every record has a field to store the *same kind* of information. If you see a field called Email Address on one record, it'll also be available for every other record.

When you're deciding what fields to put in your database, it helps to imagine, or a spreadsheet. As you've just seen,

FileMaker even lets you switch your view of the database to Table view, where your data is presented like a spreadsheet (page 50).

Spreadsheets have rows, which are equivalent to the records in your table, and they have columns, which are the equivalent of the table's fields. If you have a column in one row, obviously, it's there for every row. If you add a new column, even after you've added 100 rows, that column is available to all the rows at once.

Creating Fields

The Lease Agreement database will track the names of people to whom you lease houses and how much money you can expect to receive for rental fees over the life of each lease. Your first task is to create the fields you'll need to run your growing empire. Here's the list of fields you need:

- First Name
- Last Name
- Rental Fee
- Lease Duration
- Date Signed
- Lease Document

Here's how to create a field in Table View:

1. **Click the Create Field button.**

2. **The button's text changes to the word "Field" and the area is highlighted.**

3. **Type *First Name*, and then press Enter.**

    The first field's name is accepted.

Repeat the process once to create the Last Name field. Don't be thrown by the change in the column head's name. It only says "Create Field" on the first column. After that, it just says "Field." If you're creating lots of fields at once, you can click the "+" sign to accept a new field name and create another new field with a single click.

UP TO SPEED

A Field = Individually Significant Data

Your database tracks lease documents, and its fields will include all of the important attributes about those documents. How do you decide which fields to create?

For example, you might create a single Name field to hold lease signees' first and last names —but you'd be making a mistake. What if you need to sort your data by last name? If you've entered names the way you might type them in a word processor (first name and then last name), you'd only be able to sort by the person's first name.

It's usually a bad move to have different kinds of information in the same field. Instead, think about what elements— no matter how small—are important to how you'll search, sort, analyze, and otherwise access your records later. In database lingo, those bits of information are *individually significant*, and each one should get its own field.

For example, a US address often contains several pieces of information: street name, optional suite number, city and zip code. If you stored all that data in one field, you'd have a hard time searching for all the people in Washington state. Your search results would include records with streets or cities called Washington. So when you're deciding which fields you need, ask yourself: "Which bits of my data are *individually significant?*"

It's usually not necessary to split off a suite number from a street address field, but it's usually best to split off the city, state, and Zip code. But if you have a compelling reason to split off a bit of data (say you have to do targeted mailings to people with street numbers ranging from 1000 to 1500), then it may make sense for you to split street addresses into two, or even more, fields.

Managing Field Types

People's names are considered text, because they're made up of alphabetical characters. When you created fields using the simple technique above, you didn't have to do anything special to create a field that's ideal for storing text. But when you need to store numbers, dates or times, you should create fields meant to store those types of data. To set a field's type, repeat the steps in the tutorial above, and then click the tiny triangle to the right of the field's new name. A hierarchical menu appears that lets you change the new field's type (Figure 3-3).

To change the Rental Fee field from its original type of text to number, choose Field Type→Number. If you choose the wrong type, just go back to the menu, and then choose the type you need.

You can even change a field's type after you've started entering data in your database. But since some field types have stringent data entry requirements, some of your data can change if you do. For example, text fields can hold more data than number fields, so if you change a text field that contains a lot of data to a number field, some data could be lost when you switch field types. So it's definitely safer to make sure you've chosen the right field type before you enter data. See page 236 for more information on other field types and how to decide which field type is right for your data.

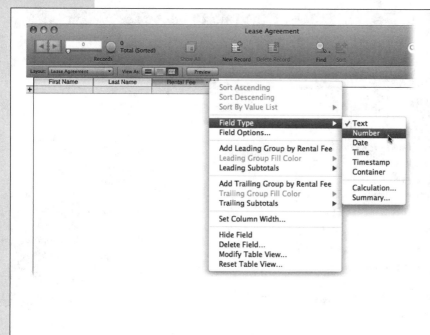

Figure 3-3:
This menu appears only when you're in Table view. The menu lets you sort the records you're viewing (page 38), manage the fields you're creating and change the design of your data screen (page 53). Choose Set Column Width to change the width of the field in Table view. You can also hide a field from view or even delete it from the database. Because deleting a field also deletes the data it contains, FileMaker gives you a chance to cancel when you choose this command.

Note: If you change a field type, don't be alarmed if you get a warning message box. FileMaker's making sure you know about the ways existing data will be changed. At this point, you don't have any data yet, so those warnings don't matter.

Now create your remaining fields and set their field types. Here's a list of the fields you need and the field type to select for each:

- Lease Duration: number

- Date Signed: date

- Lease Document: container

Creating Records in Table View

Now that you've created your fields, your first database is ready to use. Entering data in Table view isn't much different than entering in Form view (page 50) or List view. Get started by clicking in the First Name field. Notice that as soon as you click, File-Maker gets a step ahead of you by creating a place for your next new record. In other words, your Table view now looks like it has two rows.

Be careful though. That row is just a placeholder. While it looks like a new record has been created, notice the book icon in your Status toolbar. The number of records in your database hasn't increased. The record only gets created when you actually click in that new space. It might seem confusing at first, but this process keeps you from creating blank records in your database.

Tip: That new second row has a + sign to its left. This button comes in handy if you know you'll need a specific number of records. You can click the + button until you have a set number of records, and then start entering data if you want to. But if you don't like loose ends (and empty records) cluttering up your database, it's usually safest to create one record at the time.

Type this information into your first record:

- First Name: Antione
- Last Name: Batiste
- Rental Fee: 985.00
- Lease Duration: 12
- Date Signed: 7/15/2010

Notice that you can use the tab key to move from field to field. But unlike a spreadsheet, where you might expect to go a new row after you get to the last field in that row, the cursor cycles back to the first field of the record's row instead. To move down, click in the next row. And as soon as you click, FileMaker again creates space for the next record.

Inserting a File into a Container Field

Container fields can hold pictures, audio clips, videos, or even other files. Earlier you created a container field so the Lease Agreement database can store a scanned copy of each Lease Agreement for quick reference any time you need it. It's time to learn how to place a PDF in your container field.

Note: You can use any PDF file on your hard drive for the next tutorial, or you can download sample PDFs from this book's Missing CD page at *www.missingmanuals.com/cds*.

---

1. **Click in the Lease Document field.**

   The field's borders become solid to show that it's active. If a Record dialog box appears, you double-clicked the field. That dialog box lets you use your computer's microphone to record a sound clip that can be stored in the database. Click Cancel to close the Record dialog box if it appears.

2. **Choose Insert→File.**

3. **The Insert File dialog box appears. It looks like a standard Open dialog box.**

   Find, and then select the PDF file called *aBatiste.pdf* (if you downloaded the sample files for this chapter earlier). Or you can use any sample pdf file on your hard drive.

4. **Click Open.**

   A small icon and file name appear in the Lease Document field.

The PDF file is now stored inside your database. Read on to see a good reason for storing files inside your database.

Exporting Field Contents

If something ever happens to the original PDF file, you can open the Lease Document.fp7 file, find the record containing the document you need (you'd probably search by First and Last name), and then export the record. When you do, FileMaker creates a new copy of the PDF, outside of your database. Here's how it works:

1. **Click in the Lease Document field to select it.**

   You have to tell FileMaker which field contains the file you need.

2. **Choose Edit→Export Field Contents.**

   The Export Field to File dialog box appears.

3. **Navigate to the folder into which you want to save the PDF file, and then click Save.**

   You don't even need to type a new file name. FileMaker knows the file's original name and is ready to recreate it exactly as it was. Of course, you're free to change the name if you want.

See the box on page 98 for information on the handy options at the bottom of the Export Field to File dialog box.

If you had lots of records, it would be very easy to find the ones that didn't have their PDFs inserted, because the Lease Document field would be blank. If you switch to Form or List view, you can see that the file name doesn't line up properly with the data in other fields.

Inserting a File Using QuickTime

Inserting a PDF using the Insert→File command can help you turn your workplace into a paperless office. But sometimes it makes sense to link to a file without placing it into the database itself. For example, your Lease Document is saved as a PDF file. That means you can take advantage of a QuickTime feature to view your document in FileMaker without all the hassle of exporting it first.

When you use the Insert→QuickTime command, the PDF isn't stored in your database. FileMaker remembers where the document is stored and creates a link to it. Then instead of a file icon, you'll see a thumbnail image of the document, and you can use the QuickTime controller bar to flip through the document's pages.

1. **Click in the Lease Document field.**

    The field's borders become solid to show that it's active.

2. **Choose Insert→QuickTime.**

    The Insert QuickTime dialog box appears,

3. **Find, and then select the PDF file you want to link to.**

    Unlike Insert→File, only PDF documents (and QuickTime videos) are available for selection.

4. **Click Open.**

    The PDF appears as a thumbnail in the Lease Document field.

If you inserted a multiple-page PDF, you can use the field's controller bar to flip through the pages in your document. You can see the thumbnail, but it's so tiny that you can barely read it. In the next section, you'll learn how to customize your database so it looks more polished, and you'll be able to see a usable thumbnail . For that, you'll have to learn how layouts work.

Warning: Since you're storing a link to the file instead of placing it inside the database, FileMaker will lose track of the document if you move or rename it after you create the link in the container field. When the link is broken, the field can't display the thumbnail and controller. Instead you'll see a message that says "The file cannot be found:" followed by the file's name. So make sure that you have a file organization system in place before you start storing PDFs as QuickTime documents.

Understanding Layouts

Tables help you organize and store your data, but layouts determine how that data appears. Layouts determine the text formatting of your data and even where each field appears onscreen. Layouts are so critical to the way your database performs that FileMaker automatically creates a layout to go with each table you create. When you created the Lease Agreement file at the beginning of this chapter, FileMaker made a layout to hold the fields you created.

POWER USERS' CLINIC

Getting the Most Out of Your Fields

The Edit→Export Field Contents command isn't limited to container fields. With very few exceptions, you can export the contents of almost any field to a file (if you can't click in the field, then you can't export its contents, and you can't export a sound you recorded in FileMaker). To understand why you can't click in some fields, read about field behavior in Chapter 6, and about security in Chapter 16.

Here are some examples of how to export to your advantage:

- Use Edit→Export Field Contents to create a file without having to retype what you've stored in FileMaker. But if you just whiz by the Export Field to File dialog box without looking, you'll miss a couple of options that'll save you buckets of time. If you want to watch a QuickTime video at a size larger than the skimpy container field, just select the "Automatically open file" option as you export the contents of your field. FileMaker creates a duplicate video file for you, and then opens a QuickTime player for your viewing pleasure.

- In fact, FileMaker is smart enough to open the right program for whatever you've exported. You'll get a text editor for text, a PDF viewer for a PDF, or a graphics viewer for graphics. You don't have to scramble

around looking for a program that can handle your file, because FileMaker figures it out for you.

- If you want to spread the wealth around—let your colleagues know about a customer who always makes a big order at the beginning of the new quarter, for instance—then turn on the "Create email with file as attachment" option when you export your field contents. FileMaker makes a file, and then launches your email program, starts a new email message, and attaches your newly-exported file to it. All you have to do is type a name, subject, and some text, and then send the email on its merry way. FileMaker can send email through Microsoft Outlook, Outlook Express and Eudora on Windows, and through Entourage, Mail, and Eudora on the Macintosh.

Let FileMaker really impress you by clicking both options at once. You'll get a copy of the file open for reference and a fresh, shiny email nearly ready for sending. If you've got the screen real estate, you can look at both of these little jewels while you're checking out the FileMaker record that spawned them.

You already know one way that layouts give your data visual structure. For example, when you switch from Table view to Form view (page 50), the data changes from a spreadsheet-like list to a record-by-record version of your data. But a more powerful way to change your data's appearance is to use Layout Mode. There you get access to graphics and designing tools that let you change fonts, add color, paste in your logo or move your fields around so that your database can match your company's branding. Many of FileMaker's most powerful features are set up in Layout mode, so it's not just about making your database pretty.

One database file can contain as many layouts as you want. So you can create one layout for data entry and another for printing. And now that many users have very large computer monitors, it often makes sense to create one List layout for an on-screen report and a separate report layout meant for printing that same information.

Note: Layout mode has so many features that this book devotes two entire chapters to designing layouts (Chapters 7 and 14). In your real working life, you'll switch frequently between Browse and Layout modes, so this first section begins by helping you identify the basic tools and commands you'll use for layouts.

The Layout Bar

The Layout bar is tucked between the Status toolbar and the Content Area of your window. At the left of the Layout Bar is a Layout pop-up menu so you can switch between your layouts (once you get more than one layout, that is). Form, List, and Table View buttons are to the right of the Layout pop-up menu. And over at the right edge is the Edit Layout button (Detail and List view only). Click the Edit Layout button to switch from Browse mode to Layout mode. (Or you can use the View menu commands, or the Mode pop-up menu near the bottom left edge of the window.)

Tip: If you can't see the Layout bar, it may because the whole Status toolbar is hidden. Click the Status toolbar control button at the bottom of your window to show it (look between the Zoom controls and the Mode pop-up menu). Or Mac only: Click the oblong button at upper–right corner of your window to toggle the Status toolbar on and off.

The Layout Status Toolbar and Layout Mode

When you switch to Layout mode, the Layout Status toolbar also changes to show the tools you need to customize your layout. Even the menu choices and available commands have changed. Two new menus (Layouts and Arrange) have appeared, the Records menu is gone, and if you stroll through the menus that seem to have the same name, you'll see that they have many new commands in them.

Before you start designing, it makes sense to get familiar with these new tools. Figure 3-4 shows what your database looks like in Layout mode and points out the tools and objects you need to identify when you're doing basic layout design. See Chapters 7 and 14 for information on the tools not labeled in this figure.

Tip: Since the tools in Layout mode are different than in Browse mode, you can customize each toolbar separately. Choose View→Customize Status Toolbar to see the collection of buttons and tools available in each mode.

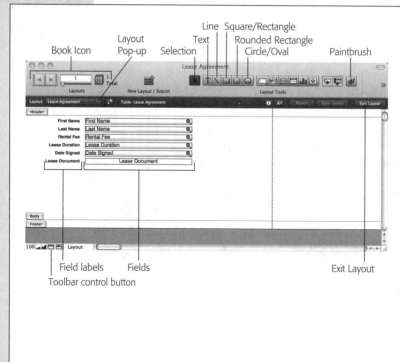

Figure 3-4:
The tools in the Status toolbar change when you switch to Layout mode. The book icon now counts your layouts instead of records as it does in Browse mode. In place of the New Record button, you now see a New Layout/Report button. The toolbar shows standard graphics tools like a pointer (also called the selection tool), type-creation and shape-drawing tools. Below the Status toolbar is the darker grey Layout bar. The Content Area shows field labels at the left (they're separate text objects), which you can select and edit as if they were text in a word processor. Fields can be moved and resized like drawn objects, plus you can change their font and color with formatting menus and tools.

Layout Objects

The items you see in the content area of a layout are called objects, and they're the basic building blocks for all layouts. You can click individual objects to move, resize, or format them. You can use your favorite technique for selecting multiple objects (see the box on page 102) and apply formatting to groups of objects at one time. There's even a Format Painter tool to copy formatting from one object to other objects of the same type.

A layout features eight types of objects, and each one has its own specific uses and behaviors. Here's an introduction to each type:

- **Text objects.** Text objects appear on nearly every layout you create. Field labels are text objects that can be moved and formatted separately from the fields they identify. All the formatting you learned about in Chapter 2 can be applied to text objects. The spell checker even works in Layout mode, except that it checks text objects instead of data inside fields. And if you're using the visual spell-checking feature (page 82), you'll see the dotted red underlines if you make a typo or misspell a word.

- **Lines and Shapes.** FileMaker has some tools for creating basic lines and shapes. You can create a colored box and place it behind a group of fields to help your database's user understand which bits of information belong together. Or add lines to reports to make them easier to read.

- **Images.** For more graphic power than FileMaker provides, use a program like Photoshop or Illustrator (or any graphics program you prefer) to create your graphics, and then place them on your layout. You can place your company's logo on a layout created to print invoices or you can use a tiny button icon next to an Email field as a visual reminder of what's inside the field.

Tip: Don't get carried away importing too many graphics onto a layout though. If you're sharing a database, either over your office network (Chapter 17) or over the Internet (page 735) your database can slow down.

- **Fields.** Fields are the heart and soul of your database, so expect to see them on every layout you create. You can easily tell the difference between fields and text objects, because fields have solid borders around them to show their shape and dimensions. Each field's name appears inside the borders, so you can tell them apart from one another. Just like text objects, you can apply text and paragraph formatting to fields, and then the formatting you choose will apply to all the data that appears in your formatted field.

Tip: Fields are so important that FileMaker's normal behavior is to add any new field you create to the layout without even asking you. That's helpful in the beginning stages of creating a database, but can become annoying after you've honed your layouts to look just so. Turn off this behavior by choosing Edit→Preferences (Windows) or FileMaker Pro→Preferences (Mac). Click the Layout tab, and then click "Add newly defined fields to current layout" to deselect it.

- **Portals.** Portals let you see records from other tables on your layout. Find out how they work on page 146.

- **Tab Controls.** Tab Controls probably aren't what they sound like (they have nothing to do with the Tab key). Instead they help you make use of the limited space on your layouts. Get the lowdown on page 155.

- **Web Viewers.** Web Viewers are like miniature web browsers. See page 612 for more information.

- **Charts.** Charts let you convert your dry data to visual form. See page 624 to learn how to create and manage them.

Note: Nearly any object on a layout can be made into a button, and there's a Button tool for creating them from scratch. But they're a bit of hybrid and not strictly a type unto themselves. See page 317 for more.

POWER USERS' CLINIC

Selecting Lots of Objects

Selecting objects on a layout is such a common task that FileMaker gives you several ways to do it. You can always click an object to select it, but you can use any of the following methods as well:

If you want to select more than one object (so you can operate on them all at once), select the first object, press Shift, and then click each additional object. As you click, each object joins the selection. If you accidentally select an object, Shift-click it again to deselect it.

To select *everything* on the layout, choose Edit→Select All or press Ctrl+A (⌘-A).

You can even select every object of a certain type (every field, for example). First select one object of the type you want. On Windows, press Shift, and then choose Edit→Select All. On Mac OS X, press Option, and then choose Edit→Select Same. FileMaker selects every object that's similar to the one you selected yourself.

If you have more than one type of object selected when you choose this command, then FileMaker selects every object like any of the selected objects. For example, to select every field *and* every text object, select one field and one text object, and then choose this command.

Finally, you can easily select objects that are close together on the layout with the selection rectangle technique. When you click an empty place on the layout and drag, FileMaker shows a dotted rectangle called the selection rectangle. Once you release the mouse button, anything inside the rectangle is selected. If you press Ctrl (⌘), then the rectangle selects every item it *touches*, not just the objects it completely surrounds.

Customizing a Layout

FileMaker gives you so many tools for customizing layouts that you can while away hours making each layout look just the way you want it to. Don't mistake this time as wasted effort. The principles of good design and software usability apply to even the most basic database. After all, if you're going to be staring at your database for hours every day, it should look and feel polished. And few databases have just one user (see Chapter 17 to learn how to share your database). So when you're customizing layouts, you have to keep other people's needs in mind, not just your own.

Good design isn't just about how things look. It's also about helping people figure out how the database works. For example, when you're storing data for Contact Management, you want to arrange objects like address fields in forms that people are familiar with. Most U.S. addresses are shown in a standard form like this:

```
Name
Street Address
City, State Zip
```

To make other people—your database's *users*—feel at home in your database, you should arrange your fields as close to that standard arrangement as possible. So a good arrangement of basic fields on your Contact layout would be to have your First Name and Last Name fields on the same line, with the Street Address on the second line, and the City, State, and Zip fields arranged on the third line and resized to the relative widths each bit of data usually takes up. That is, state names are almost always stored as two-letter abbreviations, so the State field can be very narrow compared to the City field. Finally, you'd group the name and address fields together in a "chunk" and add a little space between the name/address chunk and other chunks of data on your layout (Figure 3-5).

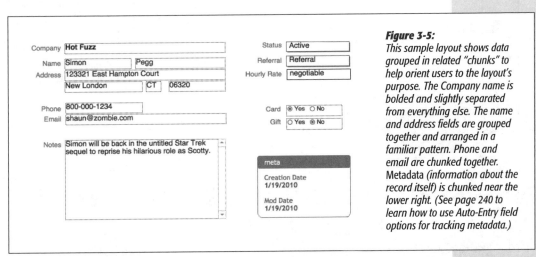

Figure 3-5:
This sample layout shows data grouped in related "chunks" to help orient users to the layout's purpose. The Company name is bolded and slightly separated from everything else. The name and address fields are grouped together and arranged in a familiar pattern. Phone and email are chunked together. Metadata (information about the record itself) is chunked near the lower right. (See page 240 to learn how to use Auto-Entry field options for tracking metadata.)

The principles for good software design have filled many books and websites. Despite their massive usefulness, most of those principles are beyond the scope of this book. However, as you're trying to decide how to arrange your layouts for maximum efficiency and impact you can take a look at FileMaker's Starter files. See the box on page 104 for more information. Of course the sample files for this book aim to keep good design principles in mind, too.

Editing Text Objects and Fields

Looking at your Lease Agreement layout, you can see that FileMaker plopped all your fields out in a column and sized them generically according to their types when it created your layout. It's up to you to arrange the objects so they make sense. You need to know how to move, resize, edit, and delete objects to chunk your name fields and labels. You also need to know how to import a logo to brand your database and add a splash of color to make it more Data 2.0 than FileMaker's stark white background. Before you get started, take a look at Figure 3-6 to see the end result you're shooting for.

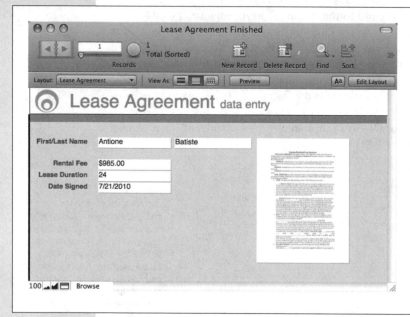

Figure 3-6:
Here's a preview of your finished layout. The layout features a logo and title, and the data has been chunked together to help make visual sense. The Lease Document container field is larger, and you can see a thumbnail version of the file itself. The Rental Fee field has been formatted for currency, and the Lease Duration and Date Signed fields have field controls that make data entry quick and consistent.

UP TO SPEED

Explore Starter Solutions

FileMaker's starter solutions are grouped in general categories, like Business, Education, and Home. They cover common database uses, like Invoices, Expense Reports, Home Budgets, Music Libraries, and Contact Management.

These starter files are a good showcase of FileMaker's features, but because they're generalized templates, they aren't meant to meet *your* specific business needs. Even if you think about starting small, these files may need a lot of retrofitting to work well as your business grows. However, poking around in these files is a great way to spark ideas about features you want to learn how to create, to get a handle on some good ways to organize your data and create layouts.

So feel free to take a look at a few starter files, and then come back to this book to learn how make a solution that's tailored to your business rules and procedures. Here's how:

1. To create a new database from a Starter Solution, choose File→New From Starter Solution.

The Starter Solution dialog box appears. Every solution template is listed automatically, but you can filter the samples by clicking any item in the list at the left of the dialog box.

2. Click the "Email Campaign Management" sample in the template window, and then click Choose.

You see a standard Save dialog box with the name of the sample you chose in the Save As field.

3. If you want to change the file's name, type the new name, and then select a location for saving the file. Finally click Save.

The new database appears onscreen.

You can start entering data and exploring the file right away. As you move through the chapters in this book, you'll be able to understand what you're seeing under the hood of these starter solutions.

Moving and resizing fields

To chunk your data on the Lease Agreement layout, it makes sense to put the First Name and Last Name fields on the same line. To save space and be more helpful, you can change the field label for the First Name field to read "First/Last Name." Here's how:

1. **Switch to Layout mode.**

   Use the Edit Layout button, the View menu, or the Layout pop-up menu.

2. **Click the First Name field to select it. Then press Shift as you click the Last Name field to add it to your selection.**

   A handle appears at each corner of both fields to show that they're selected.

3. **Click any handle on the right edge of either field, and then drag toward the left side of the layout to shorten the fields. Release the mouse when the fields are about half their original width.**

   As you drag, dotted outlines show you what size the fields will be when you release the mouse button.

4. **Shift-click the First Name field to deselect it.**

   You want to leave just the Last Name field selected.

5. **Drag the Last Name field up inline with, and a short distance to the right of the First Name field.**

   Notice that as you drag, FileMaker shows an indicator line at the bottom of the field's name to help you line it up with the First Name field.

Tip: Pressing Shift as you move an object constrains it so that it moves in one direction only—either horizontally or vertically. You determine which direction when you drag. Remember this handy tip to keep your objects nicely lined up when you want to create a little space between your data chunks.

Any object on a layout can be selected and then moved or resized. Only fields and text objects have the handy indicator line, though. Later in this section you'll learn about the Inspector, which has other tools to align objects.

Using object grids

As you were moving fields around in the previous tutorial, you may have noticed a kind of magnetic pull that helped you align the Last Name field with the First Name field as you moved it. That pull is provided by Object Grids, which are invisible 6-pixel increments that restrict an object's movement. It's a big timesaver, unless you don't want an object to align with the grid. But you can work around the grids in several ways:

- To skirt the grid temporarily, press Ctrl (⌘) as you drag the object. As long as the key is down, you can drag the object smoothly to any spot on the layout.

- Choose Arrange→Object Grids to turn the grid off. (You can always turn it on again any time you want by repeating this menu command.)

- Press any of the arrow keys to move the selected object (or objects) 1 pixel in any direction. You can press a key repeatedly to carefully nudge an object into place.

Viewing sample data

If you make a field too narrow, the data inside it will appear cut off or truncated. (Don't worry, the data's there, it just doesn't all show up.) So to help you figure out how wide a field needs to be to show its data comfortably, choose View→Show→Sample Data. The field names are replaced with data from the record that was active when you switched to Layout mode. When you want to see the field names again, choose the same command to turn the feature off.

POWER USERS' CLINIC

Exercising Constraint

FileMaker has a few tricks up its sleeve to make moving and resizing objects easier. You already know how to press Shift to constrain mouse movement (see the tip on page 105). Here are a few more goodies:

- Press the Ctrl (Windows) or Option (Mac) key while creating or resizing a rectangle, rounded rectangle, or oval to make a perfect square or circle. When working with a line, this key makes it perfectly horizontal, perfectly vertical, or exactly 45° from one of these directions.

- Change a rectangle to a square, or an oval to a circle, by pressing Ctrl (Windows) or Option (Mac) as you resize an object.

- With an object (or objects) selected, press any of the arrow keys to move the object 1 pixel in the appropriate direction.

- Duplicate an object by pressing Ctrl (Option) while you drag it. Add the Shift key to the mix to make sure the new object stays aligned with the original.

- Choose Edit→Duplicate command to create a new object that's 6 pixels to the right and 6 pixels below the original. Shortcuts are Ctrl-D (Windows) and ⌘-D (Mac).

- Choose Arrange→Object Grids to turn another alignment feature on or off. Instead of moving with pixel-by-pixel freedom—which can make things nearly impossible to line up—things on the layout automatically align themselves to an invisible grid as you drag them. You can set the spacing of this grid by choosing Layouts→Set Rulers, and then adjusting the "Grid spacing" value.

As if that weren't enough, you can use the Inspector to move objects as well. If the palette says the left edge of an object is two inches from the ruler origin, then you can type 4 into the Left Position field to move it 2 inches farther into the layout.

Note: Even if the field is too narrow to display all its data, you can still type lots of text into the field in Browse mode. The data scrolls as you type, so the field can't display all that lovely data at once (unless you widen the field, or make it multiple lines high). See page 289 to learn how to add a scroll bar to a field.

Editing text objects

The text objects you're concerned about now are field labels. They're usually created along with the fields they describe. But they're separate objects, so you can apply one font and size to a field and a different font/size combo to its label. Here's how to edit a text object:

1. **In Layout Mode, click the Text tool to select it. It's a button with a capital T on it (Figure 3-4).**

   The pointer turns to a insertion point as you move across your layout's content area.

2. **Click in the text label, between "First" and "Name."**

   A dotted outline appears around the text object to show you've hit the mark. The cursor will blink where you clicked.

3. **Edit the label to read *First/Last Name*.**

   The slash indicates that there are two separate fields provided for data entry.

4. **Click any other layout object, or onto the blank space of the Content Area to switch back to your pointer tool.**

   You've edited your text label.

The shortcut for selecting the Text tool, and then clicking into a text object, is to double-click the object. Double-click where you want the insertion point to appear. But if it's off by a character or so, just use your arrows keys to move it, and then start typing. A triple click selects a whole word within a text object.

Note: If you never edit a field label, it will stay in sync with the field name if it's changed. But once you edit the field label, that connection is broken and you'll need to edit it manually if you need it to change after you've changed the field's name.

On your layout, the name fields are in place and their label reads correctly. But now there's a stray field label taking up valuable real estate.

POWER USERS' CLINIC

Locking the Layout Tools

After you've edited a text object with the Text tool (page 107), the Selection tool is automatically reactivated. FileMaker assumes you want to work with just one text object, and saves you the trouble of switching back to the Selection tool. If you need to create or edit several objects of the same type, give the tool icon a *double-click* instead of a single-click. The icon on the button turns a slightly darker shade of gray to let you know the tool is locked. With a locked Text tool, you can create as many text objects as you want: Click to create the text box, type the text, click again for another text box, and so forth. When you're finished, click the selection tool again to make it active, or just press Esc.

If, for some reason, you don't like FileMaker always switching back to the Selection tool on your behalf, then you can instruct it to lock the drawing tools automatically—so even a single click keeps a tool active until you say otherwise. In Windows, choose Edit→Preferences; in Mac OS X, choose FileMaker Pro→Preferences. In the Preferences window, select the Layout tab, and then turn on the "Always lock layout tools" checkbox. If you're like most people, you may want to switch this checkbox off after a few minutes of working with it; just revisit the Layout tab of the preferences window, and then uncheck the preference.

Deleting objects

Delete any object on a layout by selecting it, and then pressing the Delete (or Backspace) key on your keyboard. Now that the Last Name field label is a solo act, select it, and then delete it. If you prefer using the mouse, you can select an object, and then choose the Edit→Clear command, but that's extra steps.

UP TO SPEED

Find and Replace Revisited

If your assistant thought he'd be helpful and added a ":" to the end of every field label on your layout, you don't have to visit every text object one by one to clean up the mess. Use Find/Replace to fix every field label on a layout in just one shot. When you're in Layout mode, the Find/Replace command searches through text on the layout itself rather than the data in fields and records.

The slightly pared-down dialog box you see when you choose Edit→Find/Replace→Find/Replace in Layout mode looks and works just like its Browse mode counterpart, aside from the lack of "Search across" and "Search within" options.

The other commands on the Edit→Find/Replace submenu—Find Again, "Replace & Find Again", and Find Selected—also work exactly as they do in Browse mode. (See page 72 for details on Find/Replace.)

Adding text objects

Text objects serve more purposes than just field labels. Even relatively simple databases can have many layouts, so it's helpful to put a title at the top of each layout to help you remember what the layout is for. Or you can add helpful hints, like "use the format XX-XX-XXXX" beside a date field to remind data entry folks to enter dates with a four-digit year. Here's how to add a descriptive title to your layout.

1. **In Layout mode, click the Text tool to select it, and then click near the top of the layout, where the title should appear.**

    A dotted outline with a blinking insertion point appears where you clicked.

2. **Type *Lease Agreement data entry* in the text box.**

    Your new title's text is all the same font and size.

3. **To make your layout match Figure 3-6, select the appropriate parts of the new text block, and then use the Format menu to change the text's font and size.**

    A shortcut for changing font size is to select the text, and then type the shortcut Ctrl (⌘) +Shift-< or Ctrl (⌘) +Shift->.

For short bits of text, like a title for your layout or a completely custom field label, just click, and then start typing. But if you want to add a block of text that might need paragraph-style formatting (like automatic line breaks and alignment), you should drag to define the height and width of the text block before you start typing in the new text object.

Note: You can choose any font you want from your computer's system, but every font you choose has to be installed on the computer where your database is used. If FileMaker can't find the font you choose, it'll substitute a plain one instead. So unless you're the only person who'll ever use your database, it's best to stick with the old standbys most folks are likely to have.

Using the Inspector

The Inspector is the central clearinghouse for controlling nearly every property of your layout objects (Figure 3-7). There's so much information on the Inspector that it has to be broken into three tabs worth of information. Each tab is also divided into sections that you can display or hide by clicking the white triangle to the left of the section's title. When you hide or show a section, the Inspector shrinks or grows to fit the appropriate options. And since those options change based on the object (or objects) selected, don't be alarmed if your Inspector seems to have a life of its own.

If the Inspector isn't showing on your layout, choose View→Inspector. If no information is showing in the Inspector when it appears, make sure you have at least one object selected.

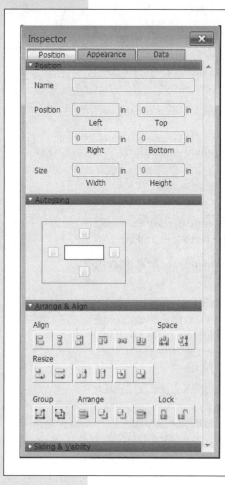

Figure 3-7:
*The Inspector shows the properties of the active object. If your
Inspector shows "0" in many of its fields or if the buttons are grayed
out, you probably don't have an object selected on your layout. Or
if you have a group of objects selected, you may see some options
dimmed because they can't be applied to some of the objects in the
group. If you don't see what you need, just change what you have
selected on your layout.*

*The Inspector is so useful that you can even create multiple ver-
sions of it, each one displaying a different tab. Choose View→New
Inspector to get a second, or even a third Inspector, and then click
the tab you want to see on each one. All Inspectors are tied to the
same object (or group of objects), so any changes you make to
any Inspector will affect every selected object. Multi-Inspectors are
meant to let you view all of an object's properties at once, without
needing to switch tabs.*

The Inspector doesn't just show you an object's properties, it lets you change them
too. For example, the layout title you created in the last tutorial might be straddling
that dotted line that separates the layout's Header part from its Body part (see page
269 for more on layout parts). You can give the title a little breathing room by making the Header a little taller. Here's how:

1. **In Layout Mode, click the Header label to select it.**

    It's on the left side of the layout content area. The Header label turns a darker
    gray to show that it's selected.

2. **If you don't have an Inspector showing, choose View→Inspector. If it's in the
    way of the objects you're focusing on, move it out of the way by dragging on
    its title bar.**

    The Inspector appears, and it's showing the Header's properties.

Formatting Text

Fields and text objects both show text. You can change the font, size, color, and style of both types of objects. First, select the objects. Then go to the Format menu. The first seven submenus let you manipulate the text formatting of the selected object.

- The Format→Font menu shows fonts installed on your computer. (In Windows, you may need to choose Format→Font→More Fonts, and then add the fonts you want to your font list. In Mac OS X, every font you have installed is automatically listed.)

- You can dress up your text in any font, size, and style you like. But don't forget that the computer your database is *used* on has to have the font installed. You have fancy $300 fonts on your computer, but your employees may be using the database on stripped-down PCs. You want to pick a font that comes standard with your operating system so everybody sees the same lovely letterforms.

- From the Format→Size menu, you can choose a size. If you don't see the one you want, choose Format→Size→Custom instead. In the window that appears, type any number from 1 to 500.

- If you're designing a database on the Mac for use on PCs, then you need to make all your text objects just a little larger than you (and FileMaker) think they need to be, because PCs display fonts larger than their Mac brethren do. You should check your layouts on a PC, because any text object that isn't wide enough flows over onto another line or may be cut off, which probably isn't what you intended.

- FileMaker includes all the standard styles (bold, italic, and so on) in the Format→Style menu. You can pick from three different types of underlines (Word Underline underlines words, but not the space between them, and Double Underline puts two lines under your text). You can also choose Upper Case, Lower Case, or Title Case to format the case of text no matter how you typed it.

- The options in Format→Align Text let you align the text left-to-right and top-to-bottom. For instance, if you choose Bottom, then the text sticks to the bottom of the text object when you make it taller. This setting makes sense only if you type multiple lines of text into a text object. For instance, you may have a paragraph of explanatory text you want to show on the layout to help people.

- Choose Format→Line Spacing→Double to apply double-spacing (or choose Format→Line Spacing→ Other to specify the spacing more precisely).

- To color your text, point to Format→Text Color. A color palette appears, and the color you select is applied to the selected text.

- The Format→Orientation menu applies only to text in Asian languages, and lets you run text either vertically or horizontally.

You can apply each of these options to an entire text object (just select the object first) or to a run of text *inside* the object. To style just a portion of the text, use the Text tool to select a portion of the text first. In this way, you can mix fonts, sizes, and styles inside a single text object.

3. **If the Position tab isn't active, click it.**

The fields you need for changing the Header's height are found on the Position tab. Measurement systems are shown in the increment label to the right of each position and size field.

4. **Click any measurement label to change the measurement system to pixels.**

   You may have to click a few times to get to the system you want. The measurement choices are: inches (in), centimeters (cm), and pixels (px). Since you're designing this layout for the screen, it makes sense to use a screen measurement system. All the labels change when you change one.

5. **In the size section of the Position tab, click in the Height field. Type *40* in the Height field, and then tab or click out of the field to make the change.**

   The Header will increase in height.

Alternatively, you could drag the dividing line between the Header and Body to resize it as you keep your eye on Inspector's display to see when you get to the right height. Either way is fine. Use the method you find easier.

You may need to move the layout title's text block now that the Header height is changed. Make sure that the text block fits completely within the Header. If it overlaps the Body part by even one pixel, you may get unintended display problems. You'll learn more about Layout Parts on page 269.

Tip: Text formatting commands are so commonly-used that they're available in the Format menu and on the Formatting Bar. But most of those commands are also grouped on the Inspector's Appearance tab.

Inserting a Picture on a Layout

You've already seen how to insert a file into a container field, but that's not the only way to use outside resources in FileMaker. You can put your company's logo on your layouts to make them look more customized and professional. Use any common graphic file format: jpeg, gif, png, eps, tiff, bmp, or wmf. Some other formats can also be used. See FileMaker Pro Help (page 851) for details.

Note: If you downloaded the sample lease documents earlier in this chapter, you have a sample logo file you can use for this tutorial. If not, go to this book's Missing CD page at *www.missingmanuals.com/cds*.

Here's how to place a graphic on a layout:

1. **In Layout Mode, click Insert→Picture, and then navigate to the folder where you've stored the sample files from this chapter.**

   If you didn't download the files earlier, you can place any .gif, .jpg, or .png file, but your results won't be the same as Figure 3-6.

2. **Select the mark.png file, and then click Open.**

   The logo appears on your layout, but it's too big. Luckily though, it's already selected.

3. **In the Inspector's Width field, type *40* and then press Tab.**

4. **Type *40* in the Height field, and then press Tab again to complete the resize.**

The logo is now small enough to fit inside the Header. Simply drag it into place.

You can use your clipboard to copy and paste a graphic onto a layout. Most of the time, it works just fine. But for some file formats, you may get unexpected results. If you do, delete the funky graphic, and then use Insert→Picture.

Adding Lines and Shapes

FileMaker has a handful of basic line and shape drawing tools, which are always available in the Status toolbar—unless you've customized it and removed them (page 99) or if your window is very narrow (just widen it to see all the tools). A companion piece to the toolbar—the Formatting bar—gives you more control over your drawn objects. If you can't see a Font pop-up menu and some alignment tools just below the Status toolbar, yours isn't showing yet. Choose View→Formatting Bar to display it. Now you're ready to draw a line at the top of the Body part. But there's a secret: this line is actually a long, short rectangle. Here's how:

1. **In Layout mode, on the Formatting bar, change the Line setting to 0 pt by choosing None. Choose a color you like from the Fill pop-up menu. Set the Effect to None.**

Not only are you telling FileMaker how the rectangle should look before you draw it, you're setting up the automatic formatting for the Rectangle tool. Any new object you draw with the Rectangle tool will have these same settings.

2. **Choose the Rectangle tool, and then drag on your layout to create a rectangle that's approximately where the bold "line" is at the top of the Body part in Figure 3-6.**

You don't have to be precise when you create the rectangle because it's easier to use the Inspector to get it in place and in shape.

3. **In the Left position field, type *0*, and in the Top position field, type *41*. Then type *577* in the Right field and *53* in the bottom field. Don't forget to press the Tab after the last setting.**

As you tab from field to field, the dimensions of your rectangle change per each new setting. Press Shift-Tab to move backwards through the fields.

Your new rectangle helps divide that plain white layout into useful chunks (Figure 3-8). The layout's title is in the header, and you're starting to create a space for your data to reside.

Tip: Presetting your automatic formatting also works for the Text tool. If your corporate font is Helvetica (beautiful, beautiful Helvetica!), make sure no layout object is selected, and then choose Helvetica from the Formatting bar's pop-up font menu or from the Format→Font menu. You've just set the automatic default for all new text blocks.

Figure 3-8:
Both these lines are the same length, according to the Inspector. But as you can see, the lighter gray line extends past its right handle. Rectangles with a line of 0 points are more predictable.

But why use a rectangle instead of a line? Because lines that are thicker than a point actually stick out past their apparent length by the amount of their thickness. That is, if you make a line 8 points tall, it's also wider at the left and right than the Inspector thinks it is. Try creating a line, and then placing it at "0" on the left. Now take a look at the line's handles – you'll see that the line actually pokes out about 8 extra pixels on the right end. If the line's by itself on your layout, it might not matter much. But when you have lots of objects with varying thicknesses of lines, using the Inspector to make items the same height or width doesn't work as you'd expect. You can make it work with some math, but it's just easier to draw a rectangle when you want a thicker line.

Formatting Fields

For most layout objects, the Inspector's Data tab is a dim, gray dud. But when a field's at stake, that third tab comes into its own (Figure 3-9). There you can set up data formatting controls that display currency, percents, and negative numbers the way you want to see them. You can also give a field a pop-up menu or drop-down list, a drop-down calendar or assign a checkbox or radio button set to the field. Chapter 7 gives details about all the Data tab's options, but you'll meet a few of them here.

Formatting a Number field

The Rental Fee field contains the amount of rent each Lease Document specifies. Because it will contain numbers, you made it a number type field when you created it. Now it's time to learn about the Inspector's suite of formatting options for number fields.

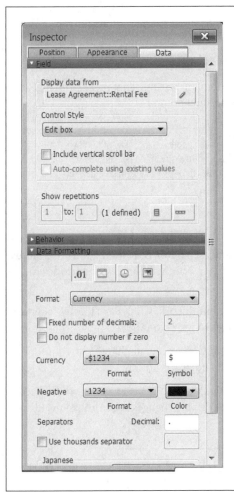

Figure 3-9:
*The Inspector's Data Tab as it appears when the Rental Fee field
is selected. The options in the Data Formatting section change,
depending on the field type of the selected field. The scroll bar
indicates that this inspector isn't tall enough to show all its options.
See Figure 3-10 for a view of the Inspector's Data tab that shows the
entire Data Formatting section.*

Since a Rental Fee is currency data, that's the format you'll apply. Number formatting
doesn't change the value in the field, it just changes the display of that data. By applying a format, you can save keystrokes and make the data more consistent. Here's
how to apply the currency format to a number field:

1. **In Layout mode, click the Rental Fee field to select it, and then click to show
   the Inspector's Data tab.**

   If the whole Inspector's disappeared, choose View→Inspector. Once the Data
   tab's selected, you'll see all the options you can apply to the Rental Fee field.
   Data Formatting is down near the bottom (Figure 3-9).

2. **Choose Currency from the Format pop-up menu.**

   The Data Formatting section changes to show all the options for the Currency format.

3. **Choose the "Fixed number of decimals" option.**

   The number 2 is the unsurprising automatic setting. That means you'll get two places to the right of the currency's decimal point.

Tip: The most common reason to change this option is to suppress the display of numbers to the right of the decimal place, even if you enter those characters. So if the entry in the field is "985.99", the field will show "986" instead. FileMaker uses normal rounding rules to display the formatted data. Enter "0" in the Fixed number of decimals fields to get this format.

---

4. **Choose the "Use thousands separator" option.**

   The standard character for a thousands separator is a comma, but you can use any other character you'd prefer. Another common choice is a period, which is used in some European countries.

5. **Switch to Browse mode to view your handiwork. Click Save if FileMaker asks whether you want to Save the changes to the layout.**

   You can tell FileMaker to stop asking you about layout changes by choosing the "Save layout changes automatically (do not ask)" option.

Click in the Rental Fee field; you can see that the data appears just as you entered it. But when you're not clicked in the field, the display changes according to the formatting options you just set.

Tip: If the Data Formatting option you want to use is dimmed, check your field's type, which has to match its format. For example, you can't apply a time format to a text field or number formatting to a container field.

Adding a field control style and a value list

Consistent data entry is critical to a well-behaved database. If you're tracking students for your school district, and the best half of your data entry folks type a school's name as "Glenwood Elementary School," and the mediocre half type "Glenwood School," and the lazy third half barely manage to peck out "Glnwod," you're going to have a mess on your hands. But you can control what users put into fields that should contain only specific bits of data.

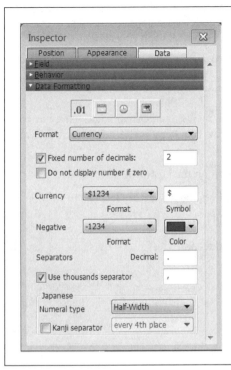

Figure 3-10:
Here, all Inspector sections except Data Formatting are closed up. Since Data Formatting is at the bottom of the Data Tab, it's helpful to close up the sections you're not focused on if you have a smaller monitor or are working on a laptop. If you don't close up the sections, you can still get to the options you need by dragging the Inspector's scrollbar. Note: the Japanese options are useful only if you're using Japanese fonts for showing Japanese number characters. Otherwise, you can safely ignore those settings.

Your database doesn't store school names, but you do limit your properties' leases to durations of 1, 2, or 3 years, and you want the data entered in months only. Here's how to create a value list that lets your data entry people know what values belong in the Lease Duration field:

1. **In Layout mode, click the Lease Duration field to select it, and then click the Inspector's Data tab.**

    If the whole Inspector's disappeared, choose View→Inspector.

2. **In the Field section of the Inspector, select "Drop-down list" from the Control style pop-up menu.**

    The "Values from" pop-up menu appears, but there's nothing in it. You have to create a value list for the field to display.

3. **Click the Pencil icon next to the "Values from" pop-up menu.**

    The Manage Value Lists for "Lease Agreement" dialog box appears.

4. **Click the New button.**

    The Edit Value List dialog box appears.

5. Type *Lease Duration* in the Value List Name field.

   A simple descriptive name is the best policy for database elements. In this case, you're matching the value list's name to the field you'll be assigning it to.

6. **Click in the "Use custom values" field, and then type the numbers** *12, 24,* **and** *36,* **without any commas and pressing Enter (Return) after 12 and 24, so each number is on its own line. (Figure 3-11).**

   You're typing the number of months in 1, 2, and 3 years, and each has to be on a separate line. Each line represents one item in the drop-down list you're creating.

7. **Click the OK button until you're back on the layout.**

   The Lease Duration value list now shows the Inspector's "Values from" pop-up.

8. **Click the "Include arrow to show and hide list" option.**

   The arrow will appear in Browse mode, and gives users a visual clue that the field contains a drop-down list.

Switch to Browse mode to see the new drop-down list in action. When you click in any field, you'll see the list's arrow appear at the right edge of the Lease Duration field. Click the arrow to see the drop-down list itself.

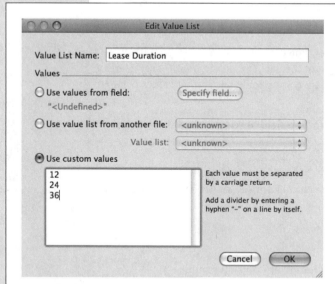

Figure 3-11:
When you name elements in your database, it helps to give them descriptive names. In this case, the new value list will be used to limit the data entry in the Lease Duration field, so even though it's the same name as the field itself, that's the best name to give the value list. Notice that each value is on its own line, and there's no trailing paragraph symbol after the last value in the list.

Editing a value list

If your business rules change and you need to change the values that display in the value list, it's easy to edit. Select the field your value list is attached to (Lease Duration, in this case), open up the Inspector to the Data tab, and then click the Pencil icon next to the value list's name. Click Edit, and then make the appropriate changes. Click OK until you're back on your layout. Finally, switch to Browse mode to see the new values.

Note: Changing the value list has no effect on any data that's already in that field. But now you have the option to select the new value going forward.

Adding a drop-down calendar to a field

FileMaker is picky about how you store dates in date fields. To make data entry easy, you can add a handy visual calendar to your date fields. Here's how.

1. **In Layout Mode, click the Date Signed field to select it, and then click the Inspector's Data tab, if it isn't visible.**

   If the whole Inspector's disappeared, choose View→Inspector.

2. **In the Field section of the Inspector, choose "Drop-down calendar" from the Control Style pop-up menu.**

   It's the last item on the list.

3. **Choose the "Include icon to show and hide calendar" option.**

   The calendar will drop down even if you don't choose this option, but this way your users can tell it's there.

Switch to Browse mode. Click in any field to activate the record. You'll see the calendar icon at the right edge of the Date Signed field (Figure 3-12). Click the icon to view the calendar pop-up menu. The calendar's left and right arrows go to the previous and next month. Its up and down arrows go to the next and previous year on the Mac or click the Month/Year title to change years on Windows. Your keyboard arrow keys move through the calendar's dates. To enter the current date, just click the Today display at the bottom of the calendar.

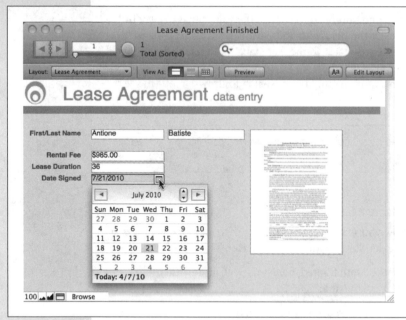

Figure 3-12:
A Drop-down calendar ensures that dates are entered according to FileMaker's rules. It appears when you click or tab into a field that's been formatted to show it. On Windows, drop-down lists or calendars may pop up instead, if the window isn't big enough to contain all their glory. You don't have to use the calendar to enter data even if a field has been formatted to show one. Just click in the field and type away, but be sure to enter a FileMaker-approved format (7/21/2010, 7.21.2010, or 7-21-2010, for example).

Controlling field borders

When you add a field control style to a field, you can see the calendar icon or the arrow on the field when the record is *active* (page 50). But you may not see those same clues in layout mode or when the record isn't active. To make them show up, you'll need to apply a border to the field.

1. **In Layout mode, use your favorite multiple-object selection technique to select the Lease Duration and Date Signed fields.**

   You can apply formatting to multiple items at the same time, so long as they can each accept the type of formatting involved.

2. **On the Inspector, click the Appearance tab, and then make sure the Object section is expanded (Figure 3-13).**

   True, the Formatting bar has a Line pop-up menu color swatch, and pattern pop-up. But the Inspector has options that give you more control. For example, when you apply a border using the Formatting bar's Line pop-up menu, you'll get borders on all four edges of your object.

3. **Click the Inspector's Right border button, and then choose Hairline from the Line thickness pop-up menu.**

   Because the field control icons appear on the right edge of the field, you don't have to have a border on all four sides of your field to get the icon to show up. Since borders on the top and left edge of a field can interfere with the legibility of the data inside the field, here less really is more.

4. **From the "Line color" pop-up menu, choose the same color you used when you drew the thick line in the tutorial on page 113.**

   Colors other than the standard black or gray can look subtler on the layout. However, the most important thing on a layout is the information it holds. Don't get carried away by choosing so many formats and colors that your data gets lost in the visual clutter.

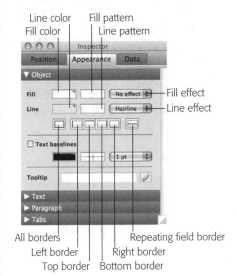

Figure 3-13:
If you're confused about what the buttons and options in this section do, hover your mouse over a button to see a helpful tip. Text blocks, fields, rectangles/squares and circle/ovals can all have borders applied to them. But not all options are available for all objects. For example, the Repeating field border applies only to fields. And Text baselines can only be applied to text blocks and to all field types except container fields.

The field control style icons show up as soon as you apply a right border to the fields. When you switch to Browse mode, each field shows its field control style icon, even if the record isn't active.

Tip: If you still can't see your fields' borders in Layout mode, choose View→Show→Field Boundaries. When this option is turned on, you'll see black borders around all the fields on your layout, no matter what formats they have. Turn this option off to see the formats themselves.

Customizing a Layout's Body Part

So far you've customized your layout by moving, resizing, and formatting layout objects. But you can also make changes to the more structural pieces of your layout, called the Layout Parts (you'll learn about them on page 269). To make your layout look more like the one in Figure 3-6, you'll add color to the Body part of the layout and adjust its size.

Adding color to a layout part

The standard layout is always white. Sure it's a nice clean color, but it can get tiresome to stare at black and white screens all day long. A little color makes the layout look more modern, and can reduce eyestrain, too, if you choose soothing colors that have enough contrast to pick out your data, but not so much that you need sunglasses to cut down the glare.

1. **In Layout mode, click the label for your Body part.**

   That's how you select a part before you can format it.

2. **In the Formatting bar, click the Fill pop-up menu. If you can't see the Formatting bar, choose View→Formatting Bar.**

   The Fill pop-up menu contains a set of premixed colors. The Other Color option lets you mix your own, using your operating system's color mixing tools.

3. **Choose a relatively light color.**

   The Missing CD sample file uses a grayish green.

Switch to Browse mode to see the changes. The Body part is colored, but so are the fields. Go back to Layout mode and use your favorite technique to highlight all the fields, and then change their Fill to white. And if you want to get sophisticated, you can change the fields' Line setting to Hairline in a calming shade of light gray.

Adjusting the Body part's height

The layout now has a nice color that makes your fields stand out. But if you want to chunk your data better (group the fields together and make the container field larger), you'll need to know how to change the Body part's size.

1. **In Layout mode, place your mouse over the bottom line of the Body part, and then hold down the mouse button.**

   If you're exactly on top of the line, the pointer changes to an equals sign with up- and down-pointing arrows.

2. **Drag the Body part until it's the height you want.**

   Since the point of resizing is to make room for a larger container field, you may need to experiment a bit to get just the effect you want.

The tutorial gives you a free-form method of changing a part's height. But if you know exactly what height you need a field to be, you can use a different technique. The Lease Document field contains a PDF, so you want the field to the same aspect ratio (height and width) as a piece of letter-size paper. Letter-size paper measures 8.5" × 11" which translates to (so you don't have to do the math) an aspect ratio of 150 × 195. Click the Lease Document field to select it, and then use the Inspector's Position tab to change the field's width to 150 pixels and the height to 195 pixels. This dimension is larger than the Body part can fit, so FileMaker wants to know if you're sure you want the field expanded (Figure 3-14).

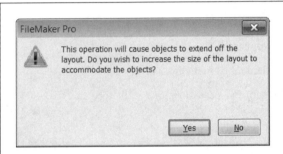

Figure 3-14:
If you use the Inspector to change an object's size, but the position and new size won't fit in the current height of the object's part, you'll see this warning. If you made the change intentionally, click Yes. Click No to abort the object's size change and the layout size change.

If you use this method, you still don't get the precise body height you need, but you get a better idea how much extra space you'll need to fit the larger object on the layout.

Tip: If you clicked Yes and got an increase that's more than you want, just choose Edit→Undo.

Creating a New Layout

Your first layout gives you a detail view of each Lease Document record. It's a good place for doing your basic data entry and viewing a thumbnail of the document's PDF. Once you have lots of data in the file, it'd be nice to have a list of all your Lease Documents. But the List view button isn't very useful, because you've got a customized body height to accommodate your container field.

What you need is a new layout that's designed with a list in mind. FileMaker has a Layout Assistant that walks you through the process. Here's how it works:

1. **In Layout mode, choose Layouts→New Layout/Report.**

    The Create a Layout/Report window of the Layout Assistant appears.

2. **Type *Lease Agreement List* in the Layout Name field.**

    Because most databases end up with lots of layouts, it's helpful to give them descriptive names.

3. **"From the Select a layout type" list, choose "List view", and then click Next.**

   The layout sample icon changes to reflect your selection and the Specify Fields window appears.

4. **Click all the available fields except the Lease Document field, and then click Move.**

   Since a list is meant to be a compact display of your records, it doesn't make a lot of sense to show a large container field on the new list. The field names appear in the "Fields shown on layout/report" list. You can use the arrows to the left of the field names to rearrange the list.

5. **Click Next.**

   The Sort Records window appears.

6. **Click the Lease Duration field, and then click Move.**

   You'll sort the list with the shortest lease durations at the top.

7. **Click Next.**

   The "Select a Theme" window appears, with the Default theme highlighted.

8. **Click Next.**

   If you've changed the original settings for your text objects and fields, FileMaker will use those new settings when it creates them. But if you don't want to use your automatic settings, choose Standard before you click Next. That restores FileMaker's original settings.

9. **In the Top left pop-up menu of the Header and Footer Information window, choose Layout Name. In the Bottom left pop-up menu, choose Current Date, and then click Next.**

   The "Create a Script for this Report" window appears.

10. **Click Next.**

    You don't need a script for this layout, so you'll skip this screen. (Chapter 10 covers the basics about scripts.)

11. **Click the "View in Layout mode" option, and then click Finish.**

    You've got some customizing to do on this layout, so go straight to Layout mode.

As usual switch to Browse mode. FileMaker has created a layout for you that's suitable for a screen list. The fields are in columns, based on the order you chose in step 4 above. There's a layout title in the Header part, and a dynamic date display in the Footer part.

Note: If you still can't see more than one record on the list layout, first make sure you have entered data for multiple records. If you have, click the List view button.

To make your new layout fit in stylistically with the custom form view you made earlier, you'll need to adjust field widths, format the Rental Fee with currency and add your field control styles (drop-down list and calendar). Make the control style changes only if you'll be using the List view for adding records and/or editing data. (Check out page 302 to learn how to change field behavior to keep data in those fields from being edited.)

The Format Painter

Your database will be more polished if your layouts look alike. Whenever possible, put some of the same elements in exactly the same place on each layout. That way, people can use those familiar objects to get oriented as they switch from one layout to another. The logo and layout title are perfect candidates for creating a sense of orientation among your layouts.

Use the Insert→Picture command to put your logo on the List layout, and then re-size it using the Inspector. To make the two layout titles look the same, you could try to remember the font, size, and color you used on the form layout's title. But it's a lot easier to let the Format Painter tool (Figure 3-15) figure that out for you. You'll use the Format Painter on a Text tool in the tutorial below, but it works for most layout objects.

Note: It won't work on imported graphics, because you can't apply any of FileMaker's formatting to them.

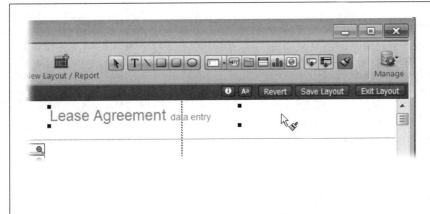

Figure 3-15:
The Format Painter tool is selected and the pointer has changed shape to show it's ready to apply its saved formats to the next object you click. Apply the format to several objects at once by drawing a selection rectangle around all the objects that you want to have the new format. Or if you double-click the tool, it retains the formats until you press Esc.

1. **In Layout mode, switch to the Lease Agreement layout, and then click the "Lease Agreement data entry" text block to select it.**

   This step tells FileMaker which item has the formatting you want to copy.

2. **Click the Format Painter tool to select it.**

   The pointer changes shape to an arrow with a brush below it. FileMaker stores the font, size, and color of the text block you highlighted.

3. **Switch to the Lease Agreement List layout, and then click the "Lease Agreement List" text block to select it.**

   The whole text block's formatting changes.

Back on page 109, you may have made the "data entry" part of your text block smaller than the rest of the text. But the Format Painter undid your work, so select it, and then make it smaller using the Ctrl (⌘)+Shift+< keystroke.

Making Two Layouts Match

Now that you've formatted two layouts—Lease Agreement and Lease Agreement List—switch back to Browse mode, and then switch between layouts. Although the text blocks and logos are now the same font and point size, you can see that they're in exactly the same spot on the two layouts. Use the Inspector to find the Left and Top position of the logo on one layout, and then switch to the other layout to apply those position measurements to the second logo. Use the same technique for matching the title text blocks.

T-Squares

Don't like typing all those numbers? You can use the T-Squares to quickly align objects between layouts. Choose View→T-Squares and you'll see a horizontal and a vertical line that intersect near the center of FileMaker's window. You can drag each line independently. To match a text block between two layouts, drag the horizontal line to the baseline and the vertical line to the left edge of the block. When you switch layouts, the T-Square stays in place, and you can drag the stray text block to the same spot on many layouts in a row. If you have lots of layouts to match up, T-Squares are the way to go.

Tip: To move an object more precisely, press the up, down, right, or left arrow keys on your keyboard. The selected object(s) move one pixel at a time.

To make the layouts match even more, you could add color to the list's Body part, too. Review page 113 for the details on adding color.

Arrange and Align Tools

Designing custom layouts requires lots of moving and resizing layout objects. It's such a frequent task that FileMaker dedicates an entire menu to helping you arrange and align the objects on a layout. You can find the same commands in a slightly different form on the Inspector. You can also find them on the Position tab, in the Arrange & Align section (Figure 3-16).

Figure 3-16:
The Inspector's Arrange and Align tools have icons that indicate their purpose. If you're not sure which tool to use, hover your mouse over a tool to see the tool's pop-up tooltip. Here the mouse is pointing to the "Resize to largest width" tool. If you get unexpected results, just choose the Edit→Undo Resize command, and all your objects return to their original sizes.

Aligning and distributing

Your database will look more organized and professional if you line up objects up with one another. When you have fields arranged in multiple columns on a layout, take care to align the fields neatly. *How* you align them depends on your layout. For example, in Figure 3-6, the tops of the First Name, Last Name, and Lease Document fields are aligned, and the left edges of the First Name, Rental Fee, Lease Duration, and Date Signed fields are aligned.

All layout objects have tops and bottoms, left and right edges, and horizontal and vertical centers. A suite of six commands (shown in Figure 3-16 or on the Arrange→ Align submenu) helps you align multiple selected objects on any of their edges or centers. When you align objects on an edge, all the objects move to align with the object that's furthest in the direction you chose. When you align objects on their centers, they line up on an invisible line through the center of every object.

Tip: To force alignment to a specific object, lock that object (page 129), and then apply the appropriate alignment command.

Fine-Tuning Aids

When you do the kind of fine-tuning work it takes to finish up a layout, you need (and probably want) all the help you can get. For instance, it sometimes helps to have rulers to guide your work. You may also want to group objects together, or lock them in place while you fine-tune things around them.

FileMaker can show you two kinds of rulers:

- Choose View→Graphic Rulers to see a ruler running along the top of the layout, and another along the left edge. As you move and resize items, markers on the rulers show you how objects line up.

- Choose View→Text Ruler to see a second ruler across the top of the layout. This ruler kicks into action when you start editing a text object. As explained on page 78, the text ruler lets you set indent levels and tab stops, which work perfectly in Layout mode too.

In addition to these rulers, you can also add dotted *ruler lines* to the layout itself. These lines appear only in Layout mode, and serve to help you gauge how things line up visually. To turn them on, choose View→Ruler Lines.

If you have a group of objects that you're done tidying up, and you want them to stick together, select them all, and then choose Arrange→Group. For instance, you can group the box, Status field, and Timestamp fields. Then, if you need to move them, you can just drag the whole group around as if it were one object. To break the group apart again, choose Arrange→Ungroup.

Other times, it's hard to work with small items because you can too easily accidentally select bigger objects nearby. You can select that bigger object, and then choose Arrange→Lock. With the object locked into place, you can't move it or change any of its properties. When you're done (or to change the object), select it, and then choose Arrange→Unlock to bring it back to life.

Grouping and locking commands are also available on the Inspector.

If the spaces between objects are uneven, use the Distribute command. Distribute works by measuring the space between the two outmost objects, and then distributing the rest of the objects between those first two. For this command to work, you have to select at least three objects. Then click the Distribute button shown in Figure 3-16, or choose Arrange→Distribute.

Resizing

Back on page 105, you learned how to "chunk" data into related bits and to align edges for better organization. A related concept is to make fields that are near one another, or in the same chunk, the same height and/or width.

You can resize any layout object manually by dragging one of its handles, using the Object Grids (page 105) or by using the Inspector to match objects by typing a measurement into a size field. But FileMaker gives you a set of menu commands and Inspector tools that make the task more efficient. You can select multiple objects and resize them to the smallest object's width or height or both. No matter where they are on the layout, selected objects aren't moved with this command; they're only resized.

Tip: See page 329 to learn how to let objects resize automatically when you resize a window.

Grouping/Locking

These commands are helpful when you have lots of objects on a layout. By grouping objects, you can control many objects as one. Locking objects makes it harder to add an unintentional format change to them. You can see the commands in Figure 3-16, or find them on the Arrange menu.

- **Group.** Select multiple objects, and then group them so you can work with them as a single object. You can copy and paste grouped objects as one item, and you can align them to another object or group of objects. You can group objects in series. That is, you can add new objects to a grouped set to create subsets of groupings. You can also group objects to control which objects appear in front of or behind other objects. See below for more information on moving objects from back to front.

- **Ungroup.** Choose a grouped object, and then select the Ungroup command to work with the objects or subgroups individually. If you've grouped objects in subsets, they'll ungroup in those same layers.

- **Lock.** Choose an object or objects, and then choose the Lock command so that the objects can't be moved, resized, reformatted or deleted. This is helpful when you have objects stacked on top of one another, like with a rectangle behind a group of fields to chunk them together. If you add a locked item to a group, the whole group becomes locked.

- **Unlock.** Choose a locked object or group of object, and then choose the Unlock command so you can move or change them.

Note: The Align, Space, Resize and Group tools work on multiple objects only. So if the commands in the Arrange menu or the buttons in the Inspector appear dimmed, make sure you have more than one object selected.

Arranging

When you create objects on a layout, each new item appears in front of the older objects in an invisible stacking order. You can change this stacking order with the stacking set of commands.

- **Arrange→Bring to Front** moves the selected object on top of everything else on the layout.

- **Arrange→Bring Forward** moves the selected object up one level in the stacking order. You may have to issue this command a few times to get the effect you want.

- **Arrange→Send to Back** moves the selected object behind all other objects.

- **Arrange→Send Backward** moves the selected object down one level in the stacking order.

Tip: The Inspector has buttons for these Arrange commands. See Figure 3-16.

Rotating

You can rotate most layout objects using the Arrange→Rotate command. Each time you choose the command, the selected object rotates 90 degrees clockwise. So to rotate a text block so it reads from top to bottom instead of left to right, issue the command three times. It's most common to rotate field blocks when you're trying to make a lot of labels fit into a tight space.

Note: Portals (page 146), Tab controls (page 155), and web viewers (page 612) can't be rotated.

You can edit rotated text blocks in Layout mode. Just click the block and it'll flip to normal orientation while you're editing. Then when you deselect the block, it flips back to the orientation you set. Oddly enough, fields do the same thing in Browse mode. But unless you're trying to confuse your users, it's usually best to leave fields in their normal orientation.

Adding Power to Your Database

I n the previous chapter, you created a custom database for storing Lease Documents. You learned how to create fields of the appropriate type to store your data, and then you customized two layouts—one for viewing the data as a form and a second for viewing the data in a list.

If you never went any further than that, you'd still have a database that tracks documents. But now that your business is more efficient, it's time to teach the database some new tricks. You're already storing the signing date and lease duration data for each lease. In this chapter, you'll create a field that lets you know when each lease is ending. Then you'll create a new table and all the supporting mechanisms for recording monthly payments.

Creating a Simple Calculation

On page 93, you learned about field types as you created them in Table view. You chose a field type based on the kind of data you wanted to enter into each field. But calculation fields can create data under their own power. For instance, your database already stores monthly Rental Fee and Lease Duration data. If you wanted to figure out the value of that lease over its life, you could enter your data into a calculator, and then manually enter the result. But a calculation field calculates and enters data automatically, and can even update if the data in either field changes. All you have to do is write a formula that tells the calculation field how to get the answer you want.

Note: This tutorial picks up where Chapter 3 left off. If you didn't complete those tutorials, or you want to start with a clean file that's already got some data in it, download the samples from this book's Missing CD page at *www.missingmanuals.com/cds*.

Creating Fields with Manage→Database

In the last chapter, you created fields in Table View using the + button (page 91). Like Table view, that's a bare-bones approach. When you need to harness all the control FileMaker gives you, call up the Manage Database window (Figure 4-1). That's how you'll create your first calculation field:

Tip: In the Manage Database window, you can delete a field by clicking the Delete button. There's a caveat though: calculation fields (like Lease Value) make reference to other fields. That is, the formula for Lease Value is "Lease Duration * Rental Fee." If you try to delete either Lease Duration or Rental Fee, FileMaker shows you a warning dialog box and refuses to delete the field. If you absolutely, positively have to delete either field you have a choice: Either change Lease Value's formula so it doesn't refer to the field you want to delete, or delete Lease Value first. Either way, FileMaker just deletes it with no warning. There's a fallback position if you delete or change fields, and then change your mind. Just click Cancel. FileMaker asks whether you want to "Discard ALL the changes made in this dialog to tables, fields, and relationships?". Click Discard, and FileMaker performs none of the changes.

---

1. **Choose File→Manage→Database, and then click the Fields tab (if it isn't already active).**

   The Fields tab is where most of your field creation takes place. (See the box on page 135 for more information about using this window.)

2. **In the Field Name field, type *Lease Value*.**

   As with other database elements, it's best to use simple, descriptive names for your new calculation field.

3. **From the Type pop-up menu, choose Calculation, and then click Create.**

   The Specify Calculation window appears. Here's where you'll write the formula that gives you the Lease Value. It's based on data in the Lease Duration and Rental Fee fields.

4. **In the Current Table list, double-click the Lease Duration field.**

   The field's name appears in the calculation area of the window. You could type the field's name, but if you make a typing error, FileMaker will bark at you, so it's usually easier to point and double-click.

5. **In the Operators section of the window, click the * sign.**

   The asterisk means multiplication.

6. **In the Current Table list, double-click the Rental Fee field.**

   The formula now reads *Lease Duration * Rental Fee*.

7. **From the "Calculation result is" pop-up menu (it's below the calculation area), choose Number.**

   Your calculation should look like Figure 4-2.

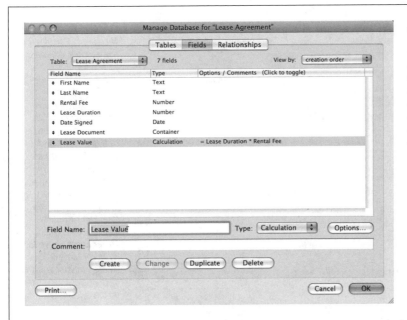

Figure 4-1:
The Manage Database window gives you everything you need to create and manage fields. You can rename a field by selecting it from the list, typing the new name, and then clicking the Change button.

Note: Forgetting to choose Number from the "Calculation result" pop-up menu is a common mistake. Some calculations don't work as you intend if you forget to set the calculation result type properly. But the fix is easy. Just return to the Manage Database dialog box, double-click the field to show the Specify Calculation dialog box, and then change the calculation result type as appropriate.

---

8. **Click OK, and then OK again to close both windows.**

   Depending on the settings in your Preferences window, you may not see the new calculation field appear immediately on your layout.

If the new calculation field appears on your layout, switch to Layout mode, and then move the field into place. Switch back to Browse mode to see the calculation in action. Change the data in the Lease Duration and Rental Fee fields to see the calculation work dynamically. If the field doesn't appear automatically, read the next section to place the field on the layout, and then try editing the data.

Tip: Now that you've created fields using the Manage Database window, you may never want to go back to creating them in Table view (page 91). Change FileMaker's Preferences by choosing FileMaker Pro→Preferences (Mac) or Edit→Preferences (Windows). Then turn on "Use Manage Database dialog to create files". The next time you create a new database, you'll get the Manage Database dialog box instead of a table.

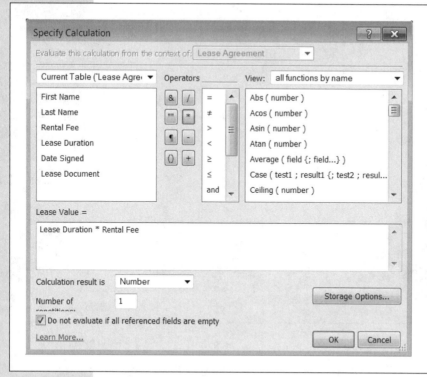

Figure 4-2:
The Specify Calculation window lets you write a formula that's attached to a calculation field. You can perform calculations on text, number, date, time, timestamp, or container fields and get results of each of those types, too. The option "Do not evaluate if all referenced fields are empty" can speed up your database, because FileMaker doesn't have to try to calculate a value if data's missing from all the fields that make up the calculation.

Adding New Fields to a Layout

You determine whether or not newly created fields appear automatically on your layout when they're created using the Manage Database dialog box. In Windows, choose Edit→Preferences; in Mac OS X, choose FileMaker Pro→Preferences and then select the Layout tab to see the "Add newly defined fields to current layout" option. When this option is turned on, FileMaker just plops the field down at the bottom of your layout and, if necessary, increases the Body part to accommodate the new field. Since developers invest a lot of time making layouts look just so, you'll usually work with this option turned off. That means you have to place any newly created fields on your layout manually.

FileMaker provides two ways to add a field to a layout, both require you to be in Layout mode. First, you can choose Insert→Field. When you do, FileMaker asks which field you want, and then drops it in the middle of the layout for you to move into place. Because you get more control with the Status toolbar's Field tool, most people prefer to use it (Figure 4-3).

UP TO SPEED

Use the Keyboard

You can get to almost everything in the Manage Database window's Fields tab from the keyboard alone. If you're a speed freak, you can avoid the mouse almost entirely. Here's how:

- On Windows, use the Tab key to move among buttons, text boxes, and pop-up menus. (On Mac OS X, you can press the Tab key to move between the field list, Field Name, and Comment boxes. Unfortunately, FileMaker doesn't honor Mac OS X's Full Keyboard Access settings.)

- While the field list is active, use the up and down arrow keys to select the next and previous fields.

- Hold down Ctrl (Control) while pressing the arrow keys, to move the selected field up or down in the list.

- Use the keyboard shortcuts for each field type. (Look in the Type pop-up menu to see them.)

- Press Alt+N (⌘-O) to see the field options dialog box for the selected field.

- Press the Delete key to delete the selected field. Then, when you're asked if you're sure you want to delete the field, press D (Windows). Mac works the same, except the D key doesn't dismiss the dialog box; you'll have to click the Delete button.

- Press the first letter of a button name in any of FileMaker's alert message boxes instead of clicking the button (Windows only). Pressing Return is the same as clicking the highlighted button on a Mac.

- To close the Manage Database window and throw away all your changes, press the Esc key, then click the Discard button

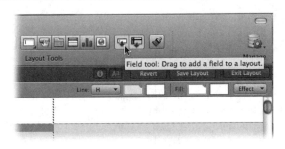

Figure 4-3:
The arrow points to the Field tool, and a tooltip identifies the tool and adds a usage tip. The Field tool works a little different from most tools. You have to drag the tool down onto the layout where you want the field to land. A blue (Mac) or dotted (Windows) outline shows you the size and shape of the field you'll create. The dotted horizontal line represents the field's baseline. Use it to line the new field up with existing fields on the layout.

To add the Lease Value field to the layout, follow these steps:

1. **Drag the Field tool down onto the layout.**

   As you drag, FileMaker shows a border and baseline that represents the new field.

2. **Drag to where you want the field to land, and then release the mouse button.**

   The Specify Field window appears (Figure 4-4), showing a list of the fields in your current table.

3. Choose the Lease Value field, and then select the "Create label" option (if it's
    not already selected).

    Although you could copy and paste an existing field label, and then change the
    text, it's usually easier to have FileMaker create the label for you, and then use
    the Format Painter to change the font and size (if the label doesn't appear in the
    same format used for your field labels).

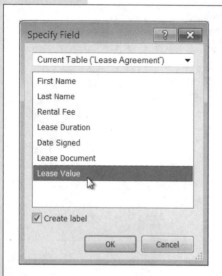

Figure 4-4:
*When you add a field to the layout, FileMaker asks which field you
want by showing you the Specify Field dialog box. Another way to
quickly create a field with the formatting you want already on it is to
copy/paste an existing field and its label. Double-click the new field to
show the Specify Field dialog box. Select the field you want, turn off the
Create label option, and then change the field's label.*

4. Click OK.

    The field and its label appear on the layout.

If necessary, adjust the field's format to match the other fields on your layout. Don't
forget to use the Inspector's Data tab to apply Currency formatting. Use the Arrange,
Resize, and Align commands if the field didn't land exactly where it needs to be.
Now you're ready to switch to Browse mode to view the data in your new calculation
field.

Creating a Related Table

Now that you've got the basic information stored for your leases, you realize that
you can centralize your data if you record rent payments in the same database as the
Lease Documents. Your first thought might be to create a field or two (Date Paid
and Amount Paid) to record each payment, but you quickly realize that since some
leases last 36 months you'll have to create 72 fields, and then place them on your
layout. Worse yet, for your 12- and 24-month leases, most of those fields are empty.

If you start signing 48-month leases, you have to create a whole new slew of fields and start rearranging your layout again. And what if your tenants make more than one payment each month? It'd be so much more efficient if each record could create only the fields it needed.

You're on the right track—instead of adding fields in the Lease Agreement table, what you need is a set of new records in a related table (see the box on page 138 for a definition of *table* and other terms you'll need to know for this section). That's where a relational database comes in. You need separate tables to store each type of information. Because when you think about it, monthly payments aren't really part of a Lease Agreement table. Date Paid and Amount Paid data pertains to a specific Lease Agreement, but it doesn't belong with the name of the tenant or the PDF of the lease agreement itself. What you need is a new Payment table, where you can add 12 records (one per month, of course) to the 12-month leases, or 24 records to the 24-month leases. With a separate table, even if you start offering 5-year leases, you'll never have to add more fields or stretch a layout to accommodate a change in the way you do business.

And you don't even have to create a new file for your new table. FileMaker lets you put dozens, even hundreds, of tables into the same file. There's an art and science surrounding how to figure out which tables you need and how to relate them to one another. You'll learn that in Chapter 5. For now, you'll learn about the tools you need to create a related table and enter monthly payment records on the Lease Agreement layout.

Understanding the Elements of a Relationship

Now that you've decided to store lease information in the Lease Agreement table and Payment information in a new Payment table, you need to make sure payments match the right Lease Agreement record? First, you start with a unique identifier called a *key field*, which uses the auto-enter field option to create a serial number that's unique for each record in the table. Then you use the *Relationships* graph to match the two tables' key fields. Finally you create a special layout object, called a *portal*, that lets you view, create and edit payment records on the same layout where you store data about each Lease Agreement.

Creating a Key Field with an Auto-Enter Serial Number

To ensure that Lease Agreements and Payments records match properly, you need a unique identifier in the Lease Agreement table. One of FileMaker's field options, called *Serial Number*, automatically assigns a unique number to each record when it's created. Here's how to create a key field, and then apply an Auto-Enter Serial number option to it:

1. **Choose File→Manage→Database, and then if it's not active, click the Fields tab.**

   The Manage Database window appears, with the Lease Agreement table's fields in a list.

UP TO SPEED

These Terms Are Relational

Before you dive into creating a relational database, you'll find it helpful to review some vocabulary and learn a few new terms:

- A *database* is a collection of tables, layouts, and other features that forms an organized system.

- A *table* holds information about one kind of thing, like your lease agreements and payments or in another database: people, products, leases and payments..

- A *record* is the collection of data in a table that described one thing. It's like a single row in a spreadsheet.

- A *field* holds one attribute of something: lease duration, the date a payment was made, the person's first or last name, the order date, the color of a product, or the supplier's address. It's like a single column in a spreadsheet.

- An *attribute* is an individual characteristic. For example, a bicycle might have several attributes: color, size, style, and price. In a database, each of these attributes gets its own field. Remember the term "individually significant" from the box on page 93?

- An *entity* is one kind of thing. If you track information about your Customers, the concept People is an entity,

so is a Payment or an Invoice or an Invoice's Line Item. Remember though, the individual thing itself isn't the entity. The person Steve Jobs isn't an entity, neither is the April 2010 payment for a specific lease. If this is confusing to you, don't get hung up on it. Focus on this: Each entity (People) gets one table in a database and each instance of an entity (Steve Jobs) gets one record in that table.

- A *key field* uniquely identifies each record so that each related record knows which record it matches, like a Social Security Number for a person. You'll create a key field using FileMaker's Auto-Enter Serial number option in this chapter, and learn about their finer points on page 198.

- A *relationship* describes how the records in two tables match each other (page 143).

The most common relationships are called *parent-child relationships*. That's because one parent record can have many children, but each child record can have only one parent. So in your database, the Lease Agreement is the parent record and each Payment record is a child.

---

2. **In the Field Name field, type *agreementID*.**

   This field name may seem odd (no spaces and a mix of upper- and lower-case letters), but it's one of many naming conventions used by developers to help them quickly identify fields that they've created to make the database work. In this naming convention, the field name starts with the name (or one-word abbreviation) of the table for which it is the key field. The "ID" at the end confirms that that the field is used as a key.

3. **From the Type pop-up menu, choose Number.**

   Key fields are most often number fields. (See page 198 for more information on choosing and creating a good key field.)

4. **Click the Create button, and then click the Options button.**

   The Options for Field "agreementID" window appears.

5. **Turn on the "Serial number" checkbox, and then click OK until you're back on the Lease Agreement layout.**

   A serial number appears in the agreementID field for each new record as it's created. See Figure 4-5.

From now on, every record you create in the Lease Agreement table will be assigned a unique number that you can use to create relationships to other tables. However, the records you've already created don't have serial numbers yet.

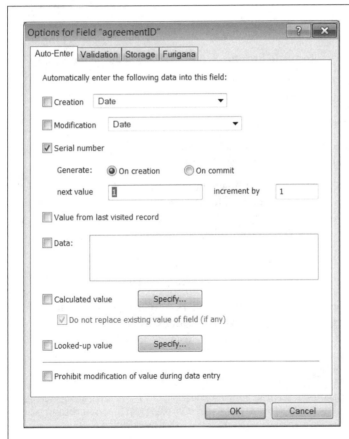

Figure 4-5:
Auto-enter serial numbers are most often created as a record is created ("On creation"), but if you choose "On commit" instead, FileMaker doesn't generate the number until the first time the user commits the record. Usually, you use this option when your database has multiple users (as you'll learn on page 730). For instance, a user might create a record, but then delete it instead of filling out its data. In that case, there would be a gap in the serial numbers, because the numbers assigned to deleted records are never reused. The next value is a running tally of where you are in the database. When you first set up an auto-enter serial number field, the next value is always "1" unless you change it. If you're importing data from another source, you should find the highest serial number in the imported data, and then set your field's "next value" to one number higher than the imported data. And while the most common "increment by" value is 1, you can make the numbers increase by any other number you choose instead.

Using Replace Field Contents to add serial numbers

When you create a key field after data's been entered, you don't have to go to each record and manually enter a serial number. You can use the Replace Field Contents command (page 70) to add in the missing serial numbers and reset the field option's "next value" counter at the same time. Since you have to have a field on a layout in order to use the Replace Field Contents command, you may have to put the agreementID field on the Lease Agreement layout if isn't already there.

1. **In Browse mode, choose Records→Show All Records.**

   Every record has to have data in its key field in order to relate to another table, so make sure you aren't looking at a found set of just some of your records.

Warning: If you're using this tutorial on a database where some records have serial numbers and some don't, find only the records without serial numbers in this step. In that case, you wouldn't want to replace the serial number in any record that already had one.

---

2. **Click in the agreementID field.**

   If you don't click into a field first, the Replace Field Contents command will be dimmed.

3. **Choose Records→Replace Field Contents.**

   The Replace Field Contents window appears. See Figure 4-6.

4. **Select "Replace with serial numbers", and then turn on "Update serial number in Entry Options", if it isn't already selected.**

   The first option tells FileMaker how you want the numbers created and the second option ensures that you don't have to find the new highest number, and then return to the Manage Database dialog box to change the "next value" setting for the agreementID field manually after the replace is done.

5. **Click Replace.**

   Serial numbers are created in all the records of your database.

Flip through the records to see the serial numbers. You can go back to the Manage Database dialog box and check the auto-entry options for the agreementID field to see that its "next value" has been updated. Create a new record to see the next value appear automatically in the agreementID field.

Tip: Because it can be cumbersome to create a key field and populate it with data months or even years later, it makes sense to create a key field in every table you create even if you have no immediate plans to relate the table to any other table. That way, you're ready to go when needs change.

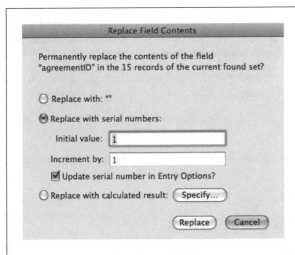

Figure 4-6:
In the Replace Field Contents dialog box, the highlighted button is not the one that does the action you've just set up. The Replace command can't be undone, so FileMaker is saving you from unintentionally destroying good data if you hit Enter too soon. Instead, Enter cancels the replacement and leaves everything as it was. Replace Field Contents is lifesaver when you have to retrofit a table with a key field after you've created records. However, replacing data after you're created relationships between tables is risky—if the value in the key field in either table changes, the child record gets disconnected from its parent.

Creating a New Table

Your Payment table needs to store information about each monthly payment for a specific Lease Agreement. The Payment table's attributes are the date the rent was paid and the amount paid. You also need a key field for hooking up Payments to the Lease Agreement table. And since it's good practice to create a key field in every table, just in case, you'll also add a paymentID field.

Two key fields in one table? It may sound crazy, but it's not uncommon for a table to have 10 or more key fields that let it relate to that many other tables. The first key field you'll create (called paymentID) uniquely identifies each Payment record, and could be used when you figure out a reason to link the Payments table (as a parent) to another table. (See page 198 for information on primary and foreign keys.) The second key field (agreementID) will hold the value that matches the value in the key field of a specific record in the Lease Agreement table. That's how a Payment record (the child) matches up with the proper Lease Agreement record (the parent).

1. **Choose File→Manage→Database, and then click the Tables tab.**

   This tab is where you create, edit and manage your tables.

2. **In the Table Name field, type *Payment*, and then click Create.**

   Remember: when you created the Lease Agreement table, you decided to use the singular case for your databases elements, so stay consistent. The Payment table appears in the Tables list.

3. **Click the Fields tab.**

   You're viewing the field list for the Payment table. FileMaker's smart like that and switched to the selected table for you. But if you need to, you can switch between tables using the Table pop-up menu above the list of fields.

4. **In the Field Name field, type *paymentID,* and then select Number from the Type pop-up menu. Click Create.**

   It's a good habit to create a table's key field first thing. That way, you won't forget to do it.

5. **Click the Options button and make the paymentID field an auto-enter serial number.**

   All your Payment records will have serial numbers because you've created a key field right at the beginning, before you create any records. And since you have no records yet, the next value should be "1".

6. **At the bottom of the Options window, turn on "Prohibit modification of value during data entry".**

   This prevents users (even you, the developer) from changing the data in a field. Protecting the data in a key field is critical to keeping your records properly related to one another.

Note: You didn't want to prohibit modification of the agreementID field when you created it because you still had to use the Replace Field Contents command to get the data into the field. Now that you know how critical this step is, don't forget to go back and make that selection in the Lease Agreement table.

---

7. **Click OK.**

   You're ready to finish creating the rest of the fields for the Payment table.

Use the skills you learned earlier in this chapter to create these fields, with the following types:

- Date Paid (Date)

- Payment Amount (Number)

- agreementID (Number)

Click OK when you're done. Because you're still viewing the Lease Agreement layout, you don't see evidence of your new table yet. But it's there.

Viewing the new table's layout

If you click the Layout pop-up menu (in either Browse or Layout mode), you'll see a new layout called Payment. FileMaker created it for you when it created your new table. And much like the boring layout you got when you created the Lease Agreement table, there's nothing there except the standard lineup of layout parts and your newly created fields. In Browse mode you can see that unlike your first table, this new table doesn't have any records yet. If you click the layout to see the fields' borders, you'll see the warning message in Figure 4-7.

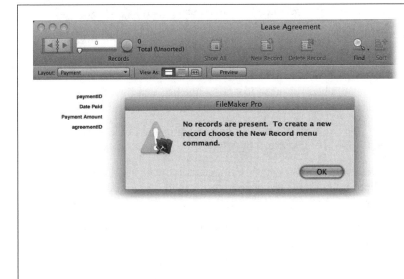

Figure 4-7:
When you see this message, just click OK. But don't bother creating a record. You'll do that later—from the Lease Agreement layout. Every time you create a new table, you'll also get a free layout just like this one. That's because tables need a place to show their fields. But once you start relating tables to one another, you'll often find that these automatically created layouts are just so much fluff. You can delete these utilitarian layouts (In Layout Mode, choose Layouts→Delete Layout), and then start from scratch using the Layout Assistant to get something more decorative.

You could dress this layout up any way you want to. For instance, you might turn it into a list layout so you can report on your payments. But since you'll be creating Payment records and entering data from the Lease Agreement table, just note that the layout's here, and go back to the Lease Agreement layout.

Creating a Relationship Between Two Table Occurrences

You just saw that when you create a table, and then add fields to it, FileMaker makes a bare bones layout for that table. It also makes a Table Occurrence for the new table on its Relationships Graph. That graph is found on the only tab of the Manage Database window that you haven't seen yet. And true to its name, that's where you create the relationship between the Lease Agreement and Payment tables.

Note: Your Relationships graph can have more than one instance of any table, and each instance is a different view into the table. Each instance of a table is called a *table occurrence*. It's important to know whether you're referring to the table itself or an occurrence of the table. A word of caution though, FileMaker isn't all that consistent about using the term in its own windows and help files, so it's not your fault if you're confused.

Also true to its name, the Relationships Graph is a visual representation of your file's tables and how they relate to one another. And you create relationships in perhaps the easiest way possible: you drag from one table to another to create a line. Here's how to create a relationship between two tables, using their key fields.

1. **Choose File→Manage→Database, and then click the Relationships tab. Or use the shortcut Ctrl+Shift+D (⌘-Shift-D)**

   You'll see two table occurrences: one for the Lease Agreement table and the other for the Payment table. You need to draw a line between the agreementID fields in each table, but that field's not visible in the Lease Agreement table occurrence.

2. **Click and hold the tiny triangle at the bottom of the Lease Agreement table occurrence.**

   That scrolls the field names so that you can see the one you need. Or you can drag the bottom border of the table occurrence to make it tall enough to show all its fields.

3. **In the Lease Agreement table occurrence, click the agreementID field, and then drag to the agreementID field in the Payment table occurrence. Release the mouse when it's pointing to the proper field.**

   As you drag, you'll see a line with a box in the middle (Figure 4-8, top). When you release the mouse, the two key fields jump above a new divider at the top of each table occurrence (Figure 4-8, bottom).

4. **Double-click the box in the middle of the relationship line.**

   The Edit Relationship window appears (Figure 4-9). The window is divided into halves, showing Lease Agreement on the left and Payment on the right.

5. **On the Payment side of the relationship, turn on "Allow creation of records in this table via this relationship" and "Delete related records in this table when a record is deleted in the other table".**

   This setup is typical of the child side of a relationship. Here's how to think about it: You'll be creating Payment records from the Lease Agreement layout, so the relationship's options need to allow record creation. And if you delete a Lease Agreement record, there probably isn't much use for the Payment records, so that second option deletes Payment records that would otherwise be "orphaned" when the parent record is deleted.

6. **Click OK until you return to the Lease Agreement layout.**

Or whichever layout you were viewing at the start of this tutorial.

If naming fields in both tables with the same name seemed confusing as you were doing it, you've just seen why it's a good idea. In a large or complex database, some tables can have many key fields for relating to other tables. But if you use the same name in the child table as the key field in the parent table, it's very easy to find the proper key field, and then drag a line between the two tables.

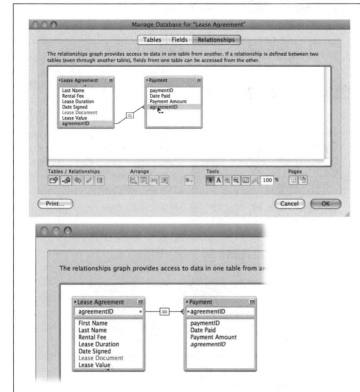

Figure 4-8:
Top: As you drag, the two selected key fields stay highlighted to help you stay oriented. The pointer has changed shape to show that you're creating a relationship. Notice that the line is straight on the Lease Agreement end and has a "fork" at the Payment end. This crow's foot helps you know which is the parent and which is the child side of the relationship. But how does FileMaker know which is which? Lease Agreement's agreementID field has the Auto-Enter Serial number option turned on, which is standard operating procedure for a field that's meant to be used as a parent table key field.

Bottom: When you release the mouse, the two key fields are listed at the top of each table occurrence with the relationship line drawn between them. Translated into plain English, this relationship means "For each Lease Agreement record, match all the Payment records where the agreementID value equals the value in the Lease Agreement's agreementID field."

Creating and Using Portals

Once your tables are related to each another, you can freely display related fields on layouts. For example, say you want the Date Paid and Amount Paid fields from the Payment table to appear on your Lease Agreement layout. You could simply add those fields to the layout, but you'd quickly find a big problem. There's only a single instance of each field, and the point of a related table is to have *multiple* records from the child table related to the parent table.

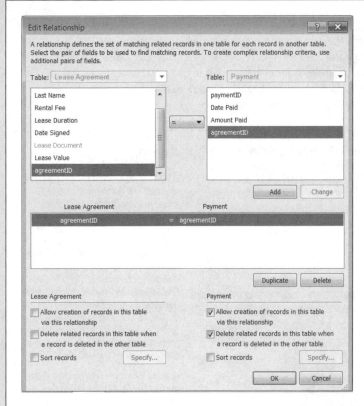

Figure 4-9:
The Edit Relationship window lets you define everything about how a relationship works. It's divided in half vertically, with one table's information on the left, and the other table's information on the right. For most people, it's easiest to visualize a relationship when the parent table is on the left and the child table is on the right. If your window is flipped (Payment on the left and Lease Agreement on the right), it's because your table occurrences are flipped on the Relationship graph. To change the display, close the Edit Relationship dialog box and then drag the table occurrences to rearrange them. In practice, it doesn't matter which side the tables appear on because relationships are bidirectional (you'll learn what that means on page 228). Just select your options very carefully.

The problem is solved with a *portal*, which is a layout object that displays multiple records from a related table. Not only can the portal display related records, you can use a portal to create, edit, and delete related records.

Adding a Portal to a Layout

A portal can display as many related records as you want, limited primarily by the size of your layout and height of the portal. As with other layout objects, you can format portals to match your database, using fills and lines the way you would with other drawn objects. Here's how to create a portal on the Lease Agreement layout:

1. **In Layout mode, drag the bottom edge of your Body part to make room for your portal.**

    Use Figure 4-10 to judge how much space you'll need.

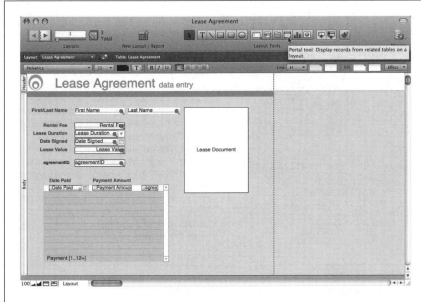

Figure 4-10:
In the upper right, you see the Portal tool. The finished portal, along with related fields and their field labels is at lower left. The portal displays information about its data along its lower-left edge. The related table's name (Payment) appears, followed by "[1...12+]." That means that the portal is tall enough to display 12 rows of related records, starting with the first record. The "+" sign means that the portal will show a active scrollbar when it contains more than 12 child records.

2. **Click the Portal tool to select it, and then drag on the layout to create a portal.**

   As with all drawn objects, it's usually easiest to start in the upper-left corner and drag to the lower right corner where you want the portal to appear. When you release the mouse, the Portal Setup window appears (Figure 4-11).

3. **From the "Show related records from" pop-up menu, choose Payment.**

   This is the Payment table occurrence you saw when you hooked up the Lease Agreement and Payment tables in the Relationships graph (page 144).

4. **Turn on "Show vertical scroll bar".**

   A scrollbar lets you see more related records in a smaller space.

5. **Turn on "Allow deletion of related portal records".**

   When this option is *turned off*, you can't delete Payment records using the portal and the regular Delete command.

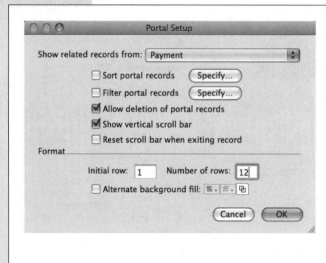

Figure 4-11:
Control a portal's options using the Portal Setup dialog box. This window appears when you first create a portal. Double-click a portal to view this window. That's how you check or change the portal's options. Of course, you can also use the Inspector to change a portal's size or position and appearance. Use the "Initial row" box to display data from a related table across multiple portals. If you need to display data that's not suitable for a list, like a large container field with a graphic (which should be tall so the graphic is visible), make several tall, single-row portals and place them side by side. Set the first portal to have an initial row of 1, the second portal to an initial row of 2, and so on. See the box on page 150 for more info.

6. **In the "Number of rows" box, type *12*, and then click OK.**

   FileMaker adjusts the portal object you drew to fit the number of rows you specify, and then opens the "Add Fields to Portal" window.

Warning: If the layout isn't tall enough to fit the adjusted portal, you'll see a warning message that tells you that the layout size needs to be increased. If you click No in that warning dialog box, the portal will stay the height you drew it. When you're done setting up the rest of your portal, you'll have to increase the layout size manually, and then try to change the row display again.

---

7. **From the list of Available fields on the left, select and move the Date Paid, Payment Amount, and agreementID fields.**

   Each field appears in the list on the right as you move it. It isn't necessary to add a related table's key field to a portal. In the real world, you *don't* usually want to see that data. But while you're learning about portals and relationships, it's very helpful to display the key field so you can see how portals work.

Tip: Pay attention to the way the field name appears in the Available fields list. You're seeing the *fully-qualified field name*. That is, the field is represented by its table name, followed by a pair of colons, and then the field name itself. It's kind of like you being called by both your first and last names. This nomenclature helps you keep the Lease Agreement and the Payment tables' agreementID fields straight.

---

8. **Click OK.**

   The related fields appear in the portal.

A portal has a few notable characteristics in Layout mode. First, no matter how many rows the portal is set to show, you only see one row of fields, and they're always in the portal's first row. Second, you can tell how high each row is because in addition to the border around the portal, there are lines between each row (unless you've turned lines off for the portal). Notice that the fields fit precisely in that top row. In fact, FileMaker used the automatic format of your fields to figure out how many rows it could fit in the space you drew with the portal tool.

The Payment fields are evenly divided within the width of your portal and their formats probably don't match the rest of the fields on your layout. You may need to adjust the fields' widths, change their text alignment and create field labels if you want your layout to match Figure 4-10.

Resizing and Moving a Portal

Just like any other layout object, a portal shows selection handles when you click to select it. But its selection handles may not be at the edges of the portal as you'd expect. They're at the bottom of the portal's first row, and not at the bottom edge of the portal. If you drag either of the portal's bottom selection handles downward, you change the row height and *not* the number of rows the portal will display. That's useful where you want to show lots of data in a portal and a single row of fields for each related record won't get the job done. You can change the width of a portal by dragging a handle or by using the Width boxes on the Inspector's Position tab.

If you move a portal, make sure you select the fields inside the portal, too. Because if the portal and its fields move out of sync and the fields overlap the portal's top row borders even a little bit you could get display problems—the fields may not show up at all, even when there are related records. If you delete a portal without deleting the related fields, they still show data (if there are related records), but you see data from just the first related record because without a portal, FileMaker can only show you one related record.

Context

Back in Browse mode, the portal appears, but there's no data in it. That's because the Payment table doesn't have any records yet. If you're thinking about choosing the New Record command, don't act on that thought, because it won't work. At least it won't create a new Payment record. It will continue to work as it always has, by creating a new Lease Agreement record. To understand why, backtrack just a bit to take a look at your layout's setup. Switch to Layout mode, and then choose Layouts→Layout Setup (Figure 4-12).

Power to the Portal

On page 148, you learned a little about how the Portal Setup dialog box works. Now it's time to dig a little deeper. To see the settings for your portal, in Layout mode, select it, and then choose Format→Portal Setup. (You can double-click the portal to get there, too.) Here's how some of the options break down:

- **Portals can be sorted by any field in the related table.** Click "Sort portal records" and you'll see a familiar Sort Records window for the related table. Sorting portal rows has no effect on the underlying table itself. That is, your Payment layout can have a completely different sort order than the Payment portal has.

- **Portals can have scroll bars.** Got 326 items on that invoice? No problem, just add a scroll bar. Portal scroll bars work like the ones in FileMaker's main window. The bar is visible no matter what, but the scroll bubble doesn't appear unless there are more related records than will fit in the number of rows you specify.

- **You can assign an "Alternate background fill" to a portal.** When you turn this option on, every even-numbered portal row has a different background color and pattern. You can make every other row green, for example. The *odd* numbered rows have whatever background color you assign to the portal itself on the layout.

- **If you change the "Initial row" value, the portal skips some rows.** For example, if you put 5 in the box on a 9-row portal, the portal shows rows 5 through 13 instead of records 1 through 9. If it suits your needs, you can put the same portal on your layout more than once, and give it different initial rows. Your layout could show the first six payments in one portal, and payments 7 through 12 in a second column, for instance.

In addition to the options in the Portal Setup dialog box, portals have other features you may find useful:

- **Each row in a portal can hold multiple fields,** and it's no problem to add an extra field after you've walked through the initial setup. You can use the field tool to create a field, and then use the Specify Field window to choose the field you want. Remember that you may have to switch Table Occurrences in the pop-up menu above the field list to see fields from the related table. Usually it's easier to copy a field that's already in the portal, and then change it to the right field because it already comes from the proper table occurrence.

- **You can draw objects and place graphics in a portal row.** Just drag or insert them into the first row, taking care that their boundaries are completely inside the first row. Because buttons (as you'll learn on page 317) are so useful, you can add them to a portal row, too. If you have a portal with a tall row height and you've arranged fields two high in that first row, you could draw a horizontal line in the portal to help organize the data.

- **Portals also have special automatic resizing powers (page 329).** If you anchor the bottom of a portal vertically, you get to decide whether FileMaker *adds more rows* or just *makes each row bigger*. Here's the trick: If anything *in* the portal is anchored on the bottom, then the portal rows get bigger. Otherwise, FileMaker keeps the rows the same height, and adds more as your window grows larger.

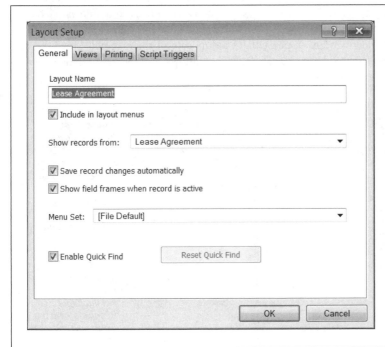

Figure 4-12:
*All layouts are tied to one, and
only one, table occurrence.
Fittingly, the Lease Agreement
layout shows records from
the Lease Agreement table
occurrence. Why all this harping
on the difference between a
table and a table occurrence?
Because you can create multiple
instances of a table on your Relationships graph–that's what a
table occurrence is–an instance
of a table. When you work with
your data (specifying fields,
creating portals, writing calculations, and other tasks), you need
to use the table occurrence for
the current context.*

When you created a portal back on page 146, you had to specify a table occurrence
for the portal to know which records to show. But the Lease Agreement table was
created for you when you created the database way back on page 89. FileMaker created the Lease Agreement table, along with a matching layout and table occurrence,
because you need all that stuff to get started and it doesn't want to bother you with
details while you're being creative. But when you start to create layouts from scratch,
you need to tell each new layout which table occurrence to draw its records from.

This concept of where you are and what records you're viewing, called *context*, is
fundamental to many aspects of your database. The context of the Lease Agreement
layout is the Lease Agreement table occurrence. In turn, the Lease Agreement layout
contains a portal whose context is the Payment table occurrence. Keep context in
mind as you're reading the next section, which covers the things you can do with
related records using a portal.

Creating Records Through a Portal

Once you've set up a portal on a layout, you can create records without going all the
way back to the actual table. On a Lease Agreement record, in Browse mode, click in
any field. All the fields, including the ones in the portal, show the dotted line that indicates they're active. You can now tab into the Payment portal's fields, just as if they
were a part of the Lease Agreement table. The fields are active even though there

aren't any related records because when you defined the relationship between the Lease Agreement and Payment tables, you chose the option that allows related records to be created (page 144). View your related table by choosing Window→New Window. A new window appears that's a duplicate of the original. Move the new window over to the side so you can see both windows, and then switch the new window to the Payment layout (Figure 4-13).

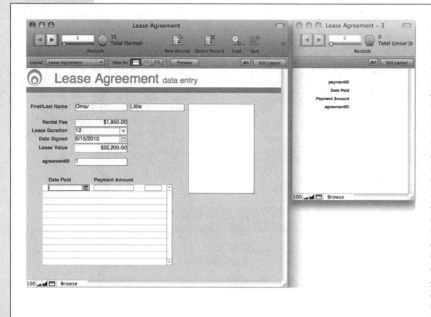

Figure 4-13:
In the window on the left, the Omar Little record is active, and you can see that the portal shows field boundaries as if there's a new record. But in the window on the right, you can see that the Payment table doesn't have any records yet. Keep your screen set up like this for the next tutorials, so you can watch how and when related records are created, edited, and deleted. This is also a good troubleshooting tip when something's wrong with a relationship and you're trying to figure out how to fix it.

1. **In your original window, in Browse mode, click in the Payment portal's Date Paid field, type a date, and then press Tab. If you've added a calendar pop-up to the field, select a date from the calendar.**

   As soon as the insertion point moves to the next field, you'll see the record appear in the Payment window. Even though you didn't enter it, the new record's agreementID field now has a value, and it matches the value in the Lease Agreement::agreementID field.

2. **Type a number in the Payment Amount field, and then press Tab again.**

   The agreementID field in the portal is active. Because it's a foreign key, it's not set up to prohibit data entry. So you can change the ID. But if you do, the Payment record won't be related to the Lease Agreement record when you commit the related record. It might even be related to the wrong parent record now. Luckily you have the Payment window open, and you can just change the key back to match the value in the parent record you're viewing. When you commit the Payment record, it will show back up in the portal.

Use the portal to create a few more payment records just to watch how the process works behind the scenes. Notice how the Tab key travels through the rows in the portal, much like a spreadsheet.

Note: Normally, you wouldn't put a foreign key field in a portal because if the value is changed, the child record disappears from the portal; it's no longer related to the parent record you're viewing. Plus it's confusing to users, since the value in every record is, as it should be, exactly the same. Still, viewing an ID field in a portal, along with a second window opened to a layout that has the context of the related records, is a good way to learn about relationships and to troubleshoot.

Editing Records Through a Portal

You edit any related record by clicking in the field you want to change, and then typing the new info. Tab to the next row, or if you're on the last row in the portal, click into blank space on the Lease Agreement record to commit the changes (see the box on page 26).

Deleting records through a portal

Unlike the New Record command, the Delete Record command *can* work on a portal—if you've formatted the portal to allow related record deletion (as you did when you set up the portal on page 146). But you have to select a portal row first to set up the context so FileMaker knows which related record you want to delete.

1. **Select the portal row you want to delete, but without clicking in any of the portal's fields.**

   Click the portal row itself (point *between* the fields in the portal, and then click). Figure 4-14 shows what selecting a portal without clicking in a field looks like.

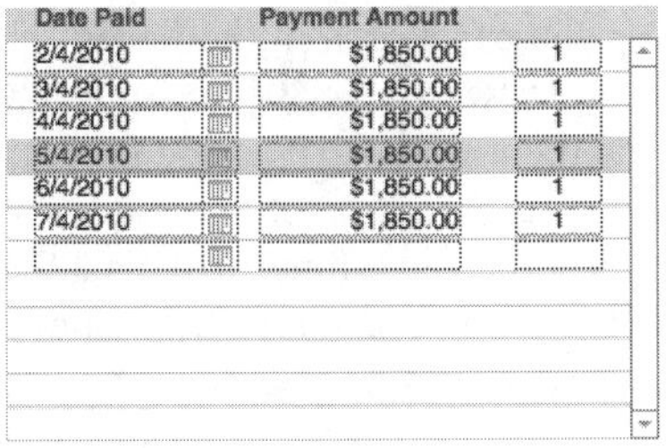

Figure 4-14:
The Payment record for May 4, 2010 is highlighted. No field in the portal row is active, but a highlight shows on the whole row. Selecting a row this way sets the context for a portal row delete. However, you can't enter or edit data in a portal row that's highlighted this way, because the insertion point isn't in a specific field.

2. **Choose Records→Delete Record.**

   The Delete Related Record Warning appears (Figure 4-15).

3. **Click Delete.**

   The related record is deleted.

Figure 4-15:
Because you can't undo a record deletion, FileMaker gives you a chance to change your mind. Click Cancel to keep the record or Delete if you're sure it's the one you mean to delete.

If you're in a field on the portal row when you choose the command, then FileMaker asks you which record you want to delete: the master record or the related record (Figure 4-16). The terms "master" and "related" are FileMaker-speak for "parent" and "child." If you're not on a portal row at all (neither an active field or a portal row highlight), the Delete Record command works exactly like it does on a layout that has no portals.

Figure 4-16:
Just clicking in a field on a portal row doesn't give FileMaker enough information about context, so it asks you which record you want to delete. Once you've made a selection (other than Cancel), you'll get a second window asking if you're sure you want to delete the record. It's easier to highlight the portal row than to interact with two windows.

Performing Finds with Related Data

You can search in related fields just as easily as you can search in the "local" table's fields. So if you wanted to find all Lease Agreements with June 2010 records for instance, just switch to Find mode, click in the Payment portal's Date Paid field, enter your search criteria, and then perform the find (page 32). You get a found set of all the Lease Agreement records that have related records dated June 2010. Each Lease Agreement record will still show all its related records, and not just the ones that match your search criteria. As you flip through your found set, you might think that some records shouldn't be in the found set. But remember, not all the related records may be showing in a portal. So if you think a record showed up when it shouldn't have, scroll down in the portal. You'll find the June 2010 Payment record in there somewhere.

But if what you wanted was a list of only the June 2010 payment records, you have to search using a layout that's set to show records from the Payment table occurrence. That way, your found set *will* contain just the records that match.

Using Tab Controls

Adding a portal to the Lease Agreement layout may streamline your workflow, but the portal's size and position don't make for a harmonious layout. Plus, the Lease Document container field would be more useful if it were larger. But if you make it *too* big, that field will dwarf all the other data on the screen, making it hard to focus on the text data.

That's where Tab Controls come in. The name makes it seems as Tab Controls have something to do with the Tab key on your keyboard, but they don't. They provide a way to organize data on a layout so you can focus on one chunk of data at a time. Tab Controls also let you put far more information on the same layout without making either a giant layout or one that's crammed with data. You've seen similar objects in other software programs, even other places in FileMaker itself. For example, the Inspector has three tabs that are used for organizing all the information it has to hold. A Layout Tab Control works much the same way (although without the collapsible sections—that would be so cool). Figure 4-17 shows the Lease Agreement layout reorganized using a Tab Control.

Creating a Tab Control

Tab Controls are easy to draw, but since it can be tricky dividing the objects on an existing layout amongst the new tabs, you'll need to do a little prep work. The process is easier on a larger monitor, but can be done even on a small one. First, expand the database's window as large as your monitor will allow. If it's not big enough to show you about double the width of space as you currently have showing, try Zooming out.

Next, follow these steps:

1. **Drag all of your fields and field labels waaaay over to the right so they're past the edge of the line that represents the edge of your layout. Use Figure 4-10 as a reference to see how far you need to move your fields.**

    If you don't move your fields, the new Tab Control will be on top of them in the layout's stacking order and it won't be easy to select them afterwards. Although you'd think that the "Send to Back" command will fix things, it doesn't always, so it's just better to empty out the space first.

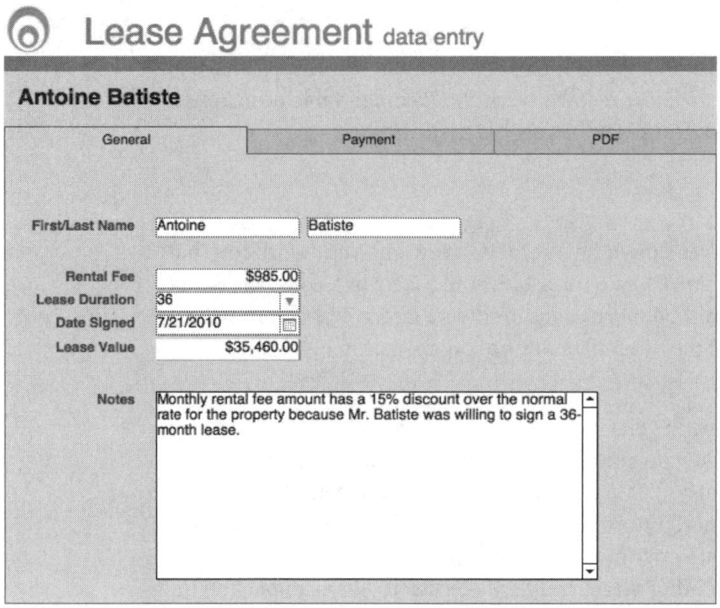

Figure 4-17:
This version of the Lease Agreement layout has a giant Tab Control covering most of its area. The Tab Control has three tabs, with the existing fields divided among them. The General tab has the basic data, plus a big new field for storing notes about the Lease Agreement. The Payment portal has been moved to the Payment tab and the Lease Document container field has been moved to the PDF tab, where it can take up lots of space and not compete with other data.

2. **In the Status toolbar, click the Tab Control tool. (It looks like a tiny tab.) Then, draw a large tab panel on the layout.**

   It should be as wide as the dividing line between the Header and the Body part and nearly the height of the Body. The Figure has the left edge of the Tab Control on the left edge of the layout, and its bottom edge is on the bottom edge of the Body part. When you finish drawing, the Tab Control Setup dialog box (Figure 4-18) appears.

3. **In the Tab Name field, type *General*, and then click Create. Repeat this step for two more tabs: Payment and PDF.**

   FileMaker adds the three tab names to the Tabs list. The first tab you create is set as the Default Front Tab. That means the General tab will be the active one whenever you switch to the Lease Agreement layout—no matter which tab was active the last time you left it.

4. **Select Full from the Tab Justification pop-up menu, and then select Square from the Appearance pop-up menu.**

   The Full option will make the tabs appear all the way across the top of the Tab Control itself. Square means the tabs won't have rounded edges.

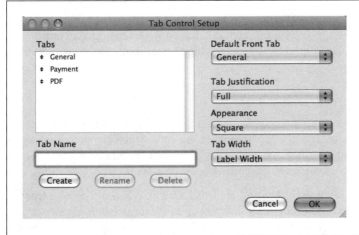

Figure 4-18:
These are the settings for the Tab Control shown in Figure 4-17. Tab widths are automatically determined by the length of their names. But you can use the Tab Width pop-up menu to add extra space, set a minimum or fixed width, or make all tabs the width of the widest label. All Tab Width options are overridden if you select Full justification, though.

5. **When you're done, click OK to close the Tab Control Setup dialog box.**

   Your new tab panel, complete with three tabs, sits highlighted in place on your layout.

Notice four selection handles, one at each corner, and a dark box around each of the tabs. Any formatting changes you make with this selection will affect all three tabs. The Tab Control in Figure 4-18 has the same background color as the Body part and a 1 pt. dark grey line. Border effects have been turned off.

Switch to Browse mode, where you'll see that your Tab Control is already working. You can click tabs, and each one comes to the front just as you'd expect. But a Tab Control without objects is pretty useless.

Switch back to Layout mode to divide your objects and move them onto their proper tabs. First, select the fields and field labels that belong on the General tab (refer back to Figure 4-17, if you need a refresher). Then drag those fields onto the General tab. Choose File→Manage→Database to create a Notes field (Text type), and then put it on the General tab, too. Use the Inspector to add a vertical scroll bar to the Notes field.

Repeat the process to move the Payment portal and its fields to the Payment tab. Double-click the portal to view the Portal Setup dialog box, and then increase the number of rows. Finally, move the Lease Document field to the PDF tab and make it larger. Try to maintain its proportions, after all it's displaying an 8.5 × 11 inch document.

Note: If you use the Arrange→Send to Back command for an object that's on a Tab Control, the selected object goes behind other objects *on the same tab,* but not behind the Tab Control itself.

Editing Tab Controls

As you just saw, you can add a Tab Control any time you need to fit more stuff on a layout. And once it's there, you can add or delete panels or change the control's appearance. Edit a Tab Control by double-clicking it in Layout Mode to summon the Tab Control Setup dialog box.

Adding, removing, and reordering tabs

In the Tab Control Setup dialog box, you can add new tabs by typing a name, and then clicking Create. The new tab appears at the end of the list of tabs, and to the right of the existing tabs in the control. You can also rename an existing tab: Select it in the list, enter a new name, and then click Rename.

To delete a tab, select it in the list, and then click Delete. When you delete a tab, you delete all the objects on that tab. (If the tab you select for deletion has any objects on it, FileMaker warns you first, and asks whether you're sure you know what you're doing.)

Finally, you can control the tab panels' order. FileMaker draws the tabs in the order they appear in the Tabs list. The leftmost tab panel is the one that appears to the top of the list, and so on. Rearrange the list using the arrows to the left of each name. FileMaker's smart enough to move the objects on each tab along with the tabs themselves when you reorder.

Default Front Tab

When you first switch to a layout but before you've clicked a tab, FileMaker needs to decide which tab to show automatically. You tell it which one by choosing the appropriate tab name from the Default Front Tab pop-up menu. While it's possible to choose any of the tab panels, be aware that most places where tabs appear, the leftmost tab is usually the front tab. If there's a compelling reason for a tab to always be in front when you first see a layout, it's pretty likely that that tab should be on the left, too.

Tab justification

If the total width of all your tabs is less than the width of the Tab Control itself *and* you haven't chosen Full justification, then FileMaker lets you choose where the grouping of tabs should be positioned. It's a lot like aligning a paragraph of text: choose from Left, Center, or Right and the tabs will bunch up according to your selection.

Note: If you have more tabs than can fit given the size of the Tab Control, then FileMaker simply doesn't show the extras. You can either force the tabs to be narrower using the Tab Width option (see below), make the Tab Control itself bigger, or make the tab names shorter.

Appearance

FileMaker can draw tabs with Rounded or Square corners. This option is purely cosmetic, so choose whichever one you like from the Appearance pop-up menu.

Note: If you're publishing your database on the web using Instant Web Publishing (page 735), rounded rectangles (tab panel tabs and buttons included) render with square corners. They *work* just fine though.

Tab width

The Tab Width pop-up menu has several choices to influence the width of the tabs:

- The standard setting, **Label Width**, makes each tab just wide enough to hold its label.

- **"Label Width + Margin of"** adds the amount of additional space you specify around the label text. The label's text will be centered within the tab.

- If you prefer all your tabs to be the same width, choose "**Width of Widest Label**". FileMaker figures out which label is biggest, sizes that tab appropriately, and then makes the others match. This setting may push some tabs out of view if they won't all fit with the new width.

- If you'd like all your tabs to be a nice consistent width, but with the ability to accommodate the odd long label, choose "**Minimum of**". Enter a minimum width (75 pixels, say), and every tab will be that width, unless the label is too big to fit, in which case that one tab will widen enough so the label fits.

- If you want the utmost in control and uniformity, choose "**Fixed Width of**", and then enter a width in the box. Every tab is exactly that width. If the label's text is too big, then FileMaker cuts it off at the edges.

POWER USERS' CLINIC

Tab in a Tab

If your layouts have more doodads than the bridge of the Enterprise, take heart. You can put a Tab Control on another tab for even more space savings. That's right. You can put tabs inside tabs inside tabs. So long as the new control sits entirely *inside* an existing tab, it behaves just like any other object on a panel. It sits there quietly behind the scenes and doesn't make an appearance until you click its enclosing panel. Only then is it visible, in all its tabbed glory. Needless to say, the more you use the tab-within-a-tab technique, the more complex your layout becomes—and the more potentially confusing to anyone using your database. Multiple nested tabs can also dramatically increase the amount of time it takes your computer to draw a layout when you're sharing a file using FileMaker Server (page 741). Use this technique sparingly.

Note: Full tab justification overrides some settings in the Tab Width pop-up menu, so if you're making changes and don't see what you expect, make sure you haven't selected Full in the Tab Justification pop-up menu.

Formatting a Tab Control

Out of the box, Tab Controls are medium gray, embossed, with a thick black border. But you can change that institutional look to match your carefully crafted layouts. In the toolbar's Formatting Bar, just use the fill and border tools to make your selections. You can even select each tab panel individually; the choices you make apply only to the currently selected tab. To select the whole Tab Control (all its tabs and all the objects on each tab), use the selection rectangle or Shift-click each tab panel.

Tip: If you accidentally format a single tab panel when you meant to format the whole tab control select your newly formatted tab and use the Format Painter (page 125) to apply formats to each unformatted tab panel.

Deleting a Tab Control

If you don't want a Tab Control after all, just select it, and then choose Edit→Clear, or press Delete or Backspace. FileMaker warns you that it's about to delete all unlocked objects on the tab panel as well. If that's all right with you, click OK. If you need to keep fields or objects on the tab panels, though, click Cancel, and then move the keepers off the panel (way to the right of your layout, perhaps) for safekeeping.

Adding Merge Fields

Your First and Last Name fields are now down on the General tab (Figure 4-17), where you can't see when you switch to the Payment or PDF tabs. It would be helpful to see which Lease Document you're dealing with as you switch tabs. You could add copies of the name fields on each tab, but there's a better way. You can create a text object that contains merge fields to display the data from each record's First Name and Last Name field. A *merge field* is a text block containing the field's name, surrounded by a pair of double angle brackets like this:

```
<<First Name>>
```

Besides being useful for displaying data on layouts, merge fields are often used for things like form letters, labels, or envelopes. Either way, merge fields expand and contract to use only the actual amount of space required by data inside the fields they represent. You can't enter or edit data using a merge field, nor can they be searched in Find mode (but the Quick Find in Browse mode will search merge fields). But that's no problem here—you'll keep and use the normal First Name and

Last Name fields for those purposes. In this case, a couple of merge fields help orient you as you switch tabs, and are a more attractive way to display data than using normal fields would be.

1. **In Layout mode, select the Text tool, and then change the formatting to 18-pt Helvetica Bold.**

   By choosing formatting before you click to create a text block, you're not only presetting the text block's format, you're changing your file's default text format.

2. **Click in the blank space above the tab control.**

   A blinking insertion point appears.

3. **Choose Insert→Merge Field., Or use the shortcut Ctrl+M (Windows) or Option-⌘-M (Mac).**

   The Specify Field dialog box appears (Figure 4-19).

4. **Double-click the First Name field, and then press the space bar.**

   The First Name merge field, "<<First Name>> ", appears inside your text block. You add the space so that the Last Name doesn't run onto the First Name.

Tip: If you know the exact name of the field(s) you want, you can type it instead of using the Insert→Merge Field command. Just be careful to get the angle brackets and name of the field exactly right. If you make a mistake, all you'll see in Browse mode is what you typed, and not the data you expect.

---

5. **Make sure that the insertion point is still blinking after the First Name and space in the text block, and then Choose Insert→Merge Field again. Double-click the Last Name field.**

   The text "<<First Name>> <<Last Name>>" now appears inside the next block.

Adjust the placement of the text block if necessary. Switch to Browse mode to see that the field's contents appear inside the merge fields there.

You can format merge fields just like any other text block. But since they also contain data, if you apply formatting from the Inspector's data tab to text blocks that contain merge fields, FileMaker displays the data according to your formatting. So if you put a merge version of the Rental Fee field on the Payment tab (so you can see what the Rental Fee's supposed to be as you record each payment), don't forget to format the text block as currency.

You can use merge fields to create a form letter (you'll get one copy for each record in the found set, with appropriate data for each record). Just type the text of the letter inside a large text block, and then insert merge fields within the text as appropriate. You'll also see heavy use of merge fields if you use the Layout/Report Assistant to create label or envelope layouts.

Using Symbols to Show Important Info

Merge fields aren't the only things FileMaker can use to show dynamic information. You use one of a handful of special *symbols*—stand-in characters that are replaced with info when you view your database in Browse or Preview mode. For example, see Figure 4-19, where each record on the Lease Agreement List layout is numbered. The record number symbol displays an automatic number for each record.

Note: *FileMaker offers a host of other symbols besides the record number symbol. See the box on the next page for details.*

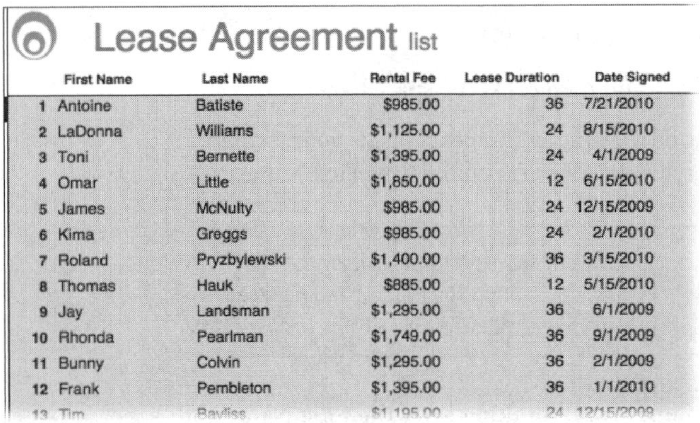

	First Name	Last Name	Rental Fee	Lease Duration	Date Signed
1	Antoine	Batiste	$985.00	36	7/21/2010
2	LaDonna	Williams	$1,125.00	24	8/15/2010
3	Toni	Bernette	$1,395.00	24	4/1/2009
4	Omar	Little	$1,850.00	12	6/15/2010
5	James	McNulty	$985.00	24	12/15/2009
6	Kima	Greggs	$985.00	24	2/1/2010
7	Roland	Pryzbylewski	$1,400.00	36	3/15/2010
8	Thomas	Hauk	$885.00	12	5/15/2010
9	Jay	Landsman	$1,295.00	36	6/1/2009
10	Rhonda	Pearlman	$1,749.00	36	9/1/2009
11	Bunny	Colvin	$1,295.00	36	2/1/2009
12	Frank	Pembleton	$1,395.00	36	1/1/2010
13	Tim	Bayliss	$1,195.00	24	12/15/2009

Figure 4-19:
The number to the left of each record on the Lease Agreement List layout comes from a special symbol placed on the layout. Sort the list, and notice that the records change order, but the record numbers themselves stay in sequence. The record number is meant to help you figure out where you are in a list, but not to identify any specific record. See page 137 for a way to assign a permanent ID number, or key, to a record.

To add a record number to your Lease Agreement List layout, choose Insert→Record Number Symbol. You now have a text object that contains "@@". You may need to format the record number merge field. Switch to Browse mode, where you see that FileMaker puts the current record number in place of the symbol.

You can also insert symbols into existing text objects. Just click into the text object first, as if to type. Then when you choose Insert→Record Number Symbol, File-Maker adds the record number symbol to the existing text.

Other Symbols

On the Insert menu, FileMaker includes symbols for several special values you may want to show on a layout. In Browse mode (or Preview mode), FileMaker replaces the symbol with the up-to-the-moment correct value. You can read about the record number symbol on the previous page. Here are the other symbols:

- The date symbol (//) is replaced by the current date. You'd include this symbol on printed reports so you can easily see when the reports were printed.-

- The time symbol (::) is replaced by the current time. If your reports needed to be identified down to the hour and minute they were printed, add this symbol to a report's header or footer.

- The user name symbol (||) is replaced by the current user's name. FileMaker takes the user name of whoever's logged into your computer (or the custom User Name if one is entered in FileMaker's Preferences). To

clarify: That's two *pipe* symbols—Shift-backslash on most keyboards—typed side by side.

- The page number symbol (##) is replaced by the page number in Preview mode and when you print. Otherwise, it just shows as a question mark.

The Insert menu has three related options as well, but unlike symbols, these don't get replaced by anything in Browse or Preview mode. When you use the Insert→Current Date command, for instance, FileMaker simply adds today's date to the text object in Layout mode. It's a static value (that is, it never changes) and shows the same date in any mode.

You can use the Insert menu to place symbols where you need them, but just like Merge fields, you can type them in manually faster and easier. So once you've seen that "##" makes a page number, forget about mousing around, and just type the two number signs.

Writing a Basic Script

Now that you have a record number on the Lease Agreement List layout, and have sorted the list, you can start to see how useful the layout really is. The Lease Agreement layout is great for revealing detail, but when the Lease Agreement List layout is sorted by Last Name, it's a cinch to scroll to the record you need without entering Find mode, typing in search criteria, and then performing a find. But it could be easier sort the records on the layout. As it is, you've got to choose Records→Sort Records, select the field you want to sort by, and then click Sort. All this stuff is easy, but efficiency is king in your world. The solution is to write a script to do these things automatically.

If you're familiar with *macros* in other programs, then you already get the idea of scripts in FileMaker—you set up scripts to perform tasks for you. The task at hand—sorting—is just one command, but it has several steps. They're all quick steps, but when you have to repeat them several times a day and so does everyone else in your office, all that wasted time adds up to real inefficiency. Also, any manual process leaves room for human error. When you make a mistake, no matter how harmless, you have to undo or redo what you just did. A script that handles your sort is more efficient and less susceptible to error.

Creating a Sort Script

Here's how to write a script that sorts the records on your list layout alphabetically by Last Name and then First Name:

1. **Choose Records→Sort Records. Set up the window to sort by Last Name and then First Name (page 38), and then click Sort.**

   Every time you open the Sort window, the last sort order is already in the window. It works the same way for scripts. So save yourself some time by performing the sort first. That way, when you write the script, the order will already be in the Sort window.

2. **Choose Scripts→Manage Scripts.**

   The Manage Scripts dialog box appears.

3. **Click New.**

   The Edit Script dialog box appears (Figure 4-20).

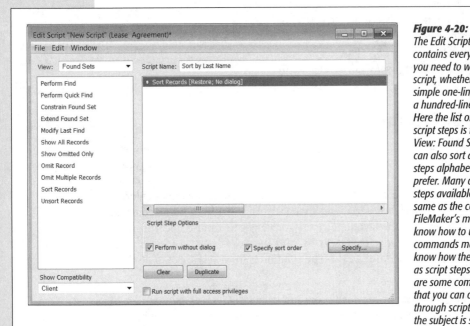

Figure 4-20:
The Edit Script window contains everything you need to write a script, whether it's a simple one-line script or a hundred-line monster. Here the list of available script steps is filtered by View: Found Sets, but you can also sort all the script steps alphabetically if you prefer. Many of the script steps available are the same as the commands in FileMaker's menus. If you know how to use those commands manually, you know how they'll behave as script steps. But there are some commands that you can only access through scripting, and the subject is so deep and wide that this book has three chapters, 10, 11, and 16, devoted to the subject.

4. **In the Script Name field, type *Sort by Last Name*.**

   As always, give everything you name in FileMaker a descriptive name. Mature databases can have hundreds of scripts, so good naming is the first step in keeping things organized.

5. **In the View pop-up menu, choose Found Sets.**

   The filters the list of script steps so you can easily pick the one you need.

6. **Double-click the Sort Records script step.**

   The Sort Records script step appears in the window's Script pane.

7. **Turn on "Perform without dialog".**

   Without this option selected, you'd see the regular Sort window every time you run the script. Don't turn on this option when you're writing a script that lets the user choose a custom sort as the script runs.

8. **Turn on "Specify sort order".**

   The regular Sort window appears, with Last Name and then First Name set up already. As you know, FileMaker remembers your most recent sort order, but it's good practice to verify *everything* when you're scripting. And if you wanted a different sort order, you can change it and the script will remember your changes.

9. **Click OK to close the Sort window, and then, in the Edit Script window, click Close.**

   FileMaker asks if you want to save the script's changes.

10. **Click Save.**

    FileMaker saves the script and closes the Edit Script window.

11. **Make sure "Include in Menu" is turned on for the Sort by Last Name script, and then close the Manage Scripts window.**

    Now that the Manage Scripts window is closed, you need some way to run the script you just wrote. Look in the Scripts menu. It appears there, along with a shortcut. You can run the script by choosing Scripts→Sort by Last Name or by using the shortcut.

Tip: Windows users can save scripts before closing the Edit Script window by choosing the Edit Script window's File→Save Script command. Both PC and Mac fans can use the Save Script shortcut Ctrl+S (⌘-S).

Now that the script is ready to go, Unsort your records (choose Records→Unsort), and then run the script.

Creating a Button

Running the script from the menu saved you a few steps, but you can make it even more convenient by attaching the script to a layout object, which then becomes a button. Then whenever you click the button in Browse mode, the script runs automatically. Here's how:

1. **In Layout mode, click the Last Name Field's label to select it.**

   It's a common convention to click a column label to sort a column, so help your users out by adopting that principle.

2. **Choose Format→Button Setup.**

   The Button Setup window appears (Figure 4-21).

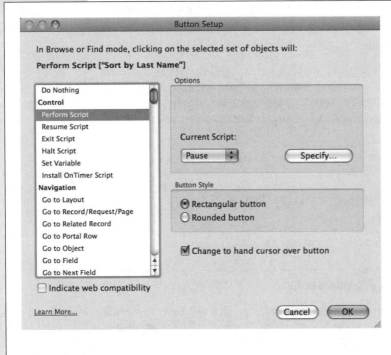

Figure 4-21:
The Button Setup window lets you choose from most of the same steps you see in the Edit Script window. The difference is that you can only choose a single script step when you define a button this way. Any time you need a process that requires two or more script steps, create a script and then attach it to the button. But even if the process is a single step, you may still want a script, so you can format it to appear in the Script menu. Even better, if you apply a script to several buttons throughout your database, you can change the script and all the buttons will run the edited script automatically. But if you had attached script actions to those buttons instead of a script, you'd have to change each one manually.

3. **In the script step list, click Perform Script.**

   This "controller" script step lets you run any script you've written by attaching it to a button.

4. **In the Options section of the window, click Specify.**

The Specify Script window appears, showing a list off all the scripts in your database. You've only got one, but it's not uncommon to have hundreds.

5. **Click the "Sort by Last Name" script, and then click OK until you're back on your layout.**

Your button is ready to use.

Switch to Browse mode, and then Unsort your records, if they're sorted. Finally, click the Last Name field label to see the script run. You haven't put anything on your layout to indicate to your users that the field label does anything useful. FileMaker changes the pointer to a hand icon when it's positioned over any button, but you have to give users a reason to wander up there with their mouses. So change the label's formatting (make it a contrasting color, or put a border around it so that it looks like a button) to help users out. (Learn more about buttons on page 317.)

Tip: Check out this chapter's Lease Agreement Finished.fp7 file to look under the hood at some formatting options and a beefed up script that can sort by different fields, depending on a script parameter (explained on page 686).

Applying a Script Trigger

The script was nice, and the button improved things, but you're still not done learning how useful and intuitive scripts can be. Since the point of going to the list layout is to quickly scan a list so you can find a particular Lease Agreement record, it'd been even more convenient if the list just knew to sort itself every time you switch to the layout. And that kind of thing is what Script Triggers are for.

You've just seen that you can run a script from the Scripts menu or from a button. But you can also tell a script to run when you do other things, like enter data in a field or go so a specific layout. Here's how to make the Sort by Last Name script run every time you go to the Lease Agreement List layout:

1. **If you're not viewing the Lease Agreement List layout, switch to it. Then in Layout mode, choose Layouts→Layout Setup.**

You'll learn about this dialog box's other options in Chapter 7. For now, you're interested in the Script Triggers tab.

2. **Click the Script Triggers tab.**

The Script Triggers tab appears (Figure 4-22).

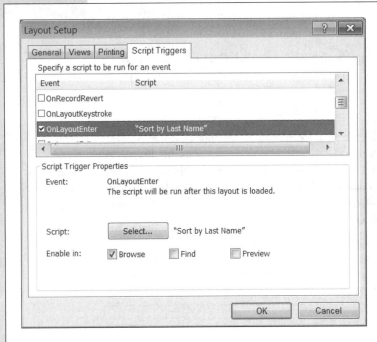

Figure 4-22:
Script triggers give you a more automated way to run a script than by using the menu or creating a button. This script trigger will run a script called "Sort by Last Name" every time the layout is visited in Browse mode. When you apply a script trigger with the Layout Setup dialog box, it only affects the layout you apply it to. Script triggers are enormously powerful and they can be tricky. Learn more about them on page 430.

3. **Select the OnLayoutEnter option in the Event list. Windows users may need to scroll the list to see that option.**

   Selecting an Event tells FileMaker *when* to run a script. Once you make a selection, the Specify Script window appears.

4. **Click the "Sort by Last Name" script to select it, and then click OK.**

   The Script Trigger tab is now set up. Notice that you're only enabling the script to run while you're viewing the layout in Browse mode.

5. **Click OK.**

   The script will run each time you switch to the Lease Agreement List layout.

To test the script trigger, Unsort your list, and then switch to the Lease Agreement layout. Then switch back to the Lease Agreement List layout. The script runs and sorts your list for you.

Creating a Dynamic Report with the Assistant

Your database is getting pretty smart now. It can do math and perform some housekeeping duties on its own. But one of the main purposes of storing data is learning how to analyze that data. You're storing information about Lease Agreements, but so far, there's no way to take a look at any trends that might show up. For instance, you offer leases of 12, 24, or 36 months. If you sort and count your leases by duration, you may be able to spot interesting trends, like people who are willing to sign longer leases are also willing to lease your more expensive properties, for example. Or, maybe the opposite is true and they're less willing. If so, you'll want to come up with some incentives to get the high rollers to sign longer leases. But you'll never know until you create a report.

You've already seen how the Layout/Report Assistant makes it a breeze to create a new layout (page 123). Many of the assistant's panels are already familiar to you. But the assistant can also build some special layout parts and create fields for you that summarize your data. Better still, the report you'll build is dynamic. If you add a new record to the list while you're viewing the onscreen report, the record is automatically sorted into place and your summary data updates immediately. Here's how to create a dynamic report:

1. **In Layout mode, choose Layouts→New Layout/Report.**

   The New Layout/Report assistant starts up and the Create a Layout/Report panel appears.

2. **In the "Show records from" pop-up menu, choose the Lease Agreement table. In the Layout Name box, type *Lease Agreement Report* and then choose Report from the "Select a layout type" list. If they're not selected, choose "Include subtotals" and "Include grand totals." Finally, click Next.**

   Watch the sample report as you make selections in the assistant's windows. You'll see clues about the type of report you're designing. After you click Next, the Specify Fields panel appears.

3. **Move the First Name, Last Name, Rental Fee, and Lease Duration fields to the "Fields shown on layout/report" box, and then click Next.**

   This should be familiar territory by now. Remember that you can use the arrow to the left of each field to move them up and down in the list on the right. After you click Next, the "Organize Records by Category" panel appears.

4. **Move the Lease Duration field into the Report categories list, and then click Next.**

   The sample report changes as you move fields into the Report categories list. After you click Next, the Sort Records panel appears.

5. **Move the Last Name and First Name fields into the Sort order list, and then click Next.**

   Lease Duration is already in the list because that's how the report will categorize the list. But you want records with the same Lease Duration value to be sorted alphabetically by Last Name and then by First Name. After you click Next, the Specify Subtotals panel appears (Figure 4-23).

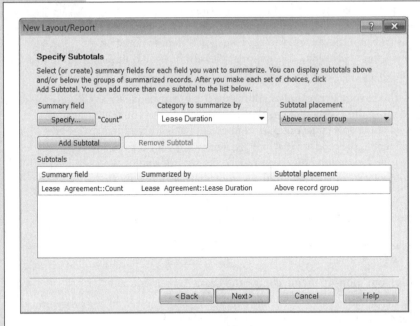

Figure 4-23:
Choices you make in this window determine how many subtotals your report will have. You can also place the subtotal above or below the records it's summarizing. You need to have at least one Subtotal line item in the bottom box for the summary to work, though, so make sure you click Add Subtotal after you create or chose a Summary field (you'll learn about them later in this tutorial).

6. **From the Subtotal Placement pop-up menu, choose "Above record group" and then click on Specify under the Summary field.**

   The Specify Field window appears.

7. **Click Add.**

   The Options for Summary Field window appears (Figure 4-24). You'll create a special field that counts the records in each category. The field will appear above the record group it summarizes because of the choice you made in the previous step.

8. **In the Summary Field Name box, type *Count*, and then select "Count of". Now choose Lease Duration from the "Choose field to summarize by" list, and then click OK until you're back on the Specify Subtotals panel. Now click Add Subtotal. When your window looks like Figure 4-23, click Next.**

   FileMaker creates a new Count field (Summary type) and at the end of this process, you'll see a Subsummary part (you'll learn how to create them manually on page 603) based on the options you just chose. The summary field counts each record in the sorted category group you selected above and displays a count of records for each group. After you click Next, the Specify Grand Totals window appears.

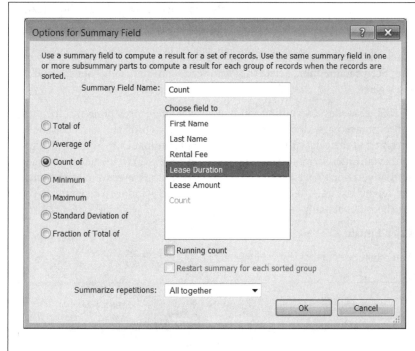

Figure 4-24:
You'd see this same window if you used the Manage Database window to create a summary field. Summary fields do just what their name implies: they summarize groups of data. You can apply one of several mathematical operations to the fields, including Totals, Averages, and Counts. You can count any field, but you can't apply math to text fields. So if you're trying to select a field, but it's grayed out, check the operation you're trying to perform. It may not be the right option for the field you want to summarize (or the field's definition may be set to the wrong type).

9. **Click Specify.**

   The Specify Field window appears. The Count field you just created appears in the list.

10. **Click the Count field to select it, and then click OK. Leave the Grand total placement pop-up menu set to "End of report", and then click Add Grand Total. Finally, click Next.**

    Make sure the Lease Agreement::Count field appears in the Grand Totals list at the bottom of the window before you click Next. Summary fields are smart enough to display different data depending on the layout part they're placed in. So you can use the same summary field in a Subsummary part and a Grand Total part, and it will display appropriate data in each part. This version of the Count field will appear at the end of the report and will give you a grand total count of all the records you're viewing. After you click Next, the Select a Theme window appears.

11. **If it isn't already selected, select Default from the Layout Themes list, and then click Next.**

    The Header and Footer Information window appears.

12. From the Header's Top left pop-up menu, choose Layout Name. From the Footer's Bottom left pop-up menu, choose Current Date. Then click Next.

   The Create a Script for this Report window appears.

13. Click the "Create a script" option, and then type *Lease Agreement Report* in the "Script name" box. Select the "Run script automatically" option, and then click Next.

   FileMaker writes a script for you that sorts your records properly (the data in subsummary parts doesn't show up unless the records are sorted by the field specified in their definition). The "Run script automatically" option attaches an OnLayoutEnter script trigger (explained on page 449) to the new report layout so that you don't have to remember to run the script every time you switch to the report layout. After you click Next, the final window tells you that you're finished. But actually, you aren't quite done.

14. Click Finish.

   Your sorted report appears (Figure 4-25).

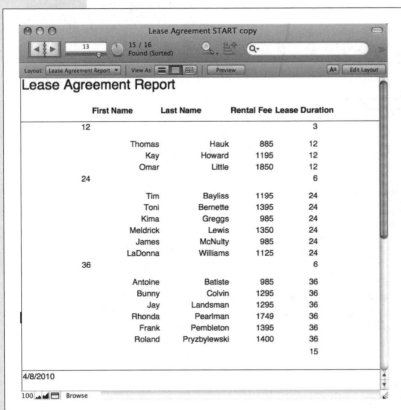

Figure 4-25:
Graphically speaking, the report as created is nothing to write home about. You'll need to put your layout design skills to use on this layout. However, the Layout Assistant gave you some nice tools to help you start analyzing your data. You can see that your current group of tenants trend toward longer leases. And it looks like your higher-priced properties are leased out, too. Except for that one guy with the $1,850 lease who's only signing on for 12 months. (While you're learning FileMaker, have your assistant find out what it'll take to get that guy signed up for another couple of years.)

There were a lot of steps and a lot of selections to make. But the hard work's been done for you. In Chapter 14, you'll learn how to create a sorted subsummary report completely by hand. Once you've done that, you'll appreciate how much easier it was to make selections in an assistant. However, you need to format your fields and generally beautify the layout so that it matches the rest of your database.

When you've got the layout looking fine, switch to Browse mode so you can see how the report updates dynamically. For example, click the New Record button in your Status toolbar, and then enter the following data in the new record:

- First Name: Janette

- Last Name: Desautel

- Rental Fee: 1295

- Lease Duration: 12

When you commit the record, it's sorted into the proper group, and the Count field is updated immediately. The same thing's true if you edit data in the field on which the sort is based (remember that this report is always sorted by the Lease Duration field). Change some data in a Lease Duration field, and then commit the record. It will sort into the proper group. If you add data that's not in an existing group (say you type *48* in the Lease Duration field), a new group will be formed with a Count of "1."

Subsummary layouts only show their summary data when your records are sorted by the field that's attached to the subsummary part (explained on page 601). So if you unsort your records, or do a sort that doesn't include the subsummary part's field (say you sorted by Last Name and First Name only), the groups and subtotals don't show on the layout. To get them back, sort the records again, and this time, make sure you include the proper field (in this case, it's Lease Duration) in the sort order.

Note: Sorted subsummary reports are great for looking at trends in your data, but you probably wouldn't usually use them as the primary way to add new records or edit exiting ones. But on those occasions when it's suitable (say the sorted report makes it clear that some data wasn't entered correctly, it's convenient that you don't have to leave the report layout to make corrections).

Creating a Trailing Group Report

The dynamic report you just created is perfect for printing out every time you want to analyze your data. Even if they don't want to print the report, your users can just switch to the Lease Agreement Report layout and get an up-to-the-minute categorized report on your properties. But what if they need a quick analysis of the data using a category that you haven't set up for them? Do they have to wait until you have time to add a new report? Or maybe you need a last-minute, one-time report that you won't be printed (you don't even have time—there's a meeting in 5 minutes and you've been told to get the data), so you don't want to bother creating a new layout and spending time making it match the rest of your database. Either way, FileMaker's Trailing Group reporting feature is the solution.

A Trailing Group report requires a Table view on a layout that shows records from the table you want to report on. It accomplishes the same thing as a dynamic sub-summary (sorts records automatically by the category you choose, with an optional summary field), but it's temporary and doesn't actually add a subsummary part to the layout.

Note: If you're using the chapter's sample files, the layout you need has already been created for you. If you continued working with the file you created in the last chapter, create a new layout that shows records using the Lease Agreement table, and then switch to Table view.

---

1. **On the Lease Agreement Table layout's Table view, click the triangle to the right of the Rental Fee's column heading. (The triangle appears when you place your mouse over the heading.) Choose "Add Trailing Group by Rental Fee" (Figure 4-26).**

   The Rental Fee field's pop-up menu appears when you click the triangle, and then when you choose the Trailing Group command, a gray summary row appears on the table and the records are automatically sorted by Rental Fee.

2. **From the Rental Fee's pop-up menu, choose Trailing Subtotals→Count.**

   The count appears in the summary row below each Trailing Group. Behind the scenes, a new summary field was created for you and its data will display on this layout.

3. **From the Rental Fee's pop-up menu, choose "Trailing Group Fill Color", and then choose a color from the pop-up menu.**

   Choose a color that helps you see the summarized data better.

FileMaker sorts and groups the records for you, so you can get the information you need from the ad hoc report without fuss. As with the dynamic report in the previous section, you have to sort the records by the Trailing Group you chose for the summaries to show up. But unlike the dynamic report, FileMaker doesn't sort the data automatically if you leave this layout and then come back to it later. Click the Rental Fee column head to sort the records and the trailing groups reappear.

If you switch to Layout mode, you'll see that the layout *doesn't* have a new part added to it. Nor does the Count field actually appear on the layout. That's why this type of report is temporary. It's meant to let you get a quick, bird's-eye view of your data and then get right back into your other tasks (or to the meeting on time and with the data you were told to have at your fingertips).

Figure 4-26:
The contextual menu for fields in table view lets you create temporary Trailing Group reports, but it also lets you change the database's schema (you can change the field's type or options, delete the field or add new summary fields) or just sort the records you're viewing. You can even change the way the Table view behaves by adding or deleting fields from the layout or changing a column's width. Or if you've made a lot of changes you want to undo, you can restore the layout's original appearance. In this case, the "Trailing Group by Rental Fee" field would disappear. But if you've created a summary field for the Trailing Group, the field isn't deleted from the table.

You can get creative with your ad hoc reports by adding multiple trailing groups at the same time. In a small database like the one you're working on, you may find that nearly every record gets its own group. But in a database with lots of records, you can use this technique to get fine-grained reports very quickly. Remove a Trailing Group by clicking the column head associated with that group. Choose "Remove Trailing Group by Rental Fee" and the group no longer shows up.

Changing the Default Account

You know that FileMaker creates a lot of elements for you when you first create a new database. One thing you may not know is that it even created a login account for you *and* it assigned that account name to be entered automatically each time you open the file. You can see that setting, and then turn it off, by choosing File→File Options (Figure 4-27).

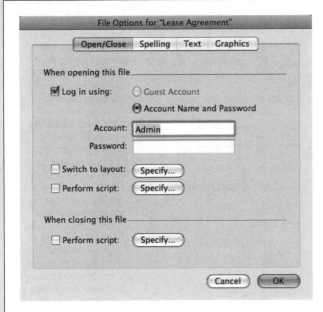

Figure 4-27:
It's not industrial-strength security, but FileMaker created an Admin account for you, and has been secretly using it every time you open the Lease Agreement database. Really it's not that much of a secret, because you have to figure that at least half of FileMaker's millions of users know about this account and the hackers amongst them would try the "Admin" account name (it doesn't even have a password), if they wanted to break into your database. One of the first things you can do to make any database more secure is turn off Log in automatically.

This default account is created in every database FileMaker creates, so to protect your new database from prying eyes, turn off the option to log in using the automatic account, and then change the default account's name and password. Here's how to change the default account:

1. **Choose File→Manage→Security.**

   The Manage Security window appears. It shows two built-in accounts, but only the Admin account is active, as shown by the checkmark in the Active column.

2. **Click the Admin account, and then click Edit.**

   The Edit Account window appears (Figure 4-28).

3. **Type your first name's initial and your last name in the account box.**

   This first initial/last name scheme is standard for creating account names. But you can use whatever scheme you like, so long as you can remember it.

4. **Type a password into the password box.**

   You know the drill by now: create a password that has a mix of letters and numbers and for extra strength, even a symbol or two. Just make sure you remember exactly what you typed, because you're about to have to retype it.

Figure 4-28:
Account Names appear in the Account Name box just as you type them, but characters in the password box are obscured by a password font. That keeps your typing safe from someone who may be looking at your computer screen over your shoulder, but it does mean that you have to be very careful as you type. Because once you add a password to an account, even you can never see what was entered in the box. (Go to Chapter 18 to read all about security.)

Note: Case does *not* matter for account names, but it *does* matter for passwords.

---

5. **Click OK until you've dismissed all the windows.**

   Before you click OK for the last time, you'll have to re-enter the new account and password you just created. And if you get it wrong, you can't close the Manage Security window. If you can't quite get the combination right, go back into the account you've just edited, and then retype your password. Once you get the combo correct, the window closes and you're back on your layout.

You know that you've got the account name and password right, because you were able to close the window. But you should test the new login account by closing the file (if you still have multiple windows open, make sure you close them all), and then opening the file again. This time, you'll be asked to enter the new account name and password.

FileMaker guesses that the account name used for each file it opens is the same as the name you entered when you first installed FileMaker. But you can change this name in the program's Preferences window. Choose Edit→Preferences (Windows) or FileMaker Pro→Preferences (Mac) to get the window shown in Figure 4-29.

Figure 4-29:
Type the account name you want to appear in the User Name box and FileMaker will use that as the automatic account name from now on. On the Mac these options are a little different. You can choose from the System's Admin Account name or choose Other, and then type a custom name. Either way, it saves you a few keystrokes every time you open the database.

Summing Up

Over the last two chapters you've created a database from scratch. In that process, you've learned the basics of FileMaker's major features. You know how to create tables and fields, and you can create relationships between them. You can create layouts and layout objects and you can change the format of the most common layout objects. You've even tried your hand at writing a script, creating some data analysis reports, and adding security to your file. Before you delve deeper into these topics, it's time to switch gears and learn more about planning a database. In the next part, you'll learn how to think like a database developer.

Part Three: Thinking Like a Developer

III

Creating and Managing a Relational Database

In Part 2, you learned the fundamentals of creating a custom database. You saw that you could create tables and fields whenever you need them. You learned how to polish layouts and add features and designs that make your data easy to maintain and analyze. You even added simple scripts for creating quick reports with the click of a button.

And you did all those things in an organic fashion; as the need arose, you created elements that gave your database more power. And you didn't have to do a lot of prep work to add that new whiz-bang feature. But as the databases you create get more sophisticated and the tasks you need them to perform get more complex, you'll find that the right kind of planning and preparation makes development go more smoothly down the road. It's time to start thinking like a database developer, so that your database can grow as your needs grow.

In this chapter, you'll learn how to create a roadmap for the tables and fields that comprise your database. (Database nerds called this map their database's *schema*.) Before you define the first table in your database, it pays to sit down and think about the kinds of data you'll be storing. Think about the basic tasks the database handles and how those tasks get carried out. This chapter shows you how to plan your database schema, and then start putting that plan into action.

Tip: Go back and read the box on page 138 if you want to review basic database and relationship terms before you plunge into the theoretical material ahead.

Understanding Relational Databases

You got your feet wet with relational databases on page 137 when you created a Payment table to track monthly payments for the Lease Document database. You needed to attach a new payment record to a specific lease document as each payment was made. So you created a second table, and then used a key field in each table to create the relationship between the two tables. Those two points are what defines any relational database:

- The database contains more than one table, and

- Those tables are related to one another by a key field.

Both conditions have to be true; just putting more than one table into a FileMaker database doesn't make it relational. Say you have a Customer table and an Antiques Collection table. There's no point putting them in the same database unless there's a relationship between those two things. But if you're selling antiques to your customers, you can create a database that tracks your inventory and sales to specific people.

Why not just keep two databases—one for customer info and one for sales tracking? The benefits of creating a relational database include:

- **You don't have to enter data twice.** When you sell an antique candelabra, you need to create a sales slip containing info about the sale plus the customer's name, phone number, and so on. Since you already have that info in the Customer table, you can save yourself retyping it into the Antiques Collection table by just connecting to the customer's record in the existing table.

    For another example, think back to the Lease Document database. Without two related tables, the Payment table would need a lot more fields in it (page 141). It would need to track the name of the person making the payment and the name of the property for which the payment is made. But because the payment record is related to a Lease Document record, that relationship tells you where the payment belongs and who signed the lease. The relationship also lets you display Payment data on the Lease Document record and vice versa.

- **Your data is easier to maintain.** Since the data really "lives" in only one table (though you can display it in any related table), you can change data in one place, and those changes are immediately reflected everywhere. When the same data is stored in unrelated tables, you may have dozens of places to find and fix data when it changes.

- **Relational databases are easier for users to understand.** Other databases (not FileMaker, lucky you) use complex queries and reports to show users their data. Spreadsheets are simpler, yet often require manipulation of rows of data to get meaningful information from it. But even a new user looking at a Lease Document record can see that the list at the bottom of the layout is for tracking payments. One reason it's so obvious is because the relationship in the database is an onscreen representation of a real-world relationship.

Keep these benefits in mind as you plan, because efficiency and clarity can help you make decisions as you draw your road map.

This chapter teaches you how to plan the schema for a database that'll track time and expenses for jobs you do for your clients, and then create invoices for those jobs. Although the database you'll design has specific sets of tasks that may not pertain to your real-world database, the concepts you'll learn can be applied to any tasks you need your custom database to do.

Modeling Your Database

When you model your database, you decide what entities you'll be tracking, which ones deserve a table, and how they relate to one another. It's easier to create the right tables and connections the first time than to go back and change them later, especially if you need to change tables that already have data in them. The point of this exercise is to build a "blueprint" to follow as you build your database. The pros call this blueprint an *entity relationship* (or ER) diagram.

Choosing Entities

First, decide what tables you need, and how they fit together. Since every table holds data about a single entity, you normally start by figuring out all the entities in your system. You probably can't list them all in one shot. Everybody forgets some that are less obvious, so start with blank paper or a word processor, and list all the things the database needs to *do*. This list will help you identify entities.

Now's the time to stretch your mind and think of every possibility. What tasks do you do every day? What do you *wish* you could do—and what information do you need to do it? What do you want your computer to show you when you sit down first thing in the morning?

Think about how your work day goes. When your workflow hits a wall, what piece of information would get you moving again? What questions do people keep asking you—and how could FileMaker answer them for you? The more your initial plan matches your real needs, the better your database will be when it's up and running. You can see a first stab at a list in Figure 5-1. At this point, your list should contain sentences or short phrases that describe the database's tasks.

With this list in hand, you can start to figure out what *entities* your database needs to track. For each item on your list, think of all the *things* it involves. Figure 5-2 shows a possible list. Add those things to each item on your list. For "Track my time", add "Tasks" and "Services", for example.

Your initial list should include all the entities you think are important. Once you have a list of entities, the next step is to figure out which ones really matter. You'll use a process of elimination to remove extraneous items from your list. For each entity, ask the following questions. This process will help you look at each entity from different perspectives as you come up with a final entity list.

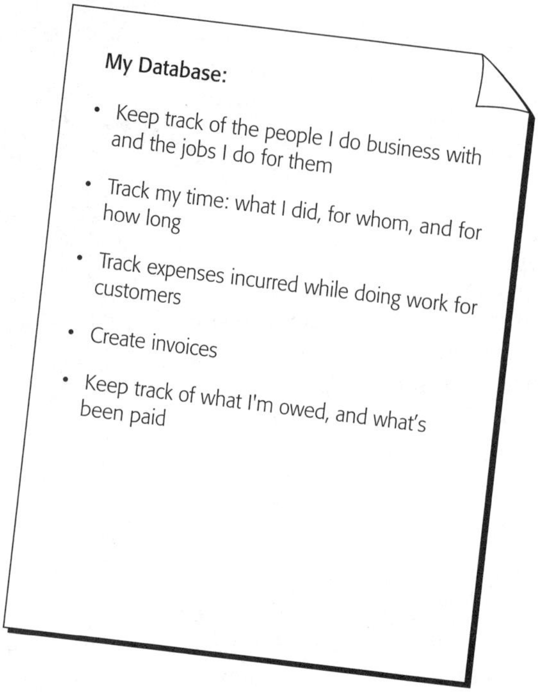

My Database:

- Keep track of the people I do business with and the jobs I do for them
- Track my time: what I did, for whom, and for how long
- Track expenses incurred while doing work for customers
- Create invoices
- Keep track of what I'm owed, and what's been paid

Figure 5-1:
Here's a list of things your database will do. A list like this helps you start figuring out your entities and possible tables. A more complex database could have a much longer list. Some big systems start with a list several pages long. Even if you think you'll start with a simple database, make this list your "blue sky" list. What are all the things you think your database will ever need to do? Sometimes starting out with a kitchen sink approach helps you focus on what's most important. And if you whittle down the list once you start to work, those deleted items often form a road map for phase two of your development.

- **Is this entity already covered?** The list in Figure 5-2 includes Checks and Payments. A check is really just a kind of payment, so you don't need to track checks separately in your database. Since a payment is more general than a check, you can eliminate Checks. Then, when you build your Payments table, you can add a field called Type, and put a value list with Check, Cash, or Credit Card on that field.

- **Is it too specific?** Sometimes you have things in your list that aren't general enough. This list shows Airline Tickets, Hotels, and Film. But you don't really need to track the details of each of these items. Instead, you're just interested in expenses in general—what they were, how much they cost, and what job they were for. To fix this problem, think of a more general word that encompasses all three things—something like Expenses. Add that to the list, and then remove the more specific versions.

- **Is it an attribute of another entity?** Do you really need an entity called Outstanding Balances? You do need to know how much each customer still owes you, but maybe you already have that information somewhere else. A customer has an outstanding balance because one or more invoices are unpaid.

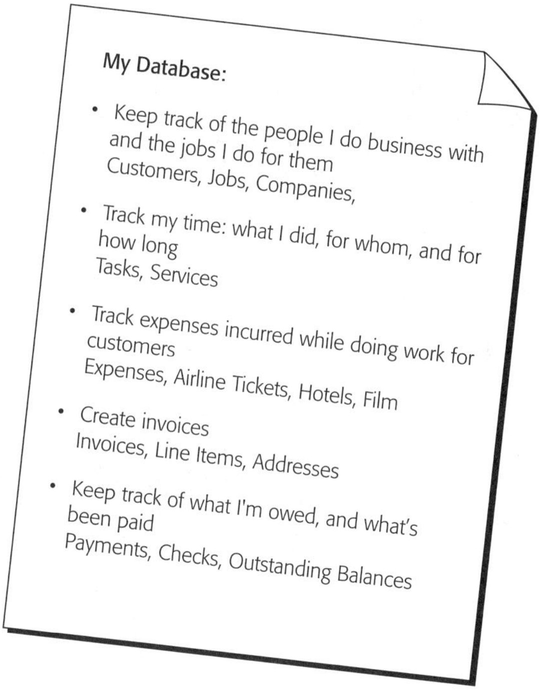

Figure 5-2:
You've now added some entities to your list. Don't worry too much about whether the entities you think of are good ones or not—right now you're just trying to get it all down so you don't leave anything out. You can start with all the nouns in the list—Customers, Tasks, Invoices—and try to think of nouns that cover other aspects of your work.

My Database:

- Keep track of the people I do business with and the jobs I do for them
  Customers, Jobs, Companies,

- Track my time: what I did, for whom, and for how long
  Tasks, Services

- Track expenses incurred while doing work for customers
  Expenses, Airline Tickets, Hotels, Film

- Create invoices
  Invoices, Line Items, Addresses

- Keep track of what I'm owed, and what's been paid
  Payments, Checks, Outstanding Balances

So to see who owes you money, you really just want to look at the balance due on any unpaid invoices. Scratch Outstanding Balances off the list. For the same reason, you can also remove Companies—they're just attributes of a customer. (For more detail, see the box on page 186.)

Note: Just because you're crossing things off your list doesn't mean those things aren't important, or don't apply to your database. It just means they don't qualify as entities that need their own table. These things may show up as *fields* in other tables, or they may just be one *type* of a more general entity, like Checks.

- **Is it important enough to track in your database?** Suppose your list has an item called Services. These services are the kinds of things you do for your customers: create a custom database, tend pets while they're away, recover a stolen computer, or whatever. You could create a Services table in your database, and put all these kinds of services in it. But what value would it add? What kind of information are you tracking about a service? Probably just its name—which doesn't really need to be *tracked*. So, as an entity, leave out Services.

Figure 5-3 shows an example of a well-edited Entities list.

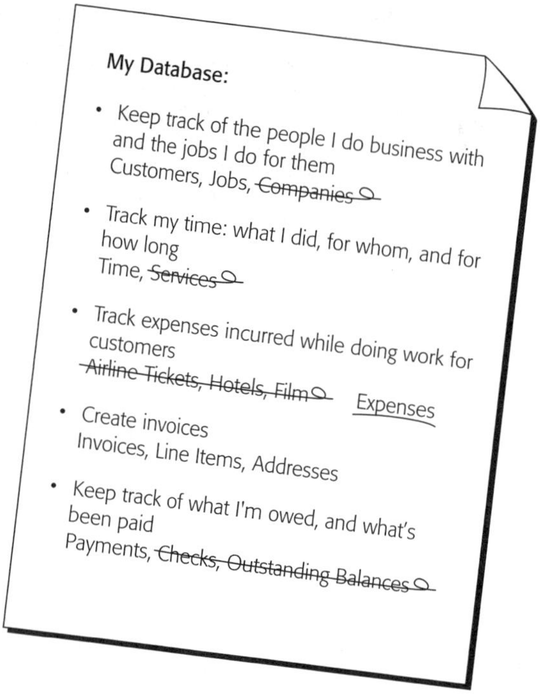

Figure 5-3:
After thinking about each entity on your list, you can remove some, and maybe add some new ones. Focus on what remains on the list after you've culled and consolidated. When you're through with this step, you have a pretty good list of the entities— and tables—in your database.

My Database:

• Keep track of the people I do business with and the jobs I do for them
Customers, Jobs, ~~Companies~~ ⟲

• Track my time: what I did, for whom, and for how long
Time, ~~Services~~ ⟲

• Track expenses incurred while doing work for customers
~~Airline Tickets, Hotels, Film~~ ⟲   Expenses

• Create invoices
Invoices, Line Items, Addresses

• Keep track of what I'm owed, and what's been paid
Payments, ~~Checks, Outstanding Balances~~ ⟲

FREQUENTLY ASKED QUESTION

No Companies?

Why is Companies just an attribute of Customers? What if my customer is a company? Don't I need to be able to keep track of that?

Your decisions about entities depend on how you intend to use the database. In this database, you're assuming that *people* hire you. Even if they hire you on behalf of some business, you put the actual person you're working for in the database, along with the name of the company that employs her.

In a different database, you may decide companies are important enough to be in their own table. If it's important to see all the people who work for one particular company, or to keep track of jobs you do by company, then you probably want a Companies table.

Finding Relationships

Now that you have a list of entities, you need to figure out how they relate to one another. To get started, just pick two of your entities—Customers and Jobs, for example—and ask yourself how they go together (if you need some guidance, see the box on page 192). You might come up with this answer: *A customer hires me to do jobs, and a job is done for a customer.* That sentence tells you two important things:

- Customers and jobs are related.

- One customer has many jobs, but each job has only one customer.

By comparing different entities in this way, you can figure out how each entity relates to other entities. Your notes as you consider these relationships might look something like Figure 5-4.

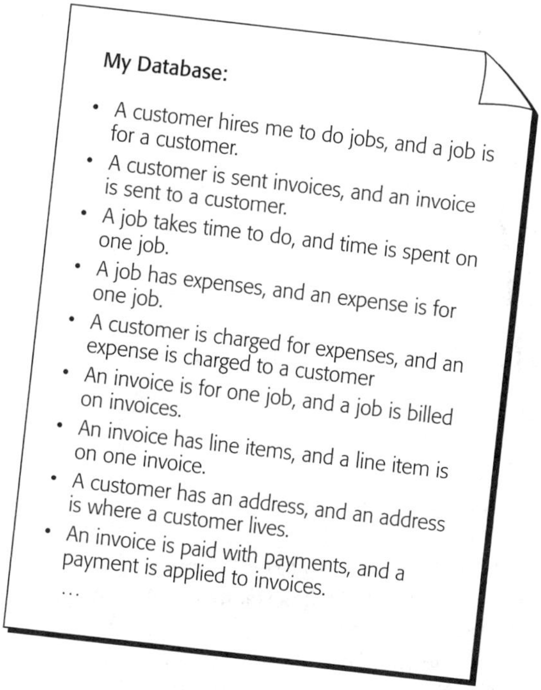

My Database:

- A customer hires me to do jobs, and a job is for a customer.
- A customer is sent invoices, and an invoice is sent to a customer.
- A job takes time to do, and time is spent on one job.
- A job has expenses, and an expense is for one job.
- A customer is charged for expenses, and an expense is charged to a customer
- An invoice is for one job, and a job is billed on invoices.
- An invoice has line items, and a line item is on one invoice.
- A customer has an address, and an address is where a customer lives.
- An invoice is paid with payments, and a payment is applied to invoices.
  ...

Figure 5-4:
Here's a series of sentences that describe relationships between entities on your list. (You may have worded things differently, or come up with some that aren't on this list.) If you're writing good subject-action sentences, they'll usually tell you what kind of relationship you'll need between the two entities.

Now you need to convert your list of sentences into a graphic representation. You can show each entity in a sentence as a box with its name in it, and then draw lines to show the type of relationship each pair will have. For example, the sentence "A customer hires me to do jobs, and a job is for a customer" makes a clear case for what's called a "one-to-many" relationship. That is, one customer can have many jobs, and each job has only one customer. The line you see in the top pair of boxes in Figure 5-5 is the visual representation of a one-to-many relationship.

As you work down the list, you can see how entities like Invoices and Customers relate to one another. (I send invoices to customers.) But the relationship with the Time entity isn't so obvious. Is "Time" plural? For that matter, if Time is an entity, then it has to be a thing, so what is a *time*? You've just discovered one of the common challenges to good relational design—choosing names that are clear and helpful.

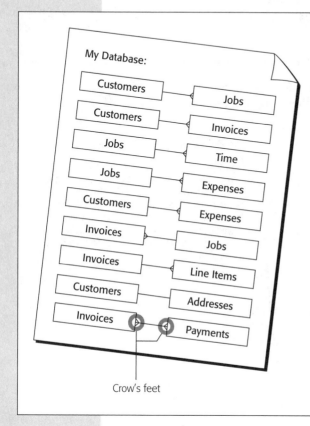

Figure 5-5:
In this picture, boxes represent entities, and the lines between them indicate relationships. The little forked end on the relationship lines (called a crow's foot) means "to-many" as in "one-to-many." If the line doesn't have a crow's foot, it's to-one. So the relationship between Payments and Invoices is many-to-many, while that between Customers and Invoices is one-to-many.

Crow's feet

You added *Time* to your list of entities because you spend time working on a job. That's a little ambiguous, though, so think about what exactly you'll be putting in the database. You'll be logging the time you spend working: what you're doing, when you started, and when you finished. You could call it a *work log entry* but that's pretty cumbersome. Because this kind of entity is quite common, database folks have made up a name for it—*timeslip*. A timeslip is sort of like one entry on a timesheet. It says what you were doing for one period of time. That unit of time will always be linked to a specific job.

Using this language, your relationship description becomes clearer:

- A job has timeslips, and a timeslip is for a job.

Now it's a lot more obvious: This relationship is one-to-many.

UP TO SPEED

Many for One and One for Many

Relationships tell FileMaker which records in two tables go together. Conceptually, relationships come in three flavors: one-to-many, many-to-many, and one-to-one. Your ER list (Figure 5-5) has examples of the first two types. One-to-many relationships are the most common.

In a one-to-many relationship, one record in the first table relates to several records in the second. For example, one invoice record has several line items, so it's a one-to-many relationship. Since relationships work both ways, a one-to-many is *always* a many-to-one as well. It's important to be clear about just what that means, though. Many different line items can be related to the same invoice, but each individual line item is only related to one invoice record.

A many-to-many relationship means something quite different. A common example is registering students for classes. Each student can be in many classes, and each class contains many students. That's a many-to-many relationship.

Finally, you can have two tables locked in a one-to-one configuration. If your database holds pictures of each product you sell, then you can create a Pictures table that would have one record for each product. Since the Products record also has one record for each product, this is a one-to-one relationship. But in practice, you might need to have multiple beauty shots for at least some of your products, which means that your one-to-one relationship quickly changes to a one-to-many. For that reason, a true one-to-one isn't very common.

FileMaker doesn't make you learn a different method for creating each type of relationship. But each type has its own set of considerations that affect the way you design your database. These concepts are discussed below.

One-to-many relationships

Most of the relationships in your diagram are one-to-many, which is normal. One-to-many relationships outnumber all other types by a large margin in almost any system. See the box above for a description of the various types of relationships.

One-to-one relationships

Your list of entities and relationships shows a one-to-one relationship between Customers and Addresses. For the purposes of this database, one customer can certainly have one address, and vice versa. But if that's the case, are they really separate entities? In fact, Address is just an attribute of the Customer entity. That makes it a prime candidate for entity-elimination. Put the address *fields* in the Customers table instead. You might argue that you *could* work for two people in the same household, and would therefore have to type the same address twice in your Customers table if you didn't have an Address table. The best answer to an argument like that is: big deal. This situation doesn't arise often enough to justify a more complicated database just to eliminate duplicating one or two addresses. Even without a separate Address table, you can still separately handle all other tasks for these two clients.

On the other hand, if you're managing a school, it's important to know which students share a home, and which parents they belong to. In that case, an Address entity makes sense. But as you start to think about the entity called Address, you start to realize that it's really a Household, and once again the Address is an attribute, but of the Household and not of the Student. This new way of thinking about your entities is one of the many realizations that can dawn on you as you're modeling your data, and it's a great example of why this sort of planning is so crucial. It's a lot better to make these type of mistakes on paper than in the database.

Tip: If you expect to have to track several addresses for each customer, then you can create a one-to-many relationship between Customers and an Addresses table. For the current example, though, you'll stick to a single address built right into the Customers table.

As a general rule, unless you can articulate a good reason for its existence, a one-to-one relationship is a mistake: It's just two tables where one would suffice. (For some clarification, see the box on page 196.) You'll almost always want to combine entities like people and their addresses into one table.

Many-to-many relationships

Ideally, you send an invoice to a customer, who pays the entire invoice with one check or credit card payment (sending an express messenger the day they receive the invoice would be a nice touch). It may even be the case that most of your customers do exactly that most of the time. But in the real world, customers will make partial payments on invoices, or sometimes they won't pay an invoice when it's due and a new one gets issued in the meantime. Then they'll cut a check to cover both invoices. Your database has to be able to track those cases, even though they aren't the norm. A many-to-many relationship lets you handle all those situations.

But many-to-many relationships pose a special challenge. To understand why, think about how they're different from a one-to-many relationship, like an Invoice and a Line Item. One Invoice can have many Line Items, but each Line Item can belong to only one Invoice. The two tables are related by a key field, which holds the same value in all the records that relate to one another. And of course each record's key field has only one value in it.

With a many-to-many relationship, you need many records in each table related to many records in the other table. But you can't put multiple values in a key field to try to make it work. Instead, you add a new special-purpose entity between the two ends of a many-to-many relationship—called a *join table*. Think of it as chopping the many-to-many line in half, and then inserting a new table in the middle. That new table has a one-to-many relationship to both of the original tables.

Here's how it works in your many-to-many relationship (Invoices and Payments): To split it up, you need to create a new entity. Since it doesn't have a decent name, just call it *Invoice Payment* (as in "This record represents one invoice payment—one payment on one invoice"). Now, instead of "An invoice is paid with payments, and a payment is applied to invoices," you can say these two things:

- An invoice is paid with invoice payments, and an invoice payment is applied to one invoice.

- A payment is divided into invoice payments, and an invoice payment is part of one payment.

Figure 5-6 shows the updated diagram.

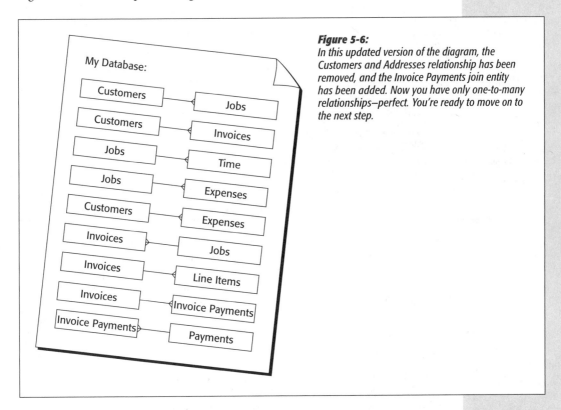

Figure 5-6:
In this updated version of the diagram, the Customers and Addresses relationship has been removed, and the Invoice Payments join entity has been added. Now you have only one-to-many relationships—perfect. You're ready to move on to the next step.

The Entity-Relationship Diagram

Now that you have a list of entities and their relationships, you're ready to assemble your master plan: the entity relationship (ER) diagram. An *ER diagram* is a picture that shows all the entities in your database, and the relationships between them. Unlike the diagram you've already drawn, each entity appears only once in an ER diagram.

Drawing the ER diagram has two purposes: First, to help you find relationships you missed, or relationships that don't belong, and second, to serve as a roadmap for your database. That is, you'll use the ER diagram when you actually create this database in FileMaker, and again if you go back to make changes later.

FREQUENTLY ASKED QUESTION

Only One Attribute

So, I'm supposed to eliminate Services as an entity because it has only one attribute (see page 184). Is that another rule? Should I remove all entities that have just one attribute?

Not necessarily. Sometimes an entity has only one attribute, but you still want to give it a table. For one thing, tables can help promote consistent data entry. Say your new database is going to track jobs, among other things. A job may have just one attribute—the Job Name—so you could just put the job name on each expense, time entry, and invoice. But what if you misspell the job name? Then you'll have expenses that should go together but don't, because FileMaker sees different job names. By creating a Jobs table, you have a central place to enter job names and use it as a value list. With a Jobs table, instead of typing the job name everywhere, you simply choose it from a list.

Wait—to do that, all you need is a value list called Jobs. Why have a table if it has just one column?

OK, wise guy. You *could* leave out the Jobs table and the job names themselves. Instead, you could just attach each expense, time log entry, or invoice to a customer. But what happens when the same customer hires you six different times? All those expenses, invoices, and entries are lumped together under that customer, and you can't track them back to the individual jobs. Sometimes a one-attribute entity exists because it gives your database greater powers of organization or categorization.

Note: The diagram you're about to create isn't, in the most technical sense, a *real* ER diagram. The real kind deals with all kinds of technical details that simply don't matter in FileMaker. So, some database big shots may chastise you for calling your beautiful picture an ER diagram. Never mind—just be glad FileMaker doesn't make you *care* about all that mumbo jumbo.

Creating an ER diagram

When you assemble an entity relationship diagram, you have to put all your entities and relationships together in one big picture. Each entity appears on the diagram just *once*, but may be connected to several other entities by lines that explain the relationship between each pair.

Your ER diagram is crucial to a successful database designing experience. First, you almost always find ways to improve your database as you create the diagram. Then, when you set out to actually *build* the database, the ER diagram guides you through the process. Finally, a couple of years from now, when you need to add more to your database design, the ER diagram will bring you—or your successor—up to speed on how your database fits together. So don't toss the diagram once you've moved from the planning phase to creation.

POWER USERS' CLINIC

It's All About the Tools

If you plan on creating more than one ER diagram, or if you have a complicated one to create, diagramming software will save you lots of time and heartache. Microsoft Visio and SmartDraw are two choices for Windows. Try Omni-Graffle or ConceptDraw for Mac OS X. If none of these fit the bill for you, many new diagramming programs have hit the online stores recently, so just do a web search for *ER diagram*. You'll even find some free, online-only diagramming tools. if that's what your budget calls for.

The beauty of all of these tools is that they *understand* ER diagrams. They can hook entities together with ease, draw crow's feet on your behalf (lots of programs just don't understand crow's feet), and keep everything connected as you move your entities around to find a good arrangement. One caveat: some of these programs have built-in database diagramming features, but they're too complex for FileMaker work. The main tools your software package needs are: drawing a box and labeling it and adding crow's feet to your lines.

If you're an unrepentant cheapskate, here's a tip: Write the entity names on a piece of paper, and cut out each one. Then arrange them on paper, draw lines, and see how it looks. You can slide the entity scraps around a few times to find a decent arrangement, and then commit the whole thing to a clean piece of paper.

Here's a description of the general process: you make one box for each entity you've identified, and then draw lines between them. First, boxes should be placed on the page so there's some open space in the middle where your lines can roam free. When that's done you can start drawing lines to represent each of the relationships you've come up with. For a simple database, you can usually get the lines in the picture without much difficulty. But creating a larger diagram without the right tools can be a real pain. If you work on paper, you end up starting half a dozen times before you get a good arrangement. If you use a typical drawing program (the drawing capabilities in Word, for example), then you spend copious hours reconnecting lines and entities, reshaping lines, and hand drawing crow's feet as you move things around. See the box above for some suggestions to solve this problem.

When you're done, you should have a single, unified diagram with each entity showing up only once, and every relationship indicated by a line. When you're thinking about relationships with just pairs of tables, you don't get the big picture. The ER diagram shows you how *everything* comes together, and when that happens, you often discover tangles of relationships just like those in Figure 5-7. Tangles like these aren't inherently bad; they're just usually completely unnecessary. Take the first tangled group—Expenses, Jobs, and Customers. The diagram tells you that customers have jobs, jobs have expenses, and customers have expenses.

UP TO SPEED

Think Relational

If you're dazed and confused trying to figure out how different entities relate, you're not alone. Understanding relational database design takes practice, plain and simple. Here are some ideas to improve your thought process:

- **Don't get hung up on technicalities.** At this point in your design, you shouldn't be thinking about database terms like primary keys, foreign keys, or join tables. Those things are all *implementation details* that you can work out later. Right now, just focus on the kinds of things you're keeping track of, and how they fit together.

- **Use familiar words.** If you're trying to figure out how customers and jobs should be related, use words familiar to you, for example: "A customer hires me to do jobs," not "A Customer entity is related to a Job entity in a one-to-many configuration." As you get the hang of it, you'll discover that the simple sentences you use every day say a whole lot about relationships. For example, if a customer hires you to do *jobs* (note the plural), then you probably have a one-to-many relationship between customers and jobs.

- **Consider individual items first.** Don't think about what *customers* do. Instead, think about what *one customer* does. The answer tells you whether a single customer has many jobs, or just one job. Then turn it around. Once you've decided a customer hires you to do jobs, ask yourself what a job has to do with customers. "I do a job for a customer." This process tells you that each job is connected to just one customer. (If you didn't follow this advice, and thought, "I do *jobs* for customers," then you're not any closer to understanding the relationship.) By combining these results, you discover that a customer has many jobs, while a job has just one customer. So Customers and Jobs have a one-to-many relationship.

- **Don't let the word "many" hang you up.** It's just a standard term to help keep things simple. (Otherwise, you could have a *one-to-quite-a-few* relationship between Jobs and Invoices, a *one-to-a-handful* relationship between Customers and Jobs, and a *usually-just-one-or-two-to-rarely-more-than-three* relationship between Payments and Invoices. Yikes!) "Many" doesn't have to mean "lots." It might mean "exactly six" or "no more than three."

But you don't need all those lines to understand all the relationships, and neither does FileMaker. Now that you have an ER diagram, you can see that the line between Customers and Expenses is entirely superfluous. Even if it weren't there, you could still see all the expenses charged to a certain customer. Just find all that customer's *jobs* first (by following the line from Customers to Jobs). Once you've found those jobs, you can look at the expenses for each job. Since customers incur expenses only by way of jobs, you get exactly what you want without an extra relationship. In other words, if two entities are connected by a path along relationship lines—even *through* other entities—then they're related as far as FileMaker's concerned. Your database can show you the expenses for a customer just as easily as it can show the jobs for that customer. Figure 5-8 shows this concept.

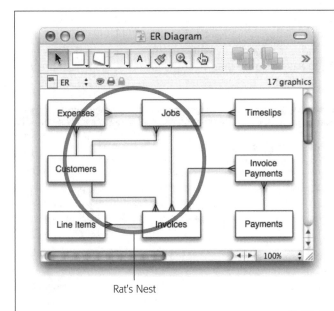

Figure 5-7:
This diagram doesn't look all that bad–except for one thing. The circled area, labeled Rat's Nest, has a lot of lines among just a few tables. Expenses, Customers, and Jobs are all interrelated–there's a relationship between Jobs and Customers, another between Customers and Expenses, and a third between Expenses and Jobs. If you look closely, the same situation exists for Customers, Jobs, and Invoices. In both cases, you have a better way.

Rat's Nest

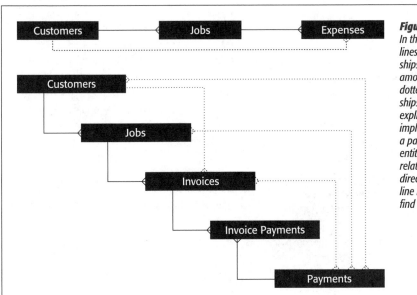

Figure 5-8:
In this picture, the solid lines represent relationships you've identified among the entities. The dotted lines show relationships you don't have to explicitly create–they're implied. As long as there's a path–any path–from one entity to another, they're related. You don't need a direct path. One implicit line is missing. Can you find where it should go?

When you're thinking about these implied relationships, pay attention to the crow's feet. If, when moving from one entity to another along the relationship lines, you *ever* go through a to-many relationship, then the larger implied relationship is itself to-many. This isn't just a clever trick; it's actually intuitive. If a customer has more than one job, and each job has expenses, then clearly a customer can have more than one expense.

WORKAROUND WORKSHOP

When to Go One-to-One

When two things—like people and addresses—have a one-to-one relationship, it usually means you've got an entity you don't need (as in the example in Figure 5-5). Every rule has exceptions, though. Here are some reasons you may see a one-to-one relationship in a database:

- **FileMaker uses record locking to prevent two people from editing the same record at the same time.** (Yes, Virginia, two people can use a database at the same time—see Chapter 18 to learn how.) Imagine you have a table of products and every time you sell something, you reduce the product's Quantity In Stock field by one. What happens if someone else is modifying the product description at the same time? FileMaker doesn't let you enter the inventory adjustment because the record is locked. Should you cancel the order? Allow the Quantity in Stock field to be wrong? Force your customer to wait while you ask your associate to get out of the record? A better solution is to put the inventory levels in a separate table. Each product has a Product record and an Inventory record, so two seemingly conflicting processes no longer lock each other out of your system.

- **Sometimes you want to divide data you store about an entity among several tables**. A database of stock photography might include high-resolution photographs in container fields. These photos make the database very large. By putting the photos in one table, and the information about the photos in another, you make managing the information easier. (This technique requires keeping each table in a separate file—learn how to connect them on page 591.) With a separate table that's in a separate file, you can back up the data file to a CD, and the photograph file to your high-capacity backup system, for example.

- **Imagine you have customers and employees.** Employees don't place orders or make payments, and customers don't have time sheets. But they both have addresses, phone numbers, and email addresses. What's more, you like to send holiday cards to all of them every year. In a situation like this, you can create three tables: People, Customers, and Employees. The People table holds all the information that customers and employees have in common—names, addresses, and so forth. Information unique to an employee (Social Security number, hire date, and such) goes in the Employee table, and information only a customer could love (referral source, membership level, and so on) stays in the Customers table. You'd have a one-to-one relationship between People and Employees, and another between People and Customers. When it comes time to send those cards, you can print envelopes right from the People table, and get customers and employees in one shot.

When you make your ER diagram, you should get rid of redundancy in your relationships. In other words, remove lines that show direct relationships when the relationship is already implied by other entities and relationships. If you don't do this now, you'll have trouble creating relationships when you finally get back to File-Maker. You see why on page 562. In your diagram, you can remove the relationship between Customers and Expenses. You can also axe one between Customers and Invoices because Customers can find their Invoices by way of Jobs. With this revision, the ER diagram now looks like Figure 5-9.

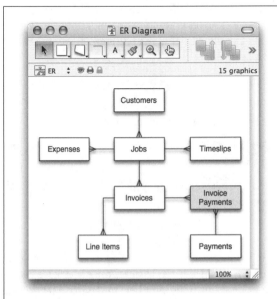

Figure 5-9:
Here's the final ER diagram that you'll use as the roadmap for creating your database. Notice that every entity is related to at least one other entity in some way. Stray, unrelated entities are so rare in a real database system that if you see one in your diagram, then you should check to make sure it belongs in your database. Or did you just forget to draw the relationships it needs?

Now's the time to take one last look over your ER diagram. Keep these points in mind as you check for errors:

- You should have no undivided many-to-many relationships.

- If you have any one-to-one relationships, make sure you can justify them (see the box on the previous page for some ideas).

- Make sure you don't have any unnecessary entities hanging out all by themselves.

- Be certain you don't have any unnecessary lines or rat's nests.

If you discover an entity that has no relationships, you may not need it in your database at all. Read back on page 184, and see if that item ought to be a field one of the other tables. Or if your diagram has two or more groups of related entities and no relationships *between* the groups, you might've forgotten to draw in a relationship, or again, you might have one or more entities that your system doesn't need. Go back and make sure you're clear on your one-to-many and many-to-many relationships.

Keys

Starting back on page 137, you created key fields and used them to relate two tables. Now it's time to look more closely at how key fields and relationships work together. Take, for example, an Invoice table and its friendly neighbor, Line Items. The Invoice table probably contains fields like Due Date, Balance Due, and Terms—all attributes of the invoice itself. Then there's the *Invoice Number* field. Unlike the other fields, it's a made-up number. It does one thing—identify a single invoice—and does it very well. Without it, you and your customers might have conversations like this: "I need a refund on one of my invoices...you know, the big one...yeah, in February...right, with three items...no, the other one...." As soon as someone mentions an invoice number, though, everybody knows exactly which invoice to look at. More important, FileMaker knows which invoice it is, too.

The invoice number is good at identifying an invoice because it has three important characteristics:

- **It's unique.** No two invoices ever have the same invoice number.

- **It's unchanging.** Invoice #24601 is #24601 today and it will be tomorrow, and the next day, and the next day.

- **It's consistent.** "Consistent" is a database term that means it's never empty. All invoice records have an invoice number.

Since it's a unique number, if you're talking about invoice #24601, and your customer is talking about invoice #24601, there's no question that you're both referring to the same invoice. Since it's unchanging, you can go back weeks, months, or even years later and find the invoice every time. And since it's consistent, you never have lonely invoices hanging out there without an identifying number. In database terms, the invoice number is called a *key*. So to sum up: a key is a field whose value uniquely, unchangingly, and consistently identifies one record.

FileMaker doesn't have a special field type for designating a key (although most key fields are number fields). As far as FileMaker's concerned, any field you use to link one table to another is a key field. Just make sure that you choose a field in which the data follows the rules you just learned.

Primary and foreign keys

When a key field is in the same table as the records it identifies, it's called a *primary key*. In the Invoice table, the Invoice Number field is the primary key because the invoice number identifies an invoice record. If you put the invoice number in some other table (like, say, the Line Items table) it's not a primary key there. Instead, it's called a *foreign key*. Foreign keys identify records in other tables.

Note: The terms "primary" and "foreign" may not seem like a match made in linguistic heaven. Wouldn't "domestic" and "foreign" make more sense? If those terms don't make sense to you, you're in good company. FileMaker avoids the terms in its software or its Help files. But developers aren't so reticent, and the concepts of primary and foreign keys are extremely important to getting your database designed properly.

Clearly every table needs a primary key, but how do you know which tables need foreign keys as well? In the Invoices database, how did you decide to put the Invoice Number field in the Line Items table? Why not create a Line Item ID key field in the Line Items table, and put it in the Invoices table? Wouldn't that accomplish the same thing? At first glance, it might seem like either method would produce the same relationship. After all, they sure *look* similar in a picture (Figure 5-10).

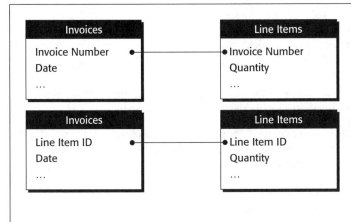

Figure 5-10:
These two relationships look similar, but they show how a simple mistake can cause big headaches. In the top example, the primary key in the Invoices table matches a foreign key (Invoice Number) in the Line Items table. This arrangement lets one invoice have many line items because the same invoice number value can be in the foreign key field in many line item records. But in the bottom example, a foreign key in the Invoice table is related to the Line Item table's primary key (Line Item ID), which would let each invoice have just one line item.

Think about what a primary key means. Each primary key value identifies one, and only one, record in the table. If you build a relationship between the Invoice and Line Item tables based on a Line Item ID key, then each invoice can have only one line item. If it had two, you'd have two line items with the same line item ID and it would no longer be unique. When you have a one-to-many relationship, you have to put the foreign key in the table on the *many* side. Luckily, keeping this information straight in your head is a breeze. Since foreign keys belong on the to-many side of a relationship, just remember this rule: When you see a crow's foot on your ER diagram, you need a foreign key in the table on the crow's foot side.

Note: That rule bears repeating: *When you see a crow's foot on your ER diagram, put a foreign key in the table on the crow's foot side.* The foreign key refers to whatever table is on the other end of the line. This is one of the very few absolute hard-and-fast rules in relational database design, so cling to this singular bit of simplicity when you start to have doubts.

Choosing a good primary key field

A primary key is most often a made-up serial number, like the one you made in your Lease Agreement database on page 137. You'll use that same technique a little later in this chapter, when you tell FileMaker to automatically make up a unique value for your primary key field each time you create a record. This kind of primary key, based on purely made-up data, is called a *surrogate key*.

Note: Unless you generate the value in your database, it's not a surrogate key, even if somebody else made it up. A surrogate key is made up *by your database*.

Occasionally, your table has a real value that meets the requirements for a key. For example, if your Product database has a field for your internal Inventory Control Number, you may be able to use that field as the primary key. If you use some real piece of data as a key, then it's called a *natural key*. Surprisingly, though, the vast majority of tables don't have a field that meets the criteria for a natural primary key. Take, for example, the Phone Number field in a contact database of people. Phone numbers are *usually* unique, and don't change *all that often*. But words like "usually" and "often" have no business in a discussion about good key fields.

In fact, in most cases the only fields that meet the requirements for a natural key are, in reality, surrogate keys from somebody else's database. For example, a Social Security Number is a value that everybody (in America) has, it never changes, and is always unique (outside of identity theft). It has these characteristics because it's a surrogate key made up by some database at the Social Security Administration. But that's OK—FileMaker databases frequently deal with information that's generated somewhere else. Your database might contain employee numbers that come from your company's payroll system, part numbers from your supplier's catalog, or document numbers from your corporate knowledge base. All these numbers are surrogate keys in some system somewhere, but they're natural keys to you.

Note: Those two caveats about Social Security Number listed above (they only apply to Americans and identity theft means you can't guarantee uniqueness) makes an SSN an unacceptable surrogate key for some developers. Others live and die on the SSN, though.

Join Tables

A many-to-many relationship is more complicated than its one-sided brethren. Back on page 190, you learned that a join table is necessary to make the many-to-many relationship work. Remember: the database you're designing tracks payments from your customers. A customer could send a check to cover *two* invoices or a check could cover *part* of an invoice only. So an invoice can have multiple payments, and a payment can be for multiple invoices: that's the concept that drives this many-to-many relationship.

Going Natural

Should I try to find natural keys for the tables in my database if I can?

This question has generated an eternal debate in the broader database world. Some ivory-tower theorists are convinced that natural keys are superior to surrogate keys for two primary reasons. First, they're *meaningful*: When you look at a natural key in your own database, it means something to you. Second, if a key is also real honest-to-goodness meaningful data, then, in a relational database situation, your table always has at least one piece of good information from the table it relates to. If that happens to be the snippet you need, you save the software the trouble of going to another table and finding the right record. Thus, the theory goes, natural keys make database programs run a little faster.

But for the kinds of databases you're likely to build with FileMaker, neither of these concerns comes up very often. If a surrogate key isn't all that meaningful to the database user, just don't put it on the layout. And as for performance, the minuscule increase in speed is almost never significant enough to matter for typical databases.

And there's a much more significant argument against trying to find an acceptable natural key: It's usually impossible.

You almost never have a normal piece of data in a record that meets all the criteria for a good primary key.

Even natural keys that really seem like great choices often turn out to be problematic. Suppose you work for a company that assigns an employee ID to each employee. You're building a database to keep track of employee stock options. Just like Social Security Number, employee ID is a surrogate key to somebody, but it's a natural key to you. You decide to make it your primary key. Then you discover you need to track stock options for employees even if they quit, and then return to the company. When they do this, their employee IDs change, and your database can't track them properly without some inconvenient upkeep. If you had used your own surrogate key instead, you wouldn't have this problem.

The penalty for a bad key choice can be huge: anything from lost connections in your data to the need for a major overhaul of the system. By contrast, surrogate keys are easy and always work. Once you accept the fact that your database will have an extra field that serves no other purpose but to be the primary key, the choice becomes a no-brainer. Don't bother with natural keys.

How do you build a relationship like this? If you put the Payment ID in the Invoices table, then a payment can be applied to more than one invoice (just put the same Payment ID in each invoice record). But an invoice can have only one payment, since it has just one Payment ID field. If you put the Invoice Number field in the Payments table, you get the same problem in the other direction. You may be tempted to try putting a foreign key field in *both* tables. In other words, add a Payment ID field to the Invoice table, and an Invoice Number field to the Payments table. Dig a little deeper, and you see that this has a whole *host* of problems:

- An invoice now has a field called Payment ID, but that field *doesn't* identify the payments for that invoice. To find the payments for an invoice, you have to search the Payments database, using the Invoice Number field. That's just plain confusing.

- Instead of one bidirectional relationship, you have two unidirectional relationships. The Payment ID in the invoice matches the Payment ID in the Payments table, but this tells you only which invoices belong to each payment. You need the other relationship (based on Invoice ID) to figure out which payments belong to each invoice. If you connect a payment to an invoice by putting the invoice number in the payment record, then you also have to put the Payment ID in the invoice record. If you forget, your data is no longer valid.

That's where a *join table* (Figure 5-11) comes in. A join table doesn't usually represent a real entity. Instead, each record in the join table represents a relationship between two records in the related tables.

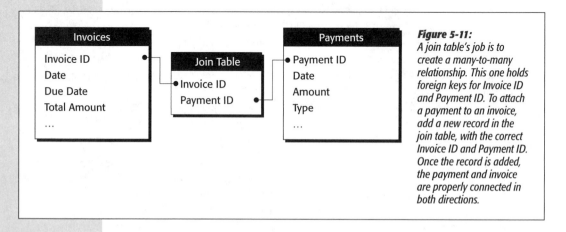

Figure 5-11:
A join table's job is to create a many-to-many relationship. This one holds foreign keys for Invoice ID and Payment ID. To attach a payment to an invoice, add a new record in the join table, with the correct Invoice ID and Payment ID. Once the record is added, the payment and invoice are properly connected in both directions.

If it helps, think of join tables this way: Invoices and Payments both have a one-to-many relationship to the join table. So one invoice can connect to many join records, each of which connects to one payment. Likewise, one payment can connect to many join records, each of which connects to one invoice. So you get many related records in both directions. A join table always contains *two* foreign keys, one from each table it's joining.

Note: The join table in the database you're building is the type that doesn't represent a real entity. But in some cases, a database may already have a real table that can act as a join table. Figure 5-12 shows an example.

Join tables can sometimes hold fields that don't quite belong in any other table. Suppose you wanted to record the portion of a payment that was applied to each invoice. For example, if a customer hands you a check for $100 and you have two outstanding invoices for that customer, for $80 and $30, then you may want to decide how to allocate the payment. Perhaps you apply $80 to the first invoice and $20 to the second.

This dollar amount applied to each invoice can't be stored in the Invoice table because an invoice can have several payments. It can't be stored in the Payment table because you have *two* amounts and only one payment record. The best place for it is right in the join table itself.

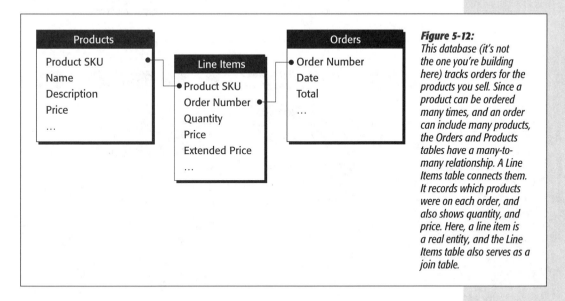

Figure 5-12:
This database (it's not the one you're building here) tracks orders for the products you sell. Since a product can be ordered many times, and an order can include many products, the Orders and Products tables have a many-to-many relationship. A Line Items table connects them. It records which products were on each order, and also shows quantity, and price. Here, a line item is a real entity, and the Line Items table also serves as a join table.

By adding a join table between Invoices and Payments, you've eliminated many-to-many relationships on your ER diagram. Now you know what foreign keys you need to make it all work. You're (finally) ready to actually build your database.

Creating a Relational Database

The planning is finally over. Now comes the fun part—actually making the database. And believe it or not, this part will go *much* more smoothly with your plan in place. You create a relational database in three steps. First, you tell FileMaker what tables you want, and then you add the fields to each table. Finally, you add relationships.

Note: Some developers cut right to the chase by creating tables with only their key fields and one or two other fields in each table to get started. For example, you might create only the primary key field and the first and last name fields in the Customer table so you don't spend hours trying to create hundreds of fields before you hook up the first relationship.

So don't be alarmed if you forget a table or miss a field. Although the point of planning is to help you figure which tables and fields you need from the start, you *can* go back at any time and make changes, even when your tables are loaded with data.

Warning: Deleting a table is a *dangerous* operation. Right now there's no risk because you're working in a brand-new database. But imagine 2 years from now, when the database is full, if you accidentally delete a table, then you lose *all* the data in it. You'll also have a lot of work to do putting your relationships and layouts back together. FileMaker warns you before it lets you delete the table, but it's worth an extra measure of caution. Because there's so much potential for danger, there's one final failsafe: In the Manage Database dialog box, if you click the Cancel button, then FileMaker discards *all* your changes, including any table deletions.

POWER USERS' CLINIC

Serial Text

As funny as it sounds, you can auto-enter serial numbers into text fields, and the values *themselves* can contain text. FileMaker looks at the text you've specified for "next value" and tries to find a number in it somewhere. When it comes time to generate a new value, it pulls that number out, increments it, and stuffs it back in its place.

Say your "next value" is C000LX, and "increment by" is set to 10. The first record you create gets C000LX. The second

gets C010LX, and then C020LX, and so on. When you get to C990LX, FileMaker doesn't just give up. Instead, it makes more room: C1000LX.

If your "next value" has more than one embedded number (C000LX22, for example), then FileMaker uses only the last number. Likewise, if you don't have a number at all, it simply adds one to the end.

Creating Relationships

Once you've defined tables and keys, you have everything you need to create your relationships. In other words, you tell FileMaker how the tables in your database fit together by matching up key fields. In the Manage Database window, click the Relationships tab, shown in Figure 5-13.

Note: You can find a starter file (JobsInvoices START.fp7) that already has the tables and some of the fields you need for the rest of this chapter on this book's Missing CD page at *www.missingmanuals.com/cds*. If you want your database name to match the figures in this chapter, change the file's name to "JobsInvoices." To change the name, make sure the file's not open, select the file, and then use your OS's method for changing a file's name.

As you learned on page 143, you define relationships between tables by dragging from one key field in a table to the key field in another. But if you just start dragging without rearranging, you may end up with a tangled mess in the graph. So take out your ER diagram and start by arranging the tables on the Relationships graph like the tables on your ER diagram. Refer to Figure 5-9 if you need a refresher. Once they're in place, it's a breeze to drag key fields from table to table. Here's a list of the relationships you need to create:

- Customers::Customer ID to Jobs::Customer ID

- Expenses::Job ID to Jobs::Job ID

- Invoices::Job ID to Jobs::Job ID

- Line Items::Invoice ID to Invoices::Invoice ID

- Invoice Payments::Invoice ID to Invoice ID

- Invoice Payments::Payment ID to Payments::Payment ID

- Timeslips::Job ID to Jobs::Job ID

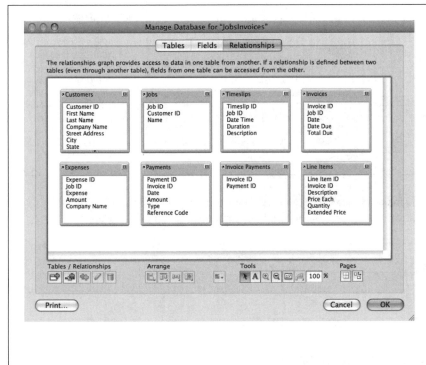

Figure 5-13:
If you create this set of tables and fields from scratch, your tables won't be in this precise order when you first view the Relationships graph. Tables appear on the graph in the order in which you create them. That's no problem, because FileMaker gives you all the tools you need to move, resize, rename, color, and of course, link up your tables. To move tables around, drag them by their title bars. Resize them by placing the mouse over the bottom or right or left edges (the pointer turns to a double-headed arrow when you hit the sweet spot), and then drag. To make the graph itself bigger, drag the bottom-right corner of the Manage Database window.

Remember, it doesn't matter whether you drag from Customers to Jobs (for example) or vice versa. What does matter is that you pick the right key fields to relate. When you're done, you should have seven relationships lines and your graph should look something like Figure 5-14.

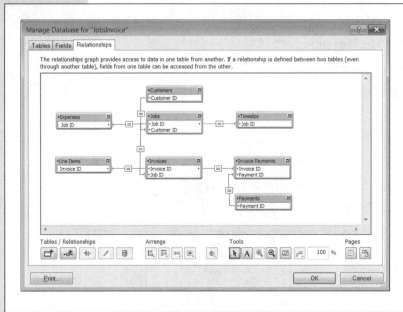

Figure 5-14:
The table occurrences (TOs) have been collapsed so you see only key fields. Change the TOs' display by clicking the button at the right of each TO's title bar. Tables toggle through three settings—open, key field only, and title bar only. On a complex graph, it's much easier to read relationships when your TOs are partly closed, as they are here. This way, you're not distracted by the other fields in each table. If you need to see a list of all the fields in a table, you can temporarily expand the appropriate TO. Or switch to the Fields tab.

If you make a mistake (say you grab the wrong field or drag to the wrong table), click the box in the middle of the relationship line, and then press Delete.

Tip: If you have a stray table occurrence (named the same as the database itself) on your Relationships graph, just select it, and then press Delete. It's a useless artifact from when the table was first created. Since this table occurrence isn't part of your ER diagram, you can safely ignore FileMaker's protestations that deleting it will break things.

Sorting a Relationship

When you drag key fields to create a relationship, you get a plain vanilla relationship. That is, the relationship links two records together when the values in their key fields match exactly. You can't create or delete records through the relationship, and it isn't sorted. Without a sort order, records will appear in the order they're created, from the first created to the last. So if you're creating Line Items for an invoice, the line items will normally appear in precisely the order in which you create them. But maybe your company likes line items to appear sorted by an internal Part Number field because it makes fulfilling the orders easier for the warehouse. Or your employees may enter their timeslips at the end of the week instead of daily and they sometimes enter them out of order.

FREQUENTLY ASKED QUESTION

FileMaker's Sixth Sense: Crow's Feet

I haven't done anything to tell FileMaker what kind of re-lationships I created. How does it know where to put the crow's feet?

You never have to tell FileMaker what type of relationship to create because it doesn't really matter. The work File-Maker performs to deal with a one-to-many relationship is no different from what it does for a one-to-one, so it doesn't care about the distinction.

However, it's useful to you as the database designer to know what kind of relationships you have. So as a spe-cial service to you, FileMaker tries to figure out where the crow's feet go. It helps you decide whether an invoice

should have room for one line item or a whole list of them, for example. So FileMaker assumes every end of every line needs a crow's foot unless it finds evidence to the contrary. Such evidence includes:

- The field used in the relationship is a serial number.
- The field used in the relationship has the "Unique validation" option turned on.

A line that connects to a field that meets either of these conditions does *not* get a crow's foot at that end. Since all your primary keys are serial numbers, FileMaker has no trouble figuring out where to leave off the crow's feet.

The Edit Relationship window lets you sort a relationship by any field in either table (when you select the option, you'll see the regular Sort Records window). You can sort the relationship by any sortable field in the table to show related records in the order you prefer, but it's far more common to sort on the to-many side.

It's important to note that sorting a relationship doesn't just change the order of records in a portal. Remember that you can show related records without using a portal, but if you do, the related field only shows one record. A relationship's sort order can change that first record, which may not be what you intended, so be care-ful about sorting relationships. See the box on page 208 for more information on sorting relationships and/or portals.

Managing the Relationships Graph

Although the JobsInvoices Relationship graph is small and easy to understand, chances are it will grow as you power up your database by adding more tables (and even as you add new features, as you'll see through the course of the next few chap-ters). As it grows, your graph can easily get messy and hard to decipher. But the Relationships graph has lots of tools for keeping things uncluttered and easy to un-derstand (Figure 5-15).

Managing table occurrences using the Tables/Relationships tools

These tools help you create and edit *table occurrences* (TOs) on the graph. A table occurrence is a representation of a table on the Relationships graph only. TOs are similar to fields on a layout in the sense that you can have more than one instance of each without changing the underlying characteristics of the real table or field. For example, you may want to have a field and a merge version of the same field on a layout so each could serve a different purpose (page 106). Similarly, you can have more than one TO on a graph without duplicating the actual table.

FREQUENTLY ASKED QUESTION

How Do I Know Where to Sort?

Back on page 206, I saw that I can choose the sort order for a portal in the Portal Setup window. Now you're saying I can set the sort order in the relationship. What's the difference? Does it matter?

When you set a sort order in the Edit Relationships window box, it applies to the relationship itself. Any time you use that relationship, the sort order applies: in portals on any layout, when showing a single related field, and when finding a set of related records (page 227).

A portal's sort order on the other hand, applies only to the portal itself. If you don't tell the portal to sort, then FileMaker uses the relationship's sort order (or if there isn't one, the order in which the records were created) instead.

If you know that every time you look at your related data it should be shown in a specific order, then set the relationship to sort. But if you think the related data ought to be sorted different ways in different contexts (and thus in different portals), then don't sort the relationship, because that's making your database do extra work—FileMaker has to sort the records for the relationship, then sort them a different way for your portal. (You don't see this process happening, but FileMaker's doing it behind the scenes.) So when you're planning on viewing data in lots of different orders, rely on sorted portals instead of sorted relationships.

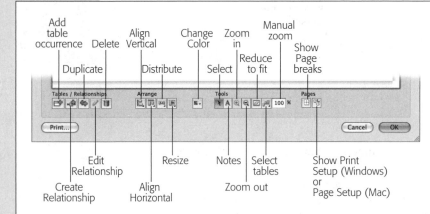

Figure 5-15:
The first group of tools helps you create and edit table occurrences and relationships. When you select more than one table occurrence, the second group, arrange and alignment tools, becomes available. The tiny triangle in the bottom-right corner shows that you can choose how the tool behaves. You also have standard zoom tools, and printing tools for getting the graph onto paper.

Tip: Don't let the Tables/Relationships label on these buttons confuse you. You have a whole tab dedicated to managing *tables*. These tools are strictly for table occurrences, not the underlying tables the occurrences refer to.

The Tables/Relationship tools lets you create new TOs or edit or delete existing ones:

- The **create table occurrence** tool lets you draw a TO, and then shows a Specify Table window so you can select the table the new occurrence should refer to. You can also give the TO a name. TO names have to be unique, so if you choose a name that's already in use, FileMaker appends a number to the end of the occurrence's name. If this happens change the name to something more descriptive right away to save yourself from confusion later.

- The **create relationship** tool shows the Edit Relationship window as you saw it first on page 146, except you now have access to pop-up menus for selecting the TOs you want to relate to one another. Dragging a relationship is super easy, but you only get one flavor. Using the button instead lets you set up multicriteria relationships (page 563) and specify whether the relationship allows creation and/or deletion of related records and if the relationship should be sorted right from the onset.

- Copy/paste doesn't work on the graph, so the **duplicate** tool is the way to go. It can duplicate whole groups of TOs, called Table Occurrence Groups (TOGs). See page 575 for details.

- The **Edit** button opens the Edit Relationships window for the selected relationship (and will open the Specify Table window if a single TO is selected). This button is grayed out, unless you have a relationship line selected. These lines are tiny, so it easier to click the box in the middle of the line to select it. Double-clicking the box both selects the line and opens the Edit Relationships window. See the box on page 231 for a special warning about using the "Delete related records in this table when a record is deleted in the other table" option.

Tip: You can tell when a relationship line is selected, because the line thickens, the box in the middle is highlighted, and the Edit tool becomes active.

- The **Delete** button has a trash can icon on it, making its purpose clear. You can also delete items by selecting them, and then pressing Delete. Because deleting items from the graph is so potentially destructive (layouts that use the TO, and all other relationships that depend on the relationship will break), you'll see a warning message to confirm that you want to remove the selected items.

If you make changes on the graph that might be destructive, or if you just change your mind, in the Manage Database window, click Cancel, and then click Discard. You'll have to redo the changes you made since you opened the window, but it's easier to redo good work than to undo bad work.

Arrange the graph

The table occurrences in the graph behave like layout objects in Layout mode. You can Shift-click or rubber band several to select them all. You can even press Ctrl+A (⌘-A) to select *all* the table occurrences. Just click empty space on the graph to de-select. Once you have some selected, you can use the arrange tools to line them up.

After you've dragged a few table occurrences around on your graph, it can look pretty sloppy. Here's how to use the tools to inflict some order on the graph:

- The **Arrange Vertical** tool lets you choose whether to align the left edges, centers, or right edges of any highlighted table occurrences.

- The **Arrange Horizontal** tool lets you align the top edges, centers, or bottom edges of the highlighted table occurrences.

- The **Distribute** tool makes the space between selected table occurrences uniform. You can choose horizontal or vertical distribution.

- The **Resize** tool makes short work of getting those manually resized table occurrences back in parade order. Select some table occurrences, and then click the resize tool to tell FileMaker whether you want all the highlighted table occurrences resized to the smallest width or height, the largest width or height, or both (as in both height and width, not both smallest and largest, as cool as that would be).

Selection tools

The Relationship graph has a few selection tricks that make life easier. To help with selecting an entire group of connected objects, you can select just one. Click the Select Tables button, and then choose "Select related tables 1-away." FileMaker automatically adds every table that's directly connected to your current selection. You can choose this same command again to extend the selection one more notch on the graph.

If you have multiple table occurrences that have the same underlying base table (you'll learn why on page 570), click the Select Tables button, and then choose "Select tables with the same source table" instead. FileMaker highlights all the table occurrences that match those you've selected.

These tools are most useful on a large and complicated graph when you know you need a specific TO, but just can't find it. Highlight one TO from the source table you're concerned with, and then click the Select Tables button. Now you only have to look at the highlighted TOs to find the one you need.

Color your table occurrences

You can change the color of any selected table occurrence(s), using a standard color pop-up menu. It looks just like the one you saw on page 113 when you learned about coloring layout objects. Adding color to table occurrences doesn't affect the database's behavior at all. It's just there to help you organize your graph. Some people like to color all TOs in a TOG the same color, and others like to color TOs from the same source table the same color, thus avoiding the need to use the selection tools above.

Adding notes

You can add comments about the graph with the Notes tool. Just select the tool, and then drag on the graph to create the note. The Edit Note dialog box appears (Figure 5-16). Type the text of the note and set its font, size, text, and background colors. If you want to edit a note, then double-click it, and the dialog reappears, ready to do your bidding.

The Note tool lets you place floating notes anywhere on your graph. Make detailed notes about individual tables, or make them as wide as the graph, with a few words describing what kind of data is in the table occurrences directly underneath. Notes always appear under a table occurrence in the window's stacking order, so you can even put one behind a set of TOs as a visual grouping (like the one behind the Invoice Payment TO in Figure 5-16).

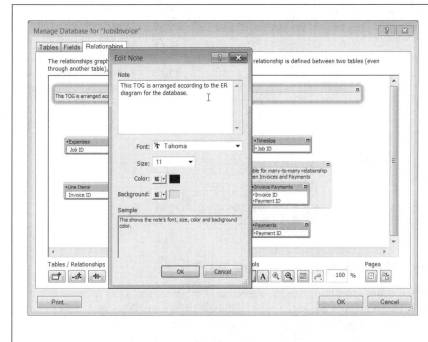

Figure 5-16:
The Edit Note dialog box lets you pick font, size, and color, and type any text you want. When you click OK, the note appears on the graph, and you can drag it around, resize it, or use the alignment tools much like you do your table occurrences. Here the Edit Note dialog box shows the setup for the highlighted note in the background. You can also see a note that appears behind the Invoice Payment table. Both notes help see how things work at a glance without poking around in each relationship.

Printing the graph

Last but not least, FileMaker offers some tools to help you print the graph. Since the graph is a roadmap to your tables, some people like to print it and tape it up beside the computer for quick reference while building layouts. Figure 5-17 shows how to lay out the graph so you can print without surprises.

Using Relational Database Power

The essence of a relational database is its multiple tables. So far this chapter has focused on planning, creating, and managing tables and relationships. But the power of multiple tables trickles throughout FileMaker. It's time to learn how to take advantage of your database's relationships as you search records, build layouts, and create value lists.

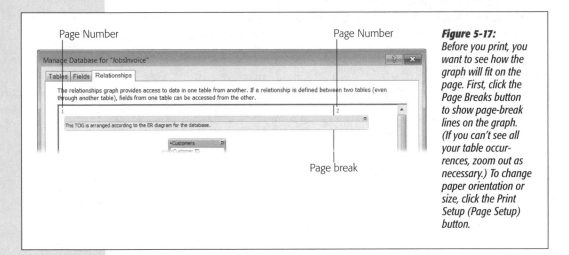

Figure 5-17:
Before you print, you want to see how the graph will fit on the page. First, click the Page Breaks button to show page-break lines on the graph. (If you can't see all your table occurrences, zoom out as necessary.) To change paper orientation or size, click the Print Setup (Page Setup) button.

Note: For a refresher on creating, editing, and deleting related records using a portal, see page 153.

One Table Occurrence, One Found Set

The most fundamental thing you should understand when using a multitable database is that each layout sees the entire database from a single perspective, or context (page 149). It's time to do a little exploration to see this concept in action. A layout is attached to an occurrence on the graph, and that's how it sees the world. This means when you're looking at a record on the Customers layout, you're seeing a customer. If you switch to Table view, then you see a list of customers. You don't see Jobs at all. To see those, you need to switch to the Jobs layout.

Since each table holds different data, the concept of a found set changes a little as well. When you perform a find, the layout you're on determines which table File-Maker searches. Your new found set is associated with that layout's table occurrence, too. Just like when you had only a single table, the found set stays the same until you perform another find, or you tell FileMaker to show you all the records for that table occurrence (Records→Show All Records). But if you switch to a different layout (one tied to a different table occurrence), your found set no longer applies.

For example, if you find the six customers from New York, and then switch to the Jobs layout, you won't have six records in your found set anymore. Instead, you have a separate *Jobs* found set. Switch back to Customers, and you see the six New Yorkers again. FileMaker remembers one found set for each table occurrence. It also re-members the *current record* for each table occurrence, so if you switch to a different layout, and then come back, then you're still on the same record that was active when you left that layout.

DON'T PANIC

Lost and Found Again

You may not see table occurrences in the Relationships graph for all the tables you create. Remain calm. You have all the right table occurrences; you just can't see them all at once. Chances are you just need to scroll the graph to the right. Unfortunately, it can be tricky to drag between two fields if you can't get them both on the screen at once. (You can do it, mind you. When you approach the edge of the graph while dragging, FileMaker automatically starts scrolling. It's just a little tedious.)

If you have a big enough computer screen, then you can simplify things by making the entire window bigger by dragging the bottom-right corner. If you still can't fit everything in, even when the window is as big as it can get, then you can zoom out on the window. Click the "Reduce to Fit" button (Figure 5-15) and FileMaker shrinks everything so it all fits on the graph at once. In this reduced view, you can still drag relationships. When you're ready to see things full-size again, in the Zoom Level box, just type 100, and then press Tab.

Don't press Enter or Return after changing the zoom level, or FileMaker thinks you meant to click the OK button and closes the Manage Database window. If you do close it accidentally, then just choose File→Manage Database again.

You can zoom in on certain parts of the graph with the Zoom In tool. First, click the tool, and then click anywhere in the graph. Use the Zoom Out tool instead if you want to zoom back out again. Unlike the zoom controls on a database window, these controls don't let you zoom in past 100 percent, but you can zoom way out—to 1 percent if you want. At that level, your tables are reduced to undifferentiated goo in the corner of the graph.

When you're done zooming, be sure to choose the Selection tool again so you can drag relationships or table occurrences.

Of course, you can have more than one layout attached to the same table occurrence—Customer List and Customer Detail, for example. The found set and current record are associated with the *table occurrence*, not the layout, so a find on the Customer List layout affects the found set on the Customer Detail layout.

Tip: If you want more than one found set or current record in the same table occurrence, don't create a new TO though. Use multiple windows, just like you learned on page 42.

If you want to see two kinds of records side by side (say Customers and Invoices), you can create a new window (Window→New Window), and then switch one of them to a different layout.

POWER USERS' CLINIC

Auto-Creation Without a Portal

You don't have to have a portal to get automatic creation of related records. Auto-creation works when you put data in *any* related field as long as the relationship is set up to allow it. Suppose you have a one-to-one relationship with one table for Bicycle Team Members and another for a photo of each racer. Both tables have a Rider ID field, but only the Riders::Rider ID field is a serial number. The relationship between the two tables is set to allow creation of related Photo records.

Your Bike Rider detail layout doesn't need a portal to create the related record in the Photo table. It just needs to display the related container field from the Photo table. Since the relationship is set to auto-create Photo records, you can insert a new picture of the rider in the Picture field, and FileMaker creates the related record for you automatically. This process works only for one-to-one relationships. You can change the picture you insert in the related record, but you can never create a second record with this technique.

If you don't have Auto-creation turned on for the relationship (page 144), then you can't click into the Picture field. FileMaker shows the dotted field outline as if the field is there and active, but doesn't let you in.

Viewing Related Fields on a Layout

Think of the layouts FileMaker made for you as starting points from which you'll put relationships to work. You saw this in action on page 145, when you put a Payment portal on the Lease Agreement layout. With this more complicated database, you have more opportunity to show related data. Portals will be very useful: you'll probably want to start by creating a Jobs portal on the Customer layout. Then edit the Customers to Jobs relationship to allow for creation and deletion of related records (page 147), so you can enter a few new Jobs records. See the box above to learn how to create related records without a portal.

After you've created a Jobs portal on the Customers layout and viewed the two jobs for Jerald Tabb (Figure 5-18), you realize that you have expenses to enter on that job. So head for the Expenses layout, where you find that Expense table has a Job ID field, but not a Job Name field, which would help you make sure you're chalking expenses up to the right job. Instead, you'll use the related fields from the Job table, and let FileMaker find the correct *related* data using the relationships you created.

1. **On the Expenses layout, switch to Layout mode.**

    That's where the tools that let you put fields on layouts are.

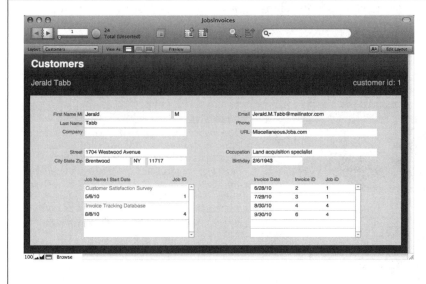

Figure 5-18:
The sample database for this chapter has been set up with data so you can focus on the relationship you're creating. To see the relationships working, make sure you're viewing the first few records in each table. Here's the first Customer record, showing one way you can arrange the new Jobs and Invoices portals you'll create as you work through the next sections. You may find it helpful to compare the finished version of the database to your work to see how all the pieces fit together.

2. **Click at the beginning of the Expenses merge field to place the insertion point in the text block.**

   You want the text block with the angle brackets around it. It reads: "<<Expenses>>". Make sure your cursor is to the left of all the angle brackets, since they belong with the Expenses merge field. You'll add a merge field for the Job Name in front of the Expense name. That way, you can tell at a glance which job an Expense is for.

3. **Choose Insert→Merge Field.**

   The Specify Field window appears, displaying a list of fields from the table you worked with the last time you opened the window.

4. **From the Current Table pop-up menu, choose Jobs.**

   Here's where you venture into unfamiliar waters. The Current Table pop-up menu lets you pick any table occurrence on your graph (Figure 5-19).

5. **Select the Name field from the Jobs table, and then click OK.**

   FileMaker adds the Jobs::Name field to the text block. It should read "<<Jobs::Name>><<Expense>>." The Expense field is local, so it doesn't have to include its table name in the text block. A name that includes both the table and field name (as Jobs::Name) is called a *fully qualified* field name. But the related field shows its full name, just so everybody's clear on where the data's coming from.

6. **Type a ":" and a space between the two merge fields.**

The text block contains the text "<<Jobs::Name>>: <<Expense>>."

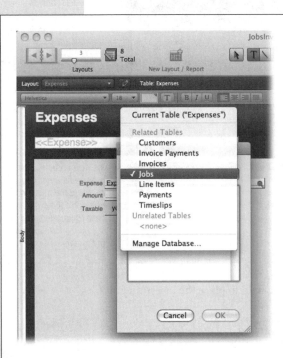

Figure 5-19:
Here you see the Specify Field dialog box's Current Table menu popped up, with a list of all the table occurrences on the graph. The ones related to the current layout are at the top and all unrelated tables are grouped below. Right now you don't have any un-related tables because the entire graph is connected in one group. The <<Expense>> merge field you're editing is visible behind the Specify Field window.

Now when you view an Expense record in Browse mode, you'll see data from the Jobs table on the Expenses layout. You could have used a regular field instead of a merge field. In fact sometimes that makes more sense, like when you might want to edit data from both contexts. But in this case, the related data appears in a text block that serves as a title for the record, plus you wouldn't want to edit a Job name while you're viewing an Expense record. So a merge field (which you can't click into in Browse mode) is the best solution. See page 303 for a way to make regular fields nonenterable.

If you use a regular field instead of merge field to display related data, you won't see the fully-qualified name in the field. Instead the name will appear as "::Name" to show its a related and not a "local" field. Select the field and view the Inspector's Data tab to see which table it comes from. The "Display data from" pop-up menu shows the field's fully qualified name.

Note: See the box on the next page for guidelines on when to use a portal and when to use a related field.

As you flip through the records, you'll see that the first few expenses show a Job name. That's because the sample database had Expense records with Job ID values in them and once you defined the relationships, the proper records were linked. But how do you go about entering a good Job ID into and Expense record as you log expenses? That's where value lists come in.

Portal or Related Field?

So far I've used a portal and a merge field to display related data on a layout. How do I know which one to use?

It's pretty simple really. Remember that most relationships are one-to-many. To keep it straight, think of the one side as the parent side, and the to-many side as the child side of a relationship. On a layout that shows the parent record, Customers for example, you used a portal because you want to show the "many" (really, it's one or more) line item records from the child table (Jobs).

Over on the child side, you wouldn't use a portal back to Customers, because there will only ever be one Customer related to any one Job. So there, you'll just use a related field or a merge field, as you did on page 214.

But the rule-of-thumb is true for any parent-child relationship (Invoice to Line Item, Jobs to Expenses, or Jobs to Timeslips). You'll almost always use a portal on the parent layout and a related field on the child layout.

Creating a Value List Based on a Related Field

You've already seen value lists based on custom values—on page 116, you created a value list to make sure only certain values were entered in the Lease Duration field. In a relational database, valid data entry is even more critical, particularly when you're not using a portal to create related records. Remember a portal automatically adds the primary key to the child table when you create a related record; that way the proper key value is created in the "to-many" side of the relationship.

But what if you don't want to use a portal for creating records? For example, even though each invoice needs to be attached to a Job record, it doesn't make sense to create an Invoice in a portal on the Jobs layout. Although you could create an *Invoice* record this way, there's no good way to create the proper *Line Item* record for the new invoice using that same portal. You really need to be viewing the Invoice record on a layout that shows Invoice records when you create the invoice's Line Item records.

Here's the solution: on the Invoices layout, create a new record, and then use a value list to enter the proper Job ID. The value list ensures that only valid values (those from existing Job records) are entered into the foreign key field in Invoices table. Here's how to create the value list you need:

1. Choose File→Manage→Value Lists, and then click New.

    Name your new value list *All Job IDs*. Since you're likely to have lots of value lists in a finished database, descriptive names help you keep things straight.

2. **Select "Use values from field".**

   The Specify Fields for Value List All Job IDs window appears (Figure 5-20).

3. **In the pop-up menu under "Use values from first field", choose Jobs.**

   This selects the table that holds the Job ID field.

4. **In the list of fields, select Job ID.**

   Job ID is the key field that relates an Invoice record to a specific Job record, so you'll use that field to make sure the information entered is accurate.

5. **Turn on the "Also display values from second field" checkbox. Then, from the right-hand field list, choose Name.**

   To avoid having to remember Job IDs, display the job's Name, too. That way, you can easily find the right Job ID. The second field's data won't be entered into the field, though—it's just for show.

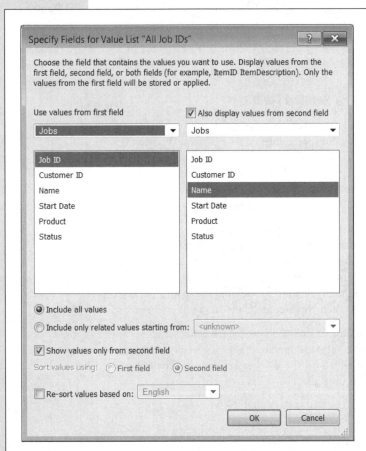

Figure 5-20:
In the "Specify Fields for Value List" window, the "Use values from field" option gives your value lists shape-shifting power: Instead of a dull list that never changes, your value lists automatically update as your data changes. So if you add a new job, it automatically shows up in the All Job IDs value list. If you delete a job, it won't appear in the value list.

Tip: The "Show values only from second field" option is really handy when you're using the value list to enter key field values, and you don't want people to be confused by a number that might not mean much to them. They see only the value in the second field, even though the field really stores the key value.

6. **In the "Sort values using" radio button set, turn on the "Second field" option.**

   It's probably easier to find the Job ID you need if it's sorted by Job Name and not Job ID.

7. **Click OK until all the windows are gone.**

   Your value list is now defined, but FileMaker isn't displaying it anywhere yet. Read on to see how to apply the list to a field.

Now that you've created the value list, you can attach it to the Job ID field in all the "to-many" layouts in the database. First, you'll put it on the Jobs ID field on the Expense layout.

1. **Switch to Layout mode, and then, if it's not already showing, choose View→ Inspector. Finally click the Inspector's Data tab to select it.**

   That's where you add a value list to a field.

2. **Click the Job ID field to select it, and then, from the Control style pop-up menu, choose Pop-up Menu.**

   The pop-up menu looks like menu choices you see in most dialog boxes, so its behavior and appearance already familiar to most users.

3. **Choose "All Job IDs" from the Values pop-up menu.**

   Job ID field's appearance changes to show that it's now a pop-up menu instead of an Edit Box.

Switch to Browse mode, and flip to a record that doesn't have a Job ID. Choose a job from the Job ID pop-up menu (Figure 5-21) and you'll see the Job name change in the merge field. (See the box on page 221 to learn how to make a value list show only related values.)

Tip: Sometimes showing just one field's data in a value list isn't the best way to find the right record–say you want to show a Customer's first and last name in a drop-down list. But the dialog box lets you pick just one field. See page 355 for a calculation that puts data from multiple fields into one field.

When you combine a relationship that allows the creation of related records, a portal and a value list from a related table, you have a solid technique for creating child records. Start to think about other places to apply the technique. For example, the Invoice layout could use a portal for creating Line Item records; similarly, you can make creating Expenses easier with an Expenses portal on the Jobs layout. You can have a portal for entering Timeslips on the Jobs layout, too. If a layout starts getting crowded, a Tab Control (page 155) might cut down on the clutter.

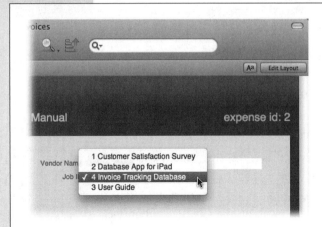

Figure 5-21:
Here's the new pop-up menu for the Jobs ID field on the Expenses layout. To attach a job to an expense, choose a Job ID from the new pop-up menu. When you do, FileMaker places the ID of the job you choose in the Expenses::Job ID field. The name is displayed in the pop-up menu to help you pick the right ID, but is not entered into the Job ID field.

Lookups

Since you have a relationship between the Jobs and Customers tables, you don't have to enter customer information on each job record. Nor do you want to store that data in both tables. If you display the customer's name and address information on the Jobs layout, and then update the customer's data, it automatically shows on the Jobs layout. This dynamic updating of related data is the essence of a relational database. However, many times you *don't* want a piece of information to change; you want FileMaker to remember the way it was at a certain point in time. *Lookup fields* use relationships to do a one-time "copy and paste" of data from one table to another. Once the looked-up data is in its new table, you can edit it, if necessary, but it doesn't change automatically if the related data changes.

Take a look at the Invoices table, for example. When you create an invoice, you attach it to a job. The job is in turn attached to a customer. When it comes time to mail the invoice, you could easily put the address fields from the Customers table occurrence on the Invoice layout, and see the customer's address. But this method is a bad idea for two reasons:

- **It doesn't allow for special circumstances.** If a customer tells you he's going to be in Majorca for a month and to please send his next invoice there, you have no way to enter an alternate address on just one invoice. You have to change the address in his customer record, send the invoice, and then change the address back.

- **It destroys relevant information.** When you *do* update the customer record with his original home address, you lose any record of where you sent the invoice. If you go back to the special-case invoice 2 years from now, it'll *look* like you sent it to his home address.

POWER USERS' CLINIC

Related Value Lists

On page 217, you saw how to make value lists that change when you add, edit, or delete records in a table. You can also decide whether the list includes values from every record in the table, or only from the related records. You start creating both types of value lists the same way: You choose a field to base the value list on, and then tell FileMaker whether you want to use values from a second field in the value list (you can even use a related field for the second value). Like regular field-based lists, you can sort the list by the first field or the second one.

But when you select the "Include only related values" radio button, the value list behaves differently. The list shows only the records related to the one you're sitting on. For example, you can use this option to show only a specific customer's Job IDs on the Invoice layout. (But you'd have to add a Customer ID field to the Invoices table to make it happen.) Then when you enter a Customer ID on an Invoice, the related value list for Job ID would show only the Jobs that have the same Customer ID value as the one you just entered.

For this method to work, FileMaker has to know which table occurrence you're using the value list on (there's that concept of *context* again). In other words, if you ask for only the related Jobs, do you mean jobs related to the Customer record or to the Invoice record? It can get confusing, but in this example, you want to use the jobs that are already related to the Customer table, even though you're using the value list on a layout that uses the context of the Invoice table occurrence. That way, the list's values change if you change the Invoice's Customer ID.

Careful, though: When you create a value list using related values only, the list works properly only when it's attached to a field on a layout associated with the same table occurrence selected in the "related values start from" menu. If you try to use it on a layout that shows records from a different TO, then FileMaker doesn't know which record to start from, and the value list doesn't show the right values.

These problems arise because invoice data is *transactional*—an invoice represents a single business transaction at one specific point in the past. But your customer record doesn't represent a single transaction with your customer: It represents an association you have with that customer. If the association changes (the customer moves and you need to store a new address), then your data should change accordingly. However, transactional data should *never* change once the transaction is complete, since it has to serve as a record of what happened during the transaction. Lookup fields solve the problem of saving transactional data.

While related fields automatically show new data, lookups use a semi-automatic approach. If you change a customer record, it *doesn't* affect the fields in existing Invoice records at all. But any new Invoice you create *does* get the updated data. You can also make lookups trigger after a record is created, using the Relookup command (page 224). Additionally, you can *change* the data in a field formatted with Auto-Enter Lookup at any time—for a one-time address change, for example. This semi-automatic approach to updating data turns out to be just the right thing for transactional data like address fields on invoices: When you change the *transaction* record, its fields update appropriately, but when you change *source* records (the address fields in your customer record), FileMaker leaves the transaction alone.

Creating Lookups

To create a lookup, you define a field normally but add an auto-enter option called *Looked-up value*. You can also add a lookup to an existing field. Simply click the field in the fields list, and then click Options. The following steps explain how to create a new lookup field:

1. **Choose File→Manage→Database, and then if necessary, click the Fields tab. Finally, from the Table pop-up menu, choose Invoices.**

   You see the fields in the Invoices table—and you're ready to add a new one. You start by adding a lookup field for the customer's street address.

2. **In the Field Name box, enter *Street Address*, and then make sure the Type pop-up menu is set to Text. Click Create.**

   FileMaker adds the new field to the field list. Right now, though, it's just an ordinary field.

3. **Click the Options button. In the Field Options dialog box, click the Auto-Enter tab.**

   The Options dialog box appears. You'll create the lookup here.

4. **Turn on the "Looked-up value" checkbox.**

   The Lookup dialog box appears (Figure 5-22).

Figure 5-22:
Here's what your Lookup dialog box looks like when you've set up the Lookup for the Invoice::Street Address field. In other circumstances, you might not want to copy over existing data if the related fields are blank. Imagine you have a table of currency exchange rates. If some currencies don't have data available the day you gather the rates, then those rate fields are blank. If you use a lookup to refresh exchange rates in your Products database, you don't want to wipe out any existing exchange rates. To keep last week's value, select the "Don't copy contents if empty" option.

5. **Make sure the "Starting with table" pop-up menu is set to Invoices.**

   It almost certainly is set properly, because in this case, the context is clear. You're defining a field in the Invoices table, so that's the field's context. If you have a table on the graph multiple times, then you might have to change the "Starting with table" pop-up menu to reflect the context of the layout on which you'll use the newly defined field, which influences how the lookup finds related data.

6. **From the "Lookup from related table" pop-up menu, choose Customers.**

   As soon as you choose a table, the "Copy value from field" list is populated with all the fields in the Customers table. You're interested in the Street Address field's value.

7. **In the "Copy value from field" list, choose Street Address. Turn off the "Don't copy contents if empty" checkbox.**

   When you turn off "Don't copy contents if empty", FileMaker dutifully copies the empty value, wiping out data in the lookup field. If you turn this option on instead, then FileMaker leaves the lookup field untouched—its value before the lookup remains in place.

8. **In the "If no exact match, then" group, turn on "use", and leave the associated text box empty.**

   If there's no customer record, the street address field should be blank. If you leave this set to "do not copy", then any existing address (for a different customer perhaps) is left in the field. (See the box on page 234 for other "If no exact match, then" options.)

9. **Click OK to close all the windows.**

   You have other fields to create, but first, you'll see how this one works.

Now switch to the Invoices layout, and then add the new field to it (page 134). When you choose a job from the Jobs table, the Invoices address field looks up the appropriate address from the Customer table. If you create an invoice and give it a valid Job ID number but no data shows up, check the Customer record to make sure you've entered addresses for your customers.

To finish your Invoices layout, create lookup fields for the remaining customer data you'll store in the Invoice table (see the list below). Use the same options as in the steps on the previous pages, or—to save clicks—duplicate the Street Address field, change its name, and then just change the field from which it looks up. That way, you get all the other lookup settings for free. Then put the new fields on the layout and create a few new records to watch the lookups in action:

- Company Name
- First Name
- Last Name

- City

- State

- Zip Code

Using a Relookup

A lookup is triggered whenever you change the data in the key field on which the relationship is based. That's why changing the Job ID field makes FileMaker look up the customer information again.

Sometimes you want a lookup to trigger *without* changing the key field. For example, suppose a new customer hires you. You work for her for 3 months, but never receive payment—despite sending three invoices. You finally decide it's time to ask her what's up, and that's when you discover you've been sending them to the *wrong address*. You mistyped her address in the Customers layout, and now all your invoices are incorrect, too. She agrees to pay you as soon as you mail the invoices to her correct address. You correct her address in the Customers table, but that doesn't affect the old invoices.

Luckily, you can easily fix them—with the Relookup Field Contents command. First, find just the three bad Invoices for your customer, and then click the field that normally triggers the lookup—the Job ID field in this case. Then choose the Records→Relookup Field Contents command. You see the message shown in Figure 5-23.

FileMaker is asking whether you want to copy the correct address onto the three bad invoices. Click OK, and FileMaker makes the correction. Then all you have to do is resend the invoices.

Figure 5-23:
When you run the Relookup Field Contents command, FileMaker shows this message. The program reminds you how many records you're updating, since you can't undo this action. If you look up new address information into old invoices accidentally, you lose historical data. If you're sure you want to proceed, click OK.

Tip: To get into the Job ID field (it has a pop-up menu controlling it), just click it, and be sure to choose the job that's already selected. Your goal is to make FileMaker think you're changing the data so the lookup retriggers without changing the data that's in the field. After you make your choice, the Relookup grabs the updated data.

Navigating Between Related Records

With pop-up menus and autocreating records, adding data to your new database is now a breeze. But you still have to do some serious work to navigate the system. For example, if you're looking at a job and you want to see details about the related customer, you have to note the Customer ID or name, switch to the Customers layout, and then find the customer. That's two steps too many.

Simplify this process with a button (page 317) on the Invoice layout—one that uses the *Go to Related Record* (GTRR) command. GTRR does the obvious, plus a little more. It goes to the related record *and* changes the layout appropriately. It can also find all the related records, and then sort them (if the relationship you're using has a sort specified). It can even create a new window, while it's at it. That's a lot of work for one little command. If that weren't enough ways to use this little powerhouse, you can also set an option that show records related to a found set instead of just the current record.

Go to Related Record

Here's one way to create a button that activates the "Go to Related Record" command. In the JobsInvoices database, the Customer's Name appears at the top of the layout in a merge field. In the following steps, you'll create a button that goes to the left of the customer name. When you click the button, it takes you to the proper customer record.

1. **Switch to the Jobs layout, and then go to Layout mode.**

    You always add buttons in Layout mode.

2. **Select the text tool, and then type a ">" symbol. Use the Format Painter (page 125) to make the symbol's font match the text block it'll sit next to. Then make it a contrasting green color and move the symbol into place.**

    The ">" symbol is a commonly-used button for revealing detail or navigating to a related page. You can draw a circle or square, or even import a graphic if you prefer. Just make it small enough to fit in the allotted space.

3. **With the text block still selected, choose Format→Button Setup.**

    The Button Setup dialog box appears.

4. **From the list's Navigation section, select the "Go to Related Record" script step. When the Options section of the window appears, click Specify.**

    The "Go to Related Records" Options dialog box appears (Figure 5-24).

5. **From the "Get related record from" pop-up menu, choose Customers.**

    You're specifying which table occurrence you want to go to.

Figure 5-24:
Use the GTRR Options window to tell File-Maker what you want to see and how you want it presented. "Get related record from" determines what table occurrence to show and "Show record using layout" determines which layout is used. In the JobsInvoices database, you have only one table occur-rence for each table, so once you choose a TO, there's only one layout to select. But in a more complex database, you might have to choose from hundreds of TOs and the doz-ens of layouts tied to the chosen TO. Later on, you'll learn how to change the found set of the target table occurrence.

6. **From the "Show record using layout" pop-up menu, choose Layout.**

    The Specify Layout window appears. In this case, there's only one layout in the list, because you only have one layout attached to the Customer TO. But in a da-tabase where there's more than one layout attached to a table, you get to choose which one to show.

7. **Click OK until you're back on the layout.**

    The button is set up. Use the View→Show→Buttons command to outline all of the layout's buttons with a dashed line.

Switch to Browse mode. Make sure you have a customer related to this job. If you don't, click the Customer ID field, and then choose one. Once you assign a customer ID to the Jobs record, the relationship is valid, and your button will work. Click it and you're transported directly to that customer's record.

Current Layout is the automatic option in the "Show record using" pop-up menu. If you forget to make a selection there, you may have trouble. After all, if you're going to a related record, it's usually from a different table occurrence. If your current lay-out can't show you the related data because it doesn't have the required fields, you'll get an error message. Check your "Show record using layout" settings, and then try again.

Note: The "Use external table's layouts" option in the GTRR Options window applies only when you're linking multiple *files* together. You'll learn about that on page 591.

Using GTRR to create a found set

If you're looking at a Customer record, then you can see all that customer's jobs, since they're right there in the Jobs portal. But what if you want to see those jobs (and only those jobs) in a sorted found set on the Jobs layout? It would take a bunch of steps if you had to do it manually. But the "Go to Related Record" command does all those steps for you—when you add a few new options to the setup you just learned.

1. **On the Customers layout, switch to Layout mode, and then select the Jobs::Name field.**

   It's in the Jobs portal.

2. **Choose Format→Button Setup. In the Button Setup dialog box, from the list, select the "Go to Related Record" command, and then click Specify.**

   The "Go to Related Record" Options window pops up.

3. **From the "Get related record from" pop-up menu, choose Jobs. From the "Show record using layout" pop-up menu, choose Layout, then choose Jobs layout, and then click OK once.**

   You need a layout that shows you meaningful data from the Jobs table. So far, this process is just like creating a related record button without a found set. The next steps make all the difference.

4. **Turn on "Show only related records".**

   When you turn on "Show only related records", FileMaker changes the found set in the target table, showing just the related records. The appropriate record will be active, and you'll be able to scroll to the other records in the found set. If the relationship has a sort order, FileMaker sorts the found set, too.

   For now, leave "Match current record only" turned on. (Selecting "Match all records in the current found set" lets you go from one found set of records to another. See the box on page 228 for more detail.)

5. **Click OK until you're back on the Customers layout.**

   You're looking at your layout again.

6. **For good measure, make the Jobs::Name field is blue and underlined (so it looks like a link).**

   Training time is cut down when you provide clues that the field is clickable.

Switch to Browse mode to admire your work. Now you have a way to move from a Job to its Customer and from a Customer to a found set of all her Jobs. To see the real power of a button in a portal, use the book icon to navigate to a customer record that has more than one related job. Click the *second* portal record. Since you're on the second row, the button takes you to the second record in your found set, not the first one. Then click the Customer Name button again and see how the results change when you click in the first portal row.

What you're seeing is another example of context. In this case the context of the *button* (the row you click) determines which record is active when the GTRR is complete. When you click the GTRR button on the Jobs layout, you see the Customer that's related to that job, but without changing the found set. But when you click a button in the Jobs portal, you get a found set of only the job records you just saw in the portal.

POWER USERS' CLINIC

GTRR on (Legal) Steroids

The "Show only related records" option of the "Go to Related Record" window lets you display a found set of records from a related table. But what if you want to do something really cool and complicated, like find a group of invoices that don't have anything in common other than being unpaid, and then see the Customers for those Invoices in a found set without writing down the list of customers and then performing a complicated search?

Here's how you do it: Make a button on your Invoice layout, and then give it a GTRR step that goes to the Customers table occurrence using the Customers layout. Then, in the Options window, select "Show only related records" *and* "Match all records in current found set".

The starting found set on the Invoice layout determines which Customer records you'll see. So if you were viewing 10 invoice records from six different customers, you'd get a found set of those six customers when you click the GTRR button. The cool thing is that you don't have to know how many customers are related to the Invoice found set, because the relationship tracks that for you. Now that you have a found set of late-paying customers, you can send them all an email letting them know they're late.

Apply GTRR (on steroids) liberally throughout your database, and people won't need to do as many complicated searches to find the data they're looking for.

Reviewing Relationship Concepts

Wrapping your head around relationships and how they work in FileMaker is a little like trying to play chess on a multilevel playing board. Though the Relationships graph is flat, it has powers that may not be apparent at first. For example, when you created Lookup fields (page 222), you used the graph to tunnel through one table to get to a table beyond, grab some data and then come back to put it in a local field. In this section, you'll go into more depth on some concepts you've touched on earlier in this chapter.

Bidirectionality

You've started to tap the power of that one little line you drew between the Customers and Jobs table. But one very important aspect of that line is worth paying extra attention to—a line describes a relationship that works in two directions. You saw that in action when you used the same relationship to make GTRR buttons that navigate between the tables at either end of one relationship.

Notice that the GTRR command behaves a little differently, depending on which table you start from, since the tables are on either end of a one-to-many relationship. But the key concept is that the relationship works both ways. That's why one Edit Relationship window (Figure 5-25) lets you set options for both tables in the relationship.

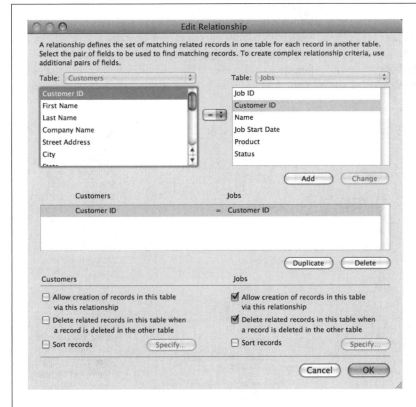

Figure 5-25:
You can set options for both tables involved in a relationship with the Edit Relationship window. It's important to understand which options make sense for which table, though. It would be extremely rare, for instance, to allow creation of a parent record from a child table for instance. And since each child record only has one parent, clicking the option to sort the records in a parent table is a waste of time.

Remember that Table Occurrences appear in the Edit Relationship window based on their relative positions on the graph. Left and right don't matter here, but if helps you to put the "one" TO on the left, then make sure it appears to the left of the "to many" TO on the graph. But because a TO might appear in the Edit Relationship window on either side of the relationship, options are shown on both sides of the window even though you'll rarely set those options on the "one" side.

Note: Here's a list of refreshers on the options you can set in the Edit Relationship window: allow creation (page 144), delete, and sort (page 146). See the box on page 231 to learn about the hidden danger of using the delete option for related records.

Implicit Relationships in Action

When you modeled the JobsInvoices database, you learned about *implicit* relationships. These relationships are when tables are connected to one another through other tables. For example, when you create a lookup field in the Invoice table that can enter data from the Customer table, you're leveraging an implicit relationship. Specifically, Invoices and Customers don't relate to one another directly (Figure 5-26). They relate to one another through the Jobs table. So you didn't create or need a Customer ID in the Invoice table to pull the data from Customers. FileMaker uses the Jobs ID field to find the right Customer, and then put the right data into the Invoice table's name and address fields. Because it can feel like having a direct pipeline into a table, using these implicit relationships is sometimes called *data tunneling*.

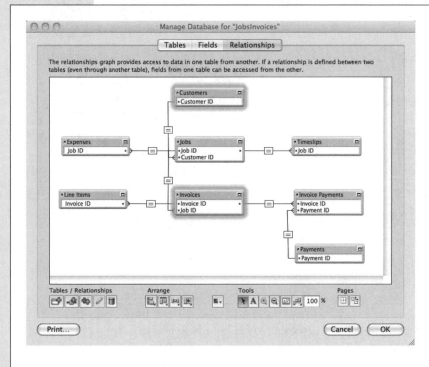

Figure 5-26:
The Invoice and Customer tables (highlighted) aren't directly related to one another, but use an implicit relationship instead. The database relationships reflect those in the real world of your business. An invoice is connected to a customer because you created an invoice for a job you did for that customer. You can use GTRR (page 225) to easily get a report for your customer about all the invoices related to a specific job. And because Invoices are tied to a job, you can even create report layouts that summarize all invoices by job for any customer (page 601).

Cascading Deletes

The "Delete related records" option can be dangerous for a couple of reasons. First, if you turn it on where it should be turned off, then you can find yourself in an odd situation: Records keep disappearing for no apparent reason. You'll get frustrated if you don't realize how this option works.

But even if you *want* it on, keep this fact in mind: File-Maker can't bring back a record you delete. It's one thing if someone accidentally deletes a Jobs record—you just have to look up the Job Name, and then enter it again, being careful to give the job the same ID it had before.

It's something else entirely if you also select the "Delete related records" option in the Jobs-to-Customers relationship, and the Customers-to-Invoices relationship, and

again in the Invoices-to-Line Items relationship. You've set up the Towering Inferno scenario called *cascading deletes*. Because now, when you delete one job record—perhaps thinking that the job is finished and you don't need the record anymore—FileMaker also obeys your "hidden" instructions and deletes the Customer record attached to that Job record, *all* the Invoices attached to the Customer, and *all* those line items, too!

Some people decide it's not worth the risk and leave the "Delete related records" option off even when it *should* be on. For a better solution to the cascading deletion problem, read up on how access privileges can limit who's allowed to delete records on page 769.

You can use data tunneling to show a list of all a customer's invoices on the Customer layout. So on the Customers layout, create an Invoice portal and place the Invoices::Date, Invoices::Invoice ID and Invoices::Job ID fields in the portal. Normally, you *wouldn't* put an ID field in a portal. In fact, it would probably be a bad idea because it would confuse users and raise the possibility that the data in a key field could get changed, thus stranding the related record or connecting it to the wrong parent record. But for this experiment, you want to see the ID fields so you can see how data tunneling works. While you're violating standard procedure, throw the Jobs::Job ID field into the Jobs portal. When you're done, your layout will look something like Figure 5-27.

Note: The sample database for this chapter has Job and Invoice records that already have IDs for Customer Jerald Tabb. If you've created Invoice records that are related to Jobs, they'll show up too, so long as the Jobs are related to a customer record.

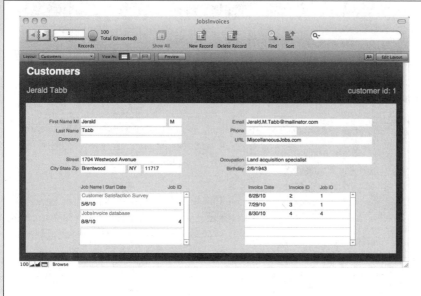

Figure 5-27:
Notice that the Invoice portal shows all invoices that are attached to either of Jerald Tabb's two jobs (Customer Satisfaction Survey and JobsInvoices database). Placing the ID fields in a portal is a good way to understand how relationships work in theory. It's also a good troubleshooting tip if a portal or relationship isn't working the way you think it should be working. Once you see the values in those ID fields, it's usually pretty easy to figure out what's happening and then fix the problem.

The records displayed in the Invoice portal shows all Invoices that are related to any of the customer's jobs. So if a customer has 20 jobs, the invoices from all those jobs appear in the portal. When you think of *this* Invoices portal, it helps to think of it as a one-to-many-*to-many* relationship. That's not a term you'll hear database developers using, but it makes the concept more clear—one Customer is related to many Jobs, which in turn are related to many Invoices.

Note: You can change the Invoices::Job ID field to show Job::Name instead. Here's how: double-click on Job ID to show the Specify Field dialog box, and then switch to the Jobs table occurrence and choose the Name field.

Context is the key. From a Customer record, the context of the Invoice table is always through the Jobs table. Because Customers are implicitly related to Invoices through Jobs, you can copy the Invoices portal from the Customer layout, and then paste it on the Jobs layout, where it will behave itself perfectly without any extra work on your part. It will show slightly different data in its new context, though. On the Invoice table, the portal shows invoices from all jobs related to the customer. On the Jobs layout the same portal shows Invoices related to the current job only. The move works because you're moving a portal along the same relationship line.

The Invoice table isn't the only one in the database that shares these properties. For example:

- You can put an Expenses, Line Item, Timeslip, or even a Payments portal on the Customers layout. For instance, you might want to see all the expenses incurred for a specific customer. And like the Invoices table, you can use calculations to sum up all those related records (page 368).

- You can put a GTRR button (page 225) on the Invoice portal so you can quickly see a found set of a Customer's invoices without performing a find.

- Using the principle of bidirectionality, you could put Customer::Full Name field on a Payment record or use a GTRR button on an Expense record to jump through hyperspace directly to the proper Customer record.

Warning: The options you set in the Edit Relationship window (Figure 5-25) don't pass through implicit relationships, with good reason. For example, the Customers-to-Jobs relationship is set to allow the creation of related Jobs records. However, when you're on a Customer record, you can't create an Invoice record from the Invoice portal unless you turn on the option to create related records for the Invoice table in the *Jobs-to-Invoices* relationship. If you do that, though, all Invoices you create through the Invoices portal on the Customer table will get the Job ID from the first record in the Jobs table. That's probably not what you want.

More likely, you'll have simultaneous jobs going on for at least some of your Customers, so you should create Invoices only when you're on a record in the Jobs table. Implicit relationships have some limitations, and you should be aware of them as you're designing.

When you're figuring out how best to add a new feature to your database, take a gander at your Relationships graph, and trace the line between all the tables that'll be affected. Take notice of the key fields in each table and the options set for each relationship. This simple preparation will often help you come up with solutions faster, and with fewer oddball behaviors.

You'll learn more advanced relationship techniques in Chapter 13. But now that you've mastered the fundamentals of relationships, you'll be switching gears to learn more about how to make fields work.

Empty Lookups

Lookup options give you some control over what happens when you don't have a matching related record. Normally, if FileMaker tries to find a related record to look up data from and it can't find one, it just leaves the lookup field alone.

That's what happens when, in the "If no exact match, then" group of radio buttons, you turn on "do not copy". Here's what the others do:

- The "copy next lower value" option looks at the closest *lower* related record. For example, if you turn it on for the Invoices::Street Address field, and there's no matching related customer, FileMaker copies the address of the customer with the next lower Customer ID alphabetically. In this case, it makes absolutely no sense.

But what if you're looking up price information based on quantity? If the customer orders 38, but you have pricing for 30 or 40, you might want to get the price for 30 items, the next lower value.

- The "copy next higher value" option works just like its similarly named counterpart. It just copies the value from the next *higher* related record instead.

- The "use" option lets you specify any value you want to substitute for a missing related value. For example, if you're looking up customer age information and you don't have an age for one person, you can tell FileMaker to use "N/A" instead.

Field Options

In Chapter 3, you learned a couple of ways to create fields, and then got your feet wet learning about some of FileMaker's eight field types. In this chapter, you'll learn more about the field types you already know, and then you'll learn about some types you haven't come across before. But type is only one of the options you can choose when you create a field. For example, lookup fields (page 222) are one way FileMaker can automatically enter data into a field, but it's not the only way. FileMaker gives you so many other ways to get automatic data into fields, the Field Options window has a whole tab dedicated to those options.

Other times, you need to restrict the types of information people can enter in a field, but a value list (page 116) is too restrictive. So FileMaker lets you decide what kind of data—date, text, or whatever—a field can accept. That's called field validation, and once again, there's a whole tab full of options.

Once you've got your data into fields, FileMaker lets you decide how to want to store it and do more advanced tricks like create a field that has the same value for every record in a table or repeat the same field multiple times on one record. And you'll learn how container fields let you store entire files from other programs within a FileMaker record.

Note: You can find a starter file, called Fields.fp7, for this chapter on this book's Missing CD page at *www. missingmanuals.com/cds*.

Understanding Field Types

FileMaker has eight different field types. Each one has its strengths and best uses. Selecting the right field type for your data is fundamental to getting your database to behave the way you want it to, so here are some tips for figuring out which field type to choose.

Text

Text fields are the automatic field type. Each text field can store about 2 GB of letters, numbers or symbols, including carriage returns, so long a your computer's memory allows that much storage. That's about one BILLION characters. The figure is approximate because it's partially based on your computer's RAM and disk space. Use text fields for names, addresses and even phone numbers.

Number

Number fields are those that you intend to do some kind of math on. If you're creating invoices, you'll need number fields so other fields can tally up the invoice total. You can type letters and even symbols in a number field, but if you do, FileMaker may change your data in unexpected ways. For instance, if you create a field to store a Part Number and then put data like 234A111, FileMaker will treat that entry as the numeric value "234111," so it's usually safest to store data with letters and symbols in text fields.

Numbers can be very large or very small. And to help people who use FileMaker for scientific or mathematic solutions, here are some limits for number fields:

- Numbers have to be between 10^{800} and -10^{800} (it's actually 9.99999999…e799, because -10^{800} itself isn't included). If you're counting something reasonable—say, the number of protons in the universe—you'll be just fine.

- You get 800 significant digits in all. In general though, any nonzero value is a significant digit. That is, the digit contributes to the number's precision. For example, the leading zeros in the number "00042" are *not* significant. That's probably all you need to know about significant digits. If you're still curious, ask a high-school algebra student.

- Only the first 400 digits are indexed in all, significant or otherwise. So if you're searching for numbers, then you have a little less precision to work with.

You can enter numbers in FileMaker as you would in most any program. Type the number and any symbols that define it, like a negative sign or a decimal point. You can also use *scientific notation*. For example, if you have a burning desire to count the air molecules in your living room, you can put 6.02E23 into a number field, which is a lot easier to type than 60,200,000,000,000,000,000,000,000. Of course, the exponent part (after the E) can be negative if really small numbers make your socks go up and down.

Number fields can't contain paragraph breaks. If you try to hit Return, FileMaker will beep at you.

Note: Number fields can also contain Boolean values. See page 644 to learn about them.

Date

Unlike text or number fields, you can only store valid Gregorian dates in date fields. Data entry has to be as month, day and year, but you can use several different punctuation marks as separators. That is you can type: "2/25/1975," "2-25-1975," or "2.25.1975."

Note: Computers in Europe and other areas use system settings that expect different day, time and number formats. FileMaker uses the settings that are in effect on the computer where the file was created. So if you ever open a file created by a Japanese user (for example), FileMaker will ask you which settings to use the first time you open that file. Choose File→File Options, and then click the Text tab to change the file's settings.

The first possible date you can store is 1/1/0001 and the current format is good until the end of the year 4000 AD, so you should be good at least until you retire. If you enter a two-digit year (like 10 or 87), FileMaker takes up your slack and puts either 19 or 20 in front. Which one you get can be hard to guess so to avoid mistakes, you're always better off entering all four digits. If you really want a two-digit year (because you're entering a date from ancient history) then enter it like this: 6/17/0034.

If the date you're entering is in the current calendar year, you can save a few keystrokes by typing the month and day only. Use only a single separator, though. For example, in 2010 you can type "11/7" to get the date November 7, 2010. Save even more time with the Insert→Current Date command. Press Ctrl (⌘), and then the hyphen key (–) to enter the current date. (This command actually works in a text field, too, or even a block of text on a layout.)

Note: Although FileMaker lets you enter and display dates in a format that we humans find meaningful (September 26, 1957 or 11/11/11), the program actually stores them as numbers (Figure 6-1). That gives you the power to perform mathematical operations on date fields when you create calculations (page 404).

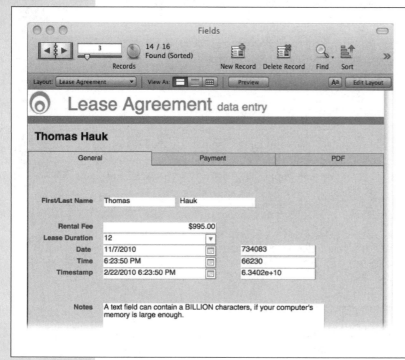

Figure 6-1:
In the left column, you see a date field, a time field, and a timestamp field. In the right column, you see the result of a calculation field that displays the value as a number instead of a date or time (the number represents the days since 1/1/0001. Timestamp values are so high that they're displayed in exponential notation and look kind of scary. But if you're planning to do math on a date, time or timestamp field, you'll get used to it. FileMaker stores timestamp data as a number—the number of seconds elapsed since 12:00:00, January 1, in the year 0001.

Time

Like date fields, time fields require precise entry. Separate hours, minutes and seconds with a colon. You don't have to enter seconds if you don't want to, but you have to include both hours and minutes. You can put "am" or "pm" in the field to indicate which 6:00 you mean, or you can use military time and enter 18:00 instead of 6:00 pm.

Time fields are most often used for time of day, like 4:30 am or 6:13:27 pm. But you can also enter a *duration* instead, like 123:38:22 (meaning 123 hours, 38 minutes, 22 seconds). You don't even have to limit yourself to a 60-minute hour. A time like 0:82:17 is perfectly valid (it means 82 minutes, 17 seconds, and is exactly equivalent to 1:22:17). (On page 311, you'll learn how to force a field to always show a valid time value in the format of your choice.)

Note: When entering time values, you *always* start with hours. If you're trying to enter just 12 minutes, 37 seconds, then you have to enter *00:12:37* or *0:12:37* so FileMaker doesn't think you mean 12 *hours*.

Time values are also quite precise. If you're recording track event times for your school, you can enter *00:00:27.180* for 27 seconds, 180 milliseconds. You can put up to six digits to the right of the decimal point. Time data is stored as numeric data and is counted by seconds elapsed since midnight of the current day.

Timestamp

A *timestamp* field is basically a date field and a time field combined. It has to hold *both* a date *and* a time. As with its companions Date and Time types, data needs to be precise. All the rules for date and time entry apply: 2/25/1975 2:45 AM. Because they're so picky, you usually don't want people typing directly into timestamp field; so use auto-enter options (page 240) to create their data instead. You can also use Insert→CurrentTime and FileMaker is smart enough to enter the data and time in a Timestamp field. .

Like its counterparts the date and time field types, a timestamp is stored as a number. A timestamp represents the number of seconds elapsed since January 1, 0001 at 12:00:00 AM (midnight).

You can use this kind of field to record when an event happened, or when it will happen. You may be tempted to use two fields (a date field and a time field), but that road only leads to heartache and pain when you try to reference those fields in calculations. If something happens on a specific date and time, you should use a timestamp field for it.

Timestamps support the same fraction-of-a-second accuracy as time fields. They're displayed as a date followed by a time with a space in between.

Note: If you're formatting a timestamp field (page 312), you have to apply *both* a date and a time format. If you apply only one type of format, it won't show up.

Container

Use container fields to store graphics, movies, sounds, or files—text documents, spreadsheets, PDFs, or even other FileMaker files. Container fields have such specific behavior that a whole section in this chapter is dedicated to explaining how to use them.

Note: Unlike with text and other kinds of fields, you can't sort records using a container field, and you can't perform finds on them. (But you can create a text field with keywords you enter manually that lets you find and sort.)

Calculation

Unlike the other field types discussed so far, you don't enter data in *calculation* and *summary* fields. The results of calculation fields do have types, too, like fields themselves.

Calculation fields' values are based on the settings you give them, when you specify a special *formula* that determine its value. For instance, if you had a field called Birth Date, you could create a calculation field that shows the person's age. The Age field automatically updates to stay correct as time goes by, so you don't have to change it. Three chapters of this book are dedicated to calculations. You'll start plumbing their depths in Chapter 8.

Summary

Calculation fields often perform math on fields that are in the same record. But Summary fields collect data from across sets of records. So even though summary fields can be defined in a table, and thus may seem as if they refer to specific record, as other fields do, summary fields get their values from found sets of records. You used the layout wizard to create a summary field in the tutorial starting on page 169 and you'll learn how to create them manually in Chapter 14.

Auto-Enter Field Options

Regardless of their type, most fields are empty when you create a new record. Often, but not always, that's what you want—a completely blank slate into which you can type all the information pertinent to a record. But auto-enter options also put data into fields for you, saving time and reducing human error. Auto-enter options can also create things like serial numbers for a primary key (page 198) or store data about your records (Figure 6-2).

Note: If you don't see any options in the Fields tab of your Manage Database window, click the Options/Comments column heading. That toggles it between showing comments and showing options.

On the Options for Field dialog box's Auto-Enter tab, the first two auto-enter options (creation values and modification values) let you create and maintain metadata. Many developers find these fields so useful for peeking behind the scenes that they create primary key fields and the four metadata fields shown in Figure 6-2 in each table before they create any other fields.

Tip: Information about records, as opposed to information about the entities you base your tables on (page 183) is called metadata. Metadata helps you do basic forensics on your database. For example, if there's a question about an Invoice, you can see at a glance who created it, and then ask the person to solve the mystery. Plus, when data entry folks know you're tracking this kind of metadata, they may start being more careful, since they know you can track their mistakes back to them.

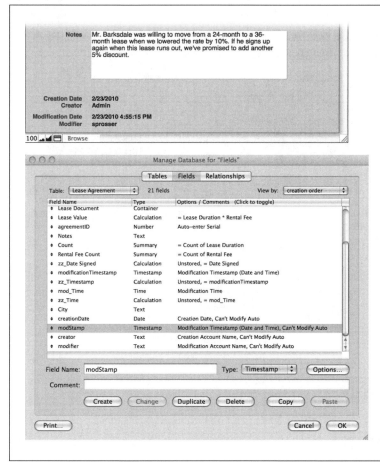

Figure 6-2:
Top: This layout shows four auto-enter fields that store information about who creates and/or modifies each record and when they do so.

Bottom: The Manage Database window's field list shows auto-enter options in the Options/Comments column. The highlighted "modStamp" field tracks the date and time that any field on any record gets changed. In conjunction with the "modifier" field, you can figure out who's entered stuff into this record and when. The names of metadata fields in this table follow a naming convention of starting with a lower case letter, and then using an upper case letters instead of a space to indicate the start of a new word. Developers often name metadata fields that way to tell them apart from fields that store user-entered data. If you're not working with FileMaker Pro Advanced, you won't have the Copy and Paste buttons shown here. See page 512 to learn about FileMaker Pro Advanced's ability to copy and paste fields from one table to another.

Creation Values

When a record is *first created*, FileMaker can enter some information about the circumstances under which it was created. It can record the date, time, or timestamp at the moment of creation, and who created the record. You can search such fields to find recently-created records, all records that are over a year old, or even records that were created on a Tuesday.

You can run through the exercises in this chapter using any database of your own. Or download a sample file from this book's Missing CD page at *www.missingmanuals.com*. You can apply an auto-enter option to a newly-created field or to one that already exists. Just make sure that the field type and option match each other. For example, make sure that an auto-enter Creation Date option is applied to a Date field. Strictly speaking, you can apply a creation date option to a text field, but if you do, the result will be sorted as text and you may not get reports sorted in the order you want.

You'll get more predictable results if you match types consistently. Here's how to set an auto-enter creation date field:

1. **In the Manage Database window, make sure a date field is selected in the Fields list, and then click the Options button.**

   The "Options for Field" dialog box appears (Figure 6-3).

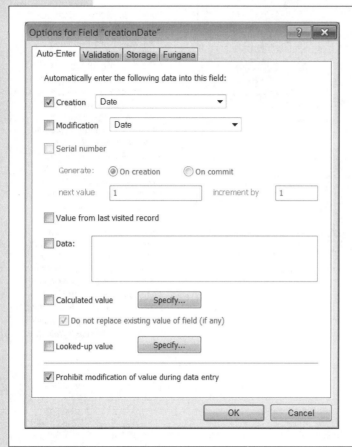

Figure 6-3:
Turn on the Creation option, and then choose Date to get a field that holds the record's date of birth. Actually, save yourself a little time and skip the Creation checkbox altogether. It turns itself on automatically when you choose an option from the pop-up menu next to it.

2. **Select the Creation checkbox.**

   You use this option for any data specifically related to the creation of a record like, say, the date and time it was created.

3. **From the Creation pop-up menu, choose Date.**

   In this case, you want the field to contain the date the record is created.

4. **Turn on the "Prohibit modification of value during data entry" checkbox.**

    Because this field automatically gets the right value, you never need to change it manually after a record is created. Plus, you don't want folks accidentally (or worse, *intentionally*) editing this data. The whole point of the exercise is to have FileMaker create an official date for each record that's incontrovertible. Figure 6-3 shows the finished product.

5. **Click OK until you're back on your layout.**

    You're now ready to test your new field. Any existing records don't have the creation date, because they were created before the field's option was set. But every record you create from here on will have a creation date.

Note: If you already have a lot of records in your table before you create the Creation Date field, you can enter dates manually by turning off the "Prohibit modification of value during data entry" option temporarily. Just be sure to turn it back on when you're done to prevent future mistakes.

In this case, a creation date is specific enough. But sometimes you need to know the Date and Time of an event. While you could create two fields (one Date field with an auto-enter creation date and a Time field with an auto-enter creation time), a Timestamp field with an auto-enter timestamp value is a lot easier to use in a calculation.

Auto-enter creation date fields are also useful for things like invoice dates. For most invoices, their date is the date they're created, so go ahead and apply an auto-enter creation date option to that field. But just make sure you don't turn on the "Prohibit modification of value during data entry" option. You want to have the ability to change the date, in case you don't have time to create an invoice the same day you delivered the product or service.

Using Creation Name and Account Name

When you're tracking who created a record, you might be tempted to choose Name on the Creation menu to store metadata about who created a record. But this options uses the FileMaker user name and has a couple of weaknesses. First, sneaky people can change their user name in the operating system (In Windows, choose Edit→Preferences; in Mac OS X, choose FileMaker Pro→Preferences). Second, someone can sit down at another user's computer and enter some information; you really only know which computer the information came from, not which person. A more reliable method of tracking the "who" part of metadata is to create database Account Names instead. To learn how to set up and manage accounts, see page 782.

Modification Values

It's useful to know when a record was *created*, but it's even more useful to know when it was *last changed*. That way, you can quickly find everything that temp you hired last week messed up, or see how stale the info you have on your best customer is. But "change" is such a pedestrian word, hardly suited to the highbrow world of database development, so FileMaker calls it *modification* instead. Making modification info available in your database is a familiar exercise:

Make a new Timestamp field called *modificationTimestamp*. *Then* in the field's Auto-Enter options, turn on the Modification checkbox, and then, from the pop-up menu, choose "Timestamp (Date and Time)".

You might hesitate to turn on the "Prohibit modification of value during data entry" option this time. After all, you want this field to change every time you enter data in a record. But don't fret. This checkbox keeps *you* from typing into the field, but FileMaker can still update its value for you. So by all means, turn the "Prohibit modification" checkbox on. Manually changing this field is just as much a problem as changing the Creation Date field.

Note: In Chapter 11, which covers scripting, you'll discover other ways to change a field that don't involve data entry. The "Prohibit modification" option applies only to the process of a human being interacting with a field in Browse mode.

Serial Number

Back in Chapter 1, you learned that record numbers can change as records get deleted or sorted. Then on page 138, you saw that when you want to assign a unique number to your record, you use the "Serial number" auto-enter option. Here's more detail on how that works: a serial number is a field whose value goes up for each new record. Typically, it goes up by a count of one, so the first record might be 1, 1001, or INV0001. In the second record you create, the serial number field would be 2, 1002, or INV0002. The numbers don't have to go up by one with each new record—you can provide any "increment by" value you want. But the value always goes up by some fixed amount.

In the Field Options dialog box, once you turn on the "Serial number" checkbox, you can specify the "next value", which is the value FileMaker uses for the next record that you create (usually, the starting value). The "increment by" value tells FileMaker how much to add with each new record.

You can specify non-numerical values for "next value" if you want. For example, if your field is a text field, you can put INV00001 in the "next value" box. Your first record would then get INV00001, followed by INV00002 and INV00003.

The Generate radio buttons under "Serial number" control *when* the serial number is assigned. If you select "On creation", then as soon as you create a record, FileMaker puts the serial number in the field. If you decide you don't want the record, even if you delete it right away, that serial number value has been *used up*, and the next record you make has a new serial number. In almost every case, losing a serial number poses no problem at all, and it's convenient to have the serial number value available before you commit the record because serial numbers are so often used as key fields when you're creating relationships (page 204).

If you select "On commit" instead, the serial number doesn't show up in the field until you exit the record. In other words, you can delete this new record without *committing*, and you haven't used up a serial number. Still, unless you have a good reason (like a stringent government regulation that requires you to record every single transaction with a string of unbroken serial numbers), you should use the "On creation" option. See the box below for more on committing records.

You use serial numbers most often when you create relationships between tables. Serial numbers also come in handy when the items in your database don't have a convenient name. In a database of invoices, it can be tough to talk about one particular invoice. ("You know, that one we sent last Thursday. No, not that one, the *other* one.") People generally use serial numbers to clarify things.

POWER USERS' CLINIC

Embracing Commitment

The word *commit* refers to a semi-technical database concept. When you create a new record, you haven't actually added a record to the table yet. Instead, you get a blank record on the screen, and the information you enter is stored in a temporary working area in your computer's memory. When you exit the record, the information in that working area is *committed*—or written—to the database.

When you edit a record, the same principle holds: As soon as you enter the record, it's copied to the working area. While you edit it, you're actually editing this copy. When you exit the record, FileMaker puts your edited copy back in the table. In general, think of *committing* a record as the same thing as *exiting* a record. When you exit the record, you commit it.

Value from Last Visited Record

Some databases need a lot of repetitive data entry. For example, if you're entering scores into a grade book database, you have to enter the same assignment information and date for each student's paper—only the grade changes. In cases like this, FileMaker's "Value from last visited record" auto-enter option is exceptionally handy. When you turn on this option, each time you make a new record, File-Maker automatically fills in those fields with the same data as the record you last created or edited.

Note: Last Visited Record has a specific meaning. It's not the last record you were *looking* at. It's the last record that was *active*. In other words, you can flip to a record and view it, but if you don't click into one of its fields, it wasn't *visited*. If you're using this option, but getting unexpected data, remember this distinction.

As with the Date option, you can easily change the values FileMaker enters after you create the record. When you do, the next record you create copies the new, changed values from the record you just edited. Entering multiple sets of repetitive information becomes a breeze—you modify the Assignment field only once per set of papers, for instance.

Data

The Data option on the Auto-Enter tab is useful when you have a field that usually has the same data in it, but occasionally needs to change. Suppose most of the properties you manage are in New Orleans. FileMaker can put *New Orleans* in a City field for you—but you can still change it when appropriate. Or if all your part numbers start with the same prefix, say "WMA-", set up your part number field to enter that data automatically, and then you can type the rest of the numbers in manually.

Calculated Value

Auto-enter calculation fields are different from calculation fields. With calculation fields, the data is entered for you, but if you need to override the value, you're out of luck. You can click into a calculation field, but if you try to type, you'll get a warning telling you the field isn't modifiable.

But auto-enter calculations give you the power of calculations, along with the ability to change the result. For example, say you have a regular calculation field called Invoice::Due Date. Its calculation—*Invoice Date + Payment Terms*—adds Payment Terms to the Invoice Date field to come up with the Due Date value. Invoice Date is set as the creation date of the record, and Payment Terms are auto-entered data (say Net 10 Days). The Due Date field is filled in when you create each Invoice record. The only way you can change the Due Date is by changing the value in the Invoice Date field or the Payment Terms field, and FileMaker updates the calculation. But you can't type the date you want directly in the Invoice::Due Date field.

Note: Yes, you can add the Payment Term field's value of "Net 10 days" to a date, *if* the Payment Terms field is defined as a number field. That way, FileMaker can ignore the text when asked to do math with the field's value. But to reduce ambiguity, stick to straight numbers in fields that are referenced by calculations.

That's where the "Calculated value" option comes in. You can specify a calculation, which enters a date when FileMaker creates the record, but then you can click into the field and change it to another date. Plus, if you convert a calculation field to another type with an auto-enter calculation, FileMaker automatically moves the formula you wrote into the auto-enter calculation box for you. You don't even have to rewrite the calculation. Even better, you can get the field's calculated value to reset later by changing the value in either the Invoice Date or Payment Terms fields. Just make sure you *don't* turn on the "Do not replace existing value (if any)" option when you set up the field (Figure 6-4).

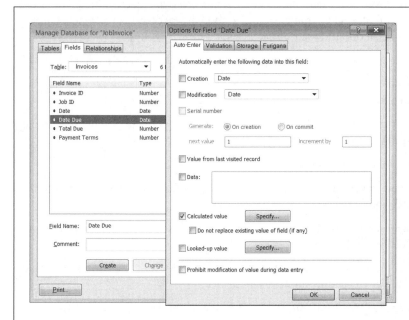

Figure 6-4:
The Auto-Enter tab of the Options for Field "Date Due" window is where you select the Calculated value option, and then turn off the automatic "Do not replace existing value (if any)" option. With these settings, if you change the value in either field referenced in the Date Due field's calculation (Invoice Date or Payment Terms), the date due value will be updated. But if you leave the "Do not replace" option turned on, the calculation only kicks in when data is entered into the referenced fields the first time. Either way, you can change the value at will unless you also choose "Prohibit modification of value during data entry", which defeats the purpose of an auto-enter calculation field.

Note: Don't worry if all this calculation talk seems mysterious. You'll learn more about how to create calculations in Chapter 8.

Looked-up Value

As you've already heard, FileMaker lets you relate multiple tables together in various ways. When you've done that, you can tell FileMaker to automatically fetch a value from a related record in another table and plop it in the field. This feature is called a *Lookup*, and it's explained on page 222.

Validation Options

Auto-enter options tell FileMaker to enter data for you. *Validation* options sort of do the opposite: They tell FileMaker what *not* to let you put in a field. You decide what kind of information *should* go there, and FileMaker warns you when you enter something that doesn't look right.

In your sample database, you may want to make sure the Zip Code field always looks like a real Zip code:

1. **Open the Field Options dialog box for the Zip Code field.**

   Don't change the field from a text field to a number field. See the box on page 251 to learn why not.

2. **Select the Validation tab.**

   As you can see in Figure 6-5, you have a lot of choices when it comes to field validation.

3. **Turn on the "Strict data type" checkbox, and then, from its pop-up menu, select Numeric Only.**

   Even though you've formatted the field as a text field, you can use validation setting to accept only numerals in the field.

4. **Click the "Maximum number of characters" checkbox, and then enter 5.**

   You can do better than just require numbers. This option tells FileMaker to accept no more than five digits in the Zip Code field.

5. **Turn on the "Display custom message if validation fails" checkbox.**

   FileMaker automatically shows a message when a value in a field doesn't match the validation settings, but it's often more considerate to give the message in your own words. That's what this setting does.

6. In the text box below this checkbox, type *The Zip Code you entered doesn't look correct. Are you sure that's what you really want?*

   FileMaker displays this message if the validation fails. (For a little guidance on what these messages should say, see the box on page 252.)

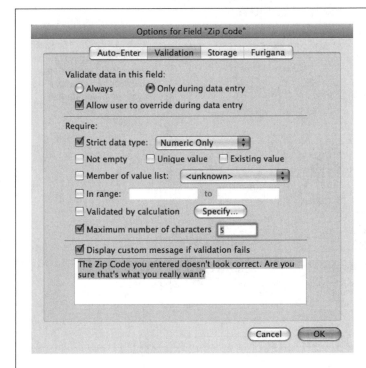

Figure 6-5:
The "Options for Field" dialog box's Validation tab lets you check for errors before placing information into fields. You can, for example, make sure only numbers are entered, or that the first name is no more than 30 characters. You can apply as many validation rules as you want, and FileMaker checks each one whenever someone modifies the field.

7. Click OK until you're back on the Lease Agreement layout.

   Switch to Browse mode (if necessary); it's time to test. Try entering too many characters into the Zip Code field, and you see your message when you exit the field, as shown in Figure 6-6.

Note: It's true that the validation settings you selected in the previous steps aren't perfect. For example, they don't allow Zip+4 codes (46077-1039). At the same time, they would let you enter something like *123*, which isn't a valid Zip code at all. To handle the nuances of the simple Zip code, you need to use the "Validate by calculation" option, which lets you set more specific validation standards by using the Specify Calculation dialog box.

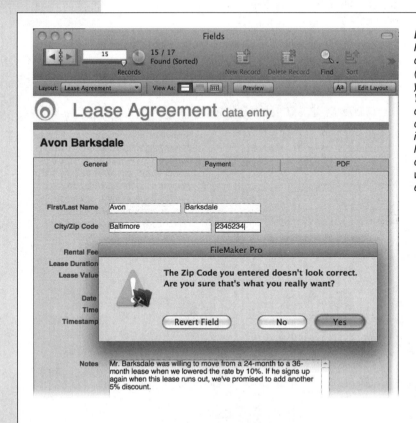

Figure 6-6:
If you enter a bogus Zip code in your database (background), you see your custom message. Click Yes to keep the invalid Zip code. If you want to fix it, click No and you'll be back in the field. If you click Revert Field, the field value changes back to what it was before you started editing.

Making Validation Stricter

Your Zip Code field validation options work pretty well, but there's a pretty glaring problem: anybody can enter just about anything they want, and then click Yes to tell FileMaker to accept the invalid data. It may help prevent mistakes, but it doesn't ensure good information.

To make FileMaker more insistent, revisit the Options for Field dialog box's Validation tab, and then turn off the "Allow user to override during data entry" checkbox (it's near the top of the window). Since this change removes the user's "Yes" and "No" choices when entering data, you also want to reword the custom message you entered. Change it to something more informative, like *Zip Codes can contain no more than five characters, which have to be numeric. Please check your data entry and try again.*

With these settings in place, if someone enters a spurious Zip code, then he sees the error message shown in Figure 6-7.

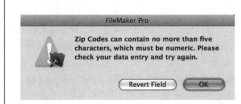

Figure 6-7:
When you turn off the "Allow user to override during data entry" validation option, FileMaker won't present a Yes to accept an invalid value. So any custom message you provide should not be phrased as a question. Instead, express the error as a statement or suggestion.

FREQUENTLY ASKED QUESTION

Numbers and Text

You have to set an awful lot of validation options to make sure people enter only Zip codes into a text field. Can't I just make the Zip Code field a number field instead?

No, you can't. Zip codes are numeric characters, but they're not *numbers*, and that makes a big difference as far as FileMaker is concerned. For example, number fields don't recognize leading zeros—like the ones at the beginning of 00501 and scores of other perfectly valid Zip codes. If you enter *00501* in a number field, FileMaker thinks you meant to type the number *501* and will treat it as the number 501 for almost all uses, including searches, sorts, and if saved to an Excel spreadsheet. But "almost all uses" may not get your mail to Holtsville, New York on time. FileMaker is kinda, sorta forgiving on this point, but when you absolutely,

positively have to rely on the Zip code entered in a field, text type (with a numeric validation) is the way to go.

The Numeric Only validation option lets the field stay a text field (which preserves all entered characters) but still accept only numerical digits on entry, which is exactly what you want for a Zip code.

Some people also assume that a phone number should be stored as a number field. Wrong again. Phone numbers contain numerals and dashes, parentheses, and sometimes other special characters—all mere text to FileMaker. As a general rule, make a field a number field only if it's expressing a mathematical value like height in inches, or the price of a bag of potatoes.

Note: The Validation tab has two more options related to this one. Under "Validate data in this field" you can choose "Always" or "Only during data entry". Data entry has the same meaning here that it had for auto-enter options. If you switch to the more strict "Always" setting, FileMaker enforces your validation rules even when data is modified by a script (Chapter 11). The Always option also enforces validation when you import data in bulk (page 837).

UP TO SPEED

Validation Messages

Custom validation messages (like the ones in Figures 6-6 and 6-7) give you a chance to communicate directly with whoever uses your database. If you don't provide a custom message when you set up field validation, then FileMaker uses a generic message of its own. This message explains the validation option that's being violated in language only a software engineer would love. This message may be confusing to whoever's using your database. By writing your own messages, you can explain things in a way that relates to the exact type of information with which you're dealing. Custom messages make your database a pleasure to use, and give it a professional quality.

Bear in mind, though, that although you can turn on as many validation options as you want, you can provide only one custom message per field. Unless you can depend upon your database users to enter the correct format every time, your message should explain exactly how to fill in the field. A message that says, "Your widget description is invalid" gives your database users no indication of how to fix the problem, and prevents them from getting their work done.

Validation Requirements

When you added validation to the Zip Code field (see page 248), you asked File-Maker to accept only numbers and allow only five digits.

But data type and character count are just two of the eight kinds of validations File-Maker has up its sleeve. In the Field Options window's Validation tab, you have six more checkboxes. Most of them work much the same way: They compare what you type against some specific condition. But one option, "Validated by calculation", offers a completely flexible way to describe exactly what you're looking for. Unfortunately, to use it, you need to learn how to perform *calculations* (mathematical or logical formulas) with your FileMaker data. They're covered starting in Chapter 8. Until then, here's what the other options do:

Strict data type

This option lets you pick one of three specific validations. You've already seen "Numeric only", which insists every character in your text field be a number. "4-digit Year Date" tells FileMaker to expect a date value, and that the year has to be four digits long (2012 instead of 12). This choice works with text, date, and timestamp fields.

"Time of day" tells FileMaker that only time values that represent real clock times are acceptable. Since time fields can hold any number of hours, minutes, and seconds, you can enter something like *237:34:11* to mean "237 hours, 34 minutes, 11 seconds." But if the field is *supposed* to be the time of your lunch meeting, that value doesn't make sense. This option prevents its entry. It applies to text and time fields (timestamp fields *always* require a time of day).

Note: The "4-digit Year Date" and "Time of day" options also work on Number fields.

Not empty

If you insist on having *something* in a field, select the "Not empty" validation option. This option makes FileMaker complain if you try to commit the record without entering *something*. This option and "Validated by calculation" are the only options that let you validate Container fields.

Unique

The "Unique value" option prevents you from putting the same value in a field for two different records. It comes in handy for things like product codes, account names, and course numbers.

Existing value

"Existing value" is just the opposite of "Unique value"; it doesn't allow any value that isn't already in that field on some record in the database. Imagine you've been using a Book database for a while, and you've built up a representative list of Category values. You can turn on the "Existing value" validation option for the Category field to be sure any books you add in the future get one of the categories you've already specified, so that typos are prevented.

This option doesn't make sense until after you've put data in your database. Like all the field options, you're free to turn it on or off whenever you want.

Member of value list

You can attach value lists to fields to restrict data entry to the values in the list (page 116). But you can also make that list a validation requirement. You'd usually do that if your users have found a way around using your value lists (like using a field on another layout that doesn't have a value list attached to it, for instance). That way, even if the value list doesn't appear on the field, you can set the validation message options as a tighter control over data input.

When you select the "Member of value list" option, a pop-up menu becomes available, from which you can choose which value list to use as a validation. You can choose an existing value list, or use the Manage Value Lists command in the pop-up menu to create a new list.

In range

"In range" lets you specify a minimum and maximum allowable value. FileMaker then protests if you enter a value outside this range. This method works for all the standard data types, since they all have a concept of order. For example, if you specify a range of *Adam* to *Johnson* for a text field, validation fails for *Schultz*. Range validation is most common, however, with number, date, and time values. You can require the Age field to be between 0 and 100, for example, or the Birth Date to be between 1/1/1900 and 12/31/2015.

Maximum number of characters

As previously mentioned, this option enforces a limit on the number of characters you can enter into a field. FileMaker fields can normally hold a huge amount of text. This option lets you keep things under control. You can use it to require specific kinds of information, like the five-digit Zip code above, or to prevent abuse of the database (for example, by limiting the First Name field to 30 characters so someone doesn't get carried away and paste the complete works of Shakespeare into it).

WORKAROUND WORKSHOP

Minimum Number of Characters

For some strange reason, FileMaker doesn't provide a simple validation option to enforce a minimum number of characters in a field. If you need this sort of thing, then you have to dip into validation calculations. Luckily, the calculation to do it is really simple. Here's a validation calculation for requiring at *least* five characters in the field:

```
Length(My Field) >= 5
```

To use this calculation, in the Validation tab, turn on the "Validated by calculation" option. In the window that appears, type the calculation.

You have to change "My Field" to the name of your field. If you want a number other than five, simply change it in the calculation. When you're done, click OK.

If you want *more than* five characters, change >= to >. If you want *exactly* five characters (no more, no less) then change >= to =. You don't need a lot of expertise for this calculation. If FileMaker gives you an error, and you can't figure it out, just click Cancel, and then try again. (See Part 4 for much more on using calculations.)

Storage Options

It's time to get a little technical. Sorry. In the Field Options dialog box, the Storage tab (see Figure 6-8) lets you control aspects of a field related to the nebulous concept of *storage*. Like a highly organized attic, FileMaker both holds onto your information *and* makes it easy to take out again. Lots of things determine how FileMaker compartmentalizes and maintains that information.

You can actually tell FileMaker to store only one value in a field, no matter how many records you have, or to allow one field to hold *more than one value* in each record. Strange, but true. Also, you get control over *indexing*, as described in the next section.

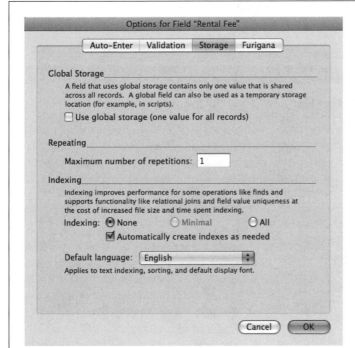

Figure 6-8:
The Storage tab is where various behind-the-scenes field settings lurk. Here, you can make a field Global so it has only one value for the whole table, or make it Repeating so it has several values in each record. Many of these options are most useful when writing scripts (Chapter 10) or for very advanced purposes.

Global Storage

"A field that uses global storage contains only one value that is shared across all records." So says the explanatory text in the dialog box, but what's that in English? When you use the "Use global storage" option, everything you learned about tables goes out the window. A *global field* isn't like a column in the table at all. Rather, it's a single bit of storage that can hold one value, no matter how many records you have. In other words, if you change the contents of a global field on one record, then File-Maker instantly changes it in every other record as well. Now every record has the same value for that field. (You'll learn a lot more about *why* you'd want to do this on page 575.)

Repeating Fields

A field can hold only a single value, right? Well, not really. If you want to, you can turn any field into a *repeating field*. These fields can hold more than one value, each kept in a separate spot (and each shown in its own little box in Browse mode). In the Storage tab section of the Field Options dialog box, you specify the maximum number of repetitions the field can hold. When would you want to use repeating fields? Almost never for normal data storage. See the box on page 256 for more info.

Note: The last tab in the Field Options dialog box applies only to Japanese text entry, and isn't covered in this book. Fortunately, should you ever need to add Furigana to your kanji, you can read how right in the dialog box.

Repeating Fields: No Substitute for Related Tables

With very few exceptions, repeating fields cause more trouble than they're worth. The truth is, they exist only because years ago when FileMaker was a youngster, it wasn't a *relational* database. That means it didn't have any way to tie multiple tables together so that they could share information and make connections between things in each table. In a database that's not relational (called a *flat file database*), you have no good way to track lots of different kinds of entities in one database, so in the bad old days FileMaker came up with the concept of repeating fields to let you store more than one kind of thing in a single record. For example, you could have an Invoice table with one record for each invoice. The line items on the invoice needed a place to live too, so you created repeating fields. That way, each individual invoice could hold, say, 20 invoice items.

But this is the 21st century, and FileMaker's come a long way. Nobody in her right mind would build an invoice database that way anymore (she'd hook together two tables instead—see page 143). Since FileMaker had repeating fields 15 years ago, and since it's really friendly about supporting all your ancient databases, it still supports repeating fields today.

That said, repeating fields are *occasionally* useful when writing calculations (Chapter 8) and scripts or for some very advanced uses like storing temporary data in arrays or storing resource graphics for use elsewhere in your file. Other than that, you should avoid them when storing most data for a few reasons:

- Repeating fields are uniquely FileMaker. If you want to take data out of your database and put it in some other program (like a spreadsheet or another database program), repeating fields can produce one serious pain in the neck. Likewise for getting data from other programs *into* repeating fields.

- Repeating fields are inherently limited: If you create a field with 20 repetitions, then you get 20 spots for data. If you need less, you're saving space for empty fields all the time. If you need more, you have to modify your fields, and then make room on your screen. A relational database, on the other hand, can grow and shrink as needed without modifying the database structure at all.

Indexing

Since you're reading this book, you're probably hoping FileMaker can help you search through volumes of information faster than you could do it yourself, especially as your database grows from a simple electronic Rolodex to a humongous mailing list. When you're looking for the three people out of 5,000,000 whose birthday is February 29, FileMaker can find them in an instant because it doesn't really look at the birthday field on each record one by one. Instead, it uses the field's *index* to skip straight to the appropriate records. It's similar to the way you'd use a book's index to go directly to the pages that mention the topic you're interested in, rather than skimming every single page in the book.

Note: FileMaker uses a field's index in other ways, too. You need an index if you want to use the "Unique value" option in the field Validation screen. You also need indexed fields to create relationships between table occurrences in your database (page 143).

FileMaker's indexing feature takes its own computerized notes about the data in your fields *in advance*, so that when you enter Find mode, the hard work's already been done, and your finds go that much faster.

Just like a book, you can have a field without an index. When FileMaker needs to find records based on what's in that field, it has to check every single record—a process that can take noticeably longer in big databases. But indexing has tradeoffs, as explained in the box below.

FREQUENTLY ASKED QUESTION

The Dark Side of Indexing

If indexing makes searching faster, why not just index every field?

Indexes have disadvantages as well. An index is useful only if it's up to date. When you change a field value, FileMaker has to store that new value in the table. If the field is indexed, FileMaker has to change the data you've typed, and it *also* has to update the index so that it knows about the changes to the field. Updating the index takes time (not much time, mind you, but it does take time).

When you're editing records in Browse mode, you *never* notice because updating the index for a handful of fields takes FileMaker less time than it takes you to realize you've pressed Enter. But if you're entering *lots* of information (like when you're *importing* records, as discussed in Chapter 19), then the index updating can slow things down noticeably.

Also, indexes take up space. A database file that has indexing turned on for every field could be much larger than the same file without indexes. For most users, this isn't an issue, but if you have a very large file, and saving space is a priority, you can turn off indexing where you don't need it, to save space.

Automatic indexing

The good news is you almost never need to think about indexing. FileMaker has a really smart way of dealing automatically with indexing: Every field starts out with no index at all, to save space and keep things as lean as possible. Later, while you're working with your database, if you do something that would be made faster with an index, like use the field in a find request, then FileMaker automatically turns indexing on for you. That first find is slow since FileMaker looks through records one by one and builds the index (showing a progress bar in really big files), but once the field is indexed, subsequent finds happen quickly. You almost always want this automatic behavior.

Controlling indexing manually

In very large databases, there may come a time when you want to adjust indexing manually. For instance, if you know you only very rarely search by a person's middle name, you can tell FileMaker not to index that field. Searches that include that field are slow, but that's OK since you hardly ever do it. On the Field Options Storage tab, select None to turn indexing off for any field.

If you want to be able to search efficiently in a field, turn on All instead. The third choice—Minimal—creates a smaller index for the field. This index has everything FileMaker needs for relationships and field uniqueness, but not enough for fast searching. If you *don't* need to search in a field, but you *do* need it indexed for other reasons, choose Minimal.

When None is selected, you can keep FileMaker's automatically-turn-it-on-when-I-need-it behavior by turning on "Automatically create indexes as needed".

Note: FileMaker uses the field index when you do a find from Find mode, but *not* when you use the Find/Replace command. The index points FileMaker to *records*, and since Find/Replace doesn't find records (it finds text inside a record or records), the index does it no good. Therefore, when you do a Find/Replace, you don't make FileMaker automatically index a field. Several actions trigger indexing, including using the field in a find request or value list, turning on Unique or Existing validation, and using the field in a relationship (page 143).

POWER USERS' CLINIC

Put Automatic Indexing to Use

FileMaker's ability to automatically index a field when it becomes necessary doesn't just save you the trouble of thinking about all this stuff. You can also use it to your advantage in some situations. Sometimes people need to distribute databases full of information.

For example, suppose you have a large parts catalog that's stored in a database, and you want your distributors to be able to use the database themselves to find parts. You can make a FileMaker database available on your website for them to download, complete with your 10,000 parts records.

If there's a lot of information about parts, then that database is pretty big. To make the download more palatable, tell FileMaker not to index *any* of the fields. But leave "Automatically create indexes as needed" turned on. This way, the database is as small as possible when people download it. However, once they get it, they can start performing finds, and FileMaker automatically indexes fields, making searches faster, and ballooning the size of the database.

Indexing language

To keep its indexes as small and tidy as possible, FileMaker doesn't actually store all a field's text in the index. Instead, it performs a little cleanup on the field values first. Most notably, it gets rid of the notion of uppercase and lowercase letters: "Peter" and "peter" become the same entry in the index.

The index also splits the field value up into individual words and removes any characters that aren't generally part of a normal word. In order to do that, it needs to know what language the text in the field is in. If your computer's regional settings are for English, then FileMaker's field indexes use English, too. Usually, that's exactly what you want. But in some cases, FileMaker's following the same language rules as your computer can cause a problem. For example, if you enter another language in a field without changing the index, then your searches can give you unexpected results. If you search in an English-indexed field for *lang* (German for "long"), then you get both "lang" and "länger" ("longer"), but if you set the index to German, you only get "lang". (In German, "ä" is a different character from "a".)

You can select an automatic language for an index using the pop-up menu on the Storage tab of the Options dialog box. A field's language setting also comes into play when you sort records. To use the example given above, when you're sorting in ascending order (from A–Z), "länger" comes before "lang" in a field indexed as German (in accordance with rules for German alphabetizing), but after it if the field's index is set to English.

Note: If the Language pop-up menu is unavailable, the field is probably not a text field. You can specify the language only for text fields.

POWER USERS' CLINIC

Unicode Indexing

One language option, called Unicode, isn't a language at all. This setting tells FileMaker to forget everything it knows about languages, and use the internal code numbers for each character as is. When indexing with this language option, FileMaker doesn't remove any special characters from the index, and it doesn't ignore uppercase and lowercase letters.

A find in such a field is *case-sensitive*. When sorting, FileMaker also uses the character code numbers. Whichever code is lower comes first in the sort order, so capital "Z" comes before lowercase "a."

You rarely want your searches and sorts to be case-sensitive, but if you do, you have the option. You're more likely to use Unicode indexing when you want to easily search for punctuation. For example, a field that holds text from a business-to-business Electronic Data Interchange (EDI) document can be well served by Unicode indexing so you can easily find the records that contain "~BIG."

The Web is full of details about Unicode characters. Do a web search for "Unicode table" if you want to find the code for a particular character.

Seeing the index

When a field is indexed, you can get a glimpse of what's in it, and even put it to use. Just click in an indexed field in Browse mode, and then choose Insert→From Index. You see the window in Figure 6-9.

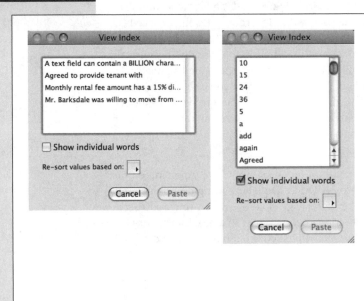

Figure 6-9:
Left: If you have indexing turned on for a field, you can click into the field, and then choose Insert→From Index. FileMaker shows this window. Here you see one line in the list for each unique value in the field. The list shows the Minimal index, also called the "Value index."

Right: If the index's storage options are set to "Automatically create indexes as needed," you can select the "Show individual words" option, and the list shows the word index instead—you see one line for each unique word or number in the field. When you show individual words, you also switch the setting in the field's storage options, even if you click Cancel after making the selection. But selecting "Re-sort values based on" a different language doesn't change the field's automatic language. It's just a way to temporarily re-sort the index.

This window is handy when you want to quickly enter something you know you've entered in a previous record. Just select the entry you want, and then click Paste to have the value inserted into the current field. This trick works in Find mode, too, where it lets you quickly see a list of things for which you may want to search. See the box on the next page to learn how to use the index to clean up inconsistent data entry.

Printing Field Definitions

Now that you've learned how to add auto-enter and validation options to your fields, you may want to have a list to keep track of what you've done. The Field Options window is the best reference for the current set of options you've applied to fields, but if something goes wrong with a calculation or auto-enter option, it helps to have a printed snapshot of your original settings so, you can see if anything's changed. Even better, you can use the printout as a map for putting things right. Or you can print a field list to send to an associate so she can send you a file with the right bits of data to be imported into your database.

To print a list of a table's fields and their options, choose File→Manage→Database, and then click Print. The printout looks like the field list, except that it's expanded to make room for *everything* about a field.

POWER USER'S CLINIC

Using the Index as a Housekeeping Tool

The View Index window is useful when you want to quickly paste data that's already in another record, but it has another power-user trick up its sleeve—helping you search out and clean up oddball values. For example, you might need to clean up the data in a Street Address field because users have entered their own unique versions of street abbreviations: St, ST, Str, Stt, Bld, Boul, and other creative variations. Here's how to do the cleanup :

1. In Find mode, use View Index to paste in a specific value (Stt, for example), and then perform the Find all the records with that value. You'll end up with a found set of just those records with the bad abbreviation.

2. Make sure you're still clicked into the Street Address field, and then choose Records→Replace Field Contents. The Specify Calculation window appears.

3. Choose the "Replace with calculated result option" to show the Specify Calculation window. In the calculation box, type *Substitute (Street Address ; "Stt" ; "St")*. This formula tells FileMaker to look inside the Street Address field and find all instances of "Stt" and then replace them with "St" instead. See page 396 for details on how this calculation works.

4. Click the OK button to close the Specify Calculation window, and then click Replace to perform the replace. The found set is clean.

5. View the field's index. The stray entry "Stt" is gone from the index.

Lather, Rinse, Repeat for each bad abbreviation.

Note: You have to select at least one field for the Print button to become clickable. Then, when you click Print, you'll get details for any field that's highlighted. To select and print just a few, Ctrl+click (⌘-click) each field you want to print, and then click Print. If you want a printout of *all* the fields in the table, first select one field, and then choose Edit→Select All. Now every field is selected, and the Print button prints them all.

Beyond Text: Container Fields

Text and numbers are the backbone of most databases, but as you saw when you placed a PDF of a lease agreement right in the record with its data (page 95) you can also store graphics and other multimedia files in your database. For example, you can store a photograph of each employee along with the personnel record, or add product shots to your inventory database. In either case, you use the graphics much like data. You could print picture badges or product catalogs using your new container fields.

Unlike all the other field types, container fields don't expect (and won't accept) typed text. Instead, you use the Insert command to insert just about any file you want, including pictures, sounds, animation, music, and movies. You can even put any file from your hard drive into a container field, like a PDF file or a Word document.

Note: The Fields database you downloaded at the beginning of this chapter has a container field on the Container Field tab that you can use to follow this section.

The Insert menu shows four commands for placing items into a container field: Picture, QuickTime, Sound, and File. Once you select a Picture, QuickTime or File, and then choose a file to insert, you can also choose whether to store the file inside FileMaker, or just store a reference to the file. In the next sections, you'll learn how you can use these commands to get what you need.

Note: This section is about *using* container fields. See page 95 to learn how to create them.

Pictures

A *picture* can be in any of more than a dozen formats, including the common kinds like JPEG, GIF, PNG, TIFF, PICT, and BMP. FileMaker will also accept Photoshop and PostScript (.eps) files. When you put a picture in a container field using the Insert→Picture command, the field displays the picture itself. But if you use the Insert→File command, you'll just see a file icon and the file name.

Copy and paste

The most obvious way to put a picture into a container field is to paste it in. You can copy a picture from a graphics program, click once in the field, and then choose Edit→Paste (Ctrl+V or ⌘-V). If the picture doesn't show up on both Mac and PC platforms, delete the graphic (click in the field, and then press Delete). Check the graphic's format for cross-platform compatibility, and then choose Insert→Picture instead of pasting.

You can also copy data from the container field back into another program. Again, simply click once on the field, and then choose Edit→Copy (Ctrl+C or ⌘-C) or Edit→Cut (Ctrl+X or ⌘-X). Whatever was in the field is now ready to paste into another field, record, or program.

Tip: Although you can't *type* text into a container field, you can *paste* it in a pinch. You can't edit the text once it's in the field, but you can copy it again or export it (page 96). Once the text is back in a text field or a word processor, you can edit the text again.

Insert→Picture

Copy and paste is simple, but sometimes doesn't work cross platform, plus it doesn't let you store only a reference to the file. To get more control, use the Insert→Picture command. Here's how:

1. **Click in the Graphic field.**

   It's on the Container Field tab in the sample database. You've now entered the record, and the Graphic field is active.

2. **Choose Insert→Picture.**

   The Insert Picture dialog box appears. This window looks almost exactly like a typical Open File dialog box in Windows or Mac OS X. You can use it to find the picture you want to insert.

3. **Select a picture or other graphic from your computer, and then select the "Store only a reference to the file" option.**

   Instead of storing the file in the container field, which can make your file sizes balloon, the path to the graphic is stored. The picture will still show in the container field, however. See the box on page 265 for information that'll help you.

4. **Click Open.**

   FileMaker grabs the file path and shows the picture you choose in the Graphic field (Figure 6-10).

Even though you've only stored a reference to the file, you can still see the graphic displayed in the container field. But it's important to remember that the real contents of the field is a text version of the path you showed FileMaker when you selected the file. So if the file is edited, your container field will display the changes in the picture. But if the file gets moved or renamed, you won't be able to see the picture unless you insert it again, from the new location or with the new name. Or you could restore the file to its original name or location.

That's why it's important to create a set of business rules for storing graphics. That is, if you're planning to store references to a lot of graphics or other files in your database, you need a predictable folder structure, preferably on a shared volume or a file server. When you're ready to place a graphic, you upload it to the server first, and then you insert it, making sure to store a reference (and not the file itself). That way, the file is visible to everyone (as long as they have access to the server), and the file isn't likely to be moved.

Note: If you need to insert *lots* of pictures into a database, you can save yourself a lot of trouble by using the File→Import Records→Folder command. See page 838 for the full explanation.

QuickTime

FileMaker uses QuickTime to help it deal with multimedia files, so you can insert any file type that QuickTime supports. Because QuickTime is frequently upgraded, the exact list of formats FileMaker supports also changes. If you're having trouble, check Apple's website for the list that matches your version of QuickTime.

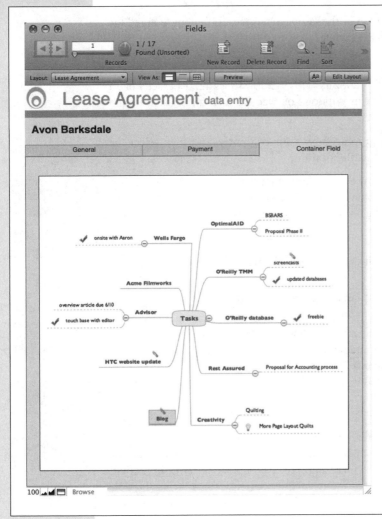

Figure 6-10:
A container field can hold any file, but what you see on the layout depends on what you place in the field. If you insert a picture into a container field, FileMaker shows you the picture. If you insert a sound file, File-Maker shows a special speaker icon that plays the sound when clicked. Music and QuickTime files give you the typical play, pause, fast-forward, and rewind controls, just like movies on the Web. For other kinds of files, FileMaker just shows you the file's icon.

When a container field holds a QuickTime file, you normally see the movie's *poster frame*, which is usually just the first frame of the movie. When you click the movie, a standard movie controller appears, so you can play, pause, fast-forward, and rewind it. The controller also has a button to adjust the volume and a little knob that shows you where you are in the movie.

Use the Insert→QuickTime menu command to select a QuickTime file from the hard drive. If the command isn't available, check to make sure you have QuickTime installed on your computer.

Note: Unlike pictures and files, FileMaker *never* stores QuickTime movies in the database. Instead, the program remembers where the original file is on your hard drive, and loads the data from it as needed. As with other files that are stored as references, if you move or delete the original file, you'll see a message in your container field telling you FileMaker can no longer find the file. And as with other lost files, you'll need to show FileMaker where the file has been moved with another Insert command.

POWER USERS' CLINIC

To Store or Not to Store

When you insert a picture or file (see page 262), the dialog box includes an option to "Store only a reference to the file." When this option is turned off, FileMaker copies the actual file into your database. You can move or delete the original file and the data will still appear in the field, because the database now contains all the inserted file's information. If you turn on "Store only a reference to the file," FileMaker doesn't copy the file into the field at all. Instead, it just remembers data about the file you select, including its name and the path to the file. Each time you look at this record, FileMaker finds the original file so it can display the data. In this respect, it works like a shortcut or alias. If the file gets moved, deleted, or renamed FileMaker can't display the file, and you'll see a short message inside the field that tells you the file can't be displayed.

There's no simple rule for when you should store the actual file, and when you should store a reference instead. Some people store files because it's easier. This is especially true when multiple people are using the database from different computers. However, here are a couple of reasons you might want to store a reference instead:

- Storing many *larger* files can make your database get big—really big—which can cause a number of problems. Performance can suffer, it takes longer to back up, and moving a huge database file from one place to another is a real pain. If you're trying to email the database to your home office, your ISP may not allow a 3 GB attachment, for example. If the inserted files aren't critical to the record data, it may make sense to leave them out of the database so it's easier to work with.

- Sometimes you want to catalog files inside FileMaker even though they might change over time. For example, if you wanted to put promotional images into a database so they're easy to locate, you probably *don't* want to make editing those images difficult. If you store a reference to these images, you can still edit the originals any time. As long as you haven't changed their name or location, when you look in FileMaker, you'll see the latest edits.

Sound

FileMaker considers a *sound* a recorded bit of audio. You can copy/paste recorded sounds right into the container field. Use sound files to keep audio notes with a project record, or record your practice speeches and save them for when you're famous. When a container field holds a sound, it displays a little speaker icon; double-click it to hear the recorded sound.

Recording sound

The Insert→Sound command doesn't bring up the same dialog box as the other Insert commands. Instead, it shows the Record (Mac) or Sound Record (Windows) dialog box (Figure 6-11). If your computer has a microphone, you can record any sound directly into the field.

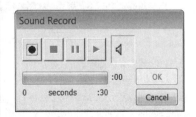

Figure 6-11:
Click in a container field, and then choose Insert→Sound (or double-click an empty container field) to record audio. Click the Record button to start, and then click the stop or pause buttons as needed. Use the Play button to check your recording. Most computers let you record any sound your computer can play.

The Record dialog box is simple, but capable. The speaker icon provides feedback about what the microphone is picking up, by showing little sound waves. The more sound waves you see, the louder the recording. In fact, the speaker icon lets you check for sound waves even when you're *not* recording, so use it to do a quick sound check ("Testing, testing, 1, 2, 3") before you start recording.

Note: The Insert→Sound command records sound directly into the field. If you already have a sound file (an MP3, for example), choose Insert→QuickTime instead. In general, if the data you're putting in the field has a *time component* (meaning it happens over time, like video or sound), treat it like a QuickTime file.

Here's how the buttons work:

- The **Record** button (a circle) starts the recording session. Click it when everything is set up: the audio you want to record has begun to play, or you've cleared your throat, reviewed your notes and are ready to speak.

- The **Stop** button (a square) stops whatever you're doing. If you're recording, the session stops immediately, and you can't add to it. If you're playing back recorded audio, clicking the Stop button stops the playback. The playback will start again at the beginning the next time you click Play.

- The **Pause** button (double lines) pauses either a recording or a playback session. Click it a second time to resume either operation.

- The **Play** button (right-pointing triangle) plays whatever you've recorded.

- Click **Cancel** to close the Sound record window.

- Click **Save** (Mac) or **OK** (Windows) to save your recording. Once you click OK (Save), you'll see the sound icon in the container field, and you can double-click the field to play the audio.

Tip: If the record dialog box won't appear, make sure you have an audio input device that works with your computer, that your computer has a sound card, and that the audio device is setup properly. For setup, use the Hardware and Sound Control Panel (Windows Vista) or Audio Devices Control Panel (Windows XP) or the Sound System Preference Pane (Mac).

File

A container field can also hold a *file*. Since FileMaker doesn't know what the file is supposed to be, it simply shows you the file's name and icon. Unfortunately, you can't do anything with a file like this while it's in FileMaker. You can't edit it. You can't even open it and view its contents while it's in FileMaker. Rather, the container field simply holds the file for you. This might sound limiting, but because you can also export the contents of any field, including container fields, FileMaker databases make good document tracking or retrieval systems.

The most common way to place a file into a container field is to use the Insert→File command. In Windows, you can also copy a file from your hard drive, and then paste it into a container field. When you insert a file, FileMaker makes no effort to figure out what's *in* the file. Even if you choose a picture, you'll still get just the name and icon. If you want to *see* the picture itself in FileMaker, choose Insert→Picture, as described on page 262.

UP TO SPEED

PDFs in Mac OS X

The ability to store pictures, movies, sounds, and files in your database can be useful for lots of reasons. For example, if you're a recruiter, you could store resumes in Microsoft Word or PDF format right in the database alongside the info about a particular candidate. In fact, the Adobe PDF format is so common that people often need to keep track of PDF files—the brochure, flyer, or documentation for each of your products, the prospectus for each of your investments, or a floor plan for each of your properties.

You already know you can use the Insert→File command to store the PDF document right in a container field (and get it back out again later to look at it). But if you're on Mac OS X, you can do one better. Choose Insert→Picture, and then select a PDF file. FileMaker shows you the PDF (the first page of it, anyway) right in the container field. If your document has more than one page, you need to export the PDF out of the container field (see below) to read the whole thing.

Or, try this unexpected twist: You can read multipage PDFs right in FileMaker if you use Insert→QuickTime instead.

This time, when you click the container field itself, the standard QuickTime movie controls appear. Using these controls, you can flip through the pages in the PDF: Fast Forward goes to the next page, Rewind goes to the previous page. If you press Play, FileMaker flips through the pages one after the other until it reaches the end of the document.

If you need to search text within a PDF file, try this. Open the PDF file, select all the text, copy it, and then paste it into a regular text field. Now, FileMaker can search the contents of the document in the text field, while you view the PDF in all it's glory from the container field.

Exporting data from container fields

Inserting files into container fields is all well and good, but it's just as important to get them back out again. To use the file in another program, click in the container field, and then choose Edit→Export Field Contents. FileMaker asks you where you want to put the file, and what to name it. Click Save, and FileMaker creates a new file that's an exact copy of the one you put in the container field. For a refresher on exporting, see the box on page 96.

Note: If you used the Insert→File command and turned on the "Store only a reference to the file" option (see the box on page 265) when you put the file into a container field, you don't need to get it back out again (after all, the file is on your hard drive somewhere). Instead, double-click the container field to open the original file in the appropriate program.

Layout Tools

In Chapter 3, you learned how easy it is to lay out a database using FileMaker's tools. You can start out with one of the program's Starter Solutions, and then customize it by moving your fields around, adding text, lines, and other fancy stuff. In this chapter, you'll delve deeper into the individual parts that make up a FileMaker layout.

By putting these parts together, you can build your own layout from the ground up. It takes longer—in some cases, a *lot* longer—than using a Starter Solution, but you get to pick your own fonts, colors, fields, and overall arrangement unencumbered by anyone else's work. In this chapter, you'll learn how to assemble layout parts; create field controls, like drop-down menus and date pickers; make your own buttons; and format fields exactly the way you want them.

Layout Parts

A layout is made up of one or more parts, each of which define how and where your data gets displayed. The Body part controls how much space to devote to each record. In Form view the Body part is usually fairly tall, so it can display fields from the same record from top to bottom. But in a list the Body will be quite short, because it generally only displays one row of fields per record. So while switching from Form to List view can help you see data in a slightly different form, it makes sense to create a list-specific layout with a very short Body part so you can see more records onscreen at a time that you could see using a layout with a large Body.

Also, layout objects can behave differently when they're placed in different parts. For example, items in a Title Header only appear at the top of the first page of a printed report, but items in a Header appear at the top of every page in that report. Here's the rundown of part types:

- **Title Header.** Put objects in the Title Header that should appear only at the top of the first page of a printed report. It only appears in Preview mode and print. Some common Title Header objects are the report's title, a company logo, large column headings, and general information about the report itself. If you make a Title Header the height of a full page, it can act like a cover page for your report.

- **Header.** Objects in a Header will appear at the top of every page in a report, unless there's a Title Header. In that case, Header objects appear from page 2 onward. When you're in Browse mode, objects in the Header appear at the top of your screen. Layout titles, column headings, and navigation buttons are generally well suited to Header parts.

- **Leading Grand Summary.** This part appears below the Header and above the Body onscreen and in print. You'll usually place special fields, called Summary fields (page 240) in a Grand Summary part.

- **Body.** The Body shows data from each record. In Form view, the body appears only once. In List or Table view, the Body repeats once for each record. Many layouts, especially those meant to be viewed onscreen, will contain only a Body part.

- **Sub-Summary.** Sub-summary parts work like Grand Summary parts, but they summarize subsets of your data. For example, a sales report showing worldwide totals in a Grand Summary, can also show a breakdown of totals by individual country. Unlike the other parts, a single layout can contain more than one Sub-summary. See page 601 for more info.

- **Trailing Grand Summary.** Just like a Leading Grand Summary, except it appears below the records it's summarizing.

- **Footer.** A Footer is like a Header, but it appears at the bottom of every screen or printed page, unless you use a Title Footer. Place page numbers, copyright notices, small report titles, and anything else you want to appear at the bottom of your screen or page.

- **Title Footer.** The Title Footer appears at the bottom of the *first* page when printed or viewed in Preview mode.

Parts in Form View

When in Browse mode, and viewing the layout as a form, you see every part (sub-summary parts are a special exception, as you'll learn in Chapter 14). You never use *all* these parts on a layout you plan on viewing in Form view. In general, if you only ever want to view a layout as a form in Browse mode, then you really need only a Body part, although if you plan to print, then you may want a Header part as well so logos, menus, and other user interface items don't repeat for every record you print.

Parts in List View

List view is a *list* because it shows several records at once. FileMaker accomplishes this magic by repeating the Body part once for each record. The layout may have several other parts, too, which appear in the same order they appear in Layout mode. (Title Headers and Title Footers don't appear in Browse mode.)

Parts in Preview Mode

A quick glance at Preview mode might lead you to believe that it shows only the Title Header and the Title Footer (exactly the opposite of List view), but that's not entirely true. Turn your eyes to Figure 7-1 for the whole story.

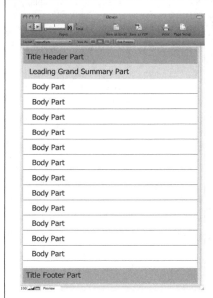 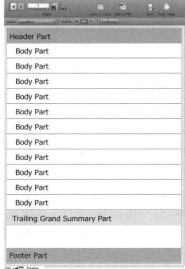

Figure 7-1:
Left: In Preview mode, the Title Header and Title Footer are at the top and bottom of the first page. The Leading Grand Summary appears right before the first record, and FileMaker adds a copy of the body for every record until it fills up the page.

Right: Every page thereafter shows the Header and Footer instead of the Title Header and Title Footer. If you don't have a Title Header, then you get the regular Header on the first page, too (and the same goes for the Title Footer). Also notice that the Trailing Grand Summary appears after the last record.

Just like List view, the Grand Summary parts place themselves before the first record and after the last record. Finally, scrolling in Preview mode just scrolls the current page. If you need to see other pages of your report while you're in Preview mode, use the book icon to move around.

POWER USERS' CLINIC

Getting Table View to Mind Its Manners

Table view is a real boon if you want a quick and easy way to make your data look like a spreadsheet. With one command, your layout displays data in rows and columns, which you can rearrange and sort. But if you dig a little deeper, then you find that you have a lot of control over how Table view works. These controls lurk under the Layout Setup command. When you click the Views tab, you see that the Table View option has a button that leads you one dialog box deeper—into Table View Properties.

- With the Grid controls, you can show or hide Table view's horizontal and vertical gridlines. Try switching off the vertical gridlines to make rows more prominent. This way, you can more easily read across the data pertaining to a single record.

- The Grid Style option comes with two familiar pop-up menus. You can choose a new color for the grids with the Color pop-up menu or apply a pattern to them from the Pattern pop-up menu. A sample swatch shows you the choices you've made.

- Under Header and Parts, you control the header, footer, and column headers. Headers and footers anchor to the top or bottom of the screen while the records scroll through long lists. Column headers are the field names at the top of each column.

- Headers and footers are normally suppressed when a layout's in Table view. Choose "Include header part" or "Include footer part" to display those parts of the layout. (For obvious reasons, these options have no effect on a layout in which you don't have those particular parts.)

- Since the column headers tell you what information you're looking at, you don't often find a reason to turn off their display. But you can do it if you want to, by unchecking "Include column headers".

- More often, you may want to turn off some of the column headers' other features. Stop users from resizing columns by unchecking "Resizable columns". Turn off "Reorderable columns" to keep folks from rearranging their order on the table. That way, nobody can move the First Name field so far away from the Last Name field that the data loses its meaning. Nobody can sort records if you uncheck "Sort data when selecting column".

- Choose "Use custom height" to set rows to a specific height.

Part Setup Dialog Box

When you choose Layout→Part Setup, FileMaker shows you the Part Setup dialog box (see Figure 7-2). This often-ignored box isn't just a slower way to get to the Part Definition window, though. From this one screen, you can create new parts, and edit, delete, and rearrange existing parts. But, as you'll see on the next page, you can do most of this work more easily *without* this window, so you won't use it very often.

To add a new part, click Create. You're presented with the Part Definition dialog box, where you can decide what kind of part to create and set various options. You can do the same thing by dragging the Part tool from the Status toolbar or choosing Insert→Part.

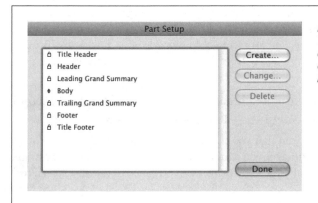

Figure 7-2:
The Part Setup dialog box is a catchall for the options pertinent to layout parts. You'll find it especially useful for rearranging parts of your layout.

To see the part definition for an existing part, select it in the Part Setup dialog box, and then click Change. This maneuver too has a shortcut: in Layout mode, just double-click any part tag.

To delete a part, select it, and then click Delete. If the part contains any objects on the layout, then FileMaker asks you if you're sure, because when you delete a part, you delete everything on it as well. You've already deleted parts without using this window, though, by selecting the part, and then choosing Edit→Clear. But if you hate menus, then you can also just press Delete.

You can also rearrange parts using the same technique you use to order fields in the Manage Database window. Just drag the arrow icon next to a part name. But some parts (most parts, in fact) have a padlock symbol instead of an arrow icon. This symbol tells you the part is *locked* in place and you can't move it. The reason is simple: It doesn't make sense to move most parts. For example, the header is always below the Title Header, and above everything else. You really only need to rearrange parts when creating *Sub-summary reports*, which Chapter 14 covers.

When to Use Each Type

While it's perfectly legal to put any parts on any layout, you've probably figured out that some arrangements are more common than others:

- Detail layouts usually have just a Body part, or some combination of header, body, and footer. These layouts may show only a single record, so there isn't much point to Summary parts since you have no list of data to summarize.

- List layouts usually have a header and a body, and sometimes a footer. Occasionally, you want a Trailing Grand Summary on your List layout as well, since it can show summary information after all the records without taking up precious space like a footer.

- Printed reports come in many forms. People often use all the parts shown on page 270 on a report: a large Title Header for the first page, and a smaller Header for each additional page; a Leading Grand Summary that shows below the Title Header and before the first record; a Body part for each record; a Trailing Grand Summary to show totals from all records; and a footer to show page numbers and the like.

- Envelopes and labels often need headers and/or footers just to get the record data to align properly on the printed page. These parts are generally empty.

- You may have a List layout that you use to browse your records, but you often print it as well. Make the layout do double duty by adding a Title Header or Title Footer. They'll show only when you print, and you can save valuable screen real estate.

Arranging Parts

The process of building a layout isn't always linear. Most people tend to bounce from task to task as they mold the layout to match their vision. You might arrange some parts, organize fields, do some decorating, and then revisit the fields. It is, after all, a creative process.

But usually, you first get the parts roughed out. Since you don't know exactly how big things are going to end up, it isn't critical that you get the parts exactly the right size right away. But you do want to decide which parts you'll be using, get them in the right places, and take a guess at how big they need to be.

Note: FileMaker lets you move objects only into parts. Sometimes, as you're arranging things, your layout can get cramped, so it's helpful to start with parts that are a little bigger than you really need. You can shrink them up again later when you've finished laying things out.

If you view your People Detail layout in Layout mode right now, then you see FileMaker has given you three parts: a header, body, and footer. If you were to print some records while on this layout, the header would appear on the top of each page, and footer on the bottom of each page. Right now, though, the header and footer are both completely empty.

Since this layout is designed to be seen onscreen in Form view, headers and footers may not be important to you. But you might consider using a Title Header just in case you decide to print this layout. That way the graphical embellishments you see on the top of the layout in Figure 4-15 print only at the top of the first page, leaving more room for record data, and using less ink. Here's how to fix it:

1. **If you haven't already, go to the People Detail layout, and then switch to Layout mode.**

   You're now ready to work on your layout.

2. **Choose Insert→Part.**

   The Part Definition dialog box appears (Figure 7-3). It wants to know what kind of part you want to add to the layout.

3. **Make sure Title Header is turned on, and then click OK.**

   FileMaker adds a Title Header part to the very top of your layout. (When you use the Insert→Part command, the part is automatically inserted in the spot that makes sense. In this case, since this is a Title Header, it goes at the very top of the layout.)

4. **Drag the Title Header part label straight down to make the Title Header larger.**

   Use Figure 7-4 as a guide.

Now that the Title Header is in place, you can get rid of the Header and Footer parts. This step is a snap:

5. **Click the Header part label once.**

   FileMaker darkens the label to indicate that it's selected.

6. **Press the Delete key.**

   Since this part is empty, it disappears right away.

Figure 7-3:
The Part Definition dialog box shows up when you add or modify a layout part. It includes a radio button for each of FileMaker's part types. You also get myriad checkboxes, most of which don't apply to a Title Header. You'll get a chance to use each of these options in time.

Warning: If you delete a part that has things on it (like the Body part on your layout), FileMaker asks you for confirmation. If you agree, then the part *and everything on it* is deleted. Exercise care when deleting parts.

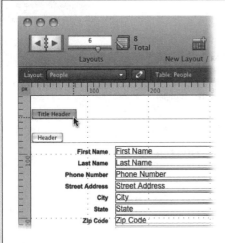

Figure 7-4:
To resize a part, you can simply drag its part label. Or, if you're deft with the mouse, you can actually drag the thin dotted line that extends from the label.

7. **Click the Footer part label to select it, and then press Delete again.**

   Once again, the part disappears.

   For more tips on arranging parts, see the box below.

FREQUENTLY ASKED QUESTION

Part Manipulation

Sometimes when I try to drag a part label up, it won't go. It seems to get stuck. What am I doing wrong?

Suppose you want to make a part *smaller*? You can probably guess how: Just drag the part label up instead of down. But sometimes you'll be surprised to discover it won't go as far as you want.

FileMaker won't let a part get smaller than the stuff on it. For example, if you try to shorten the Body part on your People Detail layout, then you discover you can't go farther north than the bottom-most field. Once the part separator touches this field, it simply doesn't go higher no matter how far you drag, because FileMaker doesn't want you to accidentally end up with the fields on a part you didn't intend.

You can most easily fix this problem when you simply move things out of the way before you resize the part. For instance, if you want a shorter body, move the fields around first, and then shorten the body.

If you want, you can press Alt (Option) while you drag instead. When you do, FileMaker changes the way it moves parts. Instead of moving everything below the part up or down to compensate for its new size, everything stays put, and just the dividing line between the two parts moves. In this way, you can move part boundaries right through other objects to, for example, resize the body to encompass newly added fields that landed on the footer.

When you're done, your layout should look like Figure 7-5.

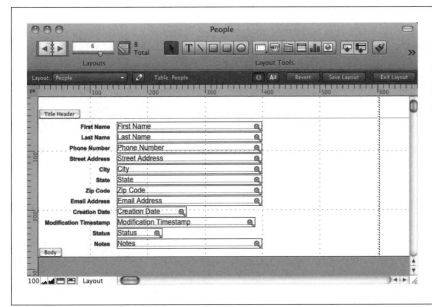

Figure 7-5:
Once you've added a Title Header and removed the header and footer, your layout should look like this example.

Layout Types

When you created the List layout in Chapter 4, you used FileMaker's Layout Assistant to speed the process along, but FileMaker fans are split on whether the assistant is the best option. Some people love the quick start you get from FileMaker, but others prefer to build a layout by hand, starting with a clean slate.

But whatever your preference, the Layout Assistant is critical for some layout types—like labels and envelopes—where lining everything up yourself can burn a lot of hours (and paper). So before you start building a layout, you'll get a brief introduction to each of the kinds of layouts FileMaker can build for you. To use them, in Layout mode, choose Layout→New Layout/Report.

Standard Form

The "Standard form" choice creates a layout just like the one FileMaker creates automatically when you start your database—a simple detail layout (see page 89). This time, though, you get to decide which fields to include. You also have some control over the fonts and colors. FileMaker calls these design controls "themes."

Table View

When you select "Table view", FileMaker creates a layout much like "Standard form", but the layout is set to Table view automatically. Actually, the pros (yourself included) know that in Browse mode, you can choose View→"View as Table" to see *any* layout in Table view, so you rarely need to create a separate layout of this type. But if you're new to this whole database thing and want a layout that looks and acts like the spreadsheets you're accustomed to, then the Table view layout is your fastest way there.

List View

If you want to show lots of records on the screen or page at one time, then choose "List view" instead. You still get to pick which fields to include and what theme to use, but FileMaker sets up the new layout as a list of records with columns of data, one per field.

Report

Report layouts are List views, with subtotals and totals to group and summarize your records. FileMaker takes you through the process of determining how you want your records grouped and tallied, then sets up the layout with any Sub-summary or Grand Summary parts required. You'll learn how to harness the power of these fields in Chapter 14.

Blank Layout

A Blank layout is both the simplest and the most flexible of the crop. You get a layout with a small header and footer, and a big body. It has nothing on it at all. If you like setting things up by hand, or your layout doesn't rightly match any of the types above, drawing a blank may be your best choice.

Labels or Vertical Labels

If you ever need to print a sheet of peel-and-stick labels from your database—to make nametags for every attendee at your conference, or address labels for all those follow-up letters—the Labels layout type is your best friend (it's shown in Figure 7-6). FileMaker is smart enough to know how to set up a layout for any of the standard Avery label types. You just pick your type, and FileMaker does all the work, producing a layout properly structured for your label dimensions. It even puts the fields you specify on the layout so that they flow together nicely. The layout may look strange to you at first, because each field is surrounded by << and >>. (These are merge fields—see page 160 for an explanation.) If you're not using Avery labels, then you can plug in your own measurements.

Note: The "Vertical labels" type applies only to databases that use Japanese text. This layout type rotates the text to create *vertical* labels.

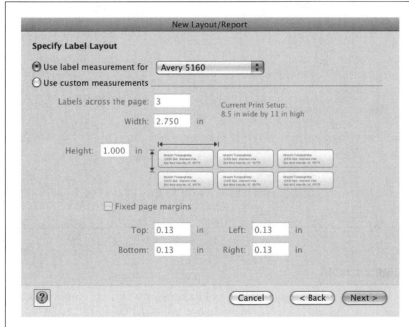

Figure 7-6:
When you create a Labels layout, FileMaker lets you pick a standard Avery label size, or key in specific dimensions (you can usually find the right numbers included with printable labels). FileMaker then creates the layout with everything in the right place to print on the labels perfectly.

Envelope

If you'd rather print right on the envelope than stick a label on it, use the Envelope layout type. FileMaker creates a layout specially designed to print on a Number 10 envelope (see Figure 7-7). You can even customize it with your company's logo and return address by adding text and pictures to the layout.

Since every printer handles envelopes a little differently, the layout needs a little adjusting to print perfectly. You can usually just delete the Header part from the layout. Also, don't forget to choose the right paper size (File→Print Setup on Windows; File→Page Setup on Mac OS X) and orientation for your envelope. On more persnickety printers, you may have to leave the header in place, and adjust its height. Getting things lined up always involves a few test prints, but once you've got it working, you never have to fuss with it again. (Well, until you get a new printer.)

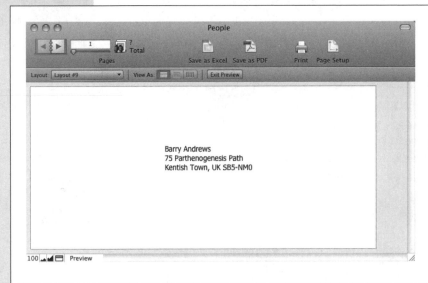

Figure 7-7:
Once you get your Envelope layout dialed in for your printer, a print run of envelopes is easy. Just find the people you want, load a stack of envelopes in your printer, and then print them out.

Renaming a Layout

If you're looking over your list of layouts and finding some of those names wanting, you're not stuck with them. To rename a layout, you need to revisit Layout mode. The Layout bar makes this easy, too:

1. **At the right end of the Layout bar, click the Edit Layout button.**

   The window switches to Layout mode. You can tell at a glance because the Layout bar turns black. It also gets several new buttons, including the one identified in Figure 7-8.

2. **Click the Layout Setup button. It looks like a little pencil.**

   If you're not the toolbar type, you can also choose Layouts→Layout Setup. Either way, you see the Layout Setup dialog box, shown in Figure 7-9.

3. **In the Layout Name box, type a more descriptive name, say, People Detail.**

   This name more clearly indicates that this layout shows full details about a person.

4. **Click OK, and then, in the Layout bar, click Exit Layout.**

   When you click Exit Layout, FileMaker asks if you want to save the change you've made to the layout.

5. **Click Save.**

   Now the Layout pop-up menu shows the new layout name.

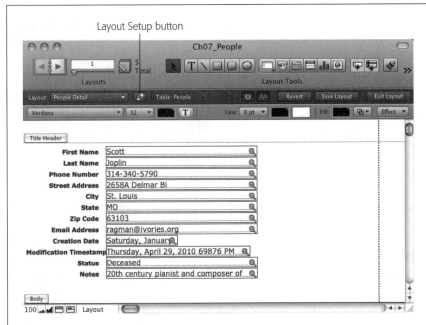

Layout Setup button

Figure 7-8:
When you switch to Layout mode to edit a layout, the Layout bar turns black. This strong visual cue helps you know where you are. It also adds several buttons, most of which you'll learn about later. To rename a layout, click the Layout Setup button, shown here.

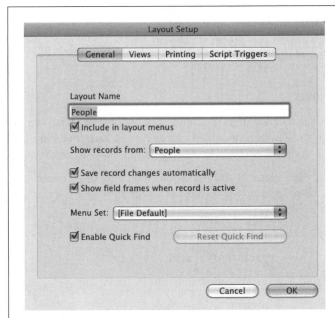

Figure 7-9:
The Layout Setup dialog box has countless under-the-hood options for your layout. You can configure which views should be allowed for the layout, how big the print margins are, and which menus appear in the menu bar. And, of course, you can type to change the layout's name.

Setting Layout View

Switch to Browse mode to admire your handiwork. If you're seeing only one record at a time, switch to List view (choose View→"View as List"). When you choose the blank layout template, you get complete freedom to make the layout look just the way you want. But one tradeoff is that you have to remember to tell the layout which view it's supposed to be in.

But there's nothing stopping you (or anybody using your database) from switching this layout back to Form view, or Table view, at some point in the future. If you don't want anyone to see the database that way, then you can tell FileMaker you want only this layout to be seen in List view:

1. **Switch to Layout mode, and then choose Layouts→Layout Setup.**

   Remember, Layout mode is the only place you can make changes to a layout. You work this particular piece of magic in the Layout Setup box.

2. **On the Views tab, turn off Form View and Table View.**

   You've just told FileMaker to make these two menu choices off-limits in Browse and Find modes. After all, they don't make much sense in a layout that's designed specifically to work as a list.

3. **Click OK to dismiss the dialog box.**

   Honestly, you have to tell some programs *everything*.

Now, when you switch to Browse mode and look at the View menu, "View as Form" and "View as Table" are grayed out. FileMaker doesn't let you accidentally switch your list to a useless view of the data.

Found Sets and Layouts

FileMaker is smart enough to know that the People List and People Detail layouts are showing the same records. In fact, you might use the People List layout to quickly find someone you want, and the switch to People Detail to make some changes.

To make switching back and forth as smooth as possible, FileMaker remembers which record you're looking at, and which records are in your found set as you switch layouts. Prove it to yourself:

1. **Switch to the People List layout.**

   Nothing new here. You see your records in a list.

2. **Perform a simple find. For instance, find someone by first name.**

   The list changes to show only the matching records.

3. **Click one of the records.**

   Even when you're in List view, FileMaker has the notion of a *current record*.

Since you can see several records at once, the program indicates which one you last clicked with a little black marker along the left edge of the record. You can see the marker in Figure 7-10.

4. **Switch to the People Detail layout.**

Notice that the record you're looking at is the one you clicked when on the List layout. Also, if you use the book icon to change records, then you see that you have a found set just like you did on the List layout. If you perform a different find now, and then switch back to People List, FileMaker lists the records that match the new find as well.

Because FileMaker keeps all this in sync, you can use multiple layouts with ease. When you want to find things, use whatever layout makes it easiest. Need to print a sheet of labels? On the List layout, find what you want first, and then go to the Labels layout and print.

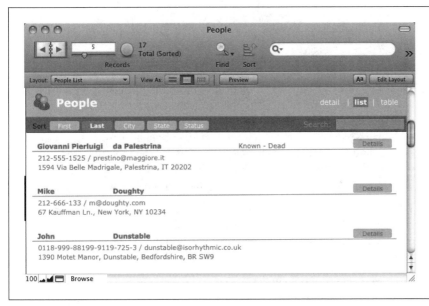

Figure 7-10:
When you're in List view (or Table view), FileMaker puts a little black marker next to the record you last clicked—Mike Doughty's record in this example. That's the current record, as far as FileMaker's concerned.

Layout Setup

FileMaker has a few more layout options that haven't appeared in this chapter so far. These options let you control overall aspects of the layout. To see them, switch to Layout mode, and then choose Layout→Layout Setup. You see the window in Figure 7-11.

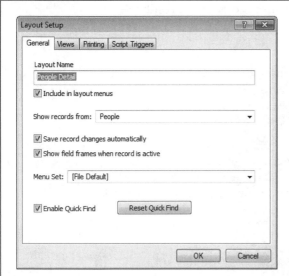

Figure 7-11:
The Layout Setup dialog box (Layout→Layout Setup) holds options that apply to the layout as a whole. They range from critical (which table's data this layout shows) to the cosmetic (whether or not FileMaker shows flashy outlines around fields when you edit records).

- The "Save record changes automatically" option is turned on with every new layout. If you turn it off instead, then FileMaker starts acting…annoying. Whenever you click out of a record after making changes on this layout, FileMaker pops up a window asking if you want to save your changes. You can opt to revert instead, and toss out all the changes you've made. You typically use this option when you're working on a small layout where you edit complex data. Normally, of course, FileMaker saves the record changes automatically with nary a word.

- When you're actively editing a record, FileMaker draws a dotted outline around enterable fields, making it immediately obvious where you can enter data because each field is outlined. But some people find this feature unsightly. Turn off "Show field frames when record is active", and FileMaker cuts it out.

- The Menu Set pop-up menu lets you pick an alternate *menu set*. You'll learn all about customizing menus in Chapter 12.

- Finally, the Enable Quick Find checkbox allows you to determine whether or not Quick Find is permitted on a given layout. If you've changed Quick Find settings for individual fields on this layout, the Reset Quick Find button can be used to negate all that customization in one shot.

Manage Layouts

Now that you know how to create new layouts, you'll find dozens of uses for them. Pretty soon, your pop-up menu of layouts will get lengthy. And, unless you're some kind of organizational genius, you probably won't create your layouts in exactly the order you want them to appear in the list. You can easily manage the list, though. Just choose File→Manage→Layouts or press Ctrl+Shift+L (⌘-Shift-L). The dialog box is shown in Figure 7-12.

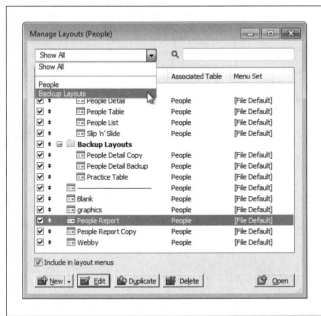

Figure 7-12:
In the Manage Layouts dialog box, drag the double-arrow to reorder the list. The checkbox in the left column lets you determine whether a layout appears in the Layout pop-up menu. The pop-up menu at the top of the window contains a list of your Layout folders. Pick a folder from that menu to temporarily hide all other folders and layouts from the list.

The Manage Layouts dialog box gives you a number of ways to tame your layout list, the simplest of which is reordering—just drag a layout to the desired position on the list. Separators provide a nice visual break between groups of related layouts. Add a separator by clicking the triangle just to the right of the "New" button and then selecting "separator" from the menu.

Perhaps the most useful organizational tool here is the Layout Folder. Once created, a layout folder can contain any number of layouts and subfolders. Simply drag a layout from the list onto a folder to place it inside. When viewing the Layout pop-up menu in the toolbar, you'll see your folders listed with a submenu of the layouts they contain as shown in Figure 7-13.

The Inspector's Data Tab

In the Inspector, the Data tab is all about fields. With few exceptions, the controls on the Data tab are available only when you've selected a field on your layout—other layout objects such as graphics and buttons don't apply. The Field section is where you specify which field's data to display and which field controls it should have. The Behavior section gives you control over user access to the field. The final section, Data Formatting, gives you a wide range of ways to present numbers, dates, times and graphics.

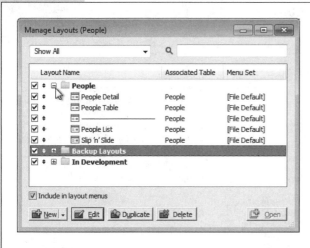

Figure 7-13:
*When you select a layout in the Manage
Layouts dialog box, the four right-hand buttons
at the bottom of the window become available.
Click Edit to open the Layout Setup dialog box
(page 283). Duplicate creates a new layout just
like the selected one with the word "Copy" appended to the layout's name. Click Delete, and
you have one opportunity to change your mind.
If you don't back out FileMaker will delete the
selected layout but good; deleting a layout is
instant and permanent. Open, off to the bottom
right of the dialog box, will bring up the selected
layout in a new window.*

Field Control

FileMaker supports all the standard controls you're used to, like pop-up menus,
checkboxes, and radio buttons. It also offers pop-up calendars. And if you want to
type with just a little assistance, it has *auto-completion*, which works just like the address bar in your web browser: As you type, FileMaker gives you options based on
other values you've typed in the field before.

All this power lives on the Inspector's Data Tab (Figure 7-14). In Layout mode,
choose View→Inspector or press Ctrl+I (⌘-I), and then click the Data tab.

In general, picking a type is simple: First select the field you want to change. Then
choose an option from the "Control style" pop-up menu on the Inspector's Data tab.

But if you choose a pop-up menu, or radio buttons, or checkboxes, how does File-
Maker know what choices to let someone pick from? The answer lies in something
you've seen just briefly so far: a *value list* (basically, a list of text values).

When you choose one of these choice-oriented field control types, you also pick a
value list. FileMaker then lets anyone using the database choose from among the
values you specify. To try it out in the People database, you can make your Status
field into a pop-up menu offering a list of the following choices:

- Active

- Retired

- Deceased

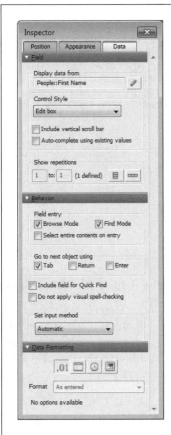

Figure 7-14:
The Data tab on the Inspector palette lets you configure the type of control people use to enter data into the field. If you only see the Field heading in the inspector, click the triangle just to the left of the word Field to reveal the controls.

Here's how:

1. **In Layout mode, on the People Detail layout, select the Status field.**

   As usual, you need to tell FileMaker which field you want to change first.

   If the Inspector isn't onscreen, choose View→Inspector or type Ctrl+I (⌘-I).

   Click the Data tab in the Inspector.

2. **From the "Control style" pop-up menu, choose "Pop-up Menu".**

   A few new options appear as shown in Figure 7-15.

Figure 7-15:
When you choose to display your field as a pop-up menu, FileMaker gives you a few new choices. Most importantly, you have to pick a value list from the "Values from" pop-up menu. You can also turn on "Allow entry of other values" to allow entry of other values if you want your pop-up menu to include an extra choice called "Other" that lets someone enter anything she wants. The second checkbox lets you add an "Edit" item to the menu so database users can edit the choices in the menu at will.

3. **Click the small button with the pencil just to the right of the "Values from" pop-up menu.**

   The Manage Value Lists dialog box appears. This window lists all the value lists you've created (you probably have only one right now). It's perfectly OK to use the same value list in more than one place, but in this case, you don't have one with the values you want, so you'll make a new one.

4. **Click New.**

   The Edit Value List window appears, ready for you to configure a fresh value list.

5. **In the Value List Name box, type *Status*.**

   You can name a value list just about anything you want. But for convenience in the future, name it something meaningful.

6. **Make sure "Use custom values" is turned on.**

   Once again, you want to specify a custom list of values. You learned about the other types on page 217.

7. **In the box under "Use custom values", type *Active, Retired,* and *Deceased* each on a separate line.**

   Make sure you press Return between each value so FileMaker knows you have three separate items in your value list, not one long item.

8. **Click OK, and then, in the Manage Value Lists window, click OK again.**

   Closing both dialog boxes gets you back to the Inspector. In the "Value from" pop-up menu, your Status value list should be selected. If it isn't, select it now.

9. **Click OK.**

Your Status field looks a little different now. It has a small drop shadow, making it look like an old-school pop-up menu.

If you switch to Browse mode now, your pop-up menu should be fully functional. Figure 7-16 shows how it looks.

Figure 7-16:
Your layout now has a functioning pop-up menu. The field looks different on the layout, with a drop shadow making the field appear to pop out of the screen a little. When you click the pop-up menu, a list of choices appears.

Your layout could use a few more field control enhancements while you're here:

- The Notes field is big, but is it big enough? You can add a scroll bar with just a few clicks. Then, if you happen to need more space, FileMaker lets you scroll through all the text you add.

- Chances are you're going to put the same stuff in the City field over and over, with a few occasional exceptions. If you turn on auto-completion, then FileMaker helps you type the common values, but stays out of your way when you type something unusual.

- The State field, on the other hand, is always a standard state abbreviation (the validation sees to that), so a pop-up menu would be good. But when you know the abbreviation you want, it's much faster to simply type it than to pick from a list. Nevertheless, the list is helpful if you can't remember whether Alaska is AK or AL. FileMaker has another control type—the drop-down list—that's sort of like a combination pop-up menu and Edit box. It lets you either choose from the list or type for yourself.

Note: You rarely use *every* field control option in any one layout, and the layout you're creating now is no exception. Fear not, though. You can read about each field control option in detail on page 291.

First up, here's how to add a scroll bar to the People database's Notes field:

1. **Select the Notes field, and, if the Inspector isn't onscreen, choose View→ Inspector or type Ctrl+I (⌘-I).**

Make sure you're on the Data tab.

2. **Turn on the "Include vertical scroll bar" checkbox.**

You're done; simple as that.

3. **Click OK, and then switch to Browse mode and behold the glory of your creation (Figure 7-17).**

   Your Notes field now has a little scroll bar along its right edge. (If you don't see this, you don't have field borders turned on. See page 120 for the steps you missed.) If you type enough data to fill up the Notes field, the scroll bar kicks into action, making it a snap to scroll up and down through as much text as you can throw at it.

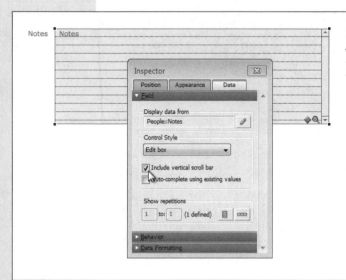

Figure 7-17:
Any field can have a scroll bar—like the Notes field here—so long as it's a standard Edit box field control.

Now you can add auto-completion to the City field. Select the field, and choose View→Inspector. This time, turn on "Auto-complete using previously entered values". When you test this control, make sure you create some records first, if you don't have any. The auto-completion is based on data in other records, so if you have no records, you'll get no auto-complete suggestions.

Assuming you do have cities entered in other records, when you start typing in the City field, FileMaker automatically fills in the full city name that starts with whatever you type. If it isn't right, you can just keep typing. If it *is* right, press Tab, and File-Maker accepts the whole value.

Now it's time to tackle the State field. You know the drill: Select the field and turn your attention to the Inspector's Data tab. from the "Control style" pop-up menu, choose the "Drop-down List" option. From the "Display values from" pop-up menu, pick your States value list While you're here, turn on "Include arrow to show and hide list". That adds an arrow icon to the field to indicate it has a drop-down list.

Once you've made this change, you may need to make the State field a little bigger to accommodate the arrow icon. You can make room by shortening the City or Zip Code field. Figure 7-18 shows the result of these changes.

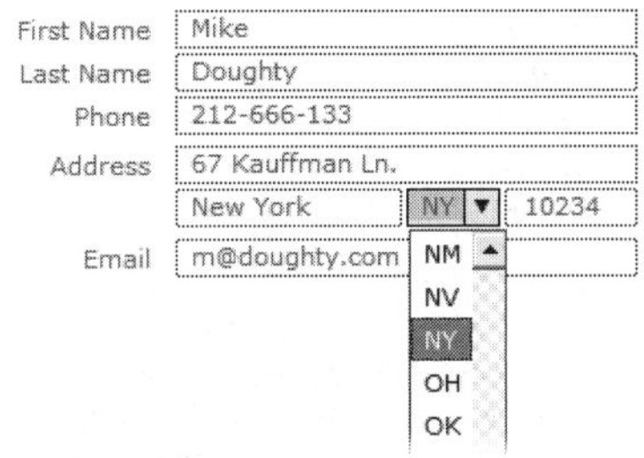

Figure 7-18:
A drop-down list works a lot like a pop-up menu. Click the arrow, and you get a list of options. But unlike a pop-up menu, you can type directly into a drop-down list. For something short like a state abbreviation, typing is often faster than picking from a list, and the field's validation ensures no bogus entries get through.

Advanced Field Controls

As you've seen throughout the last few chapters, FileMaker field controls can take on many forms. In this section you'll learn exactly how each of these works, and how you can configure them to get just the behavior you want. Each control described here is accessible via the Inspector's Data tab when in Layout mode. If the Inspector isn't onscreen, choose View→Inspector or type Ctrl+I (⌘-I).

Edit Box

Most of the fields you've used so far have been *Edit Boxes*. These fields are the click-and-type variety that normal people call a *text box*. Distinctive as always, FileMaker has its own moniker. No matter what you call it—Edit Box or text box—this sort of control isn't limited to just text. You can use an Edit Box with number fields, date fields, and so on.

When you select the Edit Box format, you have the choice of turning on the "Include vertical scroll bar" checkbox. You saw this option when you added a scroll bar to the Notes field on page 289. If you anticipate that a field will hold lots of information, a scroll bar can be a good idea, as Figure 7-19 shows.

Drop-Down List

This field type *looks* just like an Edit Box. But when you click into the field, a list of available choices appears just below it (see Figure 7-20).

The items in the list come from a value list. When you pick the Drop-down List type, you get a "Values from" pop-up menu. From this menu, choose the value list to use. You can also open the Manage Value Lists window by clicking the button with the pencil icon just to the right of the pop-up menu.

Note: If you don't apply borders to a Drop-down List, then the show/hide arrow appears only when the field is active. Add field borders (at least a right border—see page 120) to make the arrow show.

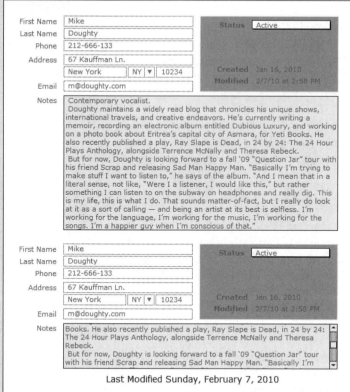

Figure 7-19:
Top: FileMaker fields can hold a lot of text. If you don't have a scroll bar, then when you click in the field, FileMaker increases its size to show all the text.

Bottom: When you tab or click out of that field, FileMaker shrinks it back to its original size, leaving no clue that more text might be hiding below the fold. If you know you're expecting lots of information, you should usually add a scroll bar.

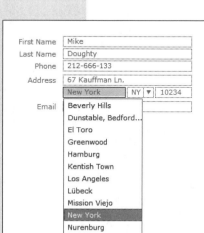

Figure 7-20:
A drop-down list like the one showing cities here gives you a list of choices to save you the trouble of typing the one you want. Just click an item in the list, and FileMaker enters it into the field. You can also use the up and down arrow keys to select an item in the list. Finally, you can type the first few letters of an item's name to select it. Once you have an item selected, press Enter (Return) to accept it.

Drop-down Lists look just like Edit Boxes until you click them or tab into the field. Then the list drops down for your data-entry pleasure. But it can get annoying to have lists flashing at you just because you happen to be tabbing through the data in a record, so FileMaker lets you stop the list waving by choosing "Include arrow to show and hide list". Now the list is a little more polite. When the field is active, the list doesn't drop down until you click the arrow. If you make a choice from the list, it disappears. Or, if you don't want to enter anything into the field after all, just click the arrow and the list goes back home.

Finally, turn on "Include Edit item to allow editing of value list" if you want your users to be able to easily modify the list of choices. When folks choose Edit (always the last item in the list), the window in Figure 7-21 shows up so they can modify the value list.

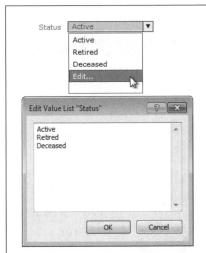

Figure 7-21:
You can include an Edit item in your Drop-down List. When folks choose it, this little Edit Value List box appears. From here, they can add new items, delete items, or edit items in the list—all by typing directly in the text box. All of this assumes your value list has "Use custom values" turned on. You can't edit the items in a value list based on field values.

Pop-Up Menu

When you format a field as a Pop-up Menu, the look changes significantly, as shown in back in Figure 7-16. Rather than type into the field, people have to click the menu and make a choice. Like Drop-down Lists, Pop-up Menus let mere mortals edit value lists, plus they up the ante by including an Other item. When people pick Other from the menu, they see the window in Figure 7-22. Entering a value in this window puts it in the field but *doesn't* add it to the value list. Turn on "Include Other item to allow entry of other values" to grant this power to the masses. (See the box on page 294 for advice on the ramifications of letting people edit or bypass your carefully crafted value lists.)

Figure 7-22:
Selecting Other opens a dialog box with plenty of space to type into at will.

UP TO SPEED

Drop Down, Pop Up, Turn On

You may wonder how a drop-down list differs from a pop-up menu. They're similar in purpose, but have three differences:

- A pop-up menu requires you to make a choice when entering data—you can't type into the field unless you specifically tell FileMaker to allow it. With a drop-down list, on the other hand, you can always dismiss the list and type directly into the field instead. When the list pops up, just click the field again to make the list go away, and then start typing. From the keyboard, press Enter (Return) to make the list go away, or press Esc to toggle the list on and off.

- Drop-down lists work just fine with *thousands* of items in them. Since the list scrolls, it doesn't much matter how long it is. Pop-up menus, by contrast, get very cumbersome with more than a dozen or so items.

- Finally, folks can make selections from a drop-down list using just the keyboard, while a pop-up menu requires a trip to the mouse. The drop-down list's keyboard ability makes it preferable in cases where speed of entry is the priority.

Checkbox Set

Figure 7-23 shows a field formatted as a Checkbox Set. With this format, people can simply click each item to turn it on or off. As they do, the data in the field changes to reflect the checked items.

Checkbox Sets can include the Other item, just like a pop-up menu. If someone enters a value that isn't in the value list, then FileMaker just turns on the Other checkbox to indicate the field has something more in it.

UP TO SPEED

A Cautionary Tale

Not even the most highly paid database developer can think of everything folks might want to enter in a database, and a drop-down list with a handy edit option seems an obvious solution. But use it with caution. When some villainous or misguided soul chooses Edit, she's doing just that: editing your *value list*, and potentially defeating the purpose for which you created it. Furthermore, if other fields in your database are formatted to use the same value list, *their* list of choices changes, too, because the underlying value list itself has changed.

So remember that value-list-based fields serve *two* purposes: simplicity and consistency. If you make it easy for folks

to add their own items to a value list, you're also making it easy for the value list to get inconsistent and disorganized.

Adding an Other item can undermine consistency even more, because it encourages quick-handed mousers to simply bypass the value list entirely.

If your value list's primary purpose is to gain consistency, then you should consider leaving the Edit and Other options turned off. You can always add new choices to the value list yourself at any time as the need arises.

Figure 7-23:
When you format a field as a Checkbox Set, it looks like the City field shown here. FileMaker adds one checkbox for each item in the value list, and arranges them to neatly fill the boundaries of the field. You can apply borders, fills, and effects to a field like this—they affect the entire area the Checkbox Set covers.

Radio Button Set

A Radio Button Set (see Figure 7-24) works much like a Checkbox Set. The only distinction is that folks can turn on only *one* item. Click one value and any previously selected value is cleared out. These buttons work much like those on car radios—only one can be selected at a time. When you change the channel from, say, smooth jazz to light rock/less talk, the station you were listening to is dropped and the new station takes its place.

___

Warning: Some sneaky malcontents out there know they can Shift-click to select multiple items in a Radio Button Set. See the box on page 379 to learn how calculations can control these people's urge to get around the system.

___

Just as with drop-down lists and Checkbox Sets, you can add an Other or Edit item to the Radio Button Set. (See the box on page 296 for more detail.)

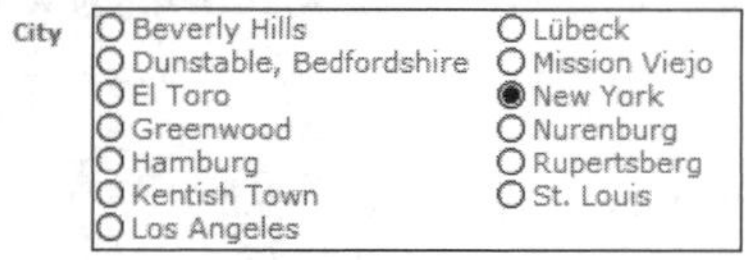

City	○ Beverly Hills	○ Lübeck
	○ Dunstable, Bedfordshire	○ Mission Viejo
	○ El Toro	● New York
	○ Greenwood	○ Nurenburg
	○ Hamburg	○ Rupertsberg
	○ Kentish Town	○ St. Louis
	○ Los Angeles	

Figure 7-24:
This time the City field is formatted as a Radio Button Set. Now you can simply click the right city to set the field, making this one of the fastest field formats for mouse-based entry.

Drop-Down Calendar

In FileMaker, you can easily read date fields, and easily set them up. But actually typing dates into them is notoriously tricky. If you don't get just the right combination of numbers and tiny little separators, FileMaker and tells you the value you've just typed isn't valid. And if somebody swipes your desk calendar, how are you supposed to know what numbers to type in the first place? FileMaker can handle both these problems. It lets you give your date fields a nifty drop-down calendar where anyone can simply point and click to enter a date.

GEM IN THE ROUGH

Checkboxes Behind the Scenes

The beauty of Checkbox Set fields is that they let folks click *more than one* checkbox. In other words, you can capture several values in one easy-to-use field. This method comes in handy when the things you're tracking in your database have fields like Available Sizes, Available Colors, Warehouses, or any other attribute of the *one or more* variety. But wait, you say—how can a single field hold *more* than one value?

Simple, if you're FileMaker. Just give each checkbox its own line. In other words, if you have a Checkbox Set showing colors, and you turn on Red, Green, and Blue, FileMaker actually thinks of the field like this:

    Red
    Green
    Blue

You can show the same field on another layout—or even the same layout if you want—without the checkbox formatting. If you do, you see the selected items: one on each line. This is called a "return-separated list." If you change what's in the field without using the checkboxes, then you could end up with lines that don't match any of the value list items. In that case, the Checkbox Set turns on its Other item if it has one. (If not, the extra items simply don't show at all.)

A final note: Checkbox Sets need to be able to put several lines in the field, so they're really suitable only for *text* fields. Other field types don't support multiline values.

When you first format a field with a drop-down calendar, FileMaker doesn't give you any visual feedback letting you know a calendar's lurking there, waiting to drop down when you tab into the field. If you want to provide a visual clue, select "Include icon to show and hide calendar". Then you see a teeny, tiny calendar at the right side of your field (see Figure 7-25). Tiny as it is, the calendar icon still takes up some room, so you may have to make the field a little wider to display the entire date plus the new icon.

Figure 7-25:
The Drop-down Calendar makes entering dates a snap. It has some sweet controls, too. When the field's empty, the current date is highlighted when the field drops down. Or, if there's data in the field already, then FileMaker highlights that date when the calendar appears.

Note: Like the show/hide arrow on drop-down lists, the calendar icon shows up in an inactive field only if the field has a border. If you're a minimalist on the field border issue, you can format your field with only a right border to force the icon to appear.

The calendar itself is a little dynamo. To enter a date, click the Month Year display at the top, and you see a pop-up menu that lets you jump to a specific month in the current calendar year.

Right-click anywhere on the calendar (or Control-click on the Mac if you don't have a two-button mouse), and the pop-up menu changes to read "Go to today". The calendar closes, and plunks the current date into the field.

You can also change the month with the right and left arrows at either side. The left arrow icon moves you backward in time, and the right one moves you forward. The up and down arrow icons change the display of years. Finally, you can move the highlighted date with your keyboard's arrow keys. Tap the down arrow key a few times to see how fast time flies.

But if you get carried away playing the controls ("Is my birthday on a Friday in 2015?"), remember that the calendar's footer always displays the current date. Just click that display to enter the current date, and then click to open up the calendar again. It reorients to today's date.

Auto-Complete

Auto-Complete is a strong ally both for database designers who care about data consistency and for data entry folk who hate to type. Unlike the other Field/Control field styles, you can apply this little beauty to a regular Edit Box. Once you've turned on the option to "Auto-complete using previously entered values", the field gets ESP and tries to figure out what you want to enter. Where do these superhuman powers come from? From that old friend, the field's index.

Auto-Complete isn't a control style in and of itself; rather, you use it in conjunction with either an Edit Box or a Drop-down List (the option isn't available for other styles). But Auto-Complete behaves a little differently on Edit Boxes than it does on Drop-down Lists. The differences are discussed in the following sections.

Auto-Complete in Edit Boxes

To turn on Auto-Complete for an Edit Box field control, visit the Inspector's Data tab and turn on "Auto-complete using previously entered values". (This checkbox only shows up when you have "Control style" set to Edit box or Drop-down list.)

UP TO SPEED

When Is Auto-Complete Not Useful?

With such a cool feature, one that seems to know what people want to type before *they* do, you may be tempted to add auto-complete powers to most of your fields. But sometimes it just isn't very helpful.

Auto-Complete depends on the index to know what to show in its list. At least one field has to have data for File-Maker to have any entries in the index. And indexes increase the size of your file, so if you index a lot of fields just for Auto-Complete, you may find that the file size balloons. Remember, this feature comes with all of indexing's dark sides as a tradeoff for its power (see the box on page 257).

Another weakness: When someone types a letter that's not used much—like X, J, or Z—Auto-Complete may not produce

a drop-down list. This lack of a list doesn't mean Auto-Complete is broken. It just means the index doesn't have any entries beginning with that letter. The index saves no time in such cases and may be confusing to the uninitiated.

Auto-Complete works best in databases with lots of records. And it's usually most effective if the records have a fairly wide range of data in them. For example, if a field is going to have only a few possible values (G, PG, PG-13, R, NC-17), then a drop-down menu or a pop-up menu is a better choice than an Auto-Complete Edit Box.

None of these cautions means that you shouldn't use Auto-Complete. Just be aware of its limitations, and the overhead it places on your file.

When you start typing into a field configured this way, FileMaker scans the field's index and drops down a list of matching entries. There *is no value list* in this case—it always draws from field values on other records. If you type *T*, for example, then you see a list of entries that begin with the letter T. If you type *R* next, then the list shortens to only words beginning with "TR". Once the list is short enough for you to find what you want, just click the list item to select it.

Note: The Auto-Complete list behaves just like a regular drop-down list, so if you prefer, you can highlight items with arrow keys, and then press Enter.

Auto-Complete in drop-down lists

If your field is formatted as a Drop-down List, you can make it even smarter by adding auto-complete behavior. Visit the Data tab of the Inspector, make sure "Control type" is set to Drop-down List, and then turn on "Auto-complete using value list." When used in conjunction with a drop-down list, Auto-Complete uses the values from the associated value list. In fact, in many ways, it works just like an ordinary drop-down list. Now, though, you get the automatic type-ahead behavior you've come to know and love: As you begin to type, FileMaker automatically narrows the list to include items that start with what you've entered so far. This can make your drop-down lists even faster and easier to use.

Note: When you click into an Auto-Complete drop-down list that's formatted with a show/hide arrow, the list doesn't appear until you click the arrow or pres the Esc key. If you want the list to display as soon as the field is entered, then don't select the "Include arrow to show and hide list" option.

WORKAROUND WORKSHOP

One or Many?

Strange as it sounds, pop-up menus and radio buttons both allow *multiple selections*, just like Checkbox Sets. Just hold down the Shift key while you select an item, and FileMaker dutifully turns it on without turning off the item that's already selected. Handy though it may be, however, chances are you don't want anyone to use this trick and choose more than one value—otherwise you use checkboxes to make it obvious that multiple choices are desirable.

Unfortunately, you don't have any direct way to turn off this feature. If you want to prevent people from picking too many items, you have to get creative. Here's one way of doing so:

Chapter 6 introduced you to auto-enter calculations (see page 246). They let you automatically change the value in a field, based on a *calculation*. You'll learn all about calculations in Part 4, so for now you just have to have some blind faith.

Here's how to limit your fields to a *single* value:

1. In the Manage Database window, select the field you want to fix, and then click Options. The Field Options dialog box appears. If it isn't already selected, click the Auto-Enter tab.

2. Turn on the "Calculated value" checkbox. The Specify Calculation dialog box appears.

3. In the big free-entry box on the bottom half of the window, type *LeftValues (Self ; 1)*. This calculation tells FileMaker you want to keep only the left-most—or *first*—value in the field.

4. Click OK. You're now back in the Field Options dialog box.

5. Turn off "Do not replace existing value (if any)", and then click OK.

You're back in your database.

Now if you try to Shift-click a second item, FileMaker immediately throws it out. In practice, it *looks* like it simply doesn't let you Shift-click.

Repetitions

On page 255, you learned about repeating fields, which let you put several values in one field, with a separate Edit Box for each one. When you put a repeating field on a layout, you get to decide how many times it shows up. Even if a field has 200 repetitions, you don't *have* to show them all on the layout. You can elect to show just the first 10. Or just the last 10. Or numbers 37 through 118.

GEM IN THE ROUGH

Tab Order and Repeating Fields

FileMaker treats each repetition of a repeating field as a separate item in the tab order. It's perfectly legal to have the *last* repetition come right after the *first*—if you're into aggravating the people using your database. But it can be a real drag to have to click each and every one of those repetitions when you set the tab order. FileMaker has a nice feature to save you the trouble.

When you click the first repetition of a repeating field (while setting tab orders), FileMaker gives it a number—and the arrow begins to flash. If you click this flashing arrow *again*, then FileMaker numbers that field's additional repetitions for you, in the logical order.

But the magic doesn't stop there: Suppose you have a series of repeating fields. The standard tab order would go *down* each column before moving to the next one, but you'd prefer to tab *across* the rows first. For example, if you're sitting in the first Quantity field, you want to tab into the Product field, then the Price field. Then once you've completed a row, you want the next tab to take you to the next one.

FileMaker can automatically do this kind of numbering for you, too. When setting the tab order, click the first Quantity field. It gets a number and begins to flash. Now click the first Product field, and then the first Price field. The arrow by the Quantity field continues to flash. Once you've done these three clicks, click the flashing arrow again. FileMaker now numbers all your repetitions properly.

In general, you click each repeating field in the order you want them tabbed to. When you're done, click the *first* one again to let FileMaker know. FileMaker fills out each row of repetitions matching this order.

To control how repeating fields display, you use the same Field Control/Setup dialog box shown in Figure 7-15. This time, focus your attention on the Show repetitions portion of the palette. Just enter the first repetition you want in the "Show repetitions" box, and the last one in the "to" box. You can't show noncontiguous repetitions here—you have to enter one beginning and one end, and FileMaker shows those and every repetition in between. But try this technique instead: Put multiple copies of the field on the layout, but specify that each copy displays a different range of repeats. You get much the same effect, as described in the box on the next page.

Tip: If the "Show repetitions" and "to" options are grayed out and you see (1 defined) it means your field isn't defined as a repeating field. You can change that by visiting File→Manage→Database, selecting the field, and then clicking Options. Under the Storage tab, set the Maximum number of repetitions to any number greater than one.

Once you've figured out which repetitions to show, you get to pick an orientation. Your choices are Horizontal and Vertical, and Figure 7-26 makes sense of them.

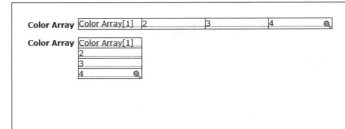

Figure 7-26:
This layout shows the same repeating field twice, once with horizontal orientation, and once with vertical. (See the box below for further advice.) In Layout mode, FileMaker numbers each repetition in a repeating field to let you know which one it is. The first repetition shows the full field name and—if there's room—the repetition number in brackets.

POWER USERS' CLINIC

Flexible Repetitions

Suppose you *want* to show noncontiguous ranges of repeating fields. Or you need something more flexible than a straight up-and-down or side-to-side orientation. For example, your layout may be easier on the eyes if it shows the first 10 repetitions in one stack, and the next 10 in another stack right beside the first set. Or you may want to show just the even-numbered repetitions. Or perhaps you're determined to see repetition number 1, then 11 through 13, then 7 and 8, and finally number 281. No matter how capricious your desires, FileMaker's up to the job.

Here's the trick: Put the field on the layout *more than once*. Or, more correctly, put several field controls on the layout, all associated with the same field. For example, suppose you have a repeating field called Dimensions. It holds all the various measurements for a particular sprocket in your catalog. Now imagine you want to show the first 10 repetitions in a vertical stack, with the next 10 beside it.

First, add the field to the layout using the Field tool. From Inspector's Data tab, configure it to show repetitions 1 through 10 in a vertical orientation, and then click OK. Now duplicate the whole shebang. Select the copy, move it to its own plot of layout land, and then visit the Inspector once more. Configure this version of the field control to show repetitions 11 through 20. If you head back to Browse mode, then you see that you have all 20 repetitions on the layout, arranged the way you wanted.

By using various combinations of repeating field controls in various configurations, you can arrange field repetitions any way you want—even if you have to add a separate control for each repetition.

Display Data From

So far, you haven't explored the topmost option in the Inspector's Data tab, where there lives an incredibly powerful feature—the "Display data from" option. With this powerful tool, you can change a field object on the layout so it's tied to a different field. This way, if you have a field that's already configured just the way you want, you can duplicate it (Edit→Duplicate), and then point the new copy to a different field in your table. This method is much faster than reconfiguring a fresh field object from scratch.

UP TO SPEED

Borders and Repeating Fields

While you've got repeating fields on the brain, there's one more formatting choice worth talking about. You can put a border around a repeating field just like any other field. But this border goes around the entire set of fields, not each individual repetition. You wind up with what looks like one big field, and it can be a surprise when you click it and discover those repetitions. Wouldn't it be nicer if you could format those repeating fields to look like a sensible set of fields?

Nicer, yes. And possible, too. In Layout mode, open an Inspector palette (Show→Inspector), and then click its Appearance tab. See that row of six rectangular buttons in the Object section of the Inspector? Click the one furthest to the right and you'll get your borderline *between* each repetition.

Field Behavior

Tabbing around the People database in Browse mode reveals another problem. You can click into (and type into) the Created and Modified fields. But these fields are strictly informational: You should be able to *see* them and *search* them, but you don't need to edit them, because FileMaker fills in the dates automatically when you create or modify a record. In fact, even though FileMaker lets you type into them, if you try to commit the record, then it displays an error message because when you created these fields, you told FileMaker to "prohibit modification of field value" (page 142). You could let people try to edit these fields and get a rude error message, but keeping them out of the fields in the first place results in a much better user experience.

If you're sharp-eyed, you might also notice that FileMaker is running its spell checker on the Email Address field. When you type an email address, which is almost never a proper word, it gets a distracting red underline.

You can fix these problems (and more) by modifying the *field behavior*. To change it, first select a field, and then turn your eyes to the Behavior section of the Inspector's Data tab (Figure 7-27).

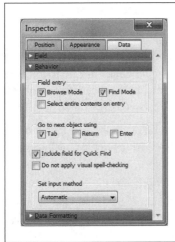

Figure 7-27:
The Inspector's Behavior section lets you control how the field acts in Browse mode. The most common setting is the first set of checkboxes, "Field entry". But each option here is useful under certain circumstances.

FileMaker lets you control five aspects of a field's behavior:

- The "Field entry" checkboxes prevent folks from being able to click into the Created and Modified fields. When you turn the Browse Mode checkbox off, clicking into the field in Browse mode doesn't work, turning the field into a visual display of data, minus human interaction. Since you often want a field that can't be edited, but can be searched, you'll most often turn off Browse Mode and turn on Find Mode. But you're free to turn on or off either checkbox in any combination that suits your needs.

Note: When you can't enter a field, then you can't select its text to copy and paste. So if you want to let people copy the information from an uneditable field, then you can leave a field enterable, but remove their ability to edit using field options (page 244) or security (page 772).

- Normally when you click into a field, the insertion point appears right where you clicked. But sometimes you *always* want to edit the entire field value. For instance, you might have a set of records you update monthly with new sales totals, and you're always typing over what's there with new numbers. In cases like this, turn on "Select entire contents on entry". Now, when you click into the field, FileMaker preselects the entire value, and you can simply start typing to replace what's there. You can always click a second time to get an insertion point, or start making a new selection. Figure 7-28 shows this subtle difference in action.

- As you learned on page 25, you can press the Tab key to jump to the next field when in Browse mode or Find mode. The Return key (or the Enter key by your main keyboard) inserts a new line into the field, and the Enter key by the number keypad commits the record and takes you out of any field. But if you prefer, you can configure any or all of these keys to go to the next record instead. Just turn on the appropriate checkbox under "Go to next object using". If you turn a checkbox *off*, then the key goes back to its normal behavior, so if you turn off the "Tab key" checkbox here, then the tab key inserts a tab into the field instead.

- FileMaker Pro 11's Quick Find searches all the fields on a given layout automatically. Uncheck "Include field for Quick Find" if you prefer leave a particular field out.

- Turn on "Do not apply visual spell checking" to turn off the dashed red lines that appear under misspelled words in that field. Many fields hold data that the spell checker doesn't like, like part numbers, email addresses, and launch codes. Since the red underlines are just a distraction in these fields, you can turn them off. You can see the change in Figure 7-28.

- The "Set input method" option deals with text entry in Asian languages. When this option is on, you can control which text "input method" is used for this field. If you need this ability, you know what it means. If not, just ignore this option.

To tidy up your layout, follow these steps:

1. **Click the Creation Timestamp field to select it.**

   The selection handles appear to let you know you're on the right track.

2. **While pressing Shift, click the Modification Timestamp field.**

   Because you pressed Shift, the Creation Timestamp stays selected, and the Modification Timestamp field is selected too.

   In the Inspector, turn off the Browse Mode checkbox (Figure 7-27).

   This prevents folks from accidentally typing in these fields.

3. **Select the Email Address field. Turn on "Select entire contents on entry".**

   An email address is exactly the kind of thing you often copy, but rarely edit.

4. **Turn on "Do not apply visual spell checking".**

   It would be awesome if FileMaker could tell you when you've mistyped an email address, but the spell checker just doesn't cut it. There's no sense spell checking something that's never going to be correct.

5. **Click OK, and then switch to Browse mode.**

   You can now try out your changes. Refer to Figure 7-28 if you're not sure what you're looking for.

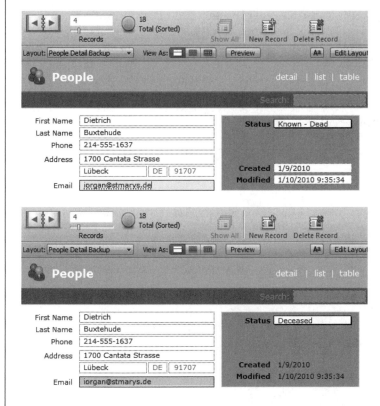

Figure 7-28:
Top: When you click a field, the flashing insertion point appears right where you clicked. In this image, you clicked at the end of the email address. Also notice that FileMaker has underlined the address because it thinks it's misspelled.

Bottom: By changing field behavior the Email Address field now behaves differently. A click selects the whole address, making it a breeze to copy or replace. And the visual spell checker has been turned off for this field, so you're no longer bothered with an underline. You'll also notice the Created and Modified dates no longer appear as editable.

Data Formatting

All this talk about how fields look and work is well and good, but what if you want to change how the *data* inside them looks? A price and a weight both go in a Number field, but they're different types of values and should *look* different. FileMaker provides a series of formatting options for the data inside fields, giving you loads of control over how numbers, dates, times, and pictures look.

FileMaker has special formatting for each kind of data a field can hold: Text, Number, Date, Time, and Container. (Timestamps are just a date and a time together, so you can format both parts separately.) You've already seen where these settings live—the old familiar Inspector's Data tab.

Number Formatting

Select a number field, and turn your attention to the Data Formatting section on the Inspector's Data tab. Click the button with the ".01" on it, as seen in Figure 7-29, to activate the number formatting options. You can use most of these in any combination, so the possibilities are vast.

Note: As with most layout settings, if you modify the formatting *without* selecting a field, then FileMaker lets you edit the *default* formats. In other words, the settings you pick apply to every number field you add to the layout thereafter.

Figure 7-29:
FileMaker has four top-level number format settings: "General", "As entered", "Boolean", and "Decimal". If you choose either of the last two, you get still more choices. If you're looking for the kind of number formatting options you're accustomed to in a spreadsheet program, then turn on "Format as decimal" and go to town.

General

If you don't tell it otherwise, FileMaker assigns the General format to any new number fields you create. Usually, this format means, "Show numbers the same way someone types them." But if your number has too many digits (either a very large number, or a number with lots of decimal places), then FileMaker rounds the number or uses scientific notation to shorten it.

As entered

If you don't want the automatic rounding and scientific notation you get with General Format, then choose leave data formatted "As entered" instead. FileMaker leaves your numbers alone, so they appear exactly as typed.

Boolean

Sometimes you use a number field simply as a Boolean value. For instance, pretend you have a field that flags customers who get holiday cards. You could use a number field for this one, with a *1* in it if you want to send a card, and a *0* if you don't. But someone looking at the layout later could mistake all those 1s and 0s for so much computer gibberish (even if that someone is yourself).

For this reason alone, the Number Format dialog box has a choice called "Format as Boolean". With this setting, a number field shows one of two text values. The first ("Show non-zero as") shows if the number field has any non-zero value. The second ("Show zero as") shows only when the field has a zero in it. In the holiday card example, you may be tempted to turn this option on, and use Send Card and Don't Send Card as the display values. Unfortunately, FileMaker lops off anything past the first *seven* characters for each display value. So you have to stick with short and sweet values, like "Yes" and "No."

Decimal

The most flexible setting is Decimal. When you choose this option, you activate a host of new settings:

- **Turn on "Fixed number of decimals"** if you want to force every number to have the same number of decimal places. Of course, FileMaker also lets you say *how many* decimal places you want. If the number in the field doesn't have a decimal part, FileMaker just fills in zeros after the decimal point. If you only want to see integers, set the number of decimals to zero.

- **Do not display number if zero.** Suppose you have a report with lots of numbers, where many of those numbers are zero. For example, a financial report that shows who owes you money (like the Aging Receivables Report) often has more zeros than anything else. All those zeros can make the report cluttered and hard to read. Turn on the "Do not display number if zero" option to make the zeros go away.

- **Notation** lets you associate a unit description with your number field. Say you're measuring temperatures. Place a degree symbol in the box, and FileMaker will display it with the numbers in your selected field. The drop-down options pertain to where you want your symbol to appear: after the number, before minus sign (if any), or after the minus sign but before the number.

- The **Negative** line gives you control over how numbers below zero are displayed. You can set a color and choose any one of six negative number formats:

  — –1234 puts a negative sign before the number in the usual fashion.

  — 1234– puts the sign on the *end* instead.

  — For that oh-so-financial look, choose (1234) instead. It puts negative numbers in parentheses.

— <1234> is similar, but it uses angle brackets instead of parentheses.

— If you're an accountant, hold onto your hat. The 1234 CR option makes you feel right at home when crediting those accounts.

— The last choice puts a small triangle before negative numbers.

Note: The "Use color" option for negative numbers may seem a little redundant considering you can get exactly the same effect using Conditional Formatting (covered in Chapter 14). Before FileMaker Pro 9, the "Use color" option was the only way to apply a different color to negative numbers. These days, you can use whichever method you prefer.

- **Numbers** use special symbols to separate their parts. For example, you usually see a decimal point between the whole and fractional parts of a number, and a comma after the thousands place. FileMaker uses whatever symbols your operating system dictates for these special purposes, but you're free to override them if you want. For instance, you can use a space instead of a comma between each third digit. In the Decimal box, type the character you want in place of a decimal point. The box accepts only a single character. FileMaker calls the comma between every third digit a "thousands separator" and you can opt to leave them out by turning on "No thousands separator". Turn on "Use thousands separator" if you want them, and feel free to enter something other than a comma in the associated box.

- The **Japanese** sub-section lets you choose among half-width, full-width, traditional kanji, or modern kanji for your numerals. You can also turn on kanji-specific separators.

Currency

Choose the Currency format, and you may think something is broken. None of the options changed! Well, currency and decimal are in fact the same set of options. But you can configure their standard settings independently so you don't loose those oddball decimal settings you so meticulously slaved over every time you need to use currency. See Figure 7-30 for more detail.

Percent

Choose Percent to turn the number into a percent value. FileMaker automatically multiplies the number by 100, and puts a percent sign after it. That way, people can enter .1 for 10 percent. (Entering the number this way makes math with percentages easier, since you can simply multiply. After all, 10 percent of 20 is 2, not 200. You'll learn how to do math in FileMaker in the next chapter.) Your other choices under Percent are drawn from the Decimal option (page 307).

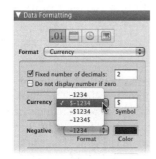

Figure 7-30:
Currency formatting offers four choices for the placement of the currency symbol (a dollar sign in this example). The first option leaves it out entirely. The second and third place it before the number and before or after the negative symbol if present. The final option places the currency symbol immediately after the number.

Date Formatting

The Date formatting works a lot like its number-oriented sister. This time, though, you tell FileMaker how you want *dates* to look. This date could be the value in a date field, or the date part of a timestamp field. For example, the date at the top of a letter may look best spelled out, while the due date on a list of 25 invoices may best be served by an abbreviated numbers-only format. Figure 7-31 shows the Date formatting section on the Inspector (no surprises here: Just click the button with the calendar icon).

Figure 7-31:
The Format pop-up menu gives you eight formats to pick from. If you choose either the second or third, you can choose something other than "/" to go between each number by typing it in the "Numeric separator" box (it's covered by the menu in this picture). You can also add a leading zero or a space to single-digit day and month numbers by picking from the Leading Characters area's pop-up menus.

As entered

When you choose "As entered" from the Format pop-up menu, FileMaker shows the date *almost* the same way you type it. If you type a two-digit year, the program changes it to four digits. Otherwise, it leaves the data alone.

Preset Styles

The next six choices in the Format pop-up menu offer the most common ways dates are formatted, as shown in Figure 7-31.

Custom

For the ultimate in control, choose Custom. When you do, a bevy of menus and boxes appear. By selecting different parts of a date from the pop-up menus and adding your own text as appropriate to the boxes, you tell FileMaker exactly how you want the date formatted. You use this option when none of the "Format as" formats (Figure 7-32) are exactly right. For example, if you're in the U.S., FileMaker suggests date formats that follow typical U.S. standards (month, then day, then year). But if people in England use your database, you may want to construct a custom format in line with their expectations (day, then month, then year).

Figure 7-32:
The Custom date format options consist of a series of text boxes and four Date Value pop-up menus. You can put anything you want in the text boxes, and it appears between portions of the date. Each pop-up menu includes the same set of choices. The first three let you show the day portion of the date. You can show the day-of-month number, or the day-of-week name as an abbreviation or full name. Next, you get the same three ways to display the month. If you're so inclined, you can add a quarter to your date in two ways. Finally, you can pick between a two-digit and a four-digit year. FileMaker strings the text and date values together to produce the final result.

When you tell FileMaker to format a date with the Custom option, it assembles the final date value piece by piece according to your specifications. Whatever you type in the Start Text box comes first, followed by the first date value. FileMaker then adds the text from the top Between Text box. Next comes another date value and more between text. This process continues until the last text box is added to the result. By mixing and matching text and date values, you can make a date look any way you want.

If you don't want to use one of the date values, from the relevant pop-up menu, choose "<none>". Likewise, to skip a between text value, clear its text box. The pop-up menu buttons to the right of each text box give you a choice of common date-related symbols for easy picking. They have a "<none>" option as well, if you want to quickly clear the associated box.

With either the "Format as" or the Custom option, in the Leading Characters area of this window, you can use the pop-up menus to tell FileMaker how to handle single-digit month and day numbers. If you want them left alone, choose "<none>". To insert a leading space, choose Space, and for a leading zero, choose Zero.

Time Formatting

Compared to dates and numbers, formatting time values is a breeze—FileMaker gives you just a few simple choices. Figure 7-33 shows the Inspector's time formatting options (click the clock icon to activate).

Figure 7-33:
To have FileMaker show your time values exactly the way you type them, choose "As entered" from the Format pop-up list. If you want to standardize the display of time values, Select one of the prepared options or "Custom" for complete control.

As entered

This time, "As entered" really means it. The time value shows exactly as you typed it.

Other Formats

All the remaining choices let you narrow down just how much detail is displayed. From the "Format" pop-up menu, choose what time information you want to include:

- **hhmmss** tells FileMaker to show hours, minutes, and seconds.

- **hhmm** says you want hours and minutes, but no seconds. If your time value has seconds, FileMaker just ignores them.

- **mmss** limits the display to just minutes and seconds. If the time value has hours, then the minutes are increased accordingly. For instance, if your field has *1:13:27* and you format it without hours, then you see *73:27*—each hour adds 60 minutes.

- **hh** gives you a field that shows just the hours. Any minutes and seconds are left off.

- **mm** tells FileMaker to show the number of minutes. Again, any hours in the time value are counted as 60 minutes, and any seconds are ignored.

- **ss** shows a time as just a number of seconds. Every minute counts as 60 seconds, and every hour as 60 minutes. They're added up along with the seconds themselves to produce the final number.

Normally time values show a colon between each number. You can change this look if you want by typing something else in the Separator box. To leave out the separator entirely, clear the box. (This method lets you make military-style times, like *0730*.)

When displaying clock time, FileMaker can use 24-hour or 12-hour notation. In other words, do you want to see *14:23* or *2:23 PM*? When you choose "24 hour notation", you can add some arbitrary text before or after the value (23:00UTC, for instance). When using 12-hour notation, you get to decide what text you want to represent a.m. and p.m. by typing in the "before noon" and "after noon" boxes.

You can choose from the pop-up menu to the right of these labels to put them on either side of the time value. Like a date value, you get to tell FileMaker how to handle single-digit numbers. Again, you can leave them a single digit, add a leading space, or add a leading zero.

Timestamp Formatting

Although FileMaker has a timestamp *field* (see page 239), the Inspector doesn't have a timestamp option. Remember that timestamp fields really contain two values: a date and a time. So, you use the Date formatting options (the button with the calendar icon) to control how the date part of a timestamp looks, and the Time formatting options (the button with the clock icon) for the time portion. Like time values, you can also use Number formatting to control decimal places and points in the seconds part.

POWER USERS' CLINIC

International Super-Date

If people all over the world use your database, you quickly discover that date formats can lead to unending confusion. A date like 1/11/07 could mean January 11 or November 1, depending on your persuasion. To avoid all this confusion, consider a date format that strikes a nice balance between efficient display and unambiguous interpretation: 11-Jan-2007.

To get this format, select a date field, head over to the Data Formatting portion of the Inspector's Data tab, and then choose the Custom option. Configure it thusly:

- In the first pop-up menu, choose the number version of the day. (It's the number in the first group of options, right below "<none>".)

- In the top text box immediately to the right, enter a hyphen (–).
- In the second pop-up menu, choose the abbreviated month name.
- In the next text box, enter another hyphen (–).
- In the third pop-up menu, choose the year (you can use either the two- or four-digit version).
- Clear the contents of the two remaining text boxes, and then, in the last pop-up menu, choose "<none>".

Now switch to Browse mode. Your date field should show this svelte-yet-satisfying format.

In order for a timestamp field to show your settings, though, you have to format *both* the date *and* the time parts. If either is set to "Leave data formatted as entered", then the timestamp field just puts its hands over its ears and hums so it can't hear you trying to format it. Once you enter both the date and the time formats, the timestamp field straightens up and follows your formatting instructions.

You *don't* have to set the number format if you don't want to. If you don't choose a number format, FileMaker leaves the decimal part of your time values formatted as people enter them.

Note: Timestamp formats are a little tough to read because the date and time just sort of run together with a scrawny single space separating them. Make a custom date format with " at" (that's *space*-a-t) in the last placeholder, and you get "Fri, May 6, 2005 at 12:30 pm". Much better.

Graphic Formatting

In Chapter 3 you learned how to put pictures, sounds, QuickTime data, and files into container fields. Remember that with pictures and QuickTime data, FileMaker actually shows the content right on the layout. When you design that layout, you have some control over how that content is displayed (see Figure 7-34).

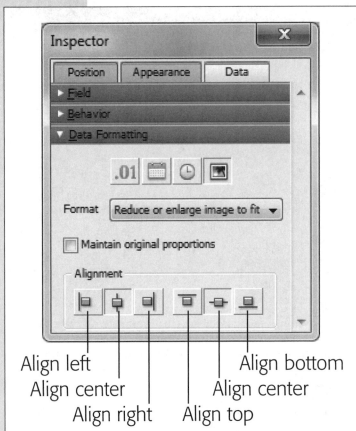

Figure 7-34:
Using the Inspector's formatting options, you can tell FileMaker to shrink and/or enlarge a picture to fit the field boundaries, or to crop it—showing only what fits. You also get to decide where the picture lives inside the field, or what part gets cropped. If you don't mind wildly skewed images, you can also tell File-Maker to stop keeping your pictures properly proportioned.

Align left
Align center
Align right
Align bottom
Align center
Align top

Note: If someone records a sound (Insert→Sound) or puts a file (Insert→File) in your container field, then you have no control over how FileMaker displays it. FileMaker automatically shows the appropriate icon and leaves it at that.

The pictures and movies you put in the field may not always be exactly the same size and dimensions as the field control itself, so FileMaker has to decide how to make things fit. Should it shrink a big picture down so it all shows, or let it get cut off on the edges? For a tiny picture, should FileMaker blow it up to use the available space, even though it may look a little blocky? For that matter, should it stretch and skew the image willy-nilly to force a fit, or leave some of the field empty? FileMaker lets you decide. With the graphic format options (the rightmost button in the Inspector's Data Formatting Section), you can control scale, position, and proportions.

Format

The Format pop-up menu for the container field lets you decide how FileMaker should handle pictures that aren't exactly the right size. Figure 7-35 illustrates a few of the possibilities:

- Choose "Crop to frame" if you want FileMaker to crop large pictures, showing only what fits.

Figure 7-35:
Here's the same image placed in container fields of three different sizes, showing the variety of picture options you have on the Inspector's Data Formatting tab.

Top: From the Format pop-up menu, choose "Crop to frame", with Center horizontal and vertical alignment.

Middle: From the Format pop-up menu, choose "Reduce or enlarge image to fit", with Center horizontal and vertical alignment.

Bottom: From the Format pop-up menu, choose "Reduce or enlarge image to fit", Center horizontal and vertical alignment. With "Maintain original proportions" turned on, FileMaker won't distort the picture even if it doesn't perfectly fit the container field.

- Choose "Reduce image to fit" if you want FileMaker to shrink large pictures to fit, but leave small pictures alone. This setting is what you automatically get if you don't change it yourself.

- Choose "Enlarge image to fit" to make small pictures grow so they fit the field but are as big as possible. (The more FileMaker has to enlarge the image, the blockier it looks.) Large pictures get cropped.

- Choose "Reduce or Enlarge image to fit" if you want FileMaker to shrink big pictures and grow small ones. This setting ensures that every picture in the field (on each record) is about the same size.

Tip: When FileMaker reduces or enlarges a picture, it keeps the picture's aspect ratio the same. In other words, a picture that's four inches by six inches may not be that *size* in the container field, but its height *is* two-thirds of its width. If you'd rather FileMaker make the picture *exactly* the size of the container field, even if it means distorting it, then turn off "Maintain original proportions".

Alignment

If the picture is small and hasn't been enlarged, the alignment buttons control *where* in the field the picture appears. For example, select the third button from the left (right-align) and the fourth (top-align) to nestle the picture in the field's top-right corner.

If a picture has been reduced or enlarged so that it fills the field, it might still be smaller than the field in one dimension. In this case, the alignment pop-up menus tell FileMaker where to put the picture along this dimension.

Finally, for large images that have been cropped, alignment controls which portion of the larger image you see. If you align to the top and left, for instance, you see as much of the top-left corner of the image as possible. You can see the same cropped picture with each possible alignment in Figure 7-36.

Align Left

Align Center

Align Right

Figure 7-36:
This window has three container fields, all containing an image that's too big to fit. Each field is set to crop, but with different alignments. On the top, the image is set to align Left. The center image is set to align Center. Finally, the bottom image is set to align Right. As you can see, FileMaker cuts off each image, but the alignment setting determines which portion of the image is visible.

Buttons

The Contact Management database template described in the box on page 104 has a pretty slick system for switching between list and detail layouts. Instead of fiddling with the tiny Layout pop-up menu, you can just click tab graphics right on the screen. Each click magically transports you to a different layout.

You can easily duplicate this magic in your own databases. Just use FileMaker's Button tool, shown in Figure 7-37. But don't let the tool's name and appearance mislead you. You're not limited to the rectangular beveled buttons this tool creates. In fact, you can turn nearly *any* object on a layout—an imported graphic or even a field—into a button. When folks click the mouse button while pointing to such an object, FileMaker highlights it so they know they're about to perform some kind of action. When they let go, something happens. You get to decide what that *something* is.

Figure 7-37:
When you're in Layout mode, you find the Button tool in the Status toolbar, right about... there. It looks like a little button being poked in the face by its big brother, or being clicked, or something.

Creating Buttons with the Button Tool

You want to add buttons to the header of your People database to switch between the Detail and List layouts. You do this in Layout mode, so open the People database, switch to the People Detail layout, and then hop over to Layout mode.

To add a button, first click the Button tool, and then *draw* the button on the layout as though you were drawing a rectangle. Figure 7-38 shows you where you may want to put it.

When you release the mouse button, FileMaker immediately pops up the Button Setup dialog box (see Figure 7-39).

You want this button to switch to a different layout whenever someone clicks it, so in the action list, find "Go to Layout", and then select it (it's right under the boldface Navigation item). When you do, the Options area shows you a pop-up menu labeled Specify. You can pick any layout in your database from this menu. For this button, choose People List.

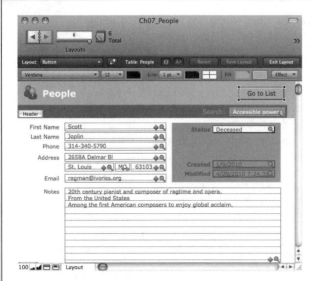

Figure 7-38:
You can put your button anywhere you want, and make it any size you want. But if it's going to look like a button with the "Go to List" label, it should be close to the size of the button shown in this window. Also, don't forget to set the button's autoresize anchors appropriately. If you put it here, then anchor it on the top and right.

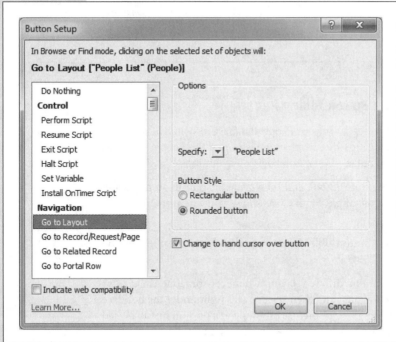

Figure 7-39:
The Button Setup dialog box shows up whenever you create a new button. You get to pick one action from the Button Action list. Most actions require a little configuration. When you pick one, its options appear in the Options area. You can come back to this box, and make changes to an existing button: Just double-click the button in Layout mode (or choose Format→Button) to open it.

If you're picky about such things, you can even control whether your button has square corners or slightly rounded corners. Four out of five dentists prefer the "Rounded button" button look for its elegance and class. (If you don't make a choice, then you get square.)

Something else changes when you select a button command: The "Change to a hand cursor over button" checkbox appears below the Button Style area. By turning this option on, you tell FileMaker to use a special pointing-finger cursor whenever someone mouses over the button. (The icon is similar to the one you usually see when you point to a link in a web browser—the universal cue that an area is clickable.)

When you're done making choices, click OK. You can now switch to Browse mode, and then give your button a try.

Note: Buttons work in Browse mode and Find mode, but not in Preview mode.

While you're in a button sort of mood, add a Detail button to the top of the People List layout. This one uses the "Go to Layout" action to bounce you back to the People Detail layout.

Turning an Existing Layout Object into a Button

Buttons are handy, but they can be redundant. Often, there's already something on your layout—like a picture or even a field—that would make a perfectly good button. For example, if you've got your company's logo in the layout's top-right corner, then you can make it link to your website's main page. A separate button reading "Go to Home Page" would be unnecessary clutter. (Incidentally, in this case you use the Open URL button action.)

Here's another common example: When you're on the List layout, it would be handy to go back to the Detail layout for a specific person. It turns out if you put a button right on the Body part of a List layout, that's exactly what happens. FileMaker notices which record you click before switching layouts. But rather than add a button to the already full Body part on the List layout, why not turn the person's name into a clickable link? When you click the name, FileMaker shows you details on that person.

Here's how:

1. **If necessary, switch to Layout mode, and to the List layout. Then, select the text object that holds the First Name and Last Name merge fields.**

   This is the object you want to turn into a button. You have to select it before you can work on it.

2. **Choose Format→Button Setup.**

   The Button Setup dialog box makes its return. This time, though, you're not making a *new* button. Instead, you're turning the selected object *into* a button.

3. **Choose the "Go to Layout" button action. When the Options area shows the Specify pop-up menu, choose People Detail.**

   This action tells the button *which* layout it should go to.

4. **Click OK.**

   The window disappears and you're back on your layout. You don't see a change because you can't normally *see* if an object has been turned into a button. If you try the button now, it works fine, but it doesn't do people much good if they don't know it's there. To make it obvious that the name links to the Detail layout, why not make it *look* like a link?

Note: When you're in Layout mode, you can choose View→Show→Buttons. When this option is turned on, FileMaker outlines every button with a thick dotted line (it shows up only in Layout mode). Choose the same command again to turn it off.

---

5. **Using any of FileMaker's text formatting tools (see the box on page 111), turn the text blue and give it an underline.**

   Now your List layout looks like the one in Figure 7-40, and it works beautifully. If you select more than one layout object before you choose the Format→Button command, then FileMaker automatically groups the objects and turns the entire group into a single button. These objects now act like any other grouped objects: Anything you do to one in Layout mode happens to all of them. If you later *ungroup* a grouped button, then FileMaker warns you, and removes the button behavior as well.

Note: If you want four *different* buttons that do the same thing (so you can work with them individually), then you have to buttonize them one at a time.

Making a Button Not a Button

If you have a layout object that's already a button, and you don't want it to be a button anymore, you need a way to *turn off* its button-ness. It's easy but not very intuitive: Select the button, and then choose Format→Button Setup (or double-click the button). In the Button Action list (Figure 7-39), choose the first item, Do Nothing, and then click OK. Now the object isn't a button anymore.

Tip: Here's a faster way, even though it's cheating. Just click a button, and then choose the Arrange→Ungroup command (or better yet, press Ctrl+Shift+R or Shift-⌘-R). Even if the button *isn't* part of a group, File-Maker pops open a message box asking if you want to remove the buttons. Just click OK, and your object is no longer a button.

People

Sort | First | Last | City | State | Status   Search:

detail | list | table

212-555-1525 / prestino@maggiore.it
1594 Via Belle Madrigale, El Toro, IT 20202

Mike Doughty   Active   Details
212-666-133 /@doughty.com
67 Kauffman Ln., New York, NY 10234

John Dunstable   Details
0118-999-88199-9119-725-3 / dunstable@isorhythmic.co.uk
1390 Motet Manor, Dunstable, Bedfordshire, BR SW9

Ella Fitzgerald   Details
310-555-3210 / elle@firstlady.com
1 Songbook St., Beverly Hills, CA 90211

Robert Johnson   Details
906-555-1212 / bluesman@delta.net
The Crossroads, Greenwood, MS 45687

Robert Johnson   Details
906-555-1212 / bluesman@delta.net
The Crossroads, Greenwood, MS 45687

Scott Joplin   Details
314-340-5790 / ragman@ivories.org
2658A Delmar Bl, St. Louis, MO 63103

Barry Manilow   Details
212-555-8888 / barry@manilow.com
50 E. 60th St., New York, NY 10020

Figure 7-40:
Your List layout (in Browse mode) should look something like this window. When you point to a name, your mouse arrow changes to the little hand icon, and when you click, the name highlights. After the button is released, you see the Detail layout for the correct person.

You can even remove the button action from the "real" buttons you create with the button tool. That's because, in reality, the button tool just creates a specially formatted text object, and automatically turns it into a button. If you switch it to Do Nothing, you're just left with a fancy text object. (You may want to deactivate a button when you're troubleshooting your database—or for a little April Fool's Day fun.)

Button Actions

The Button Setup window has dozens of available actions, as you can see at the left side in Figure 7-39. Back on page 317, you created buttons for the "Go to Layout" action, but you have many more. As you scan through these commands, you probably notice that many of them repeat the same functions you find in FileMaker's menus. Indeed, you may have already noticed that the list of actions is all but identical to the list of script steps available when editing a script. That's not just meaningless redundancy. By giving your databases buttons for lots of everyday commands, you can make FileMaker even easier to use than it already is. Design some icons (perhaps in your corporate colors), attach buttons to them, and you may find you hardly have to train your colleagues at all, because the buttons and their labels help explain what they need to do to use the database. To learn more about each button action, flip to Chapter 10—it's about scripting and the button actions are referred to as script steps. Regardless of whether you're setting up a button or writing a script, they behave just the same way.

POWER USERS' CLINIC

Making a Button Appear Grayed Out

Lots of programs on your computer include buttons you can't always click. FileMaker itself, for instance, doesn't let you click Delete in the Manage Database window's Fields tab if you don't have a field selected. The universally accepted look for a button that isn't quite ready to be clicked is a grayed-out label.

Accomplishing this feat is a breeze in FileMaker. Suppose you have a button that sends an email to the address in the Email Address field, logically labeled Send Email. But the label should be grayed out if there's no address in the field. How can you adjust the format of the button depending on what's in the field? FileMaker's conditional formatting (page 618) comes to the rescue again.

Since a button doesn't have a value of its own, you have to use the "Formula is" condition type, which you'll learn more about in Chapter 14. Here's a sneak peek to whet your appetite: Select the button, and then choose Format→Conditional Formatting. Click Add to add a new condition.

In the box next to the "Formula is" pop-up menu, type the following exactly as shown:

```
People::Email Address = ""
```

In this formula, People is the table, and Email Address is the field. In English, this formula says: *The Email Address field is equal to ""*. In other words, it's empty.

When this condition is true, use the settings in the Conditional Formatting dialog box to tell FileMaker to turn the button text gray. You can also lighten the background color of the button itself if you want. However you decide to make it look, you now have a button that automatically gives someone a visual clue when it doesn't apply.

Bear in mind that this technique only changes the button's *appearance*. Just because you grayed the text doesn't mean you'll get a different response when you click. For that, you'll have to attach your button to a script. See Chapter 10 for the skinny on scripting.

Tab Order

When you press Tab while editing a field, FileMaker automatically jumps you to the next field. But what does *next* mean? Normally, FileMaker moves through fields in a left-to-right, then top-to-bottom direction. That works well in many cases, but sometimes it falls short. For instance, on your People Detail layout, when you tab from the First Name field, it doesn't go to the Last Name field next. Instead, it goes to the Status field (a pop-up menu, so you can't type into it even if you want to), which is probably not what you want. And what if you want to be able to tab to a button? Or press return to go to the next field instead? You're going to have to customize the *tab order* yourself. In other words, you tell FileMaker exactly what order it should tab through the fields and other objects on a layout.

Customizing the Tab Order

FileMaker lets you completely customize the tab order for any layout. To fix the tab order on the Detail layout of your People database, first choose Layouts→Set Tab Order. A few things happen onscreen: You see the arrows indicating tab order, and the Set Tab Order dialog box appears (Figure 7-41). You tell FileMaker what order to use by putting appropriate numbers into the tab order arrows. Put a *1* in the arrow that points to the button or field that should get your attention when you first press Tab. Put a *2* in the next object in line, and so forth.

Figure 7-41:
When you choose Layouts→Set Tab Order, the Set Tab Order window appears. Meanwhile, FileMaker also adds arrows to the layout while this dialog box is open. From here, you can make bulk adjustments to the tab order, clear it, and start over, or manipulate the numbers one by one to get exactly the order you want.

Chances are, all the arrows that point to fields already have numbers in them reflecting FileMaker's automatic tab order. Clearing and typing into each arrow can thus be a form of digital torture. To ease the pain, FileMaker offers up the Set Tab Order window, which appears at the screen's bottom-right corner. This window lets you make a few targeted bulk changes to the tab order.

First of all, you can clear the numbers from every arrow by clicking Clear All. This trick is great because once all the arrows are empty, then you no longer have to type. Just click each arrow (or the field it points to) in succession, and FileMaker enters the numbers for you.

If you click Add, and then choose from the "Add remaining" pop-up menu, you can add unnumbered fields to the order. FileMaker numbers them for you using the same right-to-left, top-to-bottom philosophy that the automatic tab order uses. This option comes in handy if, for example, you want to set up a specific tab order for a few fields first, and then use the automatic ordering for all fields thereafter.

When you're done making changes, either in the window or by editing the arrows directly, click OK. If you decide you've caused more harm than good in this tab order editing session, then click Cancel instead, and the tab order reverts back to the way it was before you opened the Set Tab Order box.

Fixing the Tab Order in the People Database

On the People database, on the Detail layout, you want to fix the tab order so that Last Name comes after First Name. You can approach this task in several ways, but the following steps show you a trick that makes it easier. You may be tempted to Clear All, and then renumber all the arrows yourself. But since you're *removing* only a field from the tab order (the Status field) you can save yourself the trouble. Here's how:

1. **Choose Layouts→Set Tab Order.**

   The Set Tab Order window and its flock of arrows appear.

2. **Click the arrow pointing to the Status field, and then delete the number.**

   The arrow pointing to Status is now empty. Your order also now goes straight from 1 to 3, skipping right over 2. Pay no attention to this problem (that's the trick).

3. **Click OK in the Set Tab Order window.**

   If you switch to Browse mode and try out your tab order, then you see that you can now tab right from First Name to Last Name.

This trick works because FileMaker establishes the tab order by following the numbers in the arrows in order. It doesn't give a hoot whether those numbers are contiguous. You've fixed your layout with a minimum of clicks.

The same basic trick applies if you need to *insert* a field into the tab order too. For instance, if you add a new field that should go between 2 and 3 in the tab order, just give it the number 3 spot. When you do, FileMaker automatically bumps number 3 up to 4 (and so on) for you.

GEM IN THE ROUGH

Buttons and Tab Order

Since buttons are an important part of how people interact with your database, FileMaker makes the buttons as convenient as possible. It even lets folks operate them from the keyboard. When you set the tab order for your layout (Format→Set Tab Order), you can put buttons in the mix. If a button is in the tab order, you can tab to it in Browse mode (it gets a thick black outline), and then press the space bar to "click" the button.

While you're at it, you can put Tab Controls in the tab order too. Once again, the space bar switches tabs.

If you include important buttons and tabs in the tab order, then people can breeze through complex data entry tasks without separating hand and keys. They'll thank you.

Preserving the Automatic Order

As long as you never choose the Set Tab Order command on a particular layout, FileMaker automatically manages the tab order for you. For example, if you add a Middle Name field to the layout, and place it between the First Name and Last Name fields, it automatically goes into the right spot in the tab order—between First Name and Last Name. If you switch the positions of the First Name and Last Name fields, Last Name becomes the first field in the tab order, and First Name comes next.

Once you click the Set Tab Order window's OK button, though, FileMaker hands full responsibility thereafter over to you. If you add a new field to the layout, then it just gets stuck to the *end* of the tab order, no matter where you put that field on the layout. If you move fields around so that the tab order makes absolutely no sense, FileMaker doesn't care. It keeps the tab order exactly as you specified in Set Tab Order.

Merge Fields

Knowing what you know now, if you set out to build a layout yourself, you'd probably jump right for the Field tool and start dragging fields onto the layout. But look closely at Figure 7-42 first. When you put a field on a layout, you're putting it *exactly* where you want it. No matter what record you're on when you look at the layout, that field value is in the same spot. Usually, that's where you want it to be, but sometimes—like in a new List Layout—you want something a little more flexible. You want the Last Name field to start where the first name ends. Since some first names are longer than others, this spot changes from record to record.

In FileMaker, you solve this problem using *merge fields*. Merge fields work a lot like a mail merge in a word processing program. You create an ordinary text object on your layout (not a field object), and then tell FileMaker to merge different field values into the text. For example, to put the first and last names together on your new layout, you create a text object like this:

```
<<First Name>> <<Last Name>>
```

Merge fields always show up in Layout mode with angle brackets around their names, just like <<this>>. When you look at this text object in Browse mode, though, you see the value of the First Name field, then a space, and then the value of the Last Name field. Since all these values show up in a single text object, FileMaker sorts out the exact positions for you.

Note: Although you can *type* the merge field into a text object exactly as it is shown above, this method can be error-prone. If your field data isn't showing in Browse mode (and you see <<Field Name>> instead), you probably misspelled the field name. Even a stray space or missing punctuation is more than FileMaker's willing to ignore. You'll usually find it's easiest to let FileMaker type the name for you by using the Insert→Merge Field command. That's the process you'll use here.

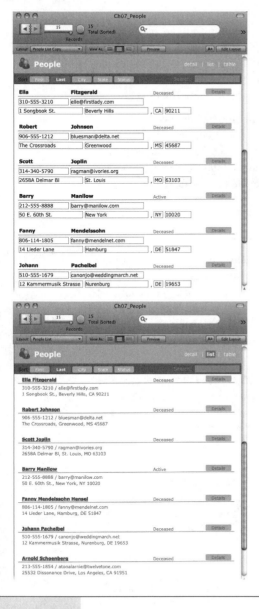

Figure 7-42:
Top: This layout uses normal fields, which are always in the same place on the layout, no matter what record you're on. Notice how the spacing between the contents of each field, particularly the First Name and Last Name fields, looks odd because it's inflexible.

Bottom: By using merge fields, you can create a more professional-looking result. Plus, it can be a lot more efficient. Since you don't have much dead space between your merge fields, you can often get more information in about the same amount of space.

Merge fields have a downside, though: They're only for display and generally best suited to layouts you intend to print rather than work with onscreen. You need a real field if you want people to be able to get in there and change its contents. Your database already has a layout with real fields just for editing data (the detail layout), so in this case, merge fields are just what the doctor ordered.

Putting merge fields into a text object is easy:

1. **In the Status toolbar, click the Text tool.**

   FileMaker activates the Text tool; it changes your mouse arrow to an I-beam, and darkens the Text tool button.

2. **Click somewhere in the Body part.**

   A new editable text box appears, ready for you to type.

3. **Choose Insert→Merge Field.**

   The Specify Field dialog box appears, listing every field in your database.

4. **Select the First Name field, and then click OK.**

   FileMaker inserts <<*First Name*>> into the text object for you.

5. **Type a single space.**

   Since you don't want the first and last name *right* next to each other, you've just added a space.

6. **Choose Insert→Merge Field again. When the Specify Field dialog box returns, select the Last Name field, and then click OK.**

   FileMaker adds the Last Name merge field to the text object.

You now have a text object that shows the first and last names with a single space between them (you can switch to Browse mode, and then try it out if you want). You just need to put it into place.

Next, you need to add a line for the phone number and email address. Using the same steps as before, add a second text object below the first, with these merge fields:

```
<<Phone Number>> <<Email Address>>
```

Finally, the address information should also be in a merge field (study Figure 7-43 to see why—they all flow together in a nicely formatted line). Repeat the steps above to build a text object like this:

```
<<Street Address>, <<City>>, <<State>> <<Zip Code>>
```

Note: You can mix and match merge fields and normal text to your heart's content. When you were setting up the first and last name, you added a space between the merge fields. This time you add even more. After the street address and city merge fields, type a comma, and then a space.

If necessary, move the new text objects so they're aligned and spaced properly, using Figure 7-43 as a guide.

Merge Variables

Merge fields are dandy, but FileMaker Pro 11 introduces a new flavor of layout text: the *Merge Variable*. A variable is like a temporary field you can create with the *Set Variable* script step. You can choose from two kinds of variable, but if you want to use yours on a layout it's got to be a Global variable (for details on the different kinds of variables, see Chapter 16). Global variables, by definition, have two dollar signs at the start of their names, *$$dayOfWeek* for example. Let's run through the steps below to create a variable and place it on a layout:

1. **Go to Scripts→Manage Scripts.**

   The Manage Scripts dialog box opens.

2. **Click New to create a new script, and name it *Set Merge Variable*. From the list of script steps on the left, double-click Set Variable.**

   FileMaker adds this step to your script and automatically selects it.

3. **Near the bottom right side of the window, click Specify.**

   The Set Variable window appears.

4. **In the Name field, type *$$dayOfWeek*. In the Value field enter the following formula:**

   ```
   DayName ( Get ( CurrentDate ) )
   ```

5. **Close the script window, being sure to save it when asked, and then close Manage Scripts.**

   You're back on your layout.

6. **Select the Text tool, and then click a blank spot to create a text box. Choose Insert→Merge Variable**

   FileMaker inserts "<<$$>>" and places your cursor just after the dollar signs.

7. **Carefully type *dayOfWeek* just as you entered it when setting the variable back in the script definition.**

   Spelling counts here.

8. **Switch to Browse mode.**

   Do you see the day of the week? Well not quite. You should see <<$$dayOf-Week>> where you placed your variable.

9. **Choose Scripts→Set Merge Variable to run the script and set the variable.**

Note: Empty variables are dead to FileMaker. When a merge variable without any value set is placed on a layout, FileMaker assumes the variable name you entered doesn't exist and helpfully shows you the merge code as a reminder. But you may have legitamate reasons for using a layout variable that is sometimes blank. Simply use a space character when you need a merge variable to appear blank—it suppresses the merge code without displaying any visible characters to the user.

Tooltips

Training people, either when you first launch a new database, or when new employees come into your workforce, is a big part of making your database successful. You can have beautiful layouts, bulletproof privilege sets, and complex, well-thought-out scripts, but if folks don't know how and when to use them, then they miss out on the benefits. To spare you the wrath of confused (or worse, frustrated) people, FileMaker Pro Advanced has a feature called *tooltips*. Like the onscreen labels that pop up in Windows and many other programs, tooltips can help guide people through the features you've created for them, and maybe even cut down on training time.

You can attach tooltips to any object, or group of objects, that you can select on a layout: fields, text, or graphics. To create a tooltip, go to Layout mode, and then choose the object you want tipped. If the Inspector isn't open, choose View→Inspector. Click the Inspector's Appearance tab, and then look for the Tooltip field. Enter the text for your tooltip here, and then switch to Browse mode, saving changes to your layout if prompted. Now people see the tooltip when the mouse hovers over the object in Browse mode. Just like tooltips in other programs, the tooltip doesn't appear immediately, so as not to inconvenience more advanced users. You can see a tooltip in action in Figure 7-43.

Just to the right of the Inspector's tooltip field is a small button with a pencil icon. Click this button, and you get all the power of calculations. The result of the calculation becomes the text of the tooltip. (If the calculation has an empty result, then FileMaker doesn't show the tooltip, so you can use the If function to make the tooltip show up only when it's relevant.)

Autoresizing

Now is a good time to step back from layout design, and scrutinize your work in Browse mode. Your layouts might not be much *prettier* than they were before, but they're neater. Things are aligned, grouped, and sized in a pleasing way. Your fields are more helpful to the data entry process than ever before.

But what about space efficiency? What happens if you make your database window bigger or smaller? Well, there's no need to guess. Have a peek at Figure 7-44 to see the not-so-great news.

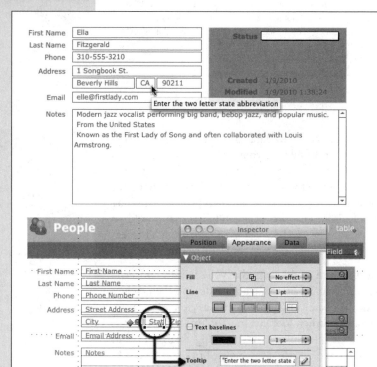

Figure 7-43:
Top: With a tooltip in place, some-one needs only to point at the State field and wait a moment to get a little help. The tooltip shows just below the mouse arrow.

Bottom: In Layout mode, you can choose View→Show→Tooltips to see which elements have a tooltip assigned. In this example, both the Notes field and the State field (circled) have a little "T" icon, indicating a tooltip has been assigned. Follow the arrow to the Tooltip portion of the Inspector where the content of your tooltip is specified.

Obviously the behavior you see right now isn't what you want. It isn't that FileMaker's dumb, though; it just needs a little guidance from you. Every object on the layout has a hidden set of *anchors*. These anchors connect the object to one or more sides of the window, so when you move and resize the window, the objects know how to move. Out of the box, FileMaker anchors each object to the top and left, meaning if you move the bottom or right edges (by making the window bigger), then nothing happens.

But you have complete control over these anchors. The Inspector holds the key—this time under its Position tab. The Autosizing section includes four checkboxes (complete with cute little anchor icons). Turn on a box, and the selected object or objects gets anchored to the associated side, as shown in Figure 7-45.

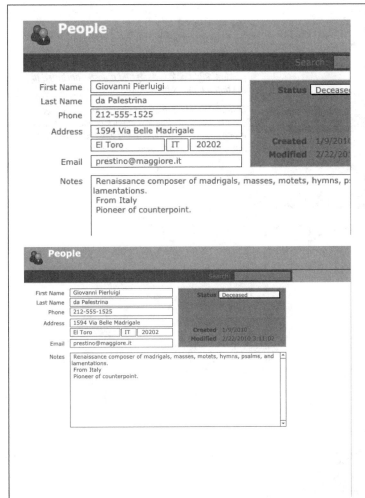

Figure 7-44:
Top: When you resize the database window, FileMaker seems to make the worst choices possible. A smaller window leaves things out—like parts of the Notes, Status, Created, and Modified fields.

Bottom: A bigger window, on the other hand, is just a waste of space. You don't get any extra room where it counts (in the fields) so your window just takes up extra space for no good reason.

You have a lot of ways you can anchor an object, and each combination is useful in one situation or another. You can even anchor an object on competing sides (both top and bottom, or both left and right, or even all four). When you do this, the object doesn't just *move* as the window gets bigger—it *grows* too, as Figure 7-46 shows.

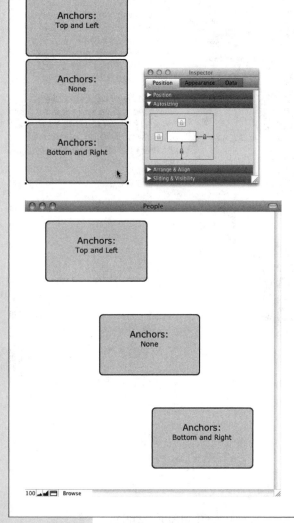

Figure 7-45:
Top: The Object Info palette (shown floating in the Top: The Autosizing control has four padlock buttons that can anchor the selected object to any side of the window. Right now the selected object is anchored to the bottom and right.

Bottom: In fact, each object's anchors are configured slightly differently (the text in each box tells you how it's anchored). As the window is enlarged, the objects move with it depending on how they're anchored.

Getting the desired results as you resize a window takes a little getting used to. The easiest approach is a four-step process:

1. **Figure out which objects should grow.**

   For instance, would it make sense for the First Name field on your layout to get *taller*? Probably not. If you let something get taller, the best candidate is probably the Notes field, since you expect it to hold a lot of text. Likewise, the Status and Timestamp fields don't benefit from extra width, so you don't want to let them grow wider. But the remaining fields could all be bigger, space permitting.

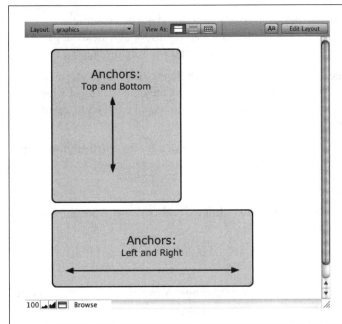

Figure 7-46:
When an object is anchored on the left and right, it stretches side to side as the window grows. Likewise, an object that's anchored top and bottom gets taller. Of course, you can anchor an object on all four sides if you want. Then it grows in both directions as the window gets bigger.

2. **Resolve conflicts among expanding objects.**

   You can have some objects stay left, some move right, and some grow. But File-Maker doesn't let any two objects grow wider in the same horizontal space, because they'll bump into each other. For instance, the City, State, and Zip Code fields all occupy the same horizontal space. So you need to decide which one should get the extra width. The obvious choice is the City field, since State and Zip Code always hold short values.

Warning: If you have a series of side-by-side fields, then you might want them all to get a little wider together. But FileMaker doesn't give you that power, so you have to be choosy. In the worst case, you can make your layout big enough to accommodate any reasonable data, and skip resizing windows altogether.

---

3. **Apply the anchors.**

   This process is tedious, but you can use the rubber band technique (page 334) to grab collections of objects, and then set them all at once.

4. **Test.**

   If you're like most of us humans, you'll miss something the first time through. So switch to Browse mode periodically, and try resizing the window. You'll instantly spot the objects that are misbehaving, and return to Layout mode to fix them.

The best anchoring approach for your layout may be as follows:

- Anchor the First Name, Last Name, Phone Number, Street Address, City, and Email Address fields on the top, left, and right. This way, the fields stay near the top of the window, and grow wider as you make the window bigger.

- Anchor the State, Zip Code, Status, and Timestamp fields on the top and right, but not the left, so they slide out of the way as the other fields get wider. You also need to anchor the Status, Created, and Modified text labels to the right for the same reason.

- The Notes field will be anchored on all four sides. It's the one field that holds a lot of information, so it benefits the most from the extra space.

Here's how to make it happen:

1. **Select the First Name, Last Name, Phone Number, Street Address, City, and Email Address fields.**

   It's probably easiest to press Shift, and then click the fields one by one. The fields should all have selection handles.

2. **If the Inspector isn't showing already, choose View→Inspector, and then select the Position tab.**

3. **In the Autoresize section, turn on the right anchor checkbox.**

   The top and left anchors are already on (if they aren't for some reason, then turn them on so that the top, left, and right anchors are all on).

4. **Using the rubber-band technique, drag a box around the Status field, the timestamps, and their three labels. Figure 7-47 shows how to do this.**

   Now the collection of fields and labels on the right side of the layout are all selected.

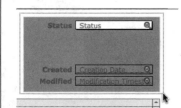

Figure 7-47:
To select several objects that are close together, you can rubber-band them. Just click above and to the left of the objects, and then drag down and right until they're all surrounded by the dotted line. When you release the mouse button, everything in the box is selected.

5. **In the Autosize controls, turn off the left anchor, and turn on the right anchor.**

   Once again, the top anchor should already be turned on, so make sure you have just the top and right anchors in play.

6. **Select the State and Zip Code fields, and then anchor them to the top and right.**

7. **Select the Notes field, and then turn on its bottom and right anchors.**

   This object should now be anchored on all four sides.

   That should do it. If you try your layout in Browse mode now, it should use space wisely when you make the window bigger. You can see for yourself in Figure 7-48.

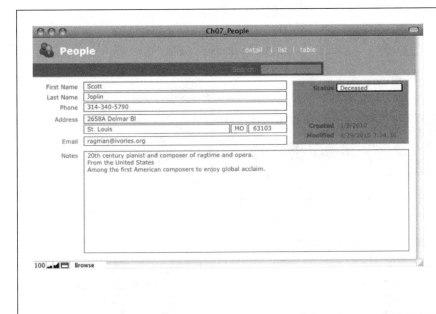

Figure 7-48:
Now when you make the window bigger, the notes and address fields (State and Zip excepting) get bigger too. If any of the expanding fields starts to overlap another object on the layout, go back into Layout mode and make sure that all the objects to the right of the expanding field are anchored to the right but not the left. Similarly, anything below a vertically expanding layout object must be anchored at the bottom but not the top.

If you make the window *smaller* now, though, then you see that the fields don't shrink beyond a certain point. FileMaker never lets the objects in Browse mode get smaller than they are in Layout mode. This fact lets you establish a minimum size for your layout to keep things from getting too small, but it limits your flexibility. In general, design your layouts to be as small as they reasonably can be. That way, people who use your database can decide how big things should be by adjusting the window size. You could probably make your People Detail layout a little more flexible by shrinking the stretchy fields down a little, like the picture in Figure 7-49.

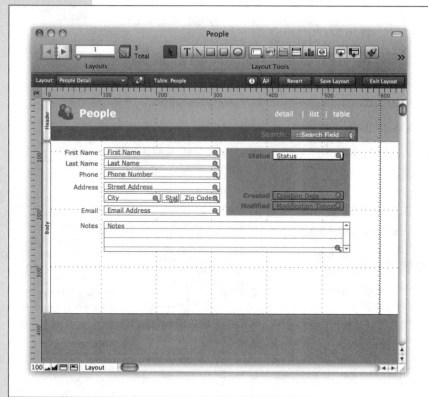

Figure 7-49:
This version of the layout looks essentially the same in Browse mode, with one subtle difference: People can make the window smaller if they want. If you make the window big, though, you get the same roomy fields you had before.

Autoresizing in List Layouts

Every good layout expects that people using the database are going to resize the window and plans accordingly, using anchors to make sure onscreen objects behave properly as the window contorts (page 330). But in List view, anchors work a little differently. In order to maximize the amount of data that can be seen in one shot, FileMaker never stretches records taller in List view. Instead, if the window gets taller, you see more records. So top and bottom anchors have no effect in List view. But left and right anchors still work as you'd expect.

To get your List layout into shape, set the anchors as follows:

- Anchor the horizontal line on the left and right so it stretches the full width of the window.

- Anchor the three text object with merge fields on the left and right. This way, if the window gets wider, then you can see more of the address, for instance.

- Anchor the Status field on the right, but not the left. This field slides to the right as the text object gets bigger so they don't bump into each other.

If you try things out in Browse mode now, as you make the window wider, the line should always span the full width, and the Status field should stay close to the right edge.

Creating Layouts for Printing

By now you've probably knocked out a few good layouts. Layouts like these meet many typical database needs: You've got your Detail layout for finding and viewing individual records, and your List layout for rapidly scanning many records at once. You also want to do *reporting*, an equally important task in a typical database. A report's no different from any other layout as far as FileMaker is concerned. But Report layouts are designed from the ground up to be *printed*. Almost no database gets by without some kind of a Report layout, and most important databases have several, from straightforward lists to powerful snapshots of your data's important statistics, like sales by region or inventory by product category.

Note: If you craft an elegant Report layout, and then discover it's only printing *one* of your records (or none of them) instead of the entire found set, you probably need to make a change in the Print dialog box. Choose File→Print, and then turn on the option called "Records being browsed". This action tells FileMaker to print all the found records. This option can be hard to find on some versions of Mac OS X. From the unnamed pop-up menu that controls which options are showing, you need to choose "File-Maker Pro".

The People database needs a reporting layout, too. In this chapter you'll create a Report layout for a simple purpose: printing a list of people. You can print a report, and then file it as a hard copy backup, take it with you on a trip, or mail it to an associate. But FileMaker's reporting powers go far beyond simple lists. Chapter 14 introduces FileMaker's powerful data summarization and reporting capabilities.

Visualize the Result in Preview Mode

First, you need a rough idea of how your layout should look. This step is especially important when you create a report, since the physical constraints of a piece of paper dictate the working space you have. When you create a Detail layout, you're free to make it large or small, tall or short, narrow or wide—whatever meets the needs of your data, and your computer's monitor. You have to live with some common restraints if you want to print your layout.

In the spirit of visualization, how about a picture? From the Preview illustration in Figure 7-50, you can get a pretty good idea of how this layout is going to come together. It has a header, a body, and a footer. The header includes a title, the date, and some column labels, and the footer has just a page number (these parts print on the top and bottom of each page). The body is the most important part: It has all the fields that show your information.

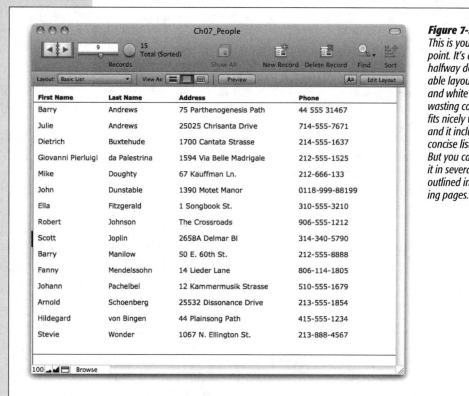

Figure 7-50:
This is your starting point. It's already a halfway decent printable layout. It's black and white to avoid wasting color ink, it fits nicely width-wise, and it includes a concise list of records. But you can improve it in several ways, as outlined in the following pages.

Note: To see your layout in Preview mode, click the Preview button in the Layout bar, or choose View→Preview Mode.

Print Margins

Margin configuration is the first problem you need to solve. Usually when you print from FileMaker, the page margins are set to the minimum size your printer allows. This arrangement provides the most usable space possible, but at a cost: The margins—and the printable area—change as you switch printers. For a report that may be printed on a variety of printers, all of which could have different margins, you don't want to deal with that kind of inconsistency.

Luckily, you can override this behavior, and set explicit margins. First, you need to make sure FileMaker is using units that make sense for page margins. Follow these steps to set the units and the margins:

1. **Choose Layouts→Set Rulers.**

   The Set Rulers window appears.

2. **From the Units pop-up menu, choose either Centimeters or Inches according to your preference, and then click OK.**

   You're back on your layout, where you've just told FileMaker your preferred unit of measurement.

3. **Choose Layouts→Layout Setup, and then click the Printing tab.**

   The printing options associated with this layout appear, as shown in Figure 7-51.

4. **Turn on the "Use fixed page margins" checkbox.**

   The Top, Bottom, Left, and Right text boxes start out grayed out. As soon as you turn on this checkbox, you can type into them.

Note: The numbers you see in these boxes (before you type anything into them, that is) are the margins associated with the printer you're hooked up to. That's why they probably look different from what you see in Figure 7-51.

---

5. **In each of the Top, Bottom, Left, and Right text boxes, type *1*.**

   Don't forget to type the decimal point. Your goal is to set the margin on all sides to one inch.

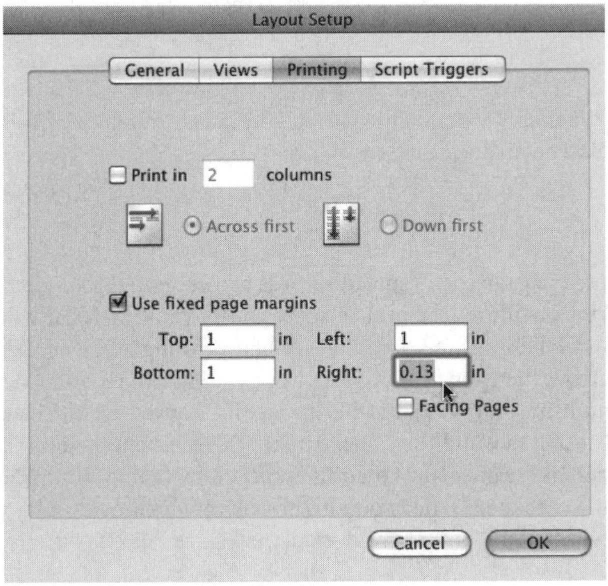

Figure 7-51:
These settings affect the way the current layout prints. For example, you can create a layout that prints in multiple columns (imagine printing sticky labels). For now, draw your attention to the "Use fixed page margins" checkbox, which you need to turn on if you want this layout to have hard-coded (and consistent) page margins.

6. **Click OK.**

If your printer's driver software hogs up even more margin space, then you see a warning message, but it doesn't tell you which margin setting is too narrow. Tweak the margins until the warning no longer appears. The Layout Setup dialog box disappears, and you're looking at your layout again. If you have sharp eyes, then you notice the page width has shrunk a bit, as shown in Figure 7-52.

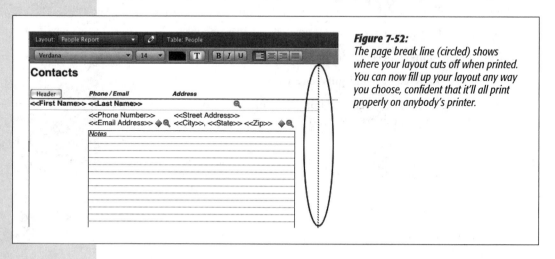

Figure 7-52:
The page break line (circled) shows where your layout cuts off when printed. You can now fill up your layout any way you choose, confident that it'll all print properly on anybody's printer.

Tip: If you like working in pixels and don't want the bother of switching units, take heart. You can probably do the math in your head even faster. Remember, you have 72 pixels per inch: A one-inch margin would be 72 pixels, and a half-inch margin would be 36. (If you like centimeters, then figure 28 pixels per centimeter.)

Now that you've fixed the usable space on the layout, you can rearrange the fields so that they fit nicely in the available width.

Columns

Occasionally your printed page needs to spread records across several *columns*. For example, when you print on address label sheets, the sheets you buy usually have two or three columns of labels on one page. Even when printing a List or Detail layout, if your data's narrow, then you can save paper by printing two records side by side. FileMaker has a built-in solution to just this problem: Choose Layout→Layout Setup, switch to the Printing tab, and then turn on the "Print in" checkbox. When you do, you can tell FileMaker *how* many columns you want by typing a number in the little entry box by the checkbox. When you turn on column printing for a layout, FileMaker shows you what's going on in Layout mode, as Figure 7-53 shows.

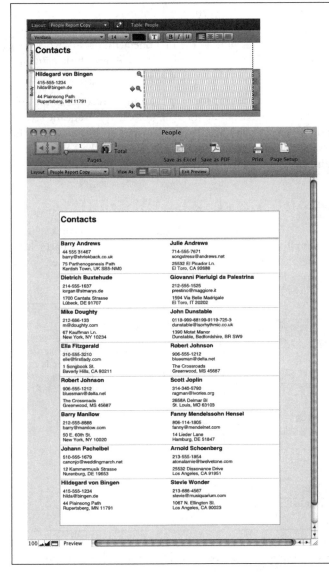

Figure 7-53:

Top: FileMaker draws a dashed line through your layout to show you where the columns land. It also covers every column but the first with a dotted pattern. This pattern is its way of saying, "Don't expect anything you put here to print." Since every column is identical, you just have to lay out the first. FileMaker repeats it for the rest.

Bottom: With the layout set to print in two columns, everything comes together in Preview mode or when you print.

The column setting has no effect on your layout in Browse or Find modes. But if you print or switch to Preview mode, then you see the effect. Instead of repeating the Body part just vertically, FileMaker *tiles* the Body part both horizontally and vertically so that it fills the page.

Every column has to be the same width (this makes sense because every column contains the same kind of information). FileMaker automatically sets the column width so that the columns perfectly divide the page. But it bases its assumptions about the size of the page on the settings in the Print Setup (Windows) or the Page

Setup (Mac OS X) dialog box at the time you turn on columns. If you later switch to a different paper size or orientation, then you probably want to resize the columns. To do so, just drag the first (leftmost) dashed line on the layout. When you finish, File-Maker makes every column the same width as the first one, with no space between them. (You can always simulate padding or a *gutter* between columns by keeping the things you add to your layout away from the column edges.)

Lastly, FileMaker gives you two choices for the way it arranges records in the columns. Choose "Across first" in the Layout Setup dialog box if you want the *second* record to be at the top of the *second* column. Choose "Down first" if it should be the second item in the *first* column. The flow arrows on the icons in the Layout Setup dialog box show how the data flows onto the printout.

Sliding Layout Objects

Suppose you want to add the Notes field to the printed report so you can use it on the road. You know enough already to get the job done. Make the Body part a little taller, and then use the Field tool to add the Notes field to the layout. When you're done, your layout might look like Figure 7-54.

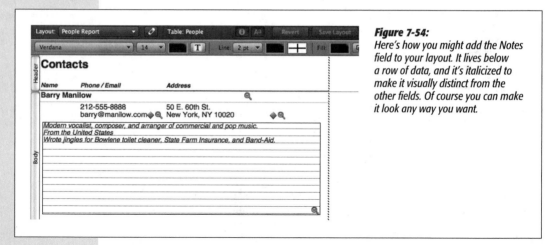

Figure 7-54:
Here's how you might add the Notes field to your layout. It lives below a row of data, and it's italicized to make it visually distinct from the other fields. Of course you can make it look any way you want.

If you preview this report, though, then you quickly spot a problem. Figure 7-55 shows the trouble.

Normally, a field on the layout takes up a fixed amount of space, no matter how much (or how little) data is inside. You might be tempted to try to fix this with a merge field, but that doesn't help here because no matter how tiny the text gets, the Body part is still just as tall as ever. You need some way for everything on the layout to *slide up* if the Notes field isn't full. Luckily, FileMaker's Inspector has the answer in the form of the Position tab's Sliding & Visibility section.

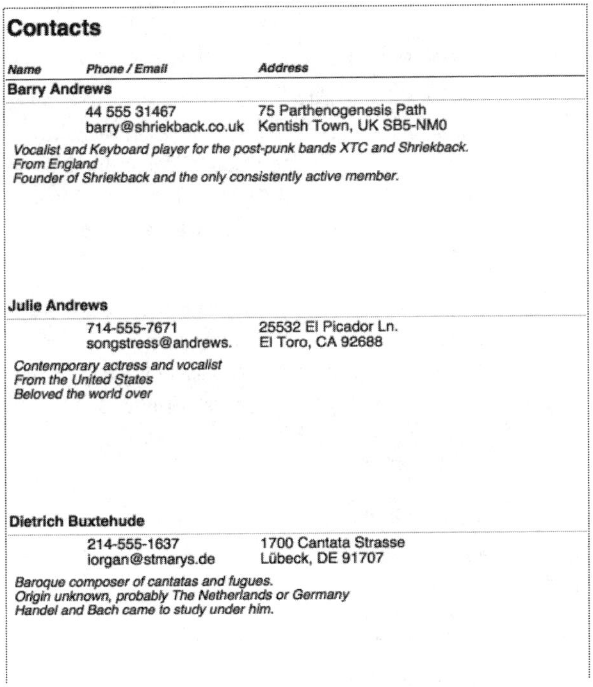

Contacts

Name	Phone / Email	Address
Barry Andrews		
	44 555 31467	75 Parthenogenesis Path
	barry@shriekback.co.uk	Kentish Town, UK SB5-NM0

Vocalist and Keyboard player for the post-punk bands XTC and Shriekback.
From England
Founder of Shriekback and the only consistently active member.

Julie Andrews

	714-555-7671	25532 El Picador Ln.
	songstress@andrews.	El Toro, CA 92688

Contemporary actress and vocalist
From the United States
Beloved the world over

Dietrich Buxtehude

	214-555-1637	1700 Cantata Strasse
	iorgan@stmarys.de	Lübeck, DE 91707

Baroque composer of cantatas and fugues.
Origin unknown, probably The Netherlands or Germany
Handel and Bach came to study under him.

Figure 7-55:
When you preview the report, you quickly see that your nice compact printout is now very space-inefficient. The Notes field is often empty, or holds just a line of text, but FileMaker reserves lots of space for it just in case. Also, if you have lots of notes in one record, then the field may not be big enough, so the text is cut off. But if you make the field even bigger, then you just waste more space. Sliding layout objects are the solution.

When to use sliding

Usually the normal field behavior doesn't cause a problem. After all, you may *want* that empty space because you're printing onto a preprinted form, and everything needs to go in just the right spot on the page, or maybe your report design counts on consistent field sizes so things line up properly. But sometimes you can't get the effect you want without adjusting the layout based on the amount of data—usually when you're trying to tighten things up on the printed page to avoid wasted paper or excessive spacing around data.

Sliding does three things to help in this situation. First, it lets fields shrink to just the right size for their data. After a field has shrunk, any object on the layout can slide up or to the left to fill the space left behind.

Choosing the objects to slide

Object sliding in FileMaker is notoriously hard to figure out. It's a bit like that board game Go. The rules take a minute to learn but a lifetime to master. Here goes.

FREQUENTLY ASKED QUESTION

Merge Fields vs. Sliding

Why should I bother with sliding? Isn't that what merge fields are for?

It's true that merge fields and sliding objects have some things in common. Both adjust the data shown on a layout, squeezing things together in the process. But they have some major differences:

- Merge fields work everywhere, even in Browse mode. Sliding objects, on the other hand, have no effect on Browse mode (or Find mode). Instead, they do their thing only in Preview mode and when printing.

- Any object on a layout, including pictures, can slide. You can't incorporate pictures into merge fields.

- Fields that slide act just like normal fields in Browse mode, in that you can edit the data in them. Merge fields are just text objects, and only for display.

Bearing all these differences in mind, you can easily figure out which method to use. If you have a few fields that you want to display as a single block of text, then use merge fields. If your needs are more complex (incorporating graphics, for instance), or you need to be able to edit data on the layout, then use sliding objects instead.

Also, there's absolutely nothing wrong with using both on one layout. In fact, the layout you just created could use merge fields for the name and address, along with the sliding to the Notes field. You can even tell a text object containing merge fields to slide if you want.

Sliding exists for only one reason: to compensate for changing field data. Therefore, unless you set at least one field to shrink, *nothing* on the layout moves. Unfortunately, you can't explicitly set a field to shrink. Instead, you set it to *slide*—and FileMaker makes sure it shrinks too. This seemingly simple principle is guaranteed to confuse you at least 36 times in the near future. You've been warned. Figure 7-56 shows how this field-shrinking business works.

Once you've figured out which fields should shrink to fit their contents, you need to decide which objects should slide. What does that mean exactly? Normally, when you add an object to a layout, you specify exactly where it goes. But when the object is set to slide, its position is no longer fixed at an exact spot on the layout.

Instead, it moves up (or to the left) if other objects above it (or to the left of it) move or shrink.

Setting sliding options

Once you have a general idea of which elements need to slide (and which fields have to shrink accordingly), you can start telling FileMaker.

Here's how to fix up your Report layout:

1. **Select the Notes field, click the Inspector's Position tab, and then locate the Sliding & Visibility section.**

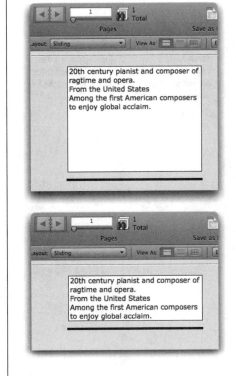

Figure 7-56:
Top: The thick black line is set to slide up and close the empty space below the text, but clearly it's not.

Bottom: After the field is also configured to slide up, it shrinks to be just tall enough for its contents and the black line can now slide up.

2. **Turn on the "Sliding up based on" checkbox.**

   If you stop here, you don't quite have your problem solved. Even though the Notes field shrinks as much as possible, the Body part itself doesn't shrink, and your report still wastes paper. To solve this problem, turn on "Also reduce the size of the enclosing part".

3. **Click OK.**

   If you view your report now, things should look much better. Figure 7-57 agrees.

Note: Once you start adding sliding to your layout, you might have trouble keeping track of which objects do what. To ease the pain, choose View→Show→Sliding Objects. When you do, FileMaker adds little up-pointing and/or left-pointing arrows to each object that slides. Now you can see at a glance what goes where.

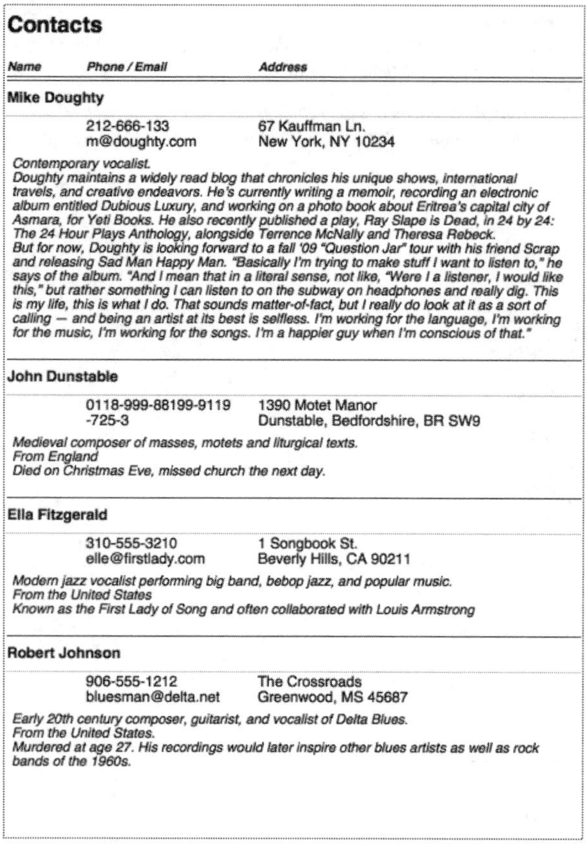

Contacts

Name	Phone / Email	Address

Mike Doughty

212-666-133
m@doughty.com

67 Kauffman Ln.
New York, NY 10234

Contemporary vocalist.
Doughty maintains a widely read blog that chronicles his unique shows, international travels, and creative endeavors. He's currently writing a memoir, recording an electronic album entitled Dubious Luxury, and working on a photo book about Eritrea's capital city of Asmara, for Yeti Books. He also recently published a play, Ray Slape is Dead, in 24 by 24: The 24 Hour Plays Anthology, alongside Terrence McNally and Theresa Rebeck.
But for now, Doughty is looking forward to a fall '09 "Question Jar" tour with his friend Scrap and releasing Sad Man Happy Man. "Basically I'm trying to make stuff I want to listen to," he says of the album. "And I mean that in a literal sense, not like, "Were I a listener, I would like this," but rather something I can listen to on the subway on headphones and really dig. This is my life, this is what I do. That sounds matter-of-fact, but I really do look at it as a sort of calling — and being an artist at its best is selfless. I'm working for the language, I'm working for the music, I'm working for the songs. I'm a happier guy when I'm conscious of that."

John Dunstable

0118-999-88199-9119
-725-3

1390 Motet Manor
Dunstable, Bedfordshire, BR SW9

Medieval composer of masses, motets and liturgical texts.
From England
Died on Christmas Eve, missed church the next day.

Ella Fitzgerald

310-555-3210
elle@firstlady.com

1 Songbook St.
Beverly Hills, CA 90211

Modern jazz vocalist performing big band, bebop jazz, and popular music.
From the United States
Known as the First Lady of Song and often collaborated with Louis Armstrong

Robert Johnson

906-555-1212
bluesman@delta.net

The Crossroads
Greenwood, MS 45687

Early 20th century composer, guitarist, and vocalist of Delta Blues.
From the United States.
Murdered at age 27. His recordings would later inspire other blues artists as well as rock bands of the 1960s.

Figure 7-57:
With the Notes field set to slide up, your layout can now show long or short notes without wasting space. (In this picture, the layout arrangement has been improved from the one in Figure 7-55 to make things look more pleasing to the eye. You can do the same with your own layouts.)

More Sliding & Visibility options

The Inspector's Sliding & Visibility section has several options to control just how the selected objects slide (and shrink if appropriate). In general, an object can slide left, up, or both.

If you want something to just slide left, you're in luck. Simply turn on the "Sliding left" checkbox, and you're done. When you print or preview the layout, the objects slide to the left when field data isn't long enough to fill the full width of the field.

Objects that slide up, on the other hand, need a little more thought. To start, turn on the "Sliding up based on" checkbox. When you turn this checkbox on, you make three more options available. The "All above" and "Only directly above" radio buttons are hard to explain. Figure 7-58, however, is worth a thousand words about sliding up.

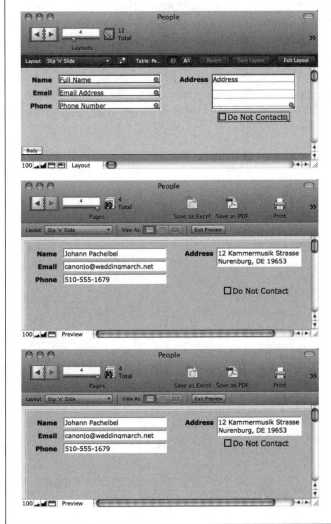

Figure 7-58:
Top: Everything on this layout is "above" the Do Not Contact checkbox. But for the purposes of sliding, only two count. From FileMaker's perspective, the Address field is directly above it, while the Phone field is simply above it. If the Address field and the Do Not Contact checkbox are both set to slide up, then the "All above" or "Only directly above" choice becomes important.

Middle: If you choose "All above", then the checkbox never slides because the Phone field doesn't.

Bottom: If you choose "Only directly above", then it sticks with the Address field, even if that means sliding up alongside the Phone field.

Finally, if you turn on "Also reduce the size of the enclosing part", then the part the object is on shrinks to fit its contents. Be sure to test and retest your layout. If you set a field to slide up and reduce the size of the enclosing part, all the layout objects below it have to be set to slide up too. If you don't, the sliding object will indeed shrink, but the non-sliding objects below will obstinately hold their ground and you'll simply end up with a gap between them.

Be cautious when sliding up based on "All above". "All above" includes items to the right of the vertical page break. When previewing and printing, FileMaker ignores layout items to the right of the vertical page break, So it's a handy spot to put on-screen notes or instructions that you don't need printed. But no matter how far to the right you place an object, it's still above any objects further down the printable area. In other words, a layout object off to the right that by definition can't be printed, can still prevent an object from sliding past it. The simplest solution is to slide based on "Only directly above".

One more Sliding & Visibility option is pretty self-explanatory. If you turn on "Do not print the selected objects", then every object you select before you open the dialog box disappears in Preview mode and when printing. This option is handy for things like navigation buttons that shouldn't show up on the printed page, or background graphics that would waste ink.

Understanding Calculations

When you learned about tables, fields, and relationships in the previous chapters, you dabbled in FileMaker's calculation dialog box. Most people first encounter the Specify Calculation window when they're creating a calculation field, so it's easy to think that's the only place it's used. True, writing formulas for calculation fields is probably the most common use of FileMaker's *calculation engine* (that's the fancy name for the code that handles math for your database), but it's far from the only use, as you'll see later in this chapter.

No matter where you run into the Specify Calculation window, it works the same way. You use that window's field list, operators and predefined functions to tell the calculation how to find the value you need. This chapter tells you how the basic concept works.

While calculations can make your database total invoices, analyze trends, and calculate dates and times, they aren't limited to number-crunching tasks. You can use them to find out about the computer your database is running on, track who's logged into the system, monitor their privileges, and then perform logical tests based on what you find. You'll start by learning how FileMaker handles calculations, and then you'll see how some common functions can take your database up to a new level of power.

Understanding Calculations

Way back on page 131, you saw how to create a field that's defined as a calculation. A calculation is a mathematical formula that manipulates the information in your database to give you the answers you need. For example, for a line item on an Invoice, you need to multiply the price of an item by the quantity to get an extended price. To hand that task over to FileMaker, you create a calculation field, and then write a formula that refers to the appropriate fields by name. FileMaker takes the information in the invoice fields, and does the math.

Note: The exercises in this chapter refer to the Jobs database from this book's Missing CD page at *www. missingmanuals.com.*

FileMaker calculations can also do more than math. For starters, you can do calculations on time, date, timestamp, container, and text fields, too. (See the box on page 352 for an example.) Calculation fields work just like any other FileMaker field, except that you can't type data into them. The calculations you give them determine what data they show. If you change the data a calculation refers to, you see FileMaker update the data automatically. Figure 8-1 shows where calculation fields can benefit your Invoice layout.

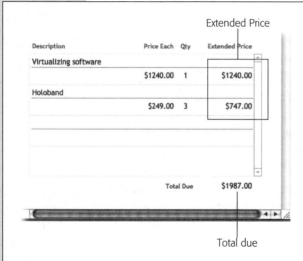

Extended Price

Total due

Figure 8-1:
*Without calculations, you have to manually calculate the extended price for each line item by multiplying the quantity times the price. And then, if the quantity changes, you have to visit your calculator again. But with calculation fields, the database does the math as soon as there's data in the fields the calculation refers to. Here the Extended Price field multiplies Price Each by Quantity (249 * 3 = 747). Plus, if data in either field changes, FileMaker updates the Extended Price automatically.*

You can use a calculation field just like any other field: Put it on a layout, use it in Find mode, and even use it in *other* calculation fields. But as a calculation field, its value always stays up-to-date automatically.

It's the fact that they change, yet update automatically that makes calculations useful for so many tasks. For example, you can use a calculation with the Records→Replace Field Contents command (see page 380). Instead of replacing the data in every record with the *same* value, a calculation can produce a unique value for each record. In the Manage Database dialog box, you can start using the Auto-Enter Calculation and Validation Calculation field options, making those features much more powerful. Scripts, as you'll learn in Chapter 10, use calculations in many of their script steps. Here are some other places you can use the Specify Calculation dialog box:

- **Auto-enter** field options let you put a calculated result in a field when someone creates a record or edits data (page 240).

- **Field validation** uses calculations to make sure the data entered in a field conforms to rules you set up (page 248).

- **Portal filtering** lets you show only some related records in a portal (page 567). For example, you can filter a portal so it only shows invoices with the status "Unpaid" or another portal could show only jobs.

- The **Send Mail** command can create email addresses or concatenate the body of an email (page 437).

- **Chart titles**, labels, and even x- and y-axes can be calculated (page 624).

- **Tooltips** can use calculations to change what's displayed in the tooltip (page 329). For example, you can show a list of related data, like the number of items remaining in inventory, or the Totals of all Invoices for a specific customer.

- **Conditional formatting** lets you apply logic to objects on a layout to change the way they look (page 618). On an invoice layout, for example, you can display the Total Due field in a bold red font *if* the invoice is more than 30 days overdue.

- **Scripts** let you use calculations to change the way script steps work. You can test conditions, create dynamic data, or even take different actions based on the results of calculations. Chapter 10 introduces you to scripts.

- The **Data Viewer** lets you preview your calculations without making a fake field or destroying a perfectly good calculation that needs tweaking. (You need FileMaker Pro Advanced to use the Data Viewer; see page 521.)

- **Accounts & Privileges** can use calculations to limit access to tables, records, and fields. Chapter 18 tells you how to use calculations for tighter database security.

Creating a Calculation

As the Jobs database now stands, when you add line items to an invoice, you have to type the quantity and price for each item. Then you have to multiply them together to get the extended price, and then you have to type the result. In this section, you'll learn how to tell FileMaker to do that all work for you, using a calculation that names your fields and uses computer shorthand to do the math:

1. **In the Jobs database, choose File→Manage Database, and then make sure you're on the Fields tab. From the Table pop-up menu, choose Line Items.**

   That's the table with your Extended Price field in it.

2. **In the field list, select the Extended Price field. From the Type pop-up menu, choose Calculation, and then click Change.**

   FileMaker warns you that when it converts the field, it changes (read: overwrites) any information already in the field. See Figure 8-2.

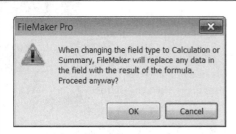

Figure 8-2:
This warning is serious. Your new calculation overwrites existing data when you close the Manage Database window. But you're safe until you click OK. If you change your mind and don't want the calculation after all, just click Cancel instead, and you get the chance to discard all the changes you've made in the dialog box.

FREQUENTLY ASKED QUESTION

Text Calculations?

Aren't calculations just for numbers?

Many people see the Manage Database window's Calculation field type and assume it's for numbers. Too bad, because calculations can do all this:

- Calculations can pick apart text and put it together in different ways (on page 613, you'll use a calculation to make a web address that links to a customer's address map). You can even modify fonts, sizes, colors, and styles (turn every occurrence of the word "credit" to bold text, for instance).

- You can do math on *dates, times,* and *timestamps.* You can find out how old someone is based on his birth date, figure out how long you worked on a job, or see which payment came first.

- If you've stored a reference to a file in a *container* field, then you can use a calculation to retrieve the *path* to the original file.

You can even convert one kind of value into another when you use calculations. For example, if you have a text field that contains "*12/29/2011*", then you can use a calculation to turn that date into a proper date value.

They're so useful that if you have a problem to solve, a calculation is likely to form at least part of the solution.

---

3. **Click OK.**

   The Specify Calculation dialog box appears, as shown in Figure 8-3.

4. **In the Calculation box, type *Price Each * Quantity.***

   You've just added a brand-new calculation that multiplies the contents of the Price Each by the contents of the Quantity field. The "*" is the same symbol you see on your computer's keypad, and it means multiply. See page 359 for details on other symbols (or operators) used for math.

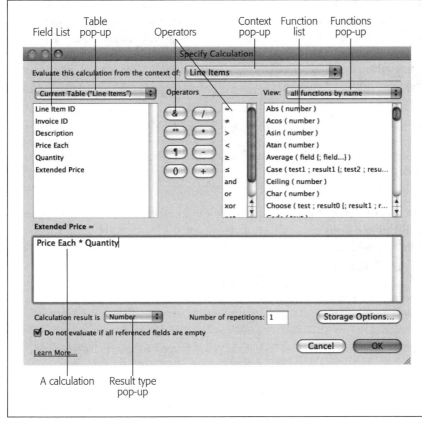

Field List | Table pop-up | Operators | Context pop-up | Function list | Functions pop-up

A calculation | Result type pop-up

Figure 8-3:
Any time you create or edit a calculation, you see a window just like this one. You have lots of tools here, all focused on helping you create a calculation. You'll learn how to use all these options in the rest of this chapter. And now that you recognize the Specify Calculation dialog box, you'll start seeing it everywhere: scripts, conditional formatting, accounts & privileges, and even custom menus.

Note: Although case doesn't matter, spelling and spacing do: You have to match the exact name of the fields you want FileMaker to handle.

---

5. **In the Manage Database window, click OK until all windows are closed.**

   You're back where you started.

Tip: If FileMaker complains about not being able to find a field when you click OK, check the spelling of your field names. And if you hate to type, you can double-click the fields in your field list instead of typing.

Switch to the Invoices layout, and then add a line item. You see that the Extended Price field updates *automatically* once there's a value in both the fields you referred to in the calculation (Price Each and Quantity).

The Structure of a Calculation

If you accidentally mistyped or misspelled a field name in the example in the previous section, you already know that FileMaker is picky about how you create a calculation. *Syntax*—the order of elements and punctuation—is critical when you're creating calculations. So before you learn more tricks, this section outlines common calculation terms and rules of thumb.

Note: Calculations are often called *calcs* for short, or *formulas*. Although some slight differences exist between a calculation and a formula, people usually use the terms interchangeably. Sometimes, a formula is so useful or common that FileMaker defines it as a reusable formula, also known as a *function* (see page 362).

In the next examples, don't focus on what the example calculation does. You'll get to that. Right now, focus on structure. A calculation can be short and simple:

```
Pi * Diameter
```

Or it can be more complicated:

```
Case ( Shape = "Circle" ; Pi * (Diameter/2) ^ 2 ;
Shape = "Rectangle" ; ShapeLength * Width ;
)
```

Note: FileMaker doesn't let you give a field the same name as an existing function. The field containing the length of a rectangular object has the unwieldy name "ShapeLength" to avoid confusion with FileMaker's *Length()* function. The field name "Width" is fine, because there's no width function.

In fact, calculations can be *really* long and complicated if you need them to be—up to 30,000 characters. Practically speaking, the only limit on the complexity of a calculation is your patience for creating it.

Regardless of its complexity, a calculation, or formula, is made up of three different elements: *field references, constants*, and *operators*. In the first example above, "Pi" is a constant, "*" is an operator, and "Diameter" is the name of a field. The second example uses a function, called a "case statement." In that example, "Shape" and "Diameter" are field references, "Circle" and "2" are constants, and "=," "*," and "^" are operators.

Field references tell the calculation engine where to find the *values* it'll be working on. When the calculation is performed or *evaluated*, first the field references are replaced with the actual values in those fields, then the operators tell FileMaker what to do to those values, and finally, FileMaker returns a *result* in your field.

Note: FileMaker uses the value *stored* in (not displayed in) a field. So if you have a number field with 3.1415926 as the stored value, but you've formatted the field on the layout to display only two decimal places, FileMaker still uses all the digits in the stored value to do its math. If you don't want to use all those digits past the decimal place, use the *round* function (see page 386).

Here are some helpful definitions of terms you'll see throughout the next chapters:

- **Field references** are just what they sound like. They refer FileMaker to the data in the field you specify. Since the data inside those fields can change on each record in your database, the values in each record can give a different result.

- **Constants** stay the same each time FileMaker does the calculation. Turn the page for details.

- **Operators** tell FileMaker what to do with the values in the calculation. See page 357 for a listing of operators and what they do.

- FileMaker has more than 180 defined **functions** that you can use as shortcuts when you create your formulas. You learn about some of the most common functions later in this chapter. Chapter 15 introduces you to more advanced functions, and shows you how to create your own reusable functions, called *custom functions*.

- Each calculation has a **result.** This result is, in a sense, the "answer" to the calculation. The result of the first calculation above is the circumference of the circle. The second calculation is a little more complex: Its result is the area of a circle *or* a rectangle, depending on the value in the Shape field. (Don't worry if this calculation doesn't make sense to you now. It will before too long.)

- The result of a calculation has a **type** (just like every field has a type). The type can be any of the standard field types—text, number, date, time, timestamp, or container—or a *Boolean (*page 644*)*. Chapter 9 goes into more detail about calculations and data types.

Note: Sometimes people call a Boolean value "True or False" or "One or Zero" instead. Which term you use doesn't matter much if you just remember that there's a yes-like value and a no-like value. See page 644 for more on Boolean values.

Using Fields in Calculations

It's very common to reference fields in calculations. For example, let's say a field has this calculation:

```
First Name & " " & Last Name
```

POWER USERS' CLINIC

Evaluating Calculations: Now or Later

When you use a calculation, you're asking FileMaker to do something with your fields, constants, and operators and come up with a result. In technical lingo, FileMaker *evaluates* the calculation. *When* the evaluation takes place depends on *where* in your database FileMaker encounters the calculation. Sometimes FileMaker evaluates right away, as when you're calculating an Extended Price. As soon as you type either a price or a quantity, FileMaker tries to multiply the value. But since one of the fields is empty, the Extended Price calculation has a result of zero (because any value times zero equals zero). When you provide the second value, FileMaker immediately does the math and shows you your result:

- If you create a new calculation field after you already have data in your database, then FileMaker updates

the data when you close the Manage Database dialog box. You may see a progress bar if you have a slower computer and a lot of records.

- When you run the Records→Replace Field Contents command, FileMaker evaluates the calculation you specify once for every record as soon as you click OK. As above, this may take a couple seconds, but it's happening just as soon as FileMaker can plow through your found set.

- Validation calculations evaluate whenever you change the field, or exit the record (you get to decide). See page 377 for more on these.

- Calculations used in scripts are evaluated when the script runs.

Note: See page 116 to learn how to use this calculation to show data from more than one field in a value list.

When FileMaker evaluates the calculation, it replaces the First Name and Last Name field names with the person's first and last names from a given record. The field type determines the calculation's automatic result type: A number field has a number value, a text field has a text value, and so forth. On page 372 you'll learn how to change the automatic result type.

Using Constants in Calculations

As handy as it is to refer FileMaker to a field to find the values in your calculations, you don't want to have to store everything in fields just to use it in a calculation. When a value is going to be the same for every record, it's time to call in a constant. You simply include that value right in the calculation.

Number constants

Sales tax is one of the most common constants. If you need to add sales tax to your order, you can just type the percentage right in the calculation, since it's the same for everybody:

```
Order Total * 1.0625
```

You can enter numbers in any of the formats supported by number fields:

- 37
- .65
- 28.3
- 6.02E23

Text constants

You can also use a constant to have FileMaker plunk some text in with your results. If you want a text value instead of a number, put it in quotes:

```
Age & " years old"
```

Everything within the quote marks is a *text constant* (some people call it a *string* as in "string of characters"). Those quote marks in the calculation are very important. Suppose you have a field called First Name, and a calculation like this:

```
"This is my First Name"
```

The quote marks enclose the text that is also a field name, so the result of this calculation is always (*constantly*) "This is my First Name". FileMaker makes no connection whatsoever between the First Name field and the words "First Name" in the text, because the text is in quote marks.

Forgetting quote marks around a text string, or putting them in the wrong place, can make FileMaker whiny. If you make the following calculation:

```
"This is" my First Name.
```

FileMaker shows you a warning message that says, "The specified field cannot be found", when you try to click OK to close the Manage Database dialog box (Figure 8-4). The characters "my First Name" are highlighted in your calculation so you can tell exactly which part of the calculation confuses FileMaker. Move your quotes appropriately, and FileMaker stops telling you that it can't find your field reference. Here's the correct formula:

```
"This is my " & First Name
```

Using Operators in Calculations

The power of calculations comes from their ability to combine various values to come up with a new and meaningful value. Here's where *operators* come in. An operator takes the values on either side of it (the *operands*) and *does something* (operates) with them.

A special symbol or word stands for each operator. This calculation uses the + (addition) operator:

```
3 + 2
```

In this case, the + operator is given 3 and 2 as operands. When the calculation evaluates, the operator and its operands combine to produce a single value.

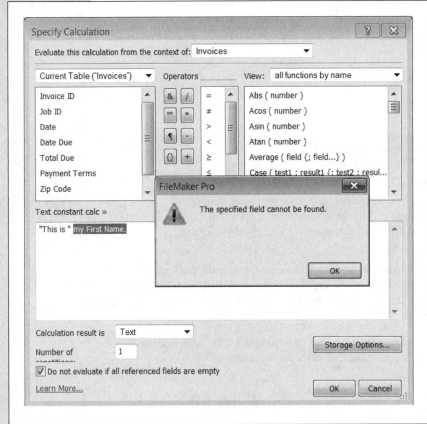

Figure 8-4:
When you click OK, FileMaker tries to evaluate your calculation. If it finds any part of the text that seems like it should be a field name, but there's no field with that name, then you see this error message. Notice that in the window behind the warning, FileMaker highlights the part of your calculation it doesn't understand.

Sometimes you've made a typing error, but sometimes the field you want is in another table.

Operators come in three flavors:

- **Mathematical and logical** operators combine two values into one. The + operator is a good example; it takes two number values, and adds them together. Its resulting value is the sum of the two numbers.

- **Comparison** operators compare two values. For example, the = operator tells you if two values are exactly the same. This kind of operator always produces a Boolean value.

- **Parenthesis** operators are used to group parts of a calculation together. Remember your eighth grade math teacher carrying on about the "order of operations"? (Working from left to right multiplication and division first, and then addition and subtraction) FileMaker remembers, too, and it uses those same rules to figure out how to evaluate calculations. If the rules don't work for you, then parentheses let you take more control.

Note: Two buttons in the Specify Calculation window's Operators section aren't really operators at all. The ¶ is a special character that tells FileMaker you want a new line in your calculation result, and the quote marks are for entering text values. See the box below to learn how to use quotes inside text.

FREQUENTLY ASKED QUESTION

Quotes in Quotes

You're saying that I should use quote marks to incorporate a word or a phrase into the results of a calculation. But what if I want to put a quote mark inside my text?

You're out of luck. No, just kidding. Just put a backslash (\) in front of the quote mark, and FileMaker pretends it doesn't exist when it analyzes your calculation. When a quote is preceded with a backslash, you say it's *escaped*, and \ is called the escape character: When you put the escape character in front of another character, it tells File-Maker to ignore any special meaning that character might have and treat it as ordinary text. It looks like this:

```
"Then Joseph Adama says, \"Balance it
out.\" That's when I got hooked on Ca-
prica."
```

This calculation is just one long text constant. The two quote marks inside it are escaped.

If you're a real troublemaker, then your next question is, "What if I want to put a real backslash *and* quote mark inside my text constant?"

Luckily, that's easy, too. Just escape the backslash, and then escape the quote:

```
"I really want this: \\\" inside my text"
```

This calculation evaluates to:

```
I really want this: \" inside my text
```

Mathematical operators

A calculation's most obvious use is to do a little math, so you'll use these operators often. Maybe your database of products includes fields for dimensions (Length, Width, and Height), and you want to know the volume. This calculation does the trick:

```
Length * Width * Height
```

It consists of three field values and two copies of the * (multiplication) operator. The result is just what you'd get if you used a calculator to multiply the three field values together.

FileMaker includes operators for basic math:

- + for addition
- – for subtraction
- * for multiplication
- / for division
- ^ for exponentiation ("to the power of" a value)

The concatenation operator

While the mathematical operators combine numbers, the "&" (concatenation) operator works with text. It hooks together two text values:

```
Length & " inches"
```

If the Length field contains 36, then the result of this calculation is *36 inches*.

Tip: FileMaker can mix numeric values and text together in the same calculation. If you use a number value or field where FileMaker is expecting text, then it just converts the number into text, and gets on with its business.

Comparison operators

You often need to compare two values to learn about them. For example, you may need to add an additional shipping charge if the total weight of an order is more than 20 pounds. All comparison operators result in a Boolean value (page 644).

FileMaker can compare things in several ways:

- = tells you if two values are the same.

- ≠ or <> tells you if the two values are different.

- > tells you if the first value is bigger than the second.

- < tells you if the first value is smaller than the second.

- ≥ or >= tells you if the first value is bigger than or equal to the second.

- ≤ or <= tells you if the first value is smaller than or equal to the second.

Logical operators

The logical operators evaluate values and come up with a Boolean (Yes/No) result (page 644). Unlike the other operators, most of them are recognizable words:

- The *and* operator tells you if both values are Yes. The calculation below uses the *and* operator. It evaluates to Yes if the length is more than 3 *and* the height is more than 5.

    ```
    Length > 3 and Height > 5
    ```

- The *or* operator tells you if *either* value is Yes. The *or* calculation below evaluates to Yes if the length is more than 3 *or* the height is more than 5.

    ```
    Length > 3 or Height > 5
    ```

- The *xor* operator's function is as offbeat as its name. It stands for *exclusive or*. The *xor* operator tells you when *only one* of your two choices is Yes. Put another way, if you find yourself thinking, "I want one of two things to be true, but *not both* of them," then *xor* saves the day. For instance, you may want to track whether you've billed a customer *or* you've marked her character rating below 3. That formula looks like this:

```
Invoice Sent = Yes xor Character Rating < 3
```

Note: If you can't think of a use for *xor*, don't worry. Most of the time when you need an "or" calculation, you can handle it with plain old *or* and not *exclusive or*.

- The last logical operator, *not*, stands alone: It works only on one value, not two like every other operator. It simply reverses the Boolean value that comes after it. So the calculation below would evaluate to Yes if the length is *not* more than 3.

```
Not Length > 3
```

Note: People usually use comparison and logical operators with *logical functions*. Chapter 9 covers those.

The ^ operator

The last—and probably least used—operator is the exponentiation, or ^ operator. This lets you use exponents in calcualtions:

```
Pi * Radius ^ 2
```

This calculation uses the exponentiation operator and squares the value in the Radius field.

Parentheses

FileMaker uses standard mathematical rules to decide in what order to evaluate things. The order of evaluation is exponentiation, then multiplication/division, then lastly addition/subtraction. If you need FileMaker to do part of your calculation *first*, before moving onto any other operators, put it in parentheses. The parentheses tell FileMaker to treat everything between them as a single unit.

In the calculation below, FileMaker multiplies 3 and 2 before adding 4, and gives you a result of 10:

```
4 + 3 * 2
```

Even though the + operator comes first in the calculation, FileMaker follows the order of calculation. If you want to add 4 and 3 before multiplying, you need to use parentheses:

```
(4 + 3) * 2
```

Thus, it sees that it needs to add 4+3 first, then multiply by 2, for a result of 14. You can see the value of parentheses in calculations like the one below, which calculates the interest on the sum of the balance and service charge. Without the parentheses, FileMaker would calculate the interest on only the service charge, and then add that to the balance due, with an entirely different result:

```
(Balance Due + Service Charge) * Interest Rate
```

Note: If you have trouble remembering (nay, understanding) the order of calculation, then just use parentheses when in doubt. It certainly doesn't hurt to be *too* explicit.

Functions

The meat of calculations is found in the Function list (which you saw briefly back in Figure 8-3). A *function* is a predefined formula, and FileMaker's list covers most common calculation purposes. If you find a function that already does what you want to do—like average all invoices—use it. When you add these tried-and-true formulas to your calculations, you save time and even help prevent errors.

For example, if you didn't know about functions, you could find your average with a series of fields. First, you'd need to create a calculation field to total all the invoices in your found set. Then you'd need another field to count the invoices in the set and a third one that divides the first field by the second. It would work, but it'd be clumsy and inefficient, since you've created at least two fields that you didn't really need.

Because you often need to find averages, FileMaker gives you a *function* that handles the math in a given field. All you have to do is tell FileMaker *which* field you want to average. The function takes care of figuring out the total of the found set, and how many records you have. It looks like this:

```
Average ( Line Item::Quantity )
```

The word "Average" is the function's name. "Line Item::Quantity" is a reference to a related field. This field reference is called a *parameter*. Parameters tell the function how to perform its specific calculation. The *average* function has only a single parameter, but many functions have two or more.

Parameters are always enclosed in parentheses. (A few functions—most notably, Random—don't need any parameters, so you leave the parentheses off all together.) When there's more than one parameter, they're separated by a semicolon, as in the date function below:

```
Date ( Month ; Day ; Year )
```

FileMaker has almost 250 functions, divided into 16 groups, as described below. Later in this chapter, you'll learn how to use some of the more common functions. (Functions come into play in Chapters 9 and 15 as well.)

Tip: FileMaker has a lengthy help file (Ctrl+? or ⌘+?) that lists each function and some sample uses. If you want to explore a function that isn't covered here, open Help, and then type the function's name.

Text functions

Dozens of *text* functions let you work with text values. You can compare them, convert them into other types (like numbers), split them up in various ways, count the number of letters, words, or lines, change case, and replace parts of them with new text values. If you're trying to slice, mix, or examine words, look here first.

Text formatting functions

Text formatting functions let you adjust the font, size, style, and color of all or part of a text value. For instance, you could make the account balance for a customer turn red if it's over $100. See page 618 for another way to format data conditionally.

Number functions

Number functions do everything with numbers—from the mundane (rounding) to the esoteric (combinatorics). In between, you can get rid of the decimal part of a number, calculate logarithms and square roots, convert signs, generate random numbers, and perform modulo arithmetic.

Date functions

Date functions make working with dates a breeze. You can safely create date values without worrying about the computer's date settings. You can also pick date values apart (for example, get just the *month* from a date), convert day and month numbers into proper names, and work with weeks and fiscal years.

Time functions

Time functions are few: They create time values from hours, minutes, and seconds, and split times up into the same parts. You use these values most frequently when you're trying to find out how long something took. For instance, if you bill your services hourly, then you can create Start Time and Finish Time fields. Then, in a Duration field, you can subtract finish time from start time to find out how long you worked on a project.

Timestamp functions

There's only one *timestamp* function: It lets you build a timestamp value from a separate date and a time. If you're creating your own data, then you already know that FileMaker needs both a date and a time for a valid Timestamp field, and you've planned accordingly. But you may receive data from an outside source in which the date and time aren't already in a single field. No problem, just use the timestamp function.

Aggregate functions

Aggregate functions calculate statistics like average, variance, and standard deviation. They can also count things, sum things, and find minimums and maximums. By definition, aggregate functions *gather up* multiple values, and find results based on the group as a whole. (See the box on page 364 for more detail.)

UP TO SPEED

Aggregate Functions

As you saw on page 363, aggregate functions work on groups of things. They can work on multiple fields within a record, a group of related records or even multiple functions. This function helps you add up the various charges on an invoice, using fields on the Invoice layout:

    Sum (Subtotal ; Sales Tax ; Shipping)

But since you can use an operator to get the same result (Subtotal + Sales Tax + Shipping), this type of use isn't very common. More often an aggregate function refers to a related field. In that case, FileMaker aggregates that field's values from *every* related record:

    Sum (Line Items::Extended Price)

An aggregate function can also reference a single repeating field, either a local one or a related one. As with a reference to a related field, a Sum function that refers to a repeating field adds the values in every repetition into a single value.

This special behavior for related or repeating fields works only if you use a single parameter. You can't, for example, sum two sets of related fields as one like this:

    Sum (Line Items::Extended Price ; Line
    Items::Shipping Charge)

If you refer to more than one field in a sum function, then it looks at only the *first* related value or repetition for each field. Of course, if you do want to total two related fields, you can do so by calling Sum twice and adding their results:

    Sum (Line Items::Extended Price) +
    Sum (Line Items::Shipping Charge)

Summary functions

You have only one *summary* function—*GetSummary()*. Its primary purpose is to let you use the value of a summary field (page 240) in your calculations. In the olden days, before FileMaker was the robust relational database it is now, the *GetSummary()* function was the best way to sort and summarize certain kinds of data. Now that FileMaker is relational, you usually use calculations through table occurrences (page 570) to do that work.

Repeating functions

Repeating functions work with repeating fields, and some of them work with *related* fields as well. You can make nonrepeating fields and repeating fields work together properly in calculations, access specific repeating values, or get the *last* non-empty value. Since repeating fields have limited uses in these days of related tables within files, so do these functions. However, these functions have a few valid uses, as you'll learn in Chapter 11.

Financial functions

Financial functions make the MBAs in the audience feel right at home. Calculate present value, future value, net present value, and payments. Non-MBAs could calculate the cost of competing loans with these functions.

Trigonometric functions

Trigonometric functions aren't common in business-related databases. But engineers and scientists know what to do with this bunch: sine, cosine, and tangent. They can also convert between radians and degrees. And if you need to, you can get Pi out to 400 decimal places.

Logical functions

Logical functions are a powerful grouping. These functions can make *decisions* based on calculated values (if the due date is more than 3 months ago, add a late fee of 10 percent). FileMaker has functions to evaluate *other* calculations inside your calculations; functions to figure out if fields are empty or contain invalid data; performance enhancing functions to create and use variables (page 689); and functions to perform lookups inside calculations (page 655). Chapter 15 is where you learn when and how to use these big dogs of the function world.

Get functions

Get functions pull up information about the computer, user, database, or FileMaker Pro itself. They make up the largest group (95 in all). You can, for example, find out the computer's screen resolution, the current layout's name, the computer's network address, the current user's name, or the size of any database window. This list just scratches the surface, though. If you're looking for information about the current state of FileMaker, the computer, or the user, then you can probably find it with a *Get* function.

Design functions

Design functions tell you about your database's structure. You can get a list of tables, fields, layouts, or value lists, or details about any of these items. You won't need most of these functions until you become an advanced database designer indeed. ValueListItems is one notable exception, which gives you a list of the values in a value list, separated by paragraph breaks.

Custom functions

If you have FileMaker Pro Advanced, then you can create your very own *custom* functions and have them show up on the list. Once you have them, you (or anyone you let create fields in your database) can choose them just like the built-in functions. (See Chapter 15 for details on creating and using custom functions.)

External functions

If you're not using plug-ins or FileMaker Server, then your *external* functions category is empty. If you've installed any plug-ins ("mini-programs" that add extra features to FileMaker), they probably brought along some functions for their own use. FileMaker stores them in this category. FileMaker Server also uses plug-ins, ironically to help you update your third-party plug-ins. (External plug-ins are covered on page 667.)

Expressions

Expression is a fancy name for a subsection of a calculation—one or more fields, functions, or constants, each connected with operators. When you made the first calculation in this chapter (page 351), you multiplied the contents of the field called Price Each by the contents of the field called Quantity. That's a calculation, but it's also an example of an *expression.*

An expression always reduces to a single value when you combine its individual values according to the operators. If you can't boil it down to a value, then it's not an expression. That's an important point, because it means you can use expressions as function parameters (page 362) just like any individual values—fields and constants. When used in a function, these expressions are called *sub-expressions.*

Here are some examples of expressions:

The following is a simple expression, which reduces to the value 6.

```
3 + 3
```

Below is a more complex expression. It might turn into something like "Shrute, Dwight K."

```
Last Name & ", " & First Name & " " & Middle Initial & "."
```

The following calculation is a function *and* it's an expression, because it reduces down to a single value:

```
Average ( L1 * W1 * H1 ; L2 * W2 * H2 ; L3 * W3 * H3 )
```

But if you look at just the stuff in parentheses, then you have this:

```
L1 * W1 * H1 ; L2 * W2 * H2 ; L3 * W3 * H3
```

That's *not* an expression because it doesn't reduce down to one value. It has three expressions in all, each separated by a semicolon. Each expression reduces to a single value—three values in all that become parameters passed to the Average function.

You can put *any valid expression* in place of a parameter in a function. In the trade, that's called *nesting* expressions. For example, you can rewrite the expression 3 + 3 like this:

```
( 1 + 1 + 1 ) + 3
```

In this case, the sub-expression (1 + 1 + 1) has replaced the original value 3. The whole thing is a new expression, and it contains one sub-expression. While the nested expression example is very simple, the concept behind it gives you a lot of power when you work with functions. Instead of using individual fields or constants in a function, you can pass along whole expressions. You can even nest functions within other functions (see page 404).

TROUBLESHOOTING MOMENT

Think Like a Machine

If you've jumped right in and started making perfect calculations every time, then you can skip this bit of arcana. But if FileMaker throws up a warning dialog box every time you try to make a halfway complex calculation, or if the syntax seems fine, but you just aren't getting the math to work out right, then you might have to try thinking like FileMaker thinks. To understand how fields, constants, functions, and operators come together to produce a single result, you have to think very logically and in a straight line that inexorably leads to the end of a problem. When FileMaker evaluates a calculation, it looks for something it can do to simplify it—fetch a field value, perform a function, or evaluate an operation.

The calculation shown in Figure 8-5 has a function (average), several operators (* and &), a constant ("cubic inches"), and six fields (L1, W1, H1, L2, W2, H2). You might think the average function is the right place to start, because it comes first. But you quickly realize you can't compute the average until you figure out what its parameters are by performing the multiplication. The * operators multiply values on either side to produce a new value—but FileMaker needs to replace these fields with their values before it can do anything else.

In step 1, FileMaker identifies six fields. Step 2 shows how the calculation looks once FileMaker replaces them with values.

Now the * operators are all surrounded by values, and FileMaker is ready to do some multiplication (step 3). Step 4 shows the calculation once all the multiplication is finished.

At last, the average function has two parameters (step 5), which is just what it needs, so FileMaker performs this function, and the new calculation looks like step 6.

You have no more fields to replace and no more functions to perform, but there's one last operator. The & operator takes two text values and puts them together, but this & operator has a number on one side. FileMaker notices this fact in step 7, and fixes it in step 8. Finally, the & operator is evaluated, and step 9 shows the calculation result.

If you apply the concepts outlined here to your problem calculations—find the answer to each step, then plod along to the next one—you can always figure out where your calculation has gone astray.

Using a Related Field in a Calculation

The invoice line items now calculate their extended prices automatically, because you created a calculation at the beginning of the chapter to handle that. But you still have to add up the extended price of each line item, and enter the total amount due on the invoice itself. Another calculation solves this problem:

1. **In the Jobs database, choose File→Manage→Databases, and then go to the Fields tab. From the Table pop-up menu, choose Invoices.**

   The field list shows all the fields in the Invoices table.

2. **In the list, select the Total Due field.**

   It's currently a Number field.

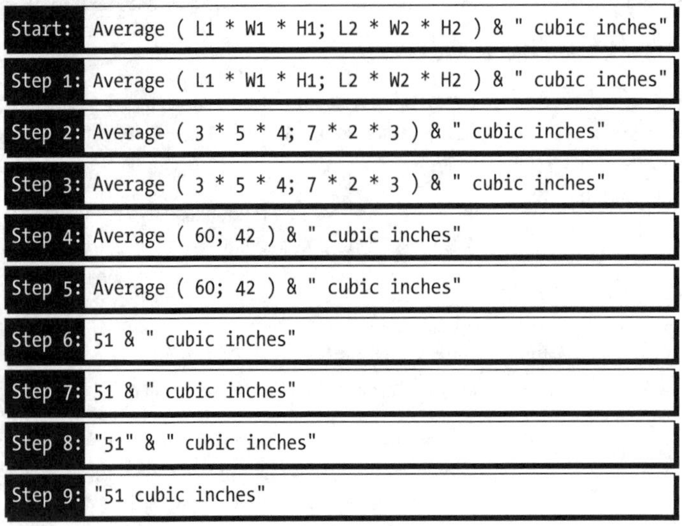

Figure 8-5:
Taking a complex calculation one bite at a time helps you get the results you expect. Just chip away at the parts, and check your logic at each stage to make sure you and FileMaker are in concert.

Start:	Average (L1 * W1 * H1; L2 * W2 * H2) & " cubic inches"
Step 1:	Average (L1 * W1 * H1; L2 * W2 * H2) & " cubic inches"
Step 2:	Average (3 * 5 * 4; 7 * 2 * 3) & " cubic inches"
Step 3:	Average (3 * 5 * 4; 7 * 2 * 3) & " cubic inches"
Step 4:	Average (60; 42) & " cubic inches"
Step 5:	Average (60; 42) & " cubic inches"
Step 6:	51 & " cubic inches"
Step 7:	51 & " cubic inches"
Step 8:	"51" & " cubic inches"
Step 9:	"51 cubic inches"

3. **From the Type pop-up menu, choose Calculation, and then click the now highlighted Change button. When FileMaker asks if you're sure you want to make this change, click OK.**

   The Specify Calculation dialog box pops up. (See page 353 for details on its many features.)

4. **From the View pop-up menu (above the function list), choose Aggregate Functions.**

   The function list now shows just the functions FileMaker uses to calculate various kinds of totals and averages. You're looking for the sum function.

5. **Double-click the "Sum (field {; field…})" function in the list.**

   FileMaker copies the full function example into the calculation box. To save you an extra step, it even selects everything between the parentheses (Figure 8-6). The next thing you type or click becomes the first parameter to the function.

Tip: Anything within curly braces in a function is optional. In the sum function in step 5, you could reference several fields that all get summed up into one glorious total. But that doesn't make sense when you're trying to summarize line items on an invoice, so you're just replacing all the highlighted material with a single field reference.

---

6. **From the pop-up menu above the field list, choose Line items to view the table occurrence you need, and then, in the list of line item fields, double-click the Extended Price field.**

   FileMaker adds this field to the calculation, placing it between the parentheses that surround the parameters to the sum function. Your calculation should now read:

   ```
   Sum ( Line Items::Extended Price )
   ```

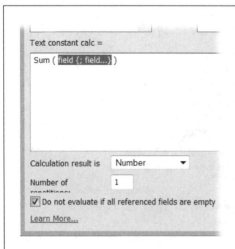

Figure 8-6:
FileMaker gives you a handy syntax reference for each function you choose from the function list. When you double-click to place the function in the calculation box, FileMaker even highlights the parameters for you, so you can start building right away. If you aren't sure what to do, click the "Learn More" link at the bottom left of the dialog box for context-sensitive help.

Tip: If you prefer the keyboard, you can use the Tab key to move from the Calculation box to the Field list, then the Operator list, and then the Function list. Once you're in one of these lists, use the up and down arrow keys to select an item (or type the first few letters of the item's name). Finally, press the space bar to add the selected item to the Calculation box.

---

7. **From the "Calculation result is" pop-up menu, choose Number.**

   Because this field was a number type before you changed it, it's probably already set to have a Number result.

8. **Click OK in each dialog box to return to your layout.**

   If you've done everything right, the Specify Calculation window disappears. If not, check the syntax of your calculation, and then try again.

Your Total Due field should now work perfectly. Since you modified an existing field that's already on your layout, you don't need to do anything else. Every layout that shows the Invoice::Total Due field now shows the new calculated value.

Switch to the Invoices layout to try for yourself. As you edit, add, or delete Line Item records, the Invoices::Total Due field changes automatically to reflect the correct total.

Result Type

Why do I have to tell FileMaker my calculation has a number result? I'm multiplying two numbers together, so isn't it obvious?

You're right; FileMaker can figure that out for itself. In fact, in a calculation where you're performing simple math, the field always has a number result. But the ability to set the result type for a field gives you a good measure of control.

For one thing, you and FileMaker may have different ideas about what type a result *should* be. Take this calculation, for example:

    1 & 1 * 3

Because you're mixing concatenation (&) and math (*) operators, it's not terribly obvious *what* that calculation will produce. A number? Or just a numerical text value? So FileMaker lets you say what you *want* it to produce. If it doesn't do what you expect, then you can easily fix the calculation, but at least you don't have to wonder what type of field you have.

Furthermore, setting the type explicitly prevents FileMaker from changing it later. Imagine if a simple change to your calculation accidentally changed the result type from number to text. If you try to reference this field in a calculation or a relationship, then you get strange results. And it might take you a while to figure out that the problem is due to FileMaker calculating a text value instead of a number, rather than a mistake in your calculation.

If you've set a result type, and your calculation doesn't naturally produce the correct type, then FileMaker converts it for you before it stores the final result. Thus, you can always tell exactly what type the field is just by looking at the Result Type pop-up menu.

Understanding the Specify Calculation Dialog Box

As you saw in the previous tutorial, whenever you create a new calculation field, File-Maker shows the Specify Calculation window (Figure 8-3). This window is loaded with options, making it seem a bit daunting—but all those buttons are there to help you. FileMaker shows you the table occurrences, fields, operators, and functions, and all you have to do is point and click to build any calculation you have in mind.

Once you learn how this box works, you can write calculations like a pro without memorizing complicated functions and/or typing out long field names. The following pages give you a guided tour of each element in the window.

Table occurrence context

Since FileMaker sees your database from the perspective of one table occurrence at a time, you have to specify which context you want the calculation to be evaluated from. The Table Occurrence pop-up menu lists every occurrence of the current table—the one you're adding a field to—on the Relationship graph. All you have to do is pick the one that works for your purposes. (If your calculation doesn't reference any related data, you can ignore the Table Occurrence pop-up menu.)

Note: Anchor-Buoy relationships (page 589) make it much easier to conceptualize calculations' context, since most calculations are created in the Anchor table occurrence, looking toward the Buoys.

Field list

Since most calculations include fields, and field names are often long and hard to remember, FileMaker lets you pick field names from a list. The Table Occurence pop-up menu shows every table occurrence in the graph, with the related tables at the top, and the unrelated tables in a group below. The list below the pop-up menu shows the fields in the selected table occurrence. A calculation can refer to any related field in the database: FileMaker follows the appropriate relationships to grab the data it needs.

Note: You can use Global fields from unrelated tables in your calculations. But if you try to use a regular field from an unrelated table, then you get a warning message when you try to close the Specify Calculation window.

If you want to put a field in the calculation itself, just double-click its name in the list, and FileMaker does the typing for you. Any time you're referring to a related field, the pop-up menu saves time and helps avoid error.

Note: When you double-click a field from the list of table occurrences, you create what FileMaker calls a "fully-qualified field reference", which contains the Table name, two colons, and the Field name (Invoices:: InvoiceID). Because you might have similar field names in several tables, a fully qualified name makes sure you refer to the right one.

Operators

To help you remember all those operators, FileMaker shows them in the Operators area. Eight buttons represent the most common operators—just click one to insert it. Other operators appear in a scrolling list, which requires a double-click.

Function list

Some functions are so short and sweet that it's faster to type them than to hunt through this very lengthy list. Or you may come to memorize the functions you use most often. But you can't beat the Function list for convenience. It shows every function FileMaker understands, *and* all the parameters each function expects, in the right order. (See the box on page 373 for more detail.)

As usual, double-click a function to add it to the calculation. If you don't fancy an alphabetical list of every function, then you can narrow down your choices using the View pop-up menu. You can pick a specific function type, and see a list of just those functions. The pop-up menu also includes three special categories. The first, "all functions by type" reorganizes the functions in the list. You can see the effect in Figure 8-7.

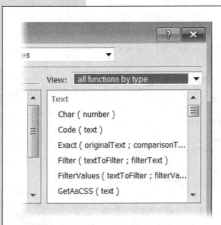

Figure 8-7:
In the function list, when you choose "all functions by type", FileMaker groups the functions by type, indents them, and then sorts them by name within each group. The type itself is shown in lighter gray bold above each group. This method is the easiest way to explore the list of functions when you're not quite sure what you're looking for but you think you know the general category your intended function should be filed under.

Tip: You can always switch back to "all functions by name" to see your functions in an alphabetical list. But despite the name, not all functions show up when you sort this way. Some of the less common functions, Get (TextRulerVisible) for example, are left out. If you need a list of all functions, sort by type. Or if you know which type your function falls under, you can filter the list that way, too.

Result Type

Just as you specify field types when you create fields (page 132), you also specify result types for your calculations. If you change a field to a calculation type field, FileMaker uses its former field type as the automatic result type. But you can use the Result Type pop-up menu to override the automatic setting. And when you create a calculation field from scratch, the Calculation result is automatically set as "Number," but that's not always what you want. Your result type should match the function type. That is, if you're using a Date function, set the result type to Date. If you're concatenating data from text fields, then Text is the result type you want. It's common to forget to change the result type when you create calculations, so if you're not getting what you expect from your calculations, check the result type setting.

UP TO SPEED

The Function List

The Function list doesn't show just a list of meaningless names—it also shows the syntax for the function. This prototype function includes everything you need to call the function in a calculation: name, the necessary parentheses, and a placeholder for each parameter. You just need to replace the placeholders with fields, constants, functions, or expressions.

Most functions are simple, and have a simple example to match:

```
Date ( month ; day ; year )
```

This function, called Date, expects three parameters: a month, day, and year. (If you're curious, it returns a date value based on the three numbers passed to it. See page 408 for more details.)

The syntax of some other functions aren't as simple, and their syntax needs some explanation (you won't learn how the functions work here, just focus on syntax for now). Some functions don't have a predetermined number of parameters. The Average function needs *at least* one parameter, but you can pass as many as you want. It looks like this in the Function list:

```
Average ( field {; field...} )
```

The first "field" parameter shows that you need to specify at least one value. The second one is inside curly braces, meaning it's optional. And it's followed by "…" meaning you can add more copies if you want.

The Case function (page 654) shows up like this:

```
Case ( test1 ; result1 {; test2 ; result2
; ... ; defaultResult} )
```

This shows that you can add additional test and result parameters, and you can put a final defaultResult parameter on the end if you want.

Finally, a few functions actually accept more than one value for a single parameter. The Evaluate function is an example:

```
Evaluate ( expression {; [field1 ; field2
;...]} )
```

It always expects one parameter, called an *expression* (see page 366). You can also specify a field to go with it. The brackets around the field show you that it can take two parameters, but the second can be a bracketed list of multiple values. In other words, you can call this function in three ways:

```
Evaluate ( "<some expression>" )
Evaluate ( "<some expression>" ; A Field )
Evaluate ( "<some expression>" ; [Field 1
; Field 2 ; Field 3] )
```

In the first case, it receives only one parameter. In both the second and third cases, you're passing *two* parameters. In the third case only, the second parameter is actually a list of values. Functions like this are rare, but a few exist.

Calculation Box

Your calculation itself goes in the Calculation box in the middle of the window (it has the field name above it as a label). You can type right into the Calculation box if you're a codehead, but mere mortals usually use the field list, operators, and function list, and let FileMaker assemble their calculations for them. When you're getting started, you probably mostly point and click, but as you get more familiar with formulas and functions, you'll start typing more often. Most people end up using a hybrid of typing and clicking to create their calculations.

Tip: You can also copy and paste into the Calculation box. If you have a calculation in another table file that's the same or similar, you can paste, and then update it for its new home, saving yourself some typing. See the Self function on page 646. It can reduce or even eliminate editing when you reuse a calculation.

Repetitions

Like any field, a calculation field can be a repeating field (see page 255). FileMaker provides this option for the rare occasion when you need to calculate repeating fields. Suppose you have a repeating field that holds five quantities, and another with five prices. You can write a calculation that multiplies the two fields, and then turn on this box. FileMaker takes care to match all the repetition numbers for you, so the third repetition of the calculation multiplies the third price and the third quantity, for instance. (You're more likely to have related tables, and use a standard single calculation to do the totals, but the option to calculate on repetitions is there if you need it.)

Changing the Standard Evaluation Behavior

At the bottom of the Specify Calculation dialog box is the standard option "Do not evaluate if all referenced fields are empty." Since the option is meant to improve performance, you'll leave it selected most of the time. When you do, the calculation field is blank.

But sometimes "blank" isn't the right value. When you create a new invoice, its Total Due value is "blank" (there's no data in the field), but it should be zero dollars and zero cents, or $0.00. First, turn off the "Do not evaluate if all referenced fields are empty" option for Invoices::Total Due. Then change that field's calculation to:

```
0+ Sum ( Line Items::Extended Price )
```

The calculation's result isn't changed by the addition of the constant value "0," but there's now a value in the fields that'll trigger evaluation of the calculation, even when the invoice has no related items (Figure 8-8).

Auto-Enter Calculations

Back on page 240, you learned about most of the auto-enter field options. Now that you know about calculations, it's time to learn how to combine the power of the calculation engine (accuracy and efficiency) with the ability to override a calculated value using auto-enter calculations. Calculation fields are fantastic—they save time, and ensure error-free results. But they have one serious limitation: You can't click into a calculation field and change its value. Of course, you can adjust the calculation itself, or the data in the fields the calculation depends on, but sometimes you need to be able to override a field's calculated value on a record-by-record basis.

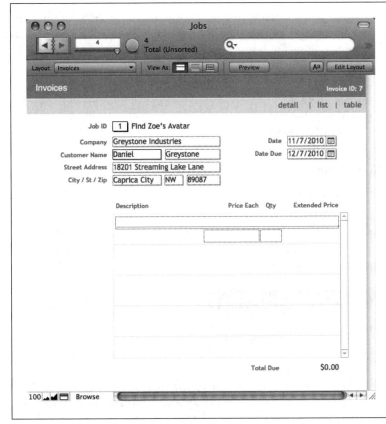

Figure 8-8:
When you first create a record, the fields referred to in your calculations are usually empty, so your calculation results are blank, until you enter data in at least one field that's referenced in the calculation. Turning off the "Do not evaluate if all referenced fields are empty" option, and then editing the calculation displays a "0" in the field instead. Use the same technique on the Line Items::Extended Price field if you want a "0" to show there, even when both Line Items::Price and Line Items::Quantity are blank.

For example, it would be nice if your invoice's Date Due field automatically showed a date 30 days after the date of the invoice itself. But sometimes you may want to make an invoice due earlier or later, based on special circumstances (like a holiday). If you make the Date Due field a calculation field, then you don't have this flexibility. Use a normal Date field with an *auto-enter calculation* (see the box on page 376).

Here's how to create an auto-enter calculation:

1. **Bring up the Manage Database window, and then switch to the now-familiar Fields tab. From the Table pop-up menu, choose Invoices.**

   The fields from the Invoices table appear.

2. **Select the Date Due field in the list, and then click Options.**

   The Field Options dialog box makes an appearance.

3. **On the Auto-Enter tab, turn on the "Calculated Value" checkbox.**

   The Specify Calculation window appears. It looks just like it did before, but this time you're *not* creating a calculation field. Instead, you're specifying the calculation used to determine the auto-enter value.

4. **Create the calculation *Date + 30*.**

   You can use any method you want to build this calculation: Click the field and operators, or type them. Notice that the calculation result is set to Date, and you don't have a pop-up menu to let you change that. Your calculation has to resolve to a valid date, or FileMaker squawks at you.

5. **Click OK three times to dismiss all the dialog boxes.**

   You return to the database itself.

   Now you can create a new invoice, and then test out your field. When you enter a date for the invoice, the Date Due field updates instantly with the date 30 days from now. Notice that you can still change the Date Due field if you want. See the box below for more on auto-enter calculations.

POWER USERS' CLINIC

Do Not Replace Existing Value

Auto-enter calculation fields don't act *exactly* like other calculation fields. If you *change* the invoice date, the due date doesn't update to reflect the change. Instead, it keeps its original value, as in the example on the previous page. That's normally the way auto-enter calculations work: It acts only when you first create a record or if the field is empty. Once the field gets a value, the calculation doesn't update it, even if the field it refers to changes.

Often, though, you *want* the calculation to change the field value every time any field used in the calculation is changed, just like a normal calculation. You can easily get this modified behavior by turning off the "Do not replace existing value of field (if any)" checkbox in the Field Options dialog box (shown in Figure 8-9). When you turn this checkbox *off*, FileMaker dutifully updates the field value whenever the calculation evaluates—in other words, when any field it uses changes.

You choose your option depending on the situation. For the Date Due field, you probably want to turn this option off. After all, if you're changing the date of an invoice, it's reasonable to assume you want to rethink the due date as well.

But suppose you have a database of products, and you use an auto-enter calculation to copy the distributor's product code into your internal product code field. If you then change the internal product code to something unique to you, then you probably *don't* want it to change again if you switch to a different distributor. In that case, you'd leave the "Do not replace existing value (if any)" option turned on, ensuring that once you've put in your own special value, it never changes.

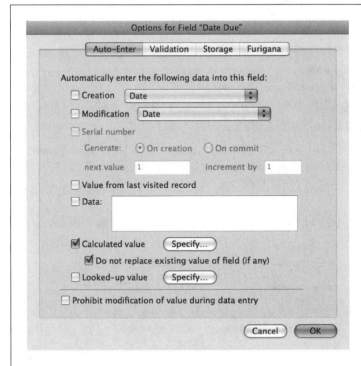

Figure 8-9:
Auto-enter calculations let you protect data that's already in a field if you change the field the calculation refers to. The verbose setting here, "Do not replace existing value for field (if any)" is turned on for you. But if want an auto-enter calculation to update any time the field(s) it refers to changes, then uncheck this option.

Validate Data Entry with a Calculation

In Chapter 6 you were introduced to several ways to validate data entered into a field. But what if the Validation tab in the Field Options dialog box doesn't have a checkbox to meet your needs? For example, you may want to use validation on the Zip Code field in the Customers table. A valid Zip code has *either* five characters or 10 characters (in other words, it can look like this: 90210, or this: 90210-1100). The closest validation option is "Maximum number of characters"—close, but not right.

This situation is just the kind where the "Validate by calculation" option comes in handy. Your job is to create a calculation with a Boolean result. It should return True when the data is valid, and False otherwise. Here's how it works:

1. **Choose File→Manage→Database, and then click the Field tab. Then switch to view the field definitions for the Customers table. Select the Zip Code field, and then click Options.**

    The Field Options dialog box pops up.

2. **Click the Validation tab, and then turn on "Validate by calculation".**

    The Specify Calculation window appears, ready for you to enter your validation calculation.

3. **From the View pop-up menu, choose "Text functions".**

   The Function list updates to show just the text functions.

4. **In the Function list, double-click "Length (text)".**

   The function appears in the Calculation box. Notice that "text" is already high-lighted, ready to be replaced. The length function returns the length of a text value. You use it here to see how many characters are in the Zip Code field.

5. **In the Field list, double-click the Zip Code field.**

   FileMaker puts this field inside the parentheses, where it becomes the parameter to the length function. Now that you have a function to tell you how long the Zip code is, you need to use the comparison operator to compare it to something.

6. **Click to the right of the closing parenthesis. Then, in the Operators list, double-click =.**

   FileMaker adds the comparison operator (=) to your calculation.

7. **After the = operator, type 5.**

   Your calculation compares the length of the Zip code to the value 5. If they're equal, then it returns True. But you also want to accept a Zip code with *10* characters.

8. **In the Operators list, double-click "or".**

   You may need to scroll down to see it. Remember that this operator connects two Boolean values, and then returns True if *either* value is true. Next, you set up the second value.

9. **Double-click the length function again, then double-click the Zip Code function again, and then double-click the = operator.**

   This second check should also compare the length to some other value.

10. **In the Calculation box, type 10.**

    Your calculation is complete. It should look like the one in Figure 8-10.

11. **Click OK until you're back on your layout.**

    You're now back in your database and ready to test. Try giving a customer a few different Zip codes to and make sure the validation works.

Most validations happen as soon as you leave the field, even if you're just moving to another field in the record. But some validation types—including most validation calculations—don't happen until you exit the *record*.

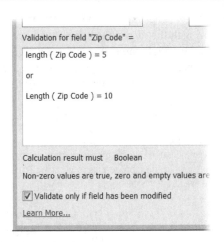

Figure 8-10:
This calculation checks for two conditions, and uses an "or" operator. One comparison checks to see if the length is five, while the other looks for a length of 10. If either is True, then your calculation is True as well, and FileMaker accepts the Zip code. If both conditions fail, then the calculation result is False, and FileMaker shows you an error message. See page 381 for an explanation of why in this calculation has extra spaces and paragraph returns. Notice that the calculation's label (where the field's name normally appears) the Specify Calculation window reminds you that you're writing a calculation for a validation, and not for the field itself.

Tip: If you're dying to know what determines when your validation occurs, here's the skinny: If, when validating a field, FileMaker looks only at the data *in the field itself*, then it performs the validation immediately. If it has to look at data in *other fields* or *other records*, then it waits until you commit the record before validating. For example, "Not empty" only requires looking at the field, so will evaluate immediately. But "Unique" requires a comparison with all the other records in the database and won't evaluate until you commit.

FREQUENTLY ASKED QUESTION

Validate Only If Field Has Been Modified

What's the "Validate only if field has been modified" checkbox for? I don't remember seeing this in the Specify Calculation window before. For that matter, where did the Result Type pop-up menu go?

Good eye. The Specify Calculation window can show up in lots of places—when defining a calculation field, when specifying an auto-enter calculation, and so on—and it can change slightly in some cases.

First, the Result Type pop-up menu shows up only when you're defining a calculation field, since it can produce any data type. Since a validation calculation always has a Boolean result, there's no need to ask you here.

In place of this pop-up menu, you often see some new option specific to the calculation type—like the "Validate only if field has been modified" checkbox in Figure 8-10.

Normally when you edit a record, FileMaker validates only the fields you actually change. Any field in the record that hasn't been changed is accepted even if it violates the validation rule. This violation can happen when you have your field set to validate "Only during data entry", and the records have been set some other way—from an import (page 826) or with a set field in a script (page 463). If you want to validate this field whenever you edit the record, not just when the field itself changes, then turn off this checkbox.

Replacing Data Using a Calculation

You've worked with the Replace command a few times now. In Chapter 2 (page 70), you used it to replace the data in every record with the same value. Then in Chapter 4 (page 140), you saw how to create data in a key field when your table had records before you created the serial number field. Finally in the box on page 261, you used a Substitute function to change only a part of the data that's in a field. That's where you really started to see the power of Replace.

Note: Replace Field Contents is a huge timesaver, but since it works on a found set of records, you can't undo it. Improperly used (with a bad calculation or the wrong found set), it can be destructive. See page 521 to learn how the Data Viewer in FileMaker Pro Advanced helps you preview the results of a calculation before you make that one-way trip through the Replace Field Contents dialog box.

The calculation you used earlier, *Substitute (Street Address ; "Stt" ; "St")*, replaced the bad abbreviation "Stt" with the good one "St" in every record in your found set. It takes a minute or so to write a calculation to do your data cleanup, but it's still a lot faster than having to flip through each record, finding and highlighting the bad text and then retyping it manually. Once you know a handful of stock functions and get quick at writing them, you can clean up thousands of records in the time it would take a human without super-calculation skills days to do.

The Substitute function is one of 45 text functions you can use to manipulate or clean up data. Take a stroll through the list to see which of them can help you with those monumental data cleansing tasks that come with just about every database.

The Proper (text) function changes every word in a field to have an Upper-case letter at its front. So if some smartie pants thinks he's e. e. cummings and won't use the shift key, you can fix the bad entries he made in a Name field with this calculation:

```
Proper ( Customer::First Name )
```

Then repeat the process for the Last Name field. (And then with any others your little poet has messed up. What you do to him afterwards is between you and your personnel department.)

Tip: FileMaker has two other functions for changing case: Upper and Lower. It probably goes without saying that Upper converts all the text to uppercase, and Lower converts it to lowercase.

Comments

Everything you can put in a calculation has some kind of value—unless it's a *comment*. Comments are chunks of text whose sole purpose is to help guide you through long calculations. Professional database developers, like all good programmers, provide lots of comments for the benefit of people who might work on the computer code months or years later. Once you have a few sets of parentheses or nested function calls, you may have trouble understanding even your *own* FileMaker calculation when you have to go back and make changes. When it evaluates the calculation, FileMaker ignores all comments completely—it's as if they weren't there. (But you'll be glad they are.)

Note: You may have noticed that this book shows some extras spaces and paragraph returns that FileMaker doesn't throw into your functions automatically. These spaces are for ease of reading, and lots of developers type them into their calculations. Like comments, FileMaker ignores those spaces, as long as all the other syntax is correct.

You can use two different styles for your comments. First, any text that comes after two consecutive slash marks (//) is considered a comment. This kind of comment goes all the way to the end of the line:

```
// this is a comment
3.14 * Diameter // and so is this
```

A comment is also any text that comes between the symbols /* and */. This symbol pair comes in handy in two places. It saves typing if you need to type a long comment across multiple lines:

```
/* this is a comment that runs across multiple
lines. To make life easier, you can use the second
comment style */
```

Also, this comment style lets you add comments *within* a line:

```
3 /*sprocket size*/ * 10 /*sprocket count*/ * 57 /*tooth count*/
```

In addition to comments, you can—and should—use whitespace to make your calculations easier to read. Calculations don't have to be strung together in one long line, even though that's the way FileMaker does it in the Specify Calculation window. Press the Return key or space bar to add space anywhere, except in a field name, function name, text constant, or number. Comments and white space can make a world of difference. Here's a long calculation that doesn't use either:

```
Let([DaysToAdd=Case(DayOfWeek(theDate)=1;1;DayOfWeek(theDate)=2;0;DayOfWeek(t
heDate)=3;-1;DayOfWeek(theDate)=4;-2;DayOfWeek(theDate)=5;-
3;DayOfWeek(theDate)=6;-4;-
5)];Date(Month(theDate);Day(theDate)+DaysToAdd;Year(theDate)))
```

The calculation works just fine, but it's a nightmare to read and worse to edit. Here's the same calculation, written with a comment and helpful spaces:

```
/*Figure out what day it is, and then add or subtract the
proper number to the DayOfWeek value to identify This Monday.*/

Let ( [ DaysToAdd =
Case (
DayOfWeek ( theDate ) = 1; 1; // Sunday
DayOfWeek ( theDate ) = 2; 0; // Monday
DayOfWeek ( theDate ) = 3; -1; // Tuesday
DayOfWeek ( theDate ) = 4; -2; // Wednesday
DayOfWeek ( theDate ) = 5; -3; // Thursday
DayOfWeek ( theDate ) = 6; -4; // Friday
DayOfWeek ( theDate ) = 7; -5) ] ; // Saturday
Date ( Month ( theDate ); Day ( theDate ) + DaysToAdd; Year ( theDate ))
)
```

Sure, it takes up a bit more space, but this way, you can much more easily pick apart the pieces to figure out what the calculation does. In the next chapter, you'll learn about the functions used in this calc.

More Calculations and Data Types

The last chapter introduced the terminology and concepts behind FileMaker's calculations. You learned how to create them using the Specify Calculation window's tools. The sheer length of the functions list shows how big a role functions play in good calculation construction. FileMaker divides that long list into types so it's easier to find the one you need, and because the types usually share some common traits that make using them easier. In this chapter, you'll learn about the most common functions for the various data types—text, number, date, time, timestamp, and container—and when to use them. To test a calculation, just create a brand new calculation field, and then start building it using the techniques you've learned so far. If it doesn't work the way you expect, or if you don't need it after your experiment is done, then just delete the field.

Number Crunching Calculations

Although they don't come first in the function list, number functions are the most obvious application of calculations, so they're a logical place to start. Plus, many concepts you'll learn for number functions apply to other functions as well.

Note: See page 359 for a refresher on mathematical operators.

Number Function Types

Since Filemaker has so many number functions, the Function list breaks them up into smaller groups with descriptive names. You can easily find the group you need (or skim by them without looking, if you might be traumatized by accidentally seeing a sine or cosine function). The function groups you use with your numeric data are:

- Number functions
- Aggregate functions
- Financial functions
- Trigonometric functions

Note: This book doesn't cover the financial and trigonometric functions, which have highly specialized uses. If you need to use these brawny functions, you probably have the mental muscle to decipher the technical terms in FileMaker's Help file, where you'll find them explained.

Using Number Functions

As you saw on page 362, most functions expect one or more parameters. Number functions' parameters have to number values, and all the number functions return a number result. In the next sections, you'll see examples of several of the most commonly used number functions. These examples are from the Number and Aggregate groups, but you might find them more easily if you sort your function list alphabetically.

Abs()

Abs is short for Absolute, and it returns the absolute value of a number, which is the positive value of the number or zero. For example, you might have a series of readings from a brainwave scan that range from negative to positive, but you just need to know how far each value is from zero. You could add an *Abs()* function to each field to find out. This calculation returns 343.7634:

    Abs (-343.7634)

This calculation returns 4:

    Abs (2 * 42 / -21)

Average()

The Average function can work with one or more: constant values, regular fields, repeating fields, all related fields in a relationship, or just the first related field. For example, if you store a series of student test scores in several related tables, then you can use an *Average()* function to round them all up. This calculation returns 10:

    Average (3 ; 6 ; 21)

When you use fields instead of numbers, FileMaker uses the values from those fields. This calculation returns the average of all tests in the related table:

    Average (Tests::Score)

This calculation returns the average for each of the first related test records:

```
Average ( AIMS::Score ; Reading::Score ; Math::Score )
```

Count()

The *Count()* function counts all non-blank values in a field, whether it's a repeating field, all related fields, or several nonrepeating fields. Because it's possible to have a record that doesn't have a value in a particular field, it's usually more accurate to count a related field that is guaranteed to have a value, like a table's ID field. This way, you can easily count related values, like the number of invoices for a customer or tests taken by a student. This calculation returns the number of invoices in the related table:

```
Count ( Invoice::InvoiceID )
```

This calculation returns the total number of changes you record for an employee's status:

```
Count ( NameChanges ; DeptChanges ; LicenseChanges )
```

Floor() and Ceiling()

The *Floor()* function is like a supercharged rounding function. It rounds any value down to the next lowest integer. It just takes a single parameter, so you can use a number, an expression, or a field reference. This calculation returns 3:

```
Floor ( 3.1416 )
```

Watch what happens with a negative number. This calculation returns –4:

```
Floor ( -3.1416 )
```

It can be awkward to show values of multiple decimal places for prices. If you want a whole dollar value instead, try this:

```
Floor ( Tax * Extended Price )
```

The *Ceiling()* function is a close relative of *Floor()*, but it rounds a number up to the next highest integer. So, this calculation returns 4:

```
Ceiling ( 3.1416 )
```

And this calculation returns –3:

```
Ceiling ( -3.1416 )
```

To figure out how to charge your customers the actual price you spent on fuel (32.987), plus a 10% surcharge (1.1), but without the weird decimal places, use this calculation for a result of 37:

```
Ceiling ( FuelExpense * 1.1 )
```

List()

This aggregate function works with numbers, but is even more useful on text. *List()* gathers up all the values you specify, and then returns them in a *return-separated list*. That is, each value appears on a line by itself, and each line has a paragraph symbol after it. So for this calculation:

```
List ( Line Items:: Description )
```

You might get:

```
Virtualizing software
Holoband
Batteries (for Serge)
```

The most common use of *List()* is to suck related data, repeating fields or a series of nonrepeating fields into a single text block for easy display, reporting, or manipulation. You could display the results of a *List()* in a tooltip (page 329). Or, if you need to grab a list of related IDs, *List()* is your go-to function.

Round()

The *Round()* function rounds a value to the number of places you set. It takes two parameters: number and precision. So if you set the precision to 3, this calculation returns 3.142:

```
Round ( 3.1416 ; 3 )
```

Tip: You might be tempted to simply use number formatting on a field to display a value to a specific number of decimal places. But remember, that method changes only what you see on a layout. If you perform math on that field, then FileMaker uses the real value (with all its decimal glory) in the calculation. But when you use the Round function, you're actually changing the value in the field, and any calculations acting on that field use the rounded value.

SetPrecision()

Some calculations demand a high degree of precision, like those that track radioactive isotopes or other scientific data with lots of places following the decimal point. The *SetPrecision()* function extends FileMaker's automatic precision of 16 decimal places, up to a maximum of 400. To get more than 16 decimals places, add a *SetPrecision()* function to the calculation that produces the value that requires precision. You can use *SetPrecision()* with all other numeric functions, except trigonometric functions, which don't accept this extended precision (Figure 9-1).

The *SetPrecision()* function requires two parameters: expression and precision. The first parameter is a number, or any expression that results in a number. The second is the number of decimal places you want to see.

Note: The *SetPrecision()* function affects your calculation's result, but not necessarily the way FileMaker displays it. To save space on your layout, you can use Number formatting on the field to show only a few decimal places until you click the field, when you see the real, stored value.

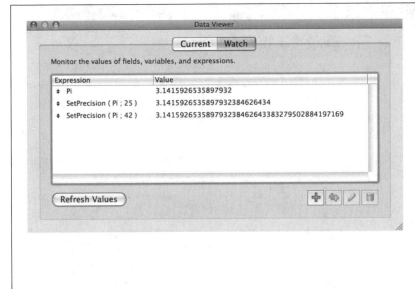

Figure 9-1:
The first item in this window shows how FileMaker normally evaluates the value of pi. In the second, the SetPrecision function shows 25 decimal places. The third item shows 42 decimal places. You can see the formula on the left, and the result on the right. This window is File-Maker Pro Advanced's Data Viewer, which lets you write a calculation and view its results without creating a field. It's a huge time saver when you're writing a hairy calc. Read about it, and other developer features on page 521.

Going Beyond Basic Calculations

In the last chapter, you created two very simple calculation fields using numbers: Extended Price and Invoice Total. Now, you'll build on those basic concepts, and use some of the number functions you've just learned to make a set of calculations that fit an upcoming sales promotion.

Note: Download the sample file for this chapter, called Function Types.fp7, from this book's Missing CD page at *www.missingmanuals.com*.

Reviewing the Data and New Business Rules

You've decided to start reselling personal security products to your customers. To help keep track of things, you have a Products table in your database. The table has these fields:

- A text field called SKU.

- A text field called Description.

- A number field called Cost.

- A number field called Price.

UP TO SPEED

The *Max()* and *Min()* Functions

Often, you need to know either the highest or lowest value in a series. The *Max()* function and its twin sister, *Min()*, fulfill these needs, and you find them in the function list's aggregate functions category. Like all the aggregate functions, these functions expect at least one parameter, and are glad to get more. Every parameter should be a number. Your parameters can be:

- Constant data
- Fields within a record
- Repeating fields
- All related fields
- The first related record of from multiple tables

The max function looks at every number referenced, and returns whichever is largest. *Min()*, on the other hand, returns the smallest value.

For example, look at this calculation:

```
Max ( 10 ; 3 ; 72 ; 19 ; 1 )
```

Its result is 72, since that's the largest parameter.

If you have a repeating field called Distances that holds the distances from your office to each Krispy Kreme store in your city, then you can use this calculation to find the closest sugar fix:

```
Min ( Distances )
```

The same is true for *related* fields too. This calculation finds the most expensive line item on an invoice:

```
Max ( Line Items::Price )
```

With both repeating fields and related fields, you pass just one field to the min or max function, but FileMaker considers *all* the values in that field. If the field is a repeating field, then FileMaker considers every repetition. If it's a related field, then its value from every related record is considered. But you can refer to multiple related tables, too. If you have several tables of updates, each with a date the update was done, then you can find the most recent update this way:

```
Min ( Name::Update ; License::Update ;
Department::Update )
```

Switch to that layout now and flip through the product records. To help drive sales to your larger clients, you want to implement a volume discount scheme; they should get a five-percent discount if they buy enough. But some of the products you sell don't have enough mark-up to justify these discounts. You want to be sure the discount never reduces your mark-up below 20 percent.

First, the lawyers say you have to add a line to all your marketing materials: "Volume discounts not available for all products." You can make this line as small as humanly possible, and hide it way down in the corner. Next, you need to fix your database so it tells you the discount price for each product.

Planning the Calculations

To implement this discount scheme, take what you need to know, and translate it into calculation terms.

- First, calculate 95 percent of the price (a five-percent discount):
  ```
  Price * .95
  ```

- Second, you also know the cost (in the Cost field) and you can figure out the lowest price by adding 20 percent to this cost:

  ```
  Cost * 1.2
  ```

- Finally, the discounted price is either the calculated discount price, *or* the cost + 20-percent price, whichever is *greater*. Put another way, you want the *maximum* of these two values:

  ```
  Max ( Price * .95 ; Cost * 1.2 )
  ```

Using the *Max()* function, the previous calculation results in either the discounted price, or the minimum price, whichever is greater (see the box on the previous page). That result is *almost* perfect. But suppose you have a product whose *normal* price is less than 20 percent above cost (hey, it's a competitive market). If you use the *Max()* calculation as it is now, then the new discounted price is *more* than the normal price. You need to go back and add to your calculation so that it takes the regular price into account, and uses *that price* if it's lower than the calculated discount. Read on to learn how to think through this calculation quandary.

Constructing the Calculation

When calculations start to get complicated like this discount price example, you can visualize the finished calculation by imagining that you have a field that contains the value you need. You can use this pretend field in your new calculation, and then, when you're all finished, put the old calculation in place of the pretend field. In this case, just pretend you have a field called Calculated Discount that holds the discount price. With that imaginary field in mind, create a calculation with this formula:

```
Min ( Calculated Discount ; Price)
```

The result of this calculation is either the calculated discount or the regular price, if it's lower. Now, just put the old calculation in place of the words "Calculated Discount" (since the old calculation *results in the calculated discount*):

```
Min ( Max ( Price * .95 ; Cost * 1.2 ) ; Price)
```

Tip: You don't even have to write the second formula in place of the words "Calculated Discount." Until you click OK, you can treat the calculation box like a big word processing page. Move the insertion point a few lines past the first calc, and then create the second calc. Then when it's correct, cut and paste it into place in the first calc.

The entire *Max()* function, complete with its two parameters, is now the *Min()* function's first parameter. You might think it looks a little confusing at first, but with practice you become accustomed to looking at functions-inside-functions like this.

If it helps, you can add white space and comments to clarify the calculation, as Figure 9-2 shows.

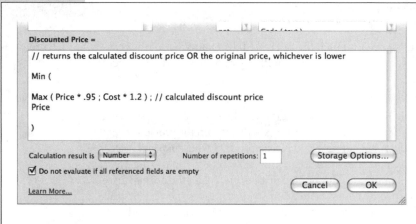

Discounted Price =

```
// returns the calculated discount price OR the original price, whichever is lower

Min (

Max ( Price * .95 ; Cost * 1.2 ) ; // calculated discount price
Price

)
```

Calculation result is [Number ▾]   Number of repetitions: [1]   (Storage Options...)
☑ Do not evaluate if all referenced fields are empty

Learn More...   (Cancel) (OK)

Figure 9-2:
You may find it hard to write nested calculations, and hard to read them if you need to come back later and tweak them. In this case, though, the calculation is formatted with copious white space and plenty of comments. Chances are you understand this version better than the one shown in the text above.

If you want to test a complicated calculation, spot-check a few records where you know the result. Sometimes the math is so complex that you just have to work it out on paper and enter dummy records to check the calculation. Usually, if a calculation isn't working, you can figure out how to fix it when you compare your math to the value in the field.

Text Calculations

Although most people think of functions for doing dry stuff like math in a spreadsheet, you can also use functions in your database's text fields. Just as you can add and subtract numbers with number functions, you can use text functions to slice and dice the words in your database. For example, you might receive data from an outside source that needs major cleanup before you can use it. This data has people's first and last names in the same field; it's even got entire email messages crammed into a field—address, subject, and body—when all you need is the email address. You can equip a temporary database with fields and text calculations to *parse* (think of it as sifting) the data into the form your better-designed database expects.

Note: Fixing data with parsing calculations is called a *calculated replace*, since you use the Replace dialog box to enter the calculation. Since Replace works on the found set of records, you do a find first, to isolate just the records that have the problem you're fixing, and then (and only then) do a calculated Replace Field Contents that fixes the error.

Repeating Fields for Multiple Results

What if one discount price isn't enough? Suppose you want to give your customers five percent off on orders of five or more, 10 percent off on orders of 10 or more, 15 percent off on orders of 15 or more, and so on. You could create more calculation fields with slight variations on the calculations you've already specified:

- Discounted Price for 10:

  ```
  Min ( Max ( Price * .90 ; Cost * 1.2 ) ;
  Price)
  ```

- Discounted Price for 15:

  ```
  Min ( Max ( Price * .85 ; Cost * 1.2 ) ;
  Price )
  ```

If you want seven price breaks, then you have to create seven fields. And if you want to change the calculation slightly (for example, to give an additional two-percent discount per break instead of five percent), then you have to change every single field's calculation.

This example is one of those cases where repeating fields come in handy. When you create a repeating calculation field, you have only one calculation, but you get multiple results. With only one calculation, though, FileMaker doesn't show you an obvious way to provide different discount rates. The secret ingredient is the *Get (CalculationRepetitionNumber)* function. It returns the repetition number being calculated at the moment. For example, when FileMaker goes to calculate the *third* value in your repeating field, this function returns 3.

With this function in mind, you can devise a single calculation that uses different discount rates depending on the repetition number:

```
Min (
 Max(
 Price[1] * (1 -
 Get(CalculationRepetitionNumber) * .05);
 Cost[1] * 1.2
 ) ;
 Price[1]
 )
```

In this calculation, you replace the constant discount rate by the expression:

```
(1 - Get(CalculationRepetitionNumber) *
.05)
```

Get (CalculationRepetitionNumber) expects to work with repeating fields. But you can use the nonrepeating Price and Cost fields by adding [1] to their names (this step tells FileMaker to grab the *first* repetition—the only one that exists in a nonrepeating field).

If you test this calculation with a few numbers, then you see it results in an extra five percent discount for each subsequent repetition. Once you've created a field like this, a lot of things become really easy:

- To add more price breaks, just change the number of repetitions in the Specify Calculation window. Going from seven breaks to 20 is a 5-second change.

- To change the discount rates for *every* break, just change one number—the .5—and you affect every calculated value.

In contrast to the wide variety of mathematical operators for working with numbers, only one pertains specifically to text—the *concatenation* operator. Represented by the "&" sign (ampersand), it strings bits of text together. (When you need to chop and divide your text in order to parse it, you use a *function* instead of an operator, as described on page 392.)

To use this operator, put it between units of text, as in the expression below:

```
"This is a " & "test"
```

The result of this calculation is *This is a test*.

The concatenation operator lets you combine text from two different fields, and make them work better together. Although you store First Name and Last Name in two separate fields, you often want to display them in a single field. When you're showing a second field in a value list (page 217), you can pick only *one* field to show along with the primary value. That example used the First Name field, but the full name would make the menu more useful. That's where concatenation comes in.

Create a new calculation field in the Customers table called *Full Name*. Set the calculation's result type to Text, and then create this calculation:

```
Last Name & ", " & First Name
```

Some results are "Greystone, Daniel" or "Adama, Joseph". Note that the calculation includes a comma and the appropriate spaces for separating data between your fields. Now you can use the Full Name field instead of First Name in a value list. Figure 9-3 shows the result.

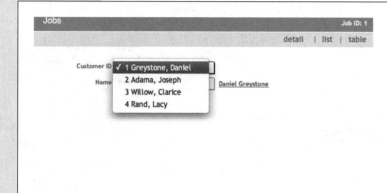

Figure 9-3:
When you switch the value list to use the new calculated Full Name field, your pop-up menu can show your Customer's full name instead of just the first name. People often use calculations to combine multiple field values for display purposes. Here the customer's last name comes first, but nothing's stopping you from making a second one with the first name followed by the last name.

Text Functions

It's surprising to database newcomers, but text requires nearly as much manipulation as numbers do. That's because data frequently comes from another source, like Excel or Access. If you're lucky, the data is already in the form you need. Often though, you have to massage the data to get it divided up to match your tables, fields, and field types. Sometimes, as with the Full Name calculation in the previous section, you just want to make the data display better. To know how to solve your problem, you need to know about text function types.

Advanced Web Viewer URLs

On page 612, you'll learn about the web viewer, a full-featured web browser you can stick right on a layout. Web viewers come configured to visit some frequently-used websites. But if you want to go beyond the basics, then you have to code your own custom URL, and that almost always requires calculations. The concatenation operator (&) will take your web viewer expertise to the next level.

In the Web Viewer Setup dialog box (page 614), in the "Choose a Web Site" list, click the first item: Custom Web Address. On the right side of the window, the configuration options disappear.

Click the Specify button, which brings up the Specify Calculation window, prefilled with a highlighted calculation. Delete it, because you'll be making a custom URL that matches the one in your browser. Find the parts of the URL that change for different sites or different pages within a website, and then convert them to a calculation. Here are a few ways to make a calculated URL:

- Your easiest solution: Store a web address in your database. Suppose you have a Home Page field in your Company database that holds the URL for a company's home page. Use this simple calculation to display the home page in your web viewer:

  `"http://" & Company::Home Page`

- If you look up a stock symbol on Yahoo Finance, then the address box in your browser shows something like this:

`http://finance.yahoo.com/q?s=AAPL`

In this case, the URL shows stock information for Apple, whose stock symbol is *AAPL*. To make the web viewer show the correct page for any symbol in your database, use this calculation (which assumes you have a field called Stock Symbol):

`"http://finance.yahoo.com/q?s=" & Company:`
`Stock Symbol`

- Finally, suppose you use the Basecamp project management system (*http://basecamphq.com/*), and you want to show the project overview page in your FileMaker billing database. Basecamp's URL looks like this:

`https://myaccount.com/projects/12345/`
`project/log`

If you look closely, then you come to the conclusion that the "12345" bit is a unique identifier for the project. Everything else looks pretty generic. So you can store just that identifier in your FileMaker database, and use this calculation to show any project in a web viewer:

`"https://myaccount.com/projects/" &`
`Project::Basecamp ID & "/project/log"`

Using the power of calculations, you can integrate just about any web content into your layout. You're no longer limited to the list of sites FileMaker provides.

Text function types

FileMaker's text-handling functions come in two flavors: *text* and *text formatting*. Text functions handle tasks like finding whether a particular string of characters occurs in a field, or changing all instances of specific characters within a field, or counting text length. Text functions can break up text in three ways: by *characters*, *words*, or *values*. When FileMaker does the dividing, it gives you three ways to decide which parts you want: *left, middle*, or *right*.

Text formatting functions change the way your text looks, like making a part of the text in a field bold and red. These functions are a lot more flexible than just making a field bold and red on your layout, because you can tell the calculation to search *inside* the field, find just the characters "Propane Sale!" and make them red, but leave all the surrounding text untouched.

POWER USERS' CLINIC

A Calculation in a Button

On page 317, you learned how to create buttons on a layout and program them to perform all kinds of database duties at a click. The only problem is, the more features you give your database, the more buttons you have to make. And some of the folks using your database need a completely different assortment of buttons. Fortunately, most button commands have one or more options you can set with a calculation. The calculation can adjust what the button does based on field data, user information, the current date or time, and so forth.

Suppose you have two different layouts to view the people in your People database. One's for the people who are *customers*, and the other's for *employees*. You might think that with two different detail layouts you'd need two buttons. But you can summon the power of calculations to make one button do double duty.

If you take a peek at the options for the "Go to Layout" button action, then you see that in addition to all the layouts in your database, the pop-up menu includes two options you haven't used before: "Layout Name by calculation" and "Layout Number by calculation".

If you pick either of these options, FileMaker presents the Specify Calculation window. You simply write a calculation that evaluates to the correct layout name (or number if that's your persuasion), and FileMaker goes to the right one. For example:

```
If ( Person::Type = "Customer", "Customer
Detail", "Employee Detail" )
```

Character functions

Parsing by character comes in handy when you have data in a predictable format, and you need to access pieces of it. You can use functions to grab the first three digits of a Social Security Number, the last four digits of a credit card number, or the style code buried inside a product number.

FileMaker can work with individual characters inside a text value. The first letter in a text value is number 1, the second is number 2, and so on. Then you can ask for the first few characters, or the last few, or just the fifth, sixth, and seventh.

Note: Every letter, number, punctuation mark, space, tab, carriage return, or other symbol counts as a character.

- The *Left()* function returns only the leftmost letters of a text value. You *pass* (that is, tell) the calculation the actual text value to parse, and the number of letters you want. For example, to get a person's initials, you can use a calculation like this:

      Left (First Name ; 1) & Left (Last Name ; 1)

  To get the first three digits of a Social Security Number, you can use this calculation:

      Left (SSN ; 3)

- The *Right()* function does the same thing but starts from the other end of the text value. If you want to record the last four digits of someone's credit card number, then you can do it like this:

      Right (Credit Card Number ; 4)

- If the information you want isn't on either end, you may need to use the *Middle()* function instead. This function expects *three* parameters. Just as when using left and right, the first parameter is the text value FileMaker's inspecting. The second parameter is the starting position. Finally, you tell FileMaker how many characters you want.

  For example, suppose you have a product database that uses a special coding system for each item. The code "SH-112-M" indicates shirt style 112, medium size. To pull out just the style number (that 112 in the middle of the product code), you want your calculation to grab three characters from the Product Number field, starting with the fourth character.

      Middle (Product Number ; 4 ; 3)

Tip: Use the Right function to pad a number with leading zeroes (or any other character). For example, the calculation *Right ("0000" & InvoiceID ; 5)* puts two zeroes in front of InvoiceID #789 (#00789), only one in front of #6789 (#06789), but none at all in front of #56789 (#56789).

Word functions

FileMaker also understands the concept of words. With word functions, you don't have to bother dealing with every single character.

In FileMaker's mind, a *word* is any stretch of letters, numbers, or the period character that doesn't have any other spaces or punctuation in it. Most of the time, this definition means FileMaker does exactly what you expect: It sees the real words in the text. For example, each of the following is one word:

- FileMaker

- ABC123

- This.is.a.word

Any sequence of other characters isn't part of a word at all. Each of these has two words:

- FileMaker Pro
- ABC 123
- A-Test
- Two *** Words

Note: If your text value doesn't have normal words (like a long URL, for example), then you may have to pay special attention to the letters-numbers-periods rule to get the results you expect.

Along the same lines as the character functions, FileMaker has three word-oriented functions called *LeftWords()*, *RightWords()*, and *MiddleWords()*. Each takes two parameters: the text value to examine, and a number to tell FileMaker which words you're interested in. You can use a word function to parse a person's first and middle names if you ever get a file with all three names unceremoniously dumped into a single field.

- *LeftWords()* returns all the text before the end of the specified word. For instance, this function:

  ```
  LeftWords ( Preamble ; 3 )
  ```

  might return *We the People*. But if Preamble contained "This *** Is *** a *** Test," it would return *This *** Is *** A* instead. In other words, it doesn't just return the words. It returns *everything* before the end of the third word.

- Likewise, *RightWords()* returns everything *after* the specified word's *beginning*, counting from the end. This calculation:

  ```
  RightWords ( Revelations ; 1 )
  ```

  returns *Amen*.

- What would *LeftWords()* and *RightWords()* be without *MiddleWords()*? You can probably guess how this function works: You pass it a text value, a starting word, and the number of words to return. It then returns everything from the beginning of the starting word through the end of the finishing word. The following calculation shows how it works; it returns "or not" because they're the third and fourth words.

  ```
  MiddleWords ( "To be, or not to be" ; 3 ; 2 )
  ```

Text editing functions

FileMaker includes dozens of text functions, but a few of them are worth special mention because you see them throughout the rest of this section, and because they're so useful for cleaning up messy data.

- The *Substitute()* function performs a find-and-replace within a text value. For example, if you want to turn all the Xs to Os in your love letter (maybe you felt like you were coming on too strong), then you can do this:

```
Substitute ( Love Letter ; "X" ; "O" )
```

FREQUENTLY ASKED QUESTION

The Middle Way

It looks like you can tell the Middle() *function to isolate characters anywhere in a text field, just by telling it which characters to count. So why do we need* Left() *and* Right() *functions when you can do the same thing with* Middle()?

As the example on this page suggests, the *Middle()* function indeed provides all the power you need to pick text values apart character by character. For example, instead of:

```
Left ( Model Number ; 3 )
```

You could do this:

```
Middle ( Model Number ; 1 ; 3 )
```

It gets a little tougher to mimic the *Right()* function, but it's possible.

In *lots* of places, one function can do the same thing as another (or a few others).

For example, you can use *Left()* and *Right()* instead of *Middle()* if you want. This calculation:

```
Middle ( Product Number ; 4 ; 3 )
```

can be rewritten like this:

```
Right ( Left ( Product Number ; 7 ) ; 3 )
```

The good news is, there's more than one *right answer*. Shorter is usually better, if only because you can often read it more easily. But if a few extra keystrokes make the calculation easier to understand, then they're usually worth it.

Substitute() is one of a few FileMaker functions that support a special *bracketed syntax*. You can perform *several* replacements on a piece of text with one substitute function. Each pair in brackets represents one search value and its replacement value. Here's how to remove all the vowels from a field:

```
Substitute ( My Field ; ["a" ; ""] ; ["e" ; ""] ; ["i" ; ""] ; ["o" ; ""]
;
["u" ; ""] )
```

Note: This example shows another nice fact about the substitute function: You can use it to *remove* something. Just replace it with empty quotes: "".

- While the substitute function can be used to change or remove what you specify, *Filter()* can remove everything you *don't* specify. For example, suppose you want to strip any non-numeric characters from a credit card number. You can *try* to think of all the possible things a person might type in a Credit Card Number field (good luck!), or you can use the filter function instead:

```
Filter ( Credit Card Number ; "0123456789" )
```

This calculation tells FileMaker to return the contents of the Credit Card Number field with everything except the numerals removed. In other words, simply put the characters you'd like to *keep* in the second parameter.

- The *PatternCount()* function tells you how many of a specific character string exist in the text. The function needs to know what you're searching, and what to look for. Consider:

  ```
  PatternCount ( Ten Commandments ; "shalt" )
  ```

  In this case, the calculation returns 10. If the pattern doesn't appear in the text, then the calc returns a 0.

- The *Trim()* function cleans up after those data entry folks who can't stop typing extra spaces before and after the important stuff. Just tell the function what to look at. From the calculation below, you get the string "Anyway" placed in your field.

  ```
  Trim ( "Anyway " )
  ```

Text value functions

If a field holds more than one chunk of text, with a paragraph symbol putting each chunk on its own line, then it's very much like a value list (page 116). The data inside the list is called *return-separated values*. Text value functions let you grab individual lines from a value list. And since you can so easily grab a particular line from a value list, you can use the *List()* function (page 385) to put your data *into* a list to make it easier to grab.

Here's a simple example to show how parsing a value list works. Suppose you have a field called Colors with a list of data like this:

- Red

- Green

- Blue

- Orange

- Yellow

The *LeftValues()* function works like its counterpart LeftWords(). It takes two parameters: the list to examine, and a number to specify how many values you want. This formula returns "Red" and "Green":

```
LeftValues ( Colors ; 2 )
```

If *LeftValues()* doesn't do the trick, try *MiddleValue()* or *RightValues()*.

Use the *GetValue()* function when you need to parse just one value from a list. The value you need has to be in a predictable place in the list, as in the whole-email-slammed-into-one-field example at the beginning of this section. Say the email comes to you like this:

- Email From

- Email To

- Subject

- Body

You could grab the Email To address with this function:

```
GetValue ( Email ; 2 )
```

You can figure out how many values in a list with *ValueCount()*. Just tell FileMaker which value list to count. The text parameter can refer to one or more fields or to static text. For example, this function returns 2:

```
ValueCount ( "Tom Cruise¶Keith Urban" )
```

Note: Notice that the value list doesn't need a paragraph symbol after the last value to return the proper count. So if you're building a return separated list in order to grab data from it, then don't worry about that last symbol.

FilterValues() works like its plain cousin *Filter()*. You specify the text, and then the values you want to allow. For example, the following function returns:

Nicole

Katie

```
FilterValues ( "Mimi¶Nicole¶Katie ; "Katie¶Nicole" )
```

FileMaker has *RightValues()* and *MiddleValues()* functions, too. See the box below for ideas on how to use them.

When Data Doesn't Comply

Sometimes the text you need to break up doesn't come in pieces that FileMaker automatically recognizes, like characters or words. For example, suppose you have a file path:

```
C:\My Documents\Product Shots\Tools\Large
Hammer.jpg
```

You need to get the name of the file (Large Hammer.jpg) and its parent folder (Tools). Unfortunately, this text value isn't divided into characters, words, or values. It's divided into *path components*, each with a backslash in between.

When you're faced with something like this, your best bet is to make it look like something FileMaker *can* deal with. If you can turn every backslash into a new line symbol (¶), then you can simply use the RightValues function to pull out the last value. In other words:

```
Substitute ( File Path ; "\ " ; "¶" )
```

The result of this expression is the list of path components, each on its own line:

```
C:
My Documents
Product Shots
Tools
Large Hammer.jpg
```

To get just the file name, you can do this:

```
RightValues ( Substitute ( File Path ; "\
" ; "¶" ) ; 1 )
```

Unless your data already contains multiple lines, you can always use the substitute function to turn any kind of delimited list into a list of values. Bear in mind, though, that the substitute function is *case-sensitive*. You can read more about case sensitivity in the box on page 653.

Text counting functions

You can also work with text by counting its individual parts. FileMaker has three related functions for finding out *how much* text your fields contain:

- The *Length()* function returns the length of a text value by counting characters.

- The *WordCount()* function tells you how many words are in a text value.

- Using the *ValueCount()* function, you can find out how many lines a field has.

These functions become powerhouses in combination with the various left, right, and middle functions. When the fields you're parsing contain varying amounts of text, you can have FileMaker count each one so you don't have to. For example, you might have a Parts Number field that contains parts numbers of varying length. Always, though, the last character is one you don't want. To return all but the last character in a field, use this calculation:

```
Left ( My Field ; Length ( My Field ) - 1 )
```

It uses the left function to grab characters from the field, and the length function (minus one) to find out how many to get. Just change the number on the end to chop off any number of junk characters from the end of a field. You're welcome.

POWER USERS' CLINIC

Outsmarting the Smarties

LeftValues() and *RightValues()* are helpful when you need to pull some items from a return-separated list. But they're also helpful when you want to protect your database from people who know a few workarounds. Say you have a sales promotion going, where your best customers get to pick one free premium from a list of four items. So you've set up a field with a value list and a set of radio buttons. Everybody knows that you can choose only one item from a radio button set, right? Apparently not, because you've got some salespeople who know they can beat the system by Shift-clicking to select multiple radio buttons.

You just have to add an auto-enter calculated value to your Premiums field. Make sure you uncheck the "Do not replace existing value (if any)" option. Here's how the calculation goes:

```
RightValues ( Premiums ; 1 )
```

Now your savvy salespeople can wear out their Shift keys, but they still can't select more than one item in the premium

field, because your calculation holds the field to a single value.

You can even add smarts to a Checkbox Set with a similar technique. Make this calculation:

```
LeftValues ( Premiums ; 2 )
```

People using the program can't select more than two checkboxes. FileMaker knows the first two items they selected, and just keeps putting those same two back into the field, no matter how many checkboxes the salespeople try to select. For another twist, change the calculation to:

```
RightValues ( Premiums ; 2 )
```

Now FileMaker remembers the last two items selected, and very cleverly deselects the oldest value, so that the field always contains the last two items selected from the Checkbox Set.

Text Formatting Functions

Normally when you see data in a calculation field, it's displayed in the format (font, size, style, color, and so on) you applied in Layout mode. Every character in the field shares the same format, unless you want to manually search through all your records selecting the words "Limited Time Only" in your Promotion Notes field, so you can make that bold and red every time it appears. Not only does that method waste your precious time (especially if you're on salary), it also plays havoc with your design when you try to print the field.

FileMaker's text formatting functions let you specify exactly what bit of text you want in 18-point, boldfaced, red Verdana. And you don't have to visit a single record in person. You just write a calculation and FileMaker does the drudgework for you, without tampering with the real data.

FileMaker has six text formatting functions, as described below.

Note: Since that big heading clearly reads "*Text* Formatting Functions," any reasonable person would assume that this formatting applies only to text. Luckily, unreasonable people rule the world. You can apply text formatting to any data type except container.

TextColor() and RGB()

The *TextColor()* function takes two parameters: some text, and a color. It returns the text you send it in the right color. Like many computer programs, FileMaker thinks of colors in RGB code, which defines all colors as combinations of red, green, and blue as expressed by numerical values. The second parameter to the *TextColor()* function is (almost) always the RGB function (and FileMaker automatically adds it when you add *TextColor()* to your formula).

This function returns a color based on three parameters: red, green, and blue. For example, if you want to change the Full Name field to show the first name in bright red, and the last name in bright blue, you use this calculation:

```
TextColor ( First Name ; RGB ( 255 ; 0 ; 0 ) )
& " " &
TextColor ( Last Name ; RGB ( 0 ; 0 ; 255 ) )
```

Tip: For a crash course in RGB code—including how to avoid using it—see the box on page 402.

TextFont()

To change the font in a calculation result, use the *TextFont()* function. You just pass it the text you want to format, and the name of the font to use. FileMaker returns the same text with the font applied:

```
TextFont ( "Dewey Defeats Truman!" ; "Times New Roman" )
```

UP TO SPEED

Color My World (with 16M Colors)

What kind of data is a *color*? The explanation isn't very, er, colorful. FileMaker understands 16,777,216 distinct colors, each subtly different from the one before, and numbered from 0 to 16,777,215. Unfortunately, *learning* all those colors by number is beyond the reach of even the most bored developer. So FileMaker uses a standard (albeit entirely unintuitive) method of specifying a color as a mixture of component colors—red, green, and blue—with varying intensities.

Each parameter to the RGB function is a number, from 0 to 255. The number says how intense—or bright—the component color should be. A zero in the first parameter means red doesn't enter into the equation at all. The number 255 means FileMaker should crank the red component to the max. The RGB function returns a number, identifying one of those 16-odd million choices. To make it doubly confusing for anyone who doesn't have a degree in computer programming or television repair, the RGB system deals with red, green, and blue as sources of *light*, not the more intuitive red-yellow-blue primary colors of paints and pigments.

When colored lights mix (like those little pixels on a monitor), red and green make…yellow. In other words, to FileMaker

and other RGB experts, it makes perfect sense to see bright yellow as the following:

    RGB (255 ; 255 ; 0)

So what's a person to do? Don't use RGB codes. Find some other tools.

If you use Mac OS X, you have just such a tool in the Utilities folder (in your Applications folder). It's called Digital Color Meter. Launch the application, and then, from the pop-up menu in its window choose RGB As Actual Value, 8-bit. Now the little blue numbers show proper red (R), green (G), and blue (B) values for any color you point to on your screen. For example, in the status area (in Layout mode), pop open the Fill Color menu, and then point to any of the colors there to see the RGB equivalent.

On Microsoft Windows, you can see RGB colors in the standard color picker window. Just go to Layout mode, and then, in the status area, click the Fill Color button. Choose Other Color. When you click a color, you see the red, green, and blue values listed in the window's bottom-right corner.

TextFont() also has a third optional parameter called fontScript. Most people can simply ignore this option. It tells FileMaker which *character set* you're interested in, and to select an appropriate font. (The character set determines which languages the font can be used for.) FileMaker accepts the following fontScript values:

- Roman
- Greek
- Cyrillic
- CentralEuropean
- ShiftJIS
- TraditionalChinese
- SimplifiedChinese
- OEM

- Symbol

- Other

Note: Unlike the font name, which is simply a text value, the script value shouldn't be in quotes. It's not a text value. Instead, you have to specify one of the above values exactly, with no quotes.

If FileMaker can't find the specific font you've asked for, then it selects another font in the specified script, so if you're on an English-based system and need to select a Chinese font, this parameter can help. (If you don't specify a script, FileMaker automatically uses the standard script on your computer. That's why you rarely have to worry about it—you automatically get what you probably want.)

TextSize()

The *TextSize()* function is simple in every case. Just pass some text, and the point size you'd like (just like the sizes in the Format→Size menu in Browse mode). FileMaker returns the resized text.

TextStyleAdd() and TextStyleRemove()

Changing text *styles* (bold, italic, and so on) is a little more complicated. After all, a piece of text can have only *one* color, *one* font, or *one* size, but it can be bold, italic, and underlined all at the same time. With text styles, you don't just swap one style for another; you need to do things like take italic text and add bold formatting or even take bold-titlecase-strikethrough text and un-strikethrough it, leaving everything else in place.

To solve these problems, FileMaker gives you *two* functions for dealing with style: *TextStyleAdd()* and *TextStyleRemove()*. You use the first to add a style to a piece of text:

```
"Do it with " & TextStyleAdd ( "style" ; Italic )
```

Likewise, the *TextStyleRemove()* function removes the specified style from the text.

```
TextStyleRemove ( My Text Field ; Italic )
```

The text style parameter goes in the calculation without quotes, just like the examples above. You can use any and every text style in FileMaker: Plain, Bold, Italic, Underline, Condense, Extend, Strikethrough, SmallCaps, Superscript, Subscript, Uppercase, Lowercase, Titlecase, WordUnderline, and DoubleUnderline. And then there's AllStyles. When you use the AllStyles parameter, it adds (or removes) *all* existing styles.

With these two functions and all these style options, you can do any kind of fancy formatting footwork imaginable. Here are some guidelines:

- When you add a style to some text using *TextStyleAdd()*, it doesn't change any style that you've already applied. The new style's simply layered over the existing styles.

- Plain style's the notable exception to the above point. Adding Plain style effectively *removes* any other styling. This style comes in handy when you need to remove a mess of styling and apply something simpler. Say your fields contain the words "Past Due", styled in uppercase, bold, italic, and double underlined, and you decide that modest italics would work just fine. Nesting the *TextStyleAdd()* function with the Plain parameter does the trick:

```
TextStyleAdd ( TextStyleAdd ( "past due" ; Plain ) ; Italic )
```

Note: As you may suspect, using *TextStyleRemove()* with the AllStyles parameter does the exact same thing as *TextStyleAdd()* with Plain. They both remove existing styling, but as you can see above, when you add Plain, you can write neater expressions.

- When you add more than one style parameter, FileMaker applies them all to the text. You can use nesting, as shown in the previous point, or simply stack them up with + signs:

```
TextStyleAdd ( "WARNING" ; Bold+Italic )
```

- If you take a bit of text that was formatted with a text formatting function, and then send it to another calculation as a parameter, then the formatting goes along with the text. With the substitute function, for example, you can format text that hasn't even been typed yet. If you add this function to a text field into which people can type letters to customers, then it changes every occurrence of "for a limited time" to bold italics.

```
Substitute ( Letter ; "for a limited time" ; TextStyleAdd ( "for a limited
time" ; Bold+Italic )
```

Date and Time Calculations

Before you start writing date and time calculations, think about how FileMaker keeps track of dates and times (page 237). FileMaker internally stores any date or time value as a single number that uniquely identifies every day and time of that day. Then, when it needs to display a date or time, it converts the number to a value people recognize, like "11/7/2009" or "10:23 AM". As with other numbers that it stores one way and displays another, FileMaker does the math on the stored value, and then converts it for your convenience.

This secret to date and time storage isn't just a technicality. It actually tells you a lot about how you can use dates and times in calculations. For example, without this knowledge, you could spend ages trying to write a calculation that gives you the first day of the month following the date an invoice is due. But it's actually pretty simple:

```
Date ( Month ( Invoice Due Date ) + 1 ; 1 ; Year ( Invoice Due Date ) )
```

To break it down, you're just adding 1 to the month in question, and then looking for the first day of that month. This section tells you what you need to know to analyze this calculation, and then use its lessons in your database.

Math with Dates and Times

Because FileMaker looks at dates and times as numbers, you're free to use them right along with other numbers and operators in all kinds of mathematical functions. By adding, subtracting, multiplying, and dividing dates, times, timestamps, and numbers, you can come up with meaningful results.

Dates

You can use the information in your database's date fields to have FileMaker figure out due dates, anniversaries, and so on. You can use date fields and numbers interchangeably. FileMaker's smart enough to figure out that you want to add whole days to the date value it's storing. Here are some general principles:

- To get a date in the future or past, add or subtract the number of days. For example, if your policy is that payments are due 10 days after invoices are presented, then, in your Date Due field, use this calculation:

      Invoice Date + 10

- Of course, you aren't limited to adding constant numbers to dates. You can add the value in a number field to the value in a date field just as easily. If your video rental database holds the checkout date and the rental duration, you can find the due date with this calculation:

      Checkout Date + Rental Duration

- To get the number of days between two dates, subtract them.

  Suppose your registration database holds arrival and departure dates. You can find the duration of the stay (in days) using this calculation:

      Departure Date - Arrival Date

Note: When you're adding a number to a date, the result is a brand-new date, and you should set the result type of your calculation accordingly. On the other hand, if you're subtracting two dates, the result is a number—the number of days between the two dates. In this case, set your calculation to return a number result.

Times

Although FileMaker's internal clock counts time as the number of seconds since midnight, a time value doesn't always have to be a time of day. Depending on the field format (page 305), a time value can be a time of day, like 2:30 p.m., or a *time* (as in duration, like 3 hours, 27 minutes).

Tip: FileMaker is savvy to the concept that time passes, but not all programs are. For instance, if you're exporting data to Excel, you may want to make calculation fields that convert time fields containing durations to a number field, and then export the new field instead.

UP TO SPEED

From Numbers to Times

If you can treat dates and times like numbers, it makes sense that you can go the other way, too. Suppose you have a field called Race Time that holds each athlete's race time as a number of seconds. If you'd rather view this time in the Hours:Minutes:Seconds (or Minutes:Seconds) format, then you can easily use a calculation to convert it to a time value:

```
GetAsTime(Race Time)
```

When you pass it a number value, the *GetAsTime()* function converts that number into the equivalent time. (If you view the field on a layout, then you can use the time formatting options to display hours, minutes, and seconds in just about any way you want, as shown on page 311.) The *GetAsTime()* function has another purpose: It can convert *text values* into times. If someone puts "3:37:03" into a text field, you can use *GetAsTime()* to convert that text into a valid time value.

FileMaker has *GetAsDate()* and *GetAsTimestamp()* functions, too, which work just the same.

In both cases, times have a numeric value, in hours:minutes:seconds format. When consider a time of day, 14:30:05 represents 5 seconds after 2:30 p.m., but if you look at it as a duration, it represents 14 hours, 30 minutes, and 5 seconds. If the time has fractional seconds (a decimal point), then the numerical value does too.

You can record how long your 5-year-old takes to find her shoes (34:26:18), or how long she takes to find the Halloween candy (00:00:02.13).

The key to doing math with any kind of time value is to remember you're always adding and subtracting amounts of *seconds*. Here are the guidelines:

- To get a time in the future or past, add or subtract a number of seconds or a time value. If you know when a student finished her exam, and you know how long the exam took in minutes (1 minute = 60 seconds), then you can figure out when she started:

  ```
  Finish Time - ( Exam Duration * 60 )
  ```

- To get the number of seconds between two times, subtract one from the other. A Test Reporting database could store start and finish times for each exam. To find the duration, use this calculation:

  ```
  Finish Time - Start Time
  ```

To get a time of day value in the future or past, add or subtract the number of seconds or a time value. Suppose you have a database of movie show times for your theater business. You use a timestamp field to record the date and time when each showing starts. You also use a time field to keep track of each movie's length. Now you need to know when each movie *ends*:

```
Showtime + Duration
```

Note: If you store the date and time the movie starts in separate date and time fields, then the movie time calculation is much more difficult. Suppose a movie starts at 11:30 p.m., and runs for 2 hours. Adding these together, you get 25:30, a perfectly valid time value, but not a valid *time of day*. When you add to time values, they don't "roll over" after midnight. Timestamps, on the other hand, work as expected: You get 1:30 a.m. on the next day.

- You can subtract one timestamp value from another. The result will be given in seconds, so you'll have to do more math on the result to get minutes or hours. For example, you use timestamps to record the start and finish times for a job. To find out how long the job took, in minutes, use this calculation:

      (Finish Time Stamp-Start Time Stamp) / 60

- To increase or decrease a time duration value, add or subtract the number of seconds, or another time duration. Say you have a related Songs table with a Song Lengths field to hold the length of each song on a CD. This calculation tells you how long the entire CD is:

      Sum (Songs::Song Lengths)

- To double, triple, halve, or otherwise scale a time duration, multiply or divide it by a number.

  If chilling your microbrew always takes twice as long as cooking, then you can determine the chilling time with this calculation:

      Cooking Time * 2

Parsing Dates and Times

Just as you can parse bits of text from text fields, FileMaker lets you pull out parts of a date or time value. For example, you can keep track of all your employees' birthdays in a normal date field, but when you're trying to get statistical data from the year they were born, you're not concerned about the month or date part of that value. You have six functions at your disposal to pick those individual components from a date, time, or timestamp value. They are *Year(), Month(), Day(), Hours(), Minutes(), Seconds().*

With a date value, you can use *Year(), Month(),* and *Day().* If you have a time, *Hours(), Minutes(),* and *Seconds()* apply. You can use all six functions with a timestamp value.

These functions all have the same form. Each takes a single parameter—the value—and returns a numerical result. For example, the day function returns the day portion of a date. This calculation returns 27:

      Day ("7/27/2009")

Tip: Just because FileMaker thinks of dates as numbers, you're not limited to using them that way. See the box below to see how to use parts of a date as text.

UP TO SPEED

Name the Day (or Month)

Even when you're using the month number to group your data, you may prefer to see months by *name*. For example, if you produce a report of sales by month, you probably want the groupings labeled January, February, March, and so on, instead of 1, 2, and 3. You can use the *Month-Name()* function to get this effect:

    MonthName (Invoice Date)

You can still sort all your invoices by the date field to get them in order, but you use your new *MonthName()* value to display in the subsummary part. See page 601 to learn how to use subsummary parts in reports.

Sometimes you need to see the day name (like Monday, Tuesday, or Wednesday). The *DayName()* function does just that. To get its numerical equivalent, use *DayOfWeek()* instead, which returns 1 for Sunday, 2 for Monday, and so forth.

Calculations that Create Dates and Times

Without even being aware of it, people do incredibly complex math every time they glance at a paper calendar or analog clock. When the boss said, "I want these invoices to go out 2 days before the end of next month," a human clerk knew exactly what to do. But how do you tell a computer to put "2 days before the end of next month" in the Invoice Date field? The answer is at the end of this section, but first you'll learn the functions to you'll need to calculate dates and times:

- The *Date()* function accepts three parameters—Month, Day, and Year—and returns the appropriate date value. For example, to put a date value of June 21, 2010 in a calculation, you use the date function like this:

      Date (6 ; 21 ; 2010)

- The *Time()* function wants three parameters as well, this time Hours, Minutes, and Seconds. It returns the time value. (The Seconds parameter can have a decimal point if necessary.) For example, you can construct the time value "8:00 p.m." like this:

      Time (20 ; 0 ; 0)

Note: For time-of-day values, the time function doesn't let you specify a.m. or p.m., so you have to use 24-hour notation.

- The *Timestamp()* function takes just two parameters: Date and Time. It combines the two into a single timestamp value. It shows June 10, 2009 at 8:30 p.m. like this:

      Timestamp (Date (6 ; 10 ; 2009) ; Time (20 ; 30 ; 0))

FREQUENTLY ASKED QUESTION

Do I Have to Use Functions?

Why can't I just put "1/10/2011" in my calculation, just like I'd put it in a date field?

Because "1/10/2011" is a text value, not a date value. When you're entering data in a date field, FileMaker knows it's a date field, and is nice enough to convert text like this into a date for you. In a calculation, though, FileMaker may not know you want a date, so it treats what you put in as text instead.

You can use the *GetAsDate()* function to convert text values like this into dates:

    GetAsDate ("1/10/2011")

But even this method isn't advisable. Remember that dates are interpreted depending on how you've configured your computer. On one computer, this calculation could produce the date value January 10, 2011, while on another machine it might result in October 1 instead. In other words, you have no safe way to ensure you get the date you really want when you use *GetAsDate()* with a text value, unless you're using text the user supplied.

The date function always expects the month, then the day, then the year. Computer settings don't affect it. So the *Date()* function is the safest way to record dates in calculations.

The secret powers of Date()

Although FileMaker doesn't look at calendars the way people do, that's not all bad. You see a calendar in absolute terms: April 30 belongs to April, May 1 belongs to May, and that's that. FileMaker, however, thinks of dates in relative terms and sees no such limitations. You can use this flexibility to your advantage in calculations—big time. You can give seemingly illogical parameters to the *Date ()* function, and have FileMaker produce a valid date anyway.

For example, this calculation actually produces a valid date:

    Date (7 ; 0 ; 2010)

You might expect a nonsense result—July 0, 2010. But FileMaker looks at the same code and says, "No problem. Zero comes before 1, so you must mean the day that comes before July 1." And so it returns June 30, 2010.

These same smarts apply to the month as well:

    Date (15 ; 11 ; 2010)

That calculation produces March 11, *2011*. In other words, 3 months into the next year, since 15 is 3 months more than 1 year.

This behavior comes in super handy when you're trying to fiddle with dates in calculations. Suppose you have order records, each one with an order date. You bill on the last day of the month in which the order was placed, so your calculation needs to figure out that date, which could be 28, 30, or 31, depending on the month, or even 29 if it's February in a leap year. That calculation would take an entire page in this book. But here's a much easier approach: Instead of calculating which day each month ends, use the fact that the *last* day of *this* month is always the day *before* the *first* day of *next* month. To start with, you can calculate next month like this:

```
Month ( Order Date ) + 1
```

So the date of the first day of next month is:

```
Date ( Month(Order Date) + 1 ; 1 ; Year(Order Date) )
```

To get the value of 2 days before the end of any month, just subtract 2 from the whole thing:

```
Date (
 Month(Order Date) + 1; // the _next_ month
 1; //the _first_ day
 Year(Order Date) // the same year
)- 2 // subtract 2 days
```

It may look a little confusing at first, but it's much shorter than the page you'd need to work the calculation out "longhand". And it works perfectly every month of every year.

Containers in Calculations

Although it isn't a typical calculation data type, you can do a few interesting things with container fields in calculations. You don't have the same vast options you do with other types. It would be great if you could subtract Cousin Clem.jpg from Family Reunion.jpg to get the scoundrel out of the picture, but alas, the technology's not quite there yet. Nevertheless, FileMaker doesn't leave containers entirely out in the cold when it comes to calculations.

Calculations with Pictures, Sounds, Movies, and Files

When you create a calculation field, you can set its result type to Container. You can't *create* container data in a calculation, but you *can* refer to other container fields. When you do, the picture, sound, movie, or file in the referenced container field shows in the new calculation field.

You can, for example, make a calculation field that shows the contents of one container field when you're in Browse mode, and another in Preview mode. This field lets you use low-resolution images when you view on the screen, and higher resolutions when you view in print. (You'll learn to do that in the next chapter, when you learn about calculations with that kind of decision-making ability.)

You may also want to use container fields in a calculated replace. Suppose you have a found set of 30 records that don't have a low-resolution image. You have to have something in that field, so you decide to take the hi-resolution image for those few records and plunk them down in the low-resolution image field. Choose Records→Replace Field Contents, and then perform this calculated replace:

```
Graphics::High Resolution Image
```

The entire calculation consists of a reference to a field of that name in the Graphics table. The calculation does the grunt work of copying the high-resolution image into the low-resolution field in each record.

Calculations with References

If a container field holds a reference to a picture, movie, sound, or file, instead of the object itself (see the box on page 265), then you can do even more. When you treat such a field as *text*, FileMaker gives you some information about the referenced file.

If you have a field called Product Shot that holds a reference to a photograph file, then you can use this calculation:

```
GetAsText ( Product Shot )
```

This calculation's result looks like this:

```
size:266,309
image:../../../../../ quilt pix/batik squares.jpg
imagemac:/Macintosh HD/current work/ quilt pix/batik squares.jpg
```

FileMaker tells you the size (width and height in pixels) and location of the file (if this weren't a picture, then you wouldn't see the "size:" line).

You can use this calculation to help you keep track of a set of images that the whole company needs to use. You really need two container fields for this purpose. One holds the graphic itself, or a low-resolution copy, if you don't want the file size to balloon. Then, when you place the graphic as a reference in the second container field, the calculation stores the graphic's original location. The calculation's not dynamic, however, so the path serves as a reference of where the file *should* be, not where it really is. Company policy about putting things back where you found them has to reinforce your good data practices.

Understanding Scripts

When you created the Lease Agreement database in Chapters 3 and 4, you wrote a script to sort records viewed in a list (page 163). That script didn't do anything you couldn't have done manually. But since it remembers a sorting setup, the script is faster to run than if you have to go to the Sort window and configure it every time you want to scan the list. To make it even more convenient, you attached the script to a button that your users could click to sort data without the need to understand how to set up a Sort window. For even more automation, you gave the list layout a script trigger that ran the Sort script every time that layout is viewed. It's almost like your database knows what your users need before they do.

That basic script introduced you to many of the advantages of scripting. Here are the main reasons to add scripts to your database:

- **Efficiency.** For just about any process, a script can run faster than you (or your users) can issue the same commands.

- **Accuracy.** Once you set it up, a script won't leave out a step or perform a series of steps out of order.

- **Convenience.** You don't have to remember how to do a process that you don't perform often.

- **Automation.** With script triggers, processes can run without you explicitly running the script. In many cases, users won't even know a script is running. They'll just see the results.

- **Complex processing.** Some processes just aren't possible (or maybe they're not feasible) without a script handling the grunt work.

Most scripts you'll write will combine more than one of these advantages. Scripts are so useful that complex databases often have hundreds of scripts (or even more). Even relatively simple databases benefit from scripts, since reports usually require a similar sequence of steps: finding records, sorting them, and showing a list layout in Preview mode. This chapter introduces you to the basics, but two more chapters (11 and 16) dive deeper into scripting.

Understanding Scripts

A *script* is a series of steps bundled together. When a script runs, FileMaker carries out all the steps on your behalf, one after the other. You can create a script to automate almost any routine task, and once it's working the way you want it to, you decide how and when the script will run.

You can run a script from the Manage Scripts window or by selecting it from the Scripts menu. But more typically, you put a button on a layout, and have FileMaker run your script when someone clicks the button. You can even use *script triggers* to make scripts run automatically in response to what someone does. For instance, you can make a script run every time someone goes to a particular layout, clicks into a certain field, or selects a tab panel in a Tab Control. Using the "Install OnTimer Script" script step, you can make a script run periodically or at a certain point in the future. Finally, you can run scripts on a schedule using FileMaker Server (see Chapter 18) to perform automated imports, send notifications, clean up data, and so on. Scripting is FileMaker's real power feature, and you have as many ways to take advantage of it as there are databases.

Scripts can be simple—just the same five steps you'd go through if you printed a report manually. Or they can be much more complicated—and handle tricky or tedious tasks you wouldn't want to do manually. Advanced scripts can even incorporate calculations to do different things in different situations by making simple decisions based on the data in your database, the current time or date, or any other condition you want to test.

Note: If you've worked with other scripting environments—like Visual Basic for Applications, AppleScript, or JavaScript—then FileMaker's scripting commands are pleasantly familiar.

Your First Script

To get a feel for how scripting works, you'll create a really simple script. Suppose you want to find all invoices with a balance due, and view them in a sorted list. The following pages show how to go about preparing your database, planning, creating, and polishing the script, and finishing off with a way to run it.

Preparing the Database

Reports usually need their fields arranged differently than, say, data entry layouts. Those summary fields have to be positioned so they're easy to see and interpret. Also, reports often need to be suitable for printing. As you're writing a script, you might realize that you need new calculation fields to get a report's summary data. FileMaker is flexible enough to let you create fields and layouts on the fly, but it's easier to focus on the script if you create all your supporting material before you even open the Manage Script window. .

Tip: In practice, you can't fully prepare a database until you've done some planning…and your preparation can reveal flaws in your plan. Work with the assumption that the plan and preparation phases of scriptwriting overlap and intertwine.

For this report, your list layout should include the Invoice ID, Job Name, Date, Date Due, and Balance Due fields. Figure 10-1 shows the List layout from the Invoices START database for this chapter. At the end of the chapter you can compare your work to the Invoices FINISHED database. Both are available on this book's Missing CD page at *www.missingmanuals.com*.

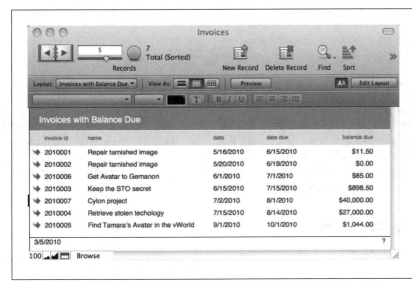

Figure 10-1:
To follow along in this chapter, you need an Invoices with Balance Due layout like this one. If you want to express your creativity, or review the process for creating layouts, feel free to roll your own report layout.

Planning Your Script

Before you dive in and create the script, you should review what you want it to do. A script is just a series of steps that FileMaker repeats for you. When you're planning a script, it often helps to manually work through the process the script should do first, so you can see whether it works. This trial run helps you clarify the steps you're scripting. Plus, some scripts are easier to write if you do the steps manually beforehand, since dialog boxes retain their settings until you change them. For example, if your script needs to sort records, the dialog box already has the settings you need when you're actually creating the script.

So let's go through the steps necessary to find Invoices with a balance due, and take notes. You probably end up with something like the following:

- **Switch to the Invoices with Balance Due layout.** This layout has the fields the script needs to create the invoice list. It's also going to display the final list, so you want to make sure the script runs in this layout.

- **Choose View→Find Mode.** The script needs to *find* all invoices with a balance due. Scripts can't click a button or even choose a menu command, but you know you need a script step that puts FileMaker into Find mode.

- **In the Balance Due field, enter ">0", and then press Enter.** This step tells FileMaker what to find, and puts it into action. When the script runs this step, FileMaker performs the find and shows the correct records, just as if you'd performed the find yourself.

Note: If none of your invoices has a balance due, just click Cancel when the error message pops up, and then choose Records→Show All Records so you can do the next step. Jot down that your script needs to account for this message box if it pops up when someone runs your script. In Chapter 15 you'll learn how to make your script account for errors like these.

- **Choose Records→Sort Records, and then sort the records ascending by Date Due.** You should now see your final list, properly sorted.

Now that you know all the steps involved, you're ready to get acquainted with the Edit Script window. Figure 10-2 shows a complete script to do the steps in this section. Even if you know nothing about scripting, you can probably look at it and get a general idea of what it does. Later scripting chapters will teach you about the other script steps and how to use them.

Creating Your Script

You create, edit, run, and delete scripts in FileMaker using the Manage Scripts window. It's the first item in the Scripts menu, and it's available from any mode, except while a script is running. When you choose this command, you see the window shown in Figure 10-3. Your window may not have scripts in it yet, but otherwise, it's the same.

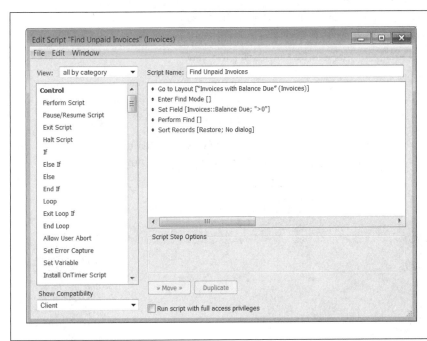

Figure 10-2:
This script tells File-Maker to switch to the Invoices with Balance Due layout, go to Find mode, put a find criteria in the Total Due field, perform the find, and sort the found records. It may not use exactly the words you'd expect, but you can tell at a glance roughly what it does.

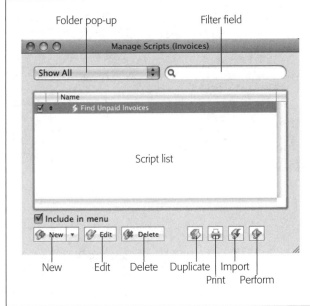

Figure 10-3:
The Manage Scripts window helps you create, organize and manage scripts. The main part of the window is a list that shows all your scripts. Tools along the bottom let you create and manage your scripts. The New pop-up menu lets you create: empty scripts, an automatic script (with basic reporting script steps), folders for organizing script, and separators. Separators show up as hyphens in the script list, and as menu separators in the Scripts menu. You'll learn more about these options in the next sections.

Now it's time to build the script. Basically, you tell FileMaker to repeat each of the steps you went through when you planned the script. Here's how:

1. **Choose Scripts→Manage Scripts, or choose File→Manage→Scripts. When the Manage Scripts window appears, click New.**

   The Edit Script window appears (Figure 10-4). Make sure to click New, and not the pop-up menu. You'll learn how and when to use the pop-up menu later.

2. **In the Script Name box, type** *Find Unpaid Invoices.*

   Your script's name is important. It's how you'll identify it when you want to run it later. As usual, a short descriptive name is the best policy.

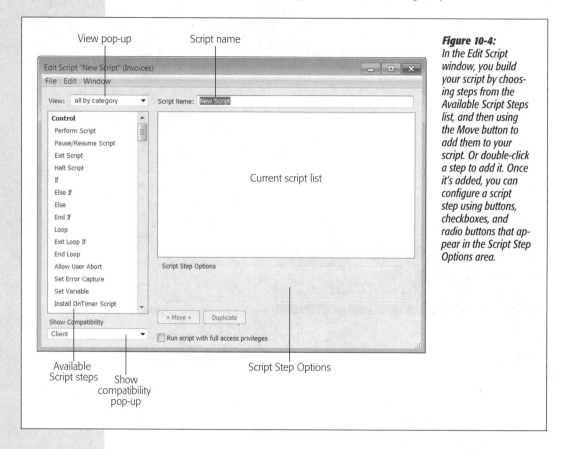

Figure 10-4:
In the Edit Script window, you build your script by choosing steps from the Available Script Steps list, and then using the Move button to add them to your script. Or double-click a step to add it. Once it's added, you can configure a script step using buttons, checkboxes, and radio buttons that appear in the Script Step Options area.

3. **Scroll the list on the left, so you can see the Navigation headline, and then choose the "Go to Layout" step to select it. Click Move.**

   The Move button doesn't become available until you've clicked a script step. When you click Move, FileMaker adds a "Go to Layout" step to the list of current steps. This step is already selected, so you can quickly make changes to its settings.

Tip: You can double-click a step in the list to avoid the trip to the Move button. When the script step list is active, you can type the first part of a step's name to scroll to it. If the script step list isn't active, then use the Tab key to move between the window's active areas.

4. **From the Specify pop-up menu (in the Script Step Options area), choose Layout. When the Specify Layout window appears, choose Invoice with Balance Due.**

   That's the report layout. Now your script has just one step, or line. If you run it as is, then it simply takes you to the Invoices with Balance Due layout. (If you're *already* on the Invoices with Balance Due layout, then it doesn't do anything.)

5. **From the View pop-up menu (top-left corner), choose "all by name" to sort the script steps alphabetically, and then scroll down until you see the Enter Find Mode step. Move it to the list.**

   FileMaker adds a second line to your script. The Script Step Options area now has new options (those that make sense with the Enter Find Mode step). Notice that the Pause option at the left side of the Script Step Options area is turned *on*.

6. **Turn off the Pause option.**

   Turning off this option tells the script not to wait for user input when it's run. (You'll learn more about pausing a script on page 484.)

7. **Add a Set Field script step to the script.**

   Use the scroll bar to skip down to the steps that start with "s" or type "set" to scroll the list without using the mouse.

   The Set Field step lets you put (or set) data in a field. You can use Set Field in Browse or Find mode. In Browse mode, it enters data; in Find mode, it specifies find requests. Since this Set Field step comes right after an Enter Find Mode step, you're specifying a find request for the invoices.

8. **In the Script Step Options area, select the "Specify target field" option.**

   The Specify Field window appears (Figure 10-5).

Tip: If you *don't* turn on the Specify target field option, then the Set Field step modifies whichever field happens to be active when the step is carried out.

9. **In the field list, select Balance Due, and then click OK.**

   The Set Field step in your script (Figure 10-6) shows the option you've selected. In the Script Step Options area, click the bottom Specify button (the one beside "Calculated result").

FileMaker shows you the Specify Calculation window, the same one you used to build calculation fields in previous chapters. Here you'll use a calculation to tell FileMaker what to put in the Invoices::Balance Due field. Remember, you're in Find mode when this script runs, so the Set Field step tells FileMaker what records you want to find.

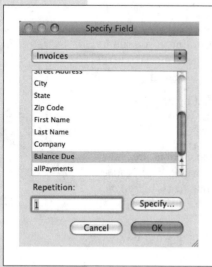

Figure 10-5:
This Specify Field dialog box looks almost exactly like the one you've seen in Layout mode. The only difference is the Repetition box at the bottom. If you select a repeating field (page 255), then you can use this box to tell FileMaker which repetition to set.

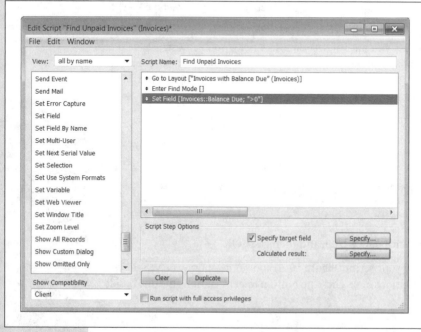

Figure 10-6:
FileMaker shows your script steps in the order they're performed. If a step has any options, then they're displayed in brackets after the step name. In this example, the Invoices::Balance Due field is modified by the Set Field step.

10. **In the Calculation box, type >0 (including the quotes), and then click OK.**

    This bit of computerese sets the Invoices::Balance Due field to the appropriate value for finding unpaid invoices. FileMaker now shows the calculation beside the Set Field step as well. (Spoken out loud, this step reads, "Set the Invoices::Balance Due field to greater than zero.")

11. **Add the Perform Find script step to your script.**

    Don't specify any options. This step carries out the find operation. It's the equivalent of clicking Find or pressing Enter if you were doing it yourself.

12. **Add the Sort Records script step to your script. Then, in the Script Step Options area, select "Perform without dialog".**

    This action tells FileMaker you want the script to go ahead and sort, instead of opening the Sort dialog box every time it runs. That way, the sort is the same every time you run the script.

13. **Turn on the "Specify sort order" checkbox.**

    If you went through the script-planning phase, as described on page 415, the Sort dialog box is already configured properly. When you add a Sort Records step to your script, FileMaker configures it to match the *last* sort you performed. If you skipped the dry run, then set the dialog box to sort by Date Due, in ascending order.

14. **In the Sort Records window, click OK.**

    Unlike some other script steps, Sort Records doesn't show its settings. It just says Restore. But if you forget, you can always click the Specify dialog box, and then check it out.

15. **Click the Edit Script window's Close button, and then click Save.**

    The Edit Script window has no Save button, but when you close it, you always see a warning dialog box that lets you save your scripts.

Tip: On Windows Vista, the Edit Script window has a File menu, from which you can choose Save Script. On Mac, use the shortcut ⌘-S. If you're writing a long or hairy script, save often because it's not uncommon to be in this window for a long time as you're working out the script's logic.

The script is now complete. But as with any new feature, you need to test your script to make sure it works as you intend. You'll learn more about the various ways to run scripts on page 428. But the most common way to run a script for testing is with the Manage Script window's Perform button (Figure 10-3).

16. **Click the Perform button.**

    It's the one with a green triangle at the bottom right. FileMaker runs your script.

Note: If the Perform button isn't highlighted, make sure that your script is selected. Even though you only have one script written, FileMaker doesn't assume it knows which one you want to perform.

You should see the correct list of invoices, or—oops!—a message telling you no records were found, if you don't have any unpaid invoices in your database right now (see the box below). In the next section, you'll refine your script to help deal with these message boxes if they pop up when someone runs the script.

Tip: You can adapt the basic structure of this script for a host of purposes. Use the Duplicate button to copy the script, give the new script a descriptive name, specify a different layout, and then change the find or sort criteria.

UP TO SPEED

To Be Continued

If your database has no unpaid invoices when you run the Find Unpaid Invoices script, then you see a message indicating that no records were found. The message is the same as the one you see if you perform the find manually, with one exception: This time you get a Continue button.

Since FileMaker was running a script when the error occurred, it gives you the choice to cancel the script (in other words, stop in the middle and return control to the user) or continue the script (keep going and pretend nothing went wrong). In this case, Cancel and Continue do the same thing since the error happened on the *last* step in the script.

If you don't want the database user to make this choice, then you can tell FileMaker to *capture* the errors as they happen, and let you deal with them inside the script. You'll learn about this process on page 694.

Improving Your Script

On the preceding pages, you created a script that mimics what you'd do to get an unpaid invoice list, step by step. Often, a script can get the results you want with *fewer* steps than it would take to do it yourself. For example, to see your unpaid invoice list, the steps boil down to the following:

- Switch to the Invoices with Balance Due layout.

- Find the right invoices.

- Sort the records.

This version has just *three* steps instead of five because it assumes you can "find the right invoices" in one step. Luckily, the Perform Find script step *really can* find what you want in one step. Here's how to revise your script to use the simpler form:

---

1. **Choose Scripts→ Manage Scripts. In the Manage Scripts window, select the Find Unpaid Invoices script, and then click Edit.**

   Or you can double-click the script instead. In the Edit Script window, the Find Unpaid Invoices script pops up.

2. **Select the second and third steps in your script (Enter Find Mode and Set Field).**

   You can select both by clicking Enter Find Mode in your script, and then Shift-clicking Set Field.

Note: Select the steps in your script (on the right-hand side of the window), not the steps in the available script steps list (on the window's left side).

---

3. **Click Clear.**

   FileMaker removes the two selected steps from the script. It now has two steps that look a lot like the simplified process on the previous page. Also notice that the Perform Find step is already highlighted, since FileMaker automatically selects the *next* step when you clear one or more steps from the script.

4. **In the Script Step Options area, turn on the "Specify find requests" checkbox.**

   The Specify Find Requests dialog box (Figure 10-7) appears, and, like the Sort script step in the previous tutorial, it's already set with the find you did when you planned your script. Since that's exactly what you want, you don't need to do anything in the Specify Find Requests dialog box. But if you skipped the recommended planning work on page 415, then you have to set your find request manually now, as described in steps 5–7.

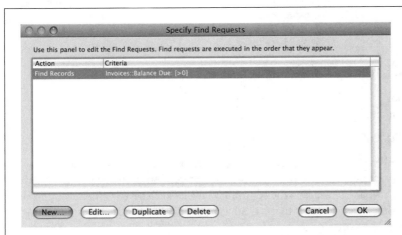

Figure 10-7:
This window shows find requests that are built into the Perform Find step. You can add or edit the find requests here. Doing your editing here is usually easier than adding Set Field steps like you did the first time 'round.

5. **Click New.**

   The Edit Find Request dialog box appears. You can see it described in Figure 10-8.

6. **In the "Find records when" pop-up menu, choose Invoices, if necessary, and then scroll through the list until you see the Balance Due field. Click to select it.**

   The Balance Due field is highlighted so you can remember which field you're telling FileMaker to search.

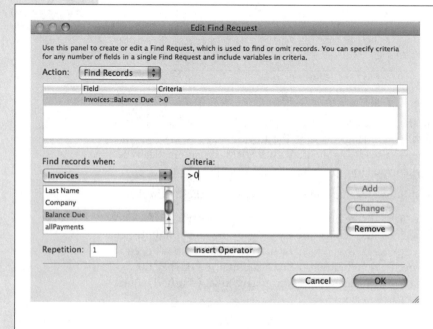

Figure 10-8:
You construct a find request in this dialog box. The list at the top shows all the fields that have criteria in the request. From the list on the left, you can pick a field, and then put something in the Criteria box to set that field in the find request. From the top list, you can also select criteria, and then edit them (click Change when you're done) or click Remove to remove them. Everything you do in this window has the same result as typing into fields in a single request in Find mode.

7. **Type *>0* in the Criteria list box, and then click OK.**

   Your search is entered at the top of the dialog box, in the Action box. (You wouldn't have all this trouble if you'd followed directions.)

8. **Click OK until you're back in the Edit Script window.**

   The Perform Find script step now has options set (Figure 10-9). Notice that the Edit Script window has a * (or asterisk) at the end of its name. That tells you you've made changes to the script that haven't been saved. Whenever you close an Edit Script window that has an asterisk, FileMaker asks if you want to save changes to your script.

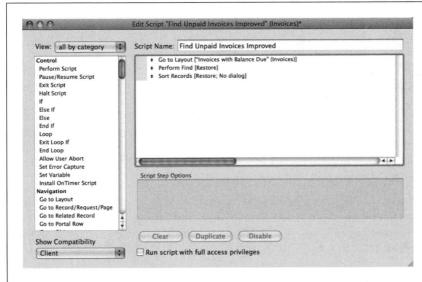

Figure 10-9:
Your finished script should look like this. It wasn't too hard to improve, and it's very easy to understand. The * at the end of the window's name tells you that the script's changes haven't been saved.

9. **Close the Edit Script window, and then, in the dialog box that follows, click Save.**

   Or choose Scripts→Save Script, or press Ctrl+S (Windows) or ⌘-S (Mac). Either way, the Edit Script window stays open, but the script is saved. You can use this command to save a script midstream while you're working on it.

Tip: The Scripts menu also has a Save All Scripts command (yes, you can work on more than one script at a time) and a Revert script command. These commands have no keyboard shortcuts, but you don't have to click the Close box on an Edit Script window to handle your save/revert chores.

---

10. **Click Perform.**

    The Manage Scripts window stays open, and your database window comes forward to show you the results of your script.

This new, simpler script does everything the first script did. It's simpler because you didn't have to script all the steps involved in performing a find: Enter Find Mode; Set Field; Perform Find. Instead, you let FileMaker do all that in one Perform Find step. You'll find that you can reduce *many* of FileMaker's common multistep operations to a single step.

Note: Later in this chapter (page 433), you'll learn more about managing and organizing scripts.

Shortcuts to the Edit Script Window

When you wrote the Find Unpaid Invoices script in the previous section, you got to the Manage Scripts window by choosing Scripts→Manage Scripts or File→Manage→Scripts. These multiple choices aren't just redundancy—they're meant to give you flexibility. In fact, you can get to the Manage Scripts window through other windows, too.

Say you want to create a button on the Customer layout that finds unpaid invoices for the customer your viewing, so you create a button (page 317). In the Button Setup dialog box, you select the Perform Script, step and then click Specify. The Specify Script window appears, but you quickly realize that the script you need isn't there (that's because you haven't written it yet).

Do you have to slow your developing momentum while closing all those windows, and then head up to the Scripts menu? Nope. You can get a direct line to the Edit Scripts window using the "+" button at the bottom of the Specify Script window (Figure 10-10).

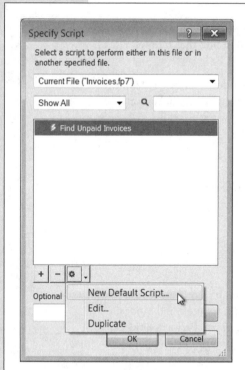

Figure 10-10:
The "+" button opens the Edit Script window. The "-" button deletes the selected script, but click it with extreme caution—you can't retrieve a deleted script. The pop-up menu (shown here) lets you create a Default Script that has basic script steps already created for you. It's a three-step script that enters find mode, goes to the layout you're on when you choose the Default Script command, and then shows all records. The Edit button lets you edit the selected script, and Duplicate creates a copy of an existing script so you can use it as the foundation for a new script.

Tip: Anywhere the Specify Script window appears you'll get these same shortcut buttons. Look for them in the File Options window (page 176), the Layout Setup's Script Trigger tab (page 447) and the Edit Custom Menu's Action Option window (page 543).

The Importance of the Layout

In a script, the active layout is very important, since it's what determines the script's *context*. Context is critical when you do things like delete records. If you write a script that simply deletes a record, without checking for context, then it deletes the current record from whatever layout someone happens to be on. That record may not be the right one at all. You could end up deleting a record from the Customer table instead of the single invoice record you meant to delete!

Take the script you've created in this chapter, for example. Before it does anything else, your Find Unpaid Invoices script goes to the Invoices with Balance Due layout— but what would happen if you left that step out? Figure 10-8 shows the options for the Perform Find script step. See if you can spot what's *missing*.

You can see that Perform Find—like most other script steps—makes absolutely no mention of which table it should act upon. Just because you're asking it to "Find records when Invoices::Balance Due > 0 doesn't mean you're looking for *invoice* records. You could be looking for customers whose attached invoices have a balance due. Or you could be looking for any line items on an unpaid invoice. FileMaker can tell what you're looking for only by the context of the layout you're on. That's why the first step in the script goes to the Invoices with Balance Due layout. That layout is attached to the Invoices table occurrence. This tells FileMaker which records to look through (those in the Invoices table) and from what perspective to resolve relationships (the Invoices table occurrence on the Relationship graph).

When to Switch

Now that you've dutifully absorbed the lesson in the previous paragraphs, don't get lured into the idea that you *always* have to switch to a layout for your script to work. The fact that a script can do something useful from more than one context can be a good thing. In general, you have three choices when you write a script, and here are some guidelines on when to use each:

- **Switch to a layout associated with the table you want to work with.** The "Go to Layout" script step makes sense when you're showing certain results from a specific context, as in the Find Unpaid Invoices script. If necessary, you can then switch *back* to the original layout at the end of the script ("Go to Layout" has an Original Layout option).

- **Don't include a "Go to Layout" script step at all.** Just let the script go about its business, whatever the context. If you use this approach, then you have to make sure the script works and makes sense from any perspective. For instance, a script could switch to Preview mode, resize the window to show the whole page, and then ask someone if he'd like to print. This script can run on nearly any layout and still do something useful: print. See the box on the next page for one example of context independent scripting.

- **Prevent the script from running on the wrong layout.** Using an If test in a script (see the box on page 517), you can make it so a script stops running if it's not working properly on the current layout. This alternative is your best bet when switching layouts within the script isn't feasible. For example, suppose you have a Refund Invoice script that carries out the steps necessary to pay someone back. Using "Go to Layout" to switch to the Invoices layout would ensure the right layout, but not the right *invoice*. It's best if this script runs only when someone's *already* open to the Invoices layout—presumably looking at the invoice she wants to refund.

Note: When a script can do damage to your database if it's run from the wrong layout, use the failsafe of the third option even if you're the only person who uses your database. If your mouse hand slips when you're insufficiently caffeinated, then the script can show you an error message rather than running at the wrong time.

Running Scripts

At this point you're probably starting to see how scripts can be really useful in your database. The fact is, most large database systems are *loaded* with scripts that do all kinds of things. But so far, the main way you've seen to run a script is pretty tedious: Chose Scripts→Manage Scripts, select the script, and then click Perform. That's lots of clicks to run a script that's supposed to *save* you time! Thankfully, you have a few *other*, more convenient, ways to run scripts, and you can set them up when you first create a script.

The Scripts Menu

You can show some or all of your scripts right in the Scripts menu. If you have a script (or two) to which you want quick access from *anywhere*, then it makes sense to put it in the Scripts menu. That way, anyone can run it by simply choosing it from the menu. FileMaker even has keyboard shortcuts for the first 10 scripts in the Scripts menu: Ctrl+1 (⌘-1) through Ctrl+9 (⌘-9) for the first nine, and Ctrl+0 (⌘-0) for number 10. Figure 10-11 shows how to assign a script to this menu in the Manage Scripts window.

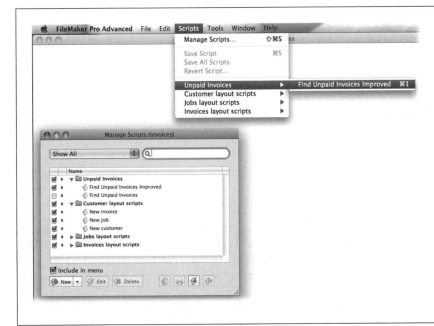

Figure 10-11:
In the Manage Scripts window, every script has a checkbox by its name. If you turn on this box, then the script appears in the Scripts menu, and you can run it simply by selecting its name. At the top, notice the Scripts menu that results from the settings above. On page 433 you'll learn how to make the folders shown here.

POWER USERS' CLINIC

Context Independence

You may be wondering why the Send Email to Customer script you create on page 436 doesn't go to the Customers layout first. After all, doesn't it only make sense from this context? Actually, this script is a perfect candidate for *context independence*. If you run this script from the Jobs layout, it creates a new email message addressed to the *related customer*. The same holds true from the Invoice layout. In fact, you can run this script from *any* layout, and get a useful result: FileMaker finds the related customer record, and addresses the message to her.

It's important to know who'll get the email if there's more than one related customer record. (Remember, the Send Email to Customer script is set to send only one email, even though the Send Mail script step lets you send multiple emails to all customers in a found set.) As you'd expect, the answer depends on the starting context when the script is run. If you run the script from the Scripts menu, FileMaker selects the *first* related customer for the active record on the current layout. If the relationship to Customers is sorted in the Relationships tab of the Manage Database window, then it's the customer that sorts to the top. Otherwise, you get the first (oldest) customer record.

But if your layout has a portal of related customers, a button on the portal determines the context from which the script runs (you created a similar navigation button in a portal on page 225). When you click this button, the script addresses the email to the customer in the portal line corresponding to the button you clicked.

The point is, you can put a button just about anywhere and tell it to run this script. FileMaker does something a little different depending on where the button is. So this example is one of those scripts that you *don't* want to associate with a specific layout.

Note: If 10 scripts in a list isn't your idea of a highly organized command center, take heart. In Chapter 19, you'll learn how to completely customize the menus in your database. You can add an item to any menu, name it whatever you want, assign a keyboard shortcut, and then have it run a script. You can remove the menus you don't want, add new items to existing menus, or even add entirely new menus. And you can completely customize the keyboard shortcuts to your liking.

Buttons

As you learned on page 317, you can add buttons to any layout—or turn existing fields, labels, pictures, and so forth into clickable buttons. At the time, you used simple single-action buttons, like a button that switches layouts. If you revisit the Specify Button dialog box now, you see the list of button commands is almost exactly like the list of available script steps. A button is, in some sense, just a one-line script.

But sometimes you want a button to do more. With almost no effort, you can get a button to run any script. Just assign the Perform Script action to the button. When you do, you can pick from among the scripts in your database. Then, when you click the button, the script runs. Buttons are an exceptionally handy way to run scripts. The button is easy to see and understand, and it's just one click away. And best of all, since buttons are on layouts, you can put just the right commands in just the right places, preventing anyone from running the wrong script, since you wouldn't put a button on a layout where it doesn't make sense.

Script Triggers

You don't have to wait for someone to click a button to make a script run. Using *script triggers*, you can tell FileMaker to automatically run a script whenever someone performs a particular action. You can apply a script trigger to a layout or an individual layout object. For instance, you might run a script when someone first switches to a particular layout. Or trigger a script when she tabs into a field. You can set up triggers in all these circumstances:

- When you view, commit, or revert a record.

- When you press a key on the keyboard when you're on a particular layout.

- When you switch to a particular layout.

- When you switch away from a particular layout.

- When you switch to or from Browse, Find, or Preview modes.

- When you switch to or from Detail, List, or Table views.

- When you enter an object. For instance, when you click or tab into a field, or highlight a tab panel or button with the Tab key.

- When you exit a field that has Field Validation options.

- When you press a key on the keyboard while in a field, or while a button or tab is selected.

- When you change the contents of a field in any way.

- When you switch from one tab panel to another.

- When you leave a field or tab away from a button or tab panel.

- When you leave a field after you've made changes to it (in other words, when FileMaker has to save changes to the field).

You'll learn how to use script triggers and more about how they behave at the end of this chapter.

Performing Scripts When a File Is Opened and Closed

You can configure a script to run each time the database is opened or closed. (These *opening* and *closing* scripts are a lot like script triggers, but FileMaker doesn't call them that.) The opening script runs when you first open the file. You can use this script if you want to be greeted with the list of unpaid invoices first thing every morning. The closing script runs when you close the *last window* for an open file. This option is a little less common, but it has its uses: If you want to make sure other related files close whenever the main file closes (even if they have open windows), then you can write a script to close them all whenever you close the main file.

UP TO SPEED

A Script Action or a Script?

Attaching a single script action to a button is so easy that it's tempting to use that technique often (page 318). But even if your buttons do only one thing, you'll still save time in the long run if you create a single-line script, and attach that to your button instead. Yes, it's a little more work upfront, but scripts have a lot more flexibility over the long haul. Here's why.

Lots of the initial development work in a database has to do with helping the users get around. So, many of the first buttons you create just go to a layout, or to a set of related records. But what if your business rules change—like from now on, only managers can see a customer's payment

history? You have to figure out how to stop unauthorized folks from seeing payment data. With an If statement (page 436) that checks Get *(PrivilegeSetName)*, a script can see who's logged in to the file before it allows the "Go to Layout" to run. So you have to write the script, and then find all the 14 places you created a button with a plain-vanilla "Go to Layout" script action. If you'd written a "Go to Layout" script, and attached that to your 14 buttons, you could handle this new wrinkle just by editing the script. No time spent finding all your "Go to Layout" buttons, or worrying about what happens if you missed one, because the script handles it all.

To make the selection, you need to visit the File Options window (File→File Options). In the File Options window, make sure the Open/Close tab is selected. In this window, you first turn on one of the "Perform script" checkboxes (there's one under "When opening this file" and another under "When closing this file"). Then you can select one of your scripts from the associated pop-up menu. Figure 10-12 shows the result.

Figure 10-12:
The Open/Close tab of the File Options window (File→File Options) lets you tell FileMaker what to do when someone opens or closes a file. Most of this window is devoted to the things that happen when a file opens. Only the last checkbox (under "When closing this file") has to do with which script should run when the file closes.

Timer Scripts

Finally, using the Install OnTimer Script script step, you can tell FileMaker to run a particular script periodically. For instance, you might set up a special computer that runs a script every 10 minutes to grab order information from your website. Or perhaps when someone switches to a sensitive layout, you want a timer to automatically switch to some place more innocuous after 5 minutes, in case he walks away from the computer.

Timer scripts are notoriously tricky, so be prepared to experiment and test thoroughly. Timer scripts are definitely not for the faint of heart. The process of setting one up, however, is simple. Just write a script that uses the "Install OnTimer Script" script step. When you configure this step, you specify a script, and then provide an interval, which is how often the script runs. You express the interval as a number of seconds using a calculation.

Organizing Your Scripts

Most mature databases end up with dozens, or even hundreds, of scripts that make life a lot easier for the folks who use it. But developers don't usually have the luxury of creating scripts in an order that makes sense for display in the Manage Scripts window. That's why FileMaker gives you a suite of tools you can use to organize your scripts.

Creating Script Folders

In Figure 10-13, you can see the Manage Scripts window from a database with a lot of scripts. The window looks a little like a window on your operating system, where documents are organized in folders. FileMaker lets you create folders for organizing your scripts that same way. Not only can you give a new folder a descriptive name, but also, like folders on your desktop, you can collapse them, so you don't have to scan a lengthy list of scripts to find those under Reports.

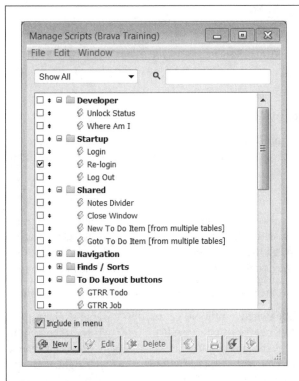

Figure 10-13:
When your database has lots of scripts, like this one, organization becomes critical. Here, the scripts are arranged in a logical order, and grouped into folders, as described in the steps starting on the next page. Some folders are open, and others are closed. Most scripts aren't set to show in the Scripts menu because this solution has buttons for users to run the scripts they need.

Script folders make the Manage Scripts window nice and tidy, but they also organize the Scripts menu. Any scripts inside a folder appear in a hierarchical (or pop-out) menu when you click the Scripts menu.

To see how all this works, you need to create a few extra scripts in your sample file. But they don't have to be real, working scripts. Just select your Find Unpaid Invoices script, and then, in the Manage Scripts window, click the Duplicate button a few times.

1. **In the Manage Scripts window, select the top script in your list, and then, at the right edge of the New button, press the little arrow that's beside the New button (see Figure 10-14).**

    The New item pop-up menu appears.

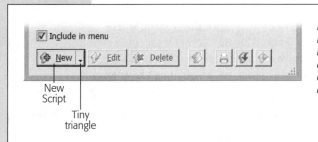

Figure 10-14:
In the Manage Scripts window, the New button makes a new script. But if you click the little arrow, then you get a pop-up menu of additional choices. You can make a new folder instead, or add a separator to the script list.

2. **Choose New Folder.**

    The Edit Folder dialog box appears.

3. **In the Folder Name box, type *Reports*.**

    Just like everything else in FileMaker, a descriptive name helps you figure out what's what. "Reports" is a little arbitrary, since this exercise is theoretical, but it's still a good habit to use descriptive names.

4. **Click OK.**

    The Reports folder appears as the second item in your list. A new group always appears just below any selected item in the list. If you forget to select a script and the new folder lands all the way at the bottom of the list, you can move it into place by dragging the double-headed arrow to the left of the folder's name.

5. **Drag the double arrow to the left of a script to move it into the Reports folder.**

    The motion can be a little twitchy until you get used to it. Drag straight up or down to move a script to a new position in the list. But drag toward the *right* to move a script into a group. If the new folder is directly above the scripts you're moving, then it's easiest to move the first script under the folder right, and then move each successive one right, also.

Tip: On the Mac, a blue line appears to help you see where a dragged item will land and folders highlight when you drag over them. Let go of the mouse button while the folder is highlighted and the script you're moving will land inside the folder.

Move a few scripts into the Reports group to get the hang of the technique. When you have some scripts in the new group, to the left of the group name, click the gray triangle (Mac) to collapse it. A second click opens the group again. (Windows shows a +/- icon to expand and collapse a folder.) Finally, click the Scripts menu to see how script groups work there.

Creating Menu Separators

Groups help you when you're plowing through a list of scripts trying to find the one you need to tweak. But you can also help people who use your database by giving them menu separators. It's a good idea to use them to organize sets of scripts that do different things. To create a menu separator, click to select the script that's just *above* where you want the separator to appear, and then, from the New item pop-up menu, choose New Separator. If a separator isn't where you want it, then you can drag it into place. (On the Mac, you can click anywhere on the separator, and then drag it, but on Windows, make sure to click the double-arrow, and then drag).

You can also use the Duplicate button to copy a whole bunch of separators with just a few clicks. Each new separator appears just below the original; just drag them into place.

A separator is really just an empty script whose name is "–", so if you like to do things the long way, you can make one manually. In Figure 10-15, you can see how a separator looks in a menu.

Branching and Looping in Scripts

Now that you have a basic foundation in what scripts do and how you can run them, it's time to see some of scripting's more powerful features. The script you created at the beginning of this chapter was the simplest kind: It goes through a series of steps from start to finish every time. Sometimes your script needs more smarts. You can add steps to the script that cause it to take different actions depending on the situation (called *branching*), or make it do the same thing over and over again (called *looping*).

Branching with If, Else If, Else, and End If

Sometimes a script needs to take action based on certain conditions in your database. When you send an email to a customer manually, you look him up in the Customers layout, copy his email address, and then go to your mail program to create, address and send the email. You'd like to add a button to the Customers layout that creates the email directly, saving you all the trouble of copying, switching, and pasting.

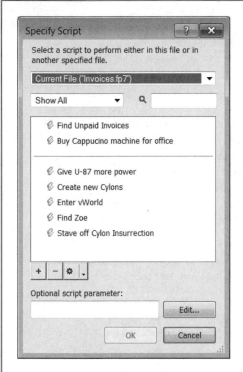

Figure 10-15:
In the Manage Scripts window, separators just show up as scripts named "–" but everywhere else, they turn into proper visual separators. Here, in the Specify Script window, the separator is right under the "Buy Cappucino machine for office" script.

A one-line script using the Send Mail script step (which is just like the File→Send Mail command) will do the trick. It's already created for you in the Invoices sample file, or see Figure 10-16 for the settings you need. If you write the script from scratch don't forget to select the "Perform without dialog" option or to save the script.

If you run the Send Email to Customer script, it creates a new email addressed to the current customer. But what happens if you *don't* have an email address for this customer? If the Customers::Email Address field is *empty*, then your script tries to send an email without a valid address through your email program, which complains mightily. Fortunately, you can head off this problem at the pass. If the Email Address field is empty, the script should let you know, and then skip the Send Mail step entirely.

The If step is the answer; it tests a condition and can take action based on the result of its test. Here's how to add an If step to the Send Email to Customer script:

1. **In the Edit Script dialog box, add the If step to your script.**

    FileMaker adds this step *after* the Send Mail step. It also adds a third step: End If. You can't have an If without an End If, so you get both automatically.

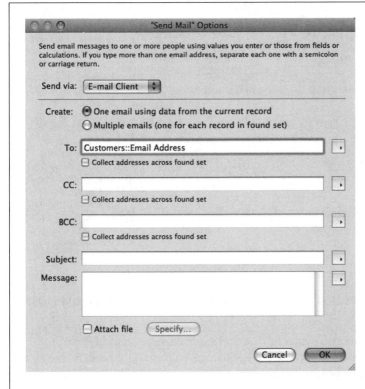

Figure 10-16:
The Send Mail Options lets you type an ordinary email address directly in the To, CC, or BCC boxes, and enter a Subject, and Message. Or, click the triangle by any box and either pick a field or enter a calculation instead. That way, you can send email to a person in the database, or fill the message with details from the current record. Turn on the "Multiple emails (one for each record in found set)" checkbox to use this script step to send email to more than one person at a time. But remember, this option must be used for good, never for evil. You'd never send spam emails, would you? See the box on page 439 to learn about the Send Via options.

Note: If you accidentally delete the End If step from your script, then FileMaker shows an error message when you try to save the script. To fix the error, you need to add the End If step back to your script, and then drag it to its proper place.

---

2. **Using the double-pointed arrow to the left of the If step, drag the step up above the Send Mail step.**

   By rearranging the steps in your script, you're telling FileMaker what order they should run in. (A script doesn't work as intended if you've got a step above something that needs to happen *first*.) Your script should look like Figure 10-17.

3. **Select the If step and, in the Script Step Options area, click Specify.**

   FileMaker shows you a standard Specify Calculation window. You use a calculation to define the *condition* of this If step. If the calculation evaluates to True, then FileMaker does the steps after the If. If the calculation evaluates to False, then FileMaker skips to the End If, and continues running the script from there.

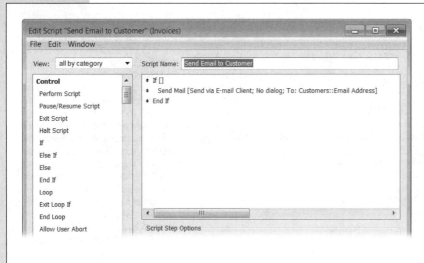

Figure 10-17:
To prevent FileMaker from making an email message when the customer has no email address, wrap the Send Mail step inside an If block as shown. Next, you'll put a condition in that If step to tell FileMaker when the message should be sent. Notice that the Send Mail step is now indented. Every step inside an If block gets indented this way.

4. **In the calculation box, enter** *Not IsEmpty(Customers::Email Address)*, **and then click OK.**

This calculation evaluates to *True*, and sends your customer an email only if the Email Address field isn't empty. See the box on page 441 for details on how this calculation makes these decisions.

Your script now checks to see if the Email Address field has something in it before running off to create the email message. But what happens when you run the script and the Email Address field is empty? Right now, nothing at all. FileMaker evaluates the If condition, sees that it's False, and skips to the End If. There's nothing after the End If, so the script just stops and your user waits in suspense, until he finally realizes that the requested email message simply isn't coming and investigates the problem on his own—or chucks his computer out the window.

In the interest of preventing property damage, your script should tell him *why* nothing's happening. For example, you can have your script show a message box saying, "You can't email this customer, since there's no email address on file", or whatever. That's what the Else step is for:

1. **In your script, select the Send Mail script step.**

When you add a *new* step, FileMaker inserts it after the selected step. You want the Else step to go right after the Send Mail step, so you select that step first.

2. **Add the Else step to the script.**

FileMaker inserts an Else step between Send Mail and End If.

POWER USERS' CLINIC

Two Ways to Send Mail

The first option in the Send Mail Options window (see Figure 10-16) is "Send via", and it gives you two options, letting you either use or bypass the email program on your computer:

- Choose **E-mail Client** to send the message using your email program. If you turn on "Perform without dialog" for the Send Mail script step, then the message goes directly into your mail program's outbox, and that program sends it the next time the send/receive mail process runs (which is automatic in most mail programs). If you leave "Perform without dialog" off, then the message goes into the Drafts folder instead. FileMaker also opens it up and switches to your mail program. This way, you get a chance to double-check the message and edit it as needed before you send it.

- Choose **SMTP Server** to send the message through your mail server. In other words, you're asking FileMaker to bypass your email program, and go straight to the network post office. You have to put in information about your mail server, including its network address and any user name and password it requires. This configuration has no "Perform without dialog" option, so you can't edit the message before FileMaker sends it off, and it doesn't show up in your sent mail folder.

Under most circumstances, you're probably best off sticking with the E-mail Client option. You can use it more easily (because you don't need to put in mail server settings). It's also more flexible since you can edit the message. Finally, you get a record of the emails you've sent from your sent mail folder.

But sometimes the E-mail Client option isn't a good choice. Sometimes you have a script that runs on the FileMaker Server (you'll learn about that in Chapter 17) or on a shared computer that has no email client. In a case like that, you're better off going straight to the server so you don't have to set up and manage a mail program.

Also, when you use the SMTP Server option, you get to specify the From name and address. If the message comes from your email client, then it comes from you. But what if you're sending shipment notifications for your company? You may want the messages to come from *orders@my-company.com*, or some other shared address instead. In a case like this, you can use the SMTP Server option, and everybody in the office can send email from the same account through FileMaker.

Finally, if you're sending lots of email, it can be faster and more reliable to send messages directly to the mail server (after all, its job is to send *lots* of email).

As a general rule, it's fine to use the E-mail Client option unless you need for the increased power (and hassle) of the SMTP Server option.

Note: Don't click the Else If step by mistake. You want the step called just Else. If you added the wrong step, select it, click Clear, and then try, try again.

3. **Right after the Else step, add the Show Custom Dialog script step to the script.**

   This step is also under Miscellaneous. Its job is to pop up a dialog box for someone. You get to decide what the box says, which buttons it includes, and which fields—if any—it should show.

4. **In the Script Step Options area, click the Specify button.**

   The "Show Custom Dialog" Options window appears (Figure 10-18).

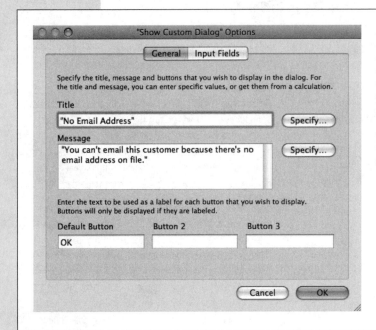

Figure 10-18:
*The Show Custom Dialog script step
lets you provide feedback, like why
an email script isn't behaving as
expected. You can give your dialog
box a title, a message, and up to
three buttons for people to click.
You can also add input fields to the
dialog box by visiting the Input Fields
tab. You'll learn about these on
page 678.*

5. **In the Title box, type** *No Email Address*.

   Whatever you type in this box appears in the title bar along the top of your custom dialog box. Punctuation marks like commas and periods look odd in title bars, but you're welcome to include them.

6. **In the Message box, type** *You can't email this customer because there's no email address on file.*

   This tells FileMaker what to put *inside* the dialog box.

7. **From the Button 2 box, select, and then delete the word Cancel.**

   A custom dialog box can have up to three buttons. In this case, you want only one: an OK button. (If you don't type anything in the Button 2 and Button 3 boxes, then those buttons don't show up.)

8. **Click OK.**

   Your script should now look like the one shown in Figure 10-19.

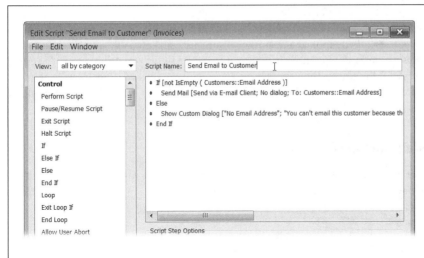

Figure 10-19:
The finished Send Email to Customer script looks like this. If you read it like a book, it says, "If the email address field is not empty, Send Mail. Otherwise show an error message to the person." The If/Else/End If steps create two branches in the script: one when the email address field is full, and one when it's empty.

UP TO SPEED

Not What?

In the script you wrote on page 438, the If script step runs the indented steps only when the whole calculation evaluates to True. To figure out when that happens, you have to deconstruct the calculation itself.

By itself, the *IsEmpty()* function returns True when the value you pass it is completely empty—in other words, when the Email Address field is empty:

    IsEmpty (Customers::Email Address)

But that action doesn't help you because you want the email sent only when there *is* data in the email field. If you have no email address entered, then the calculation above returns True, and causes the Send Email step to run. If the email address field is filled in, on the other hand, then the calculation's result is False, and FileMaker skips the Send Mail step.

This behavior is exactly the opposite of what you want. To flip the result of the calculation around, you use the Not

operator. It looks at the Boolean value to its right, and turns a True to a False, or a False to a True. Here's the calculation you need:

    Not IsEmpty (Customers::Email Address)

You can easily tell if you've got the right construction by reading the If step like a sentence: "If not is empty Email Address." It may not be grammatical perfection, but gets the logic right.

If this kind of logic makes your head spin, then you have another option. Remove the "not", and then switch your steps around. If you read the script in pseudo-English logic, it'd go like this: "If the email address is empty, show a message, else send the email." That way, you can use a more straightforward formula to test the Email Address field:

    IsEmpty (Customers::Email Address)

Now return to your database, and then try your script out: Find a customer without an email address (or just delete the email address for the Customer record you're viewing—this is just a sample database so it's OK), and choose Scripts→"Send Email to Customer". If you look at a customer record with an email address, then the script creates a email message in your mail program, ready for you to fill out. If the email address field is empty, then you see an error message instead. Finish up by creating a button for this script, and then add it to the Customers layout for the ultimate in convenience.

Testing Multiple Conditions

If you have more than one condition to consider, you can use the Else If script step. You could have a script like this, for instance:

```
If [ Get ( CurrentTime ) < Time ( 12 ; 0; 0 ) ]
  Show Custom Dialog [ "Good Morning!" ]
Else If [ Get ( CurrentTime ) < Time ( 18 ; 0 ; 0 ) ]
  Show Custom Dialog [ "Good Afternoon!" ]
Else
  Show Custom Dialog [ "Good Evening!" ]
End If
```

When this script runs, it tests each condition in turn, deciding which custom dialog box to show someone, based on the actual current time. If the current time is before noon, she sees a "Good morning" message, and the script jumps to the end (the End If script step) without needing to test the second condition.

If it isn't before noon, the script does a second test to see if it's before 6 p.m. If it is, the user sees a "Good Afternoon" message, and the script jumps to the end. But if both tests fail, no third condition is tested, and the Else just shows the "Good Evening" message, like an automatic condition in a Case statement. However, you can add other Else Ifs to test other conditions.

You can add as many Else If steps as you want, but they have to come between the If and End If steps. Each Else If can test a different condition. If you have an Else step, it should come after the If and every Else If, but before the End If. You can think of the Else condition as the default condition in a *Case()* or an *If()* statement when you write a calculation.

Tip: When you're writing multiple condition scripts, it can be hard to figure out when a condition tests as True. See the section on the Script Debugger (page 513) to learn how to watch your scripts run step by step.

Looping

Sometimes you want to do the same thing over and over again, until you reach some kind of end point. For example, people often write a script that does something to every record in the found set, one after another. This script is called a *looping script*. You make a script *loop through records* using the Loop script step.

Like the If step, the Loop step has a necessary partner called End Loop. When you put script steps between Loop and End Loop, FileMaker simply repeats them over and over, forever.

So how does a script like this end? Simple: You tell FileMaker to *exit the loop* at the right time. FileMaker has three ways to exit a loop:

- The **Go To Record/Request** step has an "Exit after last" option when you go to the next or previous record. That way, you can easily loop through all the records in the found set, exiting the loop when you get to the last one.

- The **Exit Loop If** script step lets you provide a condition formula (just like If). If the condition evaluates to True, then FileMaker immediately skips to the first step after End Loop.

- The **Exit Script** and **Halt Script** steps both end a script immediately, even if you're in a loop.

For example, a simple looping script would have this structure:

```
Loop
 # Do some stuff
 Exit Loop If [ // some condition ]
End Loop
```

Note: This script is meant for show only. If you write and then try to run it, you'll get into an *endless loop* (one that won't ever stop). This script's Exit Loop If test is commented out and so it'll never evaluate as true and stop your loop. The "#" symbol before the "Do some stuff" step is a script comment. Learn about them on page 673. Press your Escape key to stop a endless looping script.

The "Loop" step comes before the steps you want to repeat. Then you add those steps, and the Exit Loop If step, which lets you write a calculation to figure out if the loop should stop. It usually, but not always, comes at the end of the steps that'll repeat each time the loop runs. The Exit Loop If calculation is evaluated every time the loop runs, and then when the condition is met, the script stops with the End Loop step.

Using Go to Record/Request/Page to exit a loop

The most common type of looping script repeats a process on a found set of records. If you've used loops in other programs, you may think you have to devise some kind of test to figure out when you've reached the last record in your found set. You may be tempted to write a loop like this:

```
Loop
    # Your script's work goes here.
    Go to Record/Request/Page [ Next ]
    Exit Loop If [ Get ( FoundCount ) = Get (RecordNumber) ]
End Loop
    # Your script's work goes here. Again!
```

This script starts with a loop that does your task on the current record, and then moves to the next record (just as if you'd clicked the book icon's right-hand page). If the number of the record you're now on *equals* the current found count, then File-Maker exits the loop. This type of logic often requires you to repeat the steps within a loop right after it in order to get the process to run on the last record in your found set. But FileMaker has a better way. Use the "Go to Record/Request/Page" step, and select the "Exit after last" option (Figure 10-20).

A loop that works on a found set of records is called a "record loop." "Field loops" work through fields within a record. You can even nest one loop inside another, as when you need to work on a set of parent records, and then on each parent's child records. A nested loop's structure looks like this:

```
Loop
    # Work on the first parent record here
    # Open a new window containing child records
    Go to Related Record [From table: ChildTable; Using Layout: ChildLayout]
        Loop
          # Work on one set of child records here
          Go to Record/Request/Page [Next; Exit after last]
          Close Window [Current Window]
        End Loop
    # Go to the next parent record and then start the process over
    Go to Record/Request/Page [Next; Exit after last]
End Loop
```

In this nested loop, the first loop works on a parent record and is called the *outer loop*. It runs once for each parent record. The one the works on the child records is called an *inner loop* and it runs once for each child record that's related to the currently active parent record.

Note: You'll write a basic looping script on page 719.

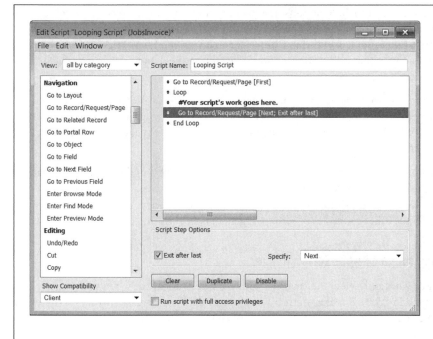

Figure 10-20:
When "Next" is selected in the Specify pop-up menu, the Go to Record/Request/ Page script step has an "Exit after last" option. When selected, "Exit after last" exits the found set (and stops the loop) after the loop's steps have run on the last record in the found set. This script will start on the first record in the found set and repeat the actions represented by the "#Your script's work goes here" comment once for each record in the found set. You can work through a found set backwards by choosing "Previous" in the Specify pop-up menu, and then selecting "Exit after last." This makes sense if you want to leave the user on the first record in a found set at the end of a loop.

Script Triggers

Scripts are all about saving you (and your users) time. And what could be less time consuming than something you don't have to do at all? As you learned earlier in this chapter, script triggers let you tell FileMaker to run a script automatically in response to something that already happens when people use your database. You'll get a brief introduction to each of FileMaker's trigger options here. Then, throughout the next chapters, you'll use these triggers in key places to make your database come alive.

Script triggers come in two flavors. *Layout triggers* apply to the layout as a whole. These triggers include actions like loading or committing a record, switching layouts, or pressing a key on the keyboard. *Object triggers* are tied to a single layout object (like a field, portal, Tab Control, or web viewer). These triggers fire when you interact with that object in some way, like editing the data in a field, or switching to a different tab panel.

In addition to the action that fires a script trigger, *timing* also comes into play. Some triggers fire before their controlling action, and some fire afterwards. As with scripting itself, the order in which a step or a whole script occurs can make or break a script.

So take care when you start to apply triggers. They're simple to apply, but can be tricky to predict unless you understand all their behaviors. So you'll start this section by applying a simple script trigger, and then you'll learn how each trigger works. You'll see other examples of script triggers in later scripting chapters.

Creating a Simple Script Trigger

Since you'd only view the Invoices with Balance Due layout when you want to find unpaid invoices, it makes perfect sense to run the Find Unpaid Invoices script every time you switch to that layout. You'll use an OnLayoutEnter script trigger to get the job done:

1. **Switch to your Invoices with Balance Due layout, and then go to Layout mode.**

   You're creating a layout trigger (that fires when you switch to the Invoices with Balance Due layout), so you need to be on the right layout.

2. **Choose Layouts→Layout Setup, and then switch to the Script Triggers tab.**

   This tab is where you configure triggers for the layout. You can see it in Figure 10-21.

3. **In the list, turn on the OnLayoutEnter checkbox.**

   The Specify Script window appears.

4. **Select the Find Unpaid Invoices script, and then click OK.**

   In the list, the OnLayoutEnter trigger is highlighted, and, in the Script column, the Find Unpaid Invoices script shows. You can also see the script's name beside the Select button in the Script Trigger Properties section of the window.

5. **Select the Browse and Preview checkboxes, and deselect the Find checkbox.**

   Since it does a Find, this script only makes sense in Browse mode and Preview mode, so you want it to trigger only in those cases.

6. **Click OK.**

   Now your trigger is installed, and ready to test.

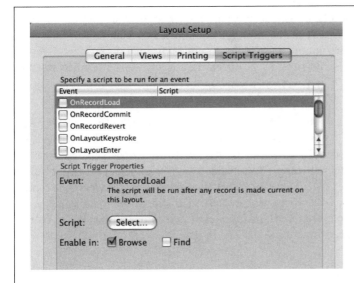

Figure 10-21:
The Layout Setup dialog box has a Script Triggers tab. From here, you can turn on various triggers, pick which scripts run, and choose which modes the triggers apply to. You can turn on as many triggers as you want, but each trigger can have only one script. If you need to do more than one thing for a trigger, just bundle them together in one script (using two or more Perform Script steps), and then run it.

To test things properly, go to the Invoices layout, and then choose Records→Show All Records. Then switch to the Invoices with Balance Due layout. If all goes well, FileMaker should automatically find only the unpaid invoices, and sort them for you.

Now that you're on the List layout, you can find again if you want to see different records, or sort in a different way. The trigger fires only when you first come to the layout from somewhere else.

Layout Triggers

As you saw in the previous section, You configure layout triggers in the Layout Setup dialog box (Layouts→Layout Setup), in the Script Triggers tab. Layout triggers are performed when an action takes place that concerns a layout itself. For example, each time a new record is viewed, that's considered a layout trigger. That makes sense, given that the layout is FileMaker's method of showing you a specific record. When you think about it, you can see that the same trigger, running the very same script, can behave slightly differently depending on whether it's run on a detail or a list type layout. Triggers can fire before their action or afterwards. Read on to learn what that means.

OnRecordLoad

The OnRecordLoad trigger fires when a record is *loaded*. In other words, when you first visit a layout, switch to a new record, make a new record, or perform a find, a record is loaded. This trigger fires after the record is loaded and works in Browse and Find modes. You'll use this trigger in the next chapter to automatically sort a set of records.

OnRecordCommit

OnRecordCommit works in Browse and Find modes. When you commit a record, the trigger fires. It doesn't matter how you commit (by clicking out of the record, switching layouts, or running a script, for instance). In each case, if this trigger is turned on, then the script runs. Even though the trigger is called "OnRecordCommit" it actually fires *after* you make the action that would normally commit the record but *before* FileMaker commits it.

That might seem like a subtle distinction, but it's actually hugely important. It means that the OnRecordCommit trigger (and any other one that fires *before* its triggering event) can be cancelled. In other words, the script that's triggered can cancel the commit operation by returning a False value (you'll learn about returning values from scripts on page 684). If you cancel the commit, then you don't leave the record, and FileMaker doesn't save your changes. You can use this power to force the person using the database to make some kind of change to a record before saving, or require some kind of extra confirmation.

OnRecordRevert

In the rare case that someone reverts a record (using the Records→Revert Record command, or the equivalent script step), the *OnRecordRevert* trigger kicks in. The trigger fires before the record is reverted and works in Browse and Find modes.

OnLayoutKeystroke

The *OnLayoutKeystroke* trigger fires every time a key is pressed. Obviously, any script you trigger should be quick, because it can be called very frequently. The trigger fires before the keystroke is applied and works in Browse, Find and Preview modes. You can use the *Get (TriggerKeystroke)* and *Get (TriggerModifierKeys)* functions to find out which key was pressed.

You can also cancel keystrokes. So if you want to stop allowing the letter L in your database, you can. Truthfully, though, keystroke triggers aren't for beginners. People can press *lots* of different keys. Your script needs to be fast, and it takes a lot of knowledge to figure out which keys were pressed. For instance, this trigger fires even if someone presses an arrow key, or the Ctrl or ⌘ key, the Tab key, or a function key. You'll learn about keystroke triggers on page 698.

Note: One exception is Ctrl or ⌘ key combinations. These *don't* fire keystroke triggers. If you want to configure keyboard shortcuts to run scripts, then use custom menus (page 538).

OnLayoutEnter

When you switch to a layout, the *OnLayoutEnter* trigger fires (you did just that on page 446). The trigger fires after the layout shows onscreen and works in Browse, Find and Preview modes. You can do some initial tab setup, or sort the records, or even bounce to a different layout if you want. OnLayoutEnter is one of the bread-and-butter triggers for an advanced database that aims to streamline people's workflows.

Tip: This trigger was called *OnLayoutLoad* in previous versions. It was changed in FileMaker Pro 11 to mirror the new function *OnLayoutExit*.

OnLayoutExit

When you switch away from a layout, *OnLayoutExit* fires. It fires before you leave the layout and works in Browse, Find, and Preview modes. It might seem as if you don't need this trigger if you've already got *OnLayoutEnter*, but it can make your scripting cleaner. That is, you can actually prevent a user from leaving a layout by checking some condition before prior to exiting the layout. That keeps you from having to write a script that remembers where the user was before they tried to switch to a new layout, and then take them back if you want to cancel that switch to keep them where they were. This way, you prevent the switch until some condition (like entering data in all the required fields on a layout) is met.

OnModeEnter and OnModeExit

The *OnModeEnter* trigger fires when you switch *to* a mode. For instance, if you switch to Find mode, then the OnModeEnter trigger fires when you get there. By contrast, the *OnModeExit* trigger fires when you *leave* a mode. As with the layout enter/exit triggers, if you use both triggers, then OnModeExit fires first, before you leave the current mode. Then OnModeEnter fires after the switch. The distinction between these two is subtle but important. First, a script triggered by OnModeEnter runs once you're in the new mode. So it can look at the current mode (using the *Get(WindowMode)* function), and act accordingly.

On the other hand, OnModeExit is cancelable. So if you choose, you can refuse to let someone leave the current mode.

OnViewChange

OnViewChange fires each time you switch between Form, List or Table views. It fires after the view is switched and works in Browse and Find modes. It doesn't activate when you first open a window or switch to a layout. Since it fires after its event, this trigger isn't cancelable.

Object Triggers

To configure an object's triggers, on the layout, first select the object, and then choose Format→Set Script Triggers. The resulting window looks familiar (Figure 10-22).

Before you look at each type, bear this in mind: You can apply triggers only to fields, Tab Controls, portals, buttons, and web viewers. You can't put a trigger on a text label, line, shape, or picture. The Set Script Triggers command will be grayed out when those objects are selected.

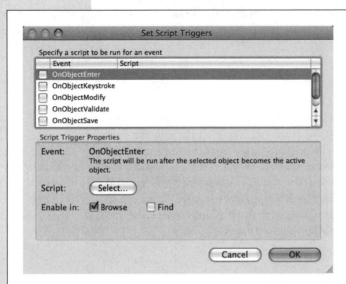

Figure 10-22:
The Format→Set Script Triggers menu command lets you configure triggers for the selected layout object. The list of triggers is smaller than for layouts, but since so many object types exist, it can be harder to make sense of them. Read on to get the full scoop.

Object triggers sound picky when you scan through their names (and to a degree they are), but that's just to give you as much control about when they fire as possible. If you read through this list, you'll see that object triggers appear in the same order as users interact with an object, in this case, say a field. So for any particular interaction with a field, the following actions might take place:

- The field is *entered*—when you click in it.

- The field is *modified*—you type new data into it.

- The field's *validation* kicks in—you click out of the field.

- The field's new data is *saved*—FileMaker's autosave makes the new data permanent.

- The field is *exited*—a new object is entered or the record is committed.

And there's even one more action that can take place on an object. As with layouts, you can have each keystroke trigger a script. As you'll see in this section, the better you understand how FileMaker handles objects, the easier it is to apply the proper object trigger.

Tip: When you're trying to tease these triggers apart, it's helpful to write a very simple script that does nothing but the Beep script step. Assign an object trigger that runs the script to a field, and then interact with the field, noticing when the beep occurs. Try each trigger—you'll soon get the picture.

OnObjectEnter

The *OnObjectEnter* trigger, generally speaking, fires after you *enter* an object. It's available in Browse and Find modes. Usually you use this trigger with a field. It fires when you enter the field, whether by clicking, tabbing, or script.

If you set an OnObjectEnter trigger on a button or Tab Control, then it fires if you put the object in the tab order, and then tab to it (causing it to get a black outline). If you use the mouse to click a button or tab, then the OnObjectEnter trigger *doesn't* fire.

For portals, the trigger fires whenever you go to a new row. For instance, if you click into a field on the portal, then the trigger fires. If you click a second field on the same row, then it *doesn't* fire again. But if you click a field on a *different* row, then it fires again. This way you can track someone as she switches from row to row.

For a web viewer, the trigger fires if you click into the web page, or tab into a field on the page.

OnObjectKeystroke

Once you're entered an object, it becomes the target for keystrokes. If you press a key on the keyboard, the object's OnObjectKeystroke trigger fires before the keystroke is entered. It can be applied in Browse and Find modes. For fields, the script runs repeatedly as you type or arrow around in the field. It also fires when you press the Tab key or Enter key to leave the field. For buttons and Tab Controls, you have to tab into the object for it to receive keystrokes. Portals and web viewers never receive keystrokes, so this trigger never fires if you assign it to one of them.

Finally, the keystroke trigger can be cancelled, which lets you, for instance, prevent entry of certain characters in a field. You'll see an example of this on page 700.

OnObjectModify

The *OnObjectModify* trigger also varies from object to object. For a field, it fires *after* something in the field changes but *while you're in the field*. For instance, if you type into the field, then the trigger fires each time you add or delete a character. But it *doesn't* fire if you just use the arrow keys to move around in the field, or if you press Tab or Enter to leave the field. It also fires once each time you cut or paste in the field. It's available for Browse and Find modes.

Warning: The OnObjectModify trigger doesn't fire if you modify the field without entering it. For instance, if a script runs the Set Field script step while you're on the layout, then the field changes but the trigger doesn't fire. New in FileMaker Pro 11, dragging text from one field into another, *does* fire the OnObjectModify trigger. Users with version 10 won't trigger, though, so take care with this trigger if you have a mix of versions.

If you attach this trigger to a Tab Control, then it fires whenever you switch tabs. OnObjectModify never fires with buttons, portals, and web viewers.

OnObjectValidate

This trigger can be applied to any object, but is only triggered for fields that have field Validation options (page 248). The trigger fires before the data in the field changes and so won't be triggered just by clicking or tabbing into the field. The trigger can be cancelled. It's available in Browse and Find modes.

Not all changes to data in validated fields will cause the trigger to fire, however. Spell Check and Find/Replace don't fire *OnObjectValidate*. Whether you run them manually or by script, Import (page 826), Replace Field Contents (page 70) and Relookup Field Contents (page 224) also don't fire this trigger.

OnObjectSave

While OnObjectModify fires as you modify a field, *OnObjectSave* fires after the field's data has been validated and saved, but before the field is exited. With this trigger, you can modify the field repeatedly without interruption. Then, when you're done and you leave the field by tabbing, pressing Enter, clicking in another field, or by any other means, the trigger fires.

This trigger fires only if you actually make a change. If you click in a field, and then leave the field without making changes, nothing is saved, and the trigger doesn't run. Once again, this trigger can be cancelled. If your script returns False, then it forces the user back into the field. It's available in Browse and Find modes. It applies to fields only.

OnObjectExit

The *OnObjectExit* trigger is exactly the opposite of OnObjectEnter. It fires when you leave an object. For fields, this means tabbing away, committing the record, and so forth. For buttons and Tab Controls, it means tabbing away. For portals, it fires when you leave a portal row in any way. Finally, for web viewers, it fires when you had previously clicked or tabbed into the page, and you then click away. Any script step that causes an object to be exited will fire the trigger.

Many actions can trigger an exit from a field, portal, or web viewer. For instance, you might leave the layout, close the window, or quit FileMaker. In every case, the trigger fires, and in every case, if the script returns False, then the action is cancelled. So you can even stop folks from closing the window before they attend to the demands of your trigger. It's available in Browse and Find modes.

Script triggers are possibly FileMaker's most powerful and complex feature. A simple trigger can be a real timesaver, and for the adventuresome, more advanced trigger scenarios can produce very powerful results.

Exploring Script Steps

N ow that you know how to create scripts, it's time to expand your repertoire. FileMaker has a script step for just about everything you can do from the menus and Status toolbar. You can use any combination of these steps with script techniques like looping, branching, custom dialog boxes, and more to automate just about anything FileMaker can do. Major areas of scripting include working with field data and records, finding, sorting, working with windows and files, and printing. This chapter is a compendium of steps—and boatloads of scripting possibilities.

Note: Download sample databases for this chapter from this book's Missing CD page at *www.missing-manuals.com*. Do the tutorials in the file called Invoices START.fp7. Use Invoices FINISHED.fp7 to compare your work, or if you want to check something as you work.

Go to Layout

The "Go to Layout" script step was introduced in the last chapter. Its purpose is simple: change layouts. It works just like making a choice from the Layout bar's Layout pop-up menu, except that the script can go to *any* layout (even if it doesn't show in the menu).

"Go to Layout" has just one option, a pop-up menu labeled Specify. In addition to every layout in your database, this menu also has three special choices:

- The original layout option causes FileMaker to switch to the layout someone was on when the script started. After all, you can run lots of scripts anywhere, especially if they're on the Script menu. Since scripts often change layouts as they run, this option makes sure folks end up back where they started.

- The "Layout Name by calculation" option lets you specify a typical FileMaker calculation. The result of the calculation has to be text, and it should exactly match the *name* of one of the layouts in the database. When the script runs, FileMaker evaluates the calculation, and then switches to the layout with the correct name.

- The "Layout Number by calculation" option is similar. You specify a calculation with a *number* result. FileMaker numbers every layout sequentially, in the order in which it's listed in Layout mode. The result of the calculation determines which layout to visit by number.

Like Record Numbers (page 162), layout numbers reflect the current state of the database and aren't reliable ways to uniquely identify a layout. First, layout numbers don't necessarily correspond to their positions in the Layout pop-up menu. Not all layouts show in the menu (you can turn off their display—see page 282), plus you can reorder them manually. To find out a layout's number reliably, you have several choices. The manual method is to switch to Layout mode, and then go to the layout in question. In the Status toolbar look at the Layout box. It shows which layout number you're on. Better yet, use the Data Viewer in FileMaker Pro Advanced.

See the box on page 458 to learn when to use "Go to Layout" with Layout Name and when to use Layout Number.

Go to Object

"Go to Object" is massively useful, because you can go to (or activate) any object on a layout, thereby setting up the context for the steps that follow. You can also use "Go to Object" to activate a Tab Control (page 155) that's not the automatic tab. Say you have a layout with a Tab Control, and the user clicks a button on the third tab. If the button's script has to leave the layout to run part of its process (say you need to run over to the Line Item layout and create a line item record before switching back to the original layout), then FileMaker will activate the automatic tab when it returns. But that's confusing and annoying to your user, who almost always wants her screen set up just like it was before she clicked a button. To smooth those ruffled feathers, name the tab where the button resides, and then add a "Go to Object" step at the end of that button's script.

Naming objects

Give objects a name with the Inspector (Figure 11-1). This name is in addition to any other name or identifier it has, such as a fully-qualified field name (Invoices::InvoiceID or Customer::Full Name) or any internal FileMaker IDs. You can name any object on a layout, but there's usually no reason to unless you need to use the name in a script.

Figure 11-1:
Name an object by selecting it and then typing a name in the Name box at the top of the Inspector's Position tab. Since you and your scripts are the only ones who'll ever see this name, you don't have to make it pretty for your users. Do make it simple and descriptive, though, so it's easy to use in a script.

Why though, would you bother naming a field when you can just use the "Go to Field" script step? If there's only one copy of a field on a layout, then you don't need to name the field. But if you have two copies of a field on a layout, but need a script to go to a specific one, then name it, and use "Go to Object" instead. A common reason for having two versions of the same field on a layout is when you have two portals from the same relationship on a layout. You might have one portal show all the records in the relationship and the other portal is filtered to show just records with "Active" in their Status fields (page 567). You might also need two or more copies of a field to show the same data on multiple tabs on a Tab Control.

Note: You should always name web viewers if you're scripting any interaction with them, because the Set Web Viewer step (page 504) requires you to address web viewers by name.

You can use any naming scheme you want, but here's a few rules to keep in mind:

- **Object names have to be unique, but only within a layout.** That is, you can't have two objects named "streetAddress" on the same layout, but every layout could have an object named "streetAddress" on it.

- **Object names aren't case sensitive.** "StreetAddress" and "streetAddress" are the same name as far as FileMaker is concerned.

- **Names can contain no more than 100 characters.** Sorry.

- **You can name objects or groups of objects.** If you group an object after you've given it a name, it retains the name, even if you name the group. You can't edit, or even see, the name of an individual object in a group unless you ungroup first.

- **You can name a locked object, but you can't edit its name unless you unlock it.**

- **If you copy an object that has a name, the name is copied also.** FileMaker appends a number after the object's name for you (streetAddress 2), since names have to be unique. If you start noticing that lots of fields have inappropriate names with numbers at the end, then you (or more likely your colleague) has unknowingly copied and pasted a named object all over the place.

FREQUENTLY ASKED QUESTION

Specifying a Layout

Filemaker has three ways to tell the "Go to Layout" step which layout to visit. Which one should I use?

The easiest way is to choose the layout directly from the Specify pop-up menu. When the script runs, FileMaker goes to your chosen layout, period (that is, unless somebody has deleted the layout since you wrote the script).

The other two options—specifying a layout by name or number—are trickier, for a couple of reasons. First, they're a pain: You have to write a calculation when you could just pick from a menu. Second, both calculation methods have soft underbellies. If you specify a layout name using a calculation, and later rename the layout, even just by adding an accidental space somewhere in the name, then the script can't find the layout any more. If you use the layout number, and then add or delete a layout, or rearrange your layout list (page 284), then the script goes to the wrong layout.

Still, these options give you greater flexibility. For example, if you use "Go to Layout" and specify by Layout Name, then you can use script parameters to name any layout in your database. With this technique, you can create a single navigation script, and use it in all sorts of routine database tasks.

If you want to create a scripted process that's like a wizard or an assistant in some programs, then Layout Number is a godsend. Create the layouts that control your process, and then make one Next button that you copy onto each layout. The button gets a "Go to Layout" script step, specifying a Layout Number that's one more than the current layout number *(Get(LayoutNumber) + 1)*. The only time this step wouldn't go to the next layout in a list is if you ran it on the *last* layout. In that case, there's no next layout to go to, so nothing will happen. But as long as you keep the layouts arranged in the proper step-by-step order, the button always takes people to the right layout.

Using Go To Object in a Script

Take care to type the object's name very carefully in the Object Name box (Figure 11-2). There's no list of named objects to choose from, so you have to type it manually and it has to be exact (except for case) in order for the script step to run.

There are some places where it doesn't matter if you rename things. FileMaker is really great about knowing that you've changed your First Name field to Name_First in the Manage Database window. But if you change a field's layout object name, any script steps that refer to that old name will fail. If all you're doing is activating a tab for user, that's not such a big deal. But the results could be disastrous if you're using "Go to Object" to set the context for doing something permanent to a bunch of records at once, like editing or deleting field data. To avoid harming your database with a bad script, avoid changing object names if at all possible.

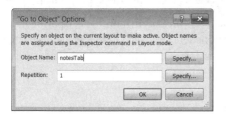

Figure 11-2:
The "Go to Object" window's Object Name field requires you to type (or calculate) the exact name of a layout object. If you're accustomed to using hard-to-type names, you can copy the object's name from the Inspector, and then paste it into the Object Name box to ensure accuracy. The Repetition option lets you go to a specific line in a repeating field. Ignore this option for all other objects.

Tip: Use the Database Design Report (DDR) in FileMaker Pro Advanced to get all the information you need about an object, including its name, before you change it (page 526).

Scripting for Fields

Most people using FileMaker spend *a lot* of their time working with field data, so it's no surprise that script steps devoted to fields abound. You can put someone in a specific field, select field text, and even play sounds and movies from container fields. You can perform a find and replace operation, run the Replace Field Contents command, and export field contents to a file. Finally, you get more than 10 ways to put data into a field.

Navigating Fields

FileMaker offers a couple of ways to field-hop—pressing Tab to move to the next field in order, or just clicking the desired field. It has script steps that mimic both techniques.

Go to Field

The simplest field navigation script step is called "Go to Field". It's really a two-purpose step, with two checkboxes to prove it. In its simplest form, you turn on the "Go to target field" checkbox, and then pick the field you want to go to. When the script runs, FileMaker puts folks in the specified field (provided it's on the layout).

Note: When you use "Go to Field" in a script, FileMaker dutifully ignores the field behavior specified on the layout, and puts people right into the field, even if they normally couldn't click into it. You can use this fact to create a field that people can get to only by using your script.

The step also has a checkbox called "Select/perform". When this option is turned on, the script either *selects* the contents of the field it goes to or *does* what's in the field—if possible. For example, if the step goes to a *container* field that holds a sound or a movie, FileMaker *plays* the contents instead. If the container field holds a *reference* to a picture or a file, FileMaker *opens* the correct file, using the appropriate program.

The mildly weird thing about "Go to Field" is you can turn on "Select/perform" and *turn off* "Go to target field". With the options set this way, "Go to Field" doesn't go to a field at all. Instead, it simply selects or performs the contents of the field you happen to be in when the script runs.

Go to Next Field and Go to Previous Field

To mimic the process of tabbing through fields, FileMaker has two more script steps. The first, called "Go to Next Field", just tabs to the next field in the tab order. You probably already figured out that "Go to Previous Field" goes to the *previous* field in the tab order. These steps don't have a "Select/perform" option—they just go to the field.

Tip: To get the effect of "Select/perform", use "Go to Next Field" or "Go to Previous Field" to get to the field you want, and then use "Go to Field" to select/perform it. When you add the "Go to Field" step, don't turn on "Go to target field", and it acts on the field you're already in.

Editing Commands

FileMaker has all the classic commands in its Edit menu: Undo, Cut, Copy, Paste, and Clear. It also has a script step for each of these commands. The Undo step is the simplest. It has no options at all, and has exactly the same effect as choosing Edit→Undo. You rarely want to undo something you just scripted, so you rarely use this script step. It's quite handy, though, if you use Custom Menus (see the box on page 528) to control access to certain menu commands.

Cut, Copy, and Clear are slightly more complicated, with two options each. The first, "Select entire contents", lets you decide which part of a field's value gets cut, copied, or cleared. If you turn this option on, then FileMaker selects the entire field before acting. If this option's turned off, then FileMaker cuts/copies/clears whatever happens to be selected in the field. (But see page 462 to learn why you should rarely use these commands.) You also get a "Go to target field" option, through which the script can tell FileMaker *which field* to act on. If it's not turned on, then it uses the *current field*—the one someone's in when the step runs.

The Paste step is the most complicated of these four. In addition to specifying the field you want, and whether or not to select everything in the field before pasting, you get an option to "Paste without style". When you turn this option on, FileMaker pastes the text on the clipboard, but throws away any style information. If you're in Windows, you get a fourth option: "Link if available" (it's there, but greyed out on the Mac). If the data on the clipboard comes from a source that supports object linking, then FileMaker embeds the linked object. Changes to the original data show up in FileMaker. Turn this option off if you want the script to just paste a *copy* of the data.

Selecting Text

FileMaker has two script steps to help you select text. The first, called Select All, selects everything in the current field, just like the Edit→Select All command. If you need more control, then use Set Selection instead. This step has two options. First, you can specify a target field so that FileMaker operates on the current field. The step also has a separate Specify button (below the one associated with "Go to target field") that brings up the Specify Set Selection window (Figure 11-3).

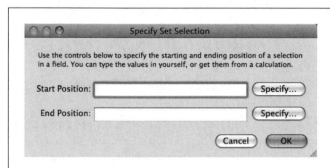

Figure 11-3:
This window lets you tell FileMaker exactly what text you want the script to select. You can type numbers directly in the Start Position and End Position boxes, or click either Specify button to bring up the Specify Calculation window.

If you imagine the text in your field as a string of letters, numbers, spaces, and punctuation, then you can pretend each of these is numbered. For instance, the word "Missing" has letters numbered one through seven. You first tell FileMaker where the selection should *start* by putting the number of the first character in the Start Position box. Next, you put the number of the *last* character in the End Position box. When the step runs, FileMaker selects these two characters and everything in between.

Editing Field Data

Editing field data is such an important part of FileMaker that it gives you 15 ways to put stuff in fields with a script step. In the last chapter, you learned that the scripted process for finding records could actually be shorter and more efficient than the manual process. Editing field data via scripts is also different from manually editing data, and the following sections cover those differences.

The first thing to understand is that, except for Set Field and Set Field by Name, the steps in this section *work only if the field is on the current layout*. This property is no problem for scripts you use to structure someone's data entry, but it can be a roadblock in other cases. Suppose you have a script that sets a "Paid in Full" flag on an invoice. You want this script to work no matter what layout you're on (as long as it's one that shows invoice records), and whether or not the field is on that layout. In that case, you need to understand the Set Field script step (or its power-user partner, Set Field by Name).

Positioning the Insertion Point

You can use the Set Selection script step to put the insertion point anywhere in a field, too. The trick is to make sure *nothing* gets selected. When you specify a Start Position and an End Position, FileMaker selects the characters at each position, plus anything in between. If these two numbers are the same, then FileMaker selects just one character.

But what if the End Position comes *before* the Start Position?

When you set the End Position one number lower than the Start Position, FileMaker doesn't select anything. Instead, it puts the little flashing insertion point right before the Start Position. Using this technique, you can get your script to put someone anywhere you want inside a field, say at the beginning of a Notes field, so she can just start typing, without needing to move the cursor.

Avoiding Cut, Copy, and Paste

Your first inclination might be to use Cut, Copy, and Paste in a script to move data from one field to another, and it usually works. You can, for example, have a script copy the Customer ID field, go to the Invoices layout, create a new invoice, and then paste it into the Customer ID field there.

But most developers don't use this approach for two reasons. First, many developers consider people's clipboards to be sacred ground. They argue you should *never* change what's on the clipboard unless someone asks you to. So it would be OK to have a Copy button by the Address fields, for example, that copies the address to the clipboard because the person would know exactly what's going into the clipboard. But what if he manually copies a long product description to the clipboard, and then runs the "Create Invoice for Customer" script? He then tries to paste the description in the invoice line item, only to find that the description's gone, replaced by the Customer ID for some odd reason. To keep from frustrating him (or yourself), you should generally avoid Cut and Copy.

Also, these steps don't work if the field isn't on the layout. People often show the customer's *name* on an invoice, but not his *ID*. But if you remove the Customer ID field from the Invoices layout, then any scripts that use Cut, Copy or Paste and the Customer ID field break. That's where the Set Field pair step in to save the day.

Set Field

Set Field is a more dependable method for editing data in a field because it works even if the field it references isn't on the layout. Set Field replaces the contents of a field with the result of a calculation. Its two options let you specify the field to set, and the calculation to use. The calculation result has to be the same type as the field you've specified. For text, date, time, and timestamp fields, Set Field is usually the step of choice: It's flexible and reliable, no matter what's on the layout.

Tip: As with many other FileMaker processes, be aware of context when you use a Set Field script step. You can edit data through a relationship using Set Field, but make absolutely certain the context is what you intend. If you aren't careful, you can edit data in the wrong record.

Like many of the steps you've seen so far, you don't have to specify a field at all. In this case, Set Field changes the field you're in *at the moment the step runs*. (This method works only with text results; otherwise, you have to specify the field so File-Maker knows what type you have in mind.)

Set Field's normal behavior is to replace all the data in a field with the data in your calculation. But you can write a calculation that appends results to existing data: Just include the field's data in the calculation. If you want to add "Esquire" to the end of the customer's last name (in the Last Name field), then just use this calculation in your Set Field step:

```
Last Name & ", Esquire"
```

Set Field by Name

Like "Go to Layout by Name," the "Set Field by Name" script step lets you make a single script more flexible because you can calculate the field's name instead of "hard-coding" it in a script. Other than that detail, though, "Set Field by Name" works just like its cousin Set Field. But how do you know which version to use?

Every once in a while, you need an extra jolt of flexibility. Suppose your script sets one of any number of possible fields, and which one varies from one running of the script to the next. For instance, imagine you have a script that puts a measurement into any one of 24 different fields in a database of statistical recordings, one for each hourly sample (with a new record for each day). When your script goes to put the data in the right place, you might feel like you're going to need a giant If/Else If block with 24 cases, and 24 nearly identical Set Field steps.

Use "Set Field by Name" instead of writing a hairy If/Else test. Instead of selecting the target field from a list, you use a calculation to produce the target field name. For instance, imagine your 24 fields are called "Measurement 1" through "Measurement 24". You could use a formula like this for your target field:

```
"Measurement " & Hour(Get(CurrentTime))
```

This formula produces the name of the field for each given hour, so a single "Set Field by Name" step can replace all those If conditions.

"Set Field by Name" has a down side, though: If you rename a field, the step stops working. To combat this problem, you have a special function called *GetField-Name()*. This function gives you the name (as a text value) of the field you pass to it. That might sound a little loopy, but consider a formula like this:

```
Choose(
Hour(Get(CurrentTime)) - 1;
GetFieldName ( Measurements::Measurement 1 )
GetFieldName ( Measurements::Measurement 2 )
GetFieldName ( Measurements::Measurement 3 )
```

```
GetFieldName ( Measurements::Measurement 4 )
GetFieldName ( Measurements::Measurement 5 )
GetFieldName ( Measurements::Measurement 6 )
GetFieldName ( Measurements::Measurement 7 )
GetFieldName ( Measurements::Measurement 8 )
GetFieldName ( Measurements::Measurement 9 )
GetFieldName ( Measurements::Measurement 10 )
GetFieldName ( Measurements::Measurement 11 )
GetFieldName ( Measurements::Measurement 12 )
GetFieldName ( Measurements::Measurement 13 )
GetFieldName ( Measurements::Measurement 14 )
GetFieldName ( Measurements::Measurement 15 )
GetFieldName ( Measurements::Measurement 16 )
GetFieldName ( Measurements::Measurement 17 )
GetFieldName ( Measurements::Measurement 18 )
GetFieldName ( Measurements::Measurement 19 )
GetFieldName ( Measurements::Measurement 20 )
GetFieldName ( Measurements::Measurement 21 )
GetFieldName ( Measurements::Measurement 22 )
GetFieldName ( Measurements::Measurement 23 )
GetFieldName ( Measurements::Measurement 24 )
)
```

Note: See page 655 to learn how the Choose function works.

This formula considers the current time, then returns the correct field name for the hour. But since it uses *GetFieldName()*, it returns the right name even if you rename a field. And as a formula in the "Set Field by Name" function, it's still a lot shorter and easier to manage than those 24 If steps. For instance, suppose you want to change what goes into the measurement field? With "Set Field by Name", you have one place to change. With 24 separate Set Field steps, you'd have to fix things in all 24 places.

Insert Calculated Result

Set Field overwrites the data in a field completely unless you calculate it to append the data instead. Insert Calculated Result lets a script put data in a field while keeping the data that's already there. It has three options. First you can specify a target field. You can also choose "Select entire contents" in the field first (in which case it overwrites the entire field, just like Set Field). Finally, you get to specify the calculation. Here are some variations on these options:

- If you *don't* turn on the "Select entire contents" option, then FileMaker inserts the calculation result *after* whatever's already in the field.

- If you *don't* specify a field at all, and you *don't* turn on "Select entire contents", then FileMaker inserts the result of the calculation into the current field. If you select data when the script step runs, then the calculation result overwrites whatever's highlighted. Otherwise, the text goes in wherever the insertion point happens to be, just as though you'd typed it from the keyboard.

Inserting other values

FileMaker has six other *Insert* script steps that work like Insert Calculated Result. Each step lets you specify a target field, and select the field contents if you want. They differ only in what gets inserted:

- **Insert Text** lets you specify any static text value and add it to the field verbatim. Use this step if you know ahead of time what you want your script to put in the field, and don't need to calculate it.

- **Insert from Index** makes your script show the same View Index window just like choosing Insert→From Index in Browse or Find mode. Someone picks a value from the list, and FileMaker inserts it into the field. This option's especially valuable in Find mode, both to keep people from having to type a value (and possibly making a typo) *and* to make sure the search always finds records, since if a value's in the index, then it's in a record somewhere.

- **Insert from Last Visited** is an interesting step. It grabs the value from the *same* field on the *last visited* record, and inserts it. This step is particularly useful on data entry layouts. Imagine, for example, you have to enter 300 people records from 15 different companies. You could use this step to create a button that pops in the *last* company you typed into the Company Name field, rather than type it over again.

Note: You can't just take a peek at a record and call it visited, though. The record has to be entered or opened (page 26). An Open Record/Request script step helps ensure you get the record you intend.

- **Insert Current Date** and **Insert Current Time** do just as they say. Unfortunately, no Insert Current Timestamp step exists; use Insert Calculated Result and the *Get (CurrentTimeStamp)* function instead.

- **Insert Current User Name** puts the user name of the person using FileMaker into the field. Your operating system normally determines this user name, but you can easily change it from FileMaker's Preferences' General Tab.

See the box on page 467 for advice on when to use Set Field and when to use an Insert step.

Putting data in container fields

On page 410, you learned that calculations can work with container data. Set Field and Insert Calculated Result are no exception: You can use either of them to move pictures, movies, sounds, and files from one container field to another. You can also use Cut, Copy, and Paste to work with container fields, provided you're willing to live with the caveats for intruding on someone's clipboard described on page 462.

But FileMaker has special commands in the Insert menu to get container data into your database in the first place, and these commands have script step equivalents:

- **Insert Picture** lets you specify the file to insert, and whether you want to "Store only a reference" (see the box on page 265 for a refresher on references). If you don't specify a file, then FileMaker asks people to pick one when the step runs.

Note: The window someone sees when he's asked to pick a picture file includes the "Store only a reference" checkbox, regardless of how you set this option on the script step itself. In a sense, your choice in the script becomes a *suggestion* to him: It determines how the checkbox is set when the dialog box pops up. He's free to change it.

- **Insert QuickTime** has only one option: the file you want to insert. Again, if no file is selected, people get to pick one when the script runs. Since QuickTime files are *always* stored as a reference, you don't get that choice this time.

- **Insert File** has the most options of all. Of course, you get to pick the file to be inserted. You also get a "Store only a reference" checkbox. This time, though, you also get a "Go to target field" checkbox. You can use it to tell FileMaker which field to put the file in.

Insert Picture and Insert QuickTime don't have an option to tell FileMaker *which field to use*, which probably seems odd. They're designed to put things in the container field that's active when the script runs. So if a user doesn't click in a container field first, that script step can't run properly. If you want more control, just use "Go to Field" first, specifying the appropriate field, and then use Insert Picture or Insert QuickTime to insert into that field.

A Field Script in Action

Suppose you decide to add a Notes field to the Customer table in your database. You use this field to hold any arbitrary information you think is important about the customer. Unfortunately, you soon realize this field is a little *too* unorganized. You have no idea if the note that says, "Customer already paid" is from last Tuesday or last year. You need a consistent way to keep track of *who* left a note, and *when*. You decide everybody should record this information along with any notes they leave. To make things even easier, you want to be sure people add *new* notes *above* older notes. Thus, when a customer record has been around for a while, the Notes field looks something like this:

```
--- 1/11/10 @ 3:30 PM by Jim ---
Called the customer, confirmed both orders were received. Placed a copy of
the order in Jello, along with Dwight's stapler, in the top drawer of his
desk.

--- 1/01/10 @ 1:25 PM by Dwight ---
Customer called saying he never got his order. I checked and we have no
record of shipment because some people are so lax! I'm shipping again.
```

```
--- 12/28/09 @ 4:58 PM by Jim ---
Order came in really close to quittin' time. I'll finish the paperwork
Monday.
```

In this example, you create a script that "forces" all added comments into that format. This script adds a separator line with the date and time (plus a couple blank lines) and leaves the insertion point under the separator. You also create a button next to the Notes field that runs this script. People just have to click, and then type.

POWER USERS' CLINIC

Set Field vs. Insert

FileMaker's field editing script steps have a lot of overlap page 460). For example, Set Field with no target field does exactly the same thing as Insert Calculated Result with no target field and the "Select entire contents" checkbox turned on. And you can use Insert Calculated Result with the appropriate calculation to do the same thing as Insert Date, Insert Time, Insert Text, and Insert Current User Name. In general, it doesn't matter one bit which one you use.

But you should think twice about using the Insert script steps with a target field specified *and* the "Select entire contents" checkbox turned on. With both options set, these script steps simply overwrite the value in some field—exactly what Set Field does.

Since these steps need the field on the layout, though, they're more *fragile:* The script can break if you make changes to a layout. You'll probably save yourself a headache tomorrow if you just use Set Field today.

Of course, if you're inserting *into* a field (without "Select entire contents" turned on), then you *have to* use an Insert step. Since you'd only use this step in a script that'll be run if someone's already in the field—you know the field's on the layout and the step will run properly.

Finally, you can't accomplish some of the Insert steps from a calculation. Specifically, you can't access the last visited record or the View Index dialog box from a Set Field step.

Note: Like almost every problem you ever solve with a script, there's more than one right way to get the job done. One way's described below, and another in the box on page 470. You may prefer a different way, and that's OK.

Before you start creating your script, think about what you need to do in sequence. Here's a breakdown:

- Put the insertion point at the start (top) of the Notes field.

- Insert two blank lines—to create some space before the previous comment.

- Put the insertion point back at the start, and add the separator line with the date and time.

- At that point, the script ends and someone can start typing.

Your next mission is to translate these plain English steps into script steps, which you'll do in the next section.

Building the script

If your Customers table doesn't already have a Notes field, create one before you write the script. Then proceed as follows:

1. **Choose Scripts→Manage Scripts. Create a new script called Add Note Separator.**

    Develop the habit of giving your scripts descriptive names so you can remember what you want them to do.

2. **Add a Set Selection script step to the script.**

    You can find this step under Editing in the list, or, from the View pop-up menu, you can choose "all by name" to see an alphabetical list. When you add the step, it appears in your script.

3. **Turn on the "Go to target field" checkbox. If necessary, from the table pop-up menu, choose Customers, choose the Notes field, and then click OK.**

    The Set Selection step in your script updates to show the target field.

Tip: If you didn't follow instructions and create the Customers::Notes field before you started this tutorial, you can do it in the Specify Field window by choosing Manage Database from the Table pop-up menu. Renegade.

---

4. **In the Script Step Options area, click the second Specify button.**

    It's not labeled, but it's *below* the first Specify button. When you click it, the Specify Set Selection window appears.

5. **In both boxes (Start Position and End Position), type *0* (zero), and then click OK.**

    Zero in both boxes tells FileMaker you want the insertion point right at the start of the field, and you don't want any text selected.

6. **Add an Insert Text step to the script, and then turn off the "Select entire contents" option.**

    You don't want the two blank lines you're about to insert to replace everything in the field.

7. **Click the bottom Specify button.**

    A window simply called Specify appears (Figure 11-4).

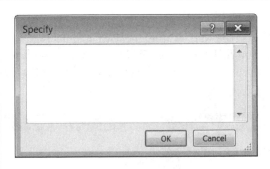

Figure 11-4:
The Specify dialog box for Insert Text may seem puzzling, because you don't have any options to click. You just type the exact text you want the script step to insert. Note that this dialog box isn't a calculation dialog box. It lets you insert only literal text. Use Insert Calculated Result if you need to insert dynamic text with a script step.

8. **In the Specify dialog box, add two empty lines (press Return or Enter twice), and then click OK.**

   That's the regular Enter key, not the one in the numerical keypad: In this dialog box, that key just clicks the OK button. Anyway, after pressing it twice, you don't see the returns you've typed in the dialog box, but, in the Insert Text script step, you do see two blank spaces inside quotes. Those returns tell FileMaker to add two blank lines to the top of the Notes field.

9. **Select the Set Selection step at the top of the script, and then, at the bottom of the window, click Duplicate.**

   FileMaker adds a second copy of the Set Selection step, right below the first.

10. **Drag either Set Selection step to the bottom of the script.**

    Keyboard junkies can use Ctrl+down arrow (⌘-down arrow) to move script steps.

    Your script now has Set Selection, then Insert Text, and then Set Selection again.

11. **Add the Insert Calculated Result step to the script, and then turn off the "Select entire contents" option.**

    Make sure the step lands *after* the last Set Selection script. If it doesn't, move it there. Turning off the selection option ensures that the calculation goes in at the insertion point (which is at the beginning of the field now).

12. **To the right of "Calculated result", click the Specify button, and then, in the Specify Calculation window, enter this calculation:**
    ```
    "--- " & Get(CurrentDate) & " @ " & Get(CurrentTime) & " by " &
    Get(AccountName) & " ---¶"
    ```
    You can use any method you want to enter the calculation, as long as your calculation looks like this one when you're done. See page 365 to learn about Get functions.

13. **Save the script.**

Your new script is ready to test.

Now you just need to add the Notes field to the Customers layout, and a button by it that runs the new script. When you click the button, FileMaker adds the separator to the field, and puts the insertion point in place. People can now type notes that are nicely organized and separated.

GEM IN THE ROUGH

Fewer Steps, Bigger Calculations

You can easily create the Add Note Separator script described on page 268, but it has one weakness: It uses four steps where two could accomplish the same thing. A more concise approach would be to first put the separator and a few blank lines at the top of the Notes field, and *then* use the Set Selection script step to put the insertion point after the separator. The drawback here is that you have more complex calculations to write. The choice is yours.

In the Insert Calculated Results step, you need a calculation that builds the separator line, adds two blank lines after it, and finally adds the *old* contents of the Notes field to the end:

```
"--- " & Get(CurrentDate) & " @ " &
Get(CurrentTime) & " by " & Get(AccountName)
& " ---¶¶¶" & Customers::Notes
```

To keep the contents of your field from being duplicated, make sure you leave the "Select entire contents" option on this time.

Now you need to get the insertion point in place after the first line, using the Set Selection script step. Use the same technique as before: Set Selection with an End Position that's *smaller* than the Start Position. FileMaker puts the insertion point *before* the character at the Start Position. Since you want it *after* the end of the first line, you need to find the first new line symbol, add *1* to it, and put *that* in the Start Position. Here's the calculation that does the trick:

```
Position ( Customers::Notes; "¶"; 1; 1 )
+ 1
```

Put this same calculation, but without the last *+1*, into the End Position field, and you're ready to test your script. You can use this script with or without the "Go to Target Field" option, as described in step 3 on page 468.

Other Steps That Work with Fields

Lots of times, you want to be able to write scripts that work on multiple records. You may need to change values across a found set of records, or you may want to let FileMaker handle the serial numbering of all the records in a table. The next script steps let you manage data in lots of records without lots of hassle.

Replace Field Contents and Relookup Field Contents

The Replace Field Contents (page 70) and Relookup Field Contents (page 224) commands let you specify a field to act upon. If you *don't* specify a field, then they act on the current field. You also get the typical "Perform without dialog" checkbox. When you turn this checkbox on, the action happens immediately when the step runs. If you leave this option off with the Replace Field Contents step, then people see the typical Replace Field Contents dialog box (with all the settings you specified in the script). With the Relookup Field Contents step, they just see a confirmation message first, asking if they really want to perform the relookup operation.

Set Next Serial Value

The Set Next Serial Value script step is invaluable—in the rare cases when anyone actually uses it. It's a one-trick pony: If a field auto-enters a serial number, then this step changes the "next value" stored in the Field Options dialog box. In other words, if you want to start your customer ID values over again, then you can use Set Next Serial Value to do it from a script. (See the box on page 474 for an example.)

Warning: Use extreme care when you change a field that's used as a key in a relationship. You risk leaving related records orphaned if you don't change their key fields, too. See the box on page 726 for a script that helps you change key fields without losing related records (or your sanity).

The step has two options. First, you can specify the field to update. As usual, if you don't specify a field, then it works on the current field. You tell FileMaker what to set the "next value" to by entering a calculation.

Perform Find/Replace

When you use the Find/Replace command yourself, you use it to replace text in one or more fields and across one or more records. But the Perform Find/Replace has *extra* powers when you use it in a script (Figure 11-5).

The new Quick Find feature is great, but it searches *all* the fields you specify on a layout and returns a found set. What if your Notes field is so widely used that some customers' notes fields are full of pages of note? Users are complaining that it's getting hard to scroll through them to find the notes you made regarding specific topics? What you need is a way to find a word or phrase that's used somewhere in the current customer's gigantic Notes field.

The script itself is simple, just two lines, but you need to do some prep work. First, create a new table in your database (page 141), and name it Globals. Give it one field: a global text field called "gSearch." Place this new field on the Customers layout above your Notes field. Set the field's behavior to be enterable in Find mode (page 302). The idea is that your users will type a word or phrase in this field, and then click a button to run the script.

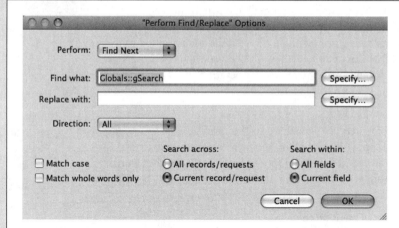

Figure 11-5:
The window behind the Specify button on a Perform Find/Replace script step looks a lot like the normal Find/ Replace window. But this version has a new pop-up menu (called Perform) and a couple of new Specify buttons that let you specify calculated values for what you're looking for and what you want to replace the found results with.

POWER USERS' CLINIC

A Reusable Notes Separator Script

The mark of a FileMaker power-scripter is someone always on the lookout for the opportunity to write *one* script that can be used in *several* places. After all, who wants to spend his life writing scripts? The fact is, you're probably so happy with your new Notes field and its separator script that you want to use it in other places—on a Job, an Invoice, a Payment, and so forth.

It would be much nicer if the Add Note Separator script could add a note separator (and place the insertion point) in *any* field you wanted. That way you could tell people to click the field they want before running the script to get the separator entered into the field of their choice.

The only thing tying your script to the Customers::Notes field is the "Go to target field" checkbox on the Set Selection steps. If you edit the script and turn this option off for *both* Set Selection steps, then it works on whatever field is active when the script runs.

If you don't like to have to click the field before running the script, then you can fix it in two ways, but both require information you haven't learned yet.

Note: If you're using the sample file for this chapter, the Globals::gSearch field has already been created for you and placed on the Customer layout. Download it from this book's Missing CD page at *www. missingmanuals.com.*

Here's how to write the script. Call it *Search Notes Field*.

1. **Add "Go to Field" as your first script step. Set it to go to the Customers::Notes field.**

   Find/Replace requires a field to be selected before it can work, so you're taking no chances with this script step.

2. **Add the Perform Find/Replace step to the script, and turn on the "Perform without dialog" checkbox. Click the Specify button.**

   You see the Perform Find/Replace Options window.

3. **Make sure the Perform pop-up menu is set to Find Next, and then, to the right of the "Find what" box, click the Specify button.**

   The Specify Calculation window appears.

4. **Double-click the Globals::gSearch field to add it to your calculation. Click OK.**

   This calculation tells FileMaker where to look when it runs the Perform Find/Replace step—whatever's in the new field, in this case. Clicking OK when you're done returns you to the Perform Find/Replace Options window.

5. **In the Direction pop-up menu, choose All.**

   This option tells FileMaker to look through the entire Notes field.

6. **Turn on the "Current record/request" and "Current field" radio buttons. Click OK until you're back in your database.**

   You don't want the search to spill into different fields or records. These options restrict it to the current record. Since the script goes to the Notes field first, FileMaker searches only that field.

To finish the job, add the new Global field, and then attach your script to the Find button on the Customers layout. Type a value into the search field, and then click he Find button to test your new script. The search word or phrase will be highlighted in the field. Click the Find button again (without changing the search terms) to find other instances of the same search criteria.

Working with Records

You can get only so far with your scripts by working with field values. Eventually you need to deal with more than one *record*. Thankfully, FileMaker has script steps for creating, duplicating, and deleting records; navigating among existing records; and even managing the process of opening and editing a record, and saving (committing) or reverting the changes. You can also work directly with portal rows on the current layout—and the records they represent.

POWER USERS' CLINIC

Why Set Next Serial Value

The Set Next Serial Value script step may seem odd to you. After all, if you want to set the next serial value for a field, you can just do it yourself from the Manage Database window. But this step can come in very handy in some situations.

Imagine you work in the auto parts business and you have 200 sister stores around the country. Each office has its own copy of your database, which gets updated periodically. You have to send a new empty database to each store with all the latest enhancements, and the folks at each store have to *import* all the data from their old databases into the new one (you'll learn about importing and exporting data in Chapter 17).

Now suppose this database includes an Orders table with an Order ID field. After the old orders have been imported, the database might have orders with IDs from one to 1000, for example. But since no *new* records have been created yet, the Order ID field still has a "next value" of *1*. The store's first thousand orders use IDs that are *already used by other records*. That's a big no-no.

The solution's obvious: You need to fix the "next value" on the Order ID field after the import's finished. To save the store manager the trouble, you can put a script in the database to fix this glitch for her. (In fact, you can make a script that does *all* the work of importing old data and fixing next serial values in every table.)

Creating, Duplicating, and Deleting Records

New Record/Request and Duplicate Record/Request have no options, and do exactly what you'd expect. The first script step creates a new record, just like the Records→New Record menu command. The second duplicates the current record. In either case, the *new* record becomes the current record, just like when you do it manually. You use these steps most often on buttons, when you're taking away menu commands from people and providing them with buttons that appear only on the layouts where you want people to be able to create records.

Note: Duplicating a record from a script step works just like doing it manually—that is, the script duplicates the static (non-calculated) values in the record, too. If calculations depend on those static values, they also get duplicated, but they change if you edit the non-calculated values later. Some auto-enter calculations, like serial numbers, are *not* duplicated, but are recalculated at the time the duplicate record is created.

The Delete Record/Request script step deletes the current record. If you turn on its "Perform without dialog" option, then the delete happens with no warning. When this option is turned off, the manager sees the same "Are you sure" message box he'd see when deleting a record manually.

Note: Each of these three script steps also works for *find requests* when a script runs in Find mode.

Navigating Among Records

Two script steps that let you switch to a different record. You can move switch with the "Go to Record/Request/Page" script step, which works a lot like the Status toolbar's book icon. Or you can switch to a related record, or a set of related records, using the "Go to Related Record" script step.

Go to Record/Request/Page

FileMaker has one script that handles changing *records, find requests, and pages.* This may seem strange at first, but it makes sense because it's exactly how the Status toolbar's book icon works: If you're in Browse mode, then the step goes to a different record. If you're in Find mode, it switches between find requests instead. Finally, if you're in Preview mode, then it flips through pages.

Note: You can't run scripts when in Layout mode, and a script *can't* go to Layout mode, so it doesn't apply here.

The "Go to Record/Request/Page" step has just one option. You get to pick *which* record, request, or page to go to from a simple list:

- First
- Last
- Previous
- Next
- By Calculation

When you lock people out of the usual display and control everything they do through the script (see the box on page 496), the First, Last, Previous, and Next options let you provide your own customized replacement for the Status toolbar and book icon. For example: Make four buttons and arrange them in a horizontal line (like on a CD player—Figure 11-6). Give each button a "Go to Record" step, and then set them up in the following order, so they mimic the tape recorder concept:

- Leftmost button: "Go to Record/Request/Page" [First]
- Second button: "Go to Record/Request/Page" [Previous]
- Third button: "Go to Record/Request/Page" [Next]
- Rightmost button: "Go to Record/Request/Page" [Last]

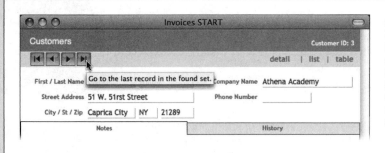

Figure 11-6:
The visual concept of these buttons is so common that people are likely to know how they work without any instructions. But a tooltip (page 329) on each button would help ensure that people understand each button's purpose.

Another common but more advanced use of this step is to provide a way for a looping script to end. When you choose the Next or Previous option, a new checkbox appears in the Script Step Options area, called "Exit after last". When it's turned on, FileMaker knows to exit the loop after it's finished with the last record (when you choose "Go to Record" [next]) or after the first record (when you choose "Go to Record" [previous]). (When to exit a loop is no small matter, as page 444 explains.)

When you choose By Calculation, you get the chance to specify a calculation with a number result. FileMaker goes to exactly that record, request, or page. You could use this option if the record number's in a field, or if you want to skip ahead 25 records each time the script is run, for example. This technique is more useful than it sounds. For example, it's an ideal way to show records in a list using Instant Web Publishing (IWP), which you'll learn about in Chapter 18. In IWP, FileMaker limits the list to 25 records at a time, so you have to give your web users some way to see the next group of records.

Go to Related Record

You were first introduced to this power step when learning about relationships (page 225). It can go to a different record, found set, layout, window, and even file—all in one step. This step's job is simple: It takes you to a related record. But carrying out that job *isn't* so simple. When you click the Specify button, you get a wealth of choices, as shown in Figure 11-7. To go to a related record, you need to tell FileMaker which related table occurrence you're interested in, by selecting it from the "Get related record" pop-up menu. For example, if you're on the Customer layout, and you want to see a related invoice, then, from the menu, you should choose Invoices.

With this done, FileMaker can find the right record. But how should it *show it to you?* If you're visiting related records, chances are you can't view them directly on the current layout (since the layout is associated with the wrong table occurrence). So a "Go to Related Record" command almost always involves changing layouts. Choose "Layout" from the "Show record using layout" pop-up menu to view the Specify Layout window, from which you pick the layout you want.

Figure 11-7:
This window's the same one you saw when you attached a "Go to Related Record" script step to a button back on page 225. But inside a script you wield a whole new level of power when you tie this command to other processes, like printing a report from a found set that changes based on whichever record someone's on when running the script.

Specify Layout shows all the layouts associated with the Invoice table occurrence you chose above, as you'd expect. But it *also* shows layouts associated with any *other* occurrence of the same table. FileMaker uses the specified table occurrence to find the right related record, and the specified layout to show it to you. You can show an invoice record from any layout that shows records from the Invoices table, no matter what *occurrence* it uses.

If the table occurrence you picked in the first menu is an occurrence of a table from a *different* file, then you can turn on "Use external table's layout" to see layouts in the file the table comes from. When you use this option from a button, FileMaker switches to a window for the other file instead of showing records in the current window. If you use this option in a script, though, then you need to add a Select Window script step (page 497) if you want the external file's window to be active.

Note: Using an external file's layout saves you from having to create a similar layout in your "local" file. But it's worth the effort of creating a local layout that shows data from that external file if you want to keep your users in the local file. They'll still need privileges to view the external file's data, though. See page 769 to learn about view privileges.

If you want a *new* window (whether you're using an external table or not), then turn on the "Show in new window" checkbox. When you do, you see the New Window Options dialog box, which is explained alongside the New Window script step on page 495.

Finally, you get to decide how to deal with the found set when the script step finishes. See the box below to help you decide when each option makes sense.

- If you don't turn on "Show only related records", then FileMaker goes to the related table, but you see all the records in the related table, not just those that are related to the formerly active record. The first related record is active in your new found set. So, from the Customer layout, GTRR without "Show only related records" shows all your invoices, and the active record is the first one for the customer that you're viewing when the GTRR script step runs.

Note: Find out which record is the first related record on page 207.

- If you turn on "Show only related records" and "Match current record only", then FileMaker returns a found set of only those records that match the active record. The customer invoice GTRR set, as described above, shows you a found set of just the invoices for the customer record that was active when the script step ran. The active record will be the first related record.

- Choosing "Show only related records" and "Match all records in current found set", is most useful when you have a found set selected before the GTRR script step runs. In this scenario, FileMaker shows a new found set in which all the records are related to at least one of the records in the old found set. So, in the Customers layout, you've found your two highest volume customers. Use GTRR, matching all records in the current found set to find all the invoices related to either of these two customers. The active record will be the first record that's related to the customer record that was active when the GTRR script step runs.

Opening, Reverting, and Committing Records

When you use your database in Browse mode, FileMaker does a lot of things automatically. When you start typing in a field, it locks the record. When you exit the record—click outside any field or press Enter—it commits the record. When you use a script, though, you're not really clicking fields and pressing Enter. So how does FileMaker know when to lock a record and when to commit? You have to tell it, by including the appropriate script steps: Open Record/Request, Revert Record/Request, and Commit Record/Request.

Open Record/Request

The Open Record/Request step tells FileMaker you're about to start editing a record. If the record is already open, then it does nothing—that is, it doesn't automatically commit the record first. It just locks the record so no other user can edit it, if it isn't locked already. But if the record is already open (by you, via another window, or by someone else), then you get a record-locking error. (See page 694 to see how you can check for errors while a script is running.)

To Show or Not to Show

How do I decide when to turn on "Show only related records" and when to leave it off?

If you don't turn on "Show only related records," FileMaker doesn't change the found set in the target table unless it has to in order to show the proper record. In other words, if the target table is showing all its records, FileMaker just makes the target record active without changing the found set. All the records are still in the found set, and the user can flip through them to see records that aren't related to the original record. But if the target table has a found set of records and your target record isn't in the set, FileMaker has to change the found set to show the target record.

But when the "Show only related records" option is turned on, the found set in the target table will always be related record(s) only. So use this option when you want to restrict the found set, either for the users' convenience, or because the script must have a found set to do its work.

The tradeoff is performance. When you turn the "Show only related records" option off, FileMaker just makes the proper record active. It doesn't worry about the found set or the sort order. When the option's turned on, though, FileMaker has to find the correct records first, and then show the one you asked for. If your relationship is sorted, then FileMaker also sorts the records. If your script just needs to visit a specific related record, do something to it, and then come right back, you can leave this option turned off to make your script run more quickly.

Whichever option you choose, you can avoid annoying your users when your untimely GTRR destroys their found set by choosing the "Show in new window" option. When you create a new window for the target table, your script won't tamper with the user's existing found set for the target table.

Commit Record/Request

Whether you've used the Open Record/Request step or just let FileMaker lock the record for you, you can explicitly commit the record with the Commit Record/Request step. It has two options:

- The "Skip data entry validation" option tells FileMaker to commit the record even if it violates field validation. This option works only when you turn on the "Only during data entry" radio button in the Validation options for the field. If you've set the validation to happen "Always", then the script *can't* get around it.

- When the "Perform without dialog" option is turned off, and, in the Layouts→Layout Setup window's General tab, you turn *off* "Save record changes automatically", FileMaker shows the message in Figure 11-8 when the step runs.

Note: You know how to handle dialog boxes when they come up, but they often confuse other people. Most database designers try to avoid requiring people to interact with FileMaker's normal dialog boxes while scripts are running, especially when people could make a choice that circumvents the purpose of the carefully crafted script.

Figure 11-8:
If the layout isn't set to save record changes (page 284), and you don't turn on the "Perform without dialog" checkbox, then you see this warning when the Commit Record/Request step runs. Click Save to commit the record. If you click Don't Save, then FileMaker reverts the record instead. The Cancel button leaves the record open and locked.

Revert Record/Request

The Revert Record/Request step has only one option: "Perform without dialog". When this option is turned off, someone sees a confirmation message. Otherwise, FileMaker reverts the record immediately when the script runs.

You can understand these script steps relatively easily, but *when* to use them is hard to figure out. Here are some things to keep in mind when you're trying to decide when you need to open or commit a record in a script:

- When you use a script step that *inserts* data into a field (and leaves someone in the field), then FileMaker locks the record when the step runs, but doesn't commit the change. You can then do *more* work with fields if you want. FileMaker commits the record later, when the user exits the record.

- If your script changes to a different layout, switches to Find or Preview mode, or closes the window, then FileMaker automatically commits the record if needed.

- If you use a script step that modifies several records—Replace Field Contents, for example—FileMaker commits the records in batches as it goes. When it's finished, every record that was modified is committed.

- If you perform a series of Set Field steps in a script, and you're *not* in the record when the script runs, then FileMaker locks the record and makes the field changes. When the script is done, you're not in the record (no field is active), but the record's still locked and uncommitted. In other words, you can use the Records→Revert Record command to revert all the changes made by the script, which probably isn't what you want. Add a Commit Records/Requests script step at the *end* of the script to avoid losing the data your script enters.

- If your script changes some records and includes a step to revert them if something goes wrong, then you should probably make sure to commit any changes someone was making before your script changes anything. That way, the script doesn't undo any of her work. Thus, put a Commit Records/Requests step at the *beginning* of your script.

Why Open a Record?

Why would I ever use the Open Record/Request step? Doesn't FileMaker automatically lock a record as soon as my script starts editing it?

For simple scripts, this step is almost always unnecessary. FileMaker does, indeed, do the right thing. But as you'll learn in Chapter 18, you can set up your FileMaker database so multiple people can use it at the same time, each on her own computer. When you set up FileMaker this way, lots of interesting things can start happening.

For example, a record can change while you're looking at it. Suppose a new area code is added in your area, and you write a script that looks at the phone number and decides, based on its exchange code, whether or not to change the area code. The script might look like this:

```
If [ "Exchange Code = 555 or Exchange Code
= 377" ]
  Set Field [ Area Code, "602"]
End If
```

You probably find this hard to believe, but technically, someone could change the Exchange Code field after the If step runs but before the Set Field happens. (Remember that other people are editing records on other computers, so they're free to make changes while the script is running on your computer.) If this scenario happens, you end up assigning the customer an incorrect phone number.

To fix this, you need to lock the record before you start looking at it:

```
Open Record/Request
If [ "Exchange Code = 555 or Exchange Code
= 377" ]
  Set Field [ Area Code, "602"]
  Commit Record/Request [No Dialog]
Else
  Revert Record/Request [No Dialog]
End If
```

Now, somebody else can't edit the Exchange Code field because the record is locked. In general, if many people use your database, then you should open a record before you start looking at it in a script.

This script reverts the record when it didn't make any changes. FileMaker does this reverting for two reasons. First, committing a record means saving the data, and that's unnecessary here. Second, suppose a field has had validation turned on since this record was created. It's possible that this unmodified record has now-invalid data. If you try to commit this data back, then you get a validation error. Reverting avoids this error since nothing's being saved. Moral of the story: Try to commit a record *only* when necessary.

And if you're still not sure if your script really needs an Open or Commit step, go ahead and open the record at the beginning of your script and commit it at the end. Sure, it takes a nanosecond or two extra to run a couple of steps that may not be strictly necessary. But what's a nanosecond on the grand scale of time when your data may be at risk?

Copying Records

FileMaker has two record-related script steps that do something you can't easily do manually in Browse mode: Copy an entire record to the clipboard. One version copies just the current record, while the other copies every record in the found set at once.

Copy Record/Request

The first, called Copy Record/Request works on one record at a time. It copies data from *every* field on the layout, and puts it on the clipboard. FileMaker puts a tab character between each field value.

If any field has *more* than one line, FileMaker converts the new line character into a funny character called a *vertical tab*. Some programs, like Microsoft Word, convert these characters back into new lines when you paste in a copied record. Figure 11-9 shows the result of pasting a customer record into Text Edit. In that example, the new line character is an "ã;" and the data's strung into one long line. Your mileage may vary.

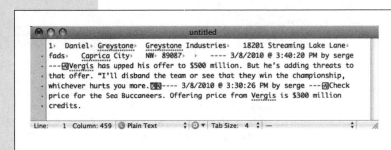

Figure 11-9:
This picture shows what you get when you copy a customer record, and then paste it into a word processor that's not great at rendering vertical tabs. It may be hard to read, but it's perfectly usable text and much easier than copying each field's data individually.

Note: As usual with FileMaker, you have more than one way to get things done. See page 819 for two other ways to export data. Remember, using a scripted Copy, Cut, or Paste command violates your sacred trust not to mess with the contents of someone's clipboard unless he knows it's happening.

Copy All Records/Requests

While Copy Record/Request copies the entire *current* record, its brother—Copy All Records/Requests—copies *every* field on the current layout for every record in the found set. Each individual record is added to the clipboard in the same format as the Copy Record/Request command produces, and FileMaker puts one record on each line.

Suppose, for example, you want to get all the Invoice IDs for a particular customer, and put them in an email to a coworker. Or perhaps you're compiling a list of all the Zip codes in Phoenix where you have customers. Using Copy All Records/Requests, you can do this job with ease.

The trick is to create a *new* layout that has only one field on it. For example, make a new layout with just the Invoice ID field, or just the Zip Code field. Write a script that switches to this layout, and then run the Copy All Records/Requests command to get a simple list of values on the clipboard.

Working with Portals

FileMaker has a script step specifically designed to go to a certain portal row. Why would you want to do that? First, when you use the "Go to Field" script step to target a field in a portal, it goes to the *first* portal row, which may not have anything to do with what someone needs at that point. If you want to put people in the field on a *different* row, you need to go to that row first.

When you use data from a related field, or put data in a related field, and you have *multiple* related records, FileMaker grabs the value from the *first* record. If you want to tell FileMaker to work with a different related record instead, then use a portal, and go to the right row. See the box below for tips (and a warning) on working with portals.

UP TO SPEED

Beware the Portal

Technically, you can do all kinds of things through a portal using a script—but it's not always wise. For example, if you want to discount every line item on an invoice by 10 percent, then you can write a looping script. It starts by visiting the first portal row, and then applying the discount. Then it can go to each additional row, applying the discount as it goes. In each pass through the loop, you're modifying the Line Items::Price field; the active portal row determines which line item is changed. Unfortunately, the active portal row is too transient to rely upon. A script can do all kinds of things that make FileMaker forget which portal row you're on (change modes, change layouts, go to another field, commit or revert the record, and so forth).

If you accidentally do confuse FileMaker like this at some point inside your loop, then you end up looping forever because you never reach the end of the portal.

It's much safer to find the appropriate records, and work with them directly. You can get the same effect by using the "Go to Related Records" script step to find all the line item records, and then looping through the records directly with "Go to Record/Request/Page", thus avoiding the perils of the portal.

Go to Portal Row

The "Go to Portal Row" script step works a lot like the "Go to Record/Request/Page" step. You can go to the First, Last, Previous, or Next portal row, or specify the row *number* with a calculation. It even has an "Exit after last" option to help when looping through portal rows.

This step includes an option you can use to make what's happening onscreen a little more obvious to people: "Select entire contents". When you turn this checkbox on, FileMaker highlights the whole portal row. Otherwise, it goes to the portal row without highlighting it onscreen. (After all, you don't always want people to see what's going on.)

One setting you *don't* find with "Go to Portal Row" is *which portal to use*. The guidelines below are how FileMaker knows which portal you have in mind:

- If the current layout only has one portal, then FileMaker uses it automatically.

- If the layout has more than one portal, then it assumes you want the portal that's currently active.

Note: In general, a portal is active whenever a person (or a script) puts the cursor in one of its fields. If you aren't sure what someone will be doing before your script runs, then throw in a "Go to Field" script step, just to be safe.

Finding Records

FileMaker has three nearly identical script steps to handle the grunt work of finding records. You can let people tell the script what to find, you can decide what the script finds (a *hard-coded* find), or you can script a dynamic find using calculations.

Deciding which one to use depends on whether people know what they're looking for—or how much work you want to save them. The upcoming sections go into this topic in detail. You'll also see a find script in action, and learn how to make a script pause and wait for information.

Performing People's Find Requests

The first, Perform Find, is the equivalent of a visit to Find mode, followed by a click of the Requests→Perform Find menu command. Perform Find's single option lets you specify what find requests to use, but, surprisingly, you can skip it entirely. If you *don't* turn this option on, then Perform Find assumes you're already in Find mode with one or more requests, and works just like the Requests→Perform Find menu command (and the Status toolbar's Find button). It looks for records that match the already defined find requests. All the matching records become the new found set.

But where do those find requests *come from?* Either someone creates them, or your script does. For example, many developers like to add special "Find" layouts to their databases. These layouts can show just the right fields, along with helpful text, to make things easier for people. Figure 11-10 shows a Find layout for the Customers table.

Next, you'll write a script that goes to the Find layout and puts someone in Find mode. The script then *pauses*, giving her a chance to enter find requests. When she's done, she clicks a button to *resume* the script, which performs the find, and then switches back to the Customers layout.

Note: The finished file for this chapter has the layout created for you. Download it from this book's Missing CD page at *www.missingmanuals.com.*.

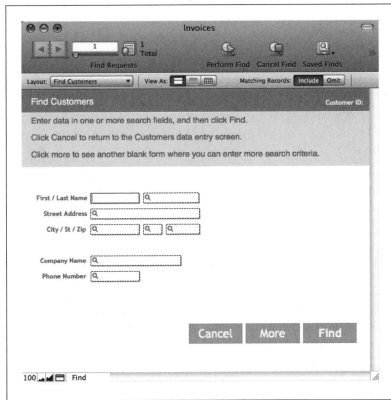

Figure 11-10:
This layout is designed specifically for Find mode. Two sets of instructions help people figure out what to do. The Find button resumes your script. The More button runs a New Record/Request script step. Since this layout is for Find mode only, make sure someone's in Find mode when she gets here, and take her to a different layout when she's done. You need a script like the one in the steps that start below.

To set this process up yourself, first create a Find Customers layout like the one shown in Figure 11-8. Then visit the Manage Scripts window, click New, and then name the script appropriately. Follow these steps to create the script itself:

1. **Add the "Go to Layout" script step, targeting the Find Customers layout.**

   You want to make sure the person's in the right context—the new Find Customers layout—before the script enters Find mode.

2. **Add the Enter Find Mode script step to the script.**

   The step already has its Pause option turned on and its "Specify find requests" option turned off. That's just what you want. This step switches to Find mode *and* pauses the script.

Note: If you want to start someone off with some basic criteria, you can specify them right in the Enter Find Mode step. FileMaker doesn't perform the find now. It just puts her in Find mode and creates the requests you specify. She's then free to *modify* or *delete* them as necessary.

---

3. **Add the Perform Find script step to the script.**

   Once the script continues, you assume she has added the necessary find requests, so you're ready to use the Perform Find step with no find requests specified. (Be careful not to choose the Perform Find/Replace script step, which isn't what you want for this script.)

4. **Add another "Go to Layout" script step to the script. This time, pick the Customers layout.**

   This step takes her back to the Customers layout once FileMaker finds the correct records.

To complete your layout, on the Find Customers layout, create a Find button. You don't even have to write a script for this button. Since the person's always in the middle of a paused script when she sees this layout, just set the button with a Resume Script action. If you're feeling adventuresome, you can also create a More button with a New Record/Request script step.

Finally, the Cancel button should run a new script that simply switches back to the Customers layout, and then uses the Enter Browse Mode step to go back to Browse mode. Since your user will click this button in the middle of a paused script, you need to think about what will happen. She will go back to the Customers layout in Browse mode, but she'll still be in the middle of a paused script. That's a recipe for confusion the next time she presses Enter.

When you assign a script to a button, you get to decide what happens to any running script, as you can see in Figure 11-11.

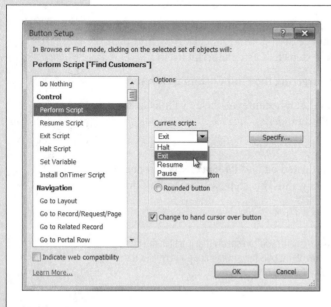

Figure 11-11:
When a button runs a script, FileMaker knows a paused script may already be running. This pop-up menu lets you decide what should happen to it. Choose Halt or Exit to have the running script immediately stop, and the new script takes over (on page 683), you'll learn about the subtle difference between these two. If you choose Resume, the button's script runs, and then the paused script resumes. If you choose Pause, then the paused script stays paused while the new script runs.

In this case, set the Current Script pop-up menu to Exit so the paused script is stopped. That way, when someone clicks Cancel, she gets back to a normal state.

Tip: It's a good idea to hide the Find Customers layout from the Layouts pop-up menu so people don't accidentally switch to it without running your script. In the Layout Setup dialog box, turn off the "Include in layouts menu" checkbox.

Triggering a Find script

Once you have your scripts and layout in place, you only need to decide how people will run it. You could put a Find button on the Customers layout. But what happens if people try to find another way (like the Mode pop-up menu on the bottom of the window, or the View→Find Mode menu command, or a keyboard shortcut, or the Status toolbar's Find button—yikes!).

In a case like this, rather than track down all the ways a person might get to Find mode and try to deal with them proactively, why not get reactive instead? It would be best if your script could simply kick in when you switch to Find mode, no matter how you do it.

Script triggers to the rescue again (page 430). Among FileMaker's many triggers is OnModeEnter, which runs whenever you enter a mode on a particular layout. You get to decide which modes you care about, and which script to run. Setting it up is a snap:

1. **Switch to Layout mode, and then go to the Customers layout.**

   Script triggers are always associated with a particular layout or object, so you need to get to the layout in question first.

2. **Choose Layouts→Layout Setup, and then switch to the Script Triggers tab.**

   You see the list of layout-oriented script triggers FileMaker supports.

3. **Scroll down the list, and then select OnModeEnter.**

   The list is too long to show every trigger, so you have to scroll just a touch to find the one you want. Once you select it, the bottom portion of the window shows you information about this trigger.

4. **Click Select, and then choose the Find Customers script you just created.**

   The Select button shows the same Select Script window you see when you're setting up buttons.

5. **Turn off the Browse and Preview checkboxes (and leave the Find checkbox turned on).**

The OnModeEnter trigger normally fires when you first go to any mode (except Layout mode, which is script-averse). In this case, you want the trigger to fire only when you enter Find mode. When you're done, the window looks like Figure 11-12.

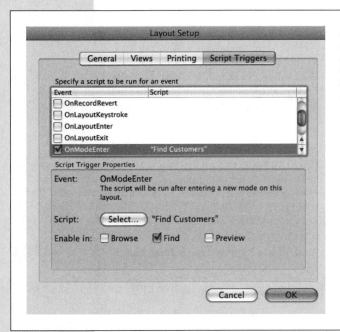

Figure 11-12:
Here's how your OnModeEnter trigger looks once you've configured it. To recap, whenever someone enters Find mode on this layout, the Find Customers script runs automatically.

When you're done, click OK to go back to the Layout Setup dialog box, save your layout, and then switch to Browse mode. Now, switch to Find mode using any of the 427 available methods and bask in the glory of script triggers, as FileMaker automatically starts your stylish find process.

Static Find Requests

With the script you created on the previous few pages, people can search for customers, by entering find requests. More often than not, you *don't* want to make people enter the find requests manually. After all, the whole point of a script is to have FileMaker do things so people don't have to. If you know ahead of time exactly what you want the script to find, use the Perform Find step all by itself: Just turn on the "Specify find requests" option, and create the settings for the request; the search options stay the same each time the script runs. When you specify find requests in a script, you see a pair of windows that let you set up a scripted request.

When you turn on the option "Specify Find Requests" or click the Specify button for the Find Request script step, you see the Specify Find Requests window (Figure 11-13). Click New and you'll see the Edit Find Request window (Figure 11-14). To edit an existing request, select it first, and then click Edit. You can also delete or duplicate the selected step using the Delete and Duplicate buttons. Using the Specify Find Requests and Edit Find Request windows, you can tell the Perform Find step to do any find you can do from Find mode.

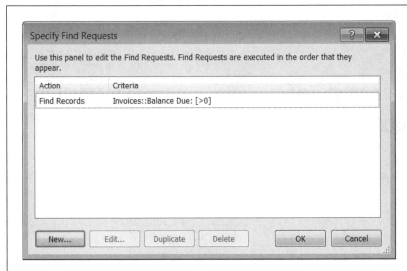

Figure 11-13:
The Specify Find Requests window shows up when you tell FileMaker you want the Perform Find script step to perform a predetermined find. (Developers call this technique hard-coding.) FileMaker automatically fills it with all the requests you used the last time you were in Find mode. If you have new requests, select them all, and then click Delete.

Tip: The Edit Find Requests dialog box is confusing until you get used to it. But there's a way you can learn how it translates requests into its own particular syntax. Perform a find manually, and then write a test script with a Perform Find script step. FileMaker sets the dialog box with the criteria for the search you just did.

To create a find request, from the "Find records when" list, select a field (if it's a repeating field, then you can specify the repetition number in the Repetition box), and then, in the Criteria box, enter text. The Insert Symbol button gives you quick access to the same symbols you see in the Status toolbar in Find mode, and the Criteria box accepts all the standard symbols. Once you've finished entering the criteria, click Add to add it to the Criteria list.

- To edit an existing item in the criteria list, select it. When you do, FileMaker automatically selects the matching field in the Field list and puts the criterion in the Criteria box. You can then make any changes necessary, and then click Change.

- To remove a criterion from the list entirely, select it, and then click Remove.

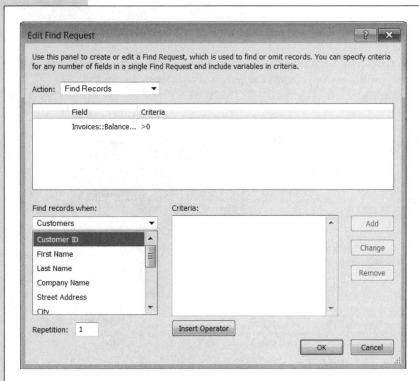

Figure 11-14:
When you add a new find request or edit an existing one, you see this dialog box. It's just a more structured way to type data in fields in Find mode. Instead of using your layouts, you use this window, which gives you direct access to every field in the database (the Fields list) and lets you easily see exactly which fields are being used in the Criteria list.

- Finally, you get to choose whether this request should be used to *find* matching records, or to *omit* them (see page 57). To turn this into an omitting find request, from the Action pop-up menu, choose Omit Records.

- When you've finished adding criteria, click OK. Just like Find mode, you can add more find requests if you want. In the Specify Find Requests window, just click the New button a second time. When you're all finished adding requests, click OK again.

Using a Variable to Create Dynamic Find Requests

As dependable as static finds are, you won't always be able to predict what someone wants to find. Or the criteria for finding the same thing over and over can change, like when you're searching in a date field. For example, suppose you want to find all the invoices created a week ago. You can easily do so in Find mode: Just put the date from a week ago in the Invoices::Date field. But what you put in that field *changes every day*. For example, if today is November 7, and you create a script to find invoices from a week ago, then you could attach this request to the Perform Find step:

```
Invoices::Date = "10/31/2010"
```

Unfortunately, as soon as November 8 rolls around, this script *won't* find week-old invoices. It always finds invoices from October 31, 2010. When you're faced with a situation like this, you can adapt your static find request process slightly. To make it work, you'll use a new script step, called "Set Variable." This step creates a temporary holding place for a value that'll be used elsewhere in the script.

POWER USERS' CLINIC

Pausing a Script

Normally when you run a script, FileMaker performs its steps one by one as fast as it can. When they're all finished, the script's done. But sometimes a script should pause, usually to wait for someone to do something (like enter Find criteria) or to show the user something (like a Preview mode for a report). The Pause/Resume Script step, and some other steps (like Enter Find Mode) can pause the script automatically when their Pause options are turned on. When FileMaker gets to a step like this, it stops executing the script, but remembers where it left off. Later, the script continues, starting with the next step in line. While a script is paused, you're free to edit records, switch modes, change layouts, and so forth. You *can't* open the Manage Database, Manage Value Lists, Manage Custom Functions, or Manage Scripts windows, though, until the script finishes running.

While a script is paused, FileMaker adds two new buttons to the Status toolbar. The Continue button causes the script to continue immediately (pressing the Enter key does the same thing). The Cancel button tells FileMaker you don't want to run the rest of the script. Your script stops, and you get back full control of the program.

If you want to, you can tell FileMaker how long to pause by clicking the Script Step Options area's Specify button when the Pause/Resume Script step is selected. The dialog box that appears has two choices: Indefinitely and For Duration. If you choose For Duration, you get to enter the number of seconds you want the script to pause, or you can click *another* Specify button to use a calculation to set the number of seconds. If you have set the script to pause for a specific duration, then you can still do things with your database while the script is paused, including click the Continue or Cancel buttons.

With a name like "Pause/Resume Script" you'd think this step can also *resume* a paused script. But then again, if the script is paused, then how can the step possibly execute? Don't be fooled: This step can only pause.

Note: You'll learn more about script variables on page 689.

Here's how to write a dynamic find script using a variable in a Find Request.

1. **Create a new script called Find This Week's Invoices.**

    Always use short descriptive names for your scripts.

2. **Move the Set Variable script step into the script list.**

    It's in the Control section of the script steps list.

3. **Click the Specify button.**

    The Set Variable Options window appears (Figure 11-15).

---

4. **Type** *$date* **into the Name field.**

   Variable's names have to start with a "$" symbol. After that it's up to you. But as with all elements, make it short, sweet and descriptive.

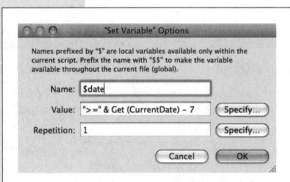

Figure 11-15:
To set a variable, you give it a name and tell it what value to hold onto. The Specify button next to the Value field leads directly to the Specify Calculation window.

5. **In the Value field, type** *">=" & Get (CurrentDate) – 7.*

   Do include the quote marks, but don't include the period at the end. You're typing the proper search criteria into the variable's value box, just as if you'd type into a date field. That is, you're telling FileMaker that the date value is "greater than or equal to today, minus 7 days."

6. **Move the Perform Find script step into the current steps list.**

   Now it's time to tell FileMaker how to use the date you've just defined.

7. **Click Specify, and then click the Specify Find Request window's New button.**

   The Edit Find Request window appears. You know it well by now.

8. **In the "Find records when" list, choose the Invoice::Date Due field.**

   That says which field to search.

9. **In the Criteria box, type** *$date.*

   FileMaker will use the dynamic date value to search each time the script is run.

10. **Click the Add button, check your window against Figure 11-16, and then click OK twice.**

    You're back in the Edit Script window.

11. **Save the script, and then close the Edit Script window.**

    Attach your script to a button on the Invoice layout and test your new button.

Tip: *If you're using this chapter's sample database, your invoice dates should be set with current dates so that the dynamic find script works, even if you haven't created new invoices. Check the "Setup Invoice Dates" script to see if you can figure out how it works.*

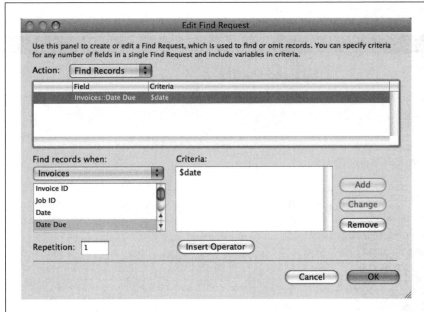

Figure 11-16:
With this setting, File-Maker can use a dynamic date value to find an invoice where the Invoice::Due Date is within the past week. The value in the $date variable will change appropriately each time the script is run.

Constraining and Extending the Found Set

You may have already noticed that Perform Find doesn't have an option for the Requests→Constrain Found Set and Requests→Extend Found Set commands. That's because each of these is a separate script step. It makes sense, really, because to constrain or extend a find, you need to do a Find first. In other words, this process always takes two separate steps to complete.

The Extend Found Set and Constrain Found Set script step options work like Perform Find. Everything you just learned about Perform Find still applies: You can hard-code the find requests, pause the script, and then let the user enter them, or build them in the script.

Omitting Records

The Omit Record script step lives a dual life. If you're in Browse mode when it runs, it simply omits the current record from the found set. If you're in Find mode, on the other hand, in the Status toolbar, it turns on the Omit checkbox.

Omit Multiple Records works only in Browse mode and does the same thing as the Records→Omit Multiple command. As usual, you can specify the number of records to omit in the script, either as a number or a calculation. You also get a "Perform without dialog" option so you can decide whether or not people get to enter the number of records to omit.

Finally, the Show Omitted Only script step has the same effect as the Records→Show Omitted Only menu command.

POWER USERS' CLINIC

Mix and Match

You have three basic options when performing a find in a script: You can let someone enter the find requests, hard-code the requests right in the Perform Find step, or use a variable to set dynamic requests. But these choices aren't mutually exclusive: You can mix and match techniques.

For example, suppose you need a relatively complex set of find requests that, for the most part, never change, but one value in one field on just one request needs to be based on the current date. It would be tedious to have to add dozens of Set Field and New Record/Request steps to your script when all but one use a hardcoded value.

Other times, it would be nice to let people specify the find requests, but add a little more to it when they're done. You can start on the Enter Find Mode script step, by turning on the "Specify find requests" option. This step tells FileMaker to go to Find mode *and* load it up with the requests you specify in a Specify Find Requests dialog box.

Once you're in Find mode, though, you're free to use Set Field, New Record/Request, and "Go to Record/Request" to modify the prefab requests to your heart's content. Just go to the right request, and use Set Field to work the dynamic date value into it.

Suppose you want to let people search for invoices. You create a Find Invoices layout and a script like the one for Find Customers, except for the Invoice layout. This time, you want to restrict people to invoices created only in the last year. Before the Perform Find step, you can add these two steps:

```
New Record/Request
Omit
Set    Field   [Invoices::Date;    "<"    &
Get(CurrentDate) - 365]
```

Now the script finds just what someone asks for, but omits records more than 365 days old. You've used the script to add a new request to the ones she created. What's more, she doesn't even know you've controlled her find.

Modify Last Find

The simplest find-related script step is Modify Last Find. It has exactly the same effect as the Records→Modify Last Find command: It puts you in Find mode with the same requests you created the *last* time you were in Find mode.

Sorting Records

After all that fuss about finding records, the sorting script steps are refreshingly simple. There are only two and you already know how to use both. The Sort Records script step behaves in a now-familiar way. All by itself, it brings up the Sort dialog box when the script runs. If you turn on its "Specify sort order" option, then you can preload the sort dialog box with a specific sort order. Finally, turn on the "Perform without dialog" option to sort the records without bothering anyone with a dialog box at all.

If the records are already sorted, then you can *unsort* them from a script. For instance, you might sort records for a report, but you want to return them to their unsorted order when the report is finished so people don't get confused. Just use the Unsort Records script step. It does its job with no options.

Sorting Records with an *OnRecordLoad* Trigger

When you first encountered a Sort script, you learned how to attach it to a layout with the *OnLayoutEnter* script trigger (page 168). That sorted your records whenever you view the List layout. But if you switch that trigger to *OnRecordLoad*, you'll get different behavior with that same script. *OnRecordLoad* fires whenever a new record is loaded, but you can still sort the records a different way any time you need to.)

If you do a find on this layout when the *OnLayoutLoad* trigger is set, the results come back unsorted. *OnRecordLoad* changes this layout to automatically sort when you first view the layout *and* when you find new records. The *OnRecordLoad* trigger fires whenever a new record is loaded, which always happens after a find. True, it happens when you switch records too, but FileMaker's smart enough to know it doesn't need to sort an already sorted list, so this doesn't cause an appreciable slowdown. But whenever you visit the Customers layout, your records are presorted. If you sort manually, then your new sort order sticks until you leave the layout and come back (or sort manually again).

Tip: Use *OnRecordLoad* for list views, where you're not likely to do much data entry. But on a Form view or a Detail layout, where you're creating lots of records, this script may trigger enough to affect performance. In that case, use *OnLayoutLoad* instead.

Working with Windows

Scripts give you complete control over the database windows on the screen. You can create new windows, close existing windows, bring any window to the front, and move or resize any window. (Why would a script need to monkey with someone's onscreen windows? See the box on page 496 for some ideas.)

Creating Windows

To make a new window on the screen, you use the New Window script step. With this step selected in your script, in Edit Script window's Step Options area, you see a Specify button. Clicking this button brings up the "New Window" Options dialog box, pictured in Figure 11-17.

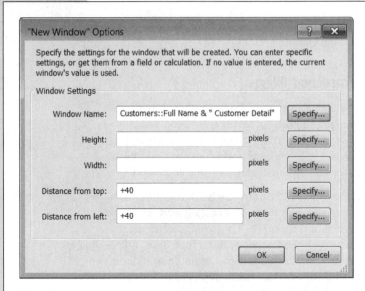

Figure 11-17:
The "New Window" Options dialog box lets your script create windows in a specific size and location on your screen. Each box in this window has a Specify button that leads to the Specify Calculation window. The settings shown here could be used in a script that runs from a list layout to show detail about a specific customer. The window will show detail for the customer record the user clicked on and the title bar will contain that customer's name. The window will be created 40 pixels down and to the right of the window that spawned it. See the box on page 498 to learn more.

POWER USERS' CLINIC

Controlling the Display

If you want to pull out all the stops, you can use a combination of layouts, Custom Menus (page 538), tooltips (page 329), and scripting to almost completely take over control of your database. You can hide and lock the Status toolbar, and then give people buttons to go to the next, previous, first, and last records. You can make it so that when you click a customer on the List layout, a new detail window pops up named after that particular customer. You can even make your script so smart that it selects an existing detail window for the customer if one exists, and makes a new one otherwise.

In this way, you give people the impression that each customer has his own window, and you make comparing customers side by side a breeze.

This kind of high-level window management takes a fair amount of work, so most people stick with the normal every-layout-in-one-window approach and let people create windows as needed. Your approach depends entirely on how much time you want to spend writing scripts and how important the multiple-window display is to you.

The first box—Window Name—gives your script control over the name of the window. (Window name is something you can control *only* from a script. When you create the window from the Window menu, FileMaker assigns it a name for you.) You can also tell FileMaker how big the window should be (Height and Width), and where to put the window on the screen ("Distance from top" and "Distance from left").

Here are some tips on using the "New Window" Options dialog box:

- If you leave any of the values blank, FileMaker uses the same value from the *current* window (it adds a number to the end of the window name so the new name is different). For example, if the current window is called "Vergis Corporation" and you run the New Window script step without specifying a name, then the new window's name is "Vergis Corporation – 2."

- If you also don't specify a size and position, FileMaker puts it right over the top of the current window (with the same size and position).

Tip: To avoid confusing people, it's usually best to offset the new window at least a little so they can see new window(s) on top of their old ones.

- You can set each value directly by typing in the box in the New Window Options dialog box, or set them from a calculation by clicking the Specify button by any box. See the box on page 498 for more info on window size and position options.

Bringing a Window to the Front

In scripting parlance, you bring a window to the front by *selecting* it. As such, you use the Select Window script step. It has one option, which lets you specify a window by name, or select the current window, as shown in Figure 11-18. You also use the Select Window script step to show a hidden window and bring it to the front.

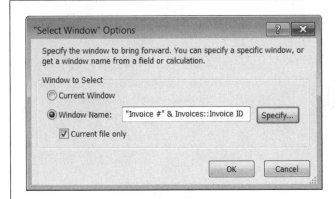

Figure 11-18:
This window appears when you click the Specify button with a Select Window script step selected. From here, you can specify the Current Window, or choose Window Name, and then put the name of the window you want in the box. This calculation looks for a window with the name "Invoice #" and the current Invoice's InvoiceID.

Note: Usually, the current window is already in the front, and you don't have to worry about this step. But when you run scripts that involve more than one database, as you'll learn in Chapter 16, you may need this step to bring forward the current window from *another file*.

Window Size and Position Calculations

The fact that you can set a new window's size and position using a calculation may seem a little strange. After all, do you really need a bigger window for someone named Bill? Do you want your windows in a different place on Thursdays?

In fact, though, you can do a lot of interesting things with window size and position calculations. FileMaker provides a handful of functions that let you find out about the size and position of the current window, and of the computer screen, and use that information in calculations:

- The *Get (WindowHeight)* function, for instance, returns the height of the current window, in screen pixels (the little dots on your screen). Its brother, *Get (WindowContentHeight)* returns the height of just the window's content area; that is, the area inside the title bar, scroll bars, and Status toolbar. The *Get (WindowWidth)* and *Get (WindowContentWidth)* functions are similar.

- *Get (WindowTop)* and *Get (WindowLeft)* functions tell you where the window is on the screen. The first returns the distance from the top of the window to the top of the screen. The second tells you the distance from the window's left edge to the screen's left side. Both distances are measured in pixels.

- The *Get (WindowDesktopHeight)* and *Get (WindowDesktopWidth)* functions tell you how much desktop space you have. On Windows, it's the area of FileMaker's main program window. On Mac OS X, it's the size of the desktop.

- Finally, *Get (ScreenHeight)* and *Get (ScreenWidth)* tell you how big the screen is. (If you have more than one screen, then they tell you about the screen the current window is on.)

By combining these functions in creative ways, you can make your scripts smart about how they size and position windows. For example, to make the new window appear slightly offset from the current window, use these settings:

- Distance from top: *Get (WindowTop) + 20*
- Distance from left: *Get (WindowLeft) + 20*

If you're paranoid, and you want to make sure the new window never hangs off the bottom of the screen, use this Let function (page 659) calculation for the "Distance from top" value:

```
Let (
    [Limit = Get(WindowDesktopHeight) -
Get(WindowHeight);
    Offset = Get(WindowTop) + 20;
    Best = Min(Limit; Offset)];

    Best
)
```

Similarly, you can use the "Distance from left" value to make sure it doesn't hang off the screen's right edge. Just substitute WindowDesktopWidth, WindowWidth, and WindowLeft for WindowDesktopHeight, WindowHeight, and WindowTop.

Closing a Window

The Close Window script step has the same options as Select Window. You tell FileMaker which window to close: the current window, or one you specify by name.

Moving and Resizing Existing Windows

FileMaker has three ways to move and resize a window. You can opt for one of its canned window maneuvers, or you can set the exact pixel size and location of the window just like you can with the New Window step. You can also *hide* the current window.

Adjust Window

The Adjust Window script step always operates on the current window, and it gives you just five simple choices:

- Choose Resize to Fit, and FileMaker makes the window exactly the right size to fit its contents.

- Choose Maximize to make the window as large as possible.

- Choose Minimize to shrink the window to a little bar (Windows) or a Dock icon (Mac OS X).

- Choose Restore to switch the window back to the *last* size it was, just before it was most recently resized.

- Choose Hide to hide the window (just like the Window→Hide Window command).

Note: The Maximize options have slightly different behavior on Mac OS X and Windows. For example, when you maximize a window in Windows, and then select a different window, the second window also gets maximized. On Mac OS X, the second window keeps its original size. Also, a maximized window on Mac OS X fills as much of the screen as possible. On Windows, it fills FileMaker's outer window, whatever size it may be, and you can't adjust the window from a script.

Arrange All Windows

The Arrange All Windows script step is the equivalent of the four window arrangement options in the Window menu. You can tile windows horizontally or vertically, or cascade them (see page 45). On Mac OS X, you can also bring all FileMaker windows to the front. This command doesn't change the active window.

Move/Resize Window

For the ultimate in window control, call upon the Move/Resize Window script step. It can move and/or resize any window with pixel-perfect precision. Its Specify button shows the dialog box in Figure 11-19, where you can choose the window's size and position. As with New Window, you can leave any of the size or position values empty. When you do, FileMaker leaves that part of the window's size or position alone. For example, if you specify a new value for Width but leave Height blank, FileMaker makes the window wider or narrower, but its height doesn't change.

Note: Move/Resize Window also selects the window it acts on, which always brings the window to the front, and, if it's a hidden window, shows it.

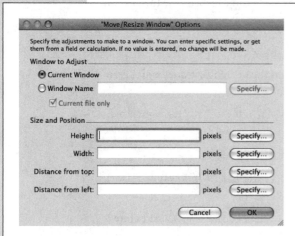

Figure 11-19:
The Move/Resize Window settings look like a combination of the Select Window settings and the New Window settings. First, you pick which window you want to work on (Current Window, or a window selected by name). You then specify the new size and position for the window.

Other Window-Related Script Steps

FileMaker has a handful of other window-related script steps, listed below. These steps come in handy if you need to exert more control over what people see (not to imply that you're a control freak or anything).

- **Freeze Window** tells FileMaker to stop showing changes in the window while the script runs. For example, if your script is looping through all the records in the found set, then you normally see each record on the screen as it runs. If you add a Freeze Window script step before the loop, then people see only the first record while it runs. When the script is finished, FileMaker updates the window again. Looping scripts that have to visit lots of records run decidedly faster when the window's frozen.

- **Refresh Window** forces FileMaker to update what's inside the window when it normally wouldn't. This action can be because you previously ran the Freeze Window step, or because FileMaker's simply being conservative. If you want to make sure someone sees a particular record or field value on the screen while a script is running, then add a Refresh Window step after making the change.

- **Scroll Window** lets you simulate a vertical scroll bar click in a window. You can scroll to the Home (top) or End of a window, or move up or down one screenful. You also get a To Selection option, which scrolls the window so that the selected record and field value both show. You'll design most of your windows so that scrolling isn't necessary, which means you may never need this step.

- **Show/Hide Status Area** lets you decide if people should see the Status Toolbar. (Unfortunately, this script step's name didn't get updated when the Status Toolbar got its new name. But it still controls the toolbar.) You can show or hide the Status Toolbar, or ask that it be *toggled* (shown if it's hidden, and hidden if it's showing). You can also turn on the Lock option to prevent people from manually changing the Status Toolbar. For example, if you never want anyone to see the Status Toolbar at all, then hide and lock it in the script that runs when your database opens. Then the Status Toolbar is locked, and its toggle icon and menu command are grayed out. More commonly, though, the Status Toolbar's turned off and locked during a process, such as a scripted find. You don't want people using the Cancel button during a Pause step to cancel a script, and then end up dumped on a layout that you meant them to see only while a script is running. If you hide the Status Toolbar, though, then you should provide a button that cancels the process, in case people change their minds. That way, they don't have to go all the way through a process if they get an urgent phone call and need to do something different from the script's agenda.

Note: If you're publishing your database online using Instant Web Publishing (IWP), you may not want users to be able to navigate at will with the Status Toolbar. Your login script can test to see if users are accessing the file over the Web (*If [PatternCount (Get (ApplicationVersion) ; "web")]*), and then hide and lock the Status Toolbar when that condition is true.

- **Show/Hide Text Ruler** can toggle, show, or hide, the Text Ruler. Unlike Show/Hide Status Toolbar, this step doesn't have a Lock option. Someone can always override your setting, so this step is rarely worth the trouble.

- **Set Window Title** lets you change any window's name. You can specify the current window, or any window by name, as well as the window's new name. FileMaker normally names a window with the file's name, but you can tailor each window to a person. Write a script that runs when the file is opened, and use the Set Window Title script step with this calculation: *Get (FileName) & " " & Get (AccountName)*.

- **Set Zoom Level** sets the window zoom level, just like the zoom controls in the window's bottom-left corner. You can pick a specific zoom level, or choose to zoom in or out to the next level. Again, you get a Lock option. If you set the zoom level, and then turn on the Lock checkbox, people can't manually change the zoom level.

- **View As** is in the Windows section of the script step list, but it isn't really a window-related step. It changes the view option for the current *layout*. You can pick Form view, List view, or Table view. You also get a choice called Cycle that tells FileMaker to switch to the *next* view setting in the list. If you really want to control how people see your database, use Layouts →Layout Setting (View Tab) to turn off the views you don't want them seeing. You can then let folks override those settings with this script step.

Working with Files

In the Script Step list, the Files section contains some of the *least often used* script steps in all of FileMaker. But if you work in a school, say, the day may come when you need to automate the process of formatting files or saving backup copies for every student in a class. You can also script the process of converting older databases to FileMaker .fp7 format and recovering damaged databases, but these processes are sensitive, and usually better handled manually.

Opening and Closing Files

Because the Open File script step lets you open another FileMaker file, it's probably used more than the others in this group. You can pick any of your existing file references (see page 592) or create a new file reference if necessary. When the step runs, the specified file opens and appears in a new window. If the file has a script set to run when it opens, it runs.

If you want the file to open, but you don't want to see a window on the screen, then turn on the "Open hidden" option for this step. The file opens, but it's listed in the Window menu's Show Window submenu, with its name in parentheses.

The Close File script step closes any open file. When you add the step, you get to pick any file reference or add a new one. You can also choose Current File to close the file the script is in. If the file is open when the script runs, then all its windows close, and its closing script runs.

Note: In general, FileMaker is very smart about when to open and close files. It opens a file when it needs to and closes it again when it no longer needs it. You usually don't need to open and close files from a script, but there's one important exception: when the file has an opening script that should run before someone can see the file. If you jump directly to a related record in another file, then FileMaker bypasses the opening script, so use an Open File script step to ensure that the open script runs.

Save a Copy As

If you need to make a copy of an open database, use the "Save a Copy As" script step. It works just like the File→"Save a Copy As" command. When you're working on a set of files and want to back them up without a lot of manual muss and fuss, just add a "Save a Copy As" script to each one. Then, from your main file, call that script in each file, and you've made a backup with one script.

Note: This script step (or menu command, for that matter) doesn't work on files shared using FileMaker Server. See page 752 to learn how to create automatic backups.

Other File-Related Script Steps

The rest of the file-related script steps are almost never used, but that doesn't mean *you* won't find a good reason to use them.

- **Convert File** lets you convert an older FileMaker database to a FileMaker 7 database. Since this process requires a lot of preparation and manual checking and is done infrequently it's rarely scripted.

- **Set Use System Formats** toggles the Use System Formats file option on or off. When you first create a database, FileMaker remembers how your system expects dates, times, and numbers to be formatted. If someone opens the file on a computer with different settings (usually a different language), then FileMaker has to decide if it should use the original format settings for the file, or those specified by the new system. You usually set this choice in the File→File Options window.

- **Recover File** runs FileMaker's automatic file repair process on a selected database. Recovering a file is a rare thing in general since FileMaker is careful to avoid damaging databases even when your computer crashes. It's even more rare, and even inadvisable, to do this on the same database so often you'd need a script to do it for you.

Printing

Printing typically involves two specific commands on Windows or Mac OS X: File→Print Setup or File→Page Setup and File→Print. The Edit Script window gives you those same two choices.

You'll use these steps often, since they're the meat and potatoes part of printing a report. Use the Print Setup script step to set the options in the Print Setup or Page Setup dialog box. Turn on "Specify print setup" or "Specify page setup" to see the standard dialog box. Pick the option you want to associate with the script step. When the script runs, FileMaker restores the options you chose. You can also turn on a "Perform without dialog" checkbox. When this option is off, a person sees—and gets a chance to configure—the dialog box when the script runs. If you just want to set the options without user intervention, turn on "Perform without dialog".

The Print script step works very similarly. You can specify which printer to use, the number of pages, and so forth or let people make the choice. Either way, when the step runs, FileMaker prints. Remember, though, you get to control which records are printed. In the Print dialog box, if you select "Records being browsed", "Current record", or "Blank record, showing fields", FileMaker remembers this setting along with all the other options. So be sure you make the right choice for people.

Note: Many of the options you can set in the Print dialog box are specific to a particular printer model. For example, some printers let you pick color or black-and-white printing or have settings for different kinds of paper. Be careful about setting these proprietary options, though. When someone uses your database and script on a different printer, then these options don't work.

Other Script Steps

You've now seen most of the often-used script steps (and a few of the not-so-often used ones). You'll see even more as they come up in the next few chapters. The rest of this chapter covers a few oddball steps that don't seem to fit in anywhere.

Open URL

You first saw the Open URL script step as a button command when learning about text calculations. When FileMaker runs this step, it asks your computer's operating system to open the URL you specify. Most often the URL is a web address (HTTP), but it can be any URL type your computer supports, including FTP, MAILTO, SSH, and even FMP7 (to open a file on a network server). As usual, you can specify the URL or let someone else do it, and you can use a calculation if needed.

Dial Phone

The Dial Phone script step tells your modem to dial the telephone using a phone number you provide. You can use a calculation to specify the phone number, or enter it directly.

Note: Because newer Macs don't have modems, this script step doesn't work on Mac OS X. If you try to chose the step, a warning message lets you know the feature's unavailable.

Set Web Viewer

Web viewers are pretty cool on their own, but the Set web Viewer script step (Figure 11-20) can make your FileMaker layouts look even more like a web browser. With this flexible script step, you can make a series of buttons:

- **Reset** sets the web viewer back to the web address that's specified in its web Viewer Setup dialog box.

- **Reload** gets you a fresh copy of the web page you're currently viewing.

- **Go Forward** lets you move forward through your web page history.

- **Go Back** lets you move backwards through the web pages you've been browsing.

- **Go to URL** lets you specify any new web address via the Specify Calculation window.

But to use this script step, you have to refer to your web viewer by name. One cool thing about referring to a web viewer by name is that you can display more than one web viewer on a layout, and then by using it's name, choose which one your scripts address. See page 450 for details on naming objects.

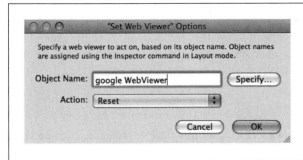

Figure 11-20:
This Set Web Viewer dialog box is set to work on a web viewer with the prosaic name of "viewer." When you select the "Go to URL…" option, you see the same Set Web Viewer dialog box that comes free with every web viewer.

Execute SQL

If you need to manipulate data in an ODBC data source, like Oracle, SQL, or MySQL, then this script step is at your service (Figure 11-21). Unlike many other script steps, this one requires some prior setup. You'll need an OBDC driver installed on any computer that runs an Execute SQL script. Each driver is a bit different, so use the drivers' documentation for installation and setting up data sources. Finally, if you don't write SQL queries, then you need help from someone who does, to make sure you get to the data you want. See page 806 to learn how you can use SQL data almost as easily as native FileMaker data.

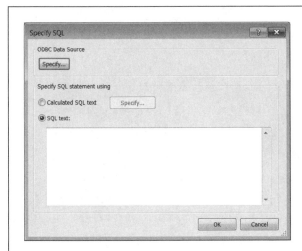

Figure 11-21:
This picture shows the Specify SQL dialog box in its unvarnished state. Once you prepare your computer, and select an ODBC Data Source, the source name shows up beside the top Specify button. Then, you can use the Calculations dialog box to assemble a query, or just type directly in the SQL text field.

Flush Cache to Disk

Unlike what you might be thinking, this script step is a good thing: it actually saves your work. Any time changes are made to a record, FileMaker records those changes in your computer's memory first, and writes the change to the hard drive later—when it gets some free time. If you want to *force* the changes to be written to disk immediately, then you can run the "Flush Cache to Disk" script step. For instance, you might add this script step after a script that creates a new customer order. That way, if your computer crashes while you're busily taking orders, then you lose only the last order you were working on.

Exit Application

Last but not least, you can have a script exit or quit the FileMaker program on your behalf. Of course, this causes every open window and file to be closed as well. People usually use this when they have just one database, and they never use FileMaker unless they're in that database. They add the Exit Application step to the very end of their database's closing script so that when they close the last database window, FileMaker goes away, too. (Of course *you* find FileMaker so useful you *never* want to close it, right?)

Tip: Use an Exit Application script as part of your logout routine when you're sharing a database on the Web. It closes out a browser's virtual windows (a temporary window some browsers draw to do behind-the-scenes work), which might otherwise keep them logged into the website, and ends the user's session. This step can free up resources for other users.

Part Four: Becoming a Power Developer

IV

Applying Developer Utilities

W ork with FileMaker for a while, and it becomes clear that this friendly, rather unassuming software lets you achieve awesome feats. When others in your organization start seeing and using your databases, requests for new features, possibly whole new databases will start coming your way. That's when you start graduating from an advanced *user* of FileMaker Pro to a *developer*. A developer isn't simply a user who knows a lot about creating databases. Developers design and build database systems that other people use in the greater world. As a FileMaker developer, you need to do a range of things:

- Construct tables and relationships that organize information while avoiding duplication and creating flexibility.

- Wield layout tools to create a display that's intuitive, attractive, and easy to use.

- Apply FileMaker's lexicon of functions in the calculations that can literally touch every part of a complex database.

- Write scripts that spare your users from repetitive work and let them work intuitively.

- Provide access to the database by employing peer-to-peer database sharing, database hosting with FileMaker Server, and web publishing.

- Secure your database to prevent unauthorized access or manipulation of the information within.

You'll develop these skills over time, but the first thing every power developer needs is the right toolbox. You don't show up at the Tour de France with a tricycle. And you don't become a power developer without FileMaker Pro Advanced. This version doesn't make your database run better, or accept more people, or hold more data. Rather, with Advanced, you can be a more productive database *developer*.

For a couple hundred dollars more ($499 for Advanced vs. $299 for Pro), you get a whole raft of developer tools to make your life easier and your databases better. If you find yourself troubleshooting long, complex scripts, then Script Debugger may save your sanity and your valuable time. The analysis tools are indispensable if you're in a consultant role, working on databases that other people created. Save and reuse your carefully crafted calculations with Custom Functions. Custom Menus give you godlike power to determine which commands are available to people who use a database. If you spend a good portion of your time building FileMaker databases, FileMaker Pro Advanced is a must-have.

Copying and Pasting Database Structure

Since a large percentage of a database designer's work is fairly repetitive, FileMaker Pro Advanced provides some tools that let you take shortcuts through the tedious process of creating tables, fields, and scripts. By copying work you've already done, you can spend less time defining fields or recreating complex scripts, and more time doing the creative work of designing a database. You can import tables and fields without copying data between tables in the same file and between different files.

FileMaker Pro Advanced also provides Copy and Paste capability in several major dialog boxes so you can reuse fields in the Manage Database window, scripts and script steps in Script Maker, and even entire tables or groups of table occurrences. (You need full access privileges in both the source file and the target file to import or copy and paste elements from file to file.)

Importing Tables and Fields

If you have a handful of tables in one file that would also be useful in another, then you can *import* the table and field information. Importing tables doesn't copy the data inside them. Rather, it copies the tables' design and structure, with all their fields, including their names, types, comments, calculations, and so on. Start by choosing File→Manage Database, and then clicking the Table tab. Click Import, and then locate the file that contains the table you want to copy.

Note: Whether you import tables or copy and paste them from another file, be aware that you're *not* importing *table occurrences* or *relationships* from the Manage Database window's Relationships tab.

Next, tell FileMaker Pro Advanced which specific tables to import in the Import Tables dialog box, shown in Figure 12-1. When FileMaker Pro Advanced has finished importing the tables and fields, it displays a dialog box similar to the one you see when you import data. You see a summary of how many tables and fields were created during the import.

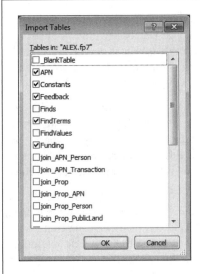

Figure 12-1:
You see a simple list of all tables in the source file from which you've chosen to import tables. Turn on the checkbox by all the tables you want to import. You don't get to specify which fields are imported—they all come in. So if you don't need a few of those fields, just delete them when the import's finished.

Note: When FileMaker Pro Advanced builds your new tables and fields, it saves a record of its progress in a log file. If you see an error in the summary window, click the Open Log File button to see what went wrong. Things might go wrong if you have calculation fields that reference table occurrences that don't exist yet, for example. When this happens, FileMaker puts the calculation in comments so you can reconstitute it later once you've added table occurrences.

Copying and Pasting Tables

If you prefer, you can copy and paste tables in the Manage Database window instead of using the Import button. In the Tables tab, just select a table, and then click Copy. If you want an exact copy in the same file, just click Paste. Alternatively, you can dismiss the Manage Database window, go to a different file, bring up its Tables tab, and then paste the table there. As usual, you can use the Shift key to select several items next to each other in the table list. Use the Ctrl (Control) key to select tables that aren't right next to each other.

Warning: When you copy a table into another database, it may include calculation fields that FileMaker can't successfully copy. For example, a calculation may reference a table occurrence that doesn't exist in the new file. In such cases, FileMaker keeps the field, but puts the entire calculation in comments (like /* this */). Be sure to check all calculation fields after pasting.

Copying and Pasting Fields

If you have complex calculations that you want to reuse in another table within the same file, or in a different file, then, on the Manage Database window's Fields tab, use the Copy and Paste buttons. Just like with tables, select one or more fields, and then click Copy. Then open the table where you want to create the new fields, and finally click Paste to do the deed.

When you copy *calculation* fields, your results may vary depending on whether you also copy the fields they reference. It usually saves time to plan ahead and make sure the field references already exist in the target table before you copy and paste. But you can always paste the calculation fields and clean up the references later, especially if you intend to use different field names anyway. Here are some general rules:

- If fields matching the references in your copied calculation don't exist in the target table, then FileMaker pastes the calculation as a comment (e.g., */*Products::Amount * LineItem::Quantity*/*), since it can't find matching fields in the new table. Simply edit the calculations to use the new field references, delete the comment markers (/* and */), and then click OK.

- To save yourself some editing work, *first* paste into the target table (or create) fields with names that match the ones in the calculation you're transferring. Then, when you paste the calculation, FileMaker resolves the field references automatically.

- If the field references are local (that is, they refer to other fields within the same table), then you can copy the fields referenced in the calculation *and* the calculation field at the same time. When you paste the set of fields, FileMaker resolves the field references automatically, and you have nothing to edit.

- If you're copying a calculation field that contains a fully qualified field reference (containing both a table name and a field name, like Expenses::Job ID), then the calculation again transfers just fine, assuming a table occurrence exists with the same name in the target file.

Copying Scripts and Script Steps

In the Manage Scripts dialog box, you can use the Import button to import whole scripts from other files, but if you have FileMaker Pro Advanced, you can avoid that cumbersome process. Simply open the file that contains the scripts you want to copy, and then, in the Manage Scripts dialog box, use Copy (Ctrl+C [⌘-C]) and Paste (Ctrl+P [⌘-P]). Copy the scripts you want to reuse, open the Manage Scripts dialog box in the *target* file, and then Paste. Check all pasted scripts to see if any field, layout, or other reference needs to be pointed to another element in its new location. Copying or importing scripts works best when you need the whole script, and all the elements referenced in your script are already in place, so that no script steps break on the way in.

You can also copy script steps individually or in chunks. In the Edit Script dialog box, select just the script steps you want, and then Copy. Then you either create a new script or open the script that needs your copied steps. Select the script step just *above* where you want the next steps to land, and then Paste. Your recycled steps appear in your script. Fix any broken references as needed.

You don't even have to move to a new script to find Copy and Paste useful. Sometimes you'll want to reuse a sequence of steps more than once in a single script. Sure, you can select the steps, and then click the Duplicate button, but then you have to move each step down into place one by one. With Copy and Paste, the pasted steps stay together and in their original order.

Script Debugger

When you write a script using FileMaker Pro, your testing and troubleshooting routine is pretty simple. You perform the script and wait to see what happens at the end. In a simple script, like one that prints a report, you can easily enough see what went wrong, and fix it: your script just went to the wrong layout, perhaps. But when you're creating a complex script that sets variables and works with different sets of records that you can't verify before the next script step whizzes past, it's devilishly hard to figure out where your script veers off course. Even simple scripts can go wrong in puzzling ways that you can't detect by reading over your steps.

That's where Script Debugger comes in. When you run scripts with Script Debugger turned on, FileMaker performs scripts at human speed, so you can see exactly what's happening, each step of the way.

Note: To run Script Debugger, it's best to be logged into the file with a password that has script editing privileges (see page 764). But if you need to figure out how a script runs for lesser accounts, then you can log in as someone else, and then use the Authenticate/Deauthenticate button (see page 516).

To see the Script Debugger, choose Tools→Script Debugger. When you do, the Script Debugger window appears on the screen (Figure 12-2). Left to its own devices, the Script Debugger window doesn't do much. It consists of a couple of blocks of empty space, and several buttons you can't click.

But it shows its true colors when you run a script. As soon as you do, it swings into action. It shows the name of the script you're running near the top, and the complete contents of that script just below. You can even see the value of any parameter that was passed to the script. But more important than all this, you can *control* the script as it runs. You can run just one line of the script at a time, dig into subscripts or back out to the calling script, skip over some steps completely, back up and run some steps over again, or stop the script in its tracks.

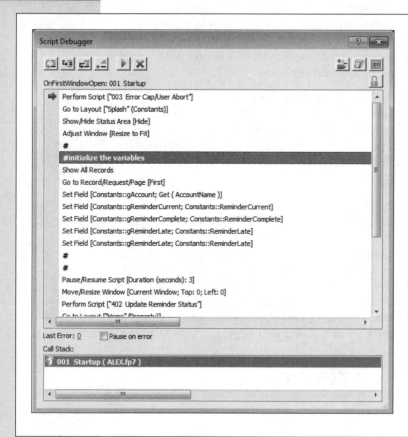

Figure 12-2:
The Script Debugger window's loaded with information about the current script. You can see the script's name at the top, and all its steps in the middle. The Call Stack at the bottom, shows you the resources that invoked this script. Scripts can be called from buttons, custom menus, triggers, and other scripts. FileMaker lists the complete history here, showing which called this one, and below it, the one that called it. If a parameter was passed to any script, then it shows up down here as well. The Script Debugger window includes a row of unlabeled buttons across the top. The buttons on the left control the running script. The buttons on the right give you quick access to other debugger features.

Controlling Script Execution

Unlike most windows, Script Debugger stays on top of your work, giving you constant feedback about running scripts. As long as Script Debugger's window is open, when a script starts running, it immediately shows up in the Script Debugger, and is essentially paused. FileMaker is asking you for permission to perform the first step. You control the running script using the buttons at the top of the window. You can see them in Figure 12-3, and read about them here:

- Click **Step Over** to execute the current script step. (FileMaker marks the current step with a blue arrow along the left edge of the script steps.) FileMaker runs that one step, moves the arrow to the next one, and then pauses, waiting for further instruction from you.

- **Step Into** works just like Step Over, with one caveat. If the current step happens to be a Perform Script script step, then Step Into goes into that script, and stops at its first line. This way you can step through the subscript line by line. The Step Over button, on the other hand, just executes the subscript in its entirety, and takes you to the next line in the calling script.

- When you click **Step Out**, FileMaker runs the current script to completion, takes you back to the script that called it, and then stops. If the script you're running wasn't called by another script, then Step Out just finishes the script normally. Use Step Out if you accidentally step into a script you don't need to see in full detail, or if you're finished investigating a subscript and want to get back to the calling script quickly.

- If you want to skip a portion of a script, or run some steps over again, select a script step, and then click **Set Next Step**. This button moves the little current step arrow to the selected step without actually running anything. For instance, if you just want to test what happens inside an If condition that you know won't be satisfied, then you can move the current step into the If, and then run its contents without the If step itself being run. You can also back up and run a section of code over again by moving the current step up in the list.

Warning: Any time you use the Set Next Step button, you're changing the normal flow of the script. The results you get when you use it may not match what would happen if you ran the script normally. For instance, if you back up and start part of a script over again, things may be different this time through because the script already did those parts. You may end up with a different found set or a different current record, for example. Or script variables may be different this time through. You may be bypassing If conditions that would otherwise apply. And you may be on a different layout from which the steps would normally run. Be careful, or you may end up sending the script in an inappropriate direction.

- If the script is paused, waiting for you to click a button, then you can click **Run/Pause** to start it running normally. It no longer stops at each step. Instead, it runs through every step in sequence. If the script is already running, then clicking this button stops the script, and lets you control its flow again. (To find out how to stop the script exactly where you want, read about *breakpoints* in the next section.)

- If you've decided you've seen enough and you just want to stop the script completely, click **Halt Script**. The Script Debugger window empties of its script-specific information and FileMaker returns to normal Browse mode behavior. The Halt Script button doesn't let the script finish running. Instead, it stops the script in its tracks, just like the Halt Script script step.

- You use the **Set/Clear Breakpoints** button to add or remove breakpoints in your script. You'll learn about these shortly.

- The **Edit Script** button is one of the Script Debugger's handiest buttons. If you're debugging a script that isn't quite working, and while it's running in the debugger you spot the problem, just click Edit Script. FileMaker opens the Edit Script window for the running script, and takes you straight to the step that's next in line (the one with the arrow pointing to it in the debugger window). You can easily make the change, and then run the script again to test it.

Note: When you click the Edit Script button, FileMaker opens the script for editing, but keeps it running in the Script Debugger. You're free to jump back to the Script Debugger window and then click any of the buttons to step the script forward further. So you can also use the Edit Script button to see more details about a script (like the exact calculation in a Set Field script step) while you're debugging. However, if you actually save a change to the script, FileMaker tells you it needs to halt the running script before it can apply the change.

- The **Open/Close Data Viewer** button shows FileMaker Pro Advanced's Data Viewer window, which is explained "The Data Viewer" later in this chapter.

- The **Authenticate/Deauthenticate** button with the padlock icon on it lets you debug a script to which you would normally not have access (because of restrictions imposed by your privilege set). Sometimes a script you create behaves differently for your users (who don't have full access to the database) than it does for you. You can log into your database as one of these restricted people to test the script, but then you can't see the contents of the script in the debugger. If you click the Authenticate/Deauthenticate button (and enter your full access account name and password), though, then FileMaker lets you see and debug the script. Importantly, the script *runs* as though you're still the restricted person. You can see exactly how it behaves for your users, and then hunt down the problem.

By using the buttons in the Script Debugger, you can watch your script in action, performing each step one by one, and examining the results as it goes. This approach makes it infinitely easier to see where a script goes wrong as you try out various iterations, squashing bugs along the way.

Tip: Each of the buttons in the Script Debugger window has a menu command counterpart in the Tools→Debugging Controls menu. If you prefer the menus, or want to learn the keyboard shortcuts, this menu is your friend.

POWER USERS' CLINIC

Conditional Breakpoints

Some programs have a feature called *conditional break-points* that let you tell the debugger to stop on a certain line only when some condition is met. For example, you may want to stop only if the $count variable is bigger than 100, or if the found count is more than 1000.

FileMaker doesn't have built-in conditional breakpoints, but you can easily set up a similar scheme. Just add an If script step to your script that checks a meaningful condition. Then put a comment inside the If block and set a break point on the comment. FileMaker goes into the only If block when the condition is met; otherwise it skips right past it and the breakpoint it contains.

For example, you might add this to a long loop in your script, so you can break only after the loop has run 100 times:

```
If [$count > 100 ]
# break here
End If
```

If you set a breakpoint on the line with the "break here" comment, then you get the desired effect.

Breakpoints

In some situations, the click-the-step-button-for-each-step approach can become unacceptably tedious. For example, you may have a long script, and you know the problem part is near the end. To make your life simpler, the Script Debugger includes *breakpoints*. You set a breakpoint on any line you want, and then click the Run/Pause button. FileMaker immediately begins cruising through the script steps, running them at full speed. When it reaches the step with the breakpoint, it immediately stops so you can begin stepping manually.

You can set a breakpoint three different ways:

- In the Script Debugger window, select the script step, and then click the Set/Clear Breakpoint button.

- In the Script Debugger window, click next to the script step in the gray stripe along the left edge of the script steps.

- In FileMaker Advanced, the same gray stripe appears in the Edit Script window. You can click next to any step when editing a script to set a breakpoint. Using this method, you can set a breakpoint in a deeply nested subscript, before you debug the main script. Then, if you click Run/Pause, FileMaker runs through the script and its subscripts until it hits your breakpoint, saving you a lot of clicking.

No matter how you get it there, the breakpoint is indicated by a red arrow to the left of the script step. To remove an existing breakpoint, just click it again (or select the line in the Script Debugger, and then click the Set/Clear Breakpoint button again). The arrow disappears.

When you click the Run/Pause button, FileMaker runs to the *next* breakpoint it encounters (even if it's in one of the subscripts this script calls). If you find you've hit a breakpoint before the one you want, just click Run/Pause again to jump to the next one. In fact, adding breakpoints at key places in a complex script (and leaving them there) can make it easy to quickly debug the script later, as you Run/Pause your way through the major chunks, stopping to step through only the parts that currently interest you.

Examining Errors

Coping with errors can be a significant part of debugging a script. As you step through your script line by line, the debugger constantly updates the Last Error display just below the list of script steps (Figure 12-3). Normally this function shows 0 (zero) because most script steps don't produce an error. But if you *do* encounter an error, the error number appears right after the step runs, making it a breeze to see what error number a certain situation produced so you can handle it in your code.

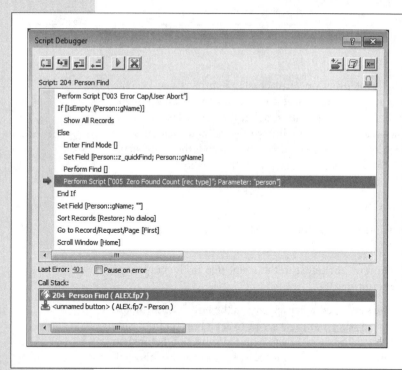

Figure 12-3:
As you step through your script, the debugger constantly updates the last error number. You can instantly see when an error happened, and what the error code is. Best of all, this error number shows up when error capture is turned on (so you can spot an otherwise silent error) and when it's turned off (so you can see the code behind the error message). So if you're looking for error numbers, watch this space. If error capture is turned on, it's the only place you can view the error condition.

You can even click the error number, which happens to look like a web link, and FileMaker shows you the help system page that explains each error code.

Pause on Error

If you know your script is producing an error *somewhere* (perhaps because an error message pops up when you run it), but you don't know where it's coming from, then the "Pause on error" checkbox is your friend. Just turn this option on, and then click Run/Pause. FileMaker runs the script full speed until any step produces an error.

When that happens, it stops so you can examine your place in the script, see the error number, and use the debugger controls to manipulate execution. You can also click the Edit Script button to jump to the trouble spot in the Edit Script window.

This feature also works whether or not error capture is turned on, so it may spot errors you're already handling. For example, a loop script that moves through a found set of records will throw an error when you get to the last record. While technically an error, FileMaker needs it to properly end the loop. When the debugger pauses on one of these, just click Run/Pause again to run to the next error. Keep going as necessary until you find the error you're looking for.

The Call Stack

The bottom part of the window shows you the Call Stack. *Call Stack* is a nerdy term for the list of actions that got you to the currently executing script. Every time a script performs another script, it moves down in the list to make room for the new script's information. FileMaker puts the topmost—and current—script in boldface at the top of the stack. Below it, you see the script that came before. If that script was itself run by another script, every thing drops one notch to accommodate the most recently called script. You can see how this looks in Figure 12-4. Of course, scripts don't run spontaneously. There has to be some action that puts things in motion. At the very bottom of a call stack, you can find that action with an icon to indicate what it is. Figure 12-5 explains each type.

Click a script in the list to switch the debugger's view to that script. The Current Position arrow changes color (white with blue outline) to indicate you're viewing a script that doesn't include the current script step.

Working with the Debugger Window

The debugger window doesn't work like FileMaker's other dialog boxes. When it's open on the screen, you can still interact with your database window. Even when a script is running (but paused waiting for you to step), you can move database windows around, switch layouts, and even type data into records. That way, you can poke around in your database while the script runs to see how things are progressing. It also lets you totally mess up your script by putting it in a state it would normally never reach, like an inappropriate layout, or a mussed-up global field. And although you can edit existing records, you can't create new records, delete records, or create new windows.

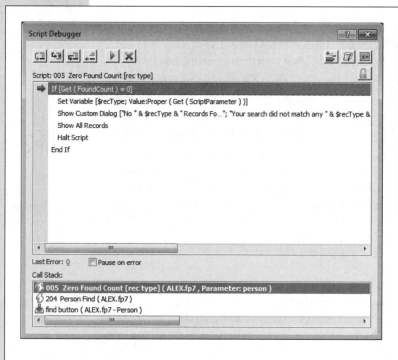

Figure 12-4:
When scripts call other scripts, FileMaker stacks the script names up in the Active Scripts list. On top— and in bold lettering—you see the name of the script you're currently looking at. Directly below each script is the name of the script that called it. If you have scripts calling scripts with more than three levels, then you have to scroll the list to see the oldest ones.

Figure 12-5:
Each kind of call gets its own icon in the Call Stack. From top: A plain scroll means the script was either selected from the Scripts menu or called as a subscript; the script name is to the right. The scroll with a star means it was invoked by a Script Trigger; the script name is to the right. The menu icon is for scripts called from a Custom Menu item; the item's name as it appears in the menus is to the right. The blue arrow is for scripts started by a layout button followed by the name of the button (if any). All stack types show the name of the file in parentheses. The button type adds the name of the layout where the button resides.

Since all this window manipulation is possible, you're free to arrange the debugger and database windows on the screen so you can see as much as possible while your script runs. You can also resize the debugger window at any time to make more space.

Warning: Before you get too hung up trying to fit your layouts on the screen so you can see field values and the like, read about the Data Viewer in the next section. It's often a better choice if you're trying to watch the data or variables change.

As long as the Script Debugger window is showing, FileMaker debugs any script that runs (even if it runs from clicking a button, or automatically when a file opens or closes). If you choose Tools→Script Debugger, then the debugger window disappears, and script execution goes back to normal. You can also simply close the debugger window to turn it off–if a script is executing at the time you close the debugger window, it will continue running until finished.

The Data Viewer

The *Data Viewer* grants you under-the-hood access to field data, variables, and calculations. It's usually the easiest way to watch things change as your script runs in the debugger. To show the Data Viewer, just choose Tools→Data Viewer, and it appears on your screen. You can also, in the Script Debugger window, click the Open/Close Data Viewer button. No matter how you get to it, though, it looks just like Figure 12-6.

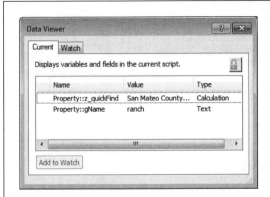

Figure 12-6:
The Data Viewer has two tabs, Current and Watch. Current shows information related to the script that's currently running in the debugger. Under Watch, you can tell FileMaker exactly what you want to see.

The Current Tab

If you open the Data Viewer (Tools→Data Viewer), and then switch to the Current tab, FileMaker strives to show you the most pertinent information about the script you're debugging. When a script starts to run in the debugger, the Data Viewer lists every field that the script uses in any way. For instance, if you use the Set Field script step to modify a field anywhere in the script, that field appears in the list in the Current tab. Likewise, if you use a field in an If condition, that field shows up, too. In addition to the name of each important field, the Data Viewer shows its current value (in the Value column) and its data type.

As you step through the script, the Data Viewer updates the value column appropriately, so it always reflects the current field value. It also helps to draw your attention to fields you should be watching, as Figure 12-7 attests.

The Current tab also shows information about script variables. Instead of showing every variable the script uses as soon as the script starts, the window shows a new line for each new variable as it's created. For example, the first time you use the Set Variable script step to set a *$customerID* variable, "*$customerID*" appears in the Data Viewer, along with its type and value.

The Current tab almost always shows you just what you need to see while you debug. It can be a huge timesaver, pointing out everything your script is using and what it's doing with data, so you don't have to run calculations in your head or scramble around different layouts. Open it early and often.

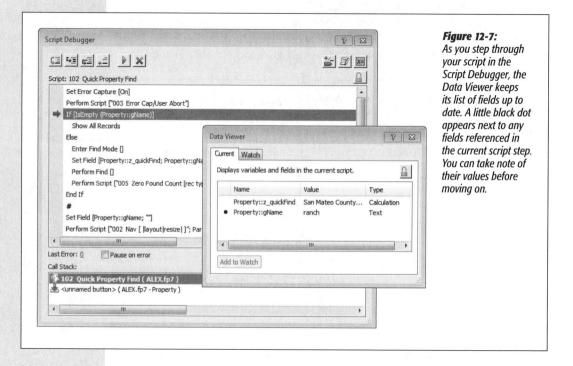

Figure 12-7:
As you step through your script in the Script Debugger, the Data Viewer keeps its list of fields up to date. A little black dot appears next to any fields referenced in the current script step. You can take note of their values before moving on.

The Watch Tab

The second tab in the Data Viewer, called Watch, shows the same kind of information as the Current tab, but you get to configure it yourself. Instead of magically showing the fields and variables your script is using, it shows the fields and variables you tell it to show. And it can show the result of arbitrary calculation expressions as well. You can see a sample Watch list in Figure 12-8.

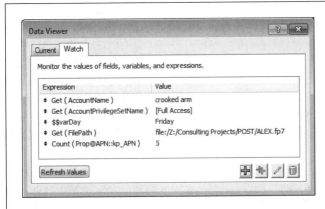

Figure 12-8:
The Data Viewer's Watch tab shows what you want to watch. You load it up with various calculation expressions, and it keeps tabs on their results for you. If you want to see a field value, then just put the field all by itself in the expression. Variables work the same way. But unlike the Current tab, you can even put variables and complex calculations here, and watch them as things change. In this window, the fourth line calculates the path to the file currently in use. Switch to a different file and the path will automatically update to the current file's path.

To add an item to the Watch list, click the Add button, it's the one with a single green plus sign. When you do, FileMaker shows you the Edit Expression dialog box (Figure 12-9). This window is almost an exact copy of the Specify Calculation window, except it has an extra text box at the bottom labeled Result, and it has two new buttons: Evaluate Now and Monitor.

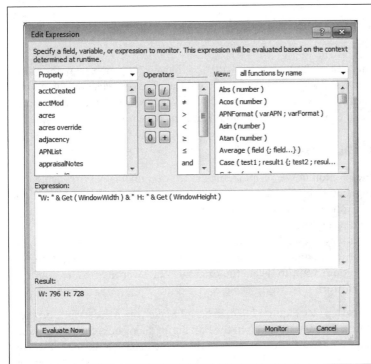

Figure 12-9:
The Data Viewer's Edit Expression window should look familiar—it's almost an exact replica of the Specify Calculation window. But this version can run the calculation in place and show you the result (just click Evaluate Now).

Differences aside, you can do anything here that you can do in the ordinary Specify Calculations window. In the Expression box, just enter any formula you want. When you click Evaluate Now, FileMaker performs the calculation and shows the result in the Result box at the bottom of the window. You can use this handy feature to test a calculation and correct it without jumping in and out of the dialog box.

When you're satisfied with the formula, click Monitor. FileMaker adds the expression to the Watch list, with its value beside it. FileMaker attempts to keep the values up to date, but it can't refresh some kinds of calculations (typically those that use Get functions). If necessary, you can click Refresh Values to automatically recalculate each Watch expression.

Note: You don't *have* to click Monitor in the Edit Expression window. It's sometimes handy to use this window when you're trying to write a calculation, even if you don't need to keep an eye on the results. Just click the Add button and fiddle with the formula until you have it right (clicking Evaluate Now whenever you need to see how it's doing). When you're happy with the results, copy the formula (Edit→Select All followed by Edit→Copy), and then click Cancel. You can now paste the tested-and-working formula into a field calculation or a script step.

The Data Viewer isn't attached to any particular file, so its Watch list contents don't change when you open and close files. The viewer can even be open while you have no databases open. Since all files and scripts share the same Watch list, it can quickly get long and hard to monitor. Select items you aren't using, and then click the Trash can icon to delete them.

Finally, if you need to see how certain calculations behave for people who don't have full access, log in as the person in question. In the Data Viewer, select the tab named "Current" then click the Authenticate icon to unlock its powers. You can now monitor values and edit expressions even though you don't have full access.

Disable Script Steps

The Set Next Step button in the Script Debugger lets you manually skip script steps while debugging, but it's not much help unless *you* remember to click it at the right time. Sometimes you have a script step (or several) that you always want FileMaker to skip. You could just delete them, but maybe you're not quite ready to. Perhaps it's code that isn't working yet, and you intend to come back later to fix it. Or perhaps you're moving the code somewhere else, and until you're sure you've got it moved and working, you don't want to delete the original. Whatever the reason, you may want to temporarily turn off a group of steps.

To turn off a script step (see Figure 12-10), in Script Maker, open the script, and then highlight the step you want to turn off. In the Edit Script dialog box, click the Disable button. FileMaker puts two slashes in front of the script steps you turned off so you can identify them. To turn a step back on again, first select it. The Disable button changes to say Enable; click it, and the step is back in business. As always, you can select *multiple* script steps at once, and turn them on or off all in one shot.

Turning script steps off is useful for debugging, but it can have long-term use, too. Any step you turn off in FileMaker Pro Advanced gets skipped whenever someone runs it—even in FileMaker Pro. So, say your company has a semi-regular promotion that creates discounts for a limited period.

GEM IN THE ROUGH

Keeping Watch

Some functions are very handy to keep in your Data Viewer's Watch tab all the time. When debugging a multi-file or multi-user database, consider giving these expressions long-term residency:

- **Get (FilePath).** Shows the name of the current database and where it resides on your drive or which server is hosting it.

- **Get (AccountName).** The account you're currently logged in with.

- **Get (AccountPrivilegeSetName).** Your current privilege set.

- **Get (LastError).** Lets you see errors even when the Script Debugger is closed.

- **Get (LayoutName).** For those times the toolbar is hidden.

- **Get (LayoutTableName).** Displays the name of the table occurrence the current layout is based on.

- **Get (WindowWidth)** and **Get (WindowHeight).** Useful to keep an eye on when designing a database for someone with a smaller screen than you.

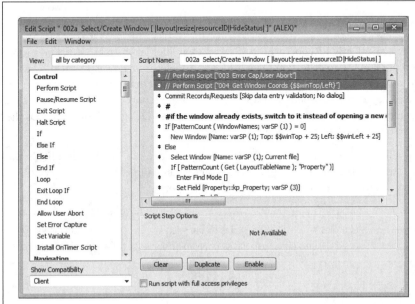

Figure 12-10:
Two steps (the Perform Script steps at the top) in this script have been turned off, as you can see by the double slashes in front of the names. When a script step you turned off is highlighted, the Disable button reads "Enable". FileMaker skips the steps you turned off when the script runs.

You don't have to write two different scripts, one with the discount and one without, and then worry about some kind of test to make them available on a button or in the script menu at the proper times. Write one script, making sure the discount creation steps are separate from the main process. Then you can turn on the pertinent steps when the promotion starts, and turn them off when it's over, with very little fuss.

The Database Design Report

Sometimes you inherit a large database from somebody else, and you simply don't see how it comes together. (OK, be honest. Sometimes *you* create a large database and still don't understand how it's put together.) While FileMaker's point-and-click display makes it easy to build databases, teasing things out later is a different story. You can look at a script, field, layout, table occurrence, or even an entire table in FileMaker Pro, and have no idea whether the database actually uses or needs it.

If you've shelled out for FileMaker Pro Advanced, however, you've got help. Its built-in internal analysis tool, the Database Design Report (affectionately called DDR), gives you an overview of your database, where you can easily see how database items are connected and other details, all in one place. You run the report, tell it what kinds of things you're interested in, and FileMaker presents the information in a series of web pages.

Unlike the reports discussed in Chapter 14, the DDR is a report about the structure of your database, not about the data inside. It tells you what tables and fields you have, which fields are used on each layout, and so on, but nothing about the information in your records and fields.

Generating the DDR

The Database Design Report window lets you tell FileMaker exactly what you want it to report on. You get to pick which files and table occurrences to include, what kinds of things you want to report on, and what format you want the report to use. You also get to decide whether you want to open the report right away, or just save it for later use. To get started, choose Tools→Database Design Report. Up pops the Database Design Report dialog box (Figure 12-11).

The Available Files list in this window shows every open file. To include a file in the report, turn on the checkbox by its name. FileMaker assumes you want every file at first, so you may have to do more turning off than on.

Tip: If you have a lot of files to turn off, you can Shift-click to select groups. Then if you turn off one file's checkbox, every selected file turns off as well. This same approach applies to tables in the list on the right.

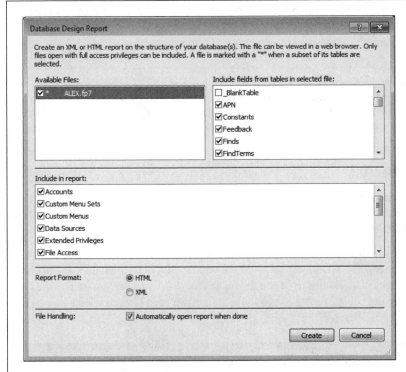

The report includes field information for tables in each file. Select a file in the list to see all its tables in the "Include fields from tables in selected file" list. Again, you can use the checkboxes in this list to tell FileMaker which tables you want included in the report.

The "Include in Report" section has a checkbox for each kind of database element the DDR can report on. Again, FileMaker assumes you want everything, but you're free to limit the report to just certain information. The less you report on, the faster the report runs, and the smaller the final files.

Normally, FileMaker saves the report in HTML format so you can read and navigate it in any web browser, but it also offers a more structured XML format. XML files aren't easy for *humans* to read, but with the help of other software, you can process the XML, and integrate information about your database into other systems. Furthermore, some companies make DDR analysis tools that process the XML version of your DDR and provide extra tools for browsing, finding, and reporting on the information it contains.

When you're done making decisions, click Create. FileMaker asks you what to name and where to save the report (For simplicity's sake, it's probably best to keep the automatic name "Summary"). The DDR is made up of several files, so you probably want to make a new folder to hold the report. The more complex your files, the longer it takes to create the DDR. In a file with dozens of tables, each of which may have dozens or even hundreds of fields, this could take a minute or more. FileMaker displays a progress bar for you, so you can gauge how long the process will take.

Note: A DDR is a snapshot of the database at the moment you create it. So it's good to make periodic DDRs as your database evolves. You can create a record of when you added or changed various parts of the database. A DDR can also help with troubleshooting broken elements.

Using the DDR

If you turned on "Automatically open report when done" when you create an HTML formatted DDR, then FileMaker launches your browser and shows you the DDR Report Overview (Figure 12-12) as soon as the progress bar disappears.

This window shows the main report file, and it has URL links that bring up the detail pages. To view the DDR later, go to where you saved it, and then open the primary file, usually called "Summary" though you can name it whatever you wish at the time you create the DDR. (You also see a folder named for each file you selected when you created the DDR.)

POWER USERS' CLINIC

Getting the Most from the DDR

At first glance, you may not appreciate the true value of the DDR. It appears to tell you the same things you can find out in other FileMaker windows, like Manage Database, Script Maker, and so on. But once you run your first DDR, you understand it has powers those flimsy boxes never dreamed of.

For example, the DDR information for a script helps you determine how the script functions in and interacts with the rest of the database. In a neat chart, you can see every field, layout, table, table occurrence, and custom function

the script uses. More importantly, you can see every script or layout button that runs this script. That kind of information would be very hard to nail down without the DDR. You'd basically have to go to each layout in your database, click anything that might be a button, and see if the script you're interested in is attached to it.

If you've created custom menus, you'd have to check them individually, too. The DDR gathers up all that information for you—not just for scripts but for tables, layouts, value lists, and other kinds of database elements as well.

On the overview page, the DDR tells you which elements you chose when you created the DDR. If you click a file name, then you see the file detail page (Figure 12-13), with lots of information about that file. The links in each column go to the same file detail page, but each link scrolls you to the relevant section. On large databases, with lots of fields, this option can save you a lot of time scrolling through the page, looking for what you want. For instance, if you click the number in the Relationships column, you see the Relationships section of the file detail page.

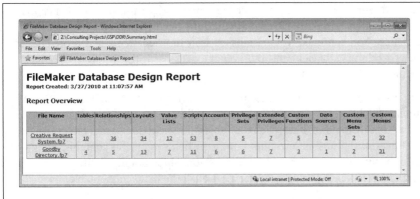

Figure 12-12:
Report Overview is the first thing you see when you open a DDR. It's a table, with one row for every file you included in the report, and a column for each option you checked when you created the DDR. Each "cell" contains a link leading to more information. Each DDR lists the time and date of its creation, so you can compare it to the current state of your database.

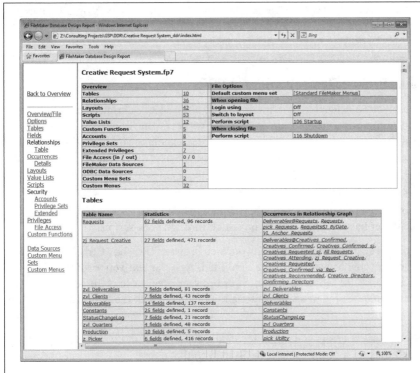

Figure 12-13:
On the Report Overview page, when you click the File Name link, you see this page. The top link on the left leads back to the Overview page. All the others just scroll the page to various important parts. The report itself is also loaded with links. You can click any link to go to more details about that item.

Use the DDR to help you figure out what parts of your database can safely be edited or deleted. Since you can so easily create tables, fields, and layouts in FileMaker, you may well end up with extras that you don't need when your database reaches completion. You can make your database easier to understand, and more efficient, by deleting these extra elements. But even if a database is the last word in efficiency, running a DDR is one of the best ways to trace the designer's thinking process.

To see if—and how—a particular element is used, look at its detail. Suppose you have a bunch of fields you'd like to delete from your database, and you want to find out whether it's safe to do so. First, click the Tables link; fields are part of tables. You see a list of tables, with information about how many fields each table contains, along with a list of occurrences of each table in the Relationships graph (Figure 12-13). Click the link for a table's fields, and you see a list of all the fields in that table.

Details appear in the Field Name, Type, and Options columns for every field. Comments, if there are any, show up in the Comments column. Any layouts or scripts that use the field are listed in the On Layouts and In Scripts columns, respectively. You see the information in the Relationship column only if it's a key field. Fields used in layouts, relationships, and scripts are called *dependencies* of those elements.

Note: Even if you don't use a "Go to Field" script step for a specific field, a field may be listed in the scripts column. "Go to Related Record", or any other step that uses a relationship, also requires the use of that relationship's key field, so it also has that field as a dependency.

Finding Broken Elements with the DDR

Suppose you've deleted a field, unaware that it's used in a script. Your script could be run numerous times, not *quite* working, without your knowledge. The DDR is a great way to check for errors like this. Say, for example, you unwittingly delete a field used in a script. If you examine that script in Script Maker, then you can see the words "<Field Missing>" right in the script:

```
Set Field [Expenses::<Field Missing>; "==" & Get (ScriptParameter)]
```

To spot every error like this, though, you have to open every script and read through it. FileMaker has no facility to let you search through your scripts.

But you *can* search the DDR page in your web browser. (Pressing Ctrl+F or ⌘-F does the trick in most browsers.) In the Find field, type the text you're looking for, and then click Next (or whatever button your browser uses) to start the search. You see the first instance of your search criteria highlighted. Click the button again to find other instances.

The whole list of errors you might search for appears below. If you have any inkling what kind of error you're looking for, start with that one:

- **<Missing Field>.** Referenced field is missing.

- **<Missing Table Occurrence>.** Referenced table occurrence set is missing.

- **<Missing Base Table>**. Referenced base table is missing.

- **<Missing File Reference>**. Referenced file reference is missing.

- **<Missing Layout>**. Referenced layout is missing.

- **<Missing Valuelist>**. Referenced value list is missing.

- **<Missing Custom Function>**. Referenced custom function is missing.

- **<Missing Script>**. Referenced script is missing.

- **<Missing Account>**. Referenced account is missing.

- **<Missing Privilege Set>**. Referenced privilege set is missing.

- **<Missing Extended Privilege>**. Referenced extended privilege is missing.

- **<Missing Custom Menu>**. Referenced custom menu is missing.

- **<Missing Custom Menu Set>**. Referenced custom menu set is missing.

Once you find a broken element, return to your database, and then fix it manually. The DDR doesn't update itself to show your fix until you run another one. And since you can't mark the electronic version of your DDR, a good way to keep track of your work is to print it out, and then mark off each item as you fix it. Then, when all the broken elements are fixed (or you've deleted all the unused stuff), run another DDR. This time it should be clean, but if it's not, you've got the tools to fix it.

POWER USERS' CLINIC

Prevention Is Worth a Pound of Cure

Why use the DDR to fix your mistakes when you can prevent them in the first place? Here's a technique you can use next time you want to delete a field, script, layout, or any other important element. If you're not completely certain you don't need the element, you can use the DDR to check for you.

First, in FileMaker, *rename* every element you plan to delete. Put something noticeable and consistent in each name. For example, you might put "TO_BE_DELETED" before each element's name.

Once you've renamed every doomed element, run a fresh DDR. Choose the HTML type. When the report is finished,

search it for the code words you put in each name ("TO_BE_DELETED," in this example). FileMaker should find each element you've marked for deletion. But it also finds this element in the list of dependencies if it's still in use. For example, a field you're pondering deleting might show up in a script. Unless that script is also marked for deletion, you have a situation you need to investigate further. Once you're sure the things you're deleting aren't used by anything else, you can delete them with confidence.

Custom Functions

No FileMaker feature is quite so pervasive as the calculation. Calculations show up in field definitions, scripts, custom menus, security settings, and conditional formatting. Chapters 8 and 15 are all about employing FileMaker's calculation engine to manipulate your data. But you, the red-hot developer that you are, can do something with FileMaker Pro Advanced that takes calculations to a whole new place.

Functions are the primary building blocks of a calculation. You can build basic calculations around two or three of FileMaker's 250 or so built-in functions, while some of the most complex may draw on a dozen or more. But as your databases grow more complex, you'll inevitably find yourself using some of the same calculations over and over again. Enter the custom function. With a custom function, you can centralize oft-used calculations and avoid rewriting them (and introducing errors) again and again. Better still, if you have to make a change to your calculation weeks or months after it was created, you won't have to track down and modify it in every place you used it. Just change the custom function, and the update ripples through your database instantly. To create and edit custom functions, you need FileMaker Pro Advanced.

You create custom functions in the Manage Custom Functions dialog box (Figure 12-14). Custom functions have to follow the same syntax as FileMaker's regular functions. That is, you provide a name and, optionally, one or more parameters.

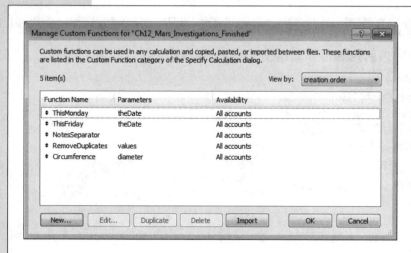

Figure 12-14:
The Manage Custom Functions window (File→Manage→Custom Functions) is where you go to create your own functions. It shows a list of any custom functions you've defined, plus buttons for creating, editing, duplicating, or deleting custom functions. As usual, you can sort the list by making a choice from the "View by" pop-up menu. Finally, when you're all done, click OK to save all your changes, or Cancel to close the window and ignore any changes you've made.

Rules for custom function names and their parameters are similar to the rules for naming tables and fields. Specifically, function and parameter names may not:

- Contain + – * / ^ & = ≠ < > ≤ ≥ (, :) [] : $ }

- Contain AND, OR, XOR, NOT

- Begin with a digit or period

- Have the same name as another function, parameter or keyword

If you violate any of these rules, FileMaker shows you a warning message. Unlike the slight leeway you get with table and field names, the program doesn't let you finish creating your custom function until you comply with the naming rules. You're safest sticking with alphanumeric characters.

Once you've created them, you can see Custom Functions in a special category of the Specify Calculation window's functions list (Figure 12-15).

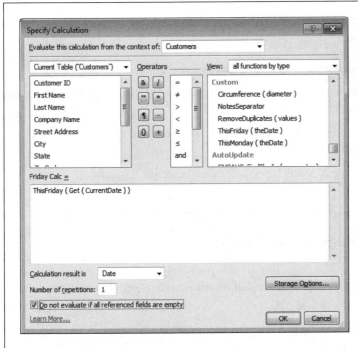

Figure 12-15:
Unless you say otherwise, all custom functions appear in the functions list of each Specify Calculation window. Here the list is arranged as "all functions by type". You can see the several custom functions from Figure 12-14 listed in alphabetical order. Just below them are the plug-in functions for a free plug-in that lets FileMaker Pro download updates from FileMaker Server. You'll learn more about plug-ins on page 667.

Defining a Custom Function

To get started, you'll add a new function that can calculate the circumference of a circle. Since a circumference is derived by multiplying the circle's diameter by Pi, it makes sense to use the words "circumference" and "diameter" in your function. That way, your formula will be easy for other people to use later.

Note: You may not actually need to calculate circumferences in your own databases much, but this example shows important concepts common to creating any custom function. Plus, it's easier to type than most real world examples. See this chapter's sample file, Custom_Functions.fp7, on this book's Missing CD page at *www.missingmanuals.com* for other examples.

---

1. **In FileMaker Pro Advanced, choose File→Manage→Custom Functions.**

   You see the window shown in Figure 12-14. If you've never created your own function before, the list is blank—but not for long.

2. **Click the New button.**

   The Edit Custom Function window appears. You can see it in Figure 12-16.

3. **In the Function Name box, type *Circumference*.**

   You've just given your function a name, which you'll call upon later when you want to use this function in calculations.

4. **In the Function Parameters box, type *diameter*, and then click the Add Parameter button (Figure 12-16).**

   FileMaker moves "diameter" into the parameter list.

Tip: When you add more than one parameter to the Function Parameters list, you can use the arrow icon by each item to move it up or down in the list. The order here's important: It determines the order in which you want the parameters to pass to the function.

---

5. **From the View pop-up menu (above the function list), choose "Trigonometric functions".**

   The function list changes to show just the relevant options.

6. **In the function list, double-click the *Pi( )* function, and then click the * operator button (or type *).**

   The function calculation area now reads *Pi **.

7. **Finally, in the parameter list, double-click "diameter".**

   FileMaker adds the word diameter to the end of the calculation, like so: *Pi * diameter*.

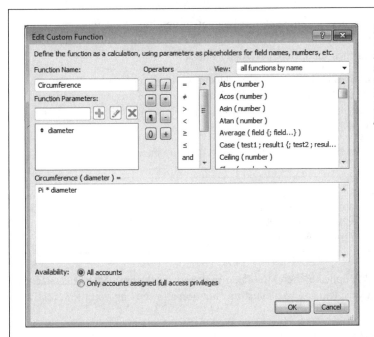

Figure 12-16:
The Edit Custom Function dialog box is very much like FileMaker's regular calculation dialog, but where the latter's shows tables and fields, this dialog box has spaces for the name of the function and its parameters.

When you're done, click OK, and then OK again to close the Edit Custom Function and Manage Custom Functions dialog boxes. The database has a brand-new function called Circumference. To use the Circumference function, create a calculation field that uses it, and point the parameter to a field that contains a diameter value.

Note: The standard setting in the Availability options lets anyone who accesses your database see and use the custom function in her own calculations. If you turn on "Only accounts assigned full access privileges", the function still works for everybody, but only superusers (page 764) can see the function in the Functions list.

Editing Custom Functions

You probably feel like a pro at the Manage Custom Functions window already, since it works a lot like other FileMaker dialog boxes. But even you could end up with a custom function that needs adjustment or repair. To edit an existing custom function, either double-click its name, or select it from the list, and then click Edit. In the Edit Custom Function window (Figure 12-16), you can modify the definition of a function as follows:

- To change its name, in the Function Name box, type a new name.

  You can add new parameters, just like you added the "diameter" parameter in the Circumference function. If you no longer need a function parameter, select it, and then click the Delete Parameter button.

- To change a parameter's name, first select it in the parameter list. When you do, FileMaker puts the parameter in the Parameter Name box, where you can edit it. When you're done, click the Edit Parameter button to apply your change to the one in the list.

- You can reorder parameters by dragging them up or down in the list.

Note: Be careful adding, reordering, or deleting parameters for an existing function. If the function is being used in a calculation somewhere, then that calculation breaks because it no longer passes the right parameters back to the function. On the other hand, it's safe to *rename* a function or its parameters—FileMaker updates any existing calculations when you do.

- If you click Duplicate, then FileMaker makes an exact copy of the selected function. That way, you can use a custom function as a starting point for creating a new one

- If you don't need a function anymore, select it, and then click Delete.

Note: Unlike built-in functions, Custom Functions can be *recursive,* meaning a custom function can run itself repeatedly until a given condition has been met. To learn about recursion, find yourself a nice, quiet place where you can concentrate and skip ahead to page 663.

Sharing Custom Functions

Custom functions reside within individual FileMaker database files. So if you've come up with a spectacular custom function you want to reuse in another database, you'll have to move it over there first. Prior to FileMaker Pro Advanced 11, moving custom functions among files was a bit tricky. Happily, you now have two easy ways to move these bundles of code between databases.

Warning: Whichever method you choose for sharing Custom Functions among databases, be certain to test each function at its new location. Custom functions can reference other custom functions, but if you copy or import one custom function without the others it relies on, *FileMaker doesn't warn you of your omission*. It does, however, comment out the imported function's calculation, a sure sign something is awry. As you bring custom functions into a new file, select each one in the Manage Custom Functions dialog box, and then click Edit. If you see the calculation wrapped in /* *comment markers* */ you've got a missing reference to track down.

The Manage Custom Functions dialog box now sports an Import button, which you can see in Figure 12-14; it's the third button from the right. Click Import, and then select another FileMaker database file to behold the Import Custom Functions dialog box, shown in Figure 12-17. It lists all of the custom functions in the selected database. Simply turn on the ones you'd like to bring into the current database file, and then click OK.

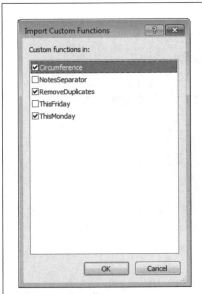

Figure 12-17:
Importing custom functions from another file is merely a matter of checking off the ones you want to bring over and clicking OK. If you have a repertoire of custom functions you frequently use, consider keeping them all in one database and importing them into your new databases as needed.

UP TO SPEED

Using Custom Functions

You can use custom functions just like any of FileMaker's built-in functions. When you're in the Specify Calculation window, choose Custom Functions from the View pop-up menu to access the functions you've made. (When you create a custom function, you're adding it to the FileMaker file you're working in. It isn't available in other files unless you add it to them as well.)

Just like other functions, custom functions can also use other custom functions to do their job.

For example, if you want to add a new function that calculates the surface area of a cylinder, then it can take two parameters (diameter and height) and use your custom Circumference function, like so:

```
Circumference (diameter) * Height
```

With this in mind, you can create functions that build upon one another—to keep each one simple, or to provide different but related capabilities.

The second, secret way to move custom functions is to simply copy and paste. It's a secret in that the Manage Custom Functions dialog box offers no Copy and Paste buttons, But if you select one or more functions and then press Ctrl+C (⌘-C), the custom function is copied to your computer's clipboard. You can then click OK, switch to another database file, choose File→Manage→Custom Functions to open the Manage Custom Functions dialog box, and then press Ctrl+V (⌘-V) to add the function to that file.

POWER USERS' CLINIC

Think Locally, Share Globally

There's a world of FileMaker developers out there and chances are that one of them has already written the Custom Function you need, or at least one like it. Here are a couple websites where you can peruse Custom Functions created by others in the FileMaker community and share your creations too.

Brian Dunning's website has over a thousand custom functions: *www.briandunning.com*.

The folks running fmfunctions.com have an entire website dedicated to custom functions: *www.fmfunctions.com*.

A terrific all-around resource, fmforums.com has a modest library of custom functions available: *http://fmforums.com*.

FileMaker Today, another discussion website, offers a custom function thread. *http://filemakertoday.com*.

Custom Menus

FileMaker's menus are all about power. Through them, you can control—and limit—people's access to the whole feature set. As the developer, you need all those commands to do your design and development of your database, but plenty of commands give too much power to people, particularly folks who don't have much computer experience or who aren't shy about experimenting with commands, even if they aren't sure what might happen at the other end of a dialog box.

Luckily, with FileMaker Pro Advanced, you can completely customize the menus people see. You can remove the Delete All Records and the Replace Field Contents commands for everyone, or you can remove them only from certain people's privilege sets. If you're the type of developer who likes to take charge of the onscreen display, custom menus are your dream come true.

Here are just a few of the things you can do:

- Remove potentially destructive items from menus: Delete All Records, for example.

- Edit menu commands: Change Modify Last Find to read Repeat Last Find, perhaps.

- Add, edit, or remove keyboard shortcuts: If you can't remember that Ctrl+S (⌘-S) does *not* mean Save in FileMaker, then you can at least prevent that pesky Sort dialog box from popping up every time.

- Remove entire menus, like the Window menu, which can be confusing for folks new to FileMaker Pro.

- Run a script from a new or edited menu item: Substitute a custom Delete Record script (complete with a custom warning) for FileMaker's normal Delete Record command.

- Change menus when a user changes layout: Create a special menu that runs commands or scripts that pertain to invoices and shows up only on the Invoice layout.

- Make one set of menus for Mac and another for Windows.

- Make menu sets that match privilege sets: Give admin-level people a special menu showing the scripts only they can run.

You can create and edit custom menus only in FileMaker Pro Advanced, but anyone can use them. These menus don't transfer to files you publish on the Web, though (Chapter 17). When you create custom menus for a database, you may want to provide a User Guide or similar documentation explaining what your custom commands do, since people can't look up the commands you add in FileMaker's help system.

UP TO SPEED

Tricky Terminology

The terms used in custom menus can be very similar, but they mean very specific things. Just in case it gets a little confusing, this mini-glossary and Figure 12-18 should help keep things straight.

- *Custom menus* refers generally to FileMaker Pro Advanced's ability to create your own menus.

- A *custom menu set* is a complete group of menus (like File, Edit, View).

- A *custom menu* is just one of the individual menus that comprise a custom menu set.

- A *custom menu item* is the thing you actually choose from the custom menu. FileMaker provides three types:

  — The *command* is the most common. When selected it performs some kind of action.

  — A *separator* is simply a horizontal line used to group similar commands within a given custom menu.

  — A *submenu* is like a custom menu nested within a custom menu. You can add menu items to a submenu that only appear onscreen when the submenu is selected.

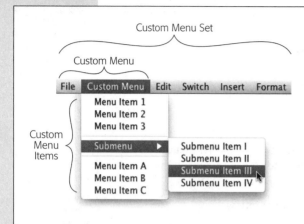

Figure 12-18:
FileMaker lets you create all kinds of custom menu items. If they all start to run into one another as you work, check back here for a refresher.

You can use custom menus to supplement, and even go beyond, privilege set features. For example, if you want to limit data entry people to using the copy and paste buttons that run your scripts, then remove the Edit menu for people with that privilege set. They can't use keyboard shortcuts to cut, copy, or paste. Removing the View menu prevents the Mode pop-up menu, toolbar, and all related keyboard shortcuts from working. (But you need to do some work providing replacement commands in your buttons and menus.)

Note: As powerful as custom menus are, they're no substitute for good security practices, as discussed in Chapter 18. For example, just because you don't see a Delete command right in front of your face doesn't mean you can't delete records. For example, if you turn off the ability to delete records using only custom menus but forget to attach your menu set to a particular layout, FileMaker's standard menus, including Delete Record will be present and available. If you need to prevent someone from doing something, *you must restrict it by privilege set.*

Editing a Menu

All new files you create use FileMaker's standard menu set unless you tell them to use a custom set. Just as each new file contains three standard privilege sets, you get one set of custom menus that you can edit to suit your needs. And as with privilege sets, some items are in brackets and can't be edited or duplicated, but you're free to create new menus with the same name, and customize them.

In this exercise in customizing menus, you want to remove menu items that may confuse people. When people are just learning FileMaker, simplified menus are less intimidating than masses of unfamiliar commands. You can also help protect your database from damage by someone unwittingly choosing the wrong command. You start the process by editing the View menu so that only a few items show up:

1. **In FileMaker Pro Advanced, choose File→Manage→Custom Menus.**

   In the Manage Custom Menus dialog box that appears (Figure 12-19), click the Custom Menus tab.

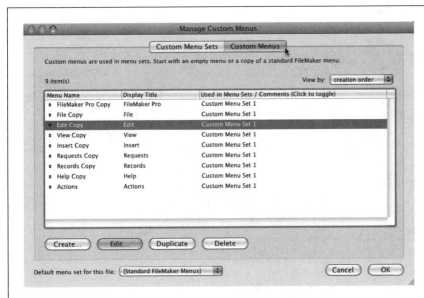

Figure 12-19:
You can reorder the items in the Custom Menu list with the "View by" pop-up menu. You can also click each of the column headers to sort the list. Probably this window's most important item is the small pop-up menu at the bottom. You can do all the editing of custom menus you like, but unless you remember to switch to your custom set, you don't see any change in your file.

2. **Double click Custom Menu Set 1, then, in the Custom Menu list, click "View copy", and then click Edit. Or you can double-click an item to edit it.**

   The Edit Custom Menu window appears (Figure 12-20). Here, you tell the custom menu what it should look like, and how it should behave.

3. **Click the radio button beside the Override Title field, and then, in the field, type Switch.**

   The Override Title option changes what someone sees in his menu bar. You changed it to Switch since the word "View" is too vague for beginners. Plus, you don't want them getting confused if they pick up FileMaker's manual (or this book) for help. The changed menu name should clue people in that they need to look at your custom documentation for help.

   The menu's name *in this dialog box* remains View Copy; that's how you know it originated from the normal View menu, not from scratch.

Warning: If you customize menus even in the slightest, consider turning off the built-in Help menu as well. It opens FileMaker's online help file, which can't answer people's questions about *your* custom menus. If you need documentation, then you can add your own Help menu that leads people to the custom-crafted help on your website, for instance.

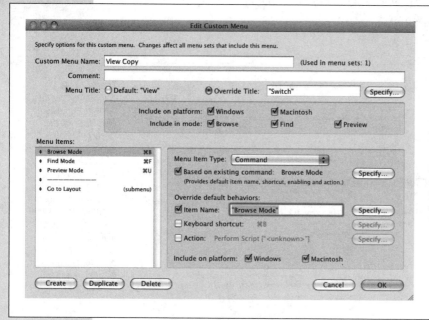

Figure 12-20:
The Edit Custom Menu dialog box has many splendors. You can specify that a menu appears only when someone's on a Mac, or only when she's in Find mode. You can add, change or remove keyboard shortcuts. You can even take the liberty of replacing a command's normal action with a script.

4. **Select the dashed line in the Menu Items list just below "Go to Layout (sub-menu)", and then press Shift as you select the last item in the list. Click the Trash can icon. Select Layout mode, and then delete it.**

   All highlighted items disappear when you click the Delete button (those hyphens represent divider lines in menus). You should be left with three mode menu items, a divider, and a "Go to Layout" menu (a total of five items) remaining in the list.

5. **Click the Browse mode menu item. As with View mode in step 2, turn on the override checkbox, and then change the title to Browse.**

   This menu item title replaces the text that appears in the list. People see a command called *"Browse,"* not Browse mode. Notice the quotation marks around "Browse". If you forget (or refuse) to type the quotes, FileMaker obstinately puts them back in for you. This behavior is your indication that FileMaker considers that text a character string, and that's a further cue that the Specify button gives you access to the Calculation dialog box.

6. **Repeat the previous step for Find mode, Preview mode, and "Go to Layout". Change Find mode's title to Find, change Preview mode's title to Print Preview, and then change the title of "Go to Layout" to Show. When you've made these changes, click OK.**

   Use terms that folks can easily comprehend. Most people already understand what Print Preview does, but Preview mode's meaning is a little murky.

7. From the "Default menu set for this file" pop-up menu, choose "Custom Menu Set 1", and then click OK.

You've just told FileMaker to display the customized version of your View menu.

The View menu now says "Switch". When you click it, you see four choices and one separator. Notice that the Edit Layout button is grayed out, and Layout mode has disappeared from the Layout pop-up menu at the bottom of your screen. Also, the commands in the pop-up menu match the changes you made in the View custom menu.

By editing menus to suppress items that might confuse those who haven't had in-depth FileMaker training, you've made your database a friendlier place to work. But don't stop there: In the next section, you'll learn how to create menus that show lists of commands, like your scripts, that you *do* want people to see.

Creating a New Menu

Using the steps described in the previous tutorial, you can edit FileMaker's menus to your heart's content, renaming them, and deleting extraneous commands to make room for new ones. If you don't necessarily want to delete any existing menus or commands, or even if you do, you can always create *additional* menus from scratch.

1. In Manage Custom Menus, select the Custom Menus tab, and then click Create. In the Create Custom Menu window that appears, choose "Start with an empty menu". Click OK.

If an existing menu is similar to what you need, you can use it as a template when you create new menus. But in this case, you don't need any existing menu commands because you'll attach your scripts to a new menu. When you click OK, the Edit Custom Menu window appears, like Figure 12-20 but without any menu items just yet.

2. In the Custom Menu Name fields, type *Invoices*. Also type *Invoices* in the Override Title field.

Since you started with an empty menu, FileMaker assumes you want a custom name. If you don't type a name, then, in your menu bar, the word "Untitled" appears.

3. Next to "Include in mode" uncheck Find and Preview.

You don't want your scripts run from either Find or Preview modes, so by telling the menu not to even *show up* in those modes, you're adding another layer of security.

4. Click the Create button.

In the set of options that appears to the right confirm that "Menu Item Type" is set to Command.

5. Turn on the Item Name checkbox, and then type *Create invoice for unbilled expenses.* Turn on the Action checkbox.

    The Specify Script Step dialog box appears,

6. Select Perform Script, and then click Specify. Select the script named Create Invoice for Job, and then click OK. Click OK once more to close the Specify Script Step dialog box.

    To add more commands to this menu, repeat the last three steps until you've created a new menu command for each script you want to make available. The arrows to the left of each item let you rearrange them.

    To add a divider line between groups of menu commands, click Create, and then set the Menu Item Type to Separator.

7. **When you've created all the commands you wish to include in your new Invoices menu, click OK.**

    You have to include your shiny new Invoices menu in a custom menu set in order to use it.

8. **In the Manage Custom Menus dialog box, click the Custom Menu Sets tab. Select "Custom Menu Set 1" in the list, and then click Edit.**

    The Edit Custom Menu Set window appears.

9. **Click Add. Down at the bottom of the menu list, you'll find Invoices (Figure 12-21). Click it, and then click Select.**

    "Invoices" appears at the bottom of the Custom Menu Set menu list.

10. **To the left of the Invoices menu, click that little double arrow, and then drag it up until it's positions between Records Copy and [Scripts].**

11. **Click OK until you're back in your database.**

The Invoices custom menu is now a part of the new custom menu set, and it appears between the Records and Scripts menus of Figure 12-22.

Using Existing Commands

While there's great power in attaching scripts to custom menu items, if you just need a menu item that's already in FileMaker's standard menu set, you can save yourself the trouble of writing a script for it. When you're creating or editing a menu item in the Edit Custom Menu dialog box, try turning on the "Based on existing command" checkbox. FileMaker offers up a list of all the built-in menu items along with the menu where each one typically resides. Figure 12-23 depicts the process. When you select an existing command, your menu item is automatically imbued with the same name, keyboard shortcut, and behaviors as the original it's based on. That's handy, but you're free to customize those settings as much as you see fit.

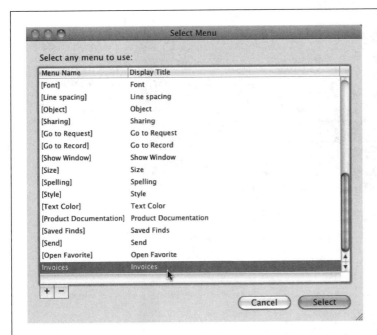

Figure 12-21:
When you select a menu to add to your custom menu set, FileMaker's built-in (and unchangeable) menus appear in square brackets: [ ]. Custom menus are unencumbered.

Figure 12-22:
This custom menu has two menu items for creating invoices and two for printing with a separator between them. The separator appears as a row of hyphens in the Edit Custom Menu dialog box, but it appears in the actual menu as a clean horizontal line.

Examine the list of existing commands closely, and you'll find that one command has a blank space in the "Normally appears on" column. FileMaker 11's new Quick Find feature comes with a Perform Quick Find command that isn't available in any standard menu. But you can use it in a custom menu item to let your database's users trigger a Quick Find. (For about a refresher on Quick Find, refer back to Chapter 4.)

Submenus

If a custom menu starts getting too lengthy, you can use submenus to consolidate its options. A submenu is a custom menu nested within a custom menu. (Flip back to Figure 12-18 to see an example of a submenu.) Creating a submenu is a combination of two things you already know how to do: making a custom menu and adding a menu item.

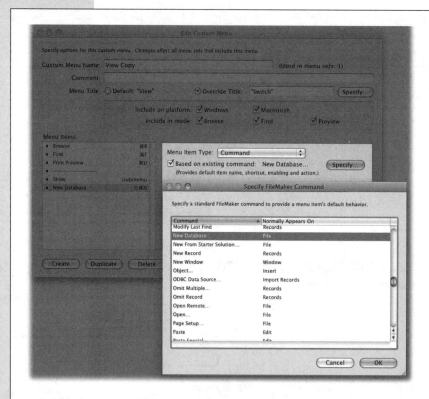

Figure 12-23:
The Specify FileMaker Command dialog box (front) automatically pops up when you turn on "Based on existing command" (highlighted in the background) in the Edit Custom Menu dialog box.

Say, for example, you have a custom menu called Reports, and you want one class of reports, we'll call them "TPS Reports" to appear in a submenu. You can do this example in any FileMaker database you'd like. First, create a new custom menu, using the steps on page 543, and then add a menu item for each report you want in the submenu. Click OK when you're finished.

1. **Back in the Manage Custom Menus dialog box, select the custom menu in which you want the submenu to reside, and then click Edit.**

    The Edit Custom Menu dialog box appears.

2. **Click Create to add a new menu item, and set the Menu Item Type to Submenu (Figure 12-24).**

3. **Click the Specify button immediately below "Menu Item Type".**

    The Select Menu dialog box appears with a list of all the built-in menus and those you've created.

4. **Scroll down to the bottom of the list to locate the "TPS Reports" custom menu you just created and double-click it.**

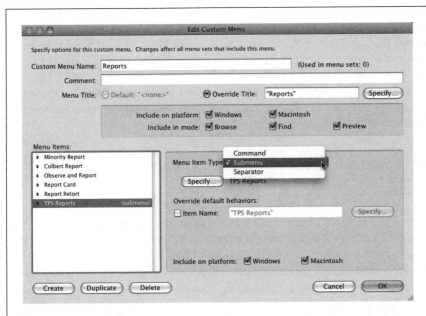

Figure 12-24:
Adding a submenu is as simple as setting the Menu Item Type to Submenu. You have to create that submenu as a custom menu first. Only then can you add it as a Submenu.

5. **Click OK until you're back to your database window.**

   With your custom menu set active, you'll see your new submenu, like the one in Figure 12-25.

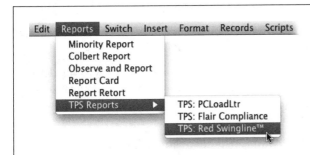

Figure 12-25:
A Submenu is simply a Custom Menu nested inside another Custom Menu. When judiciously applied, Submenus can help keep menu commands organized and accessible. That way, if you've got four bosses each of whom needs three different TPS reports, you could go ahead and come in to the office on Saturday, or you could group them neatly into subfolders and knock off work early.

So far, you've simplified one of FileMaker's menus, and created a custom menu from scratch. Now you need to get rid of a menu that strikes fear in the hearts of even experienced FileMaker users: You're going to *completely* suppress the Window menu.

Removing a Menu

At first glance through the Manage Custom Menus dialog box's Custom Menus tab, you may think you just click an item in the Custom Menu list, and then click Delete to remove it. But you run into problems if you do. Delete, say, the Help Copy menu used in Custom Menu Set 1 and you get a nasty surprise when you click OK, and then return to your file. You see the text "<Menu Missing>" inserted in the menu bar, and the Help menu stays right where it was. Despite these obstacles, you *can* remove an entire menu; you just have to dig a little deeper to do it.

Note: You can troubleshoot a file for missing menu items by running a DDR (page 526), or by checking *Get (LastError)* after you load a menu set in a script.

The Window menu can cause problems for new people. For example, the Show command lists files they may not know are open. Hiding and showing windows is also perilous for new folks if they don't understand how FileMaker manages windows. Instead of bothering people with stuff they don't need to know, you can just suppress this menu entirely by removing it from the menu bar.

1. **In the Manage Custom Menus dialog box, click the Custom Menu Sets tab. Select Custom Menu Set 1, and then click Edit.**

   The Edit Menu Set dialog box appears.

2. **In the Menu Set Name field, type *Data Entry*.**

   This descriptive name helps you remember the menu set's purpose. If you like, type additional information in the Comment box.

3. **In the "Menus in 'Data Entry'" list, click the [Window] menu. Click Remove, and then click OK until you're back in your database.**

   Usually brackets on a list item indicate you can't delete it. But you *can* delete it from the display list, as you've just done. The [Window] menu remains in the Available Custom Menus list at left. If you change your mind, you can move it back into the display list to restore it.

Back in your database, the Window menu is gone entirely from the menu bar. This menu configuration is ideal for your data entry people, but not so great for administrative people, who understand the Window menu and use it all the time. Read on to find out how to tailor *sets* of menus for people with different privilege levels.

Installing Custom Menu Sets

FileMaker Pro Advanced lets you create a set of custom menus and use it as the *standard* for a file, meaning everyone who uses your database sees it, every time. But since the people using your database may have different levels of skill (and trust), you may want your custom menus to adapt accordingly. In fact, if you've read this book's chapters on layouts and privilege sets, you have all the tools you need to make the right menus appear to the right people at the right time. It's a simple matter of assigning menu sets to these existing features. You can conceal certain menus and commands from people who don't need them, but keep them available for everybody else. Or maybe you just want menu items to show up when they make sense for the active layout.

Once you've created menu sets using the steps outlined earlier in this chapter, you can install them in any of several ways:

- **As the standard for a file.** That's what you did in the tutorial on "Editing a Menu". Unless you tell FileMaker otherwise, everybody gets the same custom menus. This option works great for a runtime file, or any situation where everyone's at the same level.

- **On individual layouts.** In this scenario, when someone switches layouts, either by menu command or through a script, the menu set changes to a layout-specific one of your choosing. Figure 12-26 shows where a menu can be attached to a layout; in Layout mode, choose Layouts→Layout Setup to get there.

- **By mode.** This option offers the ultimate in elegance. It lets you do things like create a set with only one menu and just a few items, and make it the *only* menu people see when they're in Find mode. Instead of a gaggle of buttons to perform and cancel finds, write the appropriate scripts, and display them in the one menu, short and sweet.

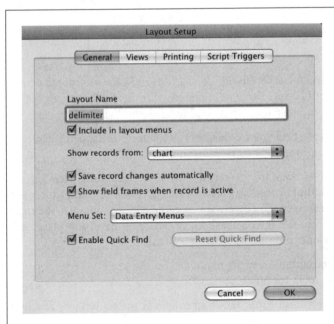

Figure 12-26:
Custom menus can be tied to particular layouts thus ensuring the user easy access to useful commands and little exposure to potentially harmful ones.

- **When a script is run.** By checking the privilege set in a script that runs when someone logs into your file, you can load a set of menus customized to that person's level of privilege. Use the *Get (PrivilegeSetName)* step to check privileges (page 796) and the Install Menu Set script step to specify which menu set installs. (If you have a re-login script, then you need to make sure the right menu set is installed each time people re-login.)

Note: Since you're effectively removing features for people when you customize menus, thorough testing is a critical part of the process. Be sure to test menus with all affected layouts, privilege sets, and scripts, and across platforms. In FileMaker Pro Advanced, choose Tools→Custom Menus to switch among sets as you test them.

Developer Utilities

The Tools→Developer Utilities command looks insignificant and benign to the unsuspecting person, but behind it lurks a vast array of powerful features. You have developer utilities for the following techniques:

- Rename one file in a system of interconnected files, and have every file reference in the *other* files automatically update to the new name.

- Turn your database into a *kiosk* system. You can use this feature to make interactive programs that run on publicly accessible computers. In this setup, FileMaker hides the menu bars, the Windows taskbar or Macintosh Dock, and all other screen decorations that aren't part of your layouts.

- Create a *runtime solution*—a special version of your database that anyone can use, even if he doesn't have FileMaker Pro.

- Permanently remove full access to files so you can send your database to people you don't know, and be sure they can't tamper with your hard work, including your scripts, table and field definitions, and Relationships graph.

- Create an error log to help you troubleshoot problems that happen when FileMaker generates runtimes.

In fact, you can (and often want to) do several of these things at once. Here's an example: You build a beautiful interactive product catalog, complete with pictures and an easy-to-use ordering screen. You then want to set up a kiosk computer at a trade show where attendees can use the database to see what you have, and place their orders. Using the developer utilities, you could do all this:

- Add "Kiosk" to the end of every file name, so you can keep this copy separate from the one you use in the office.

- Make the database run in Kiosk mode so people at the trade show can't exit FileMaker, switch to other programs, or otherwise cause mischief.

- Make the whole thing run by itself so you don't have to bother installing File-Maker on the computer you're renting just for this job.

- Lock out full access so if someone manages to steal a copy of your database while you're not looking, she can't see how it works or steal your product's beauty shots.

Using the Developer Utilities

The developer utilities' most confusing aspect is that you have to *close* your files before you work with them. So close the files you want to modify, and then choose Tools→Developer Utilities. You behold the Developer Utilities window (Figure 12-27).

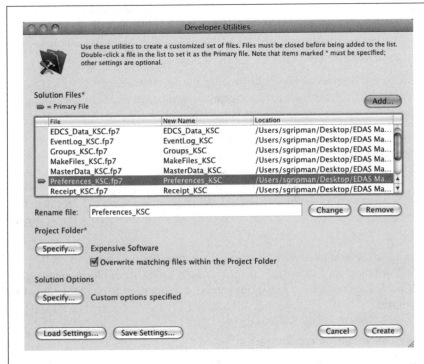

Figure 12-27:
The Developer Utilities window (Tools→Developer Utilities) lets you gather the files you want to change, and then tell FileMaker what changes to make. When you're done, click Create, and FileMaker builds new versions of your files (in a new location) with all the changes in place.

In the Developer Utilities window, you first choose which files you want to work with. Click Add to put a file on the list. In the Open File dialog box, you can select several files at once using your Shift and Ctrl (⌘) keystrokes. Keep on adding until every file you want to change is in the list. If you accidentally add the wrong file, select it, and then click Remove.

You have to pick one file to be your *main* file. This file is the one that opens first if you create a runtime solution, for example. To set the main file, in the list, just double-click it. FileMaker shows a red square—it looks surprisingly like a script break-point—by the main file.

Renaming files

Of course, you can always rename a file in Windows Explorer or the Mac's Finder. But doing this lets you change *only* the file name. Developer Utilities makes that look like child's play. When it changes a file name, it also looks inside the file, and updates any internal file references to match the file's new name. If you've ever tried to open two versions of a multiple file solution at the same time (to test some scripts that delete data and on a copy of the files, say), then you know FileMaker sometimes gets confused and keeps multiple copies open even after you try to close one set. You can eliminate the crossover problem by renaming one set in Developer Utilities. You can test your scripts without a problem, since the scripts in the copy files automatically inherit the correct new file names.

To rename a file or set of files, add them to the Solution File list (Figure 12-27). Select a file; in the "Rename file" box, type the new name, and then click Change. FileMaker shows the new name in the New Name column.

Next, you need to pick the *project folder*. FileMaker saves the finished files in this folder. Under "Project Folder", just click the Specify button, and then pick any folder you wish. If the folder already contains files with the same names as the ones you're about to create, then you get an error message—unless you turn on "Overwrite matching files within the Project Folder". When you click Create, FileMaker Pro Advanced makes copies of the files with their new names, leaving the originals untouched.

To complete the example above (your kiosk product catalog), you turn on "Create Runtime solution application(s)", "Remove admin access from files permanently", and "Enable Kiosk mode for non-admin accounts". You need to configure only the first option.

Create runtime solution application(s)

To create runtime solutions, add the files to the Solution Files list, and then select a project folder, just as you did above. Don't type a new name for the runtime in this window, though. Under Solution Options, click the Specify button. You see the Specify Solution Options dialog box, as shown in Figure 12-28.

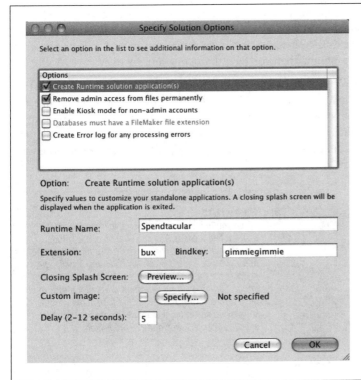

Figure 12-28:
The Specify Solution Options window lets you tell FileMaker what you want done to the files. Turn on a checkbox in the options list to tell FileMaker you want that thing done to your files. Most options need to be configured, and when you select an item in the list, the bottom half of the window lets you change the appropriate settings.

When you tell FileMaker you want to build a runtime solution, it generates a special program you need to include with your databases. This program can do most of what FileMaker Pro can do, but it can't modify tables, fields, layouts, or scripts. You get to decide what this program is called—in the Runtime Name box, just type it. Along with the runtime program, FileMaker creates new copies of each of your files to go with it, and changes all the file name extensions to something other than .fp7. Tell FileMaker which extension to use in the Extension field.

Warning: Your computer's operating system uses file name extensions to figure out which program files belong to. The Developer Utilities let you assign any extension you want, but you should avoid common extensions like .doc, .jpg, .mp3, and so on. You know computers—they get confused easily.

The new files don't just have a new name; they're also modified internally so they're *bound* to the runtime program, and the runtime program in turn can open only properly bound files. In other words, when you send people a runtime program, they can't use it to open any old FileMaker Pro file.

To facilitate the binding process, FileMaker asks you to provide a *bindkey*. FileMaker stores this value in both the runtime program and any database files in the Developer Utilities window. The value you use for the bindkey is entirely unimportant, and you don't have to keep it secret. But if you later want to bind *new* databases to the same runtime program, then you have to use the same bindkey.

Finally, when people exit the runtime program (in other words, when they close your database system), they see a "Made with FileMaker" splash screen like the customized version shown in Figure 12-29. Are you among the three percent of computer users who *enjoy* splash screens? If so, you'll be delighted to learn that the splash screen can't be turned off. However, you can't admire that screen more than 12 seconds at a time.

Figure 12-29:
When you quit a runtime solution, this window pops up for a few seconds. You can't get rid of the "Made with FileMaker" logo, but you can (as so modestly done here) override the big FileMaker Logo that usually appears in the top half of the screen. Just turn on "Custom image," and then, from your hard drive, pick a picture file. FileMaker stretches the picture to fit in the window, so to avoid distortion, you should create a picture that's exactly 382 pixels wide and 175 pixels high.

Remove admin access from files permanently

The "Remove admin access from files permanently" option doesn't actually remove the accounts that have full access. Instead, it modifies the [Full Access] privilege set so it no longer truly has full access. If you log in with an account that used to have full access, it will no longer have access to the Manage Database window, Layout mode, or Script Maker, and its access to Accounts & Privileges is limited to the Extended Privileges tab. This option has no settings.

Enable Kiosk mode for non-admin accounts

If you turn on Kiosk mode, and open the file using an account that has full access, it won't look any different. But if you log in with a lesser account, *everything* changes. The screen goes completely black, except for the content area of your database window. When you use Kiosk mode, you typically hide the Status toolbar and let people control everything using the buttons on layouts. Alternatively, you can use Custom Menus to hide all the menus and commands that would let nosy people poke around in your file. Remember to troubleshoot your file before creating a custom runtime from it, because any problems in your file (broken links, missing data, bad scripts) also show up in the runtime. Once you've suppressed all the normal FileMaker commands, folks have no way of getting around these problems.

Databases must have a FileMaker file extension

Sometimes people, Mac types especially, create databases without the .fp7 file extension, only to regret that decision later. An extension is the computer's most compatible way to identify a file. So turn on "Databases must have a FileMaker file extension", and FileMaker adds ".fp7" to the end of every file name that doesn't already have it.

Create error log for any processing errors

While FileMaker processes your files, applying your options, building runtime programs, or renaming files, it may encounter problems. Turn on "Create error log for any processing errors" so you can see what went wrong. FileMaker saves error messages in a file on your hard drive (you get to pick where it goes and what it's called).

Loading and saving settings

If you maintain a database system that other people use, you may well run your files through Developer Utilities every time you send out a new version. To save you the tedium of configuring the Database Utilities dialog box again and again, FileMaker lets you save all your settings to a special file—just click Save Settings. Later, when you're ready to process your files again, click Load Settings, and then select the same file. FileMaker sets up everything in the dialog box for you. All you have to do is click Create.

Delivering a Runtime Solution

If you build a runtime solution with FileMaker Pro Advanced in Mac OS X, it runs *only* in Mac OS X. Likewise, if you build from Windows, your runtime solution is limited to Windows. If you need a runtime solution for *both* platforms, then you have to buy FileMaker Pro Advanced for Mac OS X *and* for Windows, and build a separate runtime solution on each kind of computer.

File Maintenance

Computer files are, alas, fragile things. The more a file is open and in active use, the more opportunity there is for something to go awry. A computer crash, power surge, power outage, or malfunctioning hard drive can corrupt your digital files. FileMaker databases are just as susceptible to corruption as any other file.

File corruption may be obvious–like an error message telling you to recover the file when you try to open it, or FileMaker crashing when you navigate to a particular layout or record. There are subtler forms, too; like a gibberish text suddenly appearing in a field or a record that never sorts into the right position. With appropriate care and maintenance, however, you can head off and even repair injury to your databases.

1. **Choose File→Recover.**

   The Select Damaged File dialog box opens.

2. **Click the problematic database, and then click Select.**

   The "Name new recovered file" dialog box appears (Figure 12-30).

Figure 12-30:
Recovery doesn't fix a file in place. Rather, it reads the damaged file and builds a new copy of it, fixing as much as it can in the process.

3. **Choose a location to save the recovered file. Turn on the Use Advanced Options checkbox, and then click Specify.**

   The aptly named Advanced Recover Options dialog box opens (Figure 12-31). You see three methods for making that new copy of your file.

   - **Copy file blocks as-is.** Copies the database as-is without scanning for damage.

   - **Copy logical structure** (same as Compacted Copy). This choice creates an optimized file that takes up less space on your hard drive and operates more efficiently. It's a good choice for keeping a file in shape *before* corruption shows up, but doesn't check for structural damage.

   - **Scan blocks and rebuild file** (drop invalid blocks). The heavy hitter of the bunch, this process reads every piece of data (those are the "blocks" it refers to) and removes those that appear to be damaged. It's a blunt instrument designed to salvage data even at the cost of structure like layouts and scripts. Use this only when a file won't open normally.

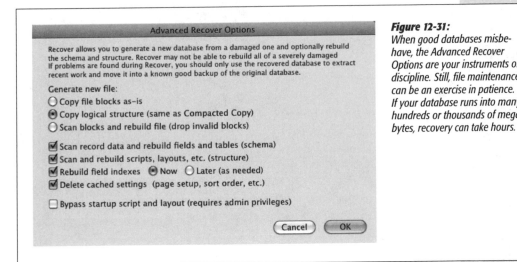

Figure 12-31:
When good databases misbehave, the Advanced Recover Options are your instruments of discipline. Still, file maintenance can be an exercise in patience. If your database runs into many hundreds or thousands of megabytes, recovery can take hours.

The next four checkboxes are automatically turned on, but you can toggle them to provide more refined control of the recovery process:

- **Scan record data and rebuild fields and tables.** A corrupt field may show gibberish where sensible text once appeared, or crash the database when clicked into, or even abruptly disappear leaving a "<field missing>" everywhere it was used. This option meticulously sifts through the damage and resurrects those wayward fields whenever possible.

- **Scan and rebuild scripts, layouts, etc.** Like the record data option, this choice provides first aid to the file structure components.

- **Rebuild field indexes.** Indexes are like invisible databases within a database. FileMaker relies on them to perform finds and sorts, display related data and execute certain calculations. A classic case of index corruption is when you perform a find for a value you're certain exists, only to have FileMaker claim no records match your request. Rebuilding the indexes typically alleviates this problem.

- **Delete cached settings.** If FileMaker keeps reverting to an old print setup (page setup on the Mac) configuration no matter how often you change it, try deleting the cached settings.

The final option is useful when a startup script isn't functioning as intended and you can't seem to stop it. "Bypass startup script and layout" ignores the corresponding settings under File→File Options thus allowing you to take corrective measures. You have to, however, possess a full access login or your attempts will be thwarted.

Advanced Relationship Techniques

I n the previous chapter, you learned how to use the tools in FileMaker Pro Advanced to make your development tasks—like debugging your database and creating custom menus—easier. That's a great start on thinking like a developer. Now it's time to turn your attention back to relationships and delve into some of the more powerful features in the Relationships graph. Your first relationships, like the ones you created on page 143, were of the most basic type: they used a single key field pair and the value in those key fields matched exactly. But you can also create relationships that work when values don't match, by using an operator other than the "=" sign. And just as you can add more criteria to a search, you can also add multiple criteria to a relationship. You do that for the same reason you add more criteria to a search: because you want the results to be more specific, as when you need a customer ID *and* a date field each to match corresponding fields in a related table. And just as you can sort a portal separately from the underlying relationship's sort order, the Portal Setup dialog box also lets you filter related records to show only some related records.

You'll also delve deeper into table occurrences. FileMaker lets you create as many instances of a table as you need on the graph. Once you know about more complex joins, you have the tools you need to start making those multiple table occurrences. But as your graph grows, so does the potential for problems, so you'll learn some organizing and structural concepts that'll help keep you on the right path as your table occurrences multiply.

Note: Sample files for this chapter are available on this book's Missing CD page at *www.missingmanuals. com*. Use the Invoices START.fp7 file to work through the chapter's tutorials. At the end of the chapter, you can compare your work to Invoices FINISHED.fp7 or use the file to get extra help as you work.

Advanced Relationships

A portal on a layout makes creating related records as simple as entering data (page 152). But another common use is to help your users avoid performing a find. Finds are relatively easy, but it can mean switching modes *and* layouts, especially when finding related records. So in addition to the relationships you create that act as your ER diagram (page 191), you'll also want to create relationships and portals that show specific related records. Then, when you add buttons or scripts that use a Go To Related Record step (page 225) to those layouts, users won't need to enter Find mode as often to see the data they need.

Self-Join Relationships

The Invoices layout of the Invoice.fp7 database has a Line Items portal and a second Payments portal. You can get a better picture of a Job's total costs by creating third portal that shows all the other invoices related to the current invoice's job. Sure, there's already such a portal on the Job layout, but if you're researching the way a particular job was billed, a button on a new portal could move you through a Job's invoice records, without needing to go back to the Jobs layout to get to the next invoice.

You'll need a special type of relationship, called a *self-join*, to make this portal. A self-join relationship is one in which a table is related to itself instead of to another table. Since you want the portal to show all invoices from the same job, you'll use the Job ID field as the key for the self-join relationship..Follow these steps to create a self-join:

1. **Choose File→Manage Database, and then click the Relationships tab.**

    The Relationships graph appears.

2. **On the Invoices table, drag the Job ID field out into the white space on your graph, and then drag it back onto Invoices::Job ID. Don't release the mouse button until you're back on the field.**

    The Add Relationship window appears (Figure 13-1). FileMaker sees that you're trying to add a relationship that could create an ambiguity in the graph, so it helpfully offers to create a new Table Occurrence (TO) for you. See page 561 for an explanation of ambiguity.

3. **In the "Name of Occurrence" box, type *Invoices_currentJob,* and then click OK.**

    The new TO appears on the graph. The "Invoices" part of the new TOs name tells you which table the TO comes from. The "_currentJob" part tells you that the relationship matches by Job. You could use the name "Invoices_jobID" instead, or any other nomenclature that makes it clear that this relationship is a special case that falls outside the set of TOs that form your ER diagram. (You can read more about naming conventions on page 579.)

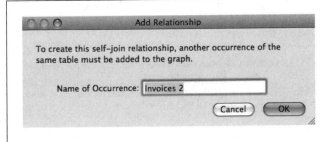

Figure 13-1:
Whenever FileMaker sees that you may be trying to create a relationship that'll cause ambiguity in the graph, you'll see this window. If you click OK, FileMaker will make a new TO and give it the name you typed in the Name of Occurrence: box. If you click the Cancel button, you don't get a new TO, but you don't get a new relationship either.

4. **If necessary, move the new TO so that it doesn't block other TOs. Click OK.**

The new relationship is ready to use on your layout.

Now that you've created the Invoices to Invoices_currentJob relationship, put a portal from the Invoices_currentJob TO on the Invoice layout (page 146). Add the Invoices_currentJob::Date and Invoices_currentJob::Total Due fields to the portal. To make the portal more functional, create a button that uses a "Go To Related Record" step (page 225) and place it in the portal. The GTRR step has to use the same relationship as the portal: Invoices_currentJob. When you're done, you can click the button to travel between all of the invoices that are related to a particular job. To show financial information for the Job below the portal, create a *Sum()* calculation (page 364) using this new relationship, and then display it on the layout below the portal.

Note: You could have avoided the warning message in step 2 by selecting the Invoice TO, and then clicking the Duplicate button to create the new TO. But it'd take more time, because you'd still have to change the TO name, and then expand the new TO to set up the match fields manually. See the box on page 563 for other ways to create relationships.

No ambiguity or circularity allowed

As you just saw, you learned that FileMaker won't let you create any relationships that would make the graph ambiguous. To understand what this means, recall the concept of *context*. That is, every TO is an instance of a particular table, which provides the context for any layout that shows records from that TO. So if you put the Jobs::Job Name field on the Invoice layout, it's as if FileMaker stands on the Invoice TO and looks through a window (or a portal...get it?) into the Jobs table to get the proper name for the job that's attached to the current invoice. Getting the job name is easy, because the Jobs TO is only one table occurrence away from the Invoices TO. But remember, you can also have FileMaker stand on the Invoices TO and get the Customer's name and address data, which is two TOs away. And to the degree that you have an unbroken line of TOs, it's possible to get data from many more "hops" away from the current context. In the sample database, you could "stand" on the

Payments TO and get data from the Customer TO, four hops away. And since most relationships are bidirectional (page 228), you could also stand on the Customer TO and view data from the Payments table or any point in between.

Tip: The Add Relationship and Edit Relationship dialog box is one of many places where FileMaker itself doesn't make the all-important distinction between tables and table occurrences. If you're not sure, take a look at the items in the Table pop-up menu. If you see names like Invoice_currentJob, or if the Table pop-up menu lists more names than you know you have tables, you can be sure that you're looking at a list of TOs, and *not* tables themselves.

Some other databases make you jump over piranha tanks and through flaming hoops to get to data that far away from your current context. But FileMaker takes its "ease of use" label seriously, so it handles the complexity for you. In exchange though, you can't create ambiguous (or circular) relationships like the faked one in Figure 13-2.

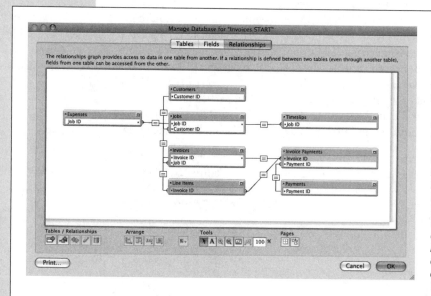

Figure 13-2:
There's a kind of a circle created by the lines representing the Invoices, Line Items, and Invoice Payment TOs in this graph. Say you're writing a calculation in the Invoices table that references the Payments table. Should FileMaker go through the Invoice Payments TO or the Line Items TO to resolve that calc? That's the ambiguity presented by circular relationships on a FileMaker graph. There's no way to specify which branch to take, so FileMaker just won't let you create a relationship like this one.

As you did in the step 2 on page 560, you can use the "no ambiguity allowed" rule to your advantage as a shortcut when creating relationships. And if you create a relationship, and then see the message shown in Figure 13-1, click OK, and then rename the new TO appropriately.

Note: Since having two table occurrences with the same name would also be ambiguous, FileMaker won't allow it. That's why your copy of the Invoice field had a "2" at the end of its name. But that's not very descriptive, so you changed it to Invoices_currentJob.

WORKAROUND WORKSHOP

When Dragging Doesn't Do It

Dragging isn't the only way to create a new relationship on the graph. Some folks like to click the Add Relationship button to start with a clean Add Relationship window. It's just like Edit Relationship, except that since it starts out blank, the Table pop-up menu at the top of the window aren't grayed out. That is, you have to start out by selecting the two table occurrences you want to relate. Then you can select your key fields and all the other options that get the relationship job done.

Using this method doesn't circumvent the rule forbidding ambiguity or circularity (page 561). FileMaker's not trying to be difficult. It's just letting you know that what you're trying to do doesn't work, and it's even going out of its way to suggest a solution. FileMaker's offering to create a new table occurrence for you. It's even smart about which table to create an occurrence for. (In the steps on page 560, you wanted a self-join relationship on the Invoices table.

So there wasn't any choice to make—you need another instance of the Invoices table.)

But say you're trying to create a new relationship between the Invoices table and the Customers table using the Add Relationship window. In that case, you'll get all the way through the process of selecting tables and key fields and operators before FileMaker can warn you that the relationship won't work and you need a new table occurrence.

You might wish the warning had been offered a little earlier in the process. But you do have control over which table gets the new occurrence. FileMaker creates the new TO for the table listed on the right side of the window. When you drag, FileMaker uses the direction you drag to decide which table to create a new occurrence for. That is, if you drag from Customers to Invoices, FileMaker will create a new TO for Invoices.

Multiple Criteria Relationships

Just as you can add extra search terms when you're performing a Find, you can also add criteria when you're defining a relationship. For example, the Invoices_Current-Job relationship is one place you might want to add another match field. Your new portal is convenient for jumping around to see the detail for other invoices related to the same job, but there's a slightly confusing element to that list. The invoice you're viewing on the layout also appears in the portal of "other" invoices. So if you're viewing Invoice #2010001, and you glance at the "other invoice" portal while you're distracted, it's easy to think that there are two invoices for $8,011.50. Just as bad, when you view a record that doesn't have any other invoices for the same job, the current invoice still appears in the list. The situation would be clearer if that list *didn't* show the current invoice. In this case, a multiple criteria relationship will remove the current invoice from the portal.

You define extra conditions in a relationship so that records only match when they're all met. In this case, you want to add another criterion to the relationship that says "don't show the record if it's the current invoice." Here's how to add a new criterion to an existing relationship:

1. **Choose File→Manage Database, and then click the Relationships tab.**

   The Relationships graph appears.

2. **Double-click the line between the Invoices and the Invoices_currentJob TOs.**

   It's easiest to double-click the box with the "=" sign in it rather than trying to hit the line itself.

   The Edit Relationship window appears. The Job ID to Job ID criteria appears in the list section.

3. **Click the Invoices::Invoice ID field, and then click the Invoices_ currentJob::Invoice ID field.**

   You're selecting the key fields for the new criterion.

4. **From the operator pop-up menu (it's between the two table occurrence lists), select the "≠" sign.**

   You want every record that has the same Job ID, but that doesn't match the current Invoice ID. In other words, don't show the current record in the "other" invoices portal. Learn more about other operators you can use on page 566.

5. **Click the Add button.**

   The new criterion appears in the list. Your window should look like Figure 13-3.

6. **Click OK.**

   Notice that the box on the line between Invoices and Invoices_currentJob has a new symbol, and both ends of the line are forked to indicate that it's a multiple criteria relationship (Figure 13-4).

7. **Click OK.**

   You're back on the Invoice layout. The current invoice no longer appears in the Invoices portal.

After you perform these steps, the portal shows invoices only where there's more than one invoice related to the same job. And the current invoice (the one you're viewing on the layout) never shows up in the portal.

If you created a *Sum()* function after the steps on page 561, you may notice that you solved one problem but have created a new one. That is, the current invoice no longer shows up in the list, and the calculation field shows the wrong total amount for the job. Because it's excluded from the relationship used by the portal, the current invoice isn't included in the sum calculation based on that relationship.

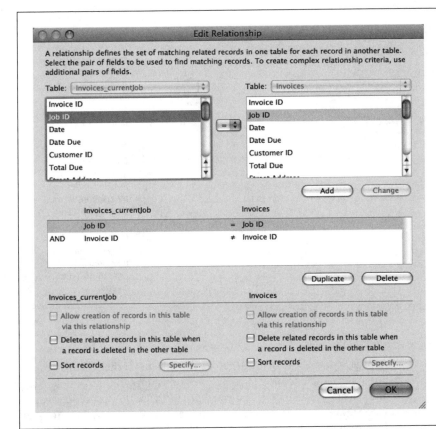

Figure 13-3:
This is a relationship with two criteria, sometimes called a multi-key (or multi-predicate) relationship, because it uses two sets of key fields in its definition. Notice the "AND" in front of the second criterion. In order for two records to relate, they have to meet both criteria. If you wanted to translate this relationships' description into words, you could say something like, "Show all records were the Job ID matches, AND where the Invoice ID does not match." It doesn't quite trip off the tongue, but it's accurate. Multiple criteria relationships are always AND conditions, never OR.

You can fix the problem by adding a new self-join relationship for the Invoice table (follow the tutorial on page 560 or copy the existing self-join TO, and then edit as appropriate). This one should be set to your original criteria of matching Invoice::Job ID to Invoice::Job ID (without the multiple criteria). Then change the *Sum()* calculation to use the relationship you just created. That way, the calculation takes the current invoice into account, and you get an accurate Job cost total, but since it uses a different relationship to show an invoice list, the portal *doesn't* include the current invoice.

And you thought you'd only ever need one table occurrence for any particular table. You have three Invoice TOs on your graph, and you've only just started finding reasons to create new ones. Later in this chapter you'll learn some techniques for organizing a graph when TOs start to multiply like rabbits.

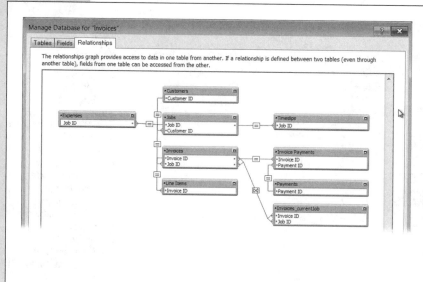

Figure 13-4:
Up until now, the relationship lines on your graph have been pretty much the same: an "=" symbol in the middle and a crow's foot on one end of the line. This line has forks on both ends, showing that two fields are involved in defining the relationship, and the odd sign (bow tie, perhaps?) in the middle of the box shows that different operators (below) were used in the criteria.

Editing a relationship's criteria

In the steps on page 564, you saw that you can easily add a new criterion to an existing relationship. It's so simple to drag to create a relationship, and then double-click on the new line's equals sign to edit it, that you'll probably use this technique even if you know you don't want a standard issue relationship right from the get-go. You can then use the Edit Relationship window to set up and add new criteria, to edit existing ones, or to delete criteria.

Tip: If you prefer, you can convert a single criterion relationship to a multiple criteria one by dragging between a new pair of fields. But you always get an "=" operator for this second pair and the Edit Relationship window doesn't open automatically when you do. So if you need anything nonstandard, you may as well just open the Edit Relationship window straightaway.

Relationship Operators

As you learned on page 564, sometimes you want a relationship to work when the values in key fields are different. But you might also want to show all Invoices after a particular date. In that case, you want to match dates when the values are greater than (>), or greater than or equal to (≥) the value in a key field. Here's a list of all the comparative operators:

- **Equals (=).** The keys on both sides of the relationship match exactly. This is the most common type of relationship.

- **Not Equals (≠).** All records but those with matching keys relate to one another. You just saw a good example: you want to show all related invoices except the one you're viewing. This operator is most often used in conjunction with another criterion.

- **Less Than (<).** Keys in the table on the left side of the dialog box have to be less than keys in the table on the right side. Use this operator to show all records with a date that's before the value in the date field on the right side.

- **Less Than or Equal To (≤).** Keys in the table on the left side of the dialog box have to be less than or equal to the keys on the right side of the table. Use this operator to show all records with a date that's before or on the value in the date field on the right side.

- **Greater Than (>).** Keys in the table on the left side of the dialog box have to be greater than keys in the table on the right side. Use this operator to show all records with a date that's after the value in the date field on the right side.

- **Greater Than or Equal To (≥).** Keys in the table on the left side of the dialog box must be greater than or equal to the keys on the right side of the table. Use this operator to show all records with a date that's after or on the value in the date field on the right side.

- **Cartesian Join (x).** All records in the table on the left are related to all records in the table on the right, regardless of the value in their key fields. A Cartesian join is the only one where it doesn't matter which fields you choose as keys. But if you like things nice and neat, pick the primary key in each table. This is the least-commonly-used operator. One example: the "Go To Related Record" step doesn't switch to the target layout if there are no records related to the record that's active when the step is run. That could leave your script running in the wrong context. If you need to switch to another context *and* it doesn't matter which records are active when you get there, you could use a relationship with a Cartesian join. As long as there's at least one record in the target table, the context will change.

As you go through the rest of this chapter, you'll see some of these operators in action. Now it's time to learn how another way to show just some of the related records in a portal.

Portal Filtering

Using a multiple criteria relationship as you did on page 564 is one way to change what displays in a portal. But when you change the relationship's definition, every portal, script or calculation that uses the relationship will change, too. But with an option in the Portal Setup dialog box, you can tell a portal to show records only under certain circumstances (say they're unpaid invoices) without changing the underlying relationship.

In the Invoices database the Customers layout has an Invoices tab, containing a portal that uses the plain-vanilla Invoices table occurrence. If you look on the Relationships graph, you can see that from the starting context of the Customers TO, the relationship travels through the Jobs TO to get to the Invoices TO. That means the portal currently shows all Invoices for all the current customer's jobs. Looking at it another way, when you view a customer record you can see all Invoices related to any job that's in turn related to the current customer.

If you wanted to see just the invoices that have a balance, you may think that adding another criterion to the relationship would do the trick. But that approach has its own problems. First, there's no direct relationship between the Customers TO and Invoices TO, so you'll have to go through the Jobs-to-Invoices relationship to change what appears on the Customer layout. If you changed that relationship's rules, everything that depends on the Jobs-to-Invoices relationship would change, too. Calculations that use the relationship would change to reflect the new rules, so the summary fields that show up at the bottom of the Jobs layout would change to show just those Invoices that are unpaid. Not only would your calculation amounts change, the Job layout's portal would change too, as would any scripts that use that relationship. Making a change to a relationship can have widespread, unintended consequences that are time-consuming to find and fix.

Or you may decide that you need a new occurrence of the Invoices table connected directly to the Customers table. You plan to use the ≥ operator on the Invoices::Balance Due field as your key for the new criterion. But you don't have an appropriate field on the Customer side to match with it. You *could* create a field called Zero, give it the calculated value of "0," and then use that as a key. But that plan adds two pieces of extra overhead (an extra field and an extra TO) to your database that don't really do anything except make a single portal work. Maybe you're willing to live with some cruft (that's the nerd term for the overhead your plan requires). But portal filtering gives you a non-cruft way to get the job done.

Here's the rule of thumb: If you want to change the records shown in a *specific* portal on a *specific* layout, portal filtering is the way to go. Much as you can sort a portal without sorting the underlying relationship (see the box on page 150), portal filtering brings the power of the Specify Calculation window to a portal without changing its underlying relationship. The *filter* part means that the relationship still determines which records are properly related to one another. But with filtering turned on, FileMaker analyzes each record individually to decide if it should show up in the portal. Think of portal filtering as a colander for your records. Some of them will get through, and some won't. You write a calculation that decides how to let records through the filter. Here's how to set up the Customer layout's Invoices portal to show only invoices that have a balance:

1. **In Layout mode, double-click the Invoices portal.**

    The Portal Setup window appears.

2. **Click the Filter portal records option.**

   The Specify Calculation window, appears. Above the Calculation box, the label reads "Each portal record will be visible when".

3. **In the calculation box, type *Invoices::Balance Due > 0*. Or if you prefer, double-click the field name to enter it into the box, and then type *> 0*.**

   However you do it, the calculation checks the value in the Invoices::Balance Due field before deciding whether to show each record in the portal.

4. **Click OK until you're back on the Customers layout.**

   The label at the bottom of the portal changes to show that it's filtered (Figure 13-5).

5. **Switch to Browse mode.**

   That's where you'll see the real changes.

Make sure you're viewing a Customer record with at least one invoice showing a Balance Due amount. Customer Daniel Greystone in your sample database will work.

Note: If the zero-balance invoice doesn't disappear immediately, you've been bitten by a portal refresh issue. Since it's based on a calculation, a portal filter kicks into effect when the values in the referenced. But changing data isn't possible or desirable here, so you can take any action that causes the window to refresh instead. Flip to the next record and right back, switch tabs, or if portal refresh bites you when you're scripting, add a "Refresh Window" script step.

You can't set up more than one filter per portal, but you can write a calculation that tests more than one condition. The calculation *Invoices::Balance Due > 0 and Invoices Total Due > 10000* would filter the portal to show only invoices with a total of over $10,000 and that still have a balance due amount. You have all the power of the calculation engine at the service of creating the filter you need. For instance, you could use a Case statement (page 654) to test a condition before deciding whether to apply a filter. You can even use a variable (page 689) to filter a portal dynamically. That is, the portal's contents could change each time the script runs if the value in the variable changes. Let your calculation wizardry rule the day.

Note: Portal filtering is most helpful where you expect the set of records to be fairly small, say fewer than a couple of hundred or so. There's no hard and fast rule, but since FileMaker has to look at every related record to decide if it can pass through your filter, performance can suffer with large numbers of related records. If a portal doesn't display records quickly, you may have to live with whatever cruft it takes to make a multiple criteria relationship to do the same job. All that extra overhead does yield some speed increase, so performance is a good determining factor in which method to use.

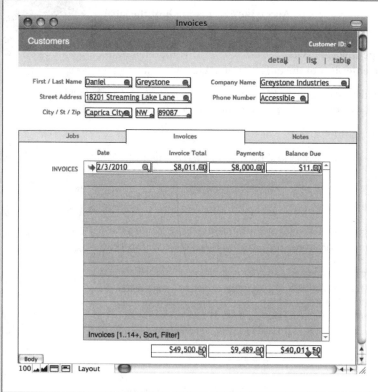

Figure 13-5:
This portal's label reads "Invoices [1..14+, Sort, Filter]. There's a lot of information packed away in those few characters. "Invoices" is the name of the related table occurrence the portal uses to show the proper records. It shows the first 14 related records (the "1..14" part) and has a scroll bar to show more (the "+" sign), where appropriate. The words "sort" and "filter" mean that you've selected those options for this specific portal. To see the sort order or the filter calculation, double-click the portal to show the Portal Setup dialog box.

Understanding Table Occurrences

As you first learned on page 144, tables and table occurrences aren't the same thing. Now it's time to dig a little deeper into that concept. At their foundations, TOs are graphical representations of the underlying table. They describe which records you can view based on your current context. Because these occurrences are representations, you can make new occurrences of a table without duplicating it (and all its data). FileMaker's not trying to confuse you; it's actually helping you relate to the same table in different ways.

Few databases can manage all their tasks without multiple occurrences of the same table. You've already seen a couple of situations that call for new TOs on the graph. But there are also functional reasons to create new TOs, too. For example, the Invoices database has an Expenses table to record things you buy to service your customers. It also has a Line Items table to record the charges you pass along to your customers. Right now these tables are connected only by way of the Jobs table (Figure 13-6).

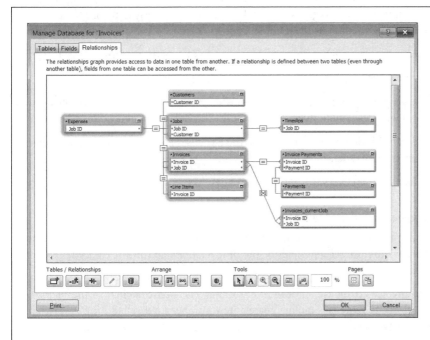

Figure 13-6:
Right now, your Relationships graph still looks a lot like your ER diagram (page 191). The Expenses, Jobs, Invoices, and Line Items tables are highlighted so you can see how they're connected, but you can look more closely at this set if you examine them in your sample database. The only relationship between an expense (which you need to be reimbursed for) and a line item (which allows for reimbursement) is through the Jobs table, and then to the Invoices table.

Even though there's no direct line between Expenses and Line Items, they *are* related. Each Expense record has a Job ID that can match an Invoice with the same Job ID. But there's no direct relationship between any single Expense item and its corresponding Line Item, so you can't look at an Expense record to see if it has been billed, or, if it has been billed, which Invoice Line Item bills it. Of course you *could* type some text into the Line Items::Description field to help you remember, but that's not very convenient from the Expenses point of view, nor would that create a relationship between the tables. You really need a whole new relationship—one that directly connects Expenses and Line Items. This new relationship lets you use "Go to Related Record" commands to toggle between expenses and invoices, and display fields from the related Line Item record on the Expenses layout to make it completely clear that the item's been billed.

Your new relationship will be "one-to-one." In other words, one Expense Line Item is related to one, and only one, Invoice Line Item. One-to-one relationships are fairly rare birds. One example you've seen in this book is a table of bike racers and a photo of each rider, with a one-to-one relationship between each. There, a photo is an attribute of the rider and just as easily could be contained in the same table. This new one-to-one relationship—Expenses to Line Items—is even rarer, in that it connects two completely different *types* of data. It's also unusual in that it's not integral to your database's structure. Unlike the other relationships in this database, you could delete it and the main part of your system would still work just fine. This relationship exists for one purpose only: to give your database a convenient way to record the Line Item on which an Expense has been billed.

To create this new relationship and make it work properly, you need three things:

- A new primary key (page 198) to hook the two tables together.

- A way to represent the new relationship in your Relationships graph without throwing the whole thing into disarray. That's right—a new table occurrence.

- New fields on one of your layouts (the Expenses layout in this case), to show the newly related data.

The next section covers the entire process.

Adding a new key field to a table

Before you can hook up the new table occurrence, you've got to make sure both tables have the proper key field for the new relationship. In this case, the Expenses table needs a Line Item ID field. (See the box below for more detail.)

In the Invoices database, choose File→Manage Database, switch to the Fields tab, then select the Expenses table. Create a new number field called Line Item ID, and then click OK when you're done. You'll use this new field to relate the Expenses table to Line Items.

UP TO SPEED

Deciding Which Table Needs a New Occurrence

When you create a new occurrence of a table, you're giving that table a new meaning in the relational structure of your database. But when you're thinking about the problem of creating a direct relationship between the Expenses and Line Item tables (see the next page), how do you know which table to make a new occurrence for? To answer that question, ask yourself this one: Which table has the information I need to see? Here are the three possible scenarios; see which one you think makes the most sense:

- If you make a new Line Item occurrence—call it Expenses_LINE ITEMS—you can access it from any table occurrence in the system. To solve the immediate problem, you could put Expenses_LINE ITEMS fields on the Expenses layout. (You *couldn't* put fields from Expenses on the Line Items layout because that layout is attached to the Line Items table occurrence, not the Expenses_LINE ITEMS occurrence.)

- If you decide to create a new occurrence of the Expenses table instead, then the opposite is true: You can't view line item information from the Expenses layout, but you *can* view expense information from the Line Item layout. In this case you've given expenses a new meaning (billed expenses, perhaps).

- If you want, you can create new occurrences of *both* tables. If you do, you can see expense information from a line item *and* line item information from an expense. But unless that plan solves a particular need, you're only creating more work for yourself.

Once you have your answer, you know which table needs a new foreign key field. In this case, you'll add a Line Item ID field to the Expenses table.

Adding a table occurrence

Since you want to access line item details while you're on the Expenses layout, you'll create a new TO for the Line Items table. And you need to make a new relationship between the Expenses TO and the Line Items TO using your new Expenses::Line Items ID key field. Figure 13-7 shows what that Relationships graph might look like with the new Line Items TO. With the new graph in mind, here's how to create that additional TO in your Customers database:

1. **On the Relationships tab of the Manage Database dialog box, click the Add Table Occurrence button (on the bottom left).**

    The Specify Table dialog box appears (Figure 13-8).

2. **Select the Line Items table from the list, and then, in the Name box, enter *Expenses_LINE ITEMS.***

    You want a descriptive name so you can pick it out of a lineup later.

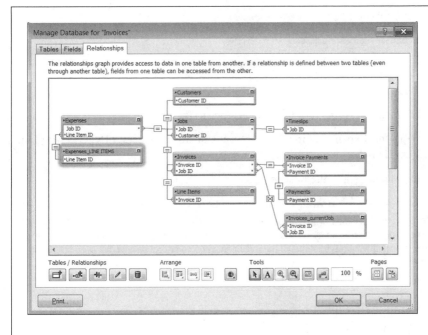

Figure 13-7:
The new occurrence of the Line Item table connects directly to the Expenses table. Two paths go from Expenses TO to the Line Items table, but because the TOs are named differently, FileMaker knows exactly which path to take to retrieve the records you need. The plain-Jane Line Items TO sits below the Invoices TO to make that relationship more clear. The new Expenses_LINE ITEMS TO is below the Expenses TO, again signifying its relationship to its "parent" table.

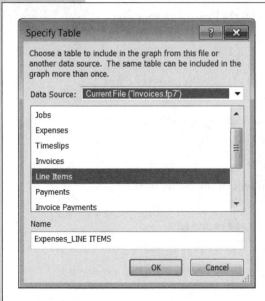

Figure 13-8:
The Specify Table box lets you tell FileMaker what table to use when you make a new table occurrence. You also get to give the new occurrence a name. When you name a new table occurrence, the goal is to help you remember the source table for the new table occurrence. The new TO's name is Expenses_LINE ITEMS. The "Expenses" part of the name tells you why you made the new TO—to help tie invoice line items to the proper expense records. "LINE ITEMS" is in all caps, so you can remember that the new TO comes from the Line Items table.

3. **Click OK.**

   FileMaker adds the new table occurrence to the graph, and selects it for you.

4. **Drag the Expenses::Line Item ID field to the Expenses_LINE ITEMS::Line Item ID field.**

   FileMaker creates the relationship.

Note: If you don't see the Line Item ID field, it may be because your table occurrences are collapsed and they show only fields used in relationships. In the upper-right corner of the TO, click the little button to expand it. Since the button cycles the TO through three states, you might have to click twice before you see all the fields.

---

5. **Click the OK button.**

   You're back on the layout.

Now it's time to add fields from your new table occurrence to the Expenses layout.

Adding fields for new table occurrences

To put your new relationship to work, you add the Invoice ID, Description, Price Each Quantity and Extended Price fields to your Expense layout. Here's how:

1. **In Layout mode, switch to the Expenses layout.**

   Or you could go to the Expenses layout, and then switch to Layout mode.

2. **Drag a new field onto the layout. When the Specify Field dialog box appears, in the pop-up menu at the top, choose Expenses_LINE ITEMS.**

   The fields from the Line Items table appear. Remember, you'll get the exact same list if you choose the plain Line Items TO, since it's the same table.

3. **From the list, choose the Invoice ID field, and then click OK.**

   This field lets you view the Invoice ID on which this expense was billed.

4. **Add the Description, Price Each, Quantity, and Extended Price fields from the Expenses_LINE ITEMS table occurrence.**

   With these fields on the Expenses layout, you can see the details of each line item, and verify that it's the right one before moving on.

5. **Add the Expenses::Line Item ID field to the layout.**

   When you enter a valid ID into this local field, your relationship is completed, and your related data shows up on the Expense record.

Back in Browse mode, you can start entering expenses. Make some expense records and some Invoices that bill those expenses out, and then put the ID of a line item in the Expenses::Line Item ID field. You may find it helpful to make a new window to view Invoices in (Figure 13-9). When you enter a valid Line Item ID, you see the associated invoice number and the details of the line item you're matching. If your fields allow data entry (page 303), then you can even edit the Invoice's Line Items right from the Expenses layout.

Table Occurrence Groups

The relationship between expenses and line items you created in the last section is *functional*, but as you added Line Item IDs, you probably discovered that it isn't very easy to work with. You had to view invoices and their line item IDs to figure out which Line Item ID to add to your Expense record. A value list of Line Item IDs might help, but as your database grows, so does the value list *and* the problems. First of all, your database could have *thousands* of line items. And even if it doesn't, line items don't have a very good name—their descriptions aren't unique, and their IDs aren't very meaningful.

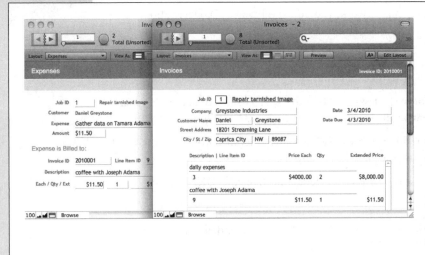

Figure 13-9:
To the left is the Expenses layout, where you can enter data about each expense you incur and assign it to a Job with a Job ID. Then, after you create an invoice record and bill for the expense, you use the Invoices layout (shown on the right) to find the Line Item ID. When you enter that number in the Expenses::Line Item ID field, the Line Item data appears on the Expenses layout.

It would improve the process if you could type an Invoice ID *right there on the Expenses layout*, and then see that invoice's Line Item IDs. A new layout called Assign Expenses (Figure 13-10) uses a new set of table occurrences, called a Table Occurrence Group (TOG) to let you manage line item data from a new Assign Expenses layout.

Listing the New Elements You'll Need

The Assign Expenses layout will provide a special set of tools, or an *interface*, to expedite a certain *process*. In this case, the process is matching line item records to expense records so you can record the Line Item ID which billed out each expense. For the new interface to work, you need several new elements. They're listed here to avoid confusion as you start creating them; you'll learn more about the role each item plays as you build the interface. You need:

- A new group of table occurrences that you'll create specifically to handle this task.

- A field in the Expenses table to type in the Invoice ID. Since this field doesn't hold information about any particular entity in your database, it's a perfect candidate for *global* storage. Global fields, as you remember from page 255, have the same value across every record of their table.

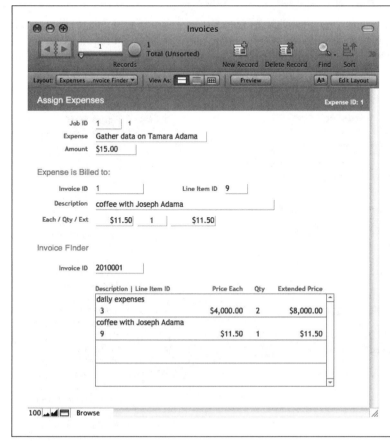

Figure 13-10:
This layout provides a nice interface for assigning line items to an expense. First, you enter an Invoice ID into a global field. Then the invoice's line items show up in a portal that shows you the data you need to choose the proper Line Item record to assign to each Expense record. As before, when you type a Line Item ID, you see the Description, Price Each, Quantity, and Extended Price that was invoiced for the Expense.

- A relationship between the Expenses table and the Invoices table, using Expenses::Global Invoice ID and Invoices::Invoice ID as the key fields.

- A new layout similar to the original Expenses layout, but with the context of your new table occurrence group and a portal showing Invoice Line Items.

To get these elements to work together, you first have to revisit your Relationships graph and decide which table occurrences to use in the new group. Read on.

Note: You can download a finished copy of the database (called Invoices FINISHED.fp7) from this book's Missing CD page at *http://missingmanuals.com*. Use the file to see how the completed process works, and as a reference as you go through the exercises that create your new layout.

Understanding Table Occurrence Groups

If you tried to add your new TOs to the existing group of table occurrences, you could easily get tangled in a mess. As you add more features that require more TOs, pretty soon you'll need a map, a GPS system, and a six-pack of aspirin to untangle all the table occurrences. See Figure 13-11 for an example of a graph gone wild.

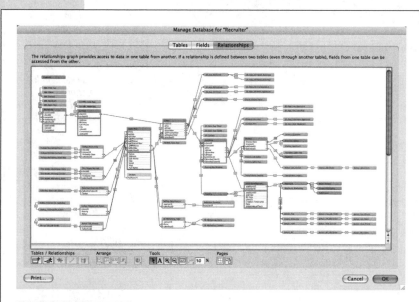

Figure 13-11:
You don't even need to be able to read the TO names in this Relationships graph (top) to see how quickly good databases become the stuff of nightmares. This database only has 19 tables, but there are nearly 100 TOs on the graph and they're all connected in a single group. If you had to tweak this database after a long absence, it could take a while to find the TO you need, and then recreate the logic you used to assemble the thing. You can't even see the whole graph at full size, so you have to either limit yourself to viewing a portion of the graph at a time, or zoom so far out that you can't read the TO names and field list. There are several spots in FileMaker that contain menus listing all your TOs. Although these TOs are named reasonably well (bottom), so that TOs that work together are grouped together alphabetically, they won't fit on the screen without scrolling. This menu is a pain to use.

The simplest way to keep things straight is to create an entirely *new* group of occurrences, called a *table occurrence group* (also known as a *TOG*), somewhere *else* in the graph. You can assemble and wire these together in any way that makes sense for your new display, without complicating or otherwise changing the existing group.

Note: You can create as many TOGs as you like without making your database any larger. Still, performance may start to suffer if you create more than about 25 occurrences of tables that contain tens of thousands of records.

To figure out which table occurrence you need to use to make the new layout, think about what you need it to do. You start by finding an expenses record on the Expenses layout, and then you need to get to the new Assign Line Items layout—via a button, perhaps. Once you're on the new layout, you'll view an Invoice and decide which Line Item goes with the current Expense. Everything takes place from an expense record's context.

Since your new layout is all about modifying an expense record, you have to attach it to an occurrence of the *Expenses* table. The other tables you need are the same ones you used to show a related Line Item on the Expense layout: Jobs, Invoices, and Line Items.

To keep things simple, you'll create new TOs of the tables needed for the new layout, and then position the new group below your other table occurrences, as shown in Figure 13-12 (top). The graph lets you work with the two distinct sets of relationships separately. That way, you can tailor each relationship to fit the specific needs of the new layout, and you get the added boon of a more organized table occurrence menu (Figure 13-12, bottom).

You can create many occurrences of a table, but each TO name has to be unique. Just as the graph can become a mess without a TOG plan, you need a TO naming scheme (or naming convention, as it's also called) to avoid creating wacky names that don't make sense in the clear light of day. Here you'll use a convention that gives each TO name a prefix identifying its TOG and that capitalizes the actual table name ("Expenses_INVOICES"). The new Expenses TO will become the context of the new layout you'll create, so it has two underscores in its name ("Expenses__EXPENSES"). That way, it appears at the top of the TOG group in a menu list, as in Figure 13-13.

Note: This naming scheme is one of many out there. Many developers use a similar scheme, but abbreviate the layout names/prefix part of the TO name (Exp_INVOICE), so the names don't get too lengthy. Others refuse to use spaces in their TO names, and use camel case instead (ExpensesINVOICE, for example). Feel free to make up your own scheme. Just use it consistently—it's your bread-crumb trail home.

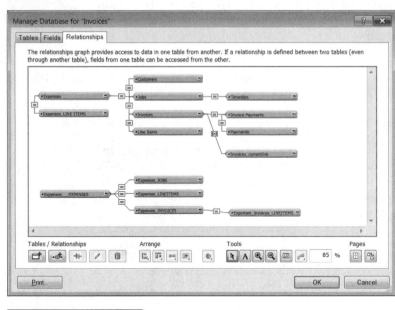

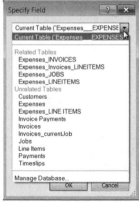

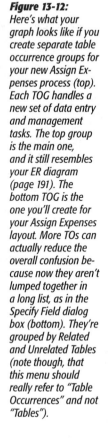

Figure 13-12:
Here's what your graph looks like if you create separate table occurrence groups for your new Assign Expenses process (top). Each TOG handles a new set of data entry and management tasks. The top group is the main one, and it still resembles your ER diagram (page 191). The bottom TOG is the one you'll create for your Assign Expenses layout. More TOs can actually reduce the overall confusion because now they aren't lumped together in a long list, as in the Specify Field dialog box (bottom). They're grouped by Related and Unrelated Tables (note though, that this menu should really refer to "Table Occurrences" and not "Tables").

Now that you've grasped the basic concept of the TOG, it's time to start the actual construction.

Customers Expenses ✓ Expenses__EXPENSES Expenses_Invoice_LINEITEMS Expenses_INVOICES Expenses_JOBS Expenses_LINE ITEMS Expenses_LINEITEMS Globals Invoice Finder__INVOICE FINDER Invoice Finder_INVOICES Invoice Finder_JOBS Invoice Payments Invoices Invoices_AllCurrentJob Invoices_currentJob Jobs Leads Line Items Payments Timeslips Manage Database…	**Figure 13-13:** *Not all menus that list TOs group them in related and unrelated chunks. By using a double underscore "__" in the name of the TO that provides the context for the new layout, it will appear at the top of its group, as you see with the Expenses__EXPENSES TO here. You can also see the result of not picking a good naming scheme earlier in your development because you have two very similarly named versions of the Expenses_Line Items TOs. Now that you know about naming conventions, you can see why it would be worth the time it takes to rename all the TOs in your ER diagram group. (Renaming TOs won't break anything, so no worries there.) Things will only get worse as your graph grows. If you renamed your ER group with an "ER" prefix, then they'd all appear together in the list, instead of scattered, as they do here, plus you'd eliminate the confusion between the two similarly named Expense Line Items TOs.*

UP TO SPEED

Managing Table Occurrences

When you use descriptive names for your TOs, they can get pretty long. Fortunately, you can easily resize any table occurrence so its entire name is visible. No matter how the table occurrence is configured, you can drag the right or left edge to make it wider or narrower. If it's set to show all its fields, then you can also drag the top or bottom edge to change its height. A table occurrence that's too short to show all its fields has little arrow icons above and below the field list. Click these arrows to scroll through the list. (When a table occurrence is set to show just the key fields or no fields at all, its height is fixed.)

To see which table an occurrence represents, just point to the arrow icon to the left of the occurrence name. FileMaker pops up an information window that tells you everything you need to know. And if long names and tooltips aren't enough, then you can use the note tool (it's the tool marked with the letter "A"). Use the note as a reminder of the purpose of your new table occurrences that's more detailed than a naming prefix. Notes behave themselves, staying in the background behind all your TOs, so some designers make large notes that enclose a new TO group to visually unite them on the graph.

Creating a New Table Occurrence Group

Before you start creating the new TOs, review your goals. Since the Assign Expenses layout needs the context of the Expenses table, it's easy to see that you need a new Expenses TO. Its purpose is to show invoice line items based on an Invoice ID you enter in a global field, and to show the job name when you've decided which line item an expense belongs to. You also want to be able to show the line item attached to that expense, so you need a second new TO for line items. With these TOs, you'll be able to see and manage the following information:

- The name of the job associated with an invoice.

- The line items attached to that invoice.

Figure 13-14 shows all the new table occurrences you need to create and the way you'll arrange them to make the new layout work.

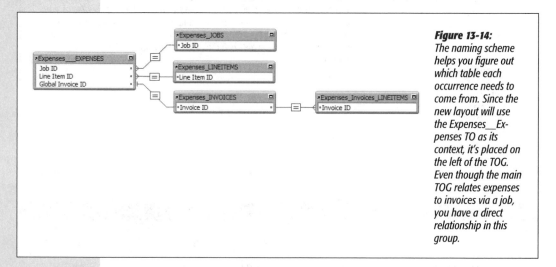

Figure 13-14:
The naming scheme helps you figure out which table each occurrence needs to come from. Since the new layout will use the Expenses__Expenses TO as its context, it's placed on the left of the TOG. Even though the main TOG relates expenses to invoices via a job, you have a direct relationship in this group.

The steps are simple if you take it one table at a time:

1. **If necessary, click the Manage Database window's Relationships tab.**

   You need to see your existing Relationships graph.

2. **Click the Add Table Occurrence button. When the Specify Table window appears, select the Expenses table.**

   When you create your layout later, it'll have the context (or viewpoint) of the Expenses table, so it makes sense to create it first.

3. **In the "Name of Table Occurrence" box, type *Expenses__EXPENSES*, and then click OK.**

   That's two underscore charaters, to put this TO at the top of the list when it's sorted alphabetically. When you click OK, FileMaker adds the new table occurrence to the middle of the graph. Move it out of the way to get ready for the next steps.

Repeat the steps above (adjust step 2 to choose the appropriate table) to create the following TOs:

- Expenses_INVOICES

- Expenses_LINE ITEMS

- Expenses_Invoices_LINEITEMS

- Expenses_JOBS

You now have five new table occurrences on your graph. Since the names are so long, you might have to stretch your new TOs so you can tell them apart.

Tip: If you use the Duplicate button to copy an existing set of TOs, you get their existing names and relationships. Then you can move the new TOG and change its names and relationships as appropriate. Or you can use a hybrid method of creating a new TO with the steps above, but copy/paste the prefix part of the name from the first TO. With practice, you'll find your own favorite style.

Once you have your TOs in place, you need to hook them together properly. Here are the relationships you need:

- From Expenses__EXPENSES to Expenses_JOBS using the Job ID fields as keys. This relationship lets you display the Job Name on the Assign Expenses layout.

- From Expenses__EXPENSES to Expenses_LINE ITEMS using the Line Item ID field as keys. The relationship will let you show a Line Item's detail on the layout.

- From Expenses_INVOICES to Expenses_Invoices_LINEITEMS using the Invoice ID fields as keys. This relationship will show an Invoice's Line Items on the new layout.

- From Expenses__EXPENSES to Expenses_INVOICES, using Global Invoice ID and Invoice ID as keys.

But as you'll notice, you don't have a Global Invoice ID field yet. That's ok; FileMaker lets you create new fields in the heat of the moment. Here's how:

1. **Switch to the Fields tab. From the Table pop-up menu, choose Expenses.**

   FileMaker shows the fields in the Expenses table.

2. **In the Field Name text box, enter *Global Invoice ID*, change its type to Number, and then click Create.**

   The new field appears in the field list.

3. **Click Options, and then, in the Field Options dialog box, click the Storage tab.**

   FileMaker shows you the field storage options. You first saw these on page 255.

4. **Turn on "Use global storage (one value for all records)", and then click OK twice to close both dialog boxes.**

   FileMaker creates the field, and it now appears in the Field list.

The Expenses::Global Invoice ID field is ready for you to use in the relationship between the Expenses__Expenses and Expenses_INVOICES TOs. As you create that relationship, notice that the global relationship shows a little bar on the Expenses side. That's to remind you there's a global field on that side of the relationship. See the box below to learn more about naming global fields.

Tip: Remember, if you like things lined up nice and neat, you have Arrange tools that let you resize and align a selected group of TOs together (page 210).

POWER USERS' CLINIC

One (Global) Field to Rule Them All

You know that fields set with global storage have the same value across every record in the table that holds them. Since these fields are so different from other fields, many database designers give them special names so that the fields stand out in a list. That way, they're less likely to get used inappropriately—say in a context where they don't have much meaning—or plopped down on a layout where someone can edit the values when they should stay static.

You can just preface the names of all your global fields with the word "global," like you did in the exercise on page 583.

But in the real world, people commonly just use a lower-case "g" as a prefix. With this scheme, you can name your global field "gInvoice ID" and save a few keystrokes. Plus, you look like a guru.

Some developers also use the lower-case "g" in the names of their TOs, to indicate that the relationship uses a global field as a key. It can be a handy extra reminder that the relationship doesn't work bidirectionally, as relationships that are based on normal fields do.

Building the Assign Expenses Layout

Now that you've finished the new table occurrence group and hooked up its relationships, you're ready to create the "Assign Expenses" layout. Since this new layout has a lot of objects, you'll have to repeat some processes a few times. Figure 13-15 shows what you're trying to accomplish.

Duplicating and editing an existing layout

Even though they're from different contexts, the Expenses and Assign Expenses layouts have many of the same objects on them. Your databases will look more polished if you copy similar elements whenever you can. In this case, duplicating a layout will keep a handful of elements in the exact same locations, so that when you switch from layout to layout, you're immediately oriented by seeing similar onscreen elements in the same spot on every layout. Here's how to copy a layout and change a field reference:

1. **Go to the Expenses layout, and then switch to Layout mode.**

   You're setting up the element you want to copy.

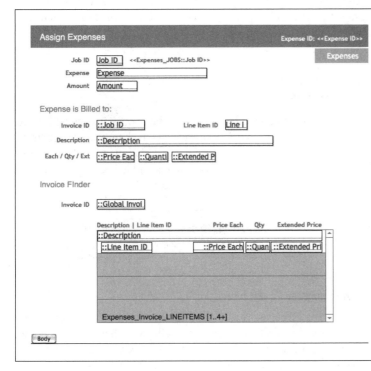

Figure 13-15:
The new layout is similar to your existing Expenses layout. To get a jumpstart, you duplicate that layout and then change some objects to fit the new context. You'll also create brand new objects from scratch. Much of your real world development will follow a similar mix of copying and editing existing elements and adding new ones from scratch.

2. **Choose Layouts→Duplicate Layout.**

   The layout is duplicated along with all its objects. The new layout has the same name as the original, except the word "Copy" is appended to the name.

3. **Choose Layouts→Layout Setup, and then change the new layout's name to "Assign Expenses."**

   That'll make it easy to remember what the layout's for when you see it in a long list later on.

4. **In the "Show records from" pop-up menu, choose the Expenses__EXPENSES table occurrence, and then click OK.**

   Now you can see another benefit of your naming convention—it's easy to spot the TO you need. All the fields on your layouts have changed from local fields to related ones. You'll have to switch each field to the proper TOG.

5. **Double-click the Job ID field.**

   The Specify Field window appears.

6. **From the "Table occurrence" pop-up menu, choose "Expenses__EXPENSES."**

   The "Table occurrence" pop-up menu is divided between related and unrelated tables. Expenses__EXPENSES is at the top of the list, and is labeled as the Current

Table (because you selected that TO in Step 3). FileMaker is well-mannered enough to know that you still want the Job ID field, so you won't have to change that part of the field name reference.

7. **Click OK.**

   The "::" disappears from the Job ID field, and you can be sure that it will now show data from the proper context now.

Repeat the process for each field on the layout. Remember, you're just switching the TO from the unrelated TO to the related TO. Don't forget to change the merge fields too. If you absolutely hate this process of switching a whole bunch fields from one TOG or TO to another, you're in good company. But to avoid it, you'll have to create all your layouts from scratch instead of duplicating and editing.

Note: Because this new layout was created for a very specific purpose, you may want to delete some items from the original Expenses layout, like the gray bar and its navigation buttons.

Copying a portal from another layout

Just as you duplicated the Expenses layout to save time and (some) trouble, you already have a Line Items portal (over on the Invoice layout) that's formatted and organized nicely. Copying it, and then changing its context, also orients your users because the portal on the Assign Expenses layout looks just like the one they use to create Invoices. They don't have to get used to a new arrangement of data just because they're performing a different task. Here's how to copy and edit a portal.

1. **Switch to Layout mode, and then go to the Invoice layout.**

   That's where the portal you need is found.

2. **Use your favorite technique for selecting multiple items. Grab the Line Items portal, all its fields and their labels. Then choose Edit→Copy or press Ctrl+C (⌘-C).**

   Make sure they're all highlighted, because it's a pain to come back here if you've missed something later on.

3. **Switch to the Assign Expenses layout. Make the Body part larger to accommodate the new portal. Click in the approximate spot you want the portal to land and then choose Edit→Paste or press Ctrl+V (⌘-V). If the layout's Body part is big enough, your copied objects will land centered on the spot where you clicked.**

   The copied items appear on the layout. Refer back to Figure 13-15 if necessary for guidance on where to place the new portal.

4. **Double-click the portal, and then choose "Expenses_Invoices_LINEITEMS" from the "Show related records from" pop-up menu.**

   The benefits of a well-chosen naming convention are well worth the extra time and thought you put into using it. You need the version of the Line Items table that goes through the Invoice table, and not the one that's directly connected to Expenses__EXPENSES.

5. **Double-click the Description field in the portal to show the Specify Field window. Change the "Show related records from" pop-up menu to the Expenses_Invoices_LINEITEMS TO.**

   Repeat the process for the portal's other fields.

The major elements of the layout are in place. Add the Expenses::Global Invoice ID field and a label to the layout, and you're ready to test the layout. Switch back to Browse mode, and then type an invoice number in the Global Invoice ID field. You may need to find an invoice in another window to make sure you have a valid ID number. When you enter the number into the field, you'll see the invoice's line items appear in the portal below the expense data. Now it's a snap to enter the appropriate line item ID value to relate expenses records and their invoice line items. See the box on page 588 to learn more about how global relationships work.

Using GTRR to switch TOGs

The layout you've just created is pretty slick, but there's one problem. Suppose you're on the *Expenses* layout looking at an expense. You decide you want to assign an invoice line item to it, so you use the Layout pop-up menu to switch to the Assign Expenses layout. Unfortunately, when you do, you won't always see the same record. That's because each table occurrence has its own current record, found set, and sort order. Users will find this situation frustrating, since they may have to do a find on the new layout to see the expense they were just viewing.

It turns out the "Go to Related Record" command has an unexpected power: It can transfer a found set—complete with current record and sort order—from one table occurrence to another. The "Go to Related Record" Options window has a "Get related record from" pop-up menu that shows every table occurrence in the database, not just the ones related to your current context. It shows layouts attached to *any* occurrence of the same table. In other words, when you ask to go to a record in the same table occurrence you're already viewing, you can pick the Assign Expenses layout, even though it's associated with a different occurrence of the Expenses table. If you want to get all geeky about it, you can call this technique "TOG Jumping" just like the pros do.

When you use this technique, FileMaker shows the records dictated by the relationship, but uses the layout you choose. To make the connection, add a button (page 225) to the Expenses layout that runs the "Go to Related Record" command. When you set up the button, choose the Expenses table occurrence and the Assign Expenses layout. Also, make sure you turn on "Show only related records". FileMaker does all the rest of the work for you.

You can also add a button to the Assign Expenses layout that transports you *back* to the Expenses layout. This time you configure the "Go to Related Record" command to use the Expenses__EXPENSES table occurrence and the Expenses layout.

FREQUENTLY ASKED QUESTION

Globals and Relationships

I don't get it. I thought relationships were supposed to hook different records together, but a global field has the same value throughout a table and isn't associated with any specific record. How come I used a global field to create a relationship?

As the Assign Expense example (page 584) shows, relationships can be created to support a display (or layout) that performs a specific task. When you use a global field in a relationship, it works just fine. Put an ID in the global field, and FileMaker makes matches to one or more records on the other side.

This kind of relationship doesn't create a permanent connection between records—it just gives you temporary access to related records when there's a value in the Expenses::Global Invoice ID field. If you clear out that field, the relationship doesn't work anymore (it's called invalid) and no line item records will show in the portal. In this case, that's an asset since you can reduce visual clutter on the layout by clearing the field's value.

Since FileMaker doesn't index global fields, the relationship doesn't work the way you'd expect when you look in the other direction—from the normal-field context back towards the global field. From the Expenses::INVOICES

direction, the relationship behaves like a Cartesian join (page 567), showing every record in the other table. That makes perfect sense, because every record in the other file has the same value in that global field. This behavior isn't important in situations like the Invoice Finder layout, because you only care what happens from the global side of a relationship. But unlike true bidirectional relationships, where you can pull data reliably from either direction, global relationships work best in only one direction. As Figure 13-14 shows, FileMaker doesn't connect the relationship line in the graph directly to the global field. This visual cue lets you know this relationship works only from the global side to the "normal" side.

One last point: You can display data in a global field in another table *without* a relationship. Since global fields aren't associated with any record, you can view and modify them from anywhere. It's common to create a table to hold values you need to use from many different tables in a global table (say, your company's logo, name, address, and other contact information), and then use those fields on printed reports. That way, if any of that data changes, you can change it in the global table, and it's immediately changed on all your reports.

Understanding Graph Arrangements

The first TOG in your graph still looks and behaves like the ER diagram you drew back on page 191, even though it has a few extra TOs in it. But you can see that the more TOs you add to this group, the quicker its intended meaning will get lost in the visual clutter. That's not to say that the TOG's behavior would change, only that you'd have a harder time seeing the main tables' relationships at a glance. Because the graph's complexity increases along with the features you add to your layout, finding an appropriate graph arrangement early in your development is critical. Without a plan, you could end up with a labyrinth, like the one in Figure 13-11.

Note: If you do end up with (or inherit) a messy graph, you can rearrange TOs or change their relationships. But calculations, script steps, and other processes that depend on the changed item could break in the process. These types of developer-introduced bugs are time-consuming to trace and fix, so most developers run a DDR (page 526) first, and then use it as a map for fixing the clutter.

Note: There's no one-size-fits-all rule for graph arrangement, but you should keep some general rules of thumb in mind. Plus, you can adapt formal data models to handle time-tested processes like inventory control or student registration databases. Those concepts are complex, though, and beyond the scope of this book. Do a Google search for *data modeling* to find out more, but don't get too bogged down in theory. As you already know, FileMaker is easier to use than most any other database out there, so some of those concepts won't apply to your FileMaker solutions.

However, FileMaker has two commonly-used graph arrangement models. First, an arrangement of TOs that looks like an ER diagram is sometimes called a *spider* because there's often a central table occurrence from which most other TOs are connected. If you're adopting this model, you may decide to keep the central spider free of extra TOs, and then create free-floating TOGs whenever you need new relationships between tables.

If you've ever worked your way through an ER diagram, you probably have a good grasp of spiders. If you're creative and experienced with scripts, you can use each TO for many purposes. (The complex script tutorial on page 704 can help you avoid the need for the Assign Expenses layout, for example.)

Another common scheme is called Anchor-Buoy; its name also comes from its appearance. The second TOG you created (page 582) follows the rules for Anchor-Bouy development. That is, the TO on the left end of the group provides the context for the TOG's layout. All the other TOs flow out to the right in lines (or buoys) that are "anchored" by the main TO. Because these lines can be three or more TOs long, they can start to look like tentacles, which is why some folks call this graph arrangement *squids* instead.

Anchor-buoy graphs have some advantages over spiders. First, they make it very clear which TOs supply the main data for layouts, because they're always the ones on the left side of the graph. Second, most calculations you write to support the TOG will use the Anchor TO's context (page 151). Third, when you're new to FileMaker development, the somewhat rigid demands of Anchor-Buoys provide predictable structure that other methods don't impose.

But Anchor-Buoys have drawbacks. They tend to require more TOs than spider models, because each TOG often requires at least one copy of each table that forms the basic ER diagram. Since nearly every layout in an Anchor-Buoy model requires

---

its own TOG, it's common to have a graph with dozens of TOGs. And since the TOGs are always arranged with layouts on the left, you lose the benefit of bidirectional relationships that spiders handle easily.

Some developers always work with one of these models, and asking them to consider change is like starting a discussion on politics or religion. If you're interested, search the Web for *anchor-buoy, FileMaker data model,* or *FileMaker relationships graph.* If you join FileMaker's TechNet (page 860), you'll get access to white papers, including one on the pros and cons of several different graph arrangement schemes for FileMaker. With time and experience, you'll find that some databases work better with one arrangement, but others work just as well with a hybrid of spider and Anchor-Buoy (Figure 13-16), or another arrangement.

Note: Rearranging your TOs doesn't change the way your tables are related, although it can change where they appear when you open a relationship's Edit Relationship dialog box.

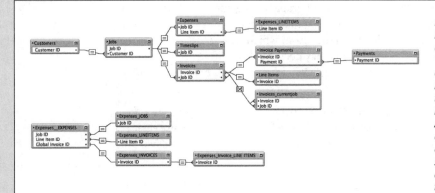

Figure 13-16:
In this rearrangement of your graph, the "spider" you created on page 206 (top) has been converted to something that looks more like an Anchor-Buoy. This arrangement retains all the benefits of the spider model, and also makes it easier to see multi-hop relationships. What's not so clear, though, is how two tables like Expenses and Invoices relate to one another. The second TOG (bottom) is fully Anchor-Buoy, in that only one of its TOGs has a layout, and the others are used merely to display related fields on that layout.

Connecting Database Files

In FileMaker, you can make two database files work together as easily as you work with multiple tables. Using the techniques you already know, you connect tables from another file (often called an *external database*) without the overhead of copying all that data into your file. You just put a table occurrence from your external file onto your Relationships graph, and that defines its context in relation to all your other tables.

For example, suppose you have a Leads database that you want to connect to the Invoice system. Your goal is to create a layout in the Invoices database so your sales department doesn't have to manually open that file while they're busy looking through invoices. You'll start by adding a table occurrence from the external file to your "local" file's Relationships graph. See the box on page 594 to learn more about why you might keep some tables in separate database files.

Note: If you downloaded the sample files for this chapter, you'll have a file called Leads.fp7. Or find the file on the book's Missing CD page at *www.missingmanuals.com*.

Adding a Table Occurrence from Another File

Once you have a Leads TO on the Invoice file's relationships graph, it begins to act like a first-class citizen in its new environment: You can create relationships to it, create layouts that are based on it, and do just about anything else you can do with the tables in this database. Here's how:

1. **In the Invoices database, choose File→Manage Database, and then click the Relationships tab. Then click the Add Table Occurrence button.**

    The Specify Table dialog box appears.

2. **From the Data Source pop-up menu, choose Add FileMaker Data Source.**

    A standard Open File dialog box appears—just like you see when you're opening a database.

3. **Browse to the Leads database, select it, and then click Open.**

    The Specify Table dialog box now shows tables from the Leads database. There's only one, and it's also called Leads. FileMaker selects the Leads table and suggests the TO name *Leads* for it. Since it doesn't duplicate any TO name in your file, you don't have to change it.

4. **Click OK.**

    FileMaker adds the new occurrence to the graph. As Figure 13-17 shows, you can tell at a glance that it's an occurrence of what FileMaker calls an *external* table because it shows you the table occurrence's name in italics.

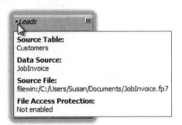

Figure 13-17:
External tables' names display in italics. To find out which database it comes from, press on the little arrow to the left of the TO's name to show the information window. FileMaker displays the source table's name, the Data Source (or file name), the Source File's path and whether the file's access protection (page 791) is turned on.

5. **Click OK.**

    Now that the Leads table is in the graph, you can use the table as freely as if it were a local table.

Unlike with new tables you create in a file, external tables don't automatically get layouts created for them. You'll have to create your Leads layout manually. Start by choosing Layouts→New Layout/Report, and then select the Leads TO from the "Show records from" pop-up menu.

Defining Data Sources Using a Path

When you added the Leads TO to your graph on page 591, FileMaker created an External Data Source reference. That's the path FileMaker uses to manage the data, so you never have to think about the connection. But these references aren't dynamic. That is, if you move the Lead.fp7 file from the location recorded in your file reference, FileMaker won't be able to show you the data in the file until you update the reference. Choose File→Manage→External Data Sources, and then double-click the file reference to edit it (Figure 13-18).

You use this same set of dialog boxes to create a Data Source manually. Give the data source a logical name, and then click the Add File button to navigate to the file's location. If you prefer typing to pointing and clicking, you can type the path from scratch, but you have to follow strict form. Acceptable form varies, based on what platform you're using and how you access the external file. You'll see examples of the acceptable File Path Formats at the bottom of the Edit Data Source dialog box.

You can even give a file reference more than one path. When you do, FileMaker looks for the file at the first path. If it doesn't find the file, then it tries the second path. The search continues until it finds the file or has tried every listed path. (If it never finds the file, then you see an error message.) Using this technique, you can have a database that opens files from different locations depending on which computer it's opened on. Or you can ask FileMaker to use your local copy of the Leads database if it finds one, but use the network copy otherwise. (You'll learn about sharing databases on a network in Chapter 19.)

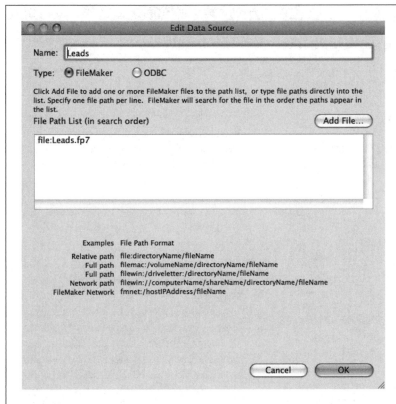

Figure 13-18:
The Data Source's name is the same as the file name, since you let FileMaker handle it when you created the TO for the external file. But you can edit the source name if you prefer. Here the file path indicates that it's in the same folder as the Invoice file. The Add File button lets you browse your system or network. In this case, you could use that button to find a file that's been moved and thus update its path.

POWER USERS' CLINIC

Going to External Records

Now that you've got a file reference and a table occurrence from an external file, what do you do with it? You *could* create a new layout attached to the Leads table occurrence, and then fill it with fields from the Leads table. But you already have a great layout for viewing the details of a Leads record: the Leads database's Leads layout.

Once again, as long as you have a valid relationship between any table and the Leads table, "Go to Related Records" comes to the rescue (see Figure 13-19). Create a button that performs the "Go to Related Record" command. In the "Go to Related Record" Options window,

choose the Leads table occurrence. Since this occurrence is from a table in another file, the "Use external table's layout" checkbox comes to life.

When this checkbox is turned on, the "Show record using layout" pop-up menu lists layouts from the Leads database rather than the current database. Turn the checkbox on, and then choose the Leads layout. Don't forget to turn on "Show only related records". Now when you click the button, the Leads database pops up and shows you the correct person's record.

POWER USERS' CLINIC

Systems with More than One Database

Just because you can put a lot of tables into a single database file, no rule says every table has to be in the same database. In fact, there are lots of good reasons to divide your system across multiple files. Chapter 5 mentioned a common reason: You might be storing large images or other files in your database. You can keep these files in an external table so the database file itself isn't so large. Then you can back up, copy, and email the information about the images without including the images themselves.

Here are some other reasons to use more than one file:

- You can create a database for each kind of layout you need. For example, if you need to track sales, you can create a database with the tables you need to store the actual data: orders, line items, customers, shipments, products, and so forth. Your company might use the database in two ways: sales people do data entry (creating and managing orders) and managers do reporting on those sales (daily, monthly, and quarterly sales reports, trend and pro-motion analysis, and so on). To keep your system as simple as possible, you can create these separate layouts as two distinct databases. Since they share the tables from the central sales database, the reporting data stays up-to-date as FileMaker processes new sales. But since they're in two databases, the layouts you need for order entry don't get in the way of the reporting layouts, and vice versa. Even better, it's easier to keep managers from seeing stuff that might confuse them because those day-to-day task layouts just don't exist in their file.

- Expanding on this first reason, one company usually has many database needs. You might have Sales, Marketing, and Engineering departments in your organization. Each of these departments has unique ways they deal with data and the database should match those needs. But the Marketing department might be very interested in sales data, and the Sales department needs access to engineering information. You can create a separate database for each department, but share some tables between systems. This way you get a layout *and* sets of tables that are tailored to each group, but the important data is shared.

- When you can use external table occurrences, you have a very flexible design metaphor. A database—or file—can hold display elements (layouts, scripts, value lists) or data (tables and fields) or both. Some developers always separate their data and display because it can make it easier to update the file when major database changes need to happen. In that case, you can replace the new display file, without needing to import masses of data into a brand new file. Data separation is a complex topic and beyond the scope of this book. To read more about it, perform a Google search for "FileMaker data separation."

You can construct the database in almost any way you see fit: one file for each table, all tables in one file, or tables in logical groupings; all the layouts in one database, or several databases to break things up. A FileMaker file is a very flexible unit of organization: Use it as you see fit.

Using Multiple Relationship Techniques

Each technique you've learned in this chapter is useful on its own, but when you combine techniques, you can really start to get creative. For example, using two global date fields and a multiple criteria relationship, you can create a layout that lets users enter dates in a pair of fields and then see a list of invoices that fall between the dates they enter. You'll call this layout an Invoice Finder.

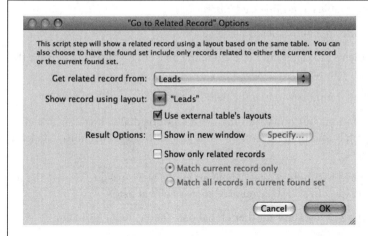

Figure 13-19:
The "Use external table's layouts" option is available only when you choose an External Table in a "Go To Related Record" command. When you choose this option, you'll see a list of layouts, from which you can choose the one you want to as your target. Reuse work you've already done by showing data in its original form—its native layout in its source file. If you also choose the "Show in new window" option, then you can leave the found set showing in your original window while you scour the external file to mine its treasures.

Creating the Invoice Finder Layout

To set up your new Invoice Finder layout, you need to create two new global fields. Since the global fields aren't associated with any particular table, it makes sense to create a *new* table to hold them. You also need a new relationship that matches fields in the Invoices table using these global fields. This sort of job benefits from its own table occurrence group. Call this group *Invoice Finder*.

To get the portal to show the right invoices, you need a relationship that uses your new global fields, and it'll have slightly more complicated rules than you've seen before:

```
Invoice Finder__INVOICE FINDER::gStart Date ≤ Invoice Finder_Invoices::Date
AND
Invoice Finder__ INVOICE FINDER::gEnd Date ≥ Invoice Finder_Invoices::Date
```

These rules say that an invoice should match if its date is *on or after* the global start date, and if the date is *on or before* the global end date.

Tip: If the logic shown here's confusing, remember that if you temporarily move the Invoice Finder__ INVOICE FINDER TO to the right of Invoice Finder_INVOICES so that the relationships read: Date ≥ gStart Date AND Date ≤ gEnd Date instead. Then when you switch the Invoice Finder__INVOICE FINDER TO back to its anchor position at the left edge of the TOG, FileMaker switches the logic for you.

Below are the steps for creating a new table, defining some global fields in that new table, and then using your creations in a new table occurrence group.

You've done most of this stuff before in other tutorials, so although you have to follow a lot of steps, they should all be familiar:

1. In the Invoices database, go to the Manage Database window's Tables tab. Create a new table called *Invoice Finder*.

   FileMaker adds the new table to the table list.

2. Click the Fields tab. Then, in the Field name box, enter *gStart Date*. Make the field a Date type, and then click Create.

   The "g" prefix reminds you that the field is a global.

3. Click the Options button. When the Field Options dialog box appears, click the Storage tab, and then turn on the "Use global storage" checkbox. Click the OK button.

   Since this field isn't holding data about an entity, but is used to change the records that display in a portal, you need to use a global field.

4. Repeat steps 2–3 to create another global date field called *gEnd Date*.

   Both fields appear in the list.

5. Switch to the Relationships tab. Drag the Invoice Finder table occurrence down below your existing TOGs. Then double-click it, and change its name to *Invoice Finder__INVOICE FINDER*.

   This new TO becomes the anchor in a new TOG, so place it near the left edge of the graph. You may also need to stretch the TO so its whole name appears.

6. Add a new occurrence of the Invoices table called Invoice Finder_INVOICES, and a new occurrence of the Jobs table called Invoice Finder_JOBS.

   Since your portal shows invoices and the job name associated with each invoice, you need these tables in your group as well.

7. Drag the Invoice Finder_INVOICES::Job ID field onto the Invoice Finder_ JOBS:: Job ID field to create a relationship.

   When an Invoice record matches a Job, the Job Name shows in the portal.

8. Click the Add/Edit Relationship button to open the Edit Relationship dialog box. From the left table's pop-up menu, choose Invoice Finder__INVOICE FINDER. Then, from the right table's pop-up menu, choose Invoice Finder_ INVOICES.

   As you select tables from the pop-up menus, their fields appear in the corresponding list.

9. From the left-hand table field list, choose "gStart Date". From the Operator pop-up menu, choose "≤".

   This symbol tells FileMaker you want the field on the left to match when it's *less than or equal* to the field you select on the right side.

10. **From the right-hand table field list, choose Date, and then click Add.**

    The Date field tells the relationship what value to compare to the Start Date in the Invoice Finder table. In other words, you want the relationship to match only when the Start Date is *before* the Invoice Date.

11. **Repeat the last two steps, but this time, from the left-hand table field list, choose the "gEnd Date" field. From the right-hand table field list, choose the Date field, and from the Operator pop-up menu, choose the "≥". Finally, click Add.**

    When you click Add, FileMaker adds the second criterion to the list. This part tells the portal to display records that are on or before the date in the gEnd Date field. Because FileMaker uses both relationships, you see only Invoices that have dates equal to or between the gStart Date and the gEnd Date. Compare your settings to Figure 13-20.

When you click OK to close both dialog boxes, FileMaker returns you to the graph.

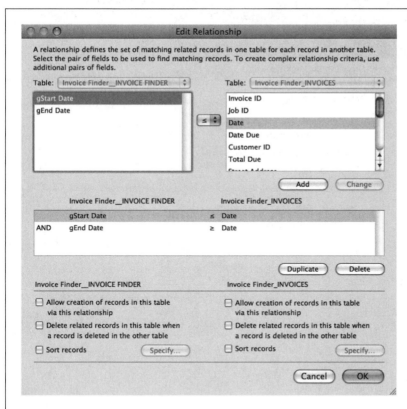

Figure 13-20:
The relationship between Invoice Finder__INVOICE FINDER and Invoice Finder_INVOICES connects two global date fields to one regular date field. An invoice has to be between the value in the gStart Date field and the value in the gEnd Date field to show up in the portal you create using this relationship. As with all relationships based on global fields, it works normally from the "left" side to the right side, but isn't truly bidirectional. Both fields have to have a valid date in them before any records show in the portal.

To test your new relationship, create a new layout, and then show records from the Invoice Finder__INVOICE FINDER table occurrence. Add the two global fields and a portal based on the Invoice Finder_INVOICES relationship. For good measure, add script triggers (page 430) to the global fields that commit the records. When it's all done, put values in the two global fields, and the portal updates to show the matching invoices. See one possible arrangement in Figure 13-21. See the box on the next page to learn another way to create this same type of relationship.

Note: The Invoice Finder table has no records. You might think this would be a problem, but it isn't. However, in some older versions of FileMaker Pro, portals don't work properly when you have no records. To clear this problem up, just create a new empty record.

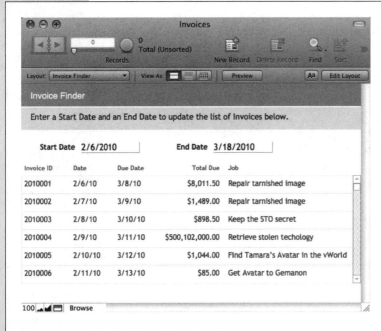

Figure 13-21:
You can create a new layout that makes it easy to see the invoices you need at a glance. As you enter new dates in the global fields, the invoice list updates on the fly, thanks to the global, multiple criteria relationship that powers it.

Global Table or Global Fields?

I've already got relationships to my Invoice table all over my graph. Why can't I use one of them instead of creating yet another Invoice TO? For example, I could put my global date fields into the Jobs table and then use a portal filtering calculation on the Jobs-to-Invoice relationship to create the same Invoice Finder. Is there a problem with that?

Not really. In fact, that approach would save you from creating the Invoice Finder table and the whole TOG that made the layout work. The Invoice Finder layout would be based on the Jobs table, and the portal filtering calculation would look a lot like the multiple criteria relationship you set up in the tutorial on page 563.

Using an existing relationship in a new way seems like a cleaner solution than adding new structure to the database and graph. If you're comfortable with the fact that gStart

Date and gEnd Date have nothing whatsoever to do with a Job record and exist only to keep the graph streamlined, then your plan will work just fine.

The main downside is that it might not be clear to another developer who has to work in your system why you made that choice (unless you make a note on the graph, of course). The benefit of creating a global field table is that as a separate table and TOG, it's completely clear what its function is. In fact, you might find other reasons to use global relationships, and then that table could become a repository for all the global fields that make similar features work. It would be rare indeed that any changes you make to the database's other structure would affect this standalone global table or any TOGs you hang off it. But it's your call.

Reporting and Analysis

A database excels at keeping track of things—itsy bitsy teeny tiny details about hundreds, thousands, even millions of little things. But people aren't so good at dealing with all that detail (hence the invention of the database). They like to see the *big picture*. If you want to understand your customer's music tastes, then a report of 200,000 individual CD sales doesn't do you much good: The information is in there somewhere, but your feeble mind stands no chance of ferreting it out. But a report that divides that information into 25 *music genres*, each with sales totals, both in aggregate and by gender, helps you interpret all those reams of data at a glance. In other words, a well-designed report *summarizes* the data for you, like the one you saw on page 169. FileMaker's not only fantastic at showing you information, it also excels at helping you see what it all *means*.

Summary Fields and Sub-summary Parts

The very cornerstone of high-level analysis in FileMaker Pro, is the summary report. To boil the values in a set of records down to totals, averages, or one of several other aggregate measures, the Summary Field is your tool. But hand-in-hand with the Summary Field are the Sub-summary and Grand Summary layout parts. A single Summary Field placed on a single Sub-summary layout part can, for example, form a report that displays one line for each city that appears in your address book database and a count of how many of your contacts live in that city.

Summary Fields

A summary field isn't associated with records like the other field types. Instead, summary fields gather up and process data from several records. Creating summary fields is much easier than describing what they do, as you can see from the following example:

1. **In the People database, choose File→Manage→Database.**

   You're about to add a field that counts the people in your database. This action is one of the most common ways to summarize database information.

2. **In the Manage Database window, choose the Fields tab. Then, in the Field Name box, type *Count of People*.**

   A summary field, like any other, has a name. You're going to use this summary field to count the people in your database.

3. **From the Type pop-up menu, choose Summary, and then click Create.**

   The "Options for Summary Field" window appears (Figure 14-1).

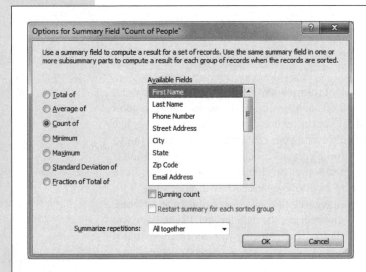

Figure 14-1:
The "Options for Summary Field" window appears when you make a new summary field. Unlike the field types you've used so far, a summary field has options that have to be set for it to be usable, so FileMaker shows you those options right away. This window also shows up if, in the Manage Database window, you select a Summary field, and then click Options.

4. **Choose the "Count of" radio button.**

   A summary field can perform one of seven summary calculations. In this case, you want it to *count* things.

5. **From the Available Fields list, choose First Name.**

   A summary field is always based on some other field in the database. For example, this field counts the First Name field. What does that mean? Simple: If a record has something in the First Name field, then it gets counted, but if the First Name field is blank, FileMaker ignores it. Since every person has a first name, this field counts every record. But beware—if you forget to type somebody's first name in a new record, then that person doesn't get included in the count.

Warning: In a simple database like this one, counting the First Name field is enough to make reasonably certain that you're counting all the records. But in the real world, you want to be certain *every* customer is counted—even if the First Name field isn't filled in.

6. **Click OK.**

   FileMaker adds the new field to the field list.

   You now have a field that helps you find out how many people are in the database. That piece of information is much more useful than it sounds; you'll be using it to find out interesting things soon.

If you squeeze this field onto the Detail layout and have a look in Browse mode, then you see something altogether unimpressive: the total number of people in the database (the Status toolbar already tells you this information). The real power of summary fields becomes apparent when you combine them with Sub-summary parts. Instead of counting all the people in your database, you might want to count how many you have in each city, or state (or both). Perhaps you need to know how many are still living, or get counts by Zip code. Or you may want to see how your contact list breaks down by city, gender, status, and mother's maiden name (assuming you have all those fields in your database).

With the help of Sub-summary parts, your humble "Count of People" summary field can tell you all this. Instead of counting all the people in the database, it can count the records in different groups, and you can define those groups based on any field value.

Suppose you want to break your People List layout down by status, with one group for Active, one for Retired, and a third for Deceased. You also want to see how many people fall in each group at a glance.

You already have the requisite summary field (the "Count of People" field you just created). Now you need a Sub-summary part:

1. **In Layout mode choose Insert→Part.**

   The Part Definition dialog box appears. Here's where you choose what kind of part you want (you saw it way back in Chapter 7).

2. **Check on the "Sub-summary when sorted by" radio button.**

   The list of fields on the right side of the window becomes active. A Sub-summary part is always hooked to a field.

3. **In the field list, select the Status field.**

   In this case, you're summarizing your records by status information.

4. **Click OK.**

   FileMaker asks if you want this part to summarize the records above it or below it. When you add group totals to your layout, they can appear before or after the records they summarize.

5. **Click Print Above.**

   FileMaker adds a new Sub-summary part to your layout, right between the header and the body. (If you had opted for Print Below, then it would be between the body and footer instead, to make it clear it comes after the records it summarizes.)

6. **Add a text object to the new part with this for content:** *Status: <<Status>> (<<Count of People>>).*

   In other words, you want a text object that merges in the Status field and "Count of People" field.

7. **Style the text object as you see fit; this part's up to you.**

If you switch to Browse mode, then you see…nothing different. The secret to Sub-summary parts is *sorting*. You *have to* sort by the field on which the Sub-summary part is based. In this case, you need to sort by Status, which, you think about it, it makes perfect sense. How can FileMaker group all the same-status records together for you if they're all mixed up? You might think FileMaker should just sort automatically in this case, but it turns out it's advantageous that you can add more than one Sub-summary part to a layout, and have them spring into action as you sort your records differently. You'll see how to do so next.

When you sort the records by the Status field, you see something like Figure 14-2.

If you scroll around, you see that each group is clearly labeled and counted.

Other Summary Field Types

The Summary Field dialog box's Options area offers several choices. Using these options, you can perform a lot of powerful analysis on your data. Figure 14-3 shows a Sub-summary report from a hypothetical sales database. This report uses several summary field options. When defining a summary field, you need to first decide which radio button to turn on. Here's what each choice does:

Total of

Use the "Total of" option to *sum* (add) number fields. In Figure 14-3, the Revenue field is a total of the Sales Amount field. For each group (state or region), you see its total.

When you have this option selected, a "Running total" checkbox appears below the Available Fields list. When you use a summary field on one of those magical layouts that produces grouping—total sales by Zip code, total sales by state, and so on—you normally see just the totals for each group in the report. If you turn on "Running total", then FileMaker changes things slightly. Instead of individual totals for each group, the totals add up from group to group, much like the Balance column in your checkbook register.

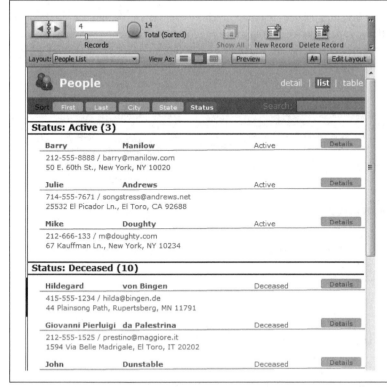

Figure 14-2:
The People List layout now summarizes by Status. As you can see here, a new visual separator appears between the group of active musicians and those who, uh, live on in our hearts. What's more, the Count of People field now shows the count just for the group because it's in a Sub summary part.

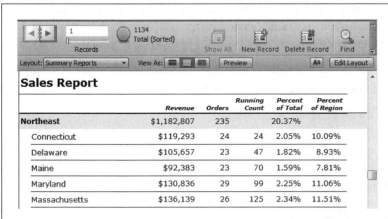

Figure 14-3:
This report shows summary fields in action. The Revenue column uses a "Total of" type summary field to add up sales numbers. Orders uses the Count type to show the total number of orders. The Running Count column, on the other hand, continues to count up the orders from one state to the next. Finally, two Percent fields use the "Fraction of Total of" summary field type to determine how much each state contributes to its region, and how much each region contributes to the total. You'll learn about all these options on the next few pages.

Average of

Obviously, the "Average of" choice calculates the average of the values in a number field. This time, you see a "Weighted average" checkbox. When you turn it on, another field list appears (see Figure 14-4). From this list, you choose the field by which to *weight* your average.

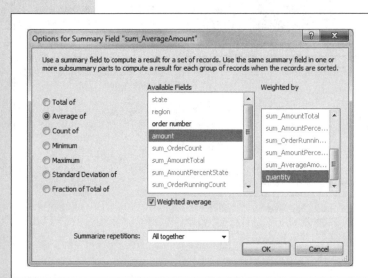

Figure 14-4:
When you turn on the "Weighted average" checkbox, FileMaker adds a second field list—"Weighted by"—to the window, where you can pick another number field. FileMaker averages the data in the first field, and weights each record's input by the second field.

You use a weighted average when the things you're averaging have an associated quantity. For example, suppose your database has a record for each product sale. It records which product was sold, how many were sold, and the unit price. If you want a summary field that calculates the average sale price, then you probably want to turn on the "Weighted average" checkbox. Imagine you have these sales figures:

- You sold three laptop computers for $2,500 each.

- You sold 18 more laptops for $2,200 each.

- You sold a single laptop for $2,800.

If you use a simple average, FileMaker tells you the average sale price for laptops is $2,500 ($2,500 + $2,800 + $2,200, divided by three). But that's not exactly right. You sold 18 of those laptops at just $2,200 each, but it counts only *once* in the calculation. In fact, you really sold 22 laptops in all, at three different prices. To calculate the correct average, you need to take quantities into consideration. In FileMaker, turn on the "Weighted average" checkbox, and then, in the "Weighted by" list, choose the Quantity field. Now it reports the correct average: $2,268.18.

Count of

Choose "Count of" to *count* items without totaling them. Since this option doesn't involve actual math, you can pick *any* field type, not just numbers. FileMaker counts each record in which that field isn't empty. If it's empty, then it simply doesn't contribute to the count. Choose a field that's *never* empty if you want to be sure you count *every* record. You can use this property to your advantage, though. If you want your count to reflect just the flagged records, then count the Flag field instead. In Figure 14-3, the Orders column uses this option.

This option gives you a "Running count" checkbox. It works like running total but has an option that running total doesn't offer. When you turn on "Running count", the "Restart summary for each sorted group" checkbox becomes available. This option lets you produce a column like Running Count in Figure 14-3. This column counts up with each state, keeping a running count. But it's set to restart numbering based on the Region field. Notice that the running count starts over with each new region.

Minimum and Maximum

If you want to know the *smallest* or the *largest* value in a group, use Minimum or Maximum. Both are very simple: Just pick the field you want to evaluate. No checkboxes, no extra lists. Number, date, time and timestamp field types are available for minimum and maximum summarization as are calculation fields with number, date, time, and timestamp results. You can use these to see the largest number of orders in your database, or the date of the earliest sale.

Standard Deviation of

If you're into statistics or just devious, use "Standard Deviation of". It gives you a field that calculates its namesake for the selected number field. It also has a "by population" checkbox, which is a little oddly named (it probably should be called "of population"). Turn this checkbox on if your records represent the entire population in your particular domain, and FileMaker uses the formula for the standard deviation of a population. Turn it off to calculate the standard deviation of a *sample*.

Note: If none of this makes sense to you, then rest assured you don't need to know what it means to use summary fields. But if you're cursed with a curious mind, Google *define:standard deviation* and go to town.

Fraction of Total of

"Fraction of Total of" is the most complex summary option. It looks at the total for the *group* you're summarizing, as well as the total for the entire database. It then reports what portion of the overall total the group represents, as a decimal number. If all your sales were in California, it shows *1*. If California accounted for only five percent of your sales, on the other hand, it says *.05*.

The Subtotaled checkbox that comes along with this option is also a little confusing. When you turn it on, FileMaker lets you pick another field from a list called "When sorted by". The name of this list serves to inform you that you have to *sort* the record by the selected field for this summary field to work. If you don't sort the records yourself before you view the report, then the field stays empty.

Warning: That problem's not as big as it may seem at first. As you learned on page 173, you have to sort records to do a lot of things with summary fields.

FileMaker looks at the selected field, figures out which records have the *same* value in them as in the current record, and calculates the fraction based only on the total of *those* records. In Figure 14-3, the "Percent of Total" field is a normal "Fraction of Total of" field, while the "Percent of Region" field uses "Fraction of Total of" subtotaled by Region.

Summarizing repetitions

When you summarize a repeating field, you have another choice to make. Do you want *one* summary value that aggregates every repetition, producing a single value? If so, then choose "All together". If you want a repeating summary value that aggregates each repetition individually instead, then choose Individually.

Warning: If you have sharp eyes, then you may notice that the "Summarize repetitions" drop-down list is available all the time, although they don't do anything unless you've selected a repeating field. Don't waste your time clicking them unless you're working with a repeating field. Just one of those FileMaker mysteries for the cocktail-party circuit.

Advanced Sub-summary Parts

So far you've been working with layouts that only contain a single Sub-summary part. But your layouts can have several sub-summaries, both above and below the Body part. You may even need a report that doesn't show the source data at all using a layout with no Body part at all.

Multiple Sub-summary parts on one layout

You can do some really creative reporting by adding multiple Sub-summary parts. Right now your layout groups by Status whenever you sort that way. But what if you want to group by city or state instead? No problem. Just add two more Sub-summary parts. Once again, the same Count of People field you already have counts the groups appropriately, so you don't need to add more fields to the layout.

Following the same basic steps you used in the previous section to add the first Sub-summary part, add two more. This time, though, attach the first to the State field and the second to the City field. In both cases, opt to "Print Above" just like you did in step 5 above. When you're done, you have three Sub-summary parts stacked up in Layout mode, as you can see in Figure 14-5.

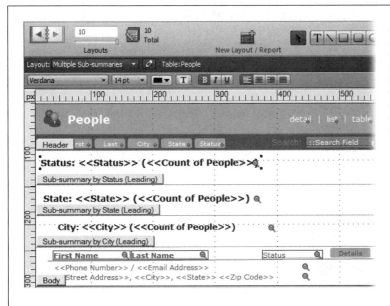

Figure 14-5:
When you add more than one Sub-summary part to your layout, FileMaker stacks them up in the order they were added. You can put the same summary fields in each one, and get totals appropriate to each group.

In the State Sub-summary part, add a text object that says "State: <<State>> (<<Count of People>>)". In the City Sub-summary part, add one with "City: <<City>> (<<Count of People>>)" instead. When you're done, your layout looks like Figure 14-6.

Note: If you're having trouble figuring out which Sub-summary part is which, you have two options. First, you can click the part label toggle to turn the part labels so they show a long and descriptive name. If you don't want to clutter your layout with long labels, then just double-click any part label instead. FileMaker opens the Part Setup dialog box again, and you can see which field the part is tied to.

When you switch to Browse mode now, your list looks just like it did before, because you're still sorted by Status. When you sort by City or State, the layout instantly switches to show the groups and totals appropriately (you can see the result in Figure 14-6).

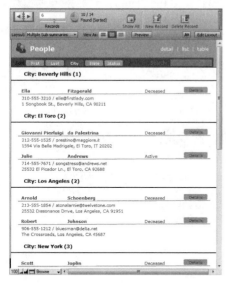

Figure 14-6:

Top: When you sort by City, the records appear in groups by city. Notice that the count of people in each city is shown in parentheses.

Bottom: Simply by changing the sort order, the layout now groups by State instead. Once again, the totals update to correctly count the new groups.

Tip: If you sort by both City and State, then you see both the associated summary parts. This feature too can be handy in a complex layout (especially a report).

Leading and Trailing Grand Summaries

Sometimes you want to see the totals for the found set as a whole. For example, you may have interesting summary fields that show averages or other statistics about your data, and you want to highlight them in your layout. FileMaker calls these layout parts *Grand Summary* parts.

If you want a grand total *above* all the records, then add a *leading Grand Summary* part to the layout, and put your summary fields in it. If you use a *trailing Grand Summary* part instead, then the grand totals appear after the last record. You can see a leading Grand Summary in Figure 14-7.

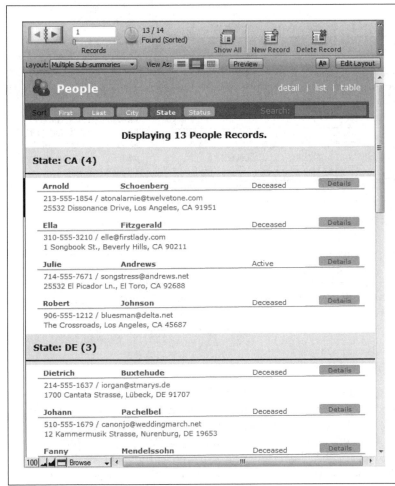

Figure 14-7:
The People List layout now has a leading grand summary part to show the overall total at the very top. If you scroll down to see more records, this total scrolls off the top of the list (unlike the header part, which never scrolls away).

Sub-summary Parts and Printing

You can use Sub-summary parts to build high-level reports that break the data down by multiple nested groups, and then roll up all the totals. For instance, your database of product sales may show order count, revenue, and share information. Using three Sub-summary parts, you can break these down by region, then state, and finally category.

For just the highest-level analysis, you can leave the Body part out of the layout entirely. When you do, FileMaker doesn't show the individual records at all. Instead, it shows just the summarized data. Figure 14-8 shows just such a layout in Layout mode.

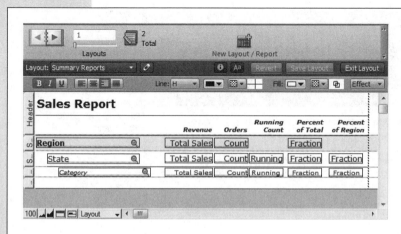

Figure 14-8:
This layout has three sub-summary parts and several summary fields. The data is intended so that when multiple Sub-summary parts show at once, you can see how the groups fit together. Also notice there's no Body part. This report shows only summarized data.

Tip: You can find the database pictured in Figure 14-8 on this book's Missing CD page at *http://missing-manuals.com/cds*.

Web Viewer Objects

Imagine you want to view a map of someone's address in your People database. Getting a map isn't a problem; they're readily available on the Web. Google Maps (*http://maps.google.com/*) and MapQuest (*www.mapquest.com/*) both give you free maps. Still, it's a lot of work to copy address information, change programs, find the right page, and then paste the address into your web browser for each record. Maybe you want to show the map right on the layout, instantly available at a glance. You could draw your own maps and store them in a container field, or even take screenshots right off of Google, and then paste them in. But that's an awful lot of work, too.

FREQUENTLY ASKED QUESTION

FileMaker's Web Browser

Is the web viewer a modern browser? Is it standards-compliant? Can it run JavaScript, or use browser plug-ins? Should I be worried about compatibility with various pages?

FileMaker doesn't actually have a web browser of its own lurking underneath your layout. Instead, it calls upon the services of the web browser engine most readily available—the one that came with your computer. In Windows, FileMaker uses Internet Explorer as its underlying browser technology. In Mac OS X, it uses Safari instead. This arrangement has a few important implications:

- FileMaker is using a tried-and-true browser technology, so you know it works well with most web pages.

It has support for all the major web technologies, just like its real web browser counterparts.

- If you install any plug-ins for your web browser, File-Maker web viewers can utilize them as well.

- If you upgrade your operating system or web browser, FileMaker's web viewer gets the benefits of the upgrade as well. For example, if you install Internet Explorer 7 (or use Windows 7), then the web viewer gets all its page-handling capabilities. If you have Internet Explorer 6 installed instead, your web viewer has its limitations.

Instead, simply ask FileMaker to go get the maps from the Internet for you. Using a FileMaker web viewer, you can get FileMaker to automatically and instantly fetch almost anything available on the Web and display it directly on the layout. FileMaker even takes care of keeping things up to date: Every time you visit a record on the layout, it checks to see if newer information is available, and automatically fetches the most up-to-date version, just like your web browser.

You create web viewers with the web viewer tool. This globe-decorated tool button lives on the Status toolbar near the field tool. It works like most FileMaker tools: First, in the Status toolbar, click the globe button, and then, on the layout, drag a rectangle to tell FileMaker where to put the web viewer, and how big to make it.

Putting a Web Viewer on a Layout

Your People database could use a map on the People Detail layout. Here's how to put one there.

1. **Switch to the People Detail layout, and then (if necessary) switch to Layout mode.**

   Since a map can be large, it makes sense to put it on the Detail layout, where you have some room to work with.

2. **Make the Body part much taller by dragging its label downward.**

   The idea is to make room for the web viewer on this otherwise crowded layout.

3. **In the Status toolbar, select the Web Viewer tool, and then draw a rectangle on the page roughly the same width as the Notes field and a few inches tall.**

As usual, you're free to tweak the exact size and position of the web viewer any time you want, so you don't have to be perfect here. As soon as you let go of the mouse button, FileMaker shows you the Web Viewer Setup dialog box (Figure 14-9).

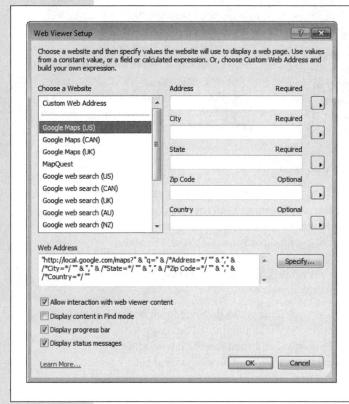

Figure 14-9:
The Web Viewer Setup dialog box has a lot of options. First, from the list on the left, pick the website you want to show. Then fill in the appropriate boxes on the right. If you choose Custom Web Address, then, at the bottom of the window, you can use the Web Address box to type any URL you want.

4. **In the "Choose a Website" list, select Google Maps (US).**

You're telling FileMaker you want this web viewer to show information from the Google Maps website. As soon as you make this selection, several entry boxes appear on the dialog box's right side.

5. **To the right of the Address entry box, click the square button, and then, from the resulting pop-up menu, choose Specify Field.**

FileMaker pops up the standard Specify Field dialog box. Here you tell File-Maker which field to pull the street address from when it goes to find a map.

6. **In the Specify Field window, select Street Address, and then click OK.**

   FileMaker now knows the first piece of information it needs to find the appropriate map. Notice that the Address box now shows People::Street Address.

7. **Repeat step 7 for the City, State, and Zip Code boxes. In each case, pick the appropriate field.**

   As you make selections, FileMaker fills in the various boxes. The Web Address box at the bottom of the window also changes, but you don't need to concern yourself with that just yet.

8. **Click OK.**

   The Web Viewer Setup window disappears, and the web viewer appears on the layout.

9. **Select the web viewer, and then anchor it to the left, bottom, and right (but not the top) using the Inspector.**

   To keep the web viewer from bumping into the expanding Notes field when the window is resized, you need to tell it to stick to the bottom of the window.

If you switch to Browse mode, and your computer is connected to the Internet, then you should see the Google Maps page with a map for the current person record (Figure 14-10). You may need to make the window bigger for the map to display properly. If you fiddle with the database a bit, then you notice a few important things:

- When you switch to a new record, the web viewer changes its contents to reflect the address information on the new record. Likewise, if you *change* the data in any of the address fields, then the map instantly updates to show the new address.

- Status information shows at the bottom of the web viewer while the page loads.

- You're free to click links in the web page, and the web viewer dutifully follows your clicks and shows a new page.

- Although the web viewer isn't a full-fledged browser (it doesn't have a Back button, for instance) you can access most typical browsing commands by right-clicking (Windows) or Control-clicking (Mac) anywhere on the web page. In fact, the menu that appears when you do is just like the one you'd see if you did the same in your real web browser. For instance, choose Back from this menu to go to the previous page.

Web Viewer Options

FileMaker offers up a few configuration options for web viewers in addition to the page they should load. The bottom of the Web Viewer Setup dialog box (Figure 14-9) includes four checkboxes to adjust the behavior of this particular web viewer.

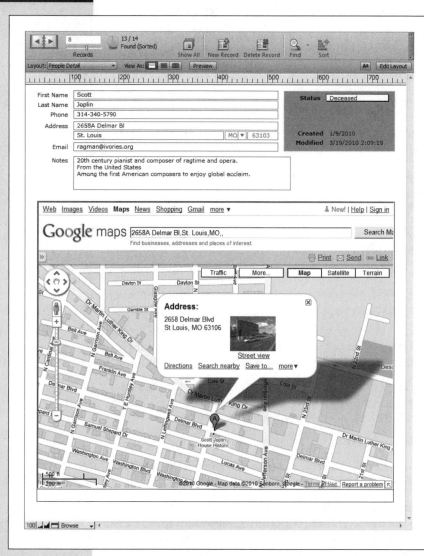

Figure 14-10:
The People database now has a Google Maps web page showing right on the detail layout. File-Maker's web viewer lets you embed any web page on the layout, so you can save countless trips to your favorite web resources. Unfortunately, web pages tend to be big. You'll learn how to give this map more breathing room without investing in a 30-inch screen on page 618.

Allow interaction with web viewer content

When the "Allow interaction with web viewer content" option is turned on (as it is for your map), FileMaker lets you actually *use* the web page it loads. Specifically, you can click a link on the page to navigate to a new page. You can also use shopping carts, send email messages, watch video, or use any other features on the page.

When you turn this option off, all page behavior is deactivated. Clicking the page produces no more response than clicking a blank spot on the layout. You can't even scroll the page. If a page is too big to fit in the space you've given it on the layout, then FileMaker simply cuts it off.

Turn this option on when the page you're showing is just a starting point (like the login screen for your Orders web page, or the first step in the application process). You should also leave this option on when the page is larger or its size is variable. On the other hand, you can turn "Allow interaction with web viewer content" off when you're showing a small page that contains all the information needed.

POWER USERS' CLINIC

Beyond the Built-in Sites

When you added a Google Maps page to your layout, you didn't have to figure out how Google expects to receive address information. Instead, you simply picked Google Maps from a list, and then filled in the blanks. This easy-to-integrate approach is possible because FileMaker already knows how to connect to Google Maps. FileMaker has built-in support for several popular websites (you see each one listed in the Web Viewer Setup dialog box). When you pick from this list, FileMaker shows a series of entry boxes appropriate for that site. For example, with Google Maps selected, the dialog box asks for Address, City, State, Zip Code, and Country. If you pick FedEx instead, FileMaker asks for a Tracking Number. In every case, you can pick a field FileMaker should use to get the data it wants, or you can type a value instead, like *USA* for Country if all your addresses are in the United States.

But don't let FileMaker's list of companion sites trick you into thinking they're the only ones that work. You can connect a web viewer to *any site*. At the top of the "Choose a Website" list, just choose Custom Web Address. Then, in the Web Address box at the bottom of the window, type any URL you want (or copy one from a web page, and then paste it in).

Unfortunately, if you want the exact page information tied to data in the record (just like the Google Maps example), then you have to supply a calculation for the Web Address. Chapters 8, 9, and 15 have everything you need to master calculations.

Display content in Find mode

Normally, when you switch to Find mode, the web viewer just goes blank. Which makes sense, since a web viewer is usually showing a page associated with data in the current record. After all, if you go to Find mode, where you're no longer necessarily looking at a particular record, then FileMaker may not be able to tell which web address goes in the web viewer.

You can change this behavior, though, by turning on "Display content in Find mode". When you do, FileMaker makes its best effort to display the web page even when you're in Find mode. For example, if you've typed a URL directly into the Web Viewer Setup dialog box, then FileMaker can continue to display the page properly no matter which mode you use (except Layout mode). If you're using a website that needs information from the database, then FileMaker feeds it the data from the find request instead. This behavior could come in handy if the web page information would be helpful to a person trying to construct a find request, but usually you want to leave this option off. It can be jarring to watch a web viewer constantly refresh itself as you enter your find criteria.

Display progress bar

Unlike everything else on your layout, web page content isn't always immediately accessible by FileMaker. The program has to go to the Internet and pull up the page, which can take some time (just as it takes time for a page to load in your browser). If you turn on "Display progress bar" (it's on until you turn it off, in fact), then File-Maker shows a subtle progress bar at the bottom of the web viewer (Figure 14-11).

Display status messages

Another option that FileMaker automatically turns on is the "Display status messages" checkbox. This option tells the web viewer to reserve a little space along its bottom edge to show status information (Figure 14-11). Status information typically means the "Loading…" messages you see at the bottom of a web browser window. Turn this option off if you'd rather not sacrifice precious layout space for not much more information than what the progress bar already gives you. That way, the web viewer can use all its space on the layout for web page content.

Conditional Formatting

Sometimes you want the formatting (color, font, style, and so forth) of a layout object to change depending on certain criteria. For example, you might want the Status field to change color depending on its value, turning red if the person is deceased. That way you easily spot this fact whenever you look at the record.

FileMaker's conditional formatting feature lets you make database objects change when, well, conditions change. It works by letting you specify a series of criteria and the specific formatting changes that go along with them. FileMaker means *condition* in the "I'll give you a hand on one condition…" sense. As long as certain restrictions are met, the formatting applies.

Conditional Formatting of Fields

You can apply conditional formatting to any text object, button, field, or web viewer. Follow these steps to make your status field more dynamic:

1. On the List layout, select the Status field, and then choose Format→Conditional.

    You see the Conditional Formatting dialog box pictured in Figure 14-12.

2. **Click Add.**

    A new condition appears in the list at the top of the window. Also, the dialog box's Condition and Format sections become active (they were grayed out until now).

3. **From the first pop-up menu under Condition, make sure "Value is" is chosen.**

    You can configure your condition in two different ways. Either you place simple rules on the value of a field, or, if your needs are more complex, you use a *formula*. You'll start with the easy kind.

Figure 14-11:
If you turn on the right options, the web viewer can show a status message (that text at the very bottom) and/or progress bar (the black line just above the status bar) as the web page loads. If you prefer a minimalist look, in the Web Viewer Setup dialog box, turn off both "Display status message" and "Display progress bar".

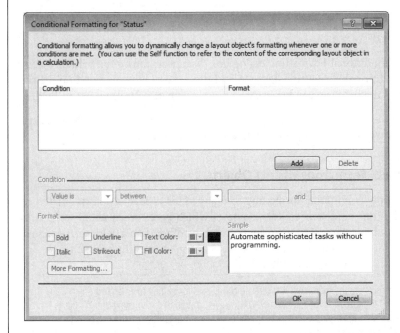

Figure 14-12:
The Conditional Formatting dialog box lets you assign formatting to a field, button, or text object that kicks in only when certain conditions are met. Simply click Add to add a new condition. Use the pop-up menus and boxes below the Condition line to tell FileMaker under what conditions the formatting should apply, and tell it what formatting you want by tweaking the options under Format.

4. **From the second pop-up menu under Condition, choose "equal to".**

   In this case, you want the conditional formatting to apply when the Status is "Deceased", so you tell FileMaker that's the kind of comparison it should do.

5. **To the right of the pop-up menu, in the box, type *Deceased*.**

   Here's where you enter the comparison value. (If you choose a comparison type other than "equal to", then the dialog box may show you different options.)

   FileMaker adjusts the display of the dialog box so that the condition line reads like a meaningful sentence: "Value is→equal to→Deceased."

6. **From the Fill Color pop-up menu, choose a dark red color. Then from the Text Color pop-up menu, choose white.**

   As soon as you make a selection from either pop-up menu, FileMaker turns on the checkbox to the left of its label. This checkbox tells FileMaker you want it to go ahead and apply this style when the condition is met. If you decide you don't want to change the fill color after all, you can simply uncheck the box.

Note: You don't have to provide any formatting rules for other values in the Status field. When none of the conditions in the Conditional Formatting dialog box apply (you can add as many as you want), FileMaker leaves the object formatted as it is in Layout mode, so you don't need to add a condition for the *normal* case.

---

7. **Click OK.**

   The Conditional Formatting dialog box disappears, and your field now sports a Conditional Formatting *badge*. That little red and blue diamond on the right side of the field lets you know Conditional Formatting is used on this field.

Although the layout looks unchanged, if you switch to Browse mode, then you see it works as advertised. Every person with a status of Deceased shows in red.

Conditional Formatting of Text Objects

You can apply conditional formatting to many kinds of layout objects—fields, text objects, buttons, and web viewers, some of which you'll learn about later in this chapter. But typically when you format something other than a field, you need to use a formula for the condition, since those objects don't have values that change.

Note: Text objects are the exception. You can use conditional formatting rules on text objects, and they apply based on the text you type into the object. However, conditional formatting of text objects is most useful when they contain symbols (page 162) or merge fields. You can set up the text object's appearance to change when its contents change.

To show a formula-based conditional formatting rule, you'll add conditional formatting to your database in a surprising place. Take a peek at Figure 14-13 to see the problem you need to fix.

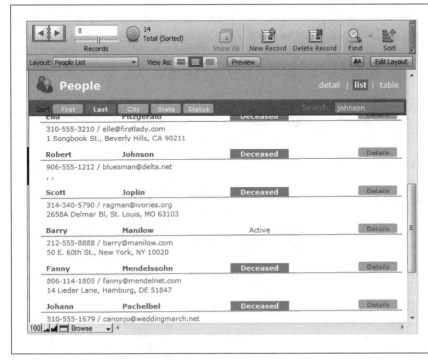

Figure 14-13:
Take a look at the text under Robert Johnson. You see two extraneous commas floating in the middle of nowhere. These commas separate the address, city, and state in the address line. In this case, all the address fields are empty, so just the commas show up.

Most people wouldn't think of it right away, but conditional formatting can help clean up a little mess like commas between empty fields. If the address fields are empty—and that's a condition—you don't want the commas to show up. FileMaker doesn't have the power to make layout objects disappear completely, but you can turn the text white. Then, even though the commas are technically there, no one can see them. Since the formatting is applied conditionally, as soon as address information is entered for a record, the data (commas and all) appears normally.

Tip: You have other ways to solve this same problem. For example, you can add a calculation field (page 131) to your database that intelligently assembles the address info into a compact line.

Using conditional formatting, you'll make the text color turn white when the address fields are empty. This tactic requires a relatively simple formula. Here are the steps:

1. **Select the text object containing the address merge fields, and then choose
   Format→Conditional.**

   The Conditional Formatting dialog box reappears.

2. **Click Add to add a new condition to the list.**

   Once again, a line appears in the list at the top of the window.

3. **Switch the first pop-up menu to "Formula is".**

   The remaining pop-up menu disappears, and a new larger box appears in its place, where you'll type your formula.

4. **In the formula box, type the following:**

   ```
   IsEmpty(People::Street Address) and IsEmpty(People::City) and
   IsEmpty(People::State) and IsEmpty(People::Zip Code)
   ```

   It's important to type the formula exactly, since typos may prevent the whole thing from working. This formula checks to see that all the address fields are empty. (Everything you need to know about formulas is in Chapter 8.)

5. **From the Text Color pop-up menu, choose the white tile, and then click OK.**

   The Conditional Formatting dialog box goes away.

Tip: If you get an error message, clear the formula box, and then try typing over the formula again.

Now if you switch to Browse mode, you see that the mysterious commas have disappeared. See Figure 14-14 for proof. This technique of hiding things is surprisingly common among more advanced FileMaker developers because it helps build more data-rich layouts with less clutter.

Advanced Conditional Formatting

In both of the previous examples, you added only one condition to the list in the Conditional Formatting dialog box. But it isn't a list if you can't add more than one. When you do, FileMaker looks at every condition on the list, and makes the formatting changes for each one that applies. As a result, you can easily create several different formats for several different conditions. For example, you can make numbers in your budget database turn red when you're getting behind, stay black when you're right on target, and turn green when you're beating expectations.

Two matching conditions can even have competing formatting rules. For instance, you can set the text color to something different in each rule, even though they both apply to the same values. In that case, FileMaker chooses the format from the condition that comes *last* in the list. You can move these conditions around using their little arrows to influence its decision. Just put the condition that should take precedence lower in the list.

Also, in the Conditional Formatting dialog box, if you don't see the formatting choice you want, just click More Formatting, and chances are you'll find what you want. This button opens a dialog box that lets you adjust additional formatting, including font, size, and a few extra styles.

Figure 14-14:
Using conditional formatting, you can "hide" text on the layout under certain conditions. Just make it turn white (or whatever your background color is). Compare this picture with Figure 14-13—no more stray commas!

Removing Conditional Formatting

If an object has conditional formatting behavior that you don't want anymore (which often happens if you duplicate one field and change it to another), then you can easily turn it off. Just select the object, choose Format→Conditional, and then delete the conditions from the list. You can Shift-click to delete them all at once, or just click the first, and then click Delete repeatedly until they're all gone.

If you spent long hours adding complex conditions and you're not quite ready to commit to losing them forever, then you can *turn them off* instead. Each condition in the list has a checkbox beside it. If you turn off a condition's checkbox, FileMaker no longer uses that condition. You can always get the condition back later by turning it back on. You can turn multiple checkboxes on or off at once as well: Just Shift-click the conditions you want to switch so they're all selected. Then turn off the checkbox beside *one* of them, and FileMaker turns all the others off as well.

Basic Charting (Found Set Charts)

Summary reports are just dandy, but there comes a time when text and numbers just don't cut it. Often, the people who want the summary information don't take the time to study and interpret those numbers. Other times, you may need to punch up the presentation to make a point. That's when charts come in handy. Consider Figure 14-15. If you're trying to impress upon the Lawnmower Museum's curator just how little enthusiasm the public is displaying for the "Pull Cords Through the Ages" exhibit, which approach do you suppose will have the greater impact?

FileMaker offers five fundamental chart types, each with some formatting options to make them your own.

Bar

The Bar chart is the classic method for visualizing data: a column for each thing you're counting and the taller it is, the more there are. You can set your Bars to be flat or 3D, shaded or solid-colored. When you have multiple data series' (see the steps on page 638), FileMaker will group and color them together.

Horizontal Bar

Distinguished by their lateral proclivities, Horizontal Bar charts are the same as the implicitly vertical Bar charts described above, just turned by 90 degrees. All the formatting options are identical.

Line

Line charts are a classic tool for showing change over time. Trending information like historical stock market performance, or annual snowfall is particularly apt for Line charts. FileMaker can draw your lines in smooth curves or sharp angles, but that's about all you can customize.

Area

A close cousin of the Line is the Area chart. In fact, it's just an angular Line chart with color filled in beneath the line. Like the Bar charts, Area charts can be flat or 3D. If the data you're plotting ever crosses (say you're showing digital music sales rising and CD sales fall) you'll want to take advantage of the "Semi-transparent" option to ensure all series' remain visible.

Pie

Unlike the other four chart choices, Pie charts always display one thing—the relative portions that make up a whole. Throw a set of data at it and FileMaker helpfully calculates each item's percentage contribution and slices the pie for you. The increasingly familiar flat/3D solid/shaded formatting choices apply here as well.

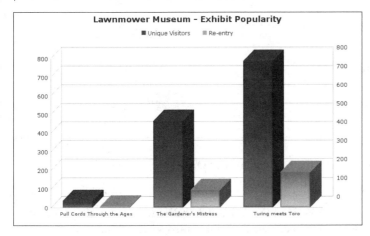

British Lawnmower Museum
Exhibit Popularity

Exhibit	Visit Date	Unique Visitors	Re-entries
Pull cords through the ages	1/16/2010	8	1
Pull cords through the ages	1/31/2010	14	2
Pull cords through the ages	2/15/2010	4	0
Pull cords through the ages	3/2/2010	6	1
Pull cords through the ages	3/17/2010	0	0
Pull cords through the ages	3/1/2010	2	0
Pull cords through the ages		**34**	**4**
The Gardener's Mistress	1/9/2010	87.5	23
The Gardener's Mistress	1/19/2010	80	13
The Gardener's Mistress	2/8/2010	85	21
The Gardener's Mistress	2/18/2010	72.5	7
The Gardener's Mistress	3/10/2010	77.5	15
The Gardener's Mistress	3/20/2010	62.5	13
The Gardener's Mistress		**465**	**92**
Turing meets Toro	1/13/2010	110	38
Turing meets Toro	1/29/2010	96	7
Turing meets Toro	2/12/2010	134	9
Turing meets Toro	2/28/2010	142	65
Turing meets Toro	3/14/2010	148	26
Turing meets Toro	3/30/2010	156	42
Turing meets Toro		**786**	**187**

Figure 14-15:
The Lawnmower museum's at-tendance figures are presented as a summary report (above) and a chart (below). It's instantly obvious which exhibit isn't drawing the crowds when the information is visualized as a chart.

For this exercise, you can download the Charts.fp7 file from this book's Missing CD page at *www.missingmanuals.com/cds*. Here's how to set up a simple Bar chart for the museum attendance database:

1. **Open the Charts.fp7 database, and then switch to the Facility layout.**

2. **In Layout Mode, select the Chart tool, and then drag to create a chart using most of the space below the fields.**

   If you don't see all your tools, it usually means you need to make the window a bit wider.

   The Chart Setup dialog box appears. Leave the Chart Type set to Bar.

3. **In the Chart Title box, type *Museum Attendance*. For the Horizontal (X) Axis, click the button to the right of the field and select Specify Field Name from the pop-up menu shown in Figure 14-16.**

   A list of fields appears.

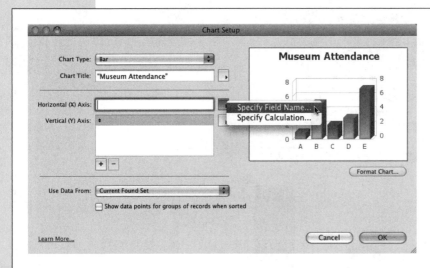

Figure 14-16:
The axes of a chart can draw their data from a particular field as shown here, or from a calculation you construct.

4. **Click the Facility field, and then click OK.**

   You see Facility::Facility Name in the Horizontal (X) Axis field.

5. **Moving down to Vertical (Y) Axis, click the button to its right, select Specify Field Name, and then choose the field named Visitor Sum. Click OK.**

   Facility::Visitor Sum appears in the Vertical (Y) Axis box.

6. **Leave all the other settings unchanged, click OK on the Chart Setup dialog box, and then switch to Browse mode.**

   You should see a chart like the one on Figure 14-17. The bars are accurate, but the chart isn't usable yet.

Gazing upon your first chart, some flaws are immediately apparent. The labels along the bottom overlap so you can't read them. The vertical axis shows no unit of measurement. And the whole thing is squished into a small space. Fortunately, File-Maker doesn't leave you without some options for whipping this chart into shape.

1. Return to Layout mode and click once on your chart to select it. Over in the Inspector window, select the Position tab and, in the Autosizing section, activate the bottom and right anchors.

   All four anchors should now be active. This will cause your chart to stretch with the size of your window when you're back in Browse mode.

2. Before you switch to Browse mode, however, select Format→Chart Setup (or simply double click the chart).

   You return to the aptly named Chart Setup dialog box.

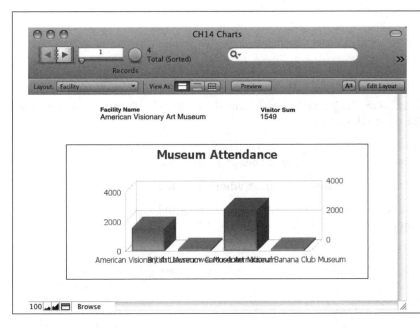

Figure 14-17:
Sure it's a chart, but is it art? This chart's X axis contains some unfortunately long museum names. FileMaker isn't quite crafty enough to sort this problem out by itself, but the tools to correct it lie in the Format Chart options.

On the right side of the dialog box, just below the example chart, click the Format Chart button (Figure 14-16).

On the left side of the Format Chart dialog box, you see five items listed: Chart Appearance, Legend, Horizontal (X) Axis, Vertical (Y) Axis, and (Y) Series 1.

3. Click Horizontal (X) Axis.

   Your chart's X Axis lists the various museums in the report.

4. In the X-Axis Title box, type *Museum Name*. Set the Label Angle pop-up menu to 45° to pretty it up.

   It looks like Figure 14-18.

5. From the list of choices on the left, click Vertical (Y) Axis. For its title, type *Attendees*.

   They Y axis graphs the number of people who attended each museum.

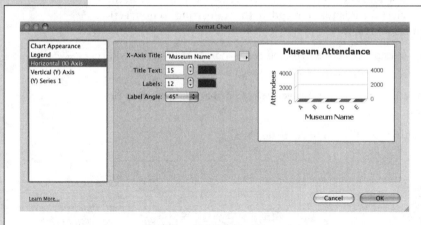

Figure 14-18:
The Format Chart dialog box is where the real magic happens. Essential components of a well-made chart like axis titles for xy charts and series legends for pie charts are configured here.

6. **Turn on the Set Y-Axis checkbox, and then enter 0 for the minimum and 3000 for the maximum.**

   Because none of the museums saw more than 3,000 visitors, you can restrict the range of the Y Axis to go no higher (Figure 14-19).

7. **Switch back into Browse mode to admire your handiwork.**

Now you've got a usable chart that's clean, readable and appropriately labeled, your chart should look something like Figure 14-20.

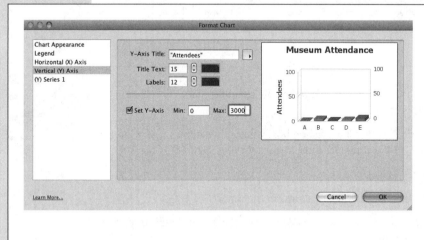

Figure 14-19:
Generally when setting the range of a Y axis, it's best to have a minimum of zero, or, if your data includes negative numbers, the lowest value in the set. The high should be just slightly higher than the largest number in your data. If your data is subject to a lot of variability, just leave this option unchecked–FileMaker does a pretty good job of setting the range automatically.

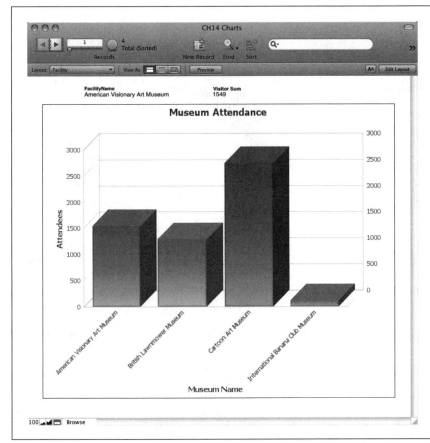

Chart Formatting

While you were working in the Format Chart dialog box in the previous section, chances are you were enticed by the Chart Appearance options. Now is a great time to try out some of those cool formatting possibilities. You can change your font, color scheme, and background. You have wide artistic latitude here, but remember, your goal is to enhance your chart and make it easier to read. Less is more.

To dig into all those possibilities, shift over to Layout mode, and then double click your chart. In the Chart Setup dialog box, click that Format Chart button on the right. Here in the Chart Appearance settings, Figure 14-21, you can ditch Helvetica for a more interesting font—but again, your goal is to be readable, not fancy. The Chart Title field just below the Font pop-up menu is the font's point size. And the dark rectangle immediately to the right of that is the font color. Click it to reveal a palette of hues to choose from.

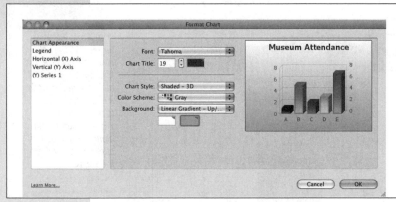

Figure 14-21:
The Chart Appearance section of the Format Chart dialog box is were you can beautify your chart. FileMaker gives you wide latitude to customize your chart however you wish, but this isn't the place to abandon restraint. Choose your font and colors carefully lest you end up with seizure-inducing contrasts.

Tip: If you're a fan of seeing sample data while working in Layout mode (View→Show→Sample Data), brace up for a little disappointment. Graphs in Layout mode will faithfully display your formatting decisions like chart type, font sizes and color schemes, but you won't see actual data until you return to Browse or Preview mode.

The Chart Style pop-up menu varies by chart type, but generally offers solid or shaded coloring, and flat or 3D style presentation. Moving down to the Color Scheme pop-up menu, you'll find that FileMaker has furnished you with 20 color schemes with florid names like Muted Rainbow and Sea Glass. If you don't see a theme you like, find one you can settle for, because this is as custom as your colors are going to get. You can't set colors for individual graph elements, and you can't create your own themes. Happily, you're not stuck with a plain white background for every chart you make. The Background pop-up menu allows you to choose your own background color, or one of eight gradient style backgrounds that fade gradually from one color to another.

Note: Those two boxes just below the Background pop-up menu are used to set the gradient colors. But they're both automatically set to white. And the gradient that transitions from white to white is no gradient at all. As you try out different gradients from the Background pop-up menu, the background in the preview remains solid white. To see a meaningful preview, simply set either of those colors to something that *isn't* white before you choose a gradient.

You can also set the background to transparent, thus allowing the chart to blend in with the background of the layout you place it on. This option helps gives your database a consistent appearance. It works really well if your layout has a quiet, subtle background. If your background is a photo of your cat, not so much.

Charting 101

Throwing together a simple chart is easy enough, but creating a *useful* and *meaningful* chart takes a little thought. Indeed, a poorly conceived chart can obscure or even contradict the information you want to communicate. Visualized data is also subject to cultural context, and more than you might think. Imagine you've invested in my ostrich ranch and I've presented you with a chart showing your financial return in the form of Figure 14-22. Would you give me the stink-eye or a hug? If you're from a western culture and read from left to right, that chart looks like bad news. Look a little closer.

Here are a few basic charting concepts to consider:

- The passage of time is usually charted in the X (horizontal) axis starting with the earliest date or time on the left and proceeding to the most recent on the right.

- Numerical values are best suited to the Y (vertical) axis with the lowest values at the bottom of the chart range. FileMaker won't even let you order values any other way. If you sort your values in descending order, the Y-axis won't change.

- Multiple items in the Y-axis of a chart are called *series*. Consider a line graph with one line showing a particular stock's performance over time and a second line showing overall market performance. The stock is one series and the overall market is the second. Series are terrific for comparing multiple entities, but

all the entities have to use the same unit of measurement. An individual stock and the whole stock market are both measured in currency (dollars, yen, euros, etc.) making them well suited to being series on the same chart. Other series just don't pair up, like a commute (measuring distance) and the capacity of a gas tank (measuring volume). One final thought about series– sometimes, even series that share the same unit of measurement don't chart well together. For example, if your database calculates the distances from various Italian cities to other Italian and South African cities, your unit of measurement will be the same. But most Italian cities are within a few hundred kilometers of each other while South Africa is at least 7,000 kilometers away. Such a vast gap between data sets doesn't generally lend itself to charting.

- Pies portray percentages. Pie charts show the proportional composition of a whole. That "whole" can be second quarter sales, Ray Bradbury's oeuvre, or your retirement savings. The slices can represent sales reps, editors, or mutual funds. The important thing is that you clearly define what the slices are and how they add up to 100 percent of something. FileMaker helps you stay clear of the temptation to use raw numbers instead of percentages for your pie charts by computing and displaying each slice's percent contribution automatically.

Charting and Reports

Charts and graphs are classic tools for boiling a whole lot of data down to easily understandable information. When it comes to FileMaker, concisely presenting a large data set is going to involve Summary fields (page 601), and Summary parts on layouts (page 608). Lucky for you, charts feel right at home in Summary reports. It's important, however, to craft your charts carefully, and then place them on the right layout parts. Take a look at Figure 14-23. Each image shows the exact same chart drawing from the exact same data. The only difference between them is the layout part they've been placed in. Now consider Figure 14-24. These images display the same chart and data set, but with different sort orders. Ultimately, producing an accurate chart comes down to three main rules: Pick the right fields, place the chart on the appropriate layout part, and use the correct sort order.

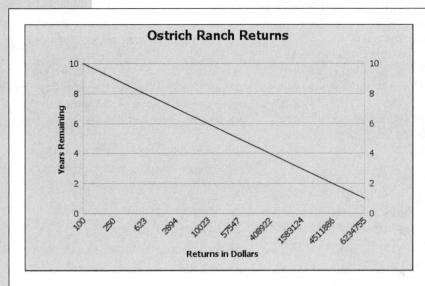

Figure 14-22:
At first glance, this chart of returns on your 10-year investment in an ostrich ranch looks pretty grim. But it's actually a perfectly valid and accurate (albeit imaginary) chart showing a return of over six million dollars! When we see a chart, we tend to assume that time is displayed horizontally from left to right and values are in the vertical axis. This ill-conceived chart runs counter to those norms and risks being gravely misinterpreted.

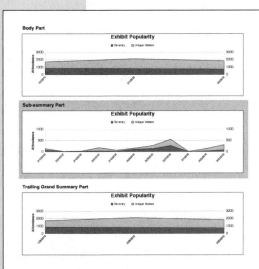

Figure 14-23:
A chart designed for use in a Sub-summary part has been copied and pasted into the Body and Trailing Grand Summary parts of the same layout. Seen here in Browse mode, it's pretty clear that what works in the Sub-summary doesn't directly translate to the other parts.

Picking the Right Fields

Picking the right fields might, on its face, seem to be a pointless rule. After all, you know which fields contain the information you want charted, right? And FileMaker won't let you make an invalid chart, so what's the problem? The problem is that no product can prevent you from creating a confusing or even meaningless chart. Choose fields that have accurate and consistent data. If your chart appears in a layout's Body part, be sure you're not trying to use a summary field for one of the axes or you'll end up displaying the same values in every record. Caution is also advised when charting fields with related data—see Advanced Charting later in this chapter for details.

Choosing an Appropriate Layout Part

Earlier in this chapter you learned how one field can display a variety of different values depending on the layout part it's in. Charts exhibit very similar behavior. Identically configured charts can display very different values whether placed in the Body, Sub-summary, or Grand Summary parts of the same layout (check out Figure 14-23). Still selecting the appropriate layout part needn't be a headache.

If you wish to graph information from a single record, or non-aggregate data from a found set of records, Body is the layout part of choice. If your aim is to visualize summarized information for groups of similar records, you'll want to set up a Sub-summary part on your layout as described on page 608 and give your chart a home there. Finally, should you want to show summarized data for the entire found set of records, you'll want to use a Grand Summary part.

Tip: When working with related data, that is, fields from another table in your database, the guidelines here don't apply quite so rigidly. For example, it's possible to display summary data for related records in a Body part using calculation fields—no Summary fields or Summary parts necessary.

Using the Correct Sort Order

Regardless of *where* you place a chart, unsorted or incorrectly sorted records can take a dandy chart and render it useless. If your chart is located in a Sub-summary part, you need only sort by the field you associated with the Sub-summary part at the time you defined it. With Body part charts, you'll generally sort by the fields charted in the X axis. See Figure 14-24 for more.

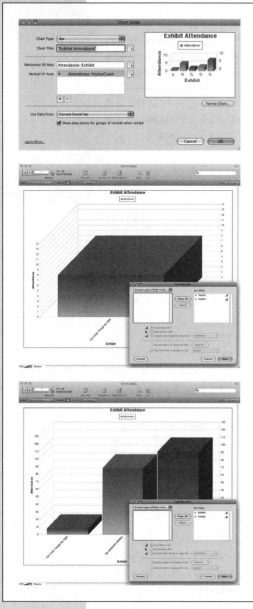

Figure 14-24:
The correct sort order is crucial to the accuracy of your charts.

Top: The Chart Setup dialog box specifies the field named "exhibit" for the X (horizontal) axis and "Show data points for groups of records when sorted" is turned on.

Middle: When the exhibit field isn't first in the sort order, you get a rather pointless one-bar chart.

Bottom: Change the sort order to put exhibit on top, and the chart instantly changes to reflect total attendance for the three exhibits in the current found set.

Advanced Charting

So far, you've been charting data from multiple records in a single table, but File-Maker offers two other data sources for visualizing—Delimited data and Related records. You can select either from the Chart Setup dialog box (Figure 14-25). To see them, enter Layout mode, and then double click any existing chart. Both are choices in the Use Data From pop-up menu.

Delimited Data

The "Current Record (delimited data)" option in the Chart Setup dialog box tells FileMaker to look at fields in the current record when drawing a chart. The data to be charted has to take the form of a *return separated list*. That is, each value has to be separated from adjacent values by a return character. When a particular character is designated to show where one list item ends and the next one begins, computer geeks call that a *delimiter*. In theory, any character, a comma, a tab, even the letter q can be a delimiter. FileMaker has settled on the return character for the purposes of charting.

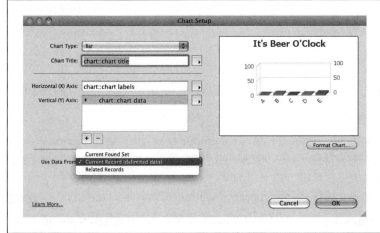

Figure 14-25:
The Use Data From pop-up menu is where you can configure your chart to draw from the current found set of records, lists of data in the current record, or records from a related table.

Note: If you have repeating fields in your database, they might seem like a natural source for delimited data. Quite often, a repeating field even looks like a return separated list on a layout. Alas, repeating fields aren't return separated, and you can't use them as such when charting.

Creating a chart of delimited data is generally straightforward. In the example database, switch over to the layout entitled "Delimited" depicted in Figure 14-26. Here you'll find two text fields with return separated lists already in them. The Chart Labels field contains the names of five Ostriches. Chart Data shows the average number of eggs each bird lays each month. You're going to chart that data.

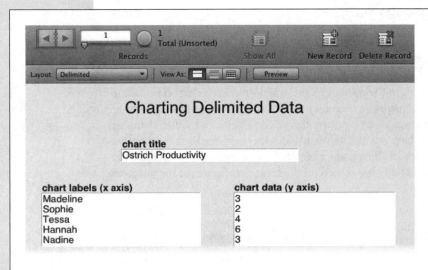

Figure 14-26:
In the FileMaker charting world, "Delimited" just means a list of values with line breaks between them. The link between the delimited values of these two fields is simply the order they're listed in. Were you to rearrange the names on the left to be in alphabetical order, the numbers on the right wouldn't automatically change with them.

1. Choose View→Layout Mode, and then select the Chart tool from the Status toolbar.

   It's the button that looks like a tiny bar chart.

2. Below the fields on the layout, drag out a box roughly the combined width of the fields already on the layout and down to about the bottom of the Body part.

   The Chart Setup dialog box appears (Figure 14-27).

3. Click the box to the right of the Chart Title field, and then select Specify Field Name from the list of fields that pops up, choose "chart title", and then click OK.

   Repeat step 3 for the X-axis, selecting the "chart labels" field and the Y-axis, choosing "chart data."

4. Finally, set the Use Data From pop-up menu to "Current Record (delimited data)", and then click OK.

   The dialog box should look like Figure 14-27.

Switch back to Browse mode to admire your chart. If you modify data in any of the fields, the chart will reflect your new data as soon as you commit the changes by clicking some empty space or pressing enter on your numeric keypad.

The beauty of charting delimited data is that you can use FileMaker's calculation tools and scripting capabilities to pull together a chart's raw data on demand. And because FileMaker draws the data exactly the way it appears in the fields, delimited data charts don't require a sorted found set.

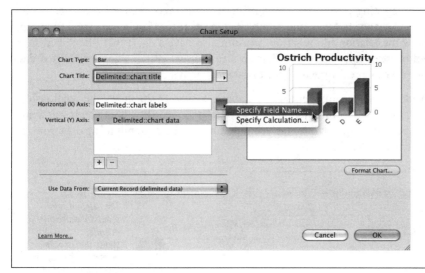

Figure 14-27:
The mechanics of charting delimited data isn't all that different from a chart based on records. The salient difference is that the fields or calculations specified here must be a list of values separated by returns.

Delimited data charts work the same way regardless of the layout part you place them in. But when placed on a part that isn't a Body, FileMaker must choose which record's data to use. Table 14-1 shows how it decides.

Table 14-1. *When a chart that's based on delimited data is placed outside of a Body layout part, File-Maker has to make an educated guess as to which record it should draw data from to create the chart.*

Layout Part	Delimited Chart Data Source
Leading Grand Summary	First record in found set
Trailing Grand Summary	Last record in found set
Header	Current selected record
Footer	Current selected record
Leading Sub-summary	First record in summary group
Trailing Sub-summary	Last record in summary group
Title Header	First record in found set
Title Footer	First record in found set

Related Records

Much of FileMaker's data mojo comes from its relational database capabilities (Chapter 5), and your charts can certainly tap into that. You can point a chart at a related table to graph the values related to the record you're viewing, which opens up some interesting possibilities. Navigating from one record to the next means your chart will change to reflect the data related to the record you're viewing. Depending on how the relationship is set up, you can also have a chart that filters its display based on selections you make. And in a multiuser setting, a chart of related data could serve as a real-time monitor to database activity.

Consider the museum attendance database. Figure 14-28 shows the relationships among the tables in this system. Charting related records will let you be on a museum's record in the Facilities table, but graph attendance trends using data from the Attendance table.

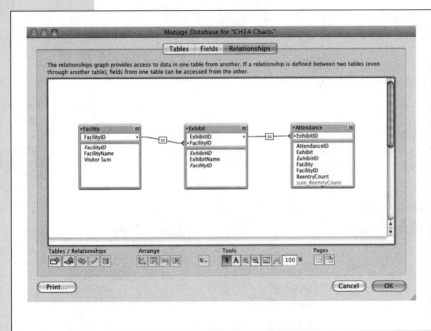

Figure 14-28:
The Relationships graph for museum attendance tracking shows the associations among its three tables. Each record Facilities represents one museum. Exhibits contains a record for each exhibit along with a Facility ID field that links the exhibit back to the Facility where it's located. Attendance records the number of visitors to a particular exhibit on a particular date, using the Exhibit ID field to maintain an association with the other two tables.

Here's how to create a chart using related records, like the one shown in Figure 14-31, using Charts.fp7 from this book's Missing CD page at *www.missingmanuals.com*:

1. **Switch to the layout named "Related Data" using the Layout pop-up menu in the Status toolbar, and then press CTRL+L (⌘-L) to enter Layout mode.**

2. **In the Status toolbar, select the Chart tool.**

    It's the button that looks like a tiny bar chart.

3. Below the fields on the layout, drag out a box about as tall as the available space in the Body part, and roughly as wide.

   The Chart Setup dialog box appears (Figure 14-29).

4. Change the Use Data From value to Related Records.

   A new Related Table pop-up menu appears.

5. From the Related Table pop-up menu, choose Attendance.

6. Turn on "Sort related records", and then double click Visit Date on the left to place it in the sort order (Figure 14-28). Click OK.

7. Back at the top of the dialog box, set Chart Type to Line. Click the square button to the right of the Chart Title field, and then select Specify Field Name.

   The Specify Field dialog box appears.

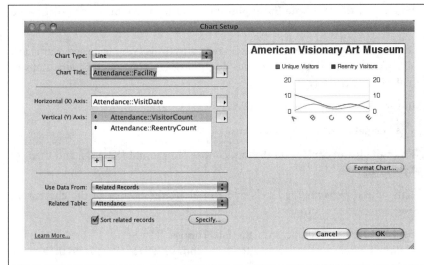

Figure 14-29:
Choosing "Related Records" for your data source isn't enough. You have to also specify which related table's records you want charted.

8. Set the pop-up menu to the first choice: Current Layout ("Related Data"). Click Facility Name, and then click OK.

   You're back in the Chart Setup dialog box.

9. Click the square button to the right of the Horizontal (X) Axis field, and then select Specify Field Name.

   In the Specify Field dialog box that appears, make sure the pop-up menu is set to Attendance.

10. From the field list, select Visit Date, and then click OK.

11. Click the square button to the right of the Vertical (Y) Axis field, and then select Specify Field Name.

    In the Specify Field dialog box that appears, make sure the pop-up menu is set to Attendance.

12. From the field list, select Reentry Count from the list, and then click OK.

13. Just below the Vertical (Y) Axis box, click the square "+" button to add a new series, click the square button to the right of the Vertical (Y) Axis field, and then select Specify Field Name.

    In the Specify Field dialog box that appears, make sure the pop-up menu is set to Attendance.

14. From the field list, select Visitor Count, and then click OK.

    You're back in the Chart Setup dialog box.

15. Finally, set the Use Data From pop-up menu to "Current Record (delimited data)", and then click OK.

    At this point, you could click OK and return to Browse mode to see your chart. You'd see a valid chart, but you need to follow a couple of additional steps to make it user friendly.

16. In the Chart Setup dialog box, click Format Chart.

    The Format Chart dialog box opens.

17. From the list of choices on the left, choose Horizontal (X) Axis, and then set Label Angle to "45°".

    This option prevents the labels that run along the bottom of the chart from overlapping one another.

18. Back in the list of choices on the left, choose "(Y) Series 1", and then type *Unique Visitors* for the Series Title. Now, choose "(Y) Series 2", and then name it Reentry Visitors.

    It should look like (Figure 14-30).

19. In the list at left click Legend from that now familiar list, and then turn on Include Legend.

    Optionally, you may change the legend formatting.

20. **Click OK to save your Format Chart settings, then click OK to save your Chart Setup.**

Hop back into Browse mode using CTRL+B (⌘-B) to admire your multiple series, related record chart.

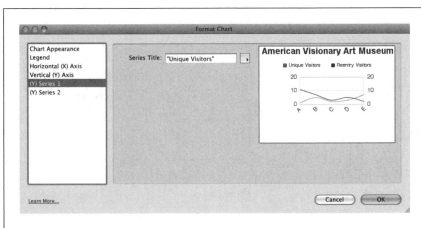

Figure 14-30:
When charting multiple data series, it's important to give each one a brief descriptive title. Users will see those titles in the chart's legend and use them to interpret the chart.

WORD TO THE WISE

Copy with Context

FileMaker merrily lets you copy and paste charts among your various layouts, but do so with care. A chart of related records that works just fine on layout A may show wildly different results or none at all when copied and pasted onto layout B. Relational context (page 151) is the reason why.

Consider this metaphor: Looking out the front window of my house, you can see about half of your next door neighbor's lawn but none of her house. If you move to a side window, you can now see almost all of her lawn and one entire side of her house. Whether your "context" was the front window or the side window, what you saw varied significantly even though it was the same property. Copying and pasting a chart of related data from one layout to another can be like moving among the windows. You won't always get the same view. If you find that you're having difficulty with related data charts, go back to page 136. A solid grounding in the fundamentals of FileMaker's relational model will serve you very well when charting.

Your new chart (Figure 14-31) shows attendance data that's related to the active Facility record. Using the flip-book in the Status Toolbar, click among the four records to see the attendance trends for each.

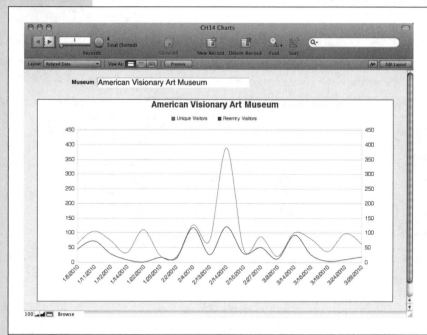

Figure 14-31:
Without this line chart you may never have noticed the Valentine's Day spike in attendance. In a multiuser setting, you'd see this chart update before your eyes as other users create or modify attendance information.

Advanced Calculations

I n the earlier calculation chapters, you learned how calculations can make your databases work harder for you. But the functions you've learned so far can't make your databases work much *smarter*. For example, what if you want to add a five-percent delinquency charge to invoices over a month old? You could create a special "past due balance" field on a special layout that you use only when you've searched for late invoices, but that's just extra complexity to create, and then maintain, if the late fee rules change later on. On the other hand, if you create a calculation that makes a *decision* based on current data, you can let the database itself can figure out when to apply late fees, and it works for every invoice, not just the late ones. This chapter shows you how to give your calculations that brainpower by using logical functions and other advanced techniques.

The calculation engine can also be used to give FileMaker features it doesn't have. You (or someone you hire) can create a *plug-in* in a programming language like C++. But you don't have to create a plug-in yourself. Lots of great ones are available from third-parties (page 670). Whether you write a plug-in or buy it, each plug-in adds new functions, like file handling, credit card processing or web services, to FileMaker's Specify Calculation window.

Note: To *create* plug-ins, you need FileMaker Pro Advanced. (Chapter 12). Once you've installed a plug-in, though, it can be *used* in any version of FileMaker.

But before you learn any of those new concepts, you'll revisit Boolean logic and learn more about how the Self function can make your calculations reusable in other fields. And you'll finally find out how and when to set a calculation field's storage options.

Tip: Download a copy of this chapter's sample file from this book's Missing CD page at *www.missing-manuals.com/cds*.

Understanding Boolean Functions

Boolean functions aren't a distinct group like Text or Number functions. Nor is "Boolean" a choice in the "Calculation Result is" pop-up menu. It's the *result* of a calculation that makes it Boolean. Regular calculations return results like 3.14 or 753 or "Dread Pirate Roberts." Boolean results refer to the theory of logic, and can always be reduced to either "true" or "false," "yes" or "no," "not empty" or "empty." Conditional Formatting calculations are always Boolean, since FileMaker needs to know if a particular condition is true before it can decide when to apply the formatting you set up. You can learn a lot about Boolean calculations by exploring the Conditional Formatting dialog box (Figure 15-1). See the box on page 647 for more on using Conditional Formatting.

The Boolean world has no shades of gray, no "maybe," and no glasses that are half full. For example, these statements are true, as most any schoolchild can tell you:

```
4 > 3
6 * 6 = 36
E = mc2
```

In Boolean terms, they're "True," but not due to any factual information they contain.

These Boolean values evaluate as "False":

```
0
False
F
f
No
N
n
Blank or ""
```

That last item in the list can make things a little murky. Typing the word *Blank* in a field doesn't make it evaluate as false; *leaving* it blank does. And that's what the "" (empty quote marks) mean. For example, in a database tracking voter opinion, even the patently false value of "widespread apathy" in the "Health Care Debate" field means "True" to a Boolean statement. If the entry isn't "0" or "False" or another item in the list above, then all the Boolean cares about is whether there's a value in the field. So you create a Conditional Formatting calculation to format the text of an Email button as gray if the Email Address field was empty:

```
Customers::Email Address = ""
```

This calculation is explicit about what it's looking for. It checks the contents of the Email Address field for blank contents. The statement evaluates to "True" when the field is blank, and to "False" when there's data in the field.

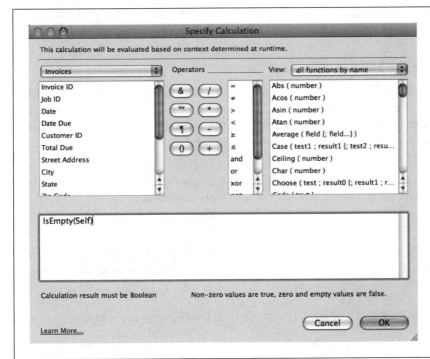

Figure 15-1:
The Specify Calculation window appears when you select "Empty" from the second pop-up menu and then change "Value is" to "Formula is" in the condition pop-up menu. The calculation engine converts the handy pop-up menu choices into calc-speak. Here you'll see heavy use of the Self function. Turn the page to learn more. Notice the text below the Calculation box: "Calculation result must be Boolean" and "Non-zero values are true, zero and empty values are false."

Note: Just remember that the Boolean calculation isn't checking the validity of the email address. You can write a calculation that tests the email address for its essential parts (using the PatternCount function) or use a plug-in (page 667) to send an email and actually test the address.

Even though it's more explicit to add the equal sign and the empty quote marks, it isn't necessary because "empty" means "False" in the Boolean world. Plus, some developers don't like the inverted logic required when you check for the presence of nothing in a field. That's why you often see Booleans written more simply, like so:

```
Customers::Email Address
```

Unlike the first example, this calculation evaluates to "True" when the field contains data, and to "False" when it's empty. But you can reinvert the logic by putting a "not" in front of a calculation:

```
not Customers::Email Address
```

This syntax means that the result is "True" when the field is empty, and "False" when the field contains data.

So is one method better than another? Probably not. But when you look at other developers' calculations, you may see all these forms, so it helps to know how they work. If you're the only developer working on your files, then you're free to use the construction that makes most sense to you. But when you develop in a team, you might want to develop a standard for constructing your Boolean calculations. In either case, it's a good idea to comment your Boolean calculations, so those who follow you can save time trying to retrace your logic.

Using the Self Function

You got a peek at the *Self()* function back in the box on page 299. The *Self()* function simply returns the contents of the object to which it's applied. FileMaker's engineers created the *Self()* function to make calculations portable—that is, you don't need to retrofit them if you move them from one field or object to another.

Here's one example of how it works. The five volunteer data entry folks keeping up with your theater group's subscription and donor list are expressing their artistic temperaments by using different formats for phone numbers. So when you print out the contact list, you've got (800) 555-1212, 800-555-1212, 800.555.1212, 555-1212, and every other variation under the sun.

FileMaker's auto-enter calculations can help you transform self-expression into standard formats. To straighten things out, you could add this calculation to your Phone field:

```
"(" & // start with an open paren sign
Left ( Filter ( Phone ; "0123456789" ) ; 3 ) & // grab the area code
") " & // finish the area code with a close paren and a space
Middle ( Filter ( Phone; "0123456789" ) ; 4 ; 3 ) & // grab the exchange
"-" & // give me a hyphen
Middle ( Filter ( Phone ; "0123456789" ) ; 7 ; 4 ) // the last four digits
```

This calculation takes the data entered into the Phone field, and imposes its own order onto the data. As the comments show, one part of the phone number format is assembled from each line of this nested calculation.

Note: This formula uses several techniques covered in Chapter 9: The *Filter()* function (page 397); *Left()*, *Middle()*, and *Right()* functions (page 395); and nested functions (page 407). Also, the Customers::Phone Number field in the sample database on this book's Missing CD page at *www.missingmanuals.com/cds/* shows you the *Self* version of the formula in action.

This calculation solves the problem for one phone field, but what if all your records contain three phone fields? Plus, you've got three phone fields in your Employees and Vendors databases, too. To transfer this calculation, you have to paste it into each field's auto-enter calculation dialog box, select each instance of "Phone", and then change it to "Mobile" or "Work Phone" so the calculation can work properly in each new context. Don't you have *real* work to do?

Separating Formatting from Data

Why would a math major like me use lowly, layout-based conditional formatting when I can make a whole bunch of very cool, very complicated calculations using text formatting functions?

It's true that conditional formatting doesn't give you a whole bunch of new options that you don't have with text formatting functions. However, you do get a giant leap closer to something that's been difficult to do in FileMaker—separating the presentation layer from the data layer of your file.

In programmer-speak, the *presentation layer* is anything having to do with showing your data. It's the layout, and all the stuff you put on a layout to make your data easy to understand. Even the fact that you can move fields around in relation to one another is part of FileMaker's sophisticated presentation layer. Boldface fields, portals, buttons, and web viewers are presentation tools, as well. Custom menus (page 538) and tooltips (page 329), which help you help your users work with their data, are also forms of presentation.

The *data layer* is just what it sounds like—the tables and fields of actual information. Most calculations also fall onto the data layer. For example, when you multiply the Quantity and Price Each fields together, using a calculation in the Extended Price field, that's the data layer.

So is adding a five percent surcharge to late payments.

Adding another five percent 30 days later, when those deadbeats have come up with more excuses, is still the data layer.

But when you use number formatting to display the results of any of those calculations with dollar signs, commas, and decimal places, then that's presentation-layer territory. And if you use a text function to display the late penalty in red, boldface at 18 points, then you're treading in the presentation layer, even if you use a sophisticated calculation to see if the penalty is due before you apply the format.

Furthermore, when you rely solely on calculations for formatting, you've got to add more *complexity* to your calculations to *simplify* some layouts. Say you use a text formatting function to display unpaid invoice totals in red after 30 days. The field *always* displays the red text where appropriate, even if that's not the purpose of the layout. For example, if the marketing department needs a list of invoices over $500 to decide who gets special offers, the red invoice amounts make no sense—and may violate customers' privacy. But if you separate presentation and data using conditional formatting, you can apply the format on a layout-by-layout basis. So all in all, it makes life easier down the road if you confine your use of calculations to mathematical operations *on* your data and use conditional formatting to handle the display *of* your data.

With the *Self()* function, which takes no parameter, and therefore doesn't need its own set of parentheses, you can write the calculation this way instead:

```
"(" &
Left ( Filter ( Self ; "0123456789" ) ; 3 ) &
") " &
Middle ( Filter ( Self; "0123456789" ) ; 4 ; 3 ) &
"-" &
Middle ( Filter ( Self ; "0123456789" ) ; 7 ; 4 )
```

The *Self()* function knows that it's referring to the field it's in, so you can copy and paste this function until the digital cows come home, and you never have to edit it for its new context. Good as it is, this calculation still has a couple of loopholes. See the box on page 661 for another way to clean up stray data entry in a Phone field.

Note: Unfortunately, *Self()* won't work in every calculation you try to use it in, for example as a script parameter (page 686). When Self won't work, FileMaker shows an error message.

Using Storage Options

Calculation fields have storage and indexing options, just as other field types do (page 254). The results of most calculations are stored when you define the calculation field and again each time the value in a field that's referenced in the calculation changes. Storage options let you control that behavior (Figure 15-2).

Understanding Stored and Unstored Calculation Fields

Values in calculation fields are updated when the value in fields referenced in their formulas change. So even though the value in a calculation field can change, it's considered a *stored* value. When you create a calculation field, the value is automatically stored and in most cases, you'll leave it that way.

But you can also require a calculation to evaluate whenever it's displayed; for example when you switch to a layout that contains the calculation field. Such calculations are considered *unstored*, and they have some special uses, as well as some drawbacks.

Whenever the data in a field changes, FileMaker also works behind the scenes, finding all the *stored* calculation fields that depend on the changed field, and *recalculates* them (even if they're aren't on your current layout), storing the new value in the field. Whether it's stored or unstored, a calculation field usually changes because a field used in the calculation has changed, as you'll see next. Understanding *when* fields recalculate and how dependencies work can help you decide whether it's appropriate to make a calculation field's value unstored.

Note: When you use a field in a calculation, you can say the calculation depends on the field (or, in other words, it has a dependency on the field).

Field dependencies

Take a look at the example in Figure 15-3 to see how FileMaker knows when to recalculate fields. Calculation fields often use other calculation fields in complex arrangements, as this hierarchy of field dependencies shows.

First Name and Last Name are the only editable fields in Figure 15-3. But they aren't the only fields that can change. When someone edits a Customer's name, FileMaker sees that it needs to recalculate Full Name, which in turn triggers a recalculation of the Full Address value. The recalculation trickles down through all the dependent fields as soon as someone makes the change, and then exits the First Name field.

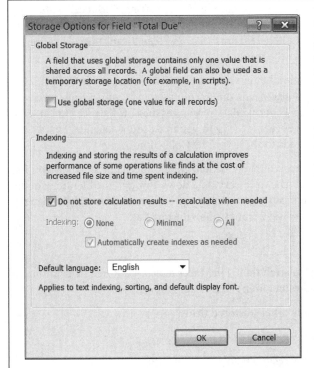

Figure 15-2:
In the Specify Calculation window, when you click the Storage Options button, you can set global storage and indexing options, just like any other field type. You also get a choice you haven't seen before: "Do not store calculation results." This example shows the storage options for the Invoice::Total Due field, which isn't stored because you want FileMaker to update if you add, delete or edit any line item on the invoice. Notice though, that you can't index unstored calculations. So finds are a little slower, and you can't use an unstored calculation as a key field (page 198).

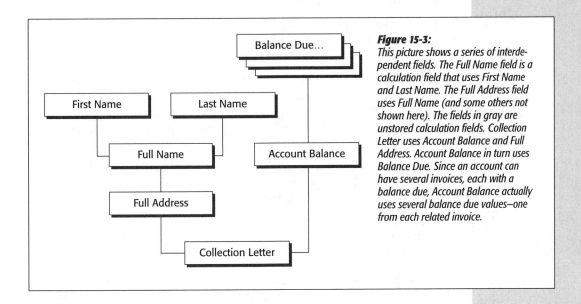

Figure 15-3:
This picture shows a series of interdependent fields. The Full Name field is a calculation field that uses First Name and Last Name. The Full Address field uses Full Name (and some others not shown here). The fields in gray are unstored calculation fields. Collection Letter uses Account Balance and Full Address. Account Balance in turn uses Balance Due. Since an account can have several invoices, each with a balance due, Account Balance actually uses several balance due values—one from each related invoice.

By contrast, since Collection Letter is an *unstored field and it's not shown on this lay-out*, FileMaker *doesn't* recalculate it right away. (It doesn't need to recalculate since you aren't displaying the value anywhere on the current layout.) Instead, the program waits until someone brings up the field onscreen, and *then* it runs the calculation on the current data, and displays the result.

That recalculates the Collection Letter value as FileMaker grabs the stored value for the Full Address field. But it also needs the Account Balance, which isn't stored. So *that* field is recalculated first. That calculation requires the new Balance Due on each invoice in turn, and then they're added up to get an Account Balance. Finally, the database has the values it needs to show you the Collection Letter.

Happily, FileMaker keeps track of these dependencies internally, so when you use *unstored* calculations, it pulls the necessary data down through the hierarchy of dependencies when your edits call for it. But if you understand how dependencies work, you can make good decisions about when to store data.

Deciding when to store

When you first create a calculation field, FileMaker makes it a stored field automatically, *if possible*. Some field values aren't eligible for storage:

- If a field depends on any other unstored fields.

- If a field depends on any global fields.

- If a field depends on any related fields.

- If a field depends on any summary fields.

If your calculation meets any of these criteria, then FileMaker automatically turns on the "Do not store calculation results—recalculate when needed" option for you, and it doesn't let you turn it off. Otherwise, FileMaker automatically stores the field.

- An unstored field has to be recalculated every time it appears onscreen or in a report. All that recalculation can slow your database down, especially if the unstored field is part of a summary field or a calculation that aggregates many records. So it's best to store a field unless you need a freshly calculated value every time you see that data.

- If you perform a find based on an unstored calculation field, then FileMaker has to go through all your records one by one, calculating each one as it goes. The result is a slow search process. If you plan on searching a field, then store it. (For more detail, see the box on the next page.)

Even if FileMaker can store a certain value, you may not always want it to. Here are some reasons you might turn *on* that "Do not store" option:

- Stored fields automatically recalculate as needed when *other fields* change. But FileMaker has no such automatic behavior for other kinds of information. For example, when you use the *Get(CurrentDate)* function in a calculation, File-Maker doesn't recalculate it when the date changes. In general, when you use any of the Get functions (page 365), you usually want to make your field unstored to "get" the most up-to-date information.

- A stored field takes up space on disk, while an unstored field doesn't. FileMaker 11 files can hold 8 TB of data, so space isn't a major consideration for most people. But if you're into slim and trim files, then you can save space by making calculations unstored.

- Lots of stored calculation fields can really slow down *record creation*. That's usually not a big deal, but if you often import data (Chapter 19) or use a script to regularly create lots of records, then you can speed things up by reducing the number of stored calculations.

Note: Obviously, you have some gray area here. When in doubt, store the field. You can always make it unstored later. Choose File→Manage Database, select your calculation field from the list, click Options, and then Storage Options to find the "Do not store calculation results–recalculate as needed" option.

FREQUENTLY ASKED QUESTION

I Want to Store My Field

What if I want to search on a field that FileMaker won't let me store?

Just because you can't store a field doesn't mean you don't wish you could. For example, in your Invoices layout, you probably do want to be able to search for invoices with a balance due. But since that field uses related data, it's not storable.

The good news is, you don't have to store a field in order to search it; the search is just a little slower. You don't notice the slowdown until you've amassed *lots* of invoice records. Sadly, there's no easy way to speed it up.

One remedy is to change the way people work with your database. You have to make your Invoice Detail layout *read only*—meaning people can't change data on the invoice directly (see page 302). Instead, they use a special layout and a script to make invoice changes.

When they're finished, your script can calculate the balance due and update a number field on the invoice appropriately. This way, the Balance Due field is a normal, nonrelated field, eligible for indexing and quick searches.

Also, remember that FileMaker can't search a calculation field that refers to related data very quickly, but it can search the related data *itself* with lightning speed. For example, to find an invoice that has payments applied to it, don't search the Amount Paid field in the invoice. Instead, search for invoices where Payments::Amount is greater than zero. That search turns up every invoice with a related payment record that's not negative. You get exactly what you want, and FileMaker can carry it out using indexed fields.

Indexing calculations

Unless they're global fields or unstored fields, you can set indexing for calculation fields just like any other field, as discussed on page 256. The available options and their effects depend on the result type of the calculation: text, number, date, or time.

Global Calculation Fields

A calculation field can use *global storage* (page 255) just like most other fields. When you turn on "Use global storage" (Figure 15-2), FileMaker calculates just one value for the entire table, rather than a value for each record. If your calculation uses other global fields—and *no* other fields—then it works just as you expect. That is, when you modify one of the global fields it depends on, FileMaker automatically recalculates its value.

If the calculation uses non-global fields, on the other hand, things get a little tricky. Whenever you change one of the fields referenced in the calculation, FileMaker recalculates the global calculation field using the values from the current record. For example, if you turn on "Use global storage" for your Full Name field, then it shows the name of the person you're looking at when you dismiss the Manage Database window. If you were on the first record, that's whose name you see in the field, just as expected. But as you flip through the records, you see that first person's name on every record. You're changing records, but with global storage, the Full Name value stays the same. That's because nothing it depends on has changed.

Now imagine you switch to the *last* record. If you then change the First Name field, Full Name recalculates. This new value displays the first and last name from the last record, since FileMaker re-evaluates the calculation in its entirety.

This behavior may seem kind of odd, but it has a really cool use. If you need to track the data in the last record you *changed*—maybe you need an informal audit of which record just got changed while you're scanning through other records—throw a global calculation field on your data entry layout. Then, no matter which record you're looking at, you see the value of the last *edited* record in that field.

Logical Functions

The logical function group is diverse and powerful. You get functions for making decisions (called *conditional functions*), learning about field values, and even evaluating calculations *inside* other calculations. This section covers all those possibilities. Along the way, you learn how to define and use *variables*, which act as placeholders while complex calculations go through their many steps.

Note: Though you learned about it at the beginning of this chapter, you find the *Self* function (page 646) in the functions list, under the Logical functions heading.

Conditional Functions

This chapter began by posing an interesting challenge: You have a calculation field in the Invoices table called Total Due. It calculates the total amount due on an invoice by subtracting the sum of all payments from the total amount of the invoice. Can you modify the Total Due calculation to add a five-percent penalty when an invoice is past due?

The answer lies in the three conditional functions. Each one lets you specify more than one possible result. The functions require one or more parameters—called *conditions* or *conditional expressions*—that tell them what result to pick. The conditional functions—*If()*, *Case()*, and *Choose()*—differ in how many possible results they support, and what kind of conditions they expect.

FREQUENTLY ASKED QUESTION

Matching Text Values

What do you mean by "First Name field matches 'Dominique'?" What constitutes a match?

When you use the = operator with text values, FileMaker compares the two values on each side, letter by letter. If every letter, number, space, punctuation and so on matches, then you get a True result. But the comparison isn't case-sensitive. In other words, this expression has a True result:

```
"TEXT" = "text"
```

If this function is too forgiving for your needs, then you can use the *Exact()* function instead.

Exact takes two text parameters, compares them, and returns

True if they match exactly—including case. This expression has a False result:

```
Exact ( "TEXT" ; "text" )
```

It's perfectly legal and quite common to use the Exact function (or any other function, field, or expression) as the first parameter of the *If()* function, like this:

```
If ( Exact ( First Name ; "Dominique" ) ;
"Free" ; "$299.00" )
```

This version of the calculation returns "$299.00" if the First Name field contains "dominique", since the case on the letter D doesn't match.

The If() function

The first and most common conditional function is simply called *If()*. The *If()* function is the basic unit of decision making in FileMaker calculations. It's the ticket when you have to decide between two choices, based on some criteria.

It looks like this:

```
If ( YourTestCondition ; True Result ; False Result )
```

When you use the *If()* function, FileMaker evaluates the condition looking for a Boolean result (True or False). If the condition has a True value, the function returns its second parameter (True result). If the condition is False, though, then it returns the False result instead. Here's an example:

```
If ( First Name = "Dominique" ; "Free" ; "$299.00" )
```

For example, the result of this calculation returns "Free" if the First Name field matches "Dominique." If it *doesn't* match, then it returns $299.00 instead. (See the box above for more details.)

The Case() function

Sometimes you need to pick from more than just two choices. Luckily, the *If()* function has a cousin named *Case()* that simply excels at such problems. For example, suppose you want to show one of these four messages on the top of your layout:

- Good Morning

- Good Afternoon

- Good Evening

- Go To Bed

FileMaker chooses a message based on the time of day. The *If()* function doesn't work very well for this problem because *If()* allows only one condition and two possible results. You *can* nest *If()* statements one inside the other, so that the False result is really another *If()* statement. But nested *If()* functions are really hard to read and even harder to tweak, so if you find that your business rules require a change in your calculation, you may rue the day you decided to use four nested *If()* functions to decide which greeting method to display.

The *Case()* function has this form:

```
Case ( test1 ; result1 ; {test2 ; result2 ; ... ; defaultResult } )
```

You can add as many parameters as you want, in pairs, to represent a condition and the result to be returned if that condition is True. Since the conditions and results are sequential and not nested, you can easily read a *Case()* statement, no matter how many conditions you pile on. You can even add an optional parameter after the last result. This parameter represents the *standard* result—the one FileMaker uses if none of the conditions were true.

Note: Since the *Case()* function accepts several conditions, more than one condition can be true at the same time. If so, FileMaker chooses the *first* True condition when it picks a result.

A calculation using the *Case()* function might look like this:

```
Case (
Get ( CurrentTime ) > Time ( 4 ; 0 ; 0 ) and Get ( CurrentTime ) < Time (
12 ; 0 ; 0 ) ;
"Good Morning" ;

Get ( CurrentTime ) > Time ( 12 ; 0 ; 0 ) and Get ( CurrentTime ) < Time (
18 ; 0 ; 0 ) ;
"Good Afternoon" ;

Get ( CurrentTime ) > Time ( 18 ; 0 ; 0 ) and Get ( CurrentTime ) < Time (
22 ; 0 ; 0 ) ;
"Good Evening" ;

"Go To Bed"
)
```

In this calculation, the *Case()* function checks first to see if the current time is between 4:00 a.m. and 12:00 p.m. If it is, then the "Good Morning" value is returned. If not, it then checks whether the time is between 12:00 p.m. and 6:00 p.m., which would produce the "Good Afternoon" message. Again, if not, it checks to see if it's between 6:00 p.m. and 10:00 p.m. If so, the user sees "Good Evening".

You don't need to specify a condition for the last result—"Go To Bed"—because if all the previous conditions are false, then it *must* be time for bed. In other words, if it *isn't* the morning, and it *isn't* the afternoon, and it *isn't* the evening, then it must be late at night. (If you need further help deciphering the above calculation, then see the box on page 656. On the other hand, if you're so far ahead that you can see a better way to do it, then see the box on page 658.)

The Choose() function

The *Choose()* function is sort of the forgotten third member of the conditional trio. People don't immediately grasp how to use it—so they don't. But if you think of it as a value list with the choices coded into a calculation, then you see how the *Choose()* function can turn an awfully ugly *Case()* function into a specimen of neatness.

It looks like this:

```
Choose ( Condition ; Result0 {; Result1 ; Result2...} )
```

Unlike the other conditional functions, *Choose()* doesn't expect a Boolean expression for its condition. Instead, it looks for a *number*. The number tells it which of the results to choose: If the Condition is zero, then the function returns Result0; if it's one, then it returns Result1; and so on.

Imagine you have a Student table, and one of its fields is called GPA. This field holds the student's current grade point average, as a number. You'd like to turn this number into a letter grade on the printed report.

Many FileMaker developers would immediately jump to the *Case()* function to solve this problem. They'd do something like this:

```
Case (
 GPA < 0.5; "F";
 GPA < 1.5; "D";
 GPA < 2.5; "C";
 GPA < 3.5; "B";
 "A"
)
```

While this calculation gets the job done, you can do it more succinctly with the *Choose()* function:

```
Choose (Round(GPA; 0); "F"; "D"; "C"; "B"; "A" )
```

First, you turn the GPA value into an integer (using the *Round()* function on page 386), so the *Choose()* function can use it. When the GPA is 3.2, FileMaker rounds it to 3, and selects the result that represents the number 3: "B." (Remember that the first result is for *zero*, so number three is actually the *fourth* result parameter. For more detail, see the box on page 659.)

Constructing a Conditional Calculation

Now that you've seen the three conditional functions, it's time to take a stab at that calculation way back from the beginning of this chapter: Add a five-percent penalty when the due date has passed.

When you're trying to come up with a logical calculation, think about what information FileMaker needs to make the decision, and what action you want FileMaker to take after it decides. Then consider how best to do that using your database's existing fields and structure. First, decide which conditional function to use.

UP TO SPEED

A Complex Case

The *Case()* function on page 654 expresses a familiar concept—do Plan A in one case, do Plan B in a different case, and so on. But you might not immediately know how you get from that simple idea to the more complicated calculations shown in this chapter. Here's how it breaks down:

Remember that semicolons separate the parameters you pass to a function. So the first parameter is *all* of this:

```
Get(CurrentTime) > Time(4;0;0) and
Get(CurrentTime) < Time(12;0;0)
```

That whole expression forms the first condition. Remember that the *and* operator works on two Boolean values. It returns a True result if the values on each side are *both true*.

So really, you can split this condition in two. First, this expression must be true:

```
Get(CurrentTime) > Time(4;0;0)
```

If that expression is true, then FileMaker checks to see if this expression is true, too:

```
Get(CurrentTime) < Time(12;0;0)
```

These sub-expressions are much simpler. Each has the same form, comparing the current time to a time you construct with the Time function. The first makes sure it's after 4:00 a.m. The second makes sure it's *before* 12:00 p.m. The other two conditions in the calculation are exactly the same—except they look at different times.

Total Due calculation #1: Using the If() function

Most people's first thought would be to use the *If()* function, since the calculation needs to check *if* one condition is true:

- Is the value of the Date Due field earlier than today's date?

The calculation then takes the result of the *If()* function, and returns one of two possible results:

- If it's *true* that the due date has passed, then add five percent (.05) of the Total Due to the value in Total Due.

- If it's *not true* that the due date has passed, then display the Total Due normally.

In plainer English, the *If()* condition checks to see if the due date has passed. If so, it adds five percent to the Total Due amount; if not, it returns the Total Due amount.

The full calculation might look like the following:

```
If ( // test

Get ( CurrentDate ) > Date Due
 and // Calculate the total due here to make sure it's not zero
Sum ( Line Items::Extended Price ) > allPayments ;

// True Result
 Sum ( Line Items::Extended Price ) + ( Sum ( Line Items::Extended Price )
 * .05 ) ; // add a 5% surcharge if Invoice is past due

// False Result
 Sum ( Line Items::Extended Price ) // display the Total Due normally
 )
```

To put this calculation to work in your sample database, delete the calculation currently in the field definition for Total Due, and then type in this one. When the due date has passed, the value in your smarter Total Due field changes to reflect a late payment penalty.

Note: Since the Total Due field already calculates the due balance, you may be tempted to create a *new* field that calculates five percent of every invoice, and then only adds that value in if the invoice is past due. But that would clutter your database with a superfluous field. Also, it's far better to have all your math in one place in case your business rules change.

Total Due calculation #2: Using the Case() function

Lots of people like the *Case()* function so much that they always use it, even in places where the *If()* function is perfectly competent. You might choose to use *Case()* if there's any chance you'll want to add some conditions to the statement later on. Instead of editing an *If()* expression later, you can save time by using *Case()* from the start.

The same calculation using *Case()* (and minus the helpful comments) looks like this:

```
Case (
 Get ( CurrentDate ) > Date Due and Sum ( Line Items::Extended Price ) >
 allPayments ;
 Sum ( Line Items::Extended Price ) + ( Sum ( Line Items::Extended Price )
 * .05 ) ;
 Sum ( Line Items::Extended Price )
 )
```

Note: With a single condition and standard result, the syntax for *If()* and *Case()* are the same. So if you do need to change an *If()* statement to *Case()* later, then simply change the word "If" to "Case", and add the new conditions.

This calculation works as advertised, but it has a couple weak points. First, it has to calculate the total amount due *three times*. That's twice too many places to make typos and places to edit the *Sum (Line Items::Extended Price)* expression if you change the calculation later.

Second, allPayments is an unstored calculation based on the sum of related records. That's one of the slowest things you can ask a calculation to do. It may not matter much in this database, but in a more complicated situation, a calculation like this could slow FileMaker to a crawl.

POWER USERS' CLINIC

Clever Case Conditions

If you were one of those students who handed in homework early and always sat in the front row, you may be jumping up and down in your chair right now, waving your hand in the air. What you're *dying* to say is, "I can make that *Case()* function simpler!" Well, you're probably right. In fact, this calculation does the same job:

```
Case (

  Get(CurrentTime) <= Time(4;0;0) or

  Get(CurrentTime) > Time(22;0;0);

  "Go To Bed";


  Get(CurrentTime) < Time(12;0;0);

  "Good Morning";


  Get(CurrentTime) < Time(18;0;0);

  "Good Afternoon";


  "Good Evening"
  )
```

This version takes advantage of the fact that the *Case()* function returns the result associated with the *first* True condition. FileMaker looks at the first condition, which checks to see if it's before 4:00 a.m. or after 10:00 p.m.

If either's true (note the "or" operator), then the function returns *Go To Bed*.

If both *aren't* true, then FileMaker moves on to the second condition, which asks if it's earlier than 12:00 p.m. If so, it returns *Good Morning*. (What if it's 3 in the morning? That *is* earlier than 12:00 p.m., but you don't see "Good Morning" because FileMaker never gets this far. If it's 3:00 a.m., then the search for truth stops after the first condition.)

If it still hasn't found a true condition, then FileMaker moves on to the next: Is it before 6:00 p.m.? Again, the structure of the case statement *implies* that it must be after noon at this point since any time before noon would've been caught in the previous conditions. So this condition is *really* looking for a time between noon and 6, even though it doesn't say exactly that.

If you're comfortable with this kind of logic, then you can save yourself some clicks and a little typing. (Technically you also make a more efficient calculation, but unless you're using the abacus version of FileMaker, you don't see a speed increase.)

Many people, on the other hand, find a calculation like this one utterly confusing. In that case, just use the longer version, and find something else in your life to brag about.

In the next section, you'll learn how FileMaker helps you write leaner calculations that are easier to read—and quicker for FileMaker to work through.

The *Let()* Function and Variables

The *Let()* function creates a temporary holder for a value, called a *variable*, which can be plugged into a calculation over and over again. You have to do a little more work upfront to set up a variable, but that effort pays off with faster calculations that are easier to read, edit, and troubleshoot.

No Zero

The Choose() *function insists that the first parameter should be for a zero condition. What if I don't want zero? My condition values start with 1.*

You're in a common predicament. Luckily, you have two equally easy ways to get what you want from the *Choose()* function. Perhaps the most obvious is to simply add a dummy zero result:

```
Choose ( Door ; "" ; "European Vacation" ;
"New Car" ; "Wah Wah Wah" )
```

In this calculation, there's no Door number zero, so you just stick "" in the spot where the zero result belongs. You could just as well put "Death by Boredom" there, since it never gets chosen anyway. Just make sure you put a set of empty quotes there, so your first real result is in the number-one spot.

If you just don't like having that dummy result in your calculation, then you can take this approach instead:

```
Choose ( Door - 1 ; "European Vacation" ;
"New Car" ; "Wah Wah Wah" )
```

This version simply subtracts one from the Door number. Now Door number one gets the zero result, and Door number two gets the one result. This approach becomes more appealing when your choices begin with an even higher number:

```
Choose ( Year - 2000 ; "Dragon" ; "Snake";
"Horse" ; "Sheep" )
```

Since this calculation uses the year as part of the condition, it would be a real drag to enter 2000 dummy values. Instead, you just subtract enough to get your sequence to start with zero.

Defining Calculation Variables

In a *Let()* function, you define a value, give it a name, and then use that name as often as you need throughout the calculation. In this case, you can calculate the amount due once, and then store the result in a variable called Amount Due.

The *Let()* function is unique among functions because it controls the way you write your calculation, not the result. Here's an example:

```
Let ( [ L = 5 ; W = 10 ; H = 3 ] ; L * W * H )
```

Like the *Substitute()* function described on page 397, *Let()* uses bracketed notation. It really takes just two parameters. The first is a list of variable definitions. Each variable gets a name and a value using this format:

```
Name = Value
```

If you have more than one variable to define (as in the example above), put a semicolon between each one, and then put them all between a pair of square brackets. You can use any calculation expression as the value.

In fact, the expression that determines the value of a variable can even use other variables defined earlier. For example, the next calculation is perfectly legal. Its Hours variable has a value of 240: 24 times the value of the Days variable:

```
Let (
[ Days = 10 ;
Hours = 24 * Days ;
Minutes = 60 * Hours ];

Minutes & " Minutes"
)
```

The second parameter can be any calculation expression. This parameter is special because you can use any of the variables you've defined inside the expression, just like fields. The first example above has three defined variables (L, W, and H); the expression then multiplies them together.

When FileMaker evaluates the *Let()* function, it determines the value of each variable just once, and then plugs this value into the expression every time that variable is used. The result of a *Let()* function is simply the result of its expression.

Total Due calculation #3: Using the Let function

Your Total Due calculation can use the *Let()* function to solve all its problems. Just put the Amount Due in a variable, and use it throughout the calculation:

```
Let ( AmountDue = Sum ( Line Items::Extended Price ) ;
If (
Get(CurrentDate) > Date Due and AmountDue > 0;
AmountDue + ( AmountDue * .05 );
AmountDue
)
)
```

This version of the calculation is simpler, easier to change, and more efficient when it evaluates. You can't beat that.

The Life of a Variable

Most variables last only as long as it takes FileMaker to work through the calculation, and then they're gone. These variables are called *local variables* because they aren't valid outside the *Let()* function that calls them into existence. But you can also create a special variable called a *global variable*, which lives beyond your calculation. Read on to see when to use each type.

Local variables

The variables you've written so far have all been local variables. Now it's time to learn that local variables having shockingly short memories.

Field Formatting Calculations

Now that you understand most of FileMaker's calculation power features, you're ready to see something really powerful. You've already seen how an auto-enter calculation can clean up a phone number during data entry (page 646). This calculation, which consolidates a lot of techniques you've covered in this section, goes one step further:

```
Let(
  cleanPhone = Filter ( Self; "0123456789"
) ;


Case (
Length( Self ) = 10 ;


"(" & Left ( cleanPhone ; 3 ) & ") " &
Middle ( cleanPhone ; 4 ; 3 ) &
```

```
"-" &

Right ( cleanPhone ; 4 ) ;

Self
)
)
```

First, the calculation uses the Filter function to remove any non-numeric characters from the entered phone number, and puts the result in a variable called "cleanPhone". Then, if cleanPhone has exactly 10 digits, the calculation breaks it apart according to the format you want. Otherwise, it just returns the phone number the way the person entered it.

To make the calculation work properly, in the Field Options dialog box, be sure you turn off "Do not replace existing value (if any)".

Local variables can lose their values even before a calculation is finished. If you write:

```
Let ( AmountDue = Sum ( Line Items::Extended Price ) ;
If (
Get(CurrentDate) > Date Due and AmountDue > Total Paid;
AmountDue + ( AmountDue * .05 );
AmountDue
)
) & If ( AmountDue < 0 ; "CR" ; "" )
```

the calculation tries to use the Amount Due variable after the end parenthesis in the *Let()* function (that's the first one in the calculation's last line). Anything that happens after that in the calculation is outside the *Let()* function's *scope (a technical term that refers to when the variable exists)*, so when you try to close the Specify Calculation window on this calculation, FileMaker complains that it doesn't know what that last Amount Due is supposed to be. Here's one way to rewrite that calculation using a local variable:

```
Let ( AmountDue = Sum ( Line Items::Extended Price ) ;
Case (
Get ( CurrentDate ) > Date Due and AmountDue > Total Paid;
AmountDue + ( AmountDue * .05 ) ;
AmountDue < 0 ; "CR" ; ""
)
)
```

In this example, you're including the last test condition within the scope of the *Let()* function, and you've switched to a *Case()* function, so that you don't have to read a set of nested *If()* functions.

If you want the local variables you set inside calculations to follow the same naming conventions as variables you set in scripts, then prefix their names with "$". In that case, you'd write the calculation you just saw like this:

```
Let ( $AmountDue = Sum ( Line Items::Extended Price ) ;
Case (
Get ( CurrentDate ) > Date Due and $AmountDue > 0;
$AmountDue + ( $AmountDue * .05 ) ;
$AmountDue < 0 ; "CR" ; ""
)
)
```

Note: When you create a variable with a "$" prefix in a calculation that evaluates while a script is running, you extend its lifespan beyond the *Let()* function. In this case, the variable's scope is now the script. This can cause problems if you accidentally give two variables the same name. In that case, one variable will overwrite the other, and your script can go off the rails. Use this technique with extreme care. See page 490 for more information on how variables work in scripts.

Notice that you have to include the prefix in the *Let()* function, *and* in the formula that follows it.

Global variables

FileMaker gives you global fields; it also gives you *global variables*. Unlike local variables, global variables hold their results after the *Let()* function is finished. To create a global variable, add a "$$" prefix to its name. Here's the same calculation rewritten with a global variable:

```
Let (
$$AmountDue = Sum ( Line Items::Extended Price ) ;
Case (
Get ( CurrentDate ) > Date Due and $$Amount Due > 0;
$$AmountDue + ( $$AmountDue * .05 ) ;
$$AmountDue < 0 ; "CR" ; ""
)
)
```

The $$ prefix is the only difference you can see in the calculation. But the practical difference is vast: Global variable values remain until you change them (through another calculation or through a script), or until you close the file.

Note: FileMaker Pro Advanced's Data Viewer (page 521) eliminates guesswork by letting you check the contents of variables, whether you create them in calculation fields or from scripts.

You could run a script that checks to see if a payment was made within 10 days of the invoice date, and if it was, apply a one-percent discount to the $$Amount Due field. Sure, you can do something similar with a straightforward calculation field, but in that case, it gets a little trickier to apply the discount to some of the records, but not to others. With a script, you can find the records you want to give a spur of the moment discount, run the script on that found set, and you're done.

Another reason to set a global variable with a calculation is to use that variable to filter portals (page 567). Portals that are filtered by variables may not always refresh when you expect them to because portals don't change their display unless a change of context (like moving to a new record) also occurs. Portal filtering by variable is usually safer in a script, because you can add a Refresh Window script step or a change of context to the script to make sure the portal refreshes when the variable is changed. But using a calculation may fit the bill in some situations, so you should know that it's possible.

Nesting Let Functions

As with other functions, you can nest *Let()* functions inside each other. In fact, you can define a variable once, and then *redefine* it inside a nested *Let()* function. The variable's value changes while inside the nested *Let()* function, and then changes back when it ends. By the same token, you can define a variable with the same name as a *field*, and FileMaker uses the variable's value while inside the *Let()* function. (These techniques aren't commonly used except by programmers who want to use the same techniques in FileMaker as they use when they write code.)

Here's a very simple example of a *Let()* function *inside* another *Let()* function:

```
Let ( X = 3 ; // only X is defined here
 Let ( Y = 4 ; // X and Y are both defined here
 X * Y
 )
 // Only X is defined here too
 )
```

You can also use the *Let()* function more than once in a single calculation without nesting:

```
Let ( X = 3; Y = 4 ; X * Y ) &
Let ( units = "inches" ; " " & units )
```

Recursion

As described in the box on page 537, you can create custom functions that call other custom functions, creating whole strings of mathematical wizardry that perform to your exact specifications. Even more interesting, a custom function can *use itself*, a technique known as *recursion*. With recursion, you can create calculations that repeat a process over and over again until they reach a result—called *iterative calculations*.

Note: Recursion is a notoriously complicated topic, and many *very* capable FileMaker developers are stymied by it. Fortunately, recursion is rarely the only solution to a given problem, so you can certainly get by without it. For example, consider using a script instead.

Imagine you need a function that removes duplicate lines from a list. For example, if a field contains a list of colors, then you want a new list with only each *unique* color name, even if it appears in the original list several times. You can't do that with a normal calculation, because you just don't know how many words you need to pull out. A recursive function solves the problem by repeating its work until it takes care of all items.

While the concept of a recursive function is simple, creating one can be tricky. To implement a recursive function, you're best off tackling the calculation in three distinct steps. First, solve the initial problem; second, call that first formula over and over again (that's the recursive part); and third, tell the formula how to stop.

Note: If you have trouble getting through the following recursion example on your own, you can download a sample database from this book's Missing CD page at *www.missingmanuals.com*.

Step 1: Solve the First Case

Rather than think about how to solve the entire problem, just figure out how to deal with the *first* line in the list. If you have a field called Values, for example, and you want to make sure the *first* line appears only once in the list, you can use this calculation (Figure 15-4):

```
LeftValues ( values ; 1 ) & Substitute ( values ; LeftValues ( values; 1 ) ;
"" )
```

Suppose the Values field contains:

```
Red
Green
Orange
Red
Orange
Yellow
```

The Substitute part of this expression does the lion's share of the work, so start with that to figure out how the formula works. The Substitute function sees that "Red" is the first item in the Values field and takes it out of the field everywhere it occurs. If Substitute were the whole shooting match, then "Red" would disappear entirely from the Values field. But the *LeftValues (values ; 1) &* piece of the expression also notices that "Red" is the first item in the Values field, and it puts "Red" back at the top of the list. When both are put together (using the "&" sign), the result is the first item in the list, then the rest of the list with the Red is removed. Here's the result you see if you make a calculation field with the formula on the previous page:

Red
Green
Orange
Orange
Yellow

Now you're ready to move on to the rest of the function, where you call the same action over and over again—and things start to get interesting.

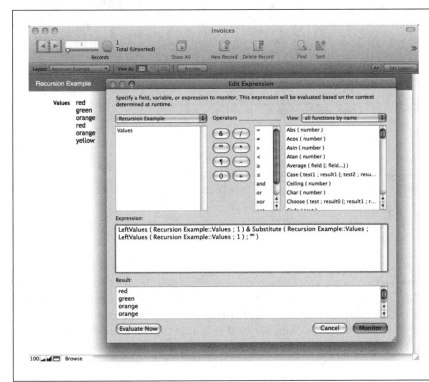

Figure 15-4:
Working through any tough calculation is much easier when you use the Data Viewer (page 521) instead of creating a calculation field. The Data Viewer has the same context as the record that's active when you open the viewer. Here the step 1 calc is working on the data in the Values field. The second instance of the value "red" is removed from the calculation's result. Use fully qualified field names in its expressions. This one changes that to a parameter when you write the custom function later in the process.

Step 2: Assume Your Function Already Works, and Use It

You're ready to take the *recursion leap of faith*. A recursive function, by definition, calls itself. So at some point, it depends on its own resources to work. But when you're *writing* the recursive custom function, it obviously doesn't work yet. You'll be at a total impasse if you don't *assume* it already works, and just get on with writing.

So since you're writing a new custom function called *RemoveDuplicates()*, write its syntax as if you already have a function called *RemoveDuplicates()* that does what you want (Figure 15-5). If such a function did exist, you could use it in the above calculation like this:

```
LeftValues ( values ; 1 ) & RemoveDuplicates ( Substitute ( values ;
LeftValues ( values ; 1 ); "" ) )
```

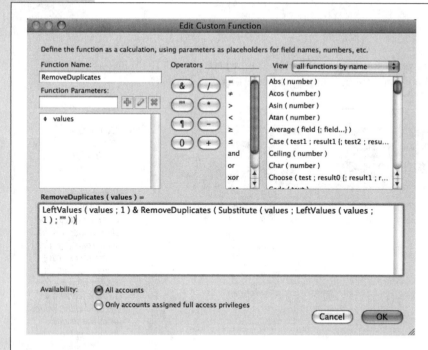

Figure 15-5:
You can switch to the Custom Function window in step 2, if you want to or you can wait until you've got the whole thing working. Like the regular Specify Calculation window, Edit Custom Function will analyze your calculation when you click OK, so make sure to define the function's parameter(s) to avoid an error message telling you that the parameters can't be found. You'll finish this function in step 3.

This new version works a lot like the last one. It first pulls the first item from the list, and then adds it to the result. It also removes duplicates of the first item from the rest of the list (using *Substitute()*). But instead of adding that to the result, it sends the entire remaining list through *RemoveDuplicates()*. If you assume *RemoveDuplicates()* already works, then it removes duplicates from the rest of the list. You take care of the *first* line using your calculation skills. Then you rely on the function itself to take care of all the rest. Notice that the new list that's passed to *RemoveDuplicates()* starts with the *second line* of the original list. So when the function runs again, the second line becomes the first, and the function takes care of it. Unfortunately, this process goes on forever, which is probably not exactly what you want.

Step 3: Find a Stopping Point

You now have two of the three critical components of a recursive function: You're manually doing the *first* part of the job, and you're telling recursion to do the rest. If you leave the function like this, though, you're in trouble. If *RemoveDuplicates()* calls *RemoveDuplicates()*, which in turn calls *RemoveDuplicates()* (ad infinitum), then you have a problem: This function just keeps going forever.

Warning: When you work on recursive functions, you inevitably create such *loops* accidentally. When you do, FileMaker thinks for several seconds, and then gives up and returns *invalid* (a question mark in the field). If FileMaker seems to be hung, wait a few seconds; recursion is limited to 10,000 cycles and FileMaker gives up eventually.

To avoid ending up in a loop, you need to figure out when to *stop* calling *Remove-Duplicates()*. Think about what happens after this function calls itself several times. Each time it's called with a slightly smaller list than the time before (because the first item—along with any copies of it—has been removed). Eventually it's going to get called with just one item (or sometimes zero items). When that happens, you no longer need the services of *RemoveDuplicates()*. Instead, you can just return that last word by itself since it obviously has no duplicates. You use an *If()* function to help the recursion figure out when to stop. The final function looks like this (with comments added):

```
// Start the result with the first item in the list
LeftValues ( values ; 1 ) &
// If there are items remaining in List...
If ( ValueCount ( values ) > 0;
// ...then remove duplicates from the remaining items
RemoveDuplicates ( Substitute ( values ; LeftValues ( values ; 1); "") );
// ...otherwise we're done
""
)
```

Now you just have to create the *RemoveDuplicates()* custom function. *RemoveDuplicates()* needs one parameter, which is the values from which you're sifting duplicates. A descriptive name, like "theList" (you can't use "list" because there's already a function with that name), helps you remember what this parameter does. Finally, create a calculation field using your new custom function, and create a reference to the field containing the list of duplicated values. See the box on page 668 to learn how to make the custom function more fool proof.

Figure 15-6 shows an example of a recursive calculation calling the *RemoveDuplicates()* custom function to remove all duplicate colors it finds in the list. (It takes four iterations to remove all the duplicates and return a unique instance of each item in the list, in the order in which they appear.)

Plug-Ins

Some things just can't be done (or can't be done *well*) using calculations and custom functions. When you run into this situation, you may consider looking into *plug-ins*, tiny applications that live inside FileMaker to help it do specific tasks that it can't do on its own.

Many plug-ins focus on doing certain things: processing credit card transactions; or interacting with special devices like cameras, bar code readers, and so on. Although plug-ins work through calculation functions, scripts (which the next section covers) generally control them.

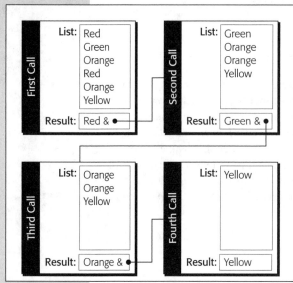

Figure 15-6:
In the top-left corner, the box shows how RemoveDu-plicates() is first called. It receives a list of colors as its one parameter. It returns the first item in the list, and the result of the second call. This time, though, Red has been removed from the list. The second call returns Green and the results of the third call. This progresses until the fourth call, when the script passes a single item to RemoveDuplicates(). This time RemoveDuplicates() simply returns the item without calling itself again. When it returns, the third call has all it needs, so it returns as well. This process goes back up the chain until the first call is reached, and the final result is returned. If you join up the results of each call, then you see the correct list.

WORKAROUND WORKSHOP

The Point of No Return

RemoveDuplicates() works great for finding unique values in a list, so long as the last item in the list has a ¶ (paragraph return) following it. If it doesn't, then the function gets confused and may not remove the last line in even if it's a duplicate. You can adjust for lists that don't have a trailing ¶ by adjusting your calculation field slightly:

    RemoveDuplicates (values & "¶")

You could also modify the custom function itself to guard against this possibility. Doing so makes the formula more complex, but here it is in case you want a challenge:

```
Let (

 [cleanList = if ( Right ( values, 1
"¶", values, values & "¶" );

 first = LeftValues ( cleanList, 1

first &

if ( ValueCount(cleanList) > 1;

 RemoveDuplicates(cleanList);

 ""

)
)
```

Plug-ins can convert, resize, and otherwise modify images in container fields, or perform complex mathematical, scientific, or financial calculations that would be difficult or inefficient in a calculation. Although this book doesn't cover any specific plug-ins, this section shows you how to access the functions provided by any plug-in you install.

Installing Plug-ins

A plug-in comes in a file bearing a special FileMaker plug-in icon (shown in Figure 15-7). In order to use plug-ins, FileMaker needs to *load* them—that is, it has to put the plug-in code into its own memory. Every time you launch the program, it searches for plug-ins in a folder called Extensions, and loads all the plug-ins it finds.

Figure 15-7:
FileMaker plug-ins come in many varieties—with many names—but they all look more or less like this. This is the Windows version of the Web plug-in you get when you perform a complete install of FileMaker. When you install a new plug-in, your job is to put the file where FileMaker can find it.

Installing a plug-in is thus a simple matter of making sure it's in the right folder:

- On Windows, it's typically C:→Program Files→FileMaker→FileMaker Pro 11→Extensions.

- On Mac OS X, it's usually Applications→FileMaker Pro 11→Extensions.

Note: If you're using FileMaker Pro Advanced, then the FileMaker folder is called FileMaker Pro 11 Advanced, not FileMaker Pro 11.

Once you've found the folder, just drag the plug-in file into it, and then restart FileMaker. To see which plug-ins FileMaker has actually loaded, visit the application preferences (FileMaker Pro→Preferences on Mac OS X or Edit→Preferences on Windows). In the Preferences window, click the Plug-ins tab, or look at Figure 15-8.

Once you've installed plug-ins, you can find their functions in the Specify Calculation dialog box by choosin "External functions" in the View pop-up menu. For details on how to use these functions, consult their developer's manuals or websites. In most cases, you use Set Field script steps (page 463) to put calculation results into global fields you create specifically for your plug-in.

Old and New Plug-ins

There are two kinds of plug-ins for FileMaker: older FileMaker 4-style plug-ins and newer FileMaker 7+-style plug-ins. FileMaker 11 works with *both* types of plug-ins, but ask your plug-in provider which type you're getting, since the FileMaker 4 plug-ins have limited abilities:

- The functions provided by FileMaker 4 plug-ins always expect *one* parameter. Even if the function doesn't need a parameter, you have to pass "", which is just an empty parameter. If the function really needs more, consult the documentation that came with the plug-in to find out how to accommodate it.

Figure 15-8:
In FileMaker's Preferences window, The Plug-ins tab shows you the configurable plug-ins you've installed. (Some plug-ins, like the Web plug-in, aren't configurable, so they don't show up in this list.) Disable a plug-in by turning off the checkbox by its name. If a plug-in requires any configuration, select it in the list, and then click Configure. When you have a plug-in selected, you see a description of it below the list.

- This single parameter's type is *always* text in a FileMaker 4 plug-in's function. If you want to pass a date, time, timestamp, or number, then you have to convert it to text first, using *GetAsText()*.

Newer FileMaker plug-ins give you a lot more options. Functions can have as many parameters as their creator cares to give them. They can also deal with all data types, including pictures, movies, and files stored in container fields. Most FileMaker plug-ins use the new capabilities, but it helps to know what to do if you run across an old-style plug-in.

Finding Plug-ins

You can hire a programmer to create a plug-in to your specifications, but you can often find one on the market that already does what you want. There's a comprehensive list of available plug-ins on FileMaker's website. Just choose Solutions→"Made for FileMaker" from the site's main navigation bar. The plug-in section is at the bottom of the page.

You can also visit the more prolific FileMaker plug-in vendors' websites:

- 24U Software (*www.24usoftware.com/*)

- 360Works (*www.360works.com/*)

- CNS Plug-ins (*www.cnsplug-ins.com/*)

- FMNEXUS (*fmnexus.com/*)

- New Millennium Communications (*www.nmci.com/*)

- Productive Computing (*www.productivecomputing.com/*)

- Qutic Development (*www.qutic.com/*)

- Troi Automatisering (*www.troi.com/*)

New vendors come up with great products all the time so if you don't see what you want, then head over to Google and get your search on.

Creating Your Own Plug-ins

If you're feeling adventurous (or have helpful programmer friends), you can create your own plug-ins. To do that, you first need FileMaker Pro Advanced (it's the only version of FileMaker that includes the *Plug-in Software Development Kit* or SDK). You also need a C++ development environment. In Windows, you're best off with Visual C++ or Visual Studio.NET. On Mac OS X, you can use XCode (it's included with the Developer Tools that came with your computer, although you have to install it yourself from the CD). Plug-in SDK includes sample projects for each of these environments—and sample plug-in code—to get you started.

Advanced Scripting

Being familiar with FileMaker's lengthy list of script steps is a great foundation, but putting together a workable script takes practice. Although some scripts are simple affairs, sometimes a script requires a lot of forethought, planning, and organization. FileMaker gives you tools to help you write scripts and troubleshoot them when they aren't working. Plus, you can organize and document your work as you go. In this chapter you'll pull these concepts together to learn how to write and manage complex scripts.

Note: Download this chapter's sample file from this book's Missing CD page at *www.missingmanuals. com/cds*. Use Invoices_START.fp7 to work inl use Invoices_FINISHED.fp7 to see the completed examples.

Commenting Scripts

When you look at a script someone else created—or you created a long time ago—you can't always tell what the script does. To help keep things clear, add comments to your script. You add each comment using a Comment script step. This step has just one option: the text of the comment itself. The Comment step is special for two reasons. First, it doesn't *do* anything. Second, it appears in bold when you view your script in the Edit Script window.

Use comments to document anything important about the script. Here are some things you may want to include in a comment or set of comments:

- What the script does.

- Who wrote the script.

- The date the script was written.

- The date, if any, the script was last edited.

- Who edited the script.

- Anything special about how or when the script should be run, like whether only some database users can run it, or if the script requires parameters to do its work (see page 686).

Documenting scripts is standard operating procedure among programmers for a couple reasons. First, if something's wrong with the script, or it needs to be changed, you've got extra information that may help. Good comments tell you exactly what the script should do and any setup necessary to make the script run properly. Plus you have a list of people who've worked on it and can give you background or pointers. Also, the date can help identify whether a particular business rule was in effect that made certain parts of a script necessary. Or if you see that script is really old, you may decide to rewrite it with some of FileMaker's newer features. Comments don't take up much space or slow down your scripts, so commenting scripts as you create them saves you time later. You can see a commented script in Figure 16-1.

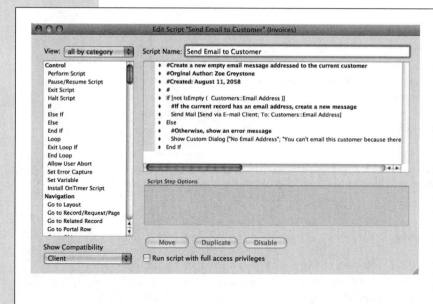

Figure 16-1:
Here's a Send Email script with comments added. Comments appear in bold and with a # symbol in front. The first comment tells what the script is supposed to do. The second and third comments say who created the script, and when. The fourth comment is blank and so makes white space to separate the script's parts. The two comments inside the script explain what the script does at critical junctures.

Tip: There's another way to indicate what your scripts are doing: Put comments in any embedded calculations. When a script has an *If()* statement that uses a complex calculation for its condition, comments in the calculation itself can demystify the calculation's purpose and the way it get its work done (page 381).

Importing Scripts

Some scripts are so handy that you want to reuse them in another FileMaker database, but you don't have to recreate them from scratch. If you have access privileges that allow you to modify scripts (page 779) in the file that contains the scripts you need, you can import scripts from one file into another.

Start in the file where you want the script(s) to appear. Open the Manage Scripts dialog box (page 417) and then click the Import button. Use the Open File dialog box to find the file that contains the script(s) you'll import. After you select the file and click Open, the Import Scripts window appears, showing a list of all the scripts in the file. Click in the checkbox to the left of each script you want to import, and then click OK.

As each script is imported, FileMaker does its best to match the referenced elements in each script step to the elements in the new file. Fields are matched using their fully qualified names (page 371). If layout names match exactly (case doesn't matter), steps pointing to them come in cleanly. FileMaker shows an Import Summary window that lets you know how many errors occurred during the import (Figure 16-2). Errors are easy to identify: you'll see "<unknown>" where the elements broke. Repoint each broken step to the proper elements in the new file. Even if no errors are reported, it's good practice to review and test the script to make sure it works properly in the new context.

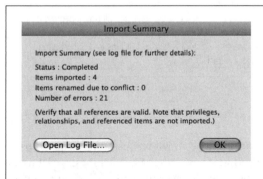

Figure 16-2:
All steps in a script are imported, but the references (tables, fields, relationships, and layouts) in the steps are not. For example, a Set Field step that targets the Invoice::Date Due in its original file will break when you import it into a file that doesn't have a field of that exact name. Each broken step is recorded as an error in the Import Summary window that appears after your import. Click the Open Log File button to get more information. For simple scripts, an import may not save you much work. But since you get all the steps in their proper order, importing scripts is a big help when the script is complex.

Tip: Reduce the number of errors that occur by creating missing elements in the target file before you import scripts.

Communicating with Database Users

Sometimes a script needs to tell people something—"There are no records to include in this report"—or ask a question—"How many copies of the report do you want?" The Show Custom Dialog script step lets you write a message and display it in a dialog box. Calling it a "Custom" dialog box may be a bit too generous—you don't have much say in how it looks—but you can at least give information to people using your database, and ask them simple questions. The Show Custom Dialog script step has three basic uses. Custom dialog boxes can:

- **Show a simple message.** Users don't get to make a choice, but like a warning dialog box, they have to click a button in response to your message.

- **Ask a Simple Question.** Users can make a choice by clicking one of the two or three buttons you provide.

- **Ask a More Complex Question.** Users can enter data into fields provided by the dialog box.

To use a custom dialog box in a script, move the Show Custom Dialog step into place in your script and set the appropriate options for the type of message you need to show. When the dialog box pops up, your script waits for user response (he has to click a button), and then continues with the next step.

Note: The title and message boxes each have a Specify button that brings up the calculation engine so you can make those items more dynamic. For instance, if someone wants to see all open invoices for a particular customer, but the script doesn't find any, you can show a calculated message that checks the Customer::Full Name fields and shows, "Tomas Vergis's account is paid in full," instead of something equally true but less helpful, like "No records were found."

Showing a Simple Message

The custom dialog box you created in the Send Email to Customer script on page 436 was a simple message with one button for user response. That message let users know that the current customer record doesn't have an email address so no email can be sent (Figure 16-3). See the box on page 681 to learn how to think like a programmer when you're showing your users a message.

Asking a Simple Question

Up one level of complexity, you can create a dialog box that asks a simple question and gives users a choice of responses. Then your script can take action based on that response. This process is very similar to the warning users get if they delete a record: FileMaker asks if the user if he wants to delete the record and gives him the option to cancel the delete action. Users are very familiar with this process, so if you have a script that posts a customer payment, you could show a custom dialog box to ask, "Are you sure you want to post a payment?," and you'd include Post Payment and Cancel buttons for feedback (Figure 16-4).

When the dialog box appears, your script waits for a click of one of its buttons, and then continues. FileMaker knows whether button 1, 2, or 3 got clicked, but your script has to tell the database what to *do* in each case. For that, you use the *Get (LastMessageChoice)* function and If statements based on its results. (The function returns *1* for the default button, 2 for Button 2, and 3 for Button 3.) In this instance, you only want the script to take action if the user clicks the Post button. Therefore, the script in Figure 16-5 uses *If [Get (LastMessageChoice) = 2]* to take action only if the function returns a value of 2. If your user clicks the default button, or hits Enter, the script does nothing, which is what she'll expect.

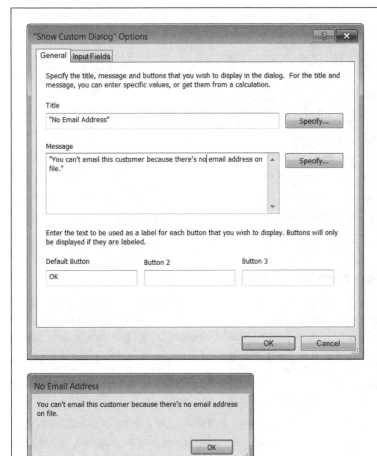

Figure 16-3:
Top: The Show Custom Dialog Options window has two tabs. You'll learn about the General tab first. It has three parts: Title, Message, and the buttons. In its most basic form, a custom dialog box shows a message with one, two, or three response buttons users can click. You must enter text in the Default Button box, but the standard text of OK makes most sense so it's not common to change this text when you only have a simple message. If you don't enter any text in the Button 2 or Button 3 boxes then those buttons don't appear in your custom dialog box.

Bottom: The dialog box that results from the settings shown above. This, the simplest version of a custom dialog box, has a title, a message, and a single button—just the basics for getting a message to folks using your database. The title appears along the top of the dialog box, the message in the middle, and the button at the bottom.

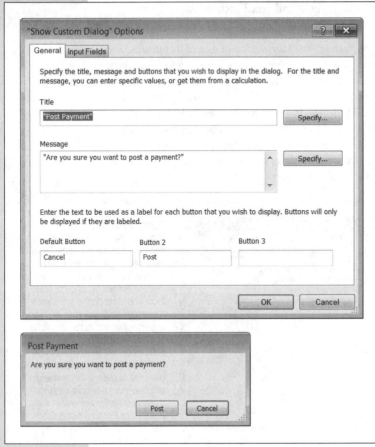

Figure 16-4:
Top: This custom dialog box is set to ask the user a question and offer two choices—Cancel and Post. Notice that the text in the Default Button box is Cancel.

Bottom: In the resulting dialog box, Cancel is automatically highlighted. This acts as a safety device, since people often reflexively hit the Return or Enter key when they see a dialog box. By making Cancel the default button, you can prevent potentially destructive processes when people fail to read your instructions. If you use this method all the time, you might even find that users start reading your dialog box messages to make sure they make the right choice.

Asking a More Complex Question

If you need user input that goes beyond two or three simple choices, you can venture into the second tab—Input Fields—in the "Show Custom Dialog" Options dialog box shown in Figure 16-6 (top). The Show Custom Dialog Options window's Input Fields tab lets you add up to three fields to your custom dialog box. To add a field to a custom dialog box, select the Input Fields tab, and then turn on one of the "Show input field" checkboxes. When you do, FileMaker shows a Specify Field dialog box, in which you can pick the field to use.

You can also give the field a label, like "Start Date" and "End Date" shown in Figure 16-5 (bottom). If you don't enter text in the label boxes, no label appears. A label can be the result of a calculation. If you turn on "Use password character" for an input field, the field works like a typical Password box: It shows * or • instead of the letters you type, so someone watching over your shoulder can't read what you're entering.

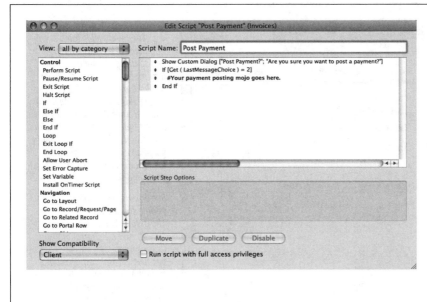

Figure 16-5:
This script asks a question using a Show Custom Dialog step, then an If statement with a Get (LastMessageChoice) function decides what to do. If someone clicks Post, then the function result is 2, and the script does whatever magic you create between the If statements. To give users two choices, plus a Cancel button, then your script needs an If statement that checks for a value of "2" and an Else If that checks for a value of "3."

The fields you add to a custom dialog box have some limitations, including the ones listed below. (For other alternatives, see the box on page 683.)

- Show Custom Dialog can have only free-entry fields like those shown in Figure 16-6. You can't use radio buttons, checkboxes, calendars or pop-up menus. You also have no control over the size of the field, so you can't specify, say, short fields for dates or tall fields for lots of text.

- "Data-entry only" validation doesn't apply to fields in custom dialog boxes. If you use a dialog box to gather data for a record, either use the Always option in the field validation, or check the validity of the data in your script (page 436).

- You *must* use the OK button as the default button when you're using input fields in a custom dialog box or FileMaker won't enter the data into a record. Consequently, you have to trust people to read the dialog box before they type information into it.

- If you're using Input Fields for actual data entry into a record, your script may need to include steps to make sure it's running in the correct context (page 151).

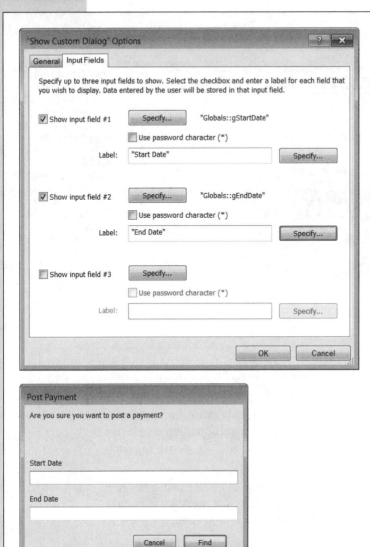

Figure 16-6:
Top: The Input Fields tab lets you add fields to a custom dialog box so users can supply more information than they could just by clicking a button. You can use input fields for actual data input into the current record, or as shown here, into global fields for use later. For instance, you might script a Find that sets fields in Find Mode using the values users enter into the custom dialog box.

Bottom: Here's the dialog box people see when the script runs. The default button (this one says "Find") isn't the Cancel button, as is normal best practice. That's because FileMaker moves data from the dialog box to the specified fields only when the default button is clicked. The other two buttons dump the data from the dialog box, so most of the time you'll just use the default button and button 2, which should let your user cancel data entry and the script.

Organizing Complex Scripts

Sometimes you need a script that does a lot. At the end of this chapter, you'll build a script that generates an invoice for a selected job. As you'll see, this process involves many steps across several tables. To do all this work in one long script can be cumbersome, especially when several levels of If and Loop steps get mixed up with each other.

Testing Multiple Conditions Redux

Back in the box on page 658, you learned how to write a script that tested multiple conditions. Now that you're familiar with setting variables, it's time to learn how to take a more advanced approach to the same problem. Instead of calling three different custom dialog boxes that are each hard-coded, you can set your message in a *local variable*, and then call a single custom dialog box that changes based on which condition tested as true.

Why go to all that trouble? It's certainly not because File-Maker gives you a limited number of Show Custom Dialog boxes and makes you ration their use.

The rationale behind this exercise is to give you a taste of the software engineer's approach to FileMaker's variables. By thinking in terms of storing data that doesn't need to last inside a local variable (which itself has a very short shelf-life), instead of as an option in a dialog box, you're well on the way to solving more advanced problems as they arise. And if you've come from another programming background, you'll be glad to see that FileMaker handles variable storage like some of the big boys in the programming world.

Here's how it looks:

```
If [ Get(CurrentTime) > Time(4; 0 ; 0) and
Get(CurrentTime) < Time(12 ; 0 ; 0) ]
  Set Variable [ $customMessage ; Value:
"Good morning!" ]
Else If [ Get(CurrentTime) > Time(12 ;
0 ; 0) and Get(CurrentTime) < Time(18 ; 0
; 0)
]
  Set Variable [ $customMessage ; Value:
"Good afternoon!" ]
Else
  Set Variable [ $customMessage ; Value:
"Go to bed" ]
End If
Show Custom Dialog [ Title: "Greetings" ;
Message: $customMessage ; Buttons:
"Thanks" ]
```

In other situations, you may need two or more scripts that do similar things. In fact, sometimes, entire sections of two scripts are identical with only minor differences. You may have a script that finds unpaid invoices so it can print a statement, and another that finds unpaid invoices to send email payment reminders.

If you build these two scripts independently, you have two problems. First, you have to write all the "find the unpaid invoices" stuff twice, which is a waste of time. More importantly, next month when you realize you need to exclude voided invoices from the list, you have to make the change in *both* places. A database that's been growing for years can be a real bear to manage if the same general business logic is implemented over and over in dozens of different scripts.

You can make your work easier and less error-prone by dividing your scripts into smaller parts. That way, you can break up a complex script into simpler scripts that each do part of the job. Also, you can make one script that finds unpaid invoices and use it in another script that prints a statement and/or sends an email payment reminder. Writing scripts in small pieces that you can then reuse in other scripts is called *modular scripting*.

The Perform Script Script Step

The key to modular scripting is the Perform Script script step. It lets one script run another script—in which case, it's called a *subscript*. When you add the Perform Script step to your script, you get only one option: a Specify button. Figure 16-7 shows how to use the Specify Script dialog box to tell your script which subscript you want to run and what file to find it in.

When one script runs another, it waits for the subscript to finish before continuing. For example, if you have a script called Find Unpaid Invoices, then a Print Statements script could start off by performing the Find Unpaid Invoices script, then, once Find Unpaid Invoices is done, Print Statements can sort and print the found invoices.

When you perform a script from another file, FileMaker uses that file's frontmost window (which is behind the user's window) to run in. If the other file doesn't have any windows, FileMaker creates one. In either case, you're in a unique scripting situation: The window your script uses isn't the one in front. Many times, that doesn't matter, because the user doesn't have to see what's going on. But if the user does need to see what's happening, use the Current Window option in the Select Window script step to bring the script's window forward.

Figure 16-7:
The Specify Script Options dialog box is where you tell the Perform Script step which script to run. You can pick any file you have a reference to from the File pop-up menu (or choose Add File Reference to add a reference to another file). The script list shows every script in the selected file, complete with its groups and separators. Just select the script you want, and then click OK. See page 686 for details on script parameters.

Halt Script and Exit Script

Normally a script ends when its last step runs. But you can force a script to end early if you want to. FileMaker actually has *two* script steps that end a script prematurely: Exit Script and Halt Script. These two steps do exactly the same thing if you run a script yourself directly. But if the current script was run by *another script*—via the Perform Script step—then they do different things. The Exit Script step tells File-Maker to stop the current script, and then continue the script that ran it. Halt Script, on the other hand, causes *all* script execution to stop immediately, no matter how the current script was started.

WORKAROUND WORKSHOP

Truly Custom Dialog Boxes

If the window that the Show Custom Dialog script step creates (Figure 15-6) doesn't meet your needs, all is not lost. You have two options: For professional-level needs (resizable dialog boxes with text you can control with a calculation, progress bars, and multiple input fields), you can get a third-party plug-in made for the task. See page 667 for more information on how to use plug-ins and where to find them. But for light duty, you can get a similar effect by assembling your own dialog box from a window, a layout, and a script.

First, you need a layout that shows the objects you need. You can use text objects on the layout to show messages, field controls to gather input, and layout buttons to run or continue a script. Once you've got the layout just the way you like it, you need a script that shows it.

To get the effect of a typical dialog box, you need to do a few things. First, you want the new layout to appear in its own window. It probably shouldn't have the status area showing. And while the window is up, your users shouldn't be able to switch to a different window. Here's how to do all these things in a script:

* Use the New Window script step to make a new window. Then use Show/Hide Status Area to hide and lock the status area, and Adjust Window with the 'Resize to Fit" option to make the new window just the right size.

* To keep the window frontmost, pause the script once the window is showing. When a script is paused, people can't switch windows. For added assurance, add the Allow User Abort script step with the Off option before you pause the script. This step prevents people from doing anything that would cancel the script.

* If someone presses Enter, FileMaker continues the script, so make one of the buttons look like a default button (bold its edges perhaps), and have the script take its action when it continues. To handle other buttons, you can have them set a variable (page 328) and resume the script. The script can then check the variable when it continues to see what action it should take.

* After the pause script step, take any steps you need to deal with the user's input, and then close the window with the Close Window script step.

This layout-based approach has some drawbacks—most notably, it lacks the convenient default Cancel button of FileMaker's built-in custom dialog boxes. If you want this behavior in a layout-based box, you have to take special measures to avoid losing valuable information if someone clicks the wrong button. For instance, you could put user-entered data into global fields, and then move that data into the real fields only when the script continues.

Exit Script (Result)

Exit Script has a powerful option that Halt Script doesn't have: a script result. With a script result, you can tie all the power of the Specify Calculation window to Exit Script. Then your main script can check the script result and decide how to proceed based on the results of the test. For example, you don't want to bother going through a sort and print process if your script doesn't find any invoices. An Exit Script step at the end of Find Unpaid Invoices will help the Print Statements script figure out whether it should sort and print. Here's how to add an Exit Script step to an existing script:

1. **In the Manage Scripts window, double-click the Find Unpaid Invoices script.**

   The Exit Script step is always added to your subscript. The Edit Script window opens.

2. **In the script step list, double-click the Exit Script step.**

   The step is added to your list. If necessary, move it to the bottom of the list. (You don't want the script stopping before all the work is done.)

3. **Click the Specify button.**

   If you don't see the specify button, make sure the exit script step is still highlighted. The Specify Calculation window appears.

4. **In the View pop-up menu, choose the Get (FoundCount) function. Or enter *Get (FoundCount)* if you prefer.**

   The function appears in the calculation field. The script will record the number of unpaid records it finds when it's done.

5. **Choose Scripts→Save Script.**

   You want to keep your work, don't you?

Exit Script Result doesn't do much on its own. You also need to test those results in the main script. Use an If test, and use the aptly-named *Get (Script Result)* function to see if any records were found that should be sorted and printed. See Figure 16-8 for a script that calls Find Unpaid Invoices, and then checks its results.

Organizing scripts that use Halt or Exit Script

The Halt Script and Exit Script steps are useful exit strategies when you want to abort a script's execution because some problem has come up. But if you're trying to stop a script to avoid a problem, you're usually better off without them. Take, for example, the two scripts shown in Figure 16-9.

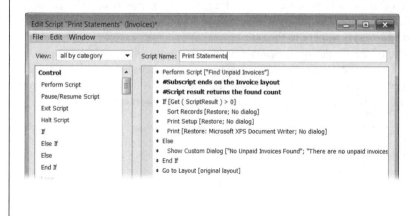

Figure 16-8:
The Print Statements script calls the subscript to which you've just added an Exit Script step. Next, a couple of comments help you remember what's going on in the subscript, so you don't have to figure it out. Then, an If test checks the results of the subscript to see whether it should sort and print invoices. If no invoices need to be printed, a dialog box tells the user what's happening, (or in this case, what's not happening).

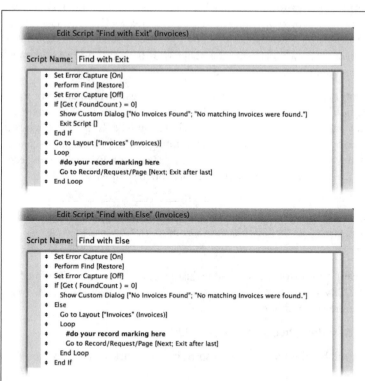

Figure 16-9:
Top: This script performs a find. Then, if it finds no records, it shows a custom dialog box and exits the script. The end point of this script might be after the last script step, which is normal, or at the Exit Script step, which is not.

Bottom: This version does the same thing, but doesn't exit the script if no records are found. Instead, it puts all the remaining script steps in the Else section of the condition. The result is the same—the extra steps run only if the script finds some records—but the bottom script always ends after the last step.

Suppose you revisit this process later and want to add some more steps to the end of the script that should happen *last*, every time the script runs—not just when records are found. If your script looks like the one on top, you have a problem. You either have to add your new steps to the script *twice* (once before the Exit Script, and again at the end of the script), or reorganize the entire script to support the changes. But the script on the bottom is easy to fix: Just add the new steps to the end. In general, if a script ends in more than one place, it will come back to bite you later. You're much better off organizing your script so it always reaches the same ending place.

Note: Halt Script has an even bigger downside. Since scripts can run other scripts, and most databases grow and change over time, you never know for sure if the script you're writing today is going to be run by another script some day in the future. It's rarely a good idea to run another script that could halt before reaching its normal end. It gives your new script no opportunity to recover if something goes wrong, so use Halt Script sparingly.

Script Parameters

When you call a script using the Perform Script step or attach the script to a button, the Specify Script window shows a box labeled "Optional script parameter." You can type a static value in the box, or you can click Edit to create a dynamic calculation that FileMaker evaluates when the script starts to run. FileMaker stores the value, and you can check it anywhere inside the script with the *Get (ScriptParameter)* function, and then branch the script based on the result.

For example, you might make a script that can sort records in three different ways. That way, three different buttons can run the same script, with three different results. The script parameter that's attached to each button tells the script which sort order to use. The benefit is similar to modular scripting: if this process has to change later, you only have one script to change, and one new button to create. This technique can drastically reduce the number of scripts you have to write.

Note: Script parameters don't automatically pass on to subscripts. If the subscript needs to know what's in your main script's parameters, use *Get (ScriptParameter)* as the subscript's optional parameter.

Suppose you want buttons on the Customer List layout to sort your Customer records by Name, City, or State. You can get the job done with just one script, You'll write a script before you add buttons:

1. **Create a new script called Sort Customer List.**

   This script will handle a few common sorts, but you start with a branch.

2. **Add the If step to the script.**

   FileMaker adds two new lines—If and End If—to your script.

3. **Click the Specify button. From the View pop-up menu, choose "Get functions".**

   The function list now shows all the *Get()* functions.

4. **Find Get (Script Parameter) in the list, and then add it to your calculation.**

   The *Get (ScriptParameter)* function returns the parameter value that was specified when this script was called. If the parameter was a calculation, it returns the *result* of the calculation, which is now in the Calculation box.

5. **In the Calculation box, after Get (ScriptParameter), type = *"Name"*, and then click OK.**

   You're back in the Edit Script window, where the If step shows your calculation. Your calculation should look like this: *Get (ScriptParameter) = "Name"*. Its result is *true* if the parameter sent to this script is "Name", and *false* otherwise.

6. **Add the Sort Records script step to the script, and then turn on "Perform without dialog".**

   Insert it after the If step and before the End If step. (If yours is somewhere else, move it between these two steps.)

Note: FileMaker inserts new script steps just below any highlighted step. If no script step is highlighted, then the new script step lands at the end of your script.

---

7. **Turn on the "Specify sort order" checkbox, add the Last Name field, and then the First Name field to the Sort Order list. Then click OK.**

   You've written your first test. The rest of the script will be variations on this theme.

8. **Add the Else If script step to the script.**

   You want Else If to come after the Sort Records step and before the End If step. (If it doesn't land there, move it.)

9. **Click Specify. In the Specify Calculation box, type *Get (ScriptParameter)* = *"City"*, and then click OK.**

   You're setting up a new test, this time checking to see if "City" is the script parameter. If it is, then you want a Sort step following this parameter to sort by—you guessed it—city.

Note: Sometimes it's quicker to copy one If test, and then paste and edit it in the Else If steps.

---

10. **Add another copy of the Sort Records script step to the script. Turn on "Perform without dialog." Set the sort order to City, and then click OK.**

    Your second test, and what to do if that test is true, is now complete.

Note: Now you can select the Else If and its Sort, and then use the Duplicate button to make copies of both steps. Then, edit the Else If test and the Sort order.

---

11. **Add one more copy of the Else If script step, this time with *Get (ScriptParameter) = "Zip"* as the calculation.**

    If the first two tests fail, your script makes this third test.

12. **Add another Sort Record step, this time set to sort by the Zip Code field. Then click OK until you're back in the database.**

    Your finished script should look something like Figure 16-10.

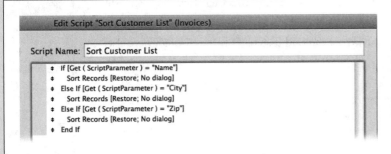

Figure 16-10:
Your finished sort script should look like this example. It has three branches (one for each of the possible sort orders). Now you need to add buttons on the Customers layout to run this script.

Note: When you're making a series of tests like the ones in this script, it's more efficient to put the condition that most often tests as true at the top. That way, the script doesn't have to test conditions that usually fail.

Now it's time to add buttons to the Customers List layout to make it easy for people to run the script.

1. **Click the button by the Last Name field label to select it, and then choose Format→Button Setup.**

    Or use the Button tool (the one that looks like a finger pushing a button). Either way, FileMaker shows you the Specify Button dialog box.

2. **Choose the Perform Script button command, and then click Specify. In the Specify Script window, select Sort Customer List.**

   That's the branching sort script you created in the last tutorial.

3. **In the "Optional script parameter" box, type *Name,* and then click OK until you're back on the Customers layout.**

   The first test of the Sort Customers script—*Get (ScriptParameter) = "Name"*—is true when people run it by clicking this button.

Note: If you check the text in the Optional script parameter box, you see that FileMaker put double quotes around "Name" for you. That's because it considers "Name" a text constant. If you like to be thorough, you can type the quote marks yourself, or you can rest easy knowing FileMaker will do it for you.

Copy the Last Name button, and then move it into place. Change its script parameter to "City", and then make another copy and change its parameter to "Zip." Switch to Browse mode to test your buttons. If one sort doesn't work, compare the spelling in your buttons' script parameters against the spelling in the script. Case doesn't matter, but spelling and spacing do.

Note: You don't have to write the script first, and then create your buttons. Lots of developers prefer to create buttons first, complete with the appropriate parameters, and then write scripts later. The order doesn't matter. Just make sure both tasks get done and that the parameters set on your buttons match up with the tests in the script.

To add a new sort to the layout you add a pair of Else If and Sort steps, and then make a button with a script parameter that matches each new test. See the box on page 692 for a way to use script parameters to extend the flexibility of the Add Note Separator script you wrote back on page 468.

Script Variables

Global fields are great for storing a value that's not tied to a specific record in a table. Script variables are similar; use them when you need to store a temporary value for your script to use, usually when you're testing a condition. But variables are better than globals in one important way: You don't have to add a field to a table to use them. Instead, variables are created as a script is running, and can vanish again when the script is finished, leaving no impact on your data's structure. (See page 659 for a refresher on using calculations to create variables.) Figure 16-11 shows you how to create a variable.

Indirection

Script parameters let you write multi-purpose scripts that you can use under many different circumstances. You just pass the script a parameter that triggers the branch that runs the parts you need, based on the circumstance (page 686).

To take your FileMaker skills to the next level, you need to learn *indirection*. That term means referring to things—usually fields, but also named objects (page 456)—without specifically naming them. The point is to make your scripts more reusable. For instance, a script that finds a record by ID needs to search the CustomerID field in the Customers table, but the InvoiceID in the Invoice table. Without indirection, you'd have to write two different find scripts, pointing to two different fields, even if every other script step is exactly the same.

A special script step called Set Field by Name lets you put data in fields by indirection. To understand how it works, look at the normal Set Field script step, which lets you specify a field to receive the result of a calculated value. For example, you might set the Zip Code field to a known value, for instance, or set the Balance Due field to the sum of costs minus the sum of payments.

By contrast, the Set Field by Name step lets you specify two calculations. The second determines the value to store, just like Set Field. But the first calc evaluates to the name of the field you want to set. In other words, if the result of the calculation is "Customers::First Name", then the step stores its value in the First Name field. If the calc returns "Customers::Last Name" instead, it puts the calculated value in the *Last* Name field. Here's a formula that assembles a field name:

```
Get(LayoutTableName) & "::First Name"
```

This formula targets the First Name field in the table associated with the current layout. So this step can work in a Customers table and an Employees table. Even better, you can use a script parameter to pass the complete field name, and then Set Field by Name uses that parameter to identify its target.

You can also fetch data from a field indirectly using the *GetField()* function:

```
GetField ( Get(LayoutTableName) & "::First
Name" )
```

This formula grabs the value from the First name field based on the current layout you're viewing.

Finally, the *GetFieldName()* function helps you grab field names reliably. Suppose you need a script that finds Invoices with today's date in either the Invoice Date or the Date Due field. You create two different buttons to run that script, and type one field's name as the script parameter in each button. Then you use *Set Field by Name* to put today's date into the specified field with *Get (ScriptParameter)*.

You've used indirection, but this approach is unsafe. Since you're passing the field name in a calculation text value, FileMaker doesn't see it as a proper field reference and won't update the script parameter if you rename the field(s). Now your scripts refer to a nonexistent field and they won't run properly. To solve this problem, use the *GetFieldName()* function. (It's in the Logical functions section.):

```
GetFieldName(Invoices::Due Date)
```

This formula returns the text value "Invoices::Due Date," which may seem like extra work to accomplish the same thing. But using the function to pass the field name instead of static text ensures that if you ever rename the field, File-Maker corrects the formula for you, and your script keeps working properly. If you ever want to pass the name of a field as a script parameter (or otherwise refer to a field's name directly in a calculation), use *GetFieldName()* to protect against name changes.

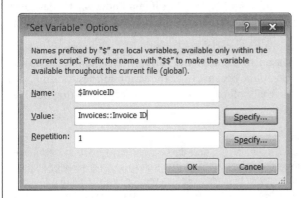

Figure 16-11:
The "Set Variable" Options dialog box lets you create a variable by giving it a name and assigning it a value. You might create a variable like this one to hold an Invoice ID while a script goes to an Invoice Line Item layout and creates a new line item tied to the current invoice.

Since you can use variables inside calculations, their naming rules are similar to those of field names. Don't use characters like a comma, +, -, *, or any other symbol that has a mathematical meaning and might confuse a calculation.

POWER USERS' CLINIC

Passing Multiple Parameters

A script can have only one parameter, and its result type is always text. But the parameter itself can be multiple values, if you're willing to use your calculation skills. To pass multiple parameters, string your values together with a separator character, and then pull them apart again in the script.

For example, if you want a script to have a pair of static values, you could type this text as the script parameter:

```
Molly¶Bloom
```

Since the separator is the "¶", each value is on its own "line," and that makes it easy to grab the bits you need using the *GetValue()* function. A calculation to pull "Molly" out from the script parameter would look like this:

```
GetValue ( Get ( ScriptParameter ) ; 1 )
```

Here's how to assemble a set of dynamic values into one script parameter:

```
Customer::First Name & "¶" & Customer::
LastName & "¶" & Customer::Phone & "¶"
& Customer::Email
```

The *GetValue()* function above can pull apart the pieces of your multivalue parameter.

The Set Script Variable script step has three options:

- **Name.** Choose a short, descriptive name. All script variable names require a $ prefix. If you forget to type the prefix, FileMaker adds it for you. But get in the habit of typing the prefix, since it determines how long the value in the variable is available. A single $ means the variable is local and lasts only while your script is running. Local variables aren't sent to subscripts. A double $$ prefix creates a global variable, and its value persists through subscripts and even after all scripts have finished running. Global variables are cleared when you close the database but are reset if called by another script or by a calculation.

- **Value.** The value you want to store in the variable. Values can be static text or the dynamic result of a calculation.

- **Repetition.** A variable can store multiple values, like a repeating field does. Repetitions are optional, and not common. But if you know what a data array is, and want to create one, variable repetitions are one way to get that job done.

Since you can pass the value in a local variable with either a script result or a script parameter, there's rarely a reason to use a global variable. Programmers consider global variables sloppy housekeeping, because once the script finishes running, variables just lay around your database full of values that don't have meaning outside a script.

Warning: Global variables are potential security risks, since the Data Viewer (page 521) in FileMaker Pro Advanced will reveal their values to anybody who knows their names and has enough privileges to run scripts. If security is a big consideration at your business, make sure you don't leave sensitive data laying around in global variables by resetting their values to "0" or "" when the script is done. In practice, though, it's usually a lot easier, and cleaner, to use only local variables and rest assured that FileMaker is cleaning up after you.

UP TO SPEED

Note Separators Revisited

In the previous scripting chapter, you learned how to make the Add Note Separator script work with any field (see the box on page 472). The only drawback is that you have to click the field you want to work with before running the script. With script parameters, you can fix this problem. Just add a series of If and Else If script steps to the top of the script. Each one checks for a Notes field (Invoice::Notes, Job::Notes, Customer::Notes, and so on) in the script parameter.

For instance, if the script parameter is "Invoice," then the script should use the "Go to Field" script step to go to the Invoices::Notes field first.

With these conditions in place, you just need to pass the right parameter from your Add Notes button. Just add tests to check the script parameter, and then use an appropriate "Go to Field" script step, depending on which button the user clicks. Use the script described on page 677 to see how to do this kind of branching.

Now if you add a new Notes field to another table, you add an Else If and a "Go to Field" step to this script. Then to change the way the note separators look or the data they contain, you can change it in one place and the change applies to every Notes field in the database.

Handling Errors

When an error occurs during a script (a Perform Find finds no records, for instance), FileMaker shows an error message almost like the one it would if you were doing the steps manually. The one difference is a button called Continue (Figure 16-12).

Figure 16-12:
When an error occurs during a script, FileMaker gives the user all the normal choices he'd usually see in a warning dialog box, plus the option to ignore the error and continue the script. This is the warning you see if no records match the request in a scripted Find. It's just like the normal Find error message, except there's also a Continue button.

If someone clicks Cancel in an error message, the script stops immediately, and leaves him wherever the script was when it stopped. If he clicks Continue instead, FileMaker ignores the error and moves on with the script. In the Perform Find example, for instance, the script continues with no records in the found set. Some errors, like when no records are found in a search, gives users a third choice. The Modify Find button goes to Find mode on the current layout, and then pauses the script.

Sometimes this error-handling approach is just fine. If the script is simple and everyone using it knows a little about FileMaker, it isn't too big a problem. But often, you need more control:

- If your system is complex—or your database's users aren't experienced with FileMaker—all sorts of confusion can result. First, the error message may make absolutely no sense to the person reading it. Maybe your script searches for a Customer record before making a new invoice. If a message complains about not finding any records, the person reading it thinks, "I just wanted to create a new invoice for this job. Who said anything about finding records?" Even worse, if she clicks Cancel, she could wind up just about anywhere: some layout in some window on some record. It could be a layout (like a developer-only layout you created to make the script run) that she's never even seen before.

- If an error happens in the middle of a larger multistep process, it might be really important that the script know about it and deal with it appropriately. But it's the *user*, not the *script*, that decides whether to continue or cancel. You may want to make sure the script *always* continues, so it can get on with important work.

Luckily, you can opt for more control over error handling if you want it. FileMaker gives you three functions for finding and dealing with errors that may happen when scripts run.

The Set Error Capture Script Step

The Set Error Capture script step lets you turn on *error capture*. That way, instead of displaying potentially confusing error messages to your database's users, FileMaker keeps track of error information (*captures* it) so you can pull it into your script and handle it there. Although error capturing is a great feature, it's not part of FileMaker's normal behavior. You have to activate it by adding the Set Error Capture step to your script, and choosing the On option. At any time in the script, you can turn it back off again by using the step a second time and switching the option off.

If a script turns error capture on, and then uses the Perform Script step to run another script, the second script also runs with error capture on. In other words, the error capture setting sticks around as long as scripts call other scripts. But as soon as script execution stops for good, FileMaker turns off error capture. Understanding this behavior helps you determine when you need an error capture script step and when it would just be redundant. Figure 16-13 shows a script that turns on error capture before performing a find, then turns it back off when it's done.

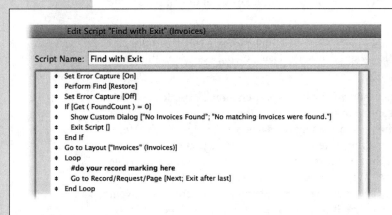

Figure 16-13:
This script turns error capture on, and then performs a find. That way, if the find fails, the script doesn't produce an error message. The script itself handles the error by checking for no found records in the If step, and then displays a more helpful, customized error message if an error did occur.

As discussed in the box on the next page, you can just turn error capture on so that your script ignores any and all errors—but that's not good script writing. The best way to use Set Error Capture is hand-in-hand with the *Get (LastError)* function, described next, to achieve error-free results.

The Get (LastError) Function

When error capture is on, FileMaker doesn't just *ignore* the errors. Rather, it remembers which error occurred and gives you the chance to ask about it if you're interested. The script in Figure 16-13, for example, *isn't* interested. It doesn't ask if an error occurred at all. Instead, it just checks to see if the find worked by counting the records in the found set.

But sometimes you can use such error information within your script, much like any other value, to trigger other script steps. To check an error, use the *Get (LastError)* function to find out what happened. This function returns an *error code*, which is always a number. If there was no error in the previous step, *Get (LastError)* returns a zero. In other words, it doesn't return the number of the last error that occurred. Instead, it returns the error number for the last step that ran. You shouldn't, therefore, put a *comment* step before the step that checks the last error, since the comment step itself always sets the last error back to zero. The same goes for End If and even Set Error Capture [Off].

WORD TO THE WISE

Keep It Off

Using Set Error Capture to eliminate those pesky dialog boxes sounds so cool, you may be tempted to turn it on at the start of every script. You can't anticipate every error, but at least you can keep FileMaker from casting doubt on your database skills by throwing error messages in people's faces. But if all your script does is turn error capture on, but then never checks to see *which* errors are happening, you're not doing your database's users—or yourself—any favors.

If odd error messages pop up, people may let you know about it (perhaps via cellphone while you're trying to relax on the beach). But that's not your best chance to figure out the problem and improve your script. With error capture turned on, a script might seem to be working because no warning dialog box shows up, but really, something's gone kablooie and error capture suppresses the dialog box that would have explained the problem.

You have little hope of figuring out what went wrong—especially if no one realizes there's been a problem until long after the script has run.

Usually, you find errors when you're developing your scripts, and you can use a custom dialog box (page 676) along with error capture to deal with them. Remember two rules for using error capture. First, don't turn error capture on unless you've already anticipated an error and figured out how your script can handle it. Second turn it off right after the error-producing part of the script has finished. That way, *unanticipated* errors don't get swept under the rug. In general, you should have just a few steps between Set Error Capture [On] and Set Error Capture [Off].

In FileMaker, just about everything that could possibly go wrong has its own error number or code. This feature gives you a lot of flexibility, but it also makes it a real pain to figure out which errors you should check for. A complete list of error codes is found in Appendix B: FileMaker Error Codes. Luckily, most of these errors are pretty obscure, and chances are you'll never have to worry about them. Here's a list of the more common error numbers you may actually be interested in:

- **Error 9, 200–217, 723–725.** Assorted security-related errors (see Chapter 18).

- **Error 112.** Window is missing (you get this error if you try to select, close, or move/resize a window that doesn't exist).

- **Error 301.** Record is in use by another user (you get this error when you try to modify a record that's locked in another window or by another user).

- **Error 400.** Find criteria are empty (if you let users enter find criteria during a script, the Perform Script step gets this error if they don't enter anything).

- **Error 401.** No records match this request (this is the actual error that happens when no records are found; most people choose to check *Get (FoundCount)* instead since it's easier to understand).

- **Errors 500–507.** Assorted field validation errors (you get these errors when you try to modify a field in a way that violates its validation setting and it's set to "always" validate).

- **Errors 718 and 719.** XML processing errors (see Chapter 19).

- **Errors 1200–1219.** Calculation-related errors (you see these errors in conjunction with the EvaluationError and Evaluate functions).

- **Errors 1400–1413.** Assorted ODBC errors (see Chapter 19).

Tip: To capture an error by number, try this: Turn on error capture before the step that's producing the error, and then add a Show Custom Dialog step right after the offending step. Set the dialog box to show *Get (LastError)*. When you run the script, instead of the error message you've been seeing, you'll see a custom dialog box with the real error number. You can then modify the script to handle this particular number.

Better Tip: But it's much easier to use the Script Debugger (page 513) in FileMaker Pro Advanced. The debugger automatically shows error numbers as they happen—no need to write junk steps into your scripts that you just have to strip out again. There's even an option to set your scripts to pause when an error occurs so you can analyze the situation and fix the problem.

The Allow User Abort Script Step

One more script step has ramifications when dealing with errors: Allow User Abort. This step lets you turn off a user's ability to cancel the script. Allow User Abort has only two options: on and off. Its normal state is to be turned on, unless you specifically turn it off with the script step. Like Set Error Capture, when you turn user abort off or back on within a script, the setting carries through any subscripts called by the main script. Allow User Abort always turns back on again when the script finishes running.

If you turn user abort off, but leave error capture on, the Cancel button in error messages is removed, so the person is forced to continue the script. Turning off user abort also prevents the user from pressing Escape (Windows) or ⌘-period (Mac) to cancel a running script. Finally, if the script pauses, he doesn't get a Cancel button in the status area. Instead, the only choice is to continue.

Note: When a script turns off user abort and pauses, the database user also can't switch to a different window, close the window, or quit FileMaker.

Advanced Script Triggers

On page 433, you got an intro to using *timers* with the Install OnTimer Script step, which lets you schedule a script to run repeatedly. Now you'll get the full Install OnTimer story, and learn how the OnKeystroke trigger lets you respond to every keystroke your user makes.

Note: These are power-user triggers that require a lot of expertise to use properly. They give you a lot of power, but they're more complex than the script steps you've seen so far. Approach them once you've got some experience under your belt.

Install OnTimer Script

The Install OnTimer Script step has two options. First, you specify the script you want to run (along with an optional script parameter). Then you specify the number of "Interval seconds." For instance, you can schedule your Find Unpaid Invoices script with an interval of 10 seconds. If you then run the script with the Install On-Timer Script step, your Find Unpaid Invoices script runs every 10 seconds forever.

Of course *forever* is a long time. How do you stop a timer like this? In two ways:

- Timers are associated with the window that was active when the timer was installed. If this window closes, the timer stops running. So you can close the database window to stop its timer.

- A window can only have one timer running. If you install a new timer in the same window, it *replaces* the one you last installed. So if you run the Install On-Timer Script step with no script specified, then you effectively turn off the timer entirely. This way, you can keep the window open, but stop its timer.

Tip: Timers can be trouble (after all, if you accidentally schedule a complicated script to run every second, it can keep your database so busy that it's tough to do anything else, including unschedule it). While you're working out the kinks in your timer-based process, make a new window to work in. Then if you accidentally get a timer running that won't stop on its own, just close the bad window.

Here are some situations where a timer might come in handy:

- You have a series of informational layouts you want to display on a wall-mounted monitor (like shop operation information or information for customers standing in line). Using a timer, you can automatically switch layouts periodically, so your monitor shows each one for 30 seconds, like a repeating slide show.

- Your editing process is time sensitive. For example, say you have lots of people working in your database, and lots of people have to edit the same record. To keep someone from keeping a record locked too long (see the box on page 44), install a timer when she switches to the edit layout. It can switch back to the read-only layout after a few minutes in case she walks away from her computer.

- You want to set up a computer to run periodic tasks. Maybe you have to import order information from your company's web server every 10 minutes, or you want to send shipment notifications every hour. You can install FileMaker on a computer, and schedule a timer to run the appropriate scripts periodically, with no intervention from anyone.

You'll see an example of a timer in action in the next section.

Keystroke Triggers

The Keystroke trigger is probably the most complex FileMaker scripting technique. The basic concept is simple though: A script runs every time any key is pressed. It's the scripting part that's complicated, since the script needs to test for all the keystrokes you want to intercept, and then take action when they're pressed. Keystroke triggers can apply to the layout, or to a specific layout *object*.

You might use an OnLayoutKeystroke trigger to add direct keyboard navigation (for example, pressing C to switch to the Contacts tab, or using the arrow keys to switch between records, and so on). An OnLayoutKeystroke trigger is also useful if you want to cancel keystrokes layout-wide. For instance, you can prevent the entry of punctuation into any field, or keep the arrow keys from working. To configure a keystroke trigger for the layout, view the Triggers tab of the Layout Setup dialog box (Layouts→Layout Setup). Select the "OnLayoutKeystroke" option, and then select the script that should run.

Most often, you apply the OnObjectKeystroke trigger to fields, where you can limit which keys your users can press, jump to the next field when they press the space bar, or some other specialized field-type action. To use an object keystroke trigger, select a layout object, and then choose Format→Set Script Triggers. Select the On-ObjectKeystroke trigger, and then select the script that should run. This time, the trigger fires only if the object has keyboard focus when the key is pressed.

Detecting which keys were pressed

Suppose you have a report you show in Preview mode. As a convenience to the people using the database, you want the up and down arrow keys to jump to the previous and next page respectively (they just can't get the hang of the book icon). It's a perfect job for an OnLayoutKeystroke trigger.

Note: If you want Ctrl or ⌘ key shortcuts for your database, you should use custom menus, not keystroke triggers. See page 538 for details.

When FileMaker calls your script from a keystroke trigger, it remembers which key the person pressed. The script uses an If statement with the *Get (TriggerKeystroke)* function to find out what key was pressed. Then the script can take appropriate action based on the value that's returned. For instance, if the "a" key is pressed, *Get (TriggerKeystroke)* returns "a" to the script. If "A" (using the Shift key) is pressed the script gets a capital "A" instead.

Note: If you care about uppercase vs. lowercase in your script, you can use the Exact function. This function compares two values, and returns *true* only if they're exactly the same, including case. So instead of this:

```
If ( Get (TriggerKeystroke) = "a"; "Yes", "No")
```

You should do this:

```
If ( Exact ( Get(TriggerKeystroke), "a"); "Yes", "No")
```

The first example results in "Yes" if the user presses "A" or "a", while the second gives you "Yes" only if she types a lowercase "a."

Testing for alphanumeric characters is old hat, but you can't put an arrow key in quotes in FileMaker's Specify Calculation window. But you can use the Code function with *Get (TriggerKeystroke)* to figure out what key was pressed. Here's the calculation for testing for the Up arrow key:

```
Code ( Get(TriggerKeystroke) ) = 29
```

The numeral 29 is the Unicode *code point* (or number) for the Up arrow key. The codes are listed in FileMaker's online help (search for "Code") or right here:

- Backspace: 8

- Tab: 9

- Enter: 10

- Return: 13

- Escape: 27

- Left Arrow: 28

- Up Arrow: 29

- Right Arrow: 30

- Down Arrow: 31

- Space: 32

- Forward Delete: 127

Tip: To find the code for an alphanumeric character or string of characters, use the Code() function. For example, *Code ("c")* returns the value 99 and *Code ("sp")* returns 11200115.

There's one more wrinkle to keystroke detection. What if someone presses Shift plus the Tab key? Since this is a common need, FileMaker has one more keystroke function: *Get (TriggerModifierKeys)*. This function, plus a little math, tells you which of the modifier keys was pressed. Once again, special codes represent each key:

- Shift: 1
- Caps Lock: 2
- Ctrl (Windows) or Control (Mac): 4
- Alt (Windows) or Option (Mac): 8
- ⌘ (Mac only): 16

This list may seem to be missing some values, like 3 and 5. That's because *Get (TriggerModifierKeys)*—and its sister function *Get (ActiveModiferKeys)*—*add* the values of all modifier keys to get their results. For example, Shift + Ctrl pressed together result in a value of 5. And, if you do some experimenting, you'll see that that's the only way to get 5. This way, every combination of modifier keys results in a unique number.

To figure out which number to test for, decide what key combination you want to trigger something in your script—Alt and Shift, say. When you write the script, add them up yourself: 8 + 1 = 9. Then you can do a check like this:

```
Get(TriggerModifierKeys) = 9
```

Note: The *Code()* function has an alter ego called *Char()*. Given a code (or series of codes) this function returns the original character equivalents. This function is far less useful than *Code()* (which is commonly used for keystroke triggers). Use it, for instance, if you need to force a tab character into a calculation—*Char(9)*—or something equally esoteric.

Creating a simple keystroke trigger

Now that you've worked through the concepts, you're ready to create your page navigation trigger. You can already use Ctrl (⌘) Up arrow and Ctrl (⌘) Down arrow to navigate through your records. But it'd be more convenient if the arrow keys worked without the modifier keys. You want to be able to use the trigger in Browse and Preview modes, so you'll need a way to short-circuit the arrow keys' behavior in Preview mode. The script you need navigates to the previous or next page, depending on which key is pressed (Figure 16-14).

Once you've written the script, you need to set up the keystroke trigger:

1. **Switch to the Customers layout, and then go to Layout mode. Choose Layouts→Layout Setup and then click the Script Triggers tab to select it.**

   Since you're applying a layout trigger, you start in Layout mode.

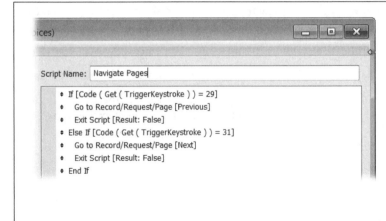

Figure 16-14:
This script checks for the key that was pressed (it's looking for the Up and Down arrow keys only) and navigates records appropriately if it detects one. Since the arrow keys already do something in Preview mode (they scroll the page up or down a bit), each test has an Exit Script step with the result of False. The Exit steps tell FileMaker to skip the normal behavior and let the scripted behavior take over. Without the Exit steps, both actions would happen.

2. **Select OnLayoutKeystroke.**

   The Specify Script Options window appears. Here's where you tell FileMaker which script to run.

Note: The sample file already has one trigger for the Customers layout. The existing trigger works only in Find mode. In this case, it's safe to apply a new trigger, because you'll set the new one to work only in Browse and Preview modes. But other triggers may not play well together, so make sure to test your custom triggers thoroughly.

---

3. **Choose the Navigate Pages script, and then click OK.**

   You're now back in the Layout Setup dialog box.

4. **If necessary, turn on the Browse and Preview checkboxes.**

   You get to tell FileMaker which modes your trigger should run in.

5. **Click OK and save your layout if necessary.**

   Now you're ready to switch to Browse mode and test your trigger.

Press the Up and Down arrow keys. If you look closely, you see FileMaker is switching from one page to the next as you do. Switch to Preview mode and test there, too.

Creating a keystroke filter

Keystroke triggers also let you limit what users can type into a field. You know how to use validation to show an error message if something inappropriate is typed in a field (page 248). But with validation, users don't get feedback until after the wrong data has been entered. Alternatively, you can write a script and set an OnObjectKeystroke trigger that can refuse certain data and beep to warn the user.

The script will check *each* key your users press, and cancel all invalid keystrokes. Careful though: writing a keystroke trigger takes special care. First of all, you have to decide what makes a keystroke invalid. Here are the rules for the Zip Code field:

- If the keystroke isn't a number (0 through 9), then don't allow it.

- If the field already has five digits in it, then cancel any keystroke.

With this in mind, switch to Layout mode, and then select the Zip Code field. Choose Format→Set Script Triggers, and then select the "OnObjectKeystroke" option. Then click the "+" button to create a new script. The new script consists of two If statements. First you check for non-number keys with a formula like this one:

```
Get ( TriggerKeystroke ) ≠ 0 and
Get ( TriggerKeystroke ) ≠ 1 and
Get ( TriggerKeystroke ) ≠ 2 and
Get ( TriggerKeystroke ) ≠ 3 and
Get ( TriggerKeystroke ) ≠ 4 and
Get ( TriggerKeystroke ) ≠ 5 and
Get ( TriggerKeystroke ) ≠ 6 and
Get ( TriggerKeystroke ) ≠ 7 and
Get ( TriggerKeystroke ) ≠ 8 and
Get ( TriggerKeystroke ) ≠ 9
```

Inside the If statement you add a beep (using the aptly-named Beep script step), and then exit the script with a result of False. Your second If statement checks for *excess* keystrokes. It has a simple calculation:

```
Length ( Customers::Zip Code ) ≥ 5
```

Once again, inside this If statement, you beep and exit with a False result. You can see this script in Figure 16-15.

When you test the Zip Code field script trigger, you'll see that the script is a little too aggressive. Since it cancels every keystroke that isn't a number, you can't use the Delete key to clear an accidental entry. Plus, it blocks the Enter, Tab, and arrow keys and you can't exit the field easily. You've created a monster—a field that can't be edited.

The fix is easy, though. If you refer back to the list of special key codes on page 699, you see that most of the special navigation keys have codes less than 31. The notable exception is the rare-but-handy Forward Delete, which is 127. So instead of adding a special case for each and every key, you can allow all the special keys in one block with a simple formula. Just wrap your entire script in a new If step with this formula:

```
Code ( Get(TriggerKeystroke) ) > 32 or Code ( Get(TriggerKeystroke) ) ≠ 127
```

You also need to improve your formula in the IF statement that checks the Zip code's length so it lets users highlight the text in order to delete it. Edit that calculation to add a new test:

```
Length ( Customers::Zip Code ) ≥ 5 and Get ( ActiveSelectionSize ) = 0
```

This tactic is perfectly safe because every normal key (letters, numbers, space, and punctuation) has code 32 or above. You can see your new and improved script in Figure 16-16.

Figure 16-15:
Your first attempt to filter keystrokes for a field might look like this one. (You can see the calculation formulas for each If step in the text above this figure.) Unfortunately, this script doesn't work quite right, since keystroke triggers fire for almost every key. This script has the nasty side effect of blocking the arrow keys, the Delete key, and even the Enter and Tab keys, which should be valid entries along with the data keys you want to allow.

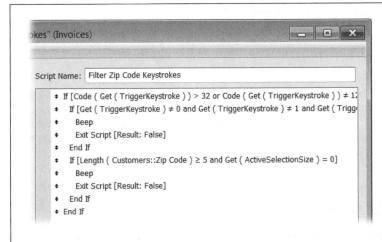

Figure 16-16:
This script improves on the one in Figure 16-15. It uses the same logic to reject non-numeric keystrokes, and any entry beyond five digits. But this time, it permits standard editing keys—those with a code below 32 and the Forward Delete key, which is code 127—to work. Now people can edit the field with ease. (Check the completed scripts in Invoices_FINISHED.fp7.)

To finish up, take a look at the modes you're applying the trigger in. You might be tempted to assign the trigger for both Find and Browse mode, but remember that you might want to find a range of Zip codes (46077...90201) or use a wildcard in your Zip Code search (852*). So you're probably best off applying this trigger only in Browse mode.

Now when you test the script trigger, you should see better behavior. If you type text or punctuation into the Zip Code field, FileMaker beeps, and nothing appears in the field. But if you type a number key, it goes right in. And once the field has five numbers, it rejects any additional entry.

Putting a Complex Script Together

Building a complicated script takes time and planning. Because scripting gives you so much flexibility, you often have many ways to solve the same problem. Your job is to find the way that best meets your business needs and is the simplest to understand, fix and maintain later. As your skills grow, the approach you take to solving problems will change.

In this section, you'll make a script that generates an invoice for a job. You want to gather all the unbilled expenses and timeslips for the job, and then add the appropriate line items to the invoice. To make a script like this, you need to cover all your bases:

- **Planning.** Before you even start writing the script, you have to decide upon a general approach. Outline all the things your script will do, and in what order. This process usually evolves from the general to the specific. The most specific version is the script itself, where you tell FileMaker *exactly* what to do.

- **Exceptions.** What kinds of things can go wrong? Think about how you'll check for errors and prevent problems.

- **Efficiency.** Are you doing the same things several places in the script? Are there other reasons to break your script into multiple smaller scripts?

Note: The rest of this chapter is one long exercise. Here, you'll get a chance to put theoretical concepts to practical use. Since each section builds on the one before it, this complex script is best digested if you work straight through from here to the end—without skipping parts or jumping around. And while you may not need this exact process in your real life databases, the techniques you'll learn are applicable to any complex scripting situations.

Planning the Script

Planning a big script is usually an iterative process. You start by outlining the steps the script will take in very general terms. You then go in and fill in more and more detail with each pass. When you're done adding detail, you know exactly what steps your script will use. Using the invoicing script as an example, you'll see how FileMaker gives you the tools to plan and execute your new script.

You can do this planning on paper, or in a word processor, or with any other tool you choose. But one good place you may *not* think of is the script itself. Since the planning process involves a series of steps, and since it naturally produces the finished script when it's done, make notes with comment script steps. As you work, replace a comment line with real script steps, and perhaps more comments explaining the process. That way, you never get lost or forget essential steps because you always have a comment to tell you what you still need to add, and where it should go. When you're done, the script is written and commented for posterity.

For this script, take a look at the script shown in Figure 16-17. To save you time, it's already created for you in the sample database for this chapter (Invoice START.fp7).

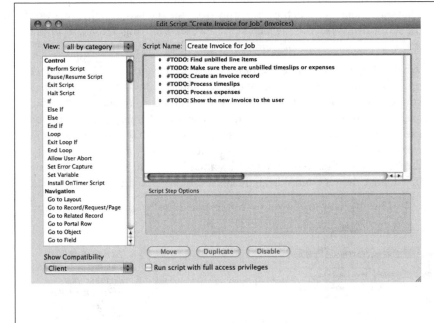

Figure 16-17:
This first draft of your script doesn't do anything yet. It's just a series of comments that map out, at the most general level, what the script is going to do. You'll add more and more details as you go. Since these comments are placeholders for the real steps and comments you'll build, each one starts with the word TODO. Use any marker you want, as long as you can easily tell these placeholder comments apart from the real comments you'll add later.

Considering Exceptions

One of the most critical steps in script writing—planning for exceptions—is often forgotten. But the old saw "A stitch in time saves nine" truly applies to scripting. Spend a few minutes at the beginning of the process thinking ahead to what might go wrong and planning how to prevent problems. These few minutes can save you hours of troubleshooting and repair work on your data later.

Look at what your script is supposed to do and try to think of reasonable *exceptions*—situations where your script might not be able to do its job. Thinking of exceptions is important for two reasons:

- If your script always assumes ideal circumstances, it can wreak havoc if your assumptions are wrong when it runs. The last thing you need is a wild script running amok in your data, changing and deleting the wrong things.

- If a script gets halfway through its job, and then discovers that it can't continue, you may be left with half-finished work. It's usually best to look for the problems up front, so the script can simply refuse to run if it won't be able to finish. (For more detail, see the box on page 707.)

For example, the Invoice creation script may run into two potential problems:

- How does the script know which job to create an invoice for? This problem is easy to solve: Make the script available only through a button on the Job layout. That way, people can run the script only from the right context. In other words, the script always runs on the job record the user is looking at. Make a comment at the top of your script that reminds you how the script is run.

- What if the job has no timeslips or expenses that haven't been billed? You wind up with an invoice that has no line items, and you don't want to send *that* to your customer nor do you want that laying around in your database. You can go ahead and create the invoice, and then delete it if it's empty. But this approach uses up an invoice number, and it means your script has to go through all the work of creating an invoice only to throw it away when it's done. Instead, have the script check first to be sure there's something to bill. Then it can display an informative message and skip all the hard work when there's nothing to bill.

Figure 16-18 shows how to edit your script to take these two problems into account.

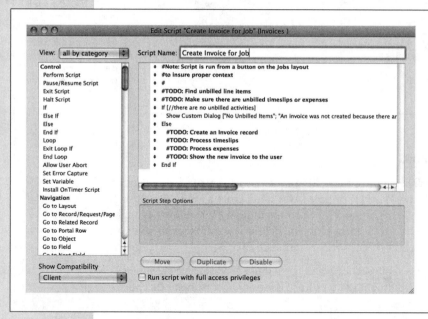

Figure 16-18:
Your first pass at editing the script shows where you'll put the test that determines whether an invoice needs to be created. And since you want to show the user a message if no invoice is made, add the Show Custom Dialog script step to the If part of the test.

- **The If step doesn't need a fully realized test yet.** Put a commented calculation (page 381) as your test for now, just to remind yourself what needs to be tested. You can put the real test in later.

- **Add feedback by putting a custom dialog step in the true part of the If step.** If you don't give feedback here, the person using the database may become confused, since nothing happens when he clicks the button to create an invoice for the job. The dialog box should explain why FileMaker isn't creating an invoice.

- **Add an Else step.** Since you don't want to create an invoice if there aren't any billable items for the job, put an Else step after the Show Custom Dialog step and put the remaining TODO items in the Else part of the If test. The End If step should be at the end of the script.

UP TO SPEED

The Problem with Problems

Although detecting problems up front is usually best, it isn't always possible. Sometimes you can't find out about problems until your script has run partway through.

Most database systems handle this problem with something called a *transaction*, a chunk of work that's held in limbo until you tell the database to make it permanent. In a nutshell, you open a transaction, and you then can do anything you want, but your changes don't get saved until you commit the record. If you decide you don't want the changes after all, you can undo the transaction.

FileMaker uses this transaction concept under the hood to handle record changes, but unfortunately you have no easy way to tap into the transaction system from a script. Here's why: When you first enter a record—using the Open Records/Requests script step, for instance—FileMaker begins a transaction for you. When you exit the record—Commit Records/Requests—FileMaker commits the transaction, writing all changes to the database. If you revert the record instead—Revert Record/Request—FileMaker essentially rolls back the transaction, leaving the database untouched. Just remember that each transaction is linked to a record. For example, you can't begin a transaction, then make changes to five different customer records and eleven invoices, and then roll back all those changes—you can only roll back the last one.

But if you create, edit, or delete records in *portal rows* while you're still in the record, all your changes happen in one transaction.

Try this exercise in the Invoices file to explore how the transaction works. Have two windows open (Choose Windows→New Window)—one showing the Invoice layout and the other showing the Line Items layout. Create a new invoice record and add a few line items. Notice that FileMaker creates the new line item records when you add items to the Line Item portal on the Invoice layout. Being very careful not to commit the record (that is, don't hit the Enter key or click anywhere outside the fields onto your layout), choose Records→Revert Record. The parent invoice record disappears, *and* all the child line items disappear, too. You've just witnessed FileMaker's version of transactions.

Knowing this, you can use the Open Record/Request script step on an invoice record, and then make changes to dozens of line items. Then if your script detects a problem, you can revert the invoice record, and toss out all your line item changes as well. If you absolutely, positively must have control over your transactions, arrange your scripts so they do everything through relationships from one single record.

Creating Subscripts

Now that you've figured out how to solve problems your script might encounter, you've come to a fork in the road. You can write a script containing all the necessary steps, but it'll be long and hard to follow. For example, the End If steps at the end of the script will be a long way from their If and Else counterparts, making it hard to figure out where they belong. The script will be easier to read if you break it up into smaller, more manageable pieces.

When you're trying to decide whether to write one long script or several shorter ones, you might consider a few other things. If you have several small scripts, you can run any one of them individually. This method gives you the chance to try out parts of the script to see if they work properly. Also, since you can pass errors, or script results (page 684) to scripts via script parameters (page 686), using subscripts to do some jobs often saves you the trouble later on. But in the end, either approach is perfectly valid. Some people really like short, simple scripts, even if it means more of them. Others prefer to put everything controlling a single process into the same script, no matter how long the script gets.

Creating subscript placeholders

For this example, you'll be creating subscripts. Use the comment steps you wrote earlier to figure out what subscripts you'll need. Then you can create placeholders for them by putting Perform Script steps underneath the appropriate comments. Figure 16-19 shows a repeat of your script-in-progress with places for subscripts clearly identified.

Each of these scripts is relatively short and easy to understand, but you'll have *five* scripts in all. (See the box on page 711 for some tips for breaking up long scripts into subscripts.)

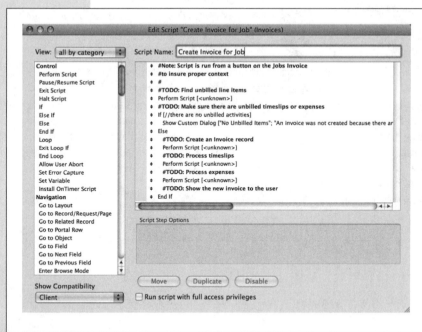

Figure 16-19:
Each empty Perform Script step marks a place for a subscript you'll create later. The first subscript will find the unbilled expenses and timeslips; the second will create the new invoice record that's related to the job; the third will loop through all the timeslips and add the necessary line items; the fourth will do the same thing for each expense.

Creating skeleton subscripts

Next, you'll create all the subscripts you need—but that doesn't mean writing them all yet. You just need to create scripts in the Manage Scripts window, and then make some placeholder comments to remind you what they should do.

Start by adding a new script called Find Unbilled Activity. You can see the Find Unbilled Activity script in its planning stage form in Figure 16-20.

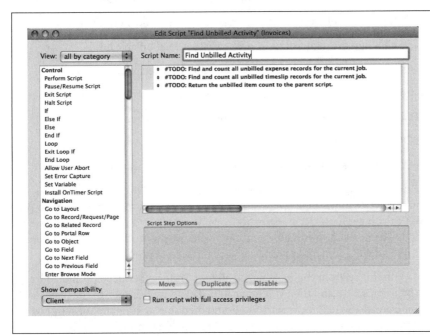

Figure 16-20:
You'll create the Find Unbilled Activity subscript first. Since a subscript is just another script, approach it like you did the "Create Invoice for Job" script: Start with a plan. You'll come back later and implement the actual script steps.

Note: Since the script you're building actually consists of several connected scripts, you can use a folder to keep things organized. Just click the little triangle by the New button in the Manage Scripts window, choose Folder, and then give your folder a nice name like "Create Invoices." Now you can keep the main script and all its helper scripts in a tidy package.

Now create the comments for the Create Invoice Record subscript. Here are the comments to help you remember the process when it's time to flesh this script out:

- TODO: Switch to the Invoice layout.

- TODO: Create a new invoice record that's related to the current Job.

- TODO: Return to the original layout.

- TODO: Send script results to the parent script.

The Process Expenses and Process Timeslips scripts are almost exactly the same. The context is different, because the data is in different tables and the data each script moves is different. But the process you'll use to find and process totals is very similar, so your comments notes can be the same for now. You'll create the custom pieces for each script in later exercises. Create those two subscripts shown now. Here are the comments you need to write for the Process Timeslips subscript:

- TODO: Check to see if there are unprocessed timeslip records.
- TODO: Make an Invoice Line Item record related to the new invoice.
- TODO: Loop through found records to gather total billable hours.
- TODO: Set the total in the new Invoices Line Item record.

Here are the comments for the Process Expenses subscript:

- TODO: Check to see if there are unprocessed expense records.
- TODO: Loop through found expense records.
- TODO: Make an Invoice Line Item record for each expense record.

These two processes are nearly the same, except they operate on different tables. To get more practice in the following section, you'll write each script from start to finish. But as you get more scripting experience, you may find that it makes sense to write one script, test it thoroughly, and then when you're sure it's perfect, duplicate the script and edit the steps appropriately for the second process.

To recap: In this section, you just created all four Perform Script steps in the Create Invoice for Job script, and then you made four skeleton subscripts. In the real world, you could create each Perform Script step, and then start writing the subscript while you're thinking about that specific process. You could even start with the last subscript and work your way backwards, if that makes sense to you. The order in which you tackle the individual steps isn't as important as finding a method that keeps you from forgetting part of a process or getting steps out of sequence.

It's also common to start out intending to write one long script, and then as it grows, realize that you've got a set of steps that deserves its own subscript. Select and copy the steps for the process (cut doesn't work in the Edit Script dialog box, unfortunately), create a new script, and then paste them into the subscript. Give the subscript a descriptive name, and then save it. Back in the parent script, delete the steps you moved to the new subscript, and then add a Perform Script step to call it. See the box on page 711 to learn when a new subscript is called for.

Note: Now that all your skeleton subscripts are finished, you *could* go back to the main script and change each empty Perform Script step to specify its proper subscript. But if you hook up each subscript as you finish it, the main script serves as a To Do list. You can tell at a glance which scripts you've done and which ones still need attention.

UP TO SPEED

The Right Way to Create Subscripts

When you think about ways to break your script into smaller pieces, you should be thinking about tasks. It makes good sense to create a smaller script to do one of the *tasks* needed in the larger script. It doesn't make sense to simply take a long script and break it in two, so that the last step in the first script simply performs the second script. Breaking scripts up that way has all the disadvantages of multiple scripts (more windows to work in, more scripts to scroll through) and none of the advantages (neither script is particularly simple or self-contained, and neither can be run individually for testing purposes). Also, as you look for places to use subscripts, look for opportunities for reuse. In other words, look for things the script has to do more than once in two different places. It almost always makes sense to use a subscript in this situation.

In almost every case, the right way to subdivide a script is to create one master script that starts *and* finishes the process. The "Create Invoice for Job" script does just that. It

starts by finding unbilled line items, and finishes by showing the invoice. Along the way, it relies on other simple scripts to get the whole job done.

There's no problem with a subscript having subscripts of its own. In fact, subscripts often do. But you should structure the entire set of scripts so that the top-level script implements the highest-level logic and behavior of the entire script itself. Each subscript should, in turn, do some particular task from start to finish. If the task is particularly complex, then the subscript itself might implement only it's highest level of logic, calling on more subscripts to handle parts of the task. Since you're in the habit of naming scripts descriptively, each subscript's name can provide nearly as much information as a comment. When you complete the "Create Invoice for Job" script, even though it's somewhat complex, you can easily follow its structure. The script almost reads like a book, describing exactly what it's doing.

Finishing the Subscripts

You've created a series of subscripts that have placeholder comments to remind you what process the script will perform. Now it's time to finish each subscript and turn them into working scripts by replacing those comments with real script steps.

The Find Unbilled Activity subscript

Before you leap into finishing this script, a short refresher about what you're trying to accomplish is in order. The Find Unbilled Activity subscript is the first step in the "Create Invoice for Job" master script, which runs when a user clicks a button on the Job layout. You'll use a script parameter to send a Job ID to the subscript, so it can find the right items. As the name says, it finds unbilled activity by searching the Timeslips and Expenses tables for items related to this job.

The first TODO item inside the script is a cinch: Just use the "Go to Layout" script step to switch to the appropriate layout. Next, for the current job, you need to find expenses that don't have a line item ID. You'll use a combination of Enter Find [Restore], "Set Field with the Job ID" (from your script's parameter), and Perform Find, to make sure you don't get items that have already been billed. Then, the script will count the found items so it can send that value back to the main script. Finally, you'll do the same thing for the Timeslips table.

1. **In the Manage Scripts window, double-click the Find Unbilled Activity script to edit it. Add the "Go to Layout" script step to the script.**

   If necessary, drag the "Go to Layout" step just below your first comment. Remember, if a script step is selected, any new step you create lands just below it.

2. **In the "Go to Layout" Script Step Options area's Specify pop-up menu, click the layout popup menu, and then choose Layout to show the Specify Layout window. Choose Expenses, and then click OK.**

   As always, context is one of the most important concepts in getting a process right.

3. **Add an Enter Find Mode script step after the Go to Layout step. Turn off the Pause checkbox, and then turn on the "Specify find requests" option.**

   The Enter Find Mode script step appears in the step list, and then the Specify Find Requests dialog box opens.

4. **If any requests are showing in the list, click Delete until they're all gone. Click the New button.**

   The Edit Find Request window appears.

5. **From the "Find records when" pop-up menu, choose Expenses, and then click the Line Item ID field.**

   The selected field is now highlighted.

6. **Click the Insert Operator button, and then choose "= match whole word (or match empty)" from the resulting menu. Click the Add button. Click OK, and then click OK again to get back to your script.**

   Just as the menu says, an equal sign, used alone, tells FileMaker you want records where the Line Item ID field matches *nothing*. These are all your expenses that haven't been billed.

7. **Add the Set Field script step to the script, and then turn on the "Specify target field" checkbox. Select the Expenses::Job ID field, and then click OK.**

   The step should appear after the Enter Find Mode step. If it doesn't, move it there now.

8. **Click the Specify button to the right of "Calculated result." In the calculation box, type `"=="` & Get (ScriptParameter). Click OK.**

   This calculation puts the Job ID (from the script parameter) into the field, with `"=="` before it, telling FileMaker you want to find records that match this ID exactly. Added to the find request above, the script finds unbilled activity for the current job.

9. **Add the Set Error Capture script step to the script, and then make sure its "On" option is selected.**

You're about to perform a find, and you don't want the database user to see an error message if there are no unbilled expenses.

10. **Add the Perform Find script step to the script.**

The script step belongs below the Set Error Capture step. Make sure you don't select Perform Find/Replace by accident.

11. **Add another copy of the Set Error Capture step to the script, this time with the "Off" option selected.**

You can select the existing Set Error Capture step, click the duplicate button, then drag the new step into place, and then set the option to "Off." Once the Perform Find step is finished, you want FileMaker to stop capturing error messages.

12. **Add a Set Variable script step below Set Error Capture [Off]. Name the variable $unbilledItems. Set its value to *Get (FoundCount)*. Save the script.**

Remember, you want to make sure you have unbilled items for this job before you create an invoice. By grabbing this value now, and passing it to the main script later on, the main script will have the information it needs to decide whether to create an invoice.

Your script should now look like the one in Figure 16-21.

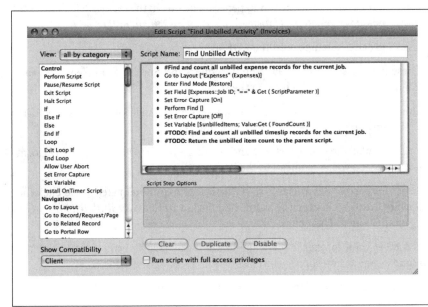

Figure 16-21:
The Find Unbilled Activity script is half done. You've got helpful comments, plus the steps to find unbilled line items that should be billed to the job for which you're creating an invoice. Refine your script further by removing the "TODO" from your first comment, so you can see that it's now an explanation of what should be happening, instead of reminders of what you still need to do.

Copying and editing existing script steps

Since the timeslips-half of the script is almost a duplication of what you did in the last tutorial, you could repeat all those steps above and you'd be done. But it's a lot faster to duplicate those steps, and then make a few changes so that your duplicated steps operate on the Timeslips table, not on the Expenses table. Here's how:

1. **Click the "Go to Layout" line in the script. With the Shift key held down, click the Set Variable step, and then click Duplicate.**

   FileMaker creates an exact copy of all the selected steps. They all wind up below the first set.

2. **Move the "TODO: Find and count all unbilled timeslip records for the current job" comment above the duplicated steps.**

   This helps you keep track of where you are in the process.

3. **Select the "Go to Layout" script step, and then change it so it goes to Timeslips instead of Expenses.**

   This time you want to work with Timeslips records, so you need to go to the Timeslips layout.

4. **Double-click the next step: Enter Find Mode. Double-click the find request in the list. Change its criterion to search the Timeslips::Line Item ID field.**

   You're changing the find request so that it searches for empty Line Item IDs in the Timeslips table instead of in Expenses. The line in the criteria list changes to show *Timeslips::Line Item ID* instead of *Expenses::Line Item ID*.

5. **Click OK, click Change, and then OK again.**

   These two clicks close the Edit Find Request and Specify Find Requests windows, respectively. You're back in the script.

6. **Double-click the next Set Field step, and then change the targeted field to Timeslips:: Job ID instead of Expenses::Job ID.**

   Your Calculated result is just fine and so are the Set Error Capture and Perform Find steps, so you skip ahead to the last step.

7. **Select the second Set Variable step (the last non-comment step), and click the Specify button. Change the value calculation to read: *$unbilledItems* + *Get (FoundCount)*. Then click OK.**

   You don't want to *replace* the value in the script variable, you want to add the found count of timeslips to the existing found count of expenses.

8. **Remove the "TODO:" from the timeslips comment.**

   When you start writing complex scripts, more comments are better. As you get more experience, you may prefer to have fewer comments.

9. After the last comment, add a "Go to Layout" step and set it to go to original layout.

Once the script is done finding things, it needs to return to the layout it started on so the script that ran this one won't be surprised by a layout change. It's usually best when a subscript puts things back the way they were when it started.

10. Add an Exit Script step at the end of the script. Click the Specify button, and then type *$unbilledItems* in the calculation box. Save and then close the script.

You're telling the subscript to pass the value in the $unbilledItems variable back to the main script.

Whew! Finally, the Find Unbilled Activity script is finished. It should look like the one in Figure 16-22.

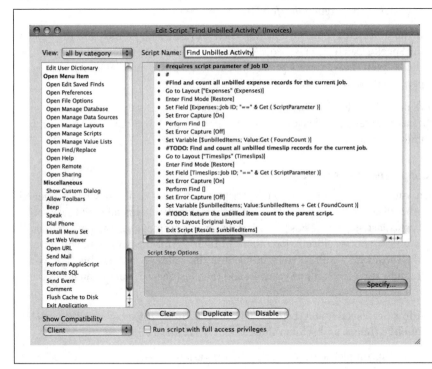

Figure 16-22:
The completed "Find Unbilled Activity" subscript. It finds and counts the expenses, and then does the same for timeslips. This serves two purposes in the final process: The $unbilledItems variable helps the "Create Invoice for Job" script decide whether it should create an invoice or not, and FileMaker uses the found sets later to create line items.

Note: Notice the highlighted comment at the top of the script. Some developers like to make a note at the top of any script that uses a script parameter telling them what should be in the parameter. It can save time later when you're troubleshooting because you can use Script Debugger and the Data Viewer to make sure the script parameter is being set and it contains the proper value.

Adding a script parameter to a Perform Script step

You've just written a script that uses a script parameter containing a Job ID when it finds unbilled timeslip and expense records. Now you have to make sure the script gets the Job ID when it runs. The main script ("Create Invoice for Job"), will be run by a button on the Job layout. You *could* set the Job ID in a script parameter on that button (page 686), but since script parameters aren't passed to subscripts, that doesn't help Find Unbilled Activity do its work. So you have to pass the Job ID to the subscript when it's run. You do that in the Perform Script step.

1. **In the Manage Scripts window, double-click the "Create Invoice for Job" script to edit it. Select the first Perform Script [<unknown>] step.**

   The Script Step Options area shows a Specify button.

2. **Click Specify. Select the Find Unbilled Activity script. In the "Optional script parameter" box, type *Jobs::Job ID*.**

   If you don't like typing field names, click Edit instead, and then add the field in the Specify Calculation window. Then, close the Specify Calculation window by clicking OK. Leave the script itself open, though. You've still got information to pass along in the next tutorial.

You've passed the Find Unbilled Items subscript a Job ID value. In turn, that subscript has a value to pass back to the Create Invoice for Job script about the number of unbilled items it found.

Checking a subscript's result

When you run a subscript, the main script often needs to know what happened when the subscript was run. That's why the Find Unbilled Items subscript set a script result as its last step (page 684). But just as script parameters aren't passed to subscripts unless you specifically pass them in their Perform Script step, you have to grab the subscript's result so you can use it in the calling script. In this case, you'll put the subscript's result into a variable, and then test the variable's contents in the If step you created back on page 706.

1. **Add a Set Variable step below the first Perform Script set. Name the variable *$unbilledItems*, and set its value to *Get (ScriptResult)*.**

   This step completes the job of passing the variable's value from the subscript up to the main script.

2. **Double-click the If test to edit it. Set its calculation to *$unbilledItems = 0*.**

   This tells the script to test the count of found items made by the subscript.

3. **Save your script.**

   Now the script can find and count unbilled activities for the current job, and then perform a test on the count so it can decide whether to create an invoice, or tell the user that no invoice is necessary (Figure 16-23).

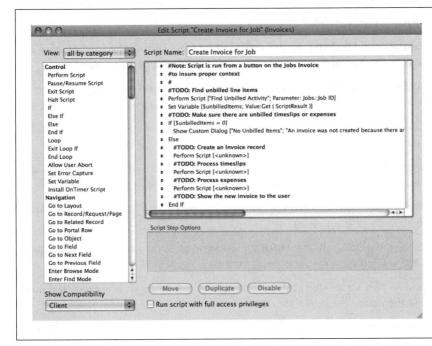

Figure 16-23:
The main script now has one completed subscript with a script parameter. It also tests the subscript's results and branches based on the value it finds. The remaining TODO comments and Perform Script [<unknown>] steps give you a perfect roadmap of the work ahead.

Finishing the Create Invoice Record subscript

The Create Invoice Record script needs to switch to the Invoices layout, create a new record, attach it to the job (by filling in its Job ID field), grab the new Invoice's ID, and then switch back to the original layout. And like the last subscript, this one needs the Job ID in its script parameter, when you hook it up.

Since you're used to removing the "TODO:" part of your existing comments and placing the appropriate script steps just below them, the remaining tutorials in this chapter will skip those instructions for simplicity's sake. Now you're ready to polish off the Create Invoice Record script itself:

1. **Double-click the Create Invoice Record script in the Manage Scripts window to edit it.**

   The Edit Script window opens. You'll replace your TODO comments with real script steps now.

2. **Add the "Go to Layout" script step at the top of the script. Set the step to go to the Invoices layout.**

   You can't add an invoice record from the Jobs layout, so you're switching to a layout attached to the Invoices table first.

3. **Add the New Record/Request step after the second comment step.**

   Keep it consistent: "real" steps go after the comments.

4. **Add the Set Field step to the script. The target field is the Invoices::Job ID field in the list, and the calculated result is *Get (ScriptParameter)*.**

   You're matching the new invoice to the Job ID. Of course this means you have to pass the Job ID to the script when you run it from the parent script.

5. **Add a Set Variable script step after the Set Field. Name the variable *$invoiceId*, and then set its value to Invoices::Invoice ID.**

   You're grabbing the new invoice's ID now, while you're still on the Invoice layout, so you can put it in the line item records later.

6. **Add the "Go to Layout" step to the script and choose "original layout" from the Specify pop-up menu.**

   Subscripts should always return the database to its previous state, so the main script doesn't get lost in the wrong context.

7. **Add an Exit Script step at the end of your script. Its result is *$invoiceID*. Save, and then close the subscript.**

   Your script will look like Figure 16-24. Since you set the new invoice's ID in a local variable, you'll pass it back to the main script with a script result.

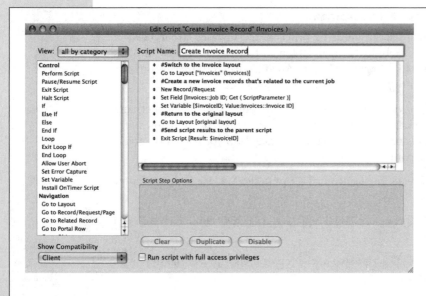

Figure 16-24:
The finished Create Invoice Record subscript has almost as many comments as it has working script steps, yet its task is relatively simple. It makes a new invoice record for a specific job. But even if you understand the process perfectly, it's good to leave comments intact. Someone else who doesn't have your experience may take over the database some day, and your comments will serve as a tutorial.

Now that the subscript is done, you have to call it from the parent script. You have to pass the Job ID along to the subscript, and then you'll need to grab the subscript's result.

1. In the "Create Invoice for Job" script, set the first Perform Script step under the Else to run the Create Invoice Record subscript, with a script parameter of Jobs::Job ID.

   You're passing the Job ID to the subscript, so it knows which job it's creating an invoice for.

2. Add a Set Variable script step below Perform Script ["Create Invoice Record"; Parameter: Jobs::Job ID]. Name the variable $invoiceId, and then set its value to *Get (ScriptResult)*. Save the script.

   The subscript will pass the ID for the invoice it's just created back to the main script so it can create related line items in the next subscripts.

Finishing the Process Timeslips subscript

Now you'll tackle the subscript that processes your unbilled timeslips. This script creates a line item record and puts the Line Item ID into the unbilled timeslip, so it's related to the line item record and won't be found next time you run the script. (Remember, your Find Unbilled Activity script looks for all timeslip and expense records that don't have a Line Item ID.) Then the script grabs the time worked from the record, and then loops through the found set of unbilled timeslips and adds the time worked from each record. After the last timeslip record is processed, the script puts the time value in the line item record.

Most steps are variations on what you've been doing—switching layouts, doing If tests, creating records, and setting data into records from variables. Working through a found set of records requires a new scripting tool: the loop. To get ready to adapt your script to a loop, use Figure 16-25 to create the basic process in your script.

Creating a looping script. A loop runs a set of script steps over and over again. There's an art to getting the right set of steps between the Loop and End Loop steps. Most times, you have to do a little prep work to get the database ready to enter the loop. Then inside the loop you put the steps that are repeated once for each record. And you must always have a way for the loop to stop. In this case, since you're working on a found set of records, you'll use a "Go to Record" step that exits after the last record (see page 444).

Here's what to do:

1. Add a "Go to Layout" step below the Set Variable step. Specify Timeslips for the target layout.

   The script was just on the Line Items layout, so you need to make sure the loop will happen in the proper context.

2. Add a "Go to Record/Request/Page" step below "Go to Layout". Make sure First is selected in the Specify pop-up menu.

   You want to make sure your loop starts with the first record in your found set. These first two steps are common preparation for starting a loop.

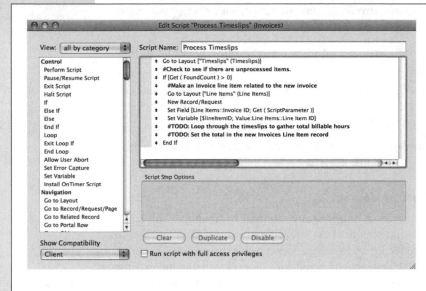

Figure 16-25:
The Process Timeslips subscript goes to the Timeslips layout to see if the Find Unbilled Items subscript found any records. If the found count contains records, the script switches to the Line Items layout and makes a new record with the Invoice ID that's passed via the subscript's parameter. Finally, it puts the new line item's ID in a variable so that you can put the ID into each timeslip record.

3. **Add a Set Variable step below "Go to Record." Name the variable *$totalHours*, and then set its value to 0.**

   This variable will add up hours as it loops through the found set of timeslip records.

4. **Add a Loop step below the Set Variable step.**

   You also get a matching End Loop step. The next few script steps will go between this pair.

5. **Add a Set Field step as the first step of your loop. The target field is Timeslips:: Line Item ID, and the calculated result is $lineItemId.**

   When you put a Line Item ID into a timeslip record, you're relating the Line Item and Timeslips table. With the right TOs, you can look at any timeslip record and see any line item related to it, and you can look at a line item record and see any timeslip related to it. You'll use this relationship later on to move data without switching layouts.

6. **Add a Set Variable step below the Set Field step. Name the variable *$total-Hours*, and then set its value to $totalHours + Timeslips::Duration.**

   The script will add the hours worked on each timeslip record to the value that's already in the variable. On the first record, the variable will have 0 in it, so the result of the first calculation will be the same as the duration. But every time the loop runs again, the value in the variable will increment by the amount in the current record.

7. **Add a "Go to Record/Request/Page" step after the Set Variable. Specify Next in the pop-up menu, and then select the "Exit after last" option.**

   Now the script goes to the next record in the found set. It exits the loop automatically after it performs the looped steps on the last record. The rest of your script steps will go after the comment following the End Loop step.

8. **Add a "Go to Layout" step below the End Loop step. Set it to go to the Line Items layout.**

   You're putting the data you gathered into your new line item record, so make sure you're back on the Line Item layout.

9. **Add a Set Field step next. Set the target field to Line Items::Price Each, and then set the calculated result to 50.**

   This step tells the line item record how much money to charge for each hour worked. If your hourly rate changes, you'll update this script step to reflect the new rate.

10. **Add a second Set Field step below the first one. Set the target field to Line Items::Quantity, and then set the calculated result to $totalHours.**

    This step tells the line item record how many hours were worked on the job.

11. **Add a third Set Field step below the second one. Set the target field to Line Items::Description, and then set the calculated result to "Labor". Edit your TODO items, and then save the script.**

    Your time line items are labeled with static text describing the charge.

12. **Add a Go to Layout step at the end of the script. Set it to go to the original layout.**

    Your looping script is finished when it returns the parent script to its starting point.

Your finished script should look like Figure 16-26. Now that you're done, change the main script's Perform Script step to run the Process Timeslips subscript and set its parameter to $invoiceID.

The Process Expenses subscript

Most of the lessons you learned in the Process Timeslips subscript apply to the Process Expenses subscript, but there are some important differences. First, according to your business rules, all labor is combined into one line item per invoice, and each expense is billed separately. So the steps that create a new line item will fall inside this script's loop. Second, you're gathering more bits of data for each expense, so the steps that set data into Line Item fields are different from what you did for Timeslips. But the overall process is still very similar. Here's what to do:

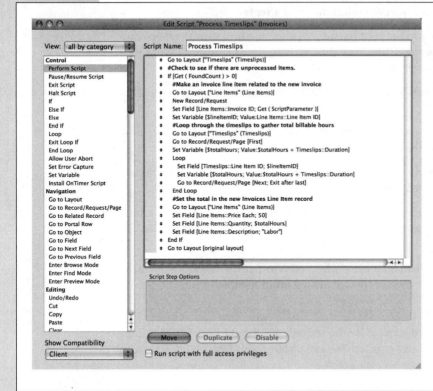

Figure 16-26:
Here's how your finished Process Timeslips script looks when you're done. The tutorial told you how to prepare the database to start the loop, which steps belong inside the loop, and what steps to take when the loop was finished. But in the real world, a good technique for writing a looping script is to create it as if it were working on a single record. Then when you've got it working properly for one record, you can add the Loop and End Loop steps to make the process repeat.

1. **Add a "Go to Layout" step to the top of your script. Set the target layout to Expenses.**

   You need to be on a layout tied to the Expenses table so you can check to see if any records need to be processed.

2. **Add an If test and set its calculation to *Get (FoundCount) > 0*. Drag the End If step down below your last comment placeholder.**

   The expense item processing steps shouldn't run if there are no expenses for the current job.

3. **Add a "Go to Record/Request/Page" step after the If step. Set the "Go to Record" option to First.**

   You want to make sure the loop begins with the first record in the found set so nothing gets missed.

4. **Add a Loop step below the "Go to Record" step.**

   You'll also get an End Loop step. Most of the rest of your script's steps will go between the Loop and End Loop steps.

5. Add a Set Variable step as the first step in the loop. Name the variable *$description*, and then set its value to *Expenses::Expense.*

   You're grabbing data to put into the new line item record you'll be creating later in this script.

6. Add a Set Variable step. Name the variable *$amount*, and then set its value to *Expenses::Amount.*

   Grab all the data you need from Expenses before you leave the layout.

7. Add a "Go to Layout" step. Set it to go to the Line Items layout.

   The context has to be right to create your new record.

8. Add a New Record/Request step.

   It doesn't have any options.

9. Add a Set Field step. The target field is Line Items::Invoice ID and the calculated result is *Get (ScriptParameter).*

   You need to remember to set this script's parameter when you hook it up to the main script later.

10. Add a Set Field step. The target field is Line Items::Description and the calculated result is *"Expense:" & $description.*

    You have to include the quote marks since you want the calculation to set the static text *Expense:* into the field, and then add the contents of your $description variable.

11. Add a Set Field step. The target field is Line Items::Price Each and the calculated result is *$amount.*

    The amount is how much you spent.

12. Add a Set Field step. The target field is Line Items::Quantity and the calculated result is *1.*

    Don't include the quotes this time, since 1 is a number. You need the value so your Extended Price can perform its math properly.

13. Add a Set Variable step. Name the variable *$lineitemID*, and set its value to *LineItems::Line Item ID.*

    You're grabbing the Line Item ID now so you can put it into the expense record next. This step creates the relationship between the Line Item and Expenses tables, and it ensures that the next time you run the script, this same expense record won't be found again.

14. Add a "Go to Layout" step. Set it to go to the Expenses layout.

    The script will return to the expense record it started the loop on.

15. **Add a Set Field step. The target is *Expenses::Line Item ID* and the calculated result is *$linteItemID*.**

    The value in *$lineItemID* links the expense record to the Line Item record the script just created.

16. **Add a "Go to Record/Request/Page" step. Specify Next in the pop-up menu, and then select the "Exit after last" option.**

    This step makes sure you're working through the found set, and can get out of the loop after the script has worked on the last record.

17. **Add a "Go to Layout" step at the end of your script. Set it to go to "original layout." Edit your TODO comments, move them into place, and then save the script.**

    Don't get so caught up in the complexity of a script that you forget to make helpful comments.

Compare your script with Figure 16-27. Now you can hook up the last Perform Script step in the "Create Invoice for Job" script (don't forget the *$invoiceID* script parameter). Then add a *Go to Layout ["Invoices" (Invoices)]* step at the end to show the new invoice. Finally, all five scripts are done! You're ready to test the script.

Testing Scripts

To test your script, first go to a job record that has unbilled timeslips and expenses (or create a new job record, plus new unbilled timeslips and expenses, if necessary). Once you're on the job record, run the "Create Invoice for Job" script. To make your testing as much like the conditions your users will see, create a button for running the script. In a flash, you should see a new invoice, properly assigned to the customer and containing line items for each unbilled item.

Note: If the script doesn't work, you have options. First, check your data to make sure you have appropriate timeslips and expenses for the script to work on. Second, you can surf over to this book's Missing CD page at *www.missingmanual.com/cds* and compare your scripts to the ones in this chapter's finished file. But if you have FileMaker Pro Advanced, you should also read about the Script Debugger and Data Viewer in Chapter 12. These tools can make hunting down script problems a breeze, and few serious scripters work without them.

In this chapter, you walked through a lengthy task where the steps and outcome were known. Out there on the mean streets of development, you won't always have a road map to follow. Still, the concepts of planning, exception handling, and efficiency will get you out of a lot of sticky script situations.

Tip: And even if your database doesn't handle invoicing, it's very common to create related records and move data via scripts so that you can retain control over data. Just adapt these scripts to meet your needs.

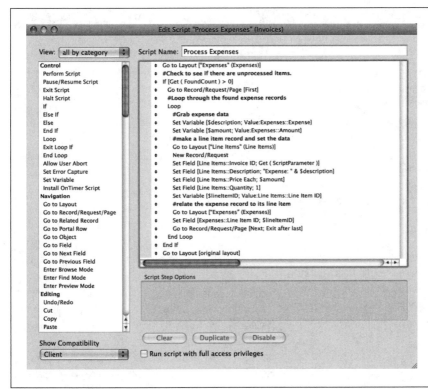

Figure 16-27:
*The finished Process
Expenses script looks
like this example.
These comments
are different from
the placeholder
comments you cre-
ated originally. Here
comments group
the script steps into
logical chunks so
it's easier to see the
reason for all the
layout changes. If
you have to grab and
set more data from
the expense record
later on, it'll be easy
to see where to grab
the new data from
and where it needs
to be set. Work out
your own system of
commenting scripts,
and then stick with it
consistently.*

When you're first scripting, or if you're attempting to do something that you aren't quite sure will work, following a approach like the one you just learned will serve you well. In addition to creating your scripts in comment and subscript form, you can break scripting down even further. Create a few script steps, and then test them to make sure they behave as you expect. If they don't work properly, tweak them until they do. Then add a few more script steps and test again. If a new problem arises, you know it's in the new steps you've just added.

Finally, don't forget that the state of your database can influence what happens when you test a script. For example, a button on the Jobs layout ensures that your users can run only the "Create Invoice for Jobs" script from the proper context. But in the heat of testing, you might accidentally run the script from the Manage Scripts window while you're on the wrong layout. If you do, the script won't have a Job ID to work with and all kinds of havoc will be loosed in the script: it won't know which unbilled items to search for and could create an Invoice that's not attached to any job at all.

As you gain experience, you'll find that planning, finding exceptions, and subscript-ing becomes second nature. You'll start envisioning scripts of increasing complexity, and soon you'll be making them your own way, without following a rigid plan.

Referential Integrity

By now, it's ingrained in your developer's brain that relationships work because there's a match between key fields in the related tables. But what if you absolutely, positively *have* to change the value in a key field? Say you inherit a file that uses telephone numbers as key fields, and you want to bring the database up to par by using a serial number field instead. You know it'll break up relationships, because as soon as you change the value in the "one" side of the relationship, all the "to-many" records are no longer related to their parent records (or to any other record). In other words, they're orphaned.

If you changed the value in key fields manually, it'd be fairly easy to figure out how to keep this from happening. You use the existing relationship to find the child records, change their keys, and only then, go back to the parent record and change its key. The record family is reunited and everybody's happy.

Here's a script that handles that grunt work for you:

```
Allow User Abort [Off]
Go to Layout ["Customers" (Customers)]
Set Variable [$newID; Value:Customers::Ne
wCustomerID]
```

```
Go to Related Record [Show only re-
lated records; From table:"Jobs"; Using
layout:"Jobs"(Jobs)]
Loop
  Set Field [Jobs::Customer ID; $newID]
  Go to Record/Request/Page [Next; Exit af-
ter last]
End Loop
Go to Layout ["Customers" (Customers)]
Set Field [Customers::Customer ID; $newID]
```

There's some brainwork that this script doesn't handle, like making sure your NewCustomerID value is unique before you use it. If you're changing your key field value, it's probably not a surrogate key (page 200), so you'll have to know how your business policy creates and insures unique key values, and then apply that logic to your script. And you need to ensure that each related record is unlocked and available for your script to change (page 44). Using this script as a foundation, add the logic you need in the appropriate spots. Work in a copy of your database until you get all the kinks worked out, and then use the Import button in the Manage Script dialog box to move the finished script into your original file.

Part Five: Integration and Security

V

Sharing Your Database

You've now got a solid foundation for building even the most complex database systems in FileMaker Pro. But your databases have so far been limited to just one user: you. Only the smallest small business, though, has only one person. Most databases are *multiuser databases*, used by lots of people, all at the same time. You can easily set up any FileMaker database for lots of people to use; you simply turn on a checkbox or two. In this chapter, you'll learn about those settings, plus some of the things you can expect from FileMaker when you're sharing databases.

Before you dive in and start changing settings, consider where you're going to keep the shared file and how other people's computers connect to it. You can choose from three types of sharing:, FileMaker Network, Internet Sharing, and FileMaker Server.

- **FileMaker Network.** This type of file sharing is also called *peer-to-peer*—that is, you don't use a server or any special software. You just use your ordinary computers to share files. Peer-to-peer sharing is limited to nine users at once. If more than nine people need to use the database at the same time, use FileMaker Server.

- **Internet Sharing.** Internet sharing has its own set of benefits and tradeoffs. On the plus side, people who need access to your files don't need a copy of FileMaker. All they need is an Internet connection and a recent-model browser. On the downside, not everything you can do in FileMaker translates to the Web, so you may have to live with fewer features. FileMaker uses a type of Internet sharing called Instant Web Publishing (IWP). It translates your layouts to web language according to settings you specify.

- **FileMaker Server** is the Big Daddy of FileMaker database sharing. FileMaker Server offers protection for your files in case of a crash, automated backups, and tremendous speed and stability boosts over peer-to-peer sharing. It also removes all restrictions on how many FileMaker users can connect at once.

Note: Another type of Internet sharing, called *Custom Web Publishing*, offers more features than IWP. Using XML/XSLT or PHP, you can build incredibly powerful web-based databases. With add-on software, you can even use other web technologies like Ruby on Rails (*www.sixfriedrice.com/wp/products/rfm/*) or Lasso (*www.lassosoft.com/*). But these technologies have steep learning curves—plus, they're beyond the scope of this book.

FileMaker Network Sharing

You can most easily share your data with *FileMaker Network Sharing*. If you already have a network in your office, and a few copies of FileMaker, then you're ready to share your database. First, you put all your databases on one computer. Then open those files, change a few settings in each file, and call that computer the *host*. Each computer that opens those files is called a *guest*, since it opens the same databases that are on the host. Up to nine guests can connect to one host.

Once you're set up, all nine people can work in the database at the same time, adding, editing, and deleting records, performing finds, printing, and running scripts. No two people can work in the same *record* at the same time, though. Once you're sharing files, you need to revisit the topic of record locking. See the box on page 44 for a refresher.

Note: You can do more than just browse data in a shared database. If your privilege set lets you, you can add or modify tables and fields, manage relationships, work in Layout mode, and even write scripts. When you do, the same one-at-a-time concept applies: Only one person can edit a particular script or layout at a time, and only one person can use the Manage→Database window. As soon as one person saves the layout or script or closes the Manage Database window, then someone else is free to hop in.

Setting Up a Host Computer

To set up the host, open the databases you want to share on one computer, and then choose File→Sharing→FileMaker Network. This opens the FileMaker Network Settings dialog box: command central for all file sharing. From the list at left, choose the database you're setting up (if it's not there, make sure the file's open). Then, as described in Figure 17-1, turn sharing on.

Once you've turned on network sharing for the host computer, you need to tell File-Maker which databases to share. The FileMaker Network Settings dialog box shows a list of each open database (if you don't see the one you want, click OK, open the database, and then choose File→Sharing→FileMaker Network again). You have to turn on network access for at least one privilege set in each file you want to share. First, from the "Currently open files" list, select a database. Then choose one of the following three settings to control who gets access to the file:

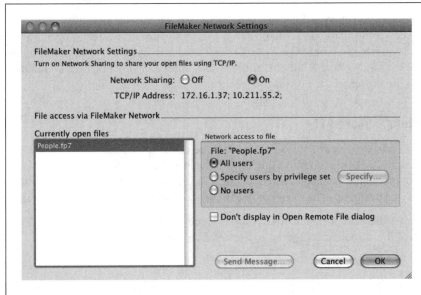

Figure 17-1:
The FileMaker Network Settings dialog box lets you set up your database host. The first step is to turn on the Network Sharing option by clicking the On radio button. When you do, FileMaker shows the computer's TCP/IP address, if it's connected to the network. (If you don't see a valid TCP/IP address, then you may have network problems.)

- **All Users** means that anybody on your network with a copy of FileMaker and a valid account can get in—up to the limit of nine concurrent users.

- **Specify users by privilege set.** When you choose this option, you see a dialog box listing all your privilege sets (see page 763). Click the checkbox to the left of each privilege set that should have access to the file.

- **No users.** If a file needs to be open on the host, but you don't want it shared, choose this option.

When you make changes to these settings, FileMaker is actually making changes to the privilege sets in the selected file. When you turn on "All users", FileMaker simply turns on the "Access via FileMaker Network" extended privilege for every privilege set. Likewise, if you choose "No users", it turns this extended privilege off for every set. When you specify people by privilege set, you get to decide which privilege sets have this extended privilege turned on. If you prefer, you can make these changes manually in the Extended Privileges tab of the Manage Accounts & Privileges window (File→Manage→Accounts & Privileges). Look for the [fmapp] extended privilege if you're setting access manually (page 788).

Note: You can control the access settings for each file even if you don't turn on network sharing. The settings you make to a file stick with that file even when you move it to another computer, so you can use this window to set the sharing options for a file *before* you send it to the host computer.

When a database is shared this way, you use the File→Open Remote command to open it from another computer (you'll learn how to do so in the next section). File-Maker then shows every available shared database. If you don't want this database to show up, then turn on the "Don't display in Open Remote File dialog" checkbox.

Why would you share a database, and then make it invisible? Suppose you have a database system that's made up of several files, but you want people to open only a specific one (because only one file has an interface and the others just hold data, for example). You want only that main file visible in the Open dialog box, so nobody opens the wrong one. However, you still need to *share* the other files.

Opening a Shared File

If you just shared your database so a colleague can access it, the easiest way to get him connected is to send him a link to your database. Just choose File→Send→Link to Database, and FileMaker creates an email in your email program with a clickable link to the database. (The recipient needs FileMaker installed for the link to work.)

But FileMaker has a more direct route to opening shared files, too. Launch File-Maker Pro on another computer on the network, and then follow these steps:

1. **Choose File→Open Remote.**

    If you're already looking at the Open File dialog box, click the Remote button instead. Either way, you see the Open Remote File dialog box (Figure 17-2).

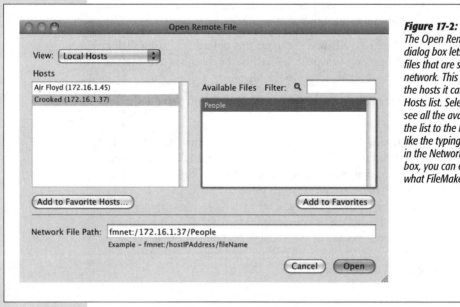

Figure 17-2:
The Open Remote File dialog box lets you find files that are shared on the network. This box lists all the hosts it can find in the Hosts list. Select a host to see all the available files in the list to the right. If you like the typing thing, then in the Network File Path box, you can enter exactly what FileMaker needs.

2. **From the Hosts list, select the appropriate host.**

   The shared files show in the Available Files list. (If the host computer you're looking for isn't listed, see the next section for advice.)

3. **Select the file you want to open from the Available Files list, and then click Open.**

   If you've added accounts to the file, FileMaker asks you for an account name and password. When you give it what it needs, the database opens.

Note: When a database opens from a host, in the window title bar, FileMaker puts the host name in parentheses to help you keep things straight. If you don't like seeing host names in your window's title bars, then use the Set Window Title step to change that name in a script that runs when the file is opened (page 501).

The Open Remote File Dialog Box

The Open Remote File dialog box (File→Open Remote) has even more tricks up its sleeve, mostly geared towards folks with a lot of databases. If you're perfectly happy with the previous instructions, then you have permission to skip this section.

Choosing a host computer

When opening a remote file, you first choose the host computer. Above the Hosts list, the View pop-up menu offers three choices:

- Choose Local Hosts, and FileMaker searches your local network and lists any host computers it finds. This view is usually the easiest way to share files in the office (or house or wherever all your computers are in one place). You can see each computer's name and IP address.

  Unfortunately, the Local Hosts option has a few weaknesses. First, it can be a little slow, which may drive you crazy if you can't stand to waste a single second. Worse, sometimes FileMaker can't find the host you want, usually because the guest computer and the host computer aren't on the same network (you might have a host computer at the office, and need to access it from home, for instance).

- If Local Hosts doesn't do the trick, from the View pop-up menu, choose Favorite Hosts instead. When you do, FileMaker doesn't show anything in the Hosts list at first. Click the Add button to summon the Edit Favorite Host dialog box, and then type the host computer's information, as shown in Figure 17-3.

  When you're done setting up the favorite host, click Save. FileMaker now shows the computer in the Hosts list. Now, whenever you visit the Open Remote File dialog box, FileMaker has Favorite Hosts preselected, with all your favorites instantly available.

Of course, you can change a favorite at any time (just select it, and then click Edit) or remove it from the list when you don't need it anymore (select it, and then click Remove).

Note: When you add a host to your favorites, FileMaker also shows it in the Quick Start dialog box. Click the Open Database icon in that window, and, in the box on the left, you see your host listed.

- The Hosts Listed by LDAP option is for the big guys. If you have a lot of FileMaker servers, and you don't want end users to have to manage their Favorites list manually, you can set up an LDAP server with available host information. Refer to the FileMaker Server documentation for details on this uncommon option.

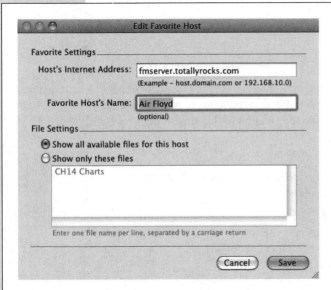

Figure 17-3:
In the Favorite Hosts list, when you add (or edit) a host, FileMaker shows this window. In the first box, type the host computer's address. You can use the IP address, or, if the computer has a name (like filemaker. mycompany.com), then you can type that instead. Next, in the Favorite Host's Name box, give it any descriptive name you want. Normally FileMaker shows every visible database from a host. You can enter specific database names if you want, though (if you routinely use just one database from a host with dozens, say). Just turn on "Show only these files", and then, in the big box below it, type one name on each line.

Choosing a file

Once you've made your host selection, you get to choose the file you want to open. Typically, each shared file is listed in the Available Files list on the window's right side, and you can just double-click one to open it (or select it, and then click Open).

If the Available Files list has *lots* of databases, then you can find the one you want by typing in the Filter box. FileMaker reduces the list to show each file whose name contains the letter or phrase you enter. For example, if you type *mars*, then you probably see only the Mars Investigations file.

If you find yourself opening the same files often (a pretty common thing), select a file, and then click "Add to Favorites". When you do, FileMaker adds this file to the Quick Start dialog box's list of favorite files (see the box on page 91).

Finally, on some occasions you may need to open a file that doesn't show in the list. For example, you might have an ancillary file that you've configured to share but not show in the Open Remote dialog box. That setup is fine for your users, who never need to open this file directly. But you, O wise developer, may need to open the file to look under the hood.

1. **From the Hosts list, select the host computer, if you haven't already.**

   In addition to showing files from the host, FileMaker adds the host's address to the Network File Path box at the bottom of the window. For example, if you select a host with the address 192.168.1.10, then FileMaker puts *fmnet:/192.168.1.10/* in the box.

2. **Add your database name to the end of the network file path (after the "/").**

   Since the file you want doesn't show in the list, you have to type its name directly. You're actually creating a FileMaker network file path, which FileMaker will use to open the file for you.

3. **Click Open.**

   If you typed the name correctly, then FileMaker opens the file.

If you get an error, check to make sure you spelled the file name correctly, and that the file really *is* shared and open on the host computer.

Tip: You don't need to put the ".fp7" in the network file path. FileMaker knows you're looking for a FileMaker database.

Sharing over the Internet

FileMaker Network Sharing is the easiest way to share your database. Folks simply open the file, and it works *exactly* like a file on their hard drives. The catch is that they need a copy of FileMaker Pro on whatever computer they're using to connect. (Of course, when you consider how cool FileMaker Pro is, you're probably doing them a favor.) If you want to open up your database to people who don't have FileMaker—and you're willing to live with a less elegant interface—you can use Instant Web Publishing. This feature turns your computer into its own web server. Like magic, it turns all your layouts into web pages, and lets anybody with an up-to-date web browser search, sort, and edit your data directly.

Turning on Web Sharing

Enabling Instant Web Publishing (IWP for short) is just as easy as turning on FileMaker Network Sharing. First, choose File→Sharing→Instant Web Publishing, and then click On. Once IWP starts up, FileMaker shows you the URL by which people access your databases. (You also get to pick a language for your web pages. This action doesn't translate the information in your database, though. Instead, it controls what language all of FileMaker's built-in buttons, labels, and links use in the web browser.)

Advanced Web Publishing Options

The Advanced Web Publishing Options window lets you configure FileMaker's built-in web server. You get to pick a *port* (more on that next) and restrict access to only certain computers, among other settings. In the Instant Web Publishing window, click Advanced Options to open the Advanced Web Publishing Options dialog box (Figure 17-4).

Network servers set up shop at a *TCP/IP Port Number*, and once you turn on IWP, your computer is a network server, too. The usual web publishing port is 80 and, if you have no other web services running on your computer, that's the one you'll usually use. But if you do need to set up your web server with multiple services, then you can change FileMaker's port number to avoid a conflict. FileMaker, Inc. has registered its very own port number just for web publishing (591). If you stick with port 591, chances are no other program's using it, and you'll avoid conflicts even if you need to add other services later on. When you assign any port other than 80, FileMaker automatically adds the port number to the URL it displays in the Instant Web Publishing dialog box, as a reminder of the link your browser uses to connect to your site.

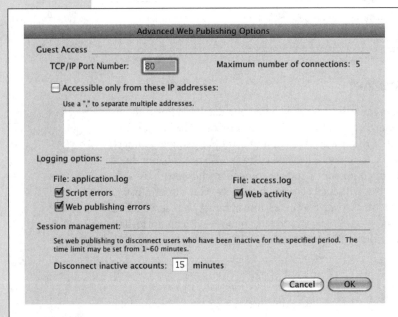

Figure 17-4:
In the Advanced Web Options dialog box, you get to decide which information FileMaker records in log files (you can refer to these files if you have problems or you're curious who's using the database). Also, you can tell FileMaker to forget about people who haven't clicked the web page for a while by setting the "Disconnect inactive accounts" value.

Note: When you use port 80, links to your site don't need to include the port number, but if you're using any other port number, then you have to make sure they do. In a URL, the port number comes right after the server name, with a colon in front, like this: *http://mycomputer:591/*.

If you don't want just anybody trying to connect to your databases, then you can turn on "Accessible only from these IP addresses". You then have to list the network address of each computer you want to allow (with commas in between). If you have a large intranet, you don't have to type dozens of IP addresses, though. You can specify a range of addresses using an asterisk. For example, 192.168.15.* lets everyone whose IP address matches the first three sets of numbers access the file.

While IWP is running, it can keep track of activity and errors. FileMaker keeps this information in log files in its Web Logs folder. The "Web activity" log records each time someone interacts with the database. The log includes the person's network address, and the URL she requested. The "Script errors" log records errors in your FileMaker scripts. The "Web publishing errors" log holds other errors that occur in IWP, like invalid requests and missing databases. You can use these logs to see if you need to fix your scripts, or to see who's been using the databases and what problems they've encountered. If you use IWP a lot, these logs can get large. Turn any or all of them off to keep FileMaker from recording this information.

Web browsers don't work exactly like FileMaker itself. Someone has to explicitly log out to tell FileMaker he's disconnecting. If he doesn't—for example, if he just quits his browser or goes to a different website—FileMaker doesn't know he's left your site. To keep people from tying up connections forever, FileMaker automatically disconnects anyone who hasn't requested a page in a while. You get to decide how long "a while" is. A smaller setting (like 15 minutes) ensures that people don't hold connections long if they forget to log out. But if they spend more than 15 minutes looking at a single record (reading a long Notes field, for instance), then they're disconnected even though they're still using the database. If you have situations like this one, set the "Disconnect inactive accounts" value to something larger (the maximum is 60 minutes).

Configuring file access

Just like FileMaker Network Sharing, you get to decide which files are shared by IWP, and which privilege sets have web access. In fact, the settings are identical: Select an open file, and then choose the appropriate access level. Finally, you manage IWP access using the [fmiwp] extended privilege.

Record Locking Revisited

Back in Chapter 1, you learned about *record locking*. When you start editing a record, FileMaker locks it, so it can't be changed in another window until you commit it in the first. At the time, this scenario probably seemed like a pretty obscure situation: How often do you try to edit the same record in two different windows? But when several people start sharing the same database, record locking takes on a whole new meaning. Now, when you start editing a record, *nobody else* can edit it. If you type a few lines in the Notes field, then dash off to Tijuana without clicking out of the record, you keep it locked all day.

When you try to edit a locked record, FileMaker warns you with a message box. It tells you the record's locked, and *who* has it locked (including the user name on his computer, *and* the account name with which he's logged in).

If you'd like to politely ask him to get out of the record, click Send Message. You see the "Send Message to Conflicting Users" window. Enter any message you want, and then click OK. A window pops up on his screen with your message, which is dandy, but it won't do you any good if he's skulking about far from his computer.

While record locking can be a minor annoyance to the user, it can be a real problem for the database developer.

If you've designed all your scripts with the mistaken notion that you can *always* edit *any* record you want, then you might get an unpleasant surprise the first time a script tries to modify a locked record.

Even worse, sometimes you build a process that simply doesn't work for multiple users. For example, suppose you expect people to flag a series of records, and then run a script that does something to all the ones they flagged. If the script *finds* the flagged records and loops through them, then FileMaker gets utterly confused when two people try to use the same script at once. The script sees everyone's marked flags, unless you take special care to make each person's flag unique. It's anybody's guess how your poor records will wind up. In this example, you could mitigate the problem by entering the person's account name in the flag field. The script could then find just that person's flagged records.

In general, you should think about how the script you write works if a record can't be edited, or if several people are using it at the same time. Or, to avoid the issue altogether, make it so only one person can use certain scripts, and use privilege sets to keep everybody else away from them.

Connecting from a Web Browser

Not all web browsers are created equal. They aren't all good at showing you websites that use Cascading Style Sheets (CSS). And since FileMaker translates your layouts into CSS when you share them via IWP, you must have a browser that understands CSS to use databases on the Web, like one of the following:

- Microsoft Internet Explorer 7.0 or 8.0 in Windows
- Safari 4.0 in Mac OS X
- Firefox 3.5 in Mac or Windows

Warning: The fact is, you can try just about any old web browser you like with IWP, and FileMaker isn't generally going to make a stink about it. If it's a reasonably current browser that supports CSS and JavaScript, chances are good it'll work just fine. However, the versions of Internet Explorer, Firefox, and Safari listed above have been tested for compatibility in FileMaker's labs. If love for your unsupported browser outweighs compatibility concerns, then go for it. If the stakes are a bit higher and you need to *know* it's going to work, stick with a browser on the list.

To connect to the database from a web browser, you need to know the URL in the Instant Web Publishing dialog box. In your web browser's Location box, type this URL. The resulting web page looks like the one in Figure 17-5.

Figure 17-5:
This screen is the first thing you see when you connect to Instant Web Publishing in your web browser. The page has a link for each shared database. You just click the link to open the database.

When you click a database link on the web page, FileMaker asks you to log into the database—even if you haven't set up accounts on your database. If you've created accounts, then enter a valid account name and password. Otherwise, enter *Admin* for the user name, and leave the password box blank. After you log in, you see what probably looks a *lot* like your real database displayed right inside the web page (Figure 17-6).

When you view your data in List view or Table view, the web page shows only a few records at a time. To see more, click the pages in the book icon, or type a record number in the Current Record box, and then click the "Go to Record" button in the Status toolbar. Since you're working on the Web, you *must* click this button to reload the page with the desired record.

The process of editing records is also different in IWP. When you first click an editable field (or, in the toolbar, click the Edit Record button), FileMaker reloads the page in editable form. The Status toolbar also changes: Submit and Cancel buttons appear, while all other tools become unavailable. After you've made changes, you have to click Submit or FileMaker doesn't save them. If you don't want to keep your changes, click Cancel instead.

Instant Web Publishing adds three buttons to the Status toolbar that aren't in File-Maker Pro (Figure 17-7). The Home button takes you out of the database and into the IWP home page of Figure 17-5. Log Out logs you out of the database—a polite thing to do if you've hit that five-user limit and someone is waiting for access. Finally, because FileMaker can't override the browser's menus, it provides a Help button, which opens a new browser window with IWP-specific information.

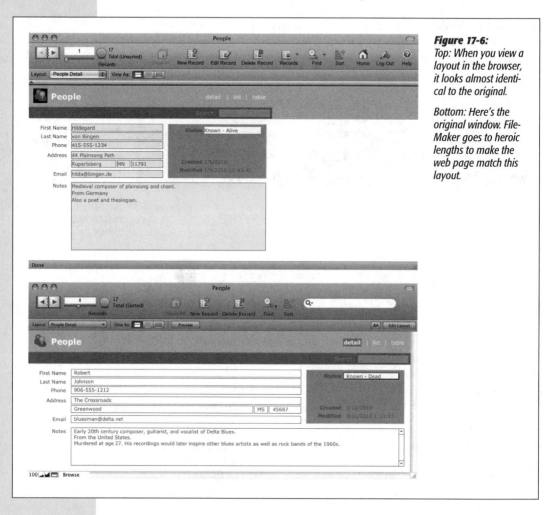

Figure 17-6:
Top: When you view a layout in the browser, it looks almost identical to the original.

Bottom: Here's the original window. File-Maker goes to heroic lengths to make the web page match this layout.

Custom Home Page

The IWP home page, shown in Figure 17-5, gets the job done, but it's not likely to match your corporate identity. And some people find it a bit confusing, since it doesn't provide them with a lot of clues about what your IWP database does. But you can make a Custom Home Page to replace it. First, take the HTML file you want to use for the home page and name it *iwp_home.html*. Then put it in FileMaker's Web folder. On Windows, you find it at Program Files→FileMaker→FileMaker Pro→Web. On Mac OS X, it's at Applications→FileMaker Pro 11→Web. If FileMaker sees a file with this name, then it automatically shows it instead of the normal IWP home page.

Of course, you'll want to include links to your databases on this page. Direct links to an IWP database look like this:

```
/fmi/iwp/cgi?-db=Database Name&-startsession
```

Just replace "Database Name" with your database's name.

Figure 17-7:
Since FileMaker can't control the Menu bar in your web browser, it has to cram everything it thinks you'll ever need into the Status toolbar instead.

FileMaker Server

Using FileMaker Pro on an ordinary desktop computer to host your files is easy and decidedly inexpensive, but it has some pretty severe drawbacks. First, it can handle no more than nine guests at once—and only five Instant Web Publishing users. If you have more, you have to find a better way. You find some less obvious problems as well, including the following:

- If somebody's working on the host computer, chances are she's doing more than just FileMaker. The more you do on a computer, the more likely it is to crash—especially after you contract the next email virus. The host in a peer-to-peer setup can sometimes be unstable. You probably don't want your database server interrupting your office workflow. But more serious than that, databases that crash often are likely to get corrupted. And that's not safe for your data.

- FileMaker Pro is designed for *using* databases, not hosting them. It does an admirable hosting job, but it simply wasn't built for speed or large numbers of simultaneous users.

- As you remember from Chapter 1, you should close databases before you back them up. But if they're open on a host computer, you have to disconnect all the guests before closing the files. This necessity makes midday backups decidedly inconvenient.

The answer to all these problems—and more—is FileMaker Server. It's a special piece of software designed for one thing: turning a dedicated computer into a lean, mean, and *stable* database host. When FileMaker Server hosts your databases, you can have *250* guests connected at once. Since it runs on a dedicated server, it tends to be much more stable (and you can put it in the closet, where nobody will pull the plug or close the files accidentally). From a performance perspective, you *can't* launch FileMaker Server and use the database directly. In fact, it has no windows, menus, or dialog boxes at all (it has an administration tool through which you can monitor the server and make changes to it, though). Instead, it's a true *server* (sometimes called a *service* or a *daemon*), designed specifically to share data over the network. Finally, it's loaded with special server-only features, including an automatic backup feature that can safely back up files while people are connected.

So what's the catch? Money. FileMaker Server costs $999, while another copy of File-Maker Pro is only $299. Don't be fooled, though. This cash is money well spent if your database is at all important to your business.

Tip: FileMaker Server comes in two flavors: *FileMaker Server* and *FileMaker Server Advanced* ($2,999). Both do a fine job with FileMaker Network Sharing and PHP-based Custom Web Publishing, if you need Instant Web Publishing or ODBC/JDBC connectivity, you'll have to go with Advanced. If you're not sure which version you need, don't sweat it. You can buy FileMaker Server today, and then trade it up to Advanced later if the need arises. This book doesn't cover the Advanced version. If you're interested in getting into big-time web publishing, check out the resources in Appendix A.

File Compatibility

As you learned back near the beginning of this book, the file extension for database files created with versions 7 through 11 is "fp7". Therefore, you can do a fair amount of version mixing between FileMaker Server, FileMaker Developer, and FileMaker Pro, and still get good results. You can develop files on FileMaker Pro Advanced 8, put them on a FileMaker 11 Server, and then let people with FileMaker Pro 10 share them. You can mix and match versions 7–11 at will.

Warning: The files open just fine across versions. However, some features, like Tab Controls, script variables, conditional formatting, script triggers, and External SQL Sources (ESS) won't work in versions that preceded the feature, so take care how you mix versions if you're using these recent additions.

However, files prior to version 7 have to be converted before you can use them with any FileMaker product that's version 7 or above. But those good folks at FileMaker, Inc. have been careful to provide support for conversion. FileMaker Pro 11 can convert files from as far back as FileMaker 3. You *can* convert even older versions, but it's tricky. You have to find someone with FileMaker 5 first, and use it to convert older files to the .fp5 format. Once the files have been updated, FileMaker Pro 11

---

can take over and get you up to .fp7-land. If you have old files to convert, be sure to download FileMaker's guide to converting: *www.filemaker.com/downloads/documentation/fm8_converting_databases.pdf.*

POWER USERS' CLINIC

Global Fields and Multiple Users

When many people share a single database, you might be worried about global fields. If one person changes a global field, does it change for *everybody*? In a word, "No." FileMaker keeps global field information on the *guest* computer. That's right: Globals are local. If one user changes the value in global field, it has no effect on what's in that global field for other people.

This characteristic is, in general, a very good thing. But it does have an annoying side effect. Since everyone has his own globals, you *can't* change them for other people even when you want to. If you open a shared database, change a global, and then close it, you lose your changes. The next time you open the database, the globals have the same values as the *host* computer.

If you're using peer-to-peer sharing, then you can change the globals on the host directly to make them stick. Since FileMaker Server has no real interface, you can't directly modify the initial value for a global field. You have to close the files on the server, move them to another computer, open them with FileMaker Pro, make the change, and then copy them back to the server. In other words, it's a pain.

If you have globals you often need to change permanently in a multiuser system, then it's often easier to simply set them from a script that runs when the database opens. Then you're sure they have the right value, and you can always modify the script if you want to change the starting value while the databases are still hosted.

Installing FileMaker Server

If you decide a FileMaker Server is the right thing for your database, then your first step is to install the software. (Although you may want to buy a good server computer first. See page 757 for some guidelines.) FileMaker Server (in both its standard and Advanced versions) includes an installer program that takes care of the basic complexities of configuration for you. When you run the installer (and after you accept the terms of the license agreement), FileMaker asks you a simple question, as shown in Figure 17-8.

If your database will be heavily used (by dozens or even a couple of hundred people) and you plan on using the web publishing capabilities of FileMaker heavily, then it probably makes sense to install different portions of the server setup on different machines. Three configurations are typical:

- **FileMaker Server and Web Server.** Install FileMaker Server and the Web Publishing Engine on one computer, and use an ordinary web server computer as the "front end" for your web publishing. This configuration works well if you already have a web server in your organization, and you want to add some FileMaker-based web content. You can keep all the FileMaker parts together in one place, with minimal impact on the web server computer.

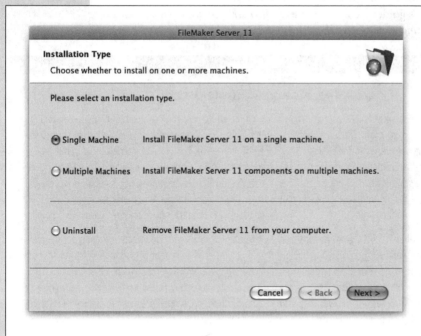

Figure 17-8:
When you install File-Maker Server, the first question you have to answer is what type of installation you want. Choose Single Machine if you want to install all server components on one computer. If you're going to use two servers (one web server and one database server, for example) then choose the second option. You should also choose Multiple Machines if you're installing FileMaker Server Advanced but you don't want all the web components just yet.

- **Web Server and Database Server.** Install FileMaker Server on one computer, and the Web Publishing Engine on another. The database server handles all your pure data serving needs. The Web Server handles both ordinary web pages and the FileMaker web publishing system.

- **Web Server, Web Publishing Engine, and Database Server.** Install the File-Maker Server on one computer, the Web Publishing Engine on another, and use a third as a web server. In this configuration, the load of the Web Publishing Engine doesn't interfere with ordinary web server tasks, and doesn't slow down the FileMaker Server. This configuration is generally the fastest for maximum load.

Note: If you aren't using FileMaker Server Advanced or you don't plan on doing any web publishing, then your decision is simple. Just do a Single Machine installation on the server computer, and you're done.

If you plan on using any of these multicomputer configurations, choose Multiple Machines when asked about Installation Type, and then click Next.

Single Machine installation

If you opted for a Single Machine installation, you're almost done. Just click Next and key in your software license code. The installer program then goes to work installing all the various parts and pieces. When it's finished, skip past the next section to Configuring Your Server to finish the installation process.

Multiple Machine installation

If you want to install on two or more machines, choose Multiple Machines. The installer takes you through the procedure for installing the components on either two or three computers. After you finish installing on the first computer, take your installer disc to the second computer, and then install the next part, again using the Multiple Machines option. If you're going for a three-piece install, just run the old installer one more time on that third computer.

Configuring your server

Once the installer has finished putting software on your computer, it asks if you want to start the Deployment Assistant. You do. If you don't run the assistant, the software sits dormant on your computer. Click Continue.

Note: If you see a security alert about an application called "FMS11-Admin Console" trying to access your computer, don't panic. The FileMaker Admin tool is triggering your computer's third-party software authentication feature. You can click to accept, or look on the warning dialog box for a link or button to display more detail. You'll see that the digital signature is from FileMaker, Inc. and has been verified.

When you first start the Deployment Assistant, it can take several minutes. FileMaker has to start up its server software, download the configuration tools to your computer, and start up the admin application. But if you exercise some patience, then you eventually see the first screen of the Deployment Assistant, as shown in Figure 17-9.

In the first screen, you're asked to set up an "admin console account." When you interact with your FileMaker Server in the future, you'll use the Admin Console application. It can tweak configuration settings, install new databases, perform backups, and more. And it can do all this from any computer on the network. To prevent unauthorized people from working with your server, you set up an account (with a name and password) for authorized administrators.

Just enter the User Name and Password you want to use. You have to type the password twice so FileMaker can be sure you didn't mistype it. Then click Next, to fill in a little information about your server (Figure 17-10).

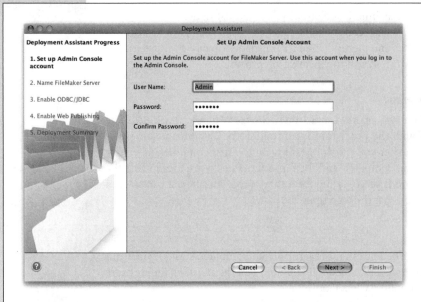

Figure 17-9:
The Deployment Assistant is divided into several steps. Once you reach the last step, your server is ready to go. Luckily, most of these steps are simple.

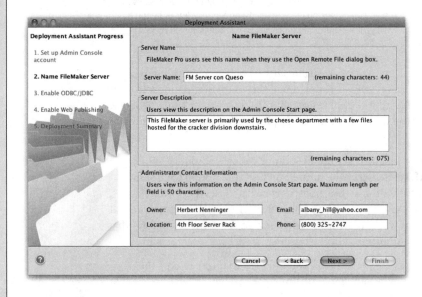

Figure 17-10:
In the Name FileMaker Server section, you give your FileMaker Server a friendly name (which people see in the Open Remote dialog box). You can also add a description, which shows up on the Admin Console page. Use this to remind you (or your administrators) where the server computer is, what it's used for, or anything else useful. Finally, you can record contact information in case an administrator ever needs to talk to you about the server.

Everything on this screen is optional except the Server Name. Fill out the parts you think will be useful, and then click Next.

For those installing FileMaker Server Advanced, the next page simply asks if you want to use ODBC/JDBC with your server. This option has nothing to do with ESS, ODBC Import, or the Execute SQL script step: You're *always* free to use these features. Instead, this setting controls whether *other* programs can talk to FileMaker using ODBC or JDBC. If you don't need this ability, keep this option turned off. (You can always turn it on later.)

Finally, FileMaker asks if you want to enable web publishing. If this is just a plain-vanilla FileMaker Server for FileMaker users only, then turn this option off. Otherwise, turn it on.

When you're through, FileMaker shows one more page, with a summary of your various settings (Figure 17-11).

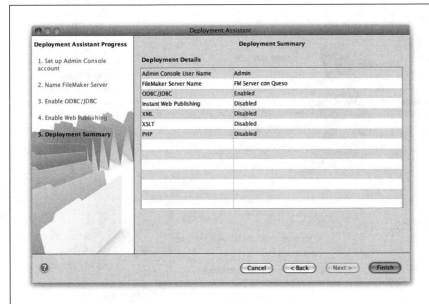

Figure 17-11:
Before it goes about deploying servers, FileMaker gives you a concise overview of the options you've selected. You can click Back if you want to change some of your choices.

When you're confident you have the server set up the way you want, click Finish. The assistant then configures all the parts of your server, and launches the Admin Console for you.

Administering FileMaker Server

Once you have a server installed and configured, you can administer it at any time using the Admin Console. On the computer where you performed the installation, you see a shortcut on the desktop that takes you to the FileMaker Server Admin Console Start Page (Figure 17-12). But you can visit this page from *any computer on your network* so you don't have to leave your desk to work with your server. If this is the first time you've accessed this page on your computer, then you have to type the URL directly. It looks like this:

```
http://myserver:16000/
```

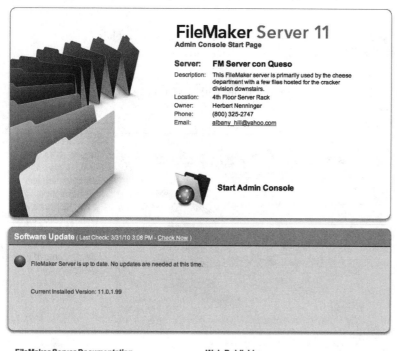

FileMaker Server 11
Admin Console Start Page

Server: **FM Server con Queso**
Description: This FileMaker server is primarily used by the cheese department with a few files hosted for the cracker division downstairs.
Location: 4th Floor Server Rack
Owner: Herbert Nenninger
Phone: (800) 325-2747
Email: albany_hill@yahoo.com

Start Admin Console

Software Update (Last Check: 3/31/10 3:08 PM - Check Now)

FileMaker Server is up to date. No updates are needed at this time.

Current Installed Version: 11.0.1.99

FileMaker Server Documentation

- Getting Started Guide
- Guide to Updating Plug-ins
- Custom Web Publishing with PHP
- Custom Web Publishing with XML and XSLT
- ODBC and JDBC Guide
- Instant Web Publishing Guide

Web Publishing

- PHP Site Assistant and XSLT Site Assistant Tools

Troubleshooting

- FileMaker Server 11 Technology Tests
- FileMaker Knowledge Base
- Customer Support Services
- Feature Requests

Figure 17-12:
The FileMaker Server Admin Console Start Page is a one-stop shop for server information. At the top, you see information about the server itself, including its name, description, and administrator contact information. The page tells you if an update is available for your FileMaker Server software (middle). It also gives you links to online server documentation and useful tools at the bottom.

In other words, use the name of your server, followed by ":16000". This URL tells your browser to access FileMaker Server's start page directly.

From the start page, you can launch the Admin Console itself. Just click the icon next to Start Admin Console. Again, the first time you use the Admin Console, it takes a few minutes to configure the software on your computer. (Later, when you come back to the Admin Console, it'll be faster.)

The sidebar in the Admin Console links to several important sections as shown by Figure 17-13:

- **Clients.** All the people who are connected to your server. Generally, they're folks who have one of your shared databases open, or are using Instant Web Publishing. You can see their FileMaker account name, the type of connection they have, their computers' network address, and even which version of FileMaker they're using. You can also send them a message, or disconnect them from the server. To do so, first select someone in the list, then pick from the Actions pop-up menu, and then click Perform Action.

- **Databases.** A list of databases being shared with this server. You can see which databases are being shared, and in what ways. And just like with Clients, you can select a database and perform any of several actions.

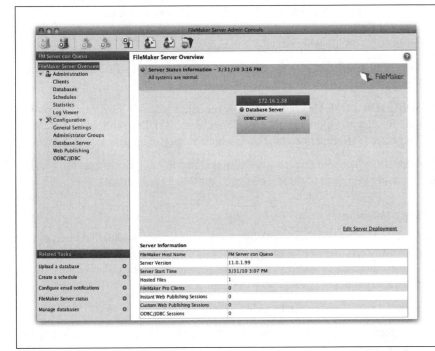

Figure 17-13:
The Admin Console is a vast application. The bar along the left side of the window lets you switch between the various sections. At the bottom of this bar, you can click links to perform important tasks. For example, you probably want to install a database on your server. To do that, click "Upload a database".

- **Schedules.** Gives you high level information about scheduled tasks on your server. You can schedule three different things on FileMaker Server: backups, scripts, and messages. Backups are the most important, and you'll see how to create a backup schedule on page 752.

- **Statistics.** Tells you about your server. The myriad numbers presented on this screen give your (or FileMaker's tech support staff) information about how much load your server encounters, and how it's performing.

- **General Settings.** Includes all the configuration options you set when you set up your server, plus some additional options. Here, you can rename your server (in the Server Information tab), tell the server to email you important information periodically (in the Email Notifications tab), change the administrator password (in the Admin Console tab), and decide if the server should start automatically when the computer boots (in the Auto Start tab).

- **Administrator Groups (FileMaker Server Advanced).** For servers with multiple constituencies, Administrator Groups provide a way to delegate a few administrative capabilities. If your server hosts databases for the Sharks and the Jets, you can set up an Administrator Group for each of them so that each can manage their own databases without gaining administrative access to the other's.

- **Database Server.** Shows configuration options specific to the database server portion of FileMaker Server. In addition to numerous parameters like how many people can connect to the server and how many databases can be installed, you can also decide where database backups are stored.

- **Web Publishing.** Settings for Custom Web Publishing and Instant Web Publishing (FileMaker Server Advanced) reside here.

- **ODBC/JDBC (FileMaker Server Advanced).** FileMaker files can be configured to accept Open Database Connectivity (ODBC) and Java Database Connectivity (JDBC) queries. This is where the pertinent options can be set up.

Below this list of console screens, the Admin Console has a list of common tasks. You'll probably visit each of these when you first set up your server.

Installing a database

When you first install your server, it's like a well of untapped potential. Although the server is ready to go, you don't have any *databases* installed. Your first job is to install at least one shared database so you can take advantage of FileMaker Server's high performance capabilities:

1. **In the Admin Console sidebar, click Databases.**

   FileMaker shows you the Databases section of the admin console, including an Actions pop-up menu.

2. **From the Actions pop-up menu, choose Upload, and then click Perform Action.**

   The Upload Database Assistant appears (Figure 17-14).

3. **Click Create Subfolder and, in the box that pops up, type *My Database System*, and then click OK.**

   FileMaker Server organizes shared databases in folders. This step is entirely optional, but if your database system has several files, or you want to share different database systems, it's helpful to keep related databases together in one folder.

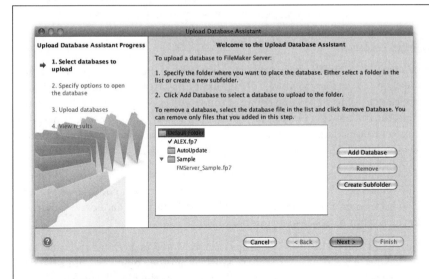

Figure 17-14:
The Upload Database Assistant makes it a breeze to install databases on your FileMaker server. You just pick the database(s) from your computer, and decide where they should go. The assistant takes care of copying them to the server, installing them in the appropriate place and setting appropriate permissions.

4. **Click Add Database.**

   You see a standard Open File dialog box. Here's where you pick the file you want to share.

5. **Navigate to the file you want to share, select it, and then click Open.**

   Make sure the database isn't already open in FileMaker Pro before you try to upload it. When you've made your choice, The Admin Console adds it to the list in the assistant window. If you have other databases to share, select a folder, and then click Add Database again.

6. **Click Next.**

   FileMaker inspects your files to be sure they're ready to share, and then asks if you want to open the files once they're uploaded. (A file can be opened and closed on the server just like on your own computer. An open file is shared and ready to be opened by other people. A closed file is on the server, but people can't access it.)

7. **Leave "Automatically open databases after upload" turned on, and then click Next.**

   The Upload Assistant uploads the databases (it shows a progress bar as they're copied), and then reports that the "Upload has completed successfully".

8. **Click Next.**

   The Upload Assistant shows you the status of each uploaded file. Generally, each file indicates "File uploaded successfully and opened". This means your database is shared and ready to be accessed in FileMaker Pro using the File→Open Remote dialog box.

When you're done uploading, click Finish. You return to the Admin Console window, where, in the Databases section, you can see your database.

Scheduling a backup

One of a true FileMaker Server's primary advantages is the ability to perform automatic backups of databases without disruption to the users. You can't overestimate the importance of this step. Some day your server will crash, perhaps because a hard drive fails, or the power goes out, or for any of a dozen other reasons. When this happens, your best course of action is to take your lumps, restore from backup, and re-enter any missing data. The more often you back up, the less difficult that'll be.

If you want, you can configure FileMaker Server to back up to a location different from the main hard drive on your server computer. It makes good sense, for example, to back up on a second hard drive. This way if the main hard drive fails, then you don't lose your database *and* your backup.

But you should also make offline backups that are stored in a remote location. This protects against natural disaster scenarios, where all the computers and drives in your office are lost. FileMaker's automated backup gets the files cleanly copied to a drive of your choice, but it's up to you to copy those backups to tape, CD, DVD, or over the network so they're stored offsite.

To configure the backup location, in the Admin Console sidebar, choose Database Server. Then switch to the Default Folders tab. At the bottom of this window, you see the backup folder location (Figure 17-15).

In the Path box, type the full path to the folder where you want backups stored. The path has to start with filewin: (Windows) or filemac: (Mac OS X), and end with a slash. When you're done typing, click Validate, and FileMaker tells you if your path is valid.

Once you've set the backup location, you're ready to schedule the backup. Like many things in FileMaker, you can do it the easy way if your needs are basic, or you can peek under the hood and make numerous configuration choices to get exactly what you want. A backup schedule runs periodically (you control how often), and backs up certain files (you control which ones). Each time FileMaker makes a backup, it puts the files in a folder with the date and time in its name so you can easily tell how old the backup file is. You also configure the schedule to keep a certain number of copies. For instance, if you choose to keep three copies, then FileMaker automatically keeps three complete backups. When the schedule runs again, it deletes the oldest and makes one more new one.

FileMaker Server includes three handy built-in schedules. If you want the most basic backup (every file, every night, keeping a week's worth of copies), then you don't have to do anything. FileMaker Server comes preconfigured to run just such a backup automatically. (You can see it in the Admin Console's Schedules section, labeled Daily.)

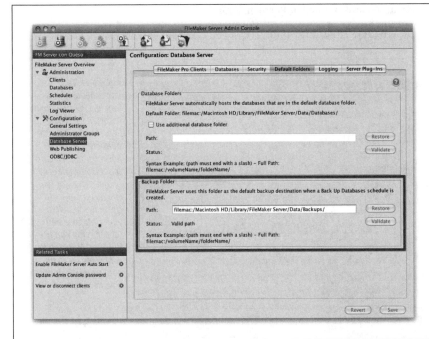

Figure 17-15:
On the Default Folders tab, you tell FileMaker where you want to store backup files. You can enter any valid path on your computer (following the syntax example). Ideally, your backups should reside on a different hard drive than the live databases.

If you want more frequent backups, turn off Daily, and turn on Hourly instead (you turn on a schedule using the checkbox by its name). This version keeps eight copies of your database, one for each hour from 8:00 a.m. to 5:00 p.m. Alternately, you can turn on Weekly if you just want backups every week (in this configuration, it keeps four copies).

It often makes sense to turn all these schedules on. That way, you get hourly backups for the current day, daily backups for the last week, and weekly backups for a month, which is a nice balance of frequent recent copies and a few old copies in case of catastrophe (imagine, for instance, you accidentally delete hundreds of older records, and don't notice for a week).

If you want to modify any of the built-in backups, in the left-side bar, just click Schedules, and then double-click any schedule. FileMaker walks you through a step-by-step configuration. You can, for instance, switch the hourly backups to run from 7:00 a.m. instead of 8:00 a.m., or tell the weekly backup to keep eight copies instead of four.

If you need a more advanced setup (maybe you want to do a special backup that your offsite backup system picks up every Friday at midnight), then you can make as many new schedules as you want:

1. **From the Actions pop-up menu at the top of the screen, choose "Create a Schedule", and then click Perform Action.**

   The Schedule Assistant window (Figure 17-16) appears.

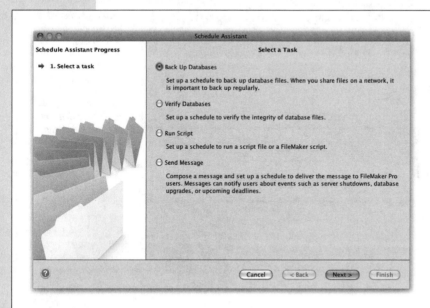

Figure 17-16:
The Schedule Assistant lets you schedule assorted FileMaker Server tasks. You can automate regular backups, schedule scripts to run directly on the server, or tell FileMaker Server to check the health of your database periodically. You can use the Send Message to tell FileMaker to announce server down time in advance.

2. **Make sure "Back up Databases" is selected, and then click Next.**

   The Schedule Assistant asks what kind of schedule you want. You can choose one of the canned schedule types listed earlier in this chapter (Hourly, Daily, or Weekly) to use as a starting point, or you can start with a clean slate by choosing Custom.

3. **Turn on Custom, and then click Next.**

   The assistant now asks which databases you want to back up. You can choose to back up all your databases, just those in a particular folder, or a single selected database.

Note: If you need to back up a specific collection of databases, you can put them into a folder in your database folder on the server computer. If that isn't an option (maybe they're already in different folders for other schedules), then you need to make a schedule for each one.

---

4. **Leave All Databases turned on, and then click Next.**

   The screen changes to show still more options (Figure 17-17).

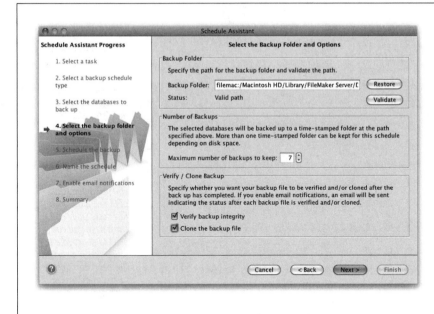

Figure 17-17:
This step in the Schedule Assistant lets you choose where to store the backup, how many copies FileMaker Server should keep, and whether or not the backup file should be verified. By "verified," FileMaker means it checks the structure of the database file to be sure it has a clean bill of health. Clone the Backup File saves a record-less copy of each file it just backed up. Clones come in very handy if you find yourself piecing together a corrupt database.

5. **In the Backup Folder, enter the full path to the folder on your server where you want the backup stored.**

   In this hypothetical example, you might have your offsite backup system configured to copy every file from a certain folder every Friday at midnight, so you would send the backup to that folder.

6. **In the "Maximum number of backups to keep" box, enter *1*.**

   You only want one to keep one weekly copy of the database in this example, since the files will be copied by your offsite backup system.

7. **Click Next.**

   The assistant now asks you when the backup should run. This screen has a lot of options (Figure 17-18).

8. **From the Frequency pop-up menu, choose Weekly.**

   The rest of the window changes to match Figure 17-18.

9. **Turn off every checkbox under "Select the days of the week you would like the schedule to run"—except Friday.**

   You've now told the assistant you want this backup to run only on Friday.

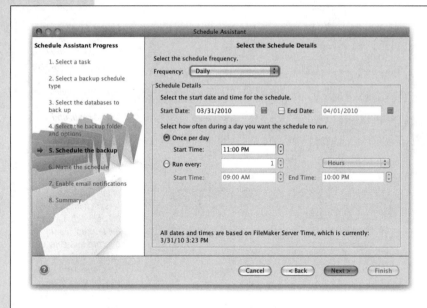

Figure 17-18:
Finally you get to tell FileMaker Server when to back up your files. First, from the Frequency pop-up menu, make a selection (your choices are Daily, "Every n days", Once Only, and Weekly). This selection determines the exact options you see in the rest of the window. In this case, Daily is chosen, so you can elect to deactivate the schedule on a certain date and decide how many times it runs each day.

10. **Turn on "Once per day", and then, in the associated box, type 11:00 PM.**

    This setting tells FileMaker Server to back up the file at 11:00 p.m. That way, the backup is finished in time for the offsite backup script at midnight. (For most databases, the backup takes just a few seconds, but this time can stretch if your database is very large or your server is very busy. You should test your backups to see how long they take, and leave a little extra time just in case.)

11. **Click Next.**

    The assistant asks you to name your schedule. This step just helps you identify it among a potentially long list of schedules you've created.

12. **In the Schedule Name box, type Friday Night Offsite, and then click Finish.**

    The Next button is grayed out at this point because you're at the last step, so Finish is the button for you. The assistant creates your new schedule, and then closes, leaving you back at the list of schedules.

In most cases, the built-in backup schedules are sufficient, but should the need arise, FileMaker's scheduling system is almost infinitely configurable.

Testing Your Server

You can test your FileMaker Server's various components at any time to be sure they're configured correctly and working. To do so, first go to the FileMaker Server Admin Console Start Page (page 747). On this page, under Troubleshooting, click the FileMaker Server 10 Technology Tests link. You can see the page in Figure 17-19.

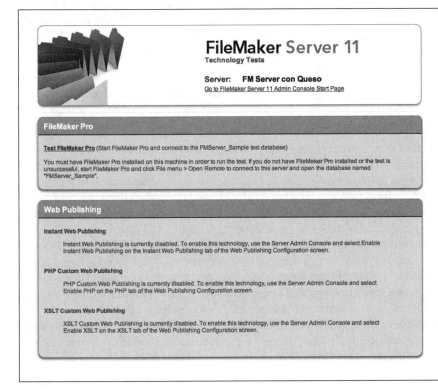

Figure 17-19:
The Technology Tests page includes a section for each of FileMaker Server Advanced's main technologies (FileMaker Sharing, Instant Web Publishing, PHP Custom Web Publishing, and XSLT Custom Web Publishing).

From this page, each section tells you if the particular sharing technology is turned on and working. You can click the link in each section to go to a test page or database. The test pages use the appropriate technology to load data from a database, so if they display successfully, then you can be confident your server is ready to publish your content.

Server Hardware

While you're spending money, why not get a better *computer*, too? If you have lots of users or lots of data (or both), your database server needs all the power you can give it. After all, FileMaker Server performs finds, edits records, sorts, imports, exports, and otherwise constantly busies itself with the work of *every user*.

The most important thing you can do to make FileMaker Server faster is give it faster access to the data on the disk. At the very least, this increased speed means you should *never* store the files on a file server. Instead, they should always be on a hard drive in the host computer. If you still find things aren't as fast as you'd like them, your best upgrade is often a faster disk system—something called a RAID, or Redundant Array of Independent Disks. A RAID is a set of two or more hard disks, usually in the same enclosure, and wired up to behave like a single hard drive. By putting several disks together, you can get faster access to your data than you would with just one disk. As important, you can get *more reliable* access as well, since the same data can be stored in more than one place in case a disk drive fails, as outlined in the box on the next page.

In addition to a fast disk system, you should consider adding plenty of RAM to the host computer. The least important component is the CPU speed itself (but that's not to say it doesn't matter; don't expect a fast server with a 500 MHz processor).

If you find all this terribly confusing, be comforted by the fact that most major computer companies sell specially configured server computers. Let them know you're setting up a database server, and you can probably buy a fantastic host computer with RAID, lots of RAM, and a fast CPU—all in one box. For all but the most basic multiuser purposes, you absolutely should consider a dedicated computer designed by the manufacturer to be used as a server. Dell, Apple, and many others have specific server-class computers. It may *seem* like one of their desktop computers has the same specs as the servers for less money, but appearances can be deceiving. Server computers may have the same processors, amount of memory, and hard drive space, but they generally use upgraded versions of key components. Everything from the hard drive to the fan that keeps things cool is designed for much more intensive use than a normal desktop computer. Consider the cost of a good server computer part of your FileMaker installation, or you'll regret it down the road when you experience poor performance, poor reliability, or (worst of all) loss of data.

Finally, no matter how reliable your server computer is, if the power goes out, it will crash. And a crashed server can lead to database corruption and a lot of lost time. To protect against this, consider purchasing an *Uninterruptible Power Supply*, or UPS. You plug one of these battery backup devices into the wall, and then plug the computer into it. If the power goes out, the battery automatically kicks in to keep the server running. Higher-quality UPS devices can even signal the computer to safely shut down when the power is out and the battery runs low, eliminating the possibility of a crash.

RAID Overview

RAID is just a generic term for any assemblage of several disks that look, to the computer, like just one disk. But the devil is in the details. It turns out there are several different *kinds* of RAID out there, and each serves a different purpose.

If speed is all you care about, there's something called *striping*. With striping, the data's spread across all disks so that when FileMaker Server reads or writes, it can usually do it to every disk at once. In general, a four-disk array with striping can shuffle data four times faster than just one disk. The trouble with striping is that every doubling of performance also produces a halving of reliability. In other words, if you expect one drive to fail sometime in the next four years, then one of the drives in your array will fail in the next year, on average. Since the data is spread across the disks, when one disk fails, you can permanently lose data (sometimes all of it).

On the other end of the spectrum is *mirroring*. This model gives you *maximum reliability*, but with no speed benefit. In a mirrored array, every piece of data is written to every drive at the same time. If one drive fails, the system can simply switch to another drive without losing any data. But you often need more performance than a mirrored array can give.

Unless you're certain you know what you're doing, you should never use just striping. The idea of maximum performance can be appealing, but data integrity and reliability are paramount. Generally, the best bet is a combination of mirroring and striping. Ideally, you create a few mirrored sets of disks, and then connect these sets into a striped super-set. If you use RAID, you should look for a system that lets you set up this kind of *striping over mirroring* configuration for the maximum in reliability and performance. You get to decide how much reliability you want (by picking the number of disks in each mirrored set) and how much speed you want (by choosing the number of mirrored sets to create).

Another type of RAID (called RAID 5) purports to give you a performance boost *and* redundancy with fewer disks. RAID 5 tends to be cheaper than true mirroring and striping systems because you can buy fewer hard drives. Unfortunately, RAID 5 is only faster when *reading* from the drives while writing can actually be *slower*, making them ill-suited for database duty. You're better off spending a little more money to get a mirrored and striped system.

Adding Security

FileMaker's all about easy access to information. But that's a double-edged sword. If you don't add security, every person who uses your database has unrestricted access and can add data, tables and scripts as freely as you can. Of course, you can take all the usual precautions (give your computer a password, install virus protection software, lock your office door, and so on). But the minute you let anyone else into the database, you have all kinds of security challenges. Mike in Accounting is free to rename or edit all your scripts if he so desires. And Kelly in Sales can delete all those "old" order records that are getting in her way. Fortunately, FileMaker has features of its own that give you a fine level of control, so you can let selected people use your database to the fullest, while keeping important information, and your database's structure, out of harm's way.

Note: You may be tempted to think you don't have to worry about security. But the best time to protect your data is *before* you have a problem. If you wait until your database grows big and complex before adding security, then it'll take you longer to build the security you need.

How Security Works

FileMaker's security system has two primary levels of control: *who* can get into your database in the first place; and *what* they can do once they're there. You determine who gets access to your database by setting up *user accounts*, and you control what each person can do by assigning *privilege sets* to each account.

Who Gets Access

FileMaker understands that different individuals access your database. The *who* part of security is important for several reasons. For instance, Dwight and Pam each need access to the database, but their manager Michael doesn't. When you give each user of your database an individual account, you can keep track of who's using the file. Plus, if Pam leaves the company, then you can keep her from accessing the database without locking anybody else out. Likewise, when Pam's replacement is hired, you can give him access, too.

You control access by creating an account for each person who uses the database. Each account has a user name and a password. Users have to type their account name and password when they open the file. If they don't know the right combination, then they can't get in.

Note: When FileMaker asks for an account name and password, propeller-heads say it's *authenticating* the user. In other words, it's making sure the user's for real. This book, for the most part, dispenses with this jargon, but you may run across the term elsewhere. Just so you know.

POWER USERS' CLINIC

Spying by Script

Once you've set up database accounts, FileMaker remembers the account name of whoever's currently signed in. Find out what FileMaker knows using the *Get (Account-Name)* function. For example, if you want to record the account name in an Access table when someone runs a particularly important script, the script can create an Access record and take notes before the script goes into its main work. To keep track, you could include a script step like this:

```
Set Field [Access::Notes ; Get(AccountName)
& " ran the script on " & Get(CurrentDate)
& " at " & Get
(CurrentTime)]
```

Then every time the script runs, FileMaker looks up the name and password of whoever's signed into the file at the moment, and puts the person's account name and the date and time in the Notes field.

FileMaker also knows the name of the privilege set used when someone logs in. The *Get (PrivilegeSetName)* function tells you which one it is.

What They Can Do

But who gets into your database is only half the story. You also control *what* they can do. You decide which layouts users can see, and which scripts they can run. You can even let them see only certain records. Each bit of access is called a privilege. Every person is unique, but you probably don't need to grant each person a unique set of privileges. For example, you may have one privilege set for Accounting and another for Sales. People with the Accounting privilege set can run reports, but they can't enter new orders. People with the Sales privilege set can enter and edit data, but they can't run reports. You can make as many—or as few—privilege sets as you need. And you can give 50 accounts the same privilege set, or make a privilege set just for one account.

Note: Usually, you create privilege sets *first*, and then add accounts for each user. When you add an account, you have to pick a privilege set to control the account access before FileMaker lets you finish the account setup. But you do have some flexibility: If you start to create an account, but don't yet have an appropriate privilege set, then you can create one right then and there, before you save the account.

Privilege Sets

When you're creating privilege sets, there's a big temptation to give people too much power. The more folks can do on their own, the less often they'll come bugging you, right? Unfortunately, this attitude invites trouble. For instance, if your database holds credit card numbers along with order records, and your Order Entry privilege set lets users export data, you may one day find yourself the subject of an FBI investigation. To be on the safe side, if you aren't *sure* someone needs a privilege, then don't give it to him.

This rule has a practical component as well. If someone has access to a feature he shouldn't have, then he's very unlikely to complain. He probably doesn't even notice, and neither do you—until someone abuses it. However, if you lock someone out of a capability he needs, you can bet you'll hear about it right away. You can easily add the needed power when it comes up. In other words, if your privilege sets start out too restrictive, then they'll naturally grow to the right level of power over time based on user feedback. FileMaker encourages this approach by creating each new privilege set without any privileges at all. Your job is to add each privilege a user needs.

You do all the work of creating and maintaining accounts and privilege sets in the Manage Security window (Figure 18-1). You can get there by way of the File→Manage→Security command.

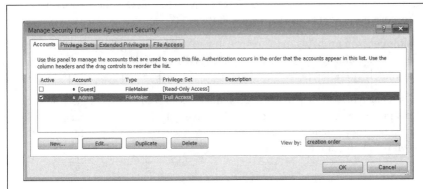

Figure 18-1:
The [Guest] and Admin accounts are added for you when you first create a new database. The checkbox to the left of the Admin account tells you that it's the only one currently active.

Understanding Privilege Sets

Every FileMaker database has three built-in privilege sets: [Full Access], [Data Entry Only], and [Read-Only Access]. You can only make a few minor edits to these sets. The brackets make it easy to pick them out of a list with your custom sets. You can see the Privilege Sets tab in Figure 18-2.

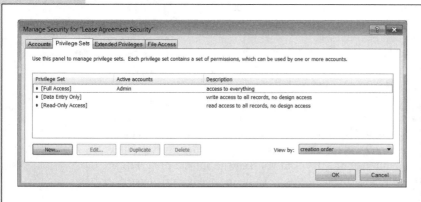

Figure 18-2:
The Privilege Sets tab of the Manage Security dialog box lists all the privilege sets in your database. Each privilege set has a name (in the Privilege Set column) and a description. The list also shows you all the accounts assigned each privilege set. Out of the box, only the [Full Access] privilege set is being used—by the Admin account.

Note: Those brackets around the default sets' names are actually part of the name, as you'll soon find out when you use the *Get (PrivilegeSetName)* function. So although they're awkward to look at and bothersome to read, get used to seeing them.

The built-in privilege sets

The standard privilege sets cover three very common access levels, and you're welcome to use them if you want, but you have to live with the way they work out of the box, because FileMaker doesn't let you edit them.

- Although you probably didn't realize it, you've been using the Full Access privilege set all along. As the name says, it gives you full access to the file with absolutely no restrictions.

- The Data Entry Only privilege set is much less powerful. Accounts assigned to this privilege set can't create or modify tables, field definitions, scripts, or layouts. But they can add, edit, and delete records in any table, print, change their own password, and export data.

- The least powerful built-in privilege set is Read-Only Access. Not only does it prevent all developer activities, but it also prevents modification of the data. Accounts with this privilege set can't create, edit, or delete records. They can *view, print or export* the data that's already there, and change their passwords.

Custom privilege sets

Those built-in privilege sets provide basic security, but they don't give you a full range of possibilities. Using just FileMaker's standard privilege sets, you can't give Dwight full control of some tables, but let him just enter data in others. In developer's lingo, you don't get a lot of *granularity*.

Note: Think of granularity as a medium for sculpture. If you're building a statue from boulders, then you can't create delicate details like the nose or eyelashes. If you're building with grains of sand (get it?), then you can work at a much finer level. Similarly, granularity in security lets you control specific access to your database.

In FileMaker, you can exercise precise, granular control over security by creating your own privilege sets, and assigning them to certain people or groups.

When you create a new privilege set, it starts out with absolutely no privileges. In other words, accounts attached to this set—if left alone—can't do *anything* in the database. You have to turn on exactly the privileges you think the user should have.

To save time, you could duplicate the [Data Entry Only] or [Read-Only Access] privilege set, and then add or remove privileges as necessary. This way is usually a little faster, but it does open up the possibility that you'll accidentally leave something turned on that shouldn't be allowed.

Note: You can't duplicate the [Full Access] privilege set. This is FileMaker's way of encouraging you to really think about the privileges you assign, and it should encourage you to give users the least access possible for them to do their jobs. If you want a privilege set that grants *almost* full access, then you have to build it up by hand.

Understanding Individual Privileges

Since FileMaker has a privilege for almost every single thing you can do, you have *lots* of them. To help you navigate the maze of privileges, the Edit Privilege Set dialog box (Figure 18-3) is divided into three primary sections:

- In the "Data Access and Design" section, you control access to the data via records and layouts. You also decide what kinds of developer operations the user can perform. For example, can she create new layouts? Or edit your scripts? Create value lists? Numerous dialog boxes and dozens of options live behind the pop-up menus in this section.

- Other Privileges includes a block of simple checkboxes controlling access to assorted database-wide features like printing, exporting, and password restrictions.

- The Extended Privileges section shows a scrolling list of checkboxes. For the most part, FileMaker adds these to control how you share your data, but you can also add your own custom extended privileges.

You'll learn more about each of these sections in the following pages.

Tip: Even if you turn a privilege off, a script that's set to run with full access privileges can work around the restriction (page 796).

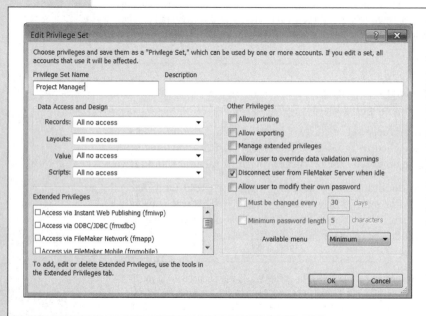

Figure 18-3:
When you create a new privilege set, you see FileMaker's granularity of control in action. Notice how many things aren't turned on, or say "All no access". You set each privilege one by one, until you've built up a set that's appropriate for the kind of user you have in mind—in this case, a Project Manager.

Other privileges

With just a set of checkboxes to turn options on or off, the Other Privileges area is the easiest section, so it's a good place to start. Here's where you select basic File-Maker features:

- **Allow printing.** Turn this option on, and the user can print layouts. If it's off, then the Print menu command is grayed out, and the Print script step fails.

- **Allow exporting.** This option lets people access the Export Records command. Again, if it's off, the menu command is grayed out, and the Export Records script step doesn't work.

- **Manage Extended Privileges.** Normally, only accounts with full access can manage security settings. Extended privileges are the exception. You'll learn more in a later section, but if this option's turned on, then people can assign extended privileges to different privilege sets themselves.

- **Allow user to override data validation warnings.** This option is a companion to the "Allow user to override during data entry" option on the Validation tab of in the Field Options dialog box (page 248), which you can turn on if you want to let people ignore the error message that's displayed if they enter invalid data in the field. But when this privilege is *not* selected, people can't override the errors even when the field options say they should be able to. In other words, this privilege trumps that field option.

- **Disconnect user from FileMaker Server when idle.** This isn't actually a privilege. It's more of an *un-privilege*, and it's turned on when you create a new privilege set. When it's on, people are kicked out of a shared database if they don't use it for a while (you get to decide how long when you configure FileMaker Server). Turn it *off* if you want to give these people the power to stay connected right through their lunch breaks.

- **Allow user to modify their own password.** FileMaker lets you implement some typical password management features. First, you get to decide if someone can change his account password at all. If you want to give him this power, then turn this option on. Once it's on, you can choose "Must be changed every", and then enter a number of days to force him to change his password periodically. You can also enforce a minimum password length.

Note: You want to turn this option off if people *share* accounts in the same database. If you have just one account for each group, for instance, then you don't want one wisenheimer changing the password on everybody else just for laughs.

- **Available menu commands.** Menu commands that users don't have privileges for are always unavailable, so this setting controls the ones you don't control elsewhere in the Edit Privilege Set window. The three levels of available menu commands are: Minimum, Editing Only, and All. Minimum is the most restrictive and it's the automatic setting for new privilege sets. Choose "Editing only" to give people access only to the Edit menu and basic formatting commands in Browse mode. "All" makes all commands that aren't covered by other settings in this window available.

Warning: Even though new accounts start with "Minimum" menu commands, the default accounts have "All" menu commands available. Since you can't change this setting, you may want to reconsider using the built-in privilege sets for this reason alone.

Creating a privilege set

In this chapter you'll start adding security to your database by creating a privilege set in your Invoice Security database for Project Managers. PMs set up jobs and create invoices for those jobs, so you'll design a privilege set with appropriate privileges. Since so many steps are involved, this exercise spans several sections.

Note: This chapter has three sample files available on this book's Missing CD page at *www.missingmanuals.com/cds*. Use the file called Invoices Security for this and the following exercises. The files called Access and No Access are for the File Access section later in this chapter.

1. **In the Invoices Security file, choose File→Manage Security. Switch to the Privilege Sets tab, and then click New.**

   The Edit Privilege Set dialog box (Figure 18-3) appears.

2. **In the Privilege Set Name box, type *Project Manager*, and in the Description box, type *create and edit jobs, create new invoices*.**

   If the privilege set name matches the department name or personnel role, it's a lot easier to apply it later on when you're creating accounts. Use the description to help you remember the basic rules for the set.

3. **Select these checkboxes:**

   - Allow printing

   - Allow user to override data validation warnings

   - Disconnect user from FileMaker Server when idle

   - Allow user to modify their own password

4. **Set the "Available menu commands" pop-up menu to "Editing only".**

   People can't get into trouble exploring if they can't even open dialog boxes that are above their pay grades.

That's it for the Other Privileges part of the dialog box. But if you leave the Project Manager privilege set with these settings, people can't do anything very useful. Next, you'll look at the section where all the granularity is hiding, so you can start adding real privileges to the list. Leave the Edit Privilege Set window open while you read through the introductory material below. The next tutorial takes up where the last one left off.

Note: You may have noticed there's no checkbox for "Allow user to manage the database", or "Allow user to create tables". Only accounts with full access can open the Manage Database window and use its features. The same goes for the Security window's Accounts and Privilege Sets tabs.

Data Access and Design privileges

The Edit Privilege Set dialog box's "Data Access and Design" section is where you control access to your specific database elements. Records, Layouts, Value Lists, and Scripts each have pop-up menus where you'll set those privileges. Right now, the Project Manager privilege set doesn't allow access to any of these. To start adding privileges, click the Records pop-up menu. Figure 18-4 shows all your choices.

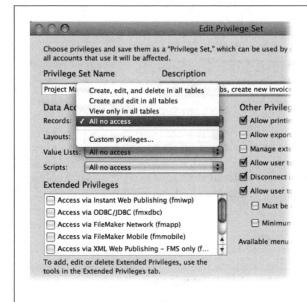

Figure 18-4:
Here you see the Records pop-up menu in the Edit Privilege Set window. Like privilege sets themselves, you get a few canned choices, the default no access option and a custom privileges dialog box. Often, one of the canned choices work just fine, but for the utmost control–like letting people see only the records they've created themselves–you have to dive into custom privileges.

Record privileges. If the three built-in privilege sets form the first level of granularity in the security system, then the options in this pop-up menu are part of the *second* level. Without much fuss, you can pick one of the accurately named prebuilt options:

- **Create, edit, and delete in all tables** is the level you're accustomed to. People can do anything they want with the records—including delete them all.

- **Create and edit in all tables** is almost as good. It just prevents people from *deleting* records.

- **View only in all tables** is for the folks who just browse your data. They can *see* anything they want, but they can't *change* anything.

- If, for some reason, you want to give somebody access to your *database* but not your *data*, then keep **All no access** selected. This option isn't commonly used, though.

Each of these options applies to *every* record in *every* table. But you may want to let some people "Create, edit, and delete" only in *some* tables, and let them "View only" in others. For instance, you can let part-timers create new customer records, but not tamper with the Expenses table. For that kind of control, choose "Custom privilege" (Figure 18-5).

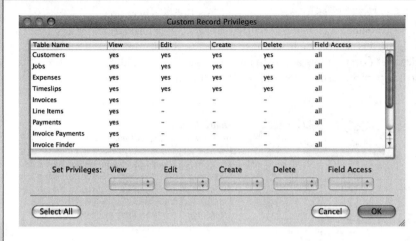

Figure 18-5:
Now you're starting to see some real granularity. The Custom Record Privileges window lets you control view, edit, create, and delete privileges on each individual table. You can also control exactly which fields people have access to by choosing options from the Field Access pop-up menu.

To modify privileges for a particular table, you first have to select it. But don't waste time: You can select *several* tables if you want to, and then modify the settings for all of them at once. FileMaker even gives you a Select All button so you can easily make a change to *every* table.

For the Project Manager privilege set, you want to give *at least* View access to every table. PMs should be able to create, edit and delete records in the Customers, Jobs, Expenses, and Timeslips tables. Here's how to set that up:

1. **From the Records pop-up menu (under "Data Access and Design"), choose Custom privileges, and then click Select All.**

   FileMaker selects every table in the list. You can apply the same privilege to them all at one time.

2. **From the View pop-up menu, choose yes.**

   In the View column the word "yes" appears for every table. Accounts with the Project Manager privilege set can see data in every table in the file.

3. **From the Field Access pop-up menu, choose "all".**

   The word "all" appears in the Field Access column. Now project managers can see the contents of every field in all of the tables.

4. **Click the list to deselect the group. Click the Customers table, and then press Shift and click Timeslips.**

   Shift-clicking selects a continuous range of items in a list. You can select a non-contiguous list by Alt-click (⌘-click).

5. **With all four tables selected, choose "yes" for each of the Edit, Create, and Delete pop-up menus.**

   Your settings should match Figure 18-5. You'll add more granularity to these settings in the next section, so leave the window open for now.

Note: The list starts out sorted into creation order. Clicking the column headings in the Custom Record Privileges dialog box re-sorts the list. Click the column heading a second time to switch the sort between ascending and descending order. The column head stays highlighted to remind you which sort is in effect.

Creating record-level access

Invoice privileges are a little more complicated. You want project managers to be able to create invoices, but invoices involve multiple tables and processes, which you have to translate into a set of privileges. They need to create invoice records, of course, but they also need to be able to create line item records. And once they've added items to an invoice, they should also be able to edit those items. You decide, however, that they *shouldn't* be able to edit items on invoices from last year. In fact, they probably shouldn't change any invoice that doesn't have today's date. You can handle even a complicated security requirement like this easily in FileMaker: Just add a simple calculation to the mix.

To limit access to individual records, FileMaker lets you use a calculation to decide which ones people can edit. This calculation gives you tremendous control over the security system. You can use data from the record itself, information about the current date, time, or account name, and even global field or global variable values. Your calculation must return a Boolean result: True if the record should be editable, and False if it shouldn't.

Here are the steps to set up the invoice privileges described above:

1. **In the Custom Record Privileges window, select the Invoices table. Then, from the Create pop-up menu, choose Yes.**

   FileMaker puts "yes" in the Create column, meaning that managers with this privilege set can create invoice records. From here on, things get more complicated.

2. **From the Edit pop-up menu, choose "limited".**

   You don't want the person to be able to edit *any* invoice record. Instead, you're giving her *limited* edit privileges. Your old friend, the Specify Calculation window, appears.

3. **In the Calculation box, enter *Date ≥ Get (CurrentDate)*.**

   This calculation returns a true result when the invoice date is on or after the current date. It's false for invoices dated before today, so FileMaker lets project managers edit today's invoices or those with a future date.

Note: This security calculation has a significant weakness: Someone can simply change the date on his computer, and bypass the restriction. Luckily, in most cases, a secured multiuser database is shared with FileMaker Server (Chapter 17). When that's the case, you can use a more robust calculation: *Date ≥ GetAsDate (Get (CurrentHostTimeStamp))*. The *Get (CurrentHostTimeStamp)* function gets the date and time from the server computer. Since you, or your IT folks, control this computer, ordinary people can't fiddle with its clock.

4. **Select the entire calculation, choose Edit→Copy, and then click OK to close the Specify Calculation window.**

   You've copied the calculation so that you can paste it into another privilege calculation. The word "limited" shows in the Edit column for Invoices.

5. **From the Delete pop-up menu, choose Limited.**

   The Specify Calculation window returns. This time, you're going to limit the managers' ability to delete invoice records. The rule is the same: They can delete only *today's* invoices.

6. **Choose Edit→Paste to use the calculation from step 3 here.**

   FileMaker adds the calculation to the Calculation box. Click OK when you're done.

7. **Repeat the above steps for the Line Items table. In this case, though, you want to let managers edit or delete line items when the invoice they're attached to contains today's date. So use the following in steps 3 and 6:**
   ```
   Invoices::Date ≥ Get ( CurrentDate )
   ```
   Project managers at your company have no business creating or editing payments or products, so you can leave Edit, Create, and Delete set to "no" for Invoice Payments, Payments, and Products. You'll add more granularity to these settings in the next section, so leave the window open for now.

Note: FileMaker shows a "–" instead of the word "no" when you turn off a privilege. The dashes make the denied privileges easier to spot when you're looking at a long list.

Field-level access. The Payments table has a field for Credit Card Number. This type of information falls into the *need-to-know* category: Unless someone *needs* it to do his job, he has no business seeing it. Even though project managers can view payment records, you can still control access to individual *fields* in that table. You're about to exercise field-level granularity:

1. **Select the Payments table, and then, from the Field Access pop-up menu, choose limited.**

   The Custom Field Privileges window appears (Figure 18-6). FileMaker offers three field-level privileges: *modifiable* means people can see *and* edit the field data; *view only* means they can see the information in the field, but can't change it; and *no access* means they can't even see it.

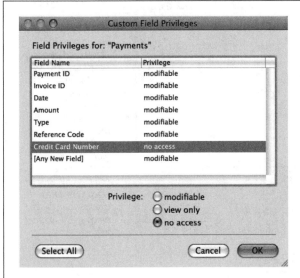

Figure 18-6:
The Custom Field Privileges window lets you control access to individual fields. Select the fields you want to change, and then select one of the Privilege radio buttons. FileMaker dutifully changes every selected field accordingly. Click Select All to quickly select every field.

2. **Click the Credit Card Number field to select it, and then choose the "no access" radio button.**

    And indeed, the words "no access" appear in the Privilege column for the selected fields.

3. **Click OK.**

    The Custom Field Privileges window closes and you can see that Field Access is now limited. Leave the Edit Privilege Set window open; you'll be adding more privileges in the next section.

Note: Even though the other fields in this list say "modifiable", the entire record isn't editable for this privilege set, so people can't change field data. The table-level security settings trump those at the field level.

The Invoice Finder table has only global fields, so it doesn't need records at all. But you still have to turn on the Edit privilege so the managers can change values in the global fields. Select it, and then, from the Edit pop-up menu, choose "yes". When you're finished, your Custom Record Privileges dialog box should look like the one in Figure 18-7.

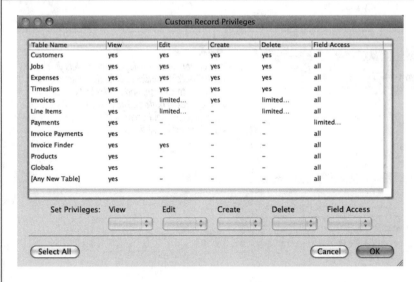

Figure 18-7:
Project managers have wide-open access to some tables, limited access to others, and view-only access to a few. Notice that if you create a new table, then PMs can view data in all its fields, but they can't edit, create or delete records. If that's not what you want, you need to edit this privilege set when your database changes. See the box on page 776 for more info.

When you're done looking, click OK to close this dialog box. Because you just made a set of complex choices, FileMaker sums up everything you just did by displaying "Custom privileges" in the Records pop-up menu in the "Data Access and Design" section of the Edit Privilege Set dialog box. To review or edit the record-level or field-level access you've set, in the Records pop-up menu, click "Custom privileges" again.

Layout privileges. If you've been following along in this section, you've given Project Managers access to data that lets them do their jobs. But if you stop now, then they still can't get very far. They don't have access to any *layouts* yet, and without layouts, a FileMaker database isn't of much use. If someone were to open the database with this privilege set now, she'd see something like Figure 18-8.

FileMaker uses layouts to display your file's data, which means you need to add layout access to your privilege sets. To give people all-important access to the various database layouts, use the Edit Privilege Set window's Layouts pop-up menu:

- **All modifiable** means people can use *and* edit every layout. (Here, "edit" means "add fields, delete portals, resize parts, and generally manipulate objects on layouts.")

- **All view only** gives people access to data on every layout, but doesn't let them change the layouts themselves.

- **All no access** prevents *any* layouts from showing, as shown in Figure 18-8.

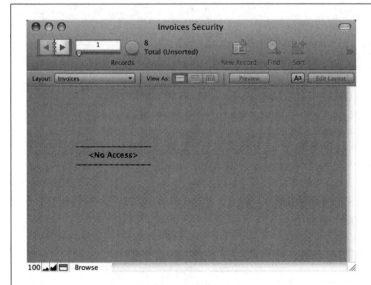

Figure 18-8:
When people try to view a layout they don't have access to, this blank screen is what they see. FileMaker tries hard to avoid this situation, though; if you haven't already removed the layouts the user can't access from the Layouts pop-up menu, it removes them for you. But your scripts can still put users somewhere they don't belong. And in this case, they don't have access to any layout, so FileMaker doesn't have much choice but to show this message.

The final option—Custom Privilege—lets you exercise the greatest control over access to specific layouts. Since layouts are a vehicle for the other database items *on* the layout, you have two distinct layers of privilege:

- **Layout.** These privileges control people's ability to view or edit the layout itself. They're basically the same as the All layout privileges described above, but they apply only to the selected layout. Choose *modifiable* if you want to let people edit the layout (enter Layout mode, and then move fields and things around), *view only* if you want them to only see it, and *no access* if you want them to see that gray screen that prompts tech support calls in Figure 18-8 instead.

- **Records via this layout.** Use this option to determine whether or not people should be able to see or edit data in fields on a particular layout. If you make records from the Customer layout "view only", then users can still edit them from the Customer List layout.

Note: If you want to prevent editing of customer data altogether, it makes more sense to use the record-level privileges instead. The "Records via this layout" setting is available just in case you want to restrict editing from one particular layout, even though the data in the table can be edited elsewhere.

UP TO SPEED

Any New Anything

The list in each Custom Privileges window has an unusual last item: [Any New Field], [Any New Table], [Any New Value List] and [Any New Script]. These privileges refer to any of those elements you create after the privilege set is created and they all start out turned to "no access." That's right—any new layout, value list or script you create is automatically unavailable to users with accounts tied to these privilege sets.

Administering security is an ongoing process, and this setting means that you can add a new feature that works perfectly well for you, but not for users whose custom privilege settings haven't been opened up for those new elements. So each time you add an element to your database, remember to select the appropriate custom options for the new element in every privilege set in your database. Yep, it's time-consuming, and you may be tempted to crank those [Any new] privileges up, thinking it'll save work. Often, though, those settings give users *too* many privileges, and it'll come back to bite you later.

Also, there's a downside to using the Select All button to make changes in the custom privileges windows—that button selects the [Any New…] item as well as the "real" items

in the list. So if you use the Select All button, you may also need to manually deselect the [Any New] item before you make changes.

Would you ever want to turn these options on intentionally? Maybe. It's fairly common to let users create new value lists, but you have to give them editing privileges on some layouts to apply their new list to a field. You might also create a privilege set for users who are allowed to create report layouts. In that case, you'll need to turn on the "Allow creation of new layouts" option at the top of the Custom Layout Privileges window, along with letting those users to modify any new layouts, which includes your new layouts. You'll also have to make sure that have access to All menu commands, so they can enter layout mode and create new layouts.

But take care when considering whether to give users privileges to create and edit scripts, which is only safe when people know what they're doing. Remember, you can let users create and edit new elements, but still keep them from editing *your* elements by setting their custom privileges to "view only."

Figure 18-9 shows the Custom Layout Privileges dialog box. This window has something else that didn't exist on the Custom Record Privileges dialog box: The "Allow creation of new layouts" checkbox lets you decide if these people can create their own new layouts. In fact, you can let people who can't even add or edit data create layouts. For example, you might have a whole class of people—the Accounting Department, say—who shouldn't be editing customer records or adding product information, but who need to create monthly and annual reports (read: layouts) *from* that data. See the box above for more info.

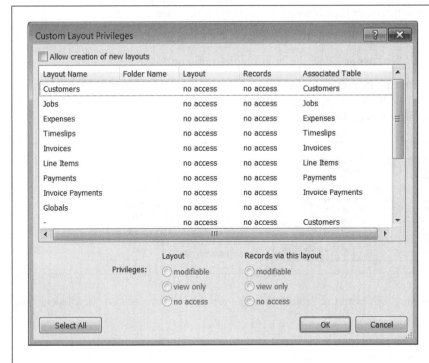

Figure 18-9:
The Custom Layout Privileges window looks a lot like its records counterpart. You get a list of layouts and some privilege choices. Fortunately, you have fewer things to do here, and thus fewer things to learn. As usual, select the layout (or layouts) first, and then make changes. This window's columns can help you set up privileges. For example, you may have hundreds of layouts, and a layout's name alone isn't enough, seeing the layout folder name (page 285) can help you remember which layout you're looking at.

In the current example, you want Project Managers to be able to use any layout (and edit records through them). But you also want them to be able to create their own layouts in case they need to do some custom reporting. These new layouts should, of course, be editable.

1. **In the Edit Privilege Set window, choose "All view only" from the Layouts pop-up menu.**

   You intend to make custom privilege settings, but when you first visit the Custom Layout Privileges dialog box, everything is turned off. Since you want most options on, save your wrist by choosing "All view only". FileMaker turns them all on for you. In the next step, you'll just turn a few options off.

2. **From the Layouts pop-up menu, choose "Custom privileges".**

   The Custom Layout Privileges window appears. Every layout, including the [Any New Layout] item, is set to "view only" with "modifiable" records.

3. **At the top of the window, select on "Allow creation of new layouts", and then, in the layout list, select the [Any New Layout] item.**

   You may have to scroll down to see it, as it's always at the bottom of the list.

4. **Under Layout, select the "modifiable" radio button.**

   Turning this setting on tells FileMaker you want new layouts to be modifiable. Click OK when you're done. See Figure 18-10 to see the warning you'll get if you forget this option.

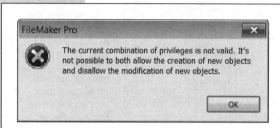

Figure 18-10:
If you select "Allow creation of new layouts" without making new layouts modifiable, then FileMaker complains that it doesn't make sense to let someone make a new layout she can't edit. You can't close the window until the privileges do match one another. Either turn off "Allow creation of new layouts" or make [Any New Layout] modifiable.

Now, anybody with the Project Manager privilege set can edit any new layouts she creates.

Value list privileges. Value lists may not seem as critical a security choice as records and layouts, but since value lists help people enter consistent data, you want to pay attention to these choices. If you put a pop-up menu on a field to limit data input, but then you give those same people the ability to modify the value list underlying the pop-up menu, then they have a way to circumvent your control.

You can see the Custom Value List Privileges window in Figure 18-11. This window lets you assign any of three privileges to each value list: modifiable, view only, or no access. You can also let somebody create new value lists with an "Allow creation of new value lists" checkbox, and set the privileges to be assigned to any new value lists.

You can control access to value lists in much the same way you manage record and layout privileges. And like record and layout privileges, you have three canned choices in the pop-up menu, plus Custom privileges:

- **All modifiable** means people can use and edit every value list.

- **All view** lets people only see and select from your value lists, but not change them.

- **All no access** prevents people from seeing value lists at all.

- **Custom privileges** gives you a dialog box where you can create your own set of privileges.

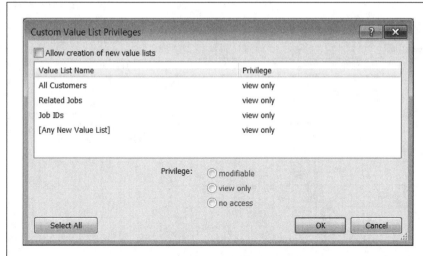

Figure 18-11:
The Custom Value List Privileges window is even simpler than the Custom Layout Privileges version. It works just like the others: Select a value list or two, and then choose a privilege as appropriate.

In the business rules you're applying to your database, project managers should have view-only access to all value lists, so, from the Value Lists pop-up menu, choose "All view only".

Note: If you select all value lists in the dialog box, and then make them "view only" there, then your settings say "Custom privileges", which may be confusing down the road.

The Value List access you assign to a privilege set overrides layout designs. That is, even if you set up a pop-up menu with the option of "Include 'Edit' item to allow editing of value list", then people with the Project Manager's privilege set can't edit values in the list.

Script privileges. The final option under "Data Access and Design" lets you control access to your scripts. As with layouts, you can have a class of people who can create new scripts, but can't edit data. If it's the accountants mentioned in the example on page 776, they need to write scripts to run the reports on the layouts you're letting them create. You could also create a privilege set that lets people at one level run most scripts, but doesn't let them run certain scripts that do destructive activities like deleting sets of records. You could save those scripts for higher-level people instead. Figure 18-12 shows the control choices you have.

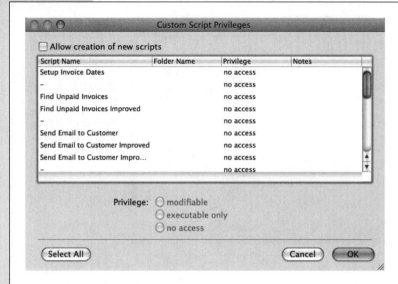

Figure 18-12:
The Folder Name column refers to the organizer folders you can create in the Manage Script window (page 416). The Notes column tells you when a script is set to "Run with full access privileges". You'll learn about this later in this chapter.

Again, the pop-up menu gives you three canned choices and a custom option:

- **All modifiable** means people can run *and* edit any script.
- **All executable** only lets folks *run* scripts, but not edit them.
- **All no access** keeps people from running any scripts at all.
- **Custom Privileges** brings up the now-familiar Custom Privileges dialog box.

Here's how to do the final settings for your Project Manager privilege set:

1. **From the Scripts pop-up menu, choose "All executable only".**

   With this change, you've finished creating your privilege set. Your window should look just like Figure 18-13.

2. **Click OK to close the Edit Privilege Set window.**

   FileMaker adds Project Manager to the list of privilege sets in the Manage Security window.

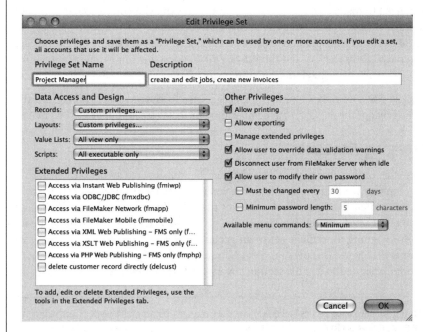

Figure 18-13:
When your privilege set is finished, it looks like this. You have so much detail there that you can't see all your settings in one screen, but the "..." in the Records and Layouts pop-up menus lets you know there's more detail to be seen if you need it. Just choose the appropriate pop-up menu if you need to review or edit.

You're done creating the Project Manager privilege set. In the past few tutorials, you created all the set's privileges. But you don't have to create everything in the same session. At any time, you can click OK to close all the Security windows, and then return to regular work. FileMaker will remember the settings you have chosen, and then you can resume setting up options later. But when you click OK to close the Manage Security window, you'll have to enter an account and password that has [Full Access] privileges. Since you haven't changed that account yet, use "Admin" as the Account name and leave the password field blank—that's the not-so-secret Admin account and password in every file. Or read page 176 to learn how to change the default account.

Note: When you give an element—a record, field, layout, value list, or script—the "All no access" setting, it disappears from the user's view. Scripts disappear from the Scripts menu, layouts from the Layouts pop-up menu, fields from sort dialog boxes, and records from lists and portals. People aren't tempted to run a script or go to a layout to which they don't have access.

Editing a privilege set

If you need to make changes to a privilege set later (maybe you've added new fields, layouts or scripts to the database, and you have to make sure all your privilege sets give each group its proper access), just come back to this window, select the privilege set you need form the list, and then click Edit. You see the Edit Privilege Set window again, and you're free to change anything you want.

You can't edit FileMaker's built-in privilege sets. To change a set, duplicate it first, and then change the duplicate. Remember, though, that you can't duplicate [Full Access].

Managing Accounts

At the start of this chapter, you learned that FileMaker security has two facets: *who* can get in and *what* they can do. So far, you've created a privilege set called Project Manager, which handles the *what* part of the security equation. But a privilege set has no effect until you tell FileMaker who gets those privileges. You handle the *who* part by assigning a privilege set to an account. As you can see in the Manage Accounts & Privileges window's Privilege Sets tab, your new privilege set has no "Active accounts" assigned to it. This section covers creating and managing accounts.

Note: You can have privilege sets that don't have active accounts, but you can't create an account without assigning a privilege set to it, which is why most developers start out by creating privilege sets before they create accounts.

The Manage Security window's Accounts tab (Figure 18-14) shows you all the accounts in your database. You never knew it, but all this time you've been using an account called Admin. FileMaker added this account when you first created your database so you'd have full access to the file without a password (see the box on page 785 for more info on this account). Unfortunately, the rest of the FileMaking world knows this little "secret" too. So your first job is to edit the Admin account.

1. **In the Manage Security window's Accounts tab, click the admin account to select it, and then click Edit (or double-click the Admin account).**

   The Edit Account window appears (Figure 18-15).

2. **In the Account Name window, type your first initial and last name.**

   That's a common Account name scheme. But Account names must be unique, so if you have a John Smith and a Jane Smith, somebody needs to use a middle initial or some other letters to make the Account Name unique.

3. **In the Password field, type any password.**

   Passwords can take any mix of alphanumeric characters and uppercase and lowercase characters you like.

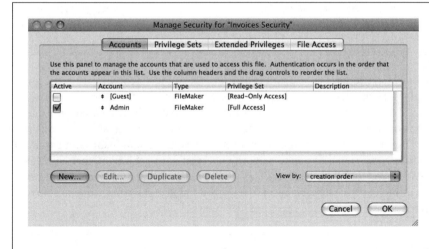

Figure 18-14:
The Accounts tab works a lot like the Privilege Sets tab. Click New to make a new account, or select an existing account, and then click Edit to change it. You can also duplicate or delete the selected account. Every account has an Active checkbox, an Account name, a type, an assigned privilege set, and an optional description.

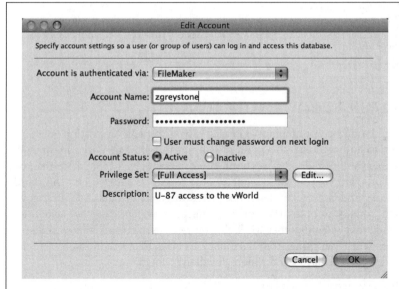

Figure 18-15:
The Edit Account window needs just three things: an account name, a password and a privilege set. You can ignore the "Account is authenticated via" pop-up menu for now. Optionally, you can make an account inactive (but that's not common when you've just created it) or add a short description to help you remember who the account belongs to.

4. **Click OK until all dialog boxes are closed.**

   When you click OK to close the Manage Security Window, FileMaker requires you to enter the new account name and password you just created. Click OK when you've done so. Now that you've assigned a password to the Admin account, the next time you open this file, FileMaker asks you for an account name and password.

Notes: Account names aren't case-sensitive, but passwords are. If the Account Name or the password includes spaces, then make sure you type them precisely or you can't log in. FileMaker gives you five chances to log in, and then it stops showing you the login dialog box. But you aren't blocked permanently. You can try again right away.

You don't have to have an account called Admin, so most people avoid the security risk and change that default account name right away. On the other hand, you *are* required to have an account with full access. If you try to close the Manage Security dialog box without one, then FileMaker will show a warning. Finally, each time you click OK, FileMaker wants to make sure you know an account name and password with full access, so it asks you to enter them. If you don't get it right, then FileMaker doesn't let you save your changes. This password box is the final layer of protection from losing your file forever, because once you forget a password, you have no way to retrieve it.

Warning: Make sure you don't forget your Full Access password. FileMaker uses industry-standard and ultra-secure techniques to manage passwords, you simply have no way to bypass them. FileMaker, Inc. may be willing to change the password in the file, but the process takes several weeks and isn't guaranteed. Also, some third-party hacks out there can promise to change your passwords for you, but steer clear of them. If you forget a more restricted password, on the other hand, then the fix is simple. Just open the database with a Full Access password, visit the Manage Accounts & Privileges dialog box, and then change the forgotten password.

Adding a New Account

You can add a new account almost as easily as you can edit an existing one. Since it's so easy to add accounts, there's no reason not to follow best security practices and give everyone an individual account. You can even give people more than one account. For example, you can designate some people as super-users who mostly do data entry and editing but sometimes need to create layouts. As much as you trust them, you just want to make sure they don't inadvertently damage layouts and scripts while they're doing other work. So you require them to log in with higher-level access when switching from data entry to tasks that require more care, like database design. (See page 797 for more detail on re-login.)

To create a new account, click New. In the Edit Account window, give the account a name and a password, and assign a privilege set. If you don't see a suitable privilege set, from the Privilege Set pop-up menu, choose New Privilege Set. You can also edit the selected privilege set by clicking Edit.

If you let each person manage his or her own password, then you can turn on "User must change password on next login". When you turn this option on, you can create an account for someone with a generic password, and then email the account information to her, with instructions to create a more secure and secret password when she first opens the database.

Note: If a user forgets his password, you can't retrieve it for him because FileMaker masks it as soon as you click OK in the Edit Account dialog box. You can *change* his password, though, so long as you have an account with full access to the file.

FREQUENTLY ASKED QUESTION

Automatic Login

If I've been using the Admin account all this time, how come FileMaker never asked me to log in? Does it just skip the authentication dialog box when some account has no password?

Actually, FileMaker's been logging in for you. Every new database is set up to log in automatically using the Admin account and a blank password. Once you give the Admin account a password for a given database, automatic login stops. But you can set your database to log in with any account automatically, or you can turn off automatic login entirely, which is a much more secure option.

The setting is behind the File→File Options command. When you choose this command, you see the File Options dialog box. Turn off the "Log in using" checkbox to stop the automatic login process. Or, you can type a different account and password in the appropriate box to log in with another account. Finally, you can have FileMaker automatically log into the file using the guest account (see the box on page 786).

If you set your file to automatically log in with an account that doesn't have full access, including the guest account, then you can't come back to this window to turn it off. You may think you've just locked yourself out of your file completely, but you haven't. If you hold down the Shift key (Option key on a Mac) while a file opens, then FileMaker asks you for an account name and password even if the file's set to automatically log in.

You can also make an account inactive. When you do, FileMaker keeps the account—and all its information—in the Accounts list, but it doesn't let people open the database using that account. For example, you can make an account inactive if someone leaves the company for an extended period of time, but plans to return. That way, you can easily reactivate the account when you need to. You can also use this option to create accounts for new employees before they start.

UP TO SPEED

The Guest Account

FileMaker has one built-in account called [Guest] that you can't rename or delete. Normally it's assigned to the [Read-Only Access] privilege set, but you can change it to any privilege set you want. The [Guest] account is also normally *inactive*. In other words, it exists, but doesn't work until you turn it on.

If you want to let some people access your database even if they don't have an account, activate the guest account by turning on the checkbox by its name. (Or you can bring

up the Edit Account dialog box and, in the Account Status option, choose "Active", but that's more steps.) When the guest account is turned on, the normal Log In dialog box includes a Guest Account radio button.

Someone can choose this option, and then click OK without entering an account name or a password. FileMaker gives her access according to the privilege set you assigned to the guest account.

Testing your new account

Creating smart security involves so many options and settings that it makes sense to test each new account and privilege set you create. And because password characters are masked as you type, you can't tell if you made a typo while creating it. So get in the habit of testing by creating a new account and assign it to the Project Manager privilege set. Then close and reopen the file. When prompted, enter the new account name and password. Now experiment. Try modifying or deleting old invoices, or editing product records. You should see your new security settings in action. When you're done, close the file again, and then open it one more time. This time use the Admin account to log in.

Tip: Write a script that lets you log in with a new account without opening and closing a file (page 797). You can even run Script Debugger (page 513) while you're testing a low-access account, but you'll have to enter a full access account name and password before you can see the debugger in action.

External Authentication

If you work for an organization that uses Windows Active Directory or Open Directory in Mac OS X, then you can take advantage of the fact that your coworkers *already* log in to their computers each morning. Since everybody already has a company-wide user name and password, you can use *external authentication*, which tells FileMaker to hand off the chore of identifying people. This setup has two advantages. First, you can save yourself the trouble of creating scads of accounts in all your database files. And when your IT department creates a new user, or removes someone who's left the company, access to FileMaker is automatically adjusted as well. Additionally, on Windows your users can take advantage of Single Sign-on: They don't have to enter a password to access FileMaker if they already logged in to their computer with their own user names and passwords.

Note: On Mac OS X, the system-wide Keychain handles automatic login for FileMaker just like every other program. You don't need to use external authentication to speed past the password dialog box. Just click "Add to keychain" the first time you log in instead.

Since these external accounts aren't actually stored in FileMaker, you don't need to add the accounts themselves to your database. Instead, you tell FileMaker which *groups* in the external system should be granted access. For example, if your Windows Active Directory already has a group for Accounting and another for Customer Service, you can tell FileMaker what privileges people in each of these groups have.

If you don't have appropriate groups in the external system, then you can have the system administrator add a new group (or several new groups) just for you. You can then assign a privilege set to each group that should be given access, and the system administrator assigns individual people to each group.

To assign a privilege set to an external group, you create a single account in File-Maker. But instead of entering a user name and password, from the "Account is authenticated via" pop-up menu, choose External Server. The Account Name and Password boxes disappear, and a new Group Name box appears instead. Just type the name of the Active Directory or Open Directory group in this box.

You can set up external authentication in two ways, but both require a working directory server and FileMaker Server (see Chapter 17):

- **Local accounts on your FileMaker server.** You can   manage account names and passwords on the server itself, and have them apply to every database. This method saves you the trouble of creating individual FileMaker accounts in every file.

- **Domain accounts.** FileMaker Server communicates with the directory server on your company's network to authenticate users. This approach centralizes account management *and* lets people log in with the same account names and passwords they use for every other computer system on your network.

Both methods require coordination with your IT department. Consult IT (or the documentation for your directory server) for more information on setting up and maintaining external authentication.

Note: You're free to use a mixture of normal FileMaker accounts and external authentication accounts. In fact, you *must* have at least one full access FileMaker account in every file. If you need to extend access to someone who's not in the directory server, then you can add a FileMaker account for that person, too. People from the directory server can log in, and so can this special person.

Extended Privileges

Extended privileges come in two flavors. A set of standard extended privileges lets you determine how people are allowed to interact with shared databases. These privileges control how your database works with other FileMaker products (primarily FileMaker Server), as covered in Chapter 17. But the short version is that if you want users to be allowed to open a database that's shared on FileMaker Server, you have to select [fmapp] extended privilege. Turn the appropriate extended privileges on in the Extended Privileges section of the Edit Privilege Set window.

Tip: Forgetting to turn this extended privilege on is the most common reason users can't see a shared database when you *can* see FileMaker Server on the network.

You can also create custom extended privileges of your own, using the Extended Privileges tab of the Manage Security dialog box. These custom extended privileges don't actually add any capability on their own. But using scripts, you can check to see whether the active privilege set has an extended privilege before you let anyone do anything important or irreversible. The next section takes you through one example.

Creating an Extended Privilege

Suppose you've decided to let project managers delete records directly, and you give them that power in their privilege set. When other people try to delete a customer record, you want FileMaker to *flag* the record instead, so that a manager can find and delete the flagged records later. To automate the process, you write a Delete script, that checks for the new extended privilege before deleting the records. Here's how to set up the extended privileges so you can use them in the script.

1. **Open the Manage Security window, click the Extended Privileges tab, and then click New.**

    You see the Edit Extended Privilege window on your screen (Figure 18-16). This extended privilege controls a user's ability to delete customer records.

2. **Type *Delete customer records directly* in the Description box. For the keyword, enter *delcust* as an abbreviation. While you're here, turn on the checkbox next to [Full Access].**

    For now, only those people with full access can delete customer records. You'll write and test an extended privileges-checking script before you add the extended privilege to the Project Manager privilege set.

3. **Click OK to close all dialog boxes.**

    You aren't prompted for Full Access credentials because you didn't edit any accounts.

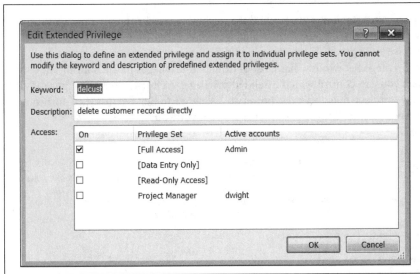

Figure 18-16:
The Edit Extended Privilege window lets you give your extended privilege a keyword and a description. The description should say what the extended privilege is for. The keyword can be anything you want; it's what you'll look for in your scripts, so if you change it later, the script may break. Activate an extended privilege by clicking the checkboxes.

Checking for an Extended Privilege

Now you need to write your script. Use the *Get (CurrentExtendedPrivileges)* function to ask FileMaker for the list of extended privileges turned on for the active privilege set (in other words, the privilege set assigned to the account name the user opened the file with). The script checks to see if this list includes "delcust", and takes the appropriate action. While creating this script, you need to add a new text field called DeleteFlag to the Customers table. You can see the finished script in Figure 18-17.

Try out your script by running it from the Customers layout. Your [Full Access] account should delete the customer record, since you have the [Full Access] privilege set. Close the database, and then open it again. This time, log in as someone assigned the Project Manager privilege set. Project Manager *doesn't* have the "delcust" extended privilege turned on, so when you run the script this time, it sets the DeleteFlag field instead of deleting the record.

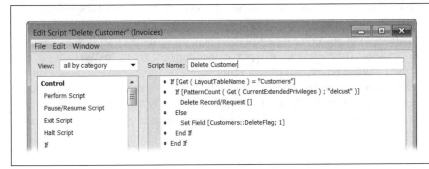

Figure 18-17:
The script checks context before running. If the context is right, it tests for the "delcust" extended privilege to decide what to do.

Assigning Extended Privileges

You have an extended privilege and the script that checks the privilege works properly. The final step gives project managers the ability to delete customers directly. You have two options: First, you can edit the Project Manager privilege set itself. The Edit Privilege Set window has a list of extended privileges in the bottom-left corner where you can control which extended privileges are turned on (see Figure 18-18). To give project managers the power to delete customer records, just turn on the checkbox next to "Delete customer records directly".

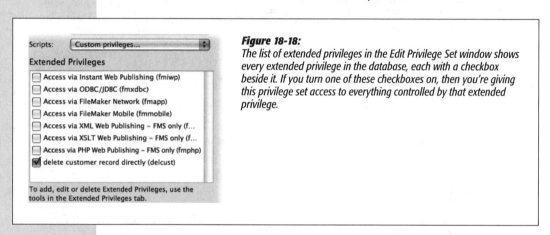

Figure 18-18:
The list of extended privileges in the Edit Privilege Set window shows every extended privilege in the database, each with a checkbox beside it. If you turn one of these checkboxes on, then you're giving this privilege set access to everything controlled by that extended privilege.

If you have a few privilege sets that need the same extended privilege, there's a faster method: Go to the Manage Security window's Extended Privileges tab, and then edit the "delcust" extended privilege instead. This way, you see all the Privilege Sets in a list. In the Edit Extended Privilege window, you can turn the extended privilege off or on for any privilege set by clicking the checkboxes in the list of privilege sets.

To test the "delcust" extended privilege, turn it on for the Project Manager privilege set, and then close the database. Then open it, log in as a project manager, and run the Delete Customer script. This time it deletes the customer right away.

Managing External File Access

FileMaker databases can take table occurrences (TOs) from other files and then use that data almost as if it "lives" in the local file. And some design functions can glean information about your file's data and metadata, even when a user doesn't have full access privileges. To prevent these types of unauthorized access to data, you can create lots of record-level and individual script access privileges to keep those external reference folks from viewing and editing data remotely. Sometimes, even if you do create restrictions in your file, motivated folks using external file references can gain access to your information. So if you have a database that contains sensitive data, you can use FileMaker Pro 11's new File Access protection. It lets you give only certain files access to a protected database.

File Access works by creating a special authorization token as part of the External Date Source. So even if a hacker tries to create a new file with the same name as the one you've authorized, it still won't work.

Warning: This authorization token changes a file's internal format. So when a file is protected, it can only be opened with FileMaker Pro 11 or FileMaker Pro Advanced 11 or later. And only FileMaker Server 11 can *host* a protected file. But if you remove the protection later, the file again becomes accessible with prior versions of FileMaker Pro.

You can't set up File Access protection for a file that's being hosted by FileMaker Server. Instead, open the file on your local computer to protect it, and then put the file back on the server. Also, turning on File Access protection doesn't lock out files that are *already* linked to the file you want to protect, so you have to be the only user of the file when you restrict external access. Finally, to enable File Access protection, you have to have [Full Access] privileges in both the file you want to protect and the file you want to authorize.

Note: For this exercise, start by opening any FileMaker Pro 11 database. You're going to authorize File Access for the Access sample file from this book's Missing CD page (*www.missingmanuals.com/cds*).

Here's how to restrict external access to a file:

1. **In the Invoices Security file, choose File→Manage Security, and then select the File Access tab.**

   Add each external file you want to authorize in this window's list.

2. **Turn on the "Prevent opening with earlier versions (pre-FileMaker 11)" checkbox.**

   Because this option blocks users with earlier versions of FileMaker from opening the file, FileMaker shows a warning and gives you a chance to change your mind.

3. **Click Yes.**

   You have to turn on version restriction before continuing; the rest of the options you need for authorizing specific files aren't available until you do.

Note: It's possible to set version restriction without setting any other options, but that doesn't protect the file.

---

4. **Turn on the "Require full access privileges to create references to this file" checkbox.**

   The Authorize button becomes available.

5. **Click Authorize.**

   A standard open window appears.

6. **Browse to and select the Access sample file you downloaded earlier (that's the one you'll authorize). Then click Open.**

   The file's login window appears.

Note: Use the Remote button if the file you need is shared using FileMaker Server (page 741). You can *authorize* shared files for access to file you're protecting, but you can't activate internal protection for shared files.

---

7. **Enter a [Full Access] Account Name and Password.**

   The Account Name and Password for this sample file are both *access* (not great for security, but suitable for testing). The Account Name and password don't have to match the protected file's Account Name and Password. However, both Accounts need to have [Full Access] to authorize any file. When you enter appropriate account info, the file name, date, and time you authorized the file and the account name you used to authorize it appear in the list (Figure 18-19).

Figure 18-19:
When a file is protected from external access, unauthorized files can't be used to sneak into a file. Without this protection, anyone with access privileges to a file can sneak around older privileges to create external references and use design functions, like ValueListItems() or ScriptNames (), to get metadata about your database.

8. **Click OK and then, when you're prompted, enter a [Full Access] Account Name and Password for the protected file.**

You're done setting up File Access is set up for the Access file.

In a closed system (one where several FileMaker databases working together), you may want to authorize other files in the protected database. Or another file (or set of files) may need its own list of authorized files. You don't have to authorize all the files in a system with one another, though. As with the rest of your security settings, take the pessimistic approach and authorize only the files that specifically need access to protected databases. You can always add more access later.

To test the Invoice database's File Access settings, close it and make sure all its windows are closed. If you open a protected database with a full-access account and then leave it open on your computer, another user could sneak into your office while you're away and authorize a file without knowing the proper account information. So if your databases contain sensitive data, take all normal precautions: close files when you leave your office, lock your door, and so on. And make sure protected files are closed when you're testing access.

Now open a nonauthorized file (use the No Access sample file: Account Name and Password are both "noaccess") and try to create a table occurrence from Invoices Security on No Access's Relationships graph (page 205). You see the standard login dialog box. The only way out of the Specify Table dialog box is to click Cancel or enter a [Full Access] account name and password. If you enter valid information for an account that doesn't have full access, you'll see a warning like the one in Figure 18-20.

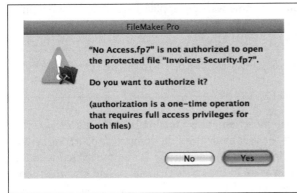

Figure 18-20:
Even if a file is authorized for access to a protected file, you have to enter a full access account name and password before creating a TO from the protected file. You see this warning if you enter an account without full access privileges.

Note: The wording in the File Access dialog box is a little confusing. You can still create an EDS reference (page 592) to a protected file from an unauthorized file without a full access password, but you can't create a TO from it, or use design functions to grab data from the file.

Now open the authorized file (Access.fp7—account name and password are both "access"). Again, enter a [Full Access] password for the Invoice file. This time, enter the account name and password you set up in the steps on page 782. Ta da! Your authorized file can create TOs and then work with the file's external data normally.

Scripts and Security

Security and script writing intersect in two areas. First, you need to take into account the level of access people have, and whether or not your scripts override some or all of their privileges (page 796). Second, FileMaker lets you automate some of the security features described earlier in this chapter with scripting. A handful of script steps are dedicated to security-related tasks, and this section shows you how to use them.

Detecting Privileges in a Script

The first way to handle security in your scripts is to deal with it directly. In the last section you learned how to check for extended privileges and take appropriate actions. If you want, then you can check for specific privilege sets, or even specific account names:

- To check the privilege set, use the *Get (PrivilegeSetName)* function. It returns the name of the privilege set assigned to the current user. Bear in mind that if you change the name of a privilege set, then you have to modify any scripts that use this function.

- If you need to restrict an action to a particular account, then use *Get (Account-Name)* instead. As you probably expect, it returns the name of the account with which the user logged in. The same warning applies here: Beware of renamed accounts.

Note: If someone logged in with external authentication, then *Get (AccountName)* gives you her real account name in the external directory server.

- Finally, FileMaker has one more tempting function: *Get (UserName)*. This function normally returns the user name from the computer's operating system (the name you use to log into the computer itself). If you use shared accounts in FileMaker, then you may want to use the user name to find out who's actually doing something. Bear in mind, though, that most people can change their user name settings to anything they want, so it isn't useful for security-related purposes because it's easy for a user to pretend to be someone else.

You can easily use these functions, but they have some drawbacks. Chances are that, at some point in the future, you'll need to change the account names, privilege sets, or users that can do certain things. Every time you do, you have to check and probably edit all your scripts.

If you want to secure a scripted process, then the extended privilege feature described on page 788 is safer and lets you much more easily update accounts and privilege sets.

Handling Security Errors

If your script tries to do something the person isn't allowed to do, then FileMaker shows the error message in Figure 18-21. If you turn error capture on in your script, then this error doesn't show on the screen. Instead, you can use the *Get (LastError)* function to check for an error (see page 694). That way, you can have the script display a custom message box, email you the name of the misbehaving person, or take some other action. The most common security-related error is number 200: "Record Access is Denied." (If you're interested in learning more about error codes, check out the resources in Appendix B: FileMaker Error Codes.)

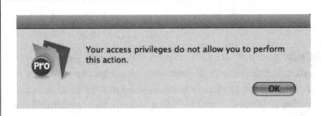

Figure 18-21:
When someone tries something your security setup doesn't allow, he sees this message—even if it's a script that's breaking the rules. Unfortunately, FileMaker doesn't tell him—or you—what the script is trying to do.

Running Scripts with Full Access Privileges

Sometimes you *want* the script to do its duty even though the user doesn't have the necessary privileges. For example, you may want to remove an accountant's ability to delete invoice records since she's not supposed to delete any orders. But you may still want to let her run a script that finds old completed invoices, exports them to an archive, and then deletes them. Since this script is careful to delete only invoices that are ready to go, the accountant can safely run it when necessary.

For those kinds of circumstances, FileMaker lets you specify when a script should run with full access privileges for *anyone*. In other words, the script overrides the normal restrictions you set up in the user's privilege set. At the bottom of the Edit Script dialog box, just turn on the "Run script with full access privileges" option. With this option turned on, the script dutifully deletes the invoices even though the accountant running it isn't allowed to delete records in the Invoice or Line Item tables with her account's privilege set.

Even when you set a script to run with full access privileges in this way, you can still prevent some folks from running it by switching it to "no access" in the Custom Script Privileges window for a privilege set (page 779). You can also make the script check for an extended privilege, and then take appropriate actions for different people.

Note: The *Get (PrivilegeSetName)* and *Get (ExtendedPrivileges)* functions may not give you what you expect if you use them while a script is running with [Full Access] privileges: The user's real privileges don't show up; the functions return [Full Access] info instead. Use *Get (AccountPrivilegeSetName)* and *Get (AccountExtendedPrivileges)* to get info about the account that opened the file.

Managing Security with Scripts

The Edit Script window (page 417) has an entire section called Accounts. It includes six steps that give you some control over the security system from your scripts. All these steps require full access privileges to work. If you don't manage a lot of accounts in your database, then you might not find much use for these steps. But if you have a large organization, or one that has lots of turnover—like a school system that's constantly adding new teachers or graduating a whole class of students who no longer need access to databases for class work—these script steps can save tons of time and effort.

Add Account

FileMaker lets you add new accounts to a database from a script—and for good reason. If you build a system that uses several databases, and you can't use external authentication, then the Add Account step is your best friend. Instead of adding each account to all your files manually, try this: Write a script that asks for the account name and password with a custom dialog box, and stores them in global fields. Then use scripts in each file to add the same account to every file at once. When you're all done, be sure to clear the password from the global field to protect it from prying eyes.

Or, if you have to populate your brand-new file with a huge number of people when you're first installing your database, then you save tons of time creating accounts if you have an electronic list of user names and passwords. Import them (page 826) into a table, and then use a looping script (page 443) to create hundreds of accounts in a few seconds.

Tip: The Add Account step lets you specify the account name and password using calculations, but you have to select a specific privilege set for all users in the loop. If you want to script the creation of accounts with different privilege sets, use the If/Else If steps and several copies of the Add Account step, each with a different privilege set selected.

Delete Account

If you're going to create accounts with a script, why not delete them, too? The Delete Account script needs only an account name—and you can supply it with a calculation. With this script, you can build the other half of your multifile account management system.

Warning: If you write a script that adds or deletes accounts, then pay special attention to its security settings. You can all too easily give a database the tightest security FileMaker allows, and then leave a gaping security hole through a script. Customize privilege sets so that only you (or a trusted few) can run the script, and *don't* put it on the Scripts menu.

Reset Account Password

If lots of people use your database, then forgotten passwords will undoubtedly become your worst nightmare. You could spend all day changing passwords for people. Why not write a script that can reset a password to something generic, and then email it to the person? If you set the script to run with full access privileges, then you can even delegate password resetting to someone else. The Reset Account Password step needs an account name and a new password to do its job.

Change Password

You'll probably use this script step only in cases where you're creating a special layout that lets people who don't have full access privileges manage security. For example, you may have someone on staff who should be able to manage accounts, but you don't want him to have full access privileges. So you can build a special layout (or two), and write scripts that run with full access privileges to manage all your security tasks. That way, you can even do special workarounds like allowing some members of a privilege set to change their passwords without giving this power to each of them. To do so, you usually need a user's table with a field that controls who can and can't run your Change Password script.

Enable Account

Once you've created a bunch of new accounts using the Add Account step, the Enable Account step lets you turn them on and off at will. That way, you can create accounts for, say, an entire class of students, and later turn on accounts for those who've arrived on campus. This step sets the appropriate Account Status, and it works only when there's a valid account name that matches your script settings.

Re-Login

The most exciting step in the Accounts section is Re-Login. It provides a function that doesn't exist anywhere else in FileMaker. It lets you switch to a different account without closing the file, which makes testing security settings a lot more convenient. Instead of opening and closing the files until your mouse button wears out, just run a Re-Login script. Add steps in the script that set global fields on pertinent layouts to *Get (AccountName)* and *Get (PrivilegeSet)* so you can keep track of what you're testing as you re-login over and over. To get the most realistic testing conditions, make sure your Re-login script calls any script that runs when your file opens.

You can also use Re-Login when someone inevitably calls you to his desk to show you a problem in the database. Just re-login as an account with full access, and then you can poke around and find out what's happening *on his computer*. When you re-login, you're not just saving time by not closing and reopening the file: You can actually work in the same window, on the same record, with the same found set and sort order without all the trouble of recreating the situation back at your desk.

Tip: If you have a login script that changes that setup, turn on Script Debugger before you run the Re-Login script. Then skip over the parts of the login script that would change that all-important setup.

Since you can re-login only from a script, most developers add a Re-Login script to the Scripts menu in every database they create.

Sharing Data with Other Systems

Building a big database can make you feel like a slave to your computer, but the point of a database is to let you manage information more efficiently. Nothing shows this point better than FileMaker's ability to pull data into your database from various sources, and dump it back out again in assorted ways.

If you have data in almost any kind of program—spreadsheets full of figures, lists of names and phone numbers, electronic orders in XML, folders full of pictures or text documents—FileMaker can *import* it directly into your database. If your data is already in FileMaker, then you can *export* it to lists, other databases, XML, or almost any other format imaginable. FileMaker takes a wonderfully flexible approach: It lets you handle simple imports and exports with just a click or two, and provides the features to tackle the most complex cases as well—if you (or some hired help) are willing to do the necessary work.

If your company uses one of the vast corporate databases—Oracle, Microsoft SQL Server, or MySQL—FileMaker can integrate directly with them, bringing its powerful (and easy) developer tools to bear on their complex-yet-oh-so-speedy data. You can put your corporate SQL data right on the FileMaker layout, perform FileMaker finds, write scripts, and even add calculation fields, all without writing a single line of SQL code.

Sharing Your Data with Others

Most database systems don't live in a vacuum. Chances are your information is important to someone else, or important to you some*where* else. You may want to transfer job information to your Accounting software, or send the sales report to your associate across town. Luckily, FileMaker provides options for getting the data out of your database in all kinds of forms.

Save/Send Records As

If your data is destined for a person (rather than some other computer program), then you want a format that's easy to look at and to work with on almost any computer. FileMaker lets you save your data in two ubiquitous formats, an Excel spreadsheet and a PDF document, and the unique Snapshot Link. Choose Excel if you want to be able to work with the data (perform analysis, combine it with other data, create graphs, and so forth). If you want the output to look just like it looks in FileMaker, and you don't need it to be editable, then a PDF is the perfect choice. Snapshot links direct other FileMaker users to a particular set of records in your database.

Saving as Microsoft Excel

If people need to work with the data you send them, but they aren't lucky enough to have FileMaker, you can create an Excel file for them. (And presumably, if they're working with data, they have either Excel or a program that can open Excel spreadsheets.) Just choose File→Save/Send Records As→Excel. When you do, FileMaker shows the window in Figure 19-1.

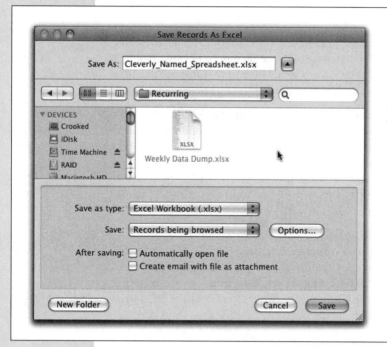

Figure 19-1:
The Save Records As Excel window lets you tell FileMaker where to save the spreadsheet file. It also gives you the option of automatically opening the file you're creating, so you don't have to go rummaging around your hard drive looking for it.

The Save pop-up menu lets you choose whether you want to save all the "Records being browsed" (that is, the found set) or just the "Current record." Turn on "Automatically open file" if you want to see the spreadsheet as soon as FileMaker finishes saving it. When you do, FileMaker automatically launches Excel and shows you the spreadsheet. You also have the option to "Create email with file as attachment," so it's easy to check your work and create a quick email with the data your boss just asked you to email her. Once you save, FileMaker creates a new email message in your email program, attaches the spreadsheet, and opens the message so you can add recipients, a subject, and any message you want.

If you click Options, you can set up some basic details for your new Excel file. For example, you can choose whether you want your FileMaker field names to appear in the first row of the spreadsheet. You can also type a worksheet name and a title, subject, and author (each of which appear in the spreadsheet in the appropriate places). One option you *don't* have is which FileMaker fields are included in the Excel file. All the fields that appear on the layout you're currently viewing (including merge fields) will become columns in the Excel file.

Saving as Portable Document Format (PDF)

Just about anybody with a computer can view PDF files. With PDF, you get to choose exactly how the data looks, since this format preserves your beautifully crafted layouts. With FileMaker's layout tools, your keen design sense, and the "Save/Send Record as PDF" command, you could use email to distribute invoices, product catalogs, sales brochures, or annual reports. You can even send vision-impaired people a file their software can read aloud. Even if all you need to do is send people data they can see but can't change, then a PDF file is just what the software engineer ordered.

Tip: The most common PDF viewer, Adobe Reader, is a free download at *www.adobe.com/products/acrobat/readstep2.html*. Mac OS X also comes preloaded with its own PDF viewer, called Preview.

The basic choices are the same as for Excel. You choose between sending just the current record or the whole found set. And, whether the file opens in a PDF viewer or attaches to a new, blank email just as soon as FileMaker creates it. But behind the Options button you find a much richer set of choices. There are three tabs—Document (Figure 19-2), Security (Figure 19-3), and Initial View (Figure 19-4). Starting with the Document tab, you can set:

- **Title.** This title isn't the name you give the file in the dialog box. It's an additional title that becomes part of the properties of the document. Most, but not all, PDF viewer programs let you see a file's properties.

- **Subject.** This document property helps you tell a series of similar documents apart from each other.

- **Author.** This document property is usually your name, but may also be the name of your company or department. Again, it helps you organize a bunch of similar files.

- **Keywords.** Some file management programs can search these keywords to locate documents.

- **Compatibility.** Choose from Acrobat 5, 6, or 7 and later. If you think your recipient might not have the latest and greatest PDF viewer, pick a lower number.

- **Number pages from.** You can make a different numbering system than the one you have in FileMaker. Keep in mind, though, if your layout displays page numbers in FileMaker, this setting won't change them. You could create a document where the PDF viewer says you're on page 5 but the number displayed on the page is 7.

- **Include.** You can set a limited page-number range with these options, so that only a part of the found set is included in the PDF file. You may have to go to Preview mode in FileMaker first, though, to help you set the page range properly.

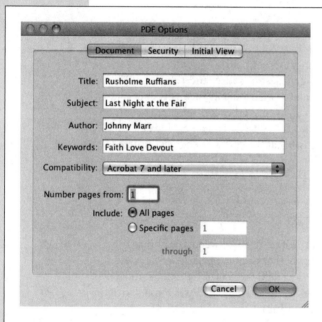

Figure 19-2:
The PDF Options dialog box shows up when you choose File→Save/Send Records As→PDF, and then click Options. The Document tab lets you add information to the PDF document. The first four options become part of the document's properties, as described in the note below.

Tip: You can see the PDF file's Title, Subject, and Author in Adobe Acrobat's PDF viewer's Document Properties Summary window. In Mac OS X's Preview program, choose Tools→Inspector instead.

In the Security tab (Figure 19-3), you can decide how much access you give your recipients when they receive your file. You can choose:

- **Require password to open the file.** Click the checkbox to turn this option on, and then enter a password. This checkbox is useful if you're selling a catalog and provide passwords only to people who've paid to receive it. Then, of course, there's the standard use; you just don't want every Malcolm, Reese, and Dewey poking around in your PDF files.

- **Require password to control printing, editing and security.** Click the checkbox to turn this option on and enter a password. You might want your PDF freely distributed, but not so freely used. If so, don't require a password to open the file, but lock it down so nobody without a password can use the material without your permission. With this option checked, a whole raft of new options becomes available. You can set:

  — *Printing.* Choose from Not Permitted, Low Resolution (150 dpi), or High Resolution. These options would protect photographic or other artwork images that you want to send in a catalog but don't want people to reprint freely. You also may want someone to *see* your document onscreen, but not print it and risk having it fall into the wrong hands.

  — *Editing.* Although PDF files are generally considered view-only, with the right software, they can actually be edited. If you don't want to allow this (or want to restrict what can be done), choose options from the Editing pop-up menu. For example, if you're sending a contract for review, and you want to be sure no new clauses are snuck in while it's away, you can choose Not permitted.

  — *Enable copying of text, images and other content.* With this option checked, recipients can copy and paste material from your PDF file.

  — *Allow text to be read by screen reading software.* This option lets people with vision or reading problems have their screen reading programs read your document out loud. Seems like turning this off would be pretty uncool.

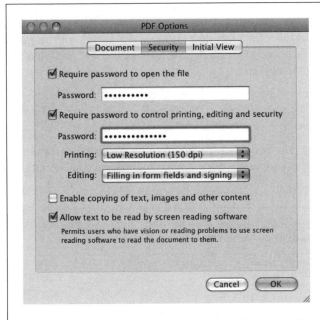

Figure 19-3:
The Security tab lets you lock down your PDF file if you need to prevent inappropriate use. Some older PDF reading programs may not recognize all these options. If someone's PDF reader doesn't have security features, it can't open the PDF file at all, so your data is still safe.

Note: Looking for absolute, iron-clad control of your information? Handwrite it on paper and store it in a secret vault. Vast amounts of money and time have been spent trying to secure digital information from unauthorized access and reuse. Ask the record companies how that worked out for them. The old chestnut about the lock only keeping the honest man honest applies here, too. PDF security settings are deterrents to unwanted use of your intellectual property, but they're all surmountable. When you use these tools, you're managing risk, not eliminating it.

The final tab in the PDF Options window is probably the one you'll use the least. But if you like to control which PDF viewer options are visible when your recipient first opens your PDF file, then Initial View (Figure 19-4) is the panel for you:

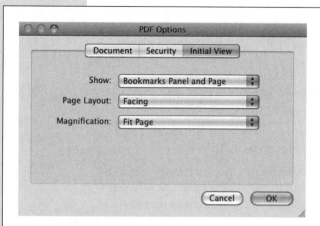

Figure 19-4:
You get to decide what the user sees when she first opens the PDF containing your database info. Once again, not all these options work in older versions of PDF software, so consider your settings here a suggestion.

- **Show.** Your choices include Page Only (just the FileMaker layout, with no extra tools or panels), Bookmarks Panel and Page, or Pages Panel and Page to offer viewers some navigation options.

- **Page Layout.** Control the way the PDF viewer displays multipage documents. If you choose *Default*, your recipients' preferred view remains in force. But you can also specify Single Page, Continuous, or Continuous-Facing.

- **Magnification.** Here you can define an automatic magnification as either a fixed percentage of the document's native size or automatically adjusted to fit the window.

Warning: These Initial View options may or may not actually take effect, depending on what program and what version of that program the PDF is opened with.

Snapshot Link

At times, collaborating with other users of the same database can get complicated. You may answer a question by saying "go to the monthly report layout, find the records for last May, and then sort by region," and be met with a vacant stare. Hey, not everyone has your FileMaker mojo! But if your colleague knows how to click, Snapshot Links can help lead the way.

A Snapshot Link is a little package of instructions saved as a small file. Send that file to your less-savvy colleague, and with a double-click, the database opens to the layout and found set of records you chose.

Setting up the Snapshot Link is easy. Switch to the layout you want to share, find and sort the records, and then select File→Save/Send Records As→Snapshot Link. The Snapshot Link dialog box appears Figure 19-5, looking much like a Save dialog box. Choose where you want to save it, whether to include the current record, or the whole found set and if you want FileMaker to attach it to a new, outgoing email message for you. With that, FileMaker saves a Snapshot Link file, with a .fpsl filename extension.

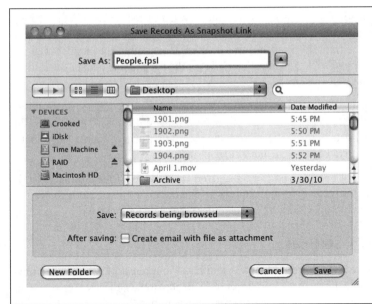

Figure 19-5:
The Snapshot Link dialog box looks suspiciously similar to any old Save dialog box. And it does indeed save a file, just one without any actual data.

Snapshot Links are simply XML files that contain eight pieces of information about your database that FileMaker uses to recreate the state of the database at the time the Snapshot was taken.

- **The paths to the database.** Yes, that's plural. The snapshot records your database's location on your hard drive, as well as any potential network paths to the file. So long as the database is available through FileMaker Network sharing, Snapshot Link users on your network can access it.

- **The found set of records, listed by their internal record IDs.**

- **The current layout.** The Snapshot link records the layout's internal ID number, not its name. You can rename that layout all day, but unless you delete it outright, the Snapshot Link is going to find it.

- **View state.** Whether you're looking at the layout as a form, a list, or a table, the link's recipient will, too.

- **Current record.** If you want to draw attention to a particular record in the found set, make sure that record is the active record when you create the link. That record will be selected when the Snapshot Link is opened.

- **Toolbar state.** Either showing or not.

- **Mode.** Create the Snapshot Link in Preview mode and, you guessed it, that's what the user will see. Create it while in Browse or Layout mode, and the user will get Browse mode. You can't create Snapshot Links in Find mode.

- **Sort Order.** However you last sorted the current found set is retained.

Snapshot Links are slick, but it's important to understand what they don't include.

- **Your last find.** The Snapshot Link contains a list of record IDs. That list may be the result of a find for every customer who bought a pogo stick, but it's only current at the time the Snapshot was created. If you open that snapshot in six weeks, new pogo stick customers won't be on the list and any deleted customers won't be magically restored.

- **Data.** Snapshot Links are instructions for FileMaker, not unlike a script. They tell FileMaker something like "go this layout, show me records 1, 3, and 5, and sort them by date". They don't possess any record data at all. When using a Snapshot Link, you always see the *most current* data.

- **Privileges.** Just because *you* can see a given layout, doesn't mean others can. If the recipient of your Snapshot Link lacks the database permissions to see the layout or records specified in the link, FileMaker won't allow it.

External SQL Sources

If you don't know MySQL from MySpace, and have no interest in taking your humble FileMaker skills to the hard-core level of IT professionals, then feel free to skip right past this section. But if you have to cross between these worlds or need to bring the power and capability of industrial-grade database servers into your systems, FileMaker's *External SQL Sources* (or ESS) feature will seem like magic.

In a nutshell, you point your FileMaker database in the general direction of an Oracle, Microsoft SQL Server, or MySQL (pronounced "my sequel") database (hereafter referred to as a SQL database). FileMaker then takes in information about that database, learning all it needs to know to make those normally complicated systems almost as easy to use as FileMaker. You can create table occurrences in your Relationships graph that are actually references to the tables in the SQL database. You can draw relationship lines between SQL tables, and even between your FileMaker tables and the SQL tables. You can create a layout based on a SQL table, drop a few fields on the layout, and then jump to Find mode, where FileMaker searches the real honest-to-goodness SQL data and shows you a found set of records.

POWER USERS CLINIC

Behind the Data

Snapshot Links are simply XML files. XML or *eXtensible Markup Language,* is a computer language designed to give different computer systems and programs a flexible way to share information among one another. XML can be very complex, but it's also fantastically flexible. You can muck about in a Snapshot Link's XML code if you wish. Just use a text editor or XML authoring program to open a .fpsl file and you see something like this example. Even if you don't know XML, you can probably see that you can change the Snapshot Link's view by changing <view type="form"></view> to <view type="list"></view>.

While changing Snapshot Link XML code can't cause any harm to your database, it can very easily render the Snapshot Link itself unusable. That's OK, because you're working on a backup copy, *right?*

```
<?xml version="1.0" encoding="UTF-8"?>
<fpsl>
<uistate>
  <universalpathlist>
  filemac:/Macintosh HD/Users/Charts.fp7
  </universalpathlist>
  <rows type="nativeIDList" rowcount="66"
  basetableid="130">
```

```
    &#10;<![CDATA[1-66]]>&#10;
</rows>
<layout id="6"></layout>
<view type="form"></view>
<selectedrow type="nativeID" id="1"></se-
lectedrow>
<statustoolbar    visible="True"></status-
toolbar>
<mode value="browseMode"></mode>
<sortlist value="True">
  <sort type="Ascending">
    <primaryfield>
            <field  tableid="1065090"
table="Attendance"
      id="2" name="Facility">
      </field>
    </primaryfield>
  </sort>
</sortlist>
</uistate>
</fpsl>
```

With few exceptions, a SQL table works just like any other FileMaker table. But instead of storing the data on your hard drive, the SQL database stores and manages the data. You don't need to know a lick of SQL programming to work with it. When you add a record using the Records→New Record command, FileMaker sends the right secret code that adds the record to the SQL database. Just type in a field, and then press Enter, and FileMaker updates the SQL database. It just doesn't get more seamless than this.

Setting Up ODBC

Before you can take advantage of ESS, you need to set up a few things. This business of getting things installed and configured is the hardest part—and it's not FileMaker's fault.

The SQL database server

First of all, you need a SQL database. To integrate as seamlessly as it does, FileMaker needs to know exactly which database you're using:

- Microsoft SQL Server 2008

- Microsoft SQL Server 2005

- Microsoft SQL Server 2000

- Oracle 11g

- Oracle 10g

- Oracle 9i

- MySQL 5.1 Community Edition

- MySQL 5.0 Community Edition

If your SQL database isn't in this list, you have to upgrade or migrate to one that is. Trying to make a different type of database work is futile—just ask someone who's tried. Luckily, this list represents recent versions of three very popular database systems. If you don't have a SQL database, but you want to get one, you need to research which is best for you. But if you just want to experiment, start with MySQL. For most purposes (including real commercial use), it's completely free. To get MySQL for Mac OS X or Windows, visit *www.mysql.com/* and look for the MySQL Community Server link.

The rest of this section assumes you have a working SQL database server, and that you have access to at least one database on that server.

Installing the ODBC driver

In order for FileMaker to communicate with the SQL database, you need an ODBC driver. This software acts as the bridge between programs on your computer and the SQL database server software. The driver is specific to your database server. If you're using Oracle, you need an Oracle ODBC driver, for instance. If you use Microsoft Windows, this step is usually a breeze. Each of the supported SQL databases has an ODBC driver provided by the manufacturer. Just visit their website and find out how to get the driver you need.

Note: If you're not sure what you need, try searching the Web for *microsoft sql server odbc driver download*. The first site listed is probably the download page you need. (Substitute *oracle* or *mysql* for microsoft sql server, as appropriate.)

Mac OS X users aren't so lucky. The big database developers don't provide free ODBC drivers for the Mac. Instead, head over to *www.actualtechnologies.com/*, and then purchase the right driver (they're cheap and work beautifully). FileMaker, Inc. worked directly with Actual to ensure maximum compatibility, and they provide the drivers of choice. (For MySQL, choose the driver called *ODBC Driver for Open Source Databases*.)

Once you've acquired the correct driver, install it on your computer. After you've installed the driver, you have to configure it.

Configuring the data source

Your computer's operating system has the ODBC system built in. You use a special program on your computer to tell it which SQL databases you want to work with. The configuration process is entirely different on Mac OS X and Windows, so go directly to the section that applies to you.

Configuring data sources on Windows. You configure your Windows machine for ODBC in the Control Panel (Start→Control Panel). The control panel looks a little different in various Windows versions:

- On Windows 7, look for "System and Security". Open this category, and then click Administrative Tools. If you don't have "System and Security", look for Administrative Tools right in the Control Panel window, and then open it there.

- On Windows Vista, you may see a category called "System and Maintenance." Open this category, and then click Administrative Tools at the bottom of the list. If you don't see "System and Maintenance", look for Administrative Tools in the Control Panel window, and then open it there.

- On Windows XP, you may see a category called "Performance and Maintenance". Open this category, and then click Administrative Tools. If you don't have "Performance and Maintenance", look for Administrative Tools right in the Control Panel window, and then open it there.

Assuming you've found the Administrative Tools window, look inside it, and then open *Data Sources (ODBC)*. You should see something on your screen that looks like Figure 19-6.

In this window, you add a *DSN (data source name)* for each SQL database you want FileMaker to work with. A DSN can be one of two flavors: A *System* DSN is available to everyone who uses your computer; and a *User* DSN is available only to the person who created it. FileMaker works only with the System DSN variety, so to get started, switch to the System DSN tab. Unfortunately, you may not have permission to define these computer-wide data sources on your work computer. If Windows doesn't let you add a system DSN, contact your system administrator.

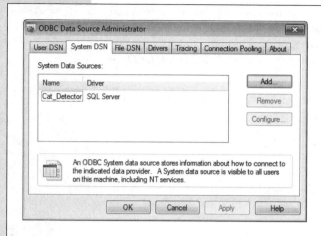

Figure 19-6:
The ODBC Data Source Administrator on Windows lets you configure the SQL databases your computer has access to. The acronym DSN stands for Data Source Name, since you name each data source you define here, and then refer to it by name in FileMaker.

Once you're on the System DSN tab, click Add. Windows shows you a list of available ODBC drivers. Select the appropriate one, and then click Finish. (Don't get too excited by the label on this button; you're nowhere near finished.)

Note: You may get a little confused by the list of available drivers on Windows. First, you may see many drivers whose names are apparently in a foreign language. Just scroll right past them. Also, you may be tempted to select the driver called SQL Server. After all, every database FileMaker works with could legitimately be called a SQL database server. But this driver is specifically for *Microsoft* SQL Server. If you use one of the other database systems, keep looking.

From this point forward, configuration works a lot like Mac OS X. Skip ahead to "Finishing ODBC data source configuration" below.

Configuring data sources on Mac OS X. On Mac OS X, you configure ODBC data sources using a program called ODBC Administrator. You can find this program in your Applications→Utilities folder. When you launch the program, you see the window in Figure 19-7.

When you open ODBC Administrator, first click the padlock icon in the bottom-left corner to unlock it. Then click the System DSN tab. (FileMaker works only with system-wide data sources.) Next, click Add. A sheet slides down showing a list of ODBC drivers installed on your computer. Select the one you want, and then click OK.

At this point, the exact configuration will vary based on the driver you're using.

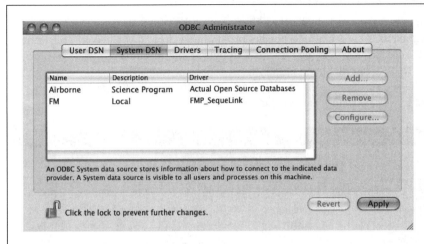

Figure 19-7:
The ODBC Administrator on Mac OS X lets you create ODBC data sources. You need to log in to your computer as an administrator to create the kind of data source FileMaker needs. You also may need to click the padlock icon in the bottom-left corner of this window before you can make changes.

Finishing ODBC data source configuration

The exact setup procedure varies with each ODBC driver, but a few things remain constant:

- On Mac OS X, even though you're in the System DSN tab, you have the option of creating either a *user* or a *system* DSN. Make sure you choose *system*.

- Give the data source any name you like. You'll use this name later when you connect FileMaker to the database. But bear in mind if you *change* a name here, you'll have to update every FileMaker database that uses it or the connections will break.

- The description isn't important. Leave it blank, or leave a note for yourself.

- You need to know the address (IP address or host name) of the database server, as well as a user name and password. You also need to know the name of the database you're connecting to (not Oracle or MySQL, but the name of the actual database on the server, like Products or Financial).

- Your driver may ask lots of questions, but you can usually accept the pre-entered answers for most of them. If you're not sure, talk to your database administrator. If you don't have a database administrator, make friends with one.

- On the last page of the setup process, you get a chance to test data source. Click this button—it tells you whether all the info you just entered is correct. Better to find out now than when FileMaker gets confused later on.

Once you're finished, you see your data source listed in the System DSN tab of your ODBC configuration program. Go ahead and close the window. Your configuration work is finished.

Connecting FileMaker to a SQL Data Source

Suppose you've decided to harness the power of the Web to grow your private investigation business. You hired a hotshot programmer to build you a sweet little website that's sure to put you at the top of the Google search results. Even better, visitors to your website can fill out an inquiry form asking for your help. The programmer set up the site so the form submissions go directly into a MySQL database. Now you want to work with that data in FileMaker.

WORKAROUND WORKSHOP

The Case of the Missing Driver

A bug in the MySQL ODBC driver installer can leave your ODBC system in a confused state where it stops showing new ODBC drivers you've installed (even non-MySQL drivers). If you installed your driver but it isn't in the list, don't beat yourself up. You didn't do anything wrong.

The fix requires a trip to the RegEdit program, where non-technical folks rarely dare to tread. Luckily, the steps are straightforward. Just follow them exactly, and you'll be fine. If you're worried, show this page to your nerdiest friend (or anyone under 20) and ask for help.

1. Run the RegEdit program.
2. On Windows 7 or Windows Vista, click the Start button and, in the search panel, type *regedit*. Then click regedit.exe at the top of the Start menu. On Windows XP, click Start→Run, type *regedit* in the box that pops up, and then click OK.
3. Choose File→Export and save your current registry someplace safe.
4. On the off chance you mess up here, you can restore your old settings by running RegEdit again and using the File→Import command.

5. In the folder list on the left side of the window, click the plus signs to expand each of these folders in succession: HKEY_LOCAL_MACHINE, SOFTWARE, ODBC, and ODBCINST.INI.
6. The Windows registry works like a hierarchy of folders, and you're digging your way down to the thing you need to change.
7. Select the ODBC Drivers folder inside ODBCINST.INI.
8. RegEdit fills the list on the right with what looks a lot like the list of ODBC drivers.

At this point, you need to look for the problem. At the top of the list on the right side, you see an entry called "(Default)" (with parentheses and all). In the Data column for that line, it should say "(value not set)." If the top row of the data column is empty, or has a pair of quotation marks, then you're a victim of the bug. Just select the "(Default)" item, and then press the Delete key on your keyboard. The words "(value not set)" should appear where they weren't before.

Close RegEdit and, if prompted, agree to save the changes. Now exit the Data Sources control panel, and then open it again. You should see your driver.

You've acquired all the necessary information from the programmer, and configured an ODBC data source. Your next step is to tell your FileMaker database about the SQL database:

1. **Open the FileMaker database you've been building, or download a copy from** *www.missingmanuals.com/.* **Then choose File→Manage→External Data Sources.**

   Here's where you tell your database about other places it can find data. You used this same window to connect one FileMaker database to another (see page 592). This time, though, you're going to connect to a non-FileMaker database.

---

2. **Click New.**

   FileMaker shows you the Edit Data Source window.

3. **In the Name box, type Web Leads.**

   You can name the data source anything you want. This name will show up when you're choosing tables to add to the Relationships graph.

4. **Click the ODBC radio button below the Name box.**

   FileMaker revamps the dialog box so it looks like the one in Figure 19-8.

5. **Click Specify.**

   You see a list of all the system ODBC data sources defined on your computer.

6. **Choose the data source you want to connect to, and then click OK.**

   FileMaker puts the data source name in the box next to DSN.

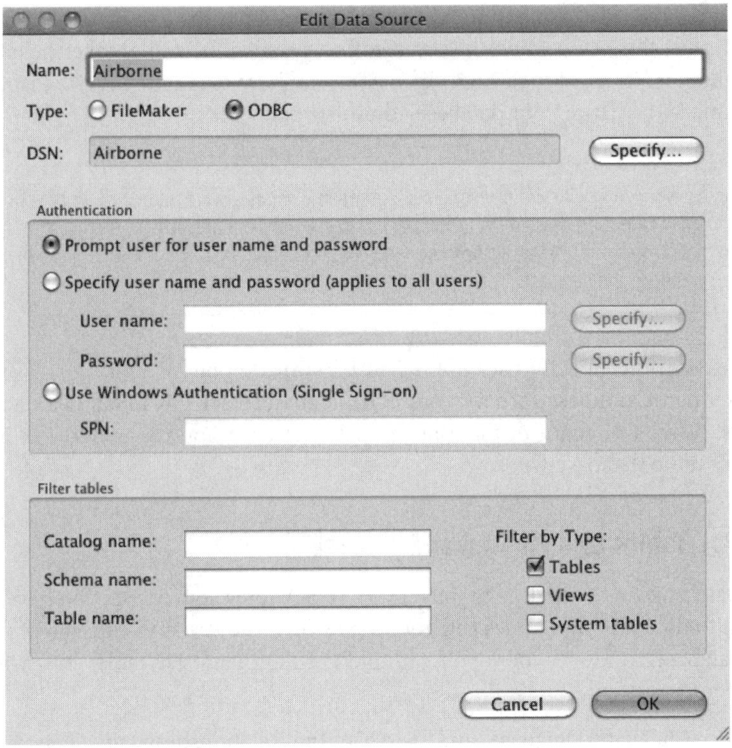

Figure 19-8:
When you select ODBC as the Type for your new data source, the Edit Data Source window takes on a whole new look. Instead of just the path to a FileMaker database, you tell FileMaker which ODBC data source to connect to, the user name and password to use, and which SQL objects you want to see. Don't worry if these terms don't make sense yet. You'll learn about them later in this chapter, and many of them don't matter much anyway.

At this point you have a decision to make. When someone opens this database, how does it log in to the remote database? You have three options here:

- Turn on **"Prompt user for user name and password"** if you want people to enter the login information when FileMaker makes the connection. This option means everyone has to log in to the SQL database every time they open the FileMaker database (in addition to any password they need to open the FileMaker file).

- Turn on **"Specify username and password (applies to all users)"** if you want FileMaker to automatically log in to the SQL database on everyone's behalf. When you do, you can enter a calculation to determine either value, so you can hard code a text value, automatically use the current user's FileMaker account name (with the *Get (AccountName)* function) or any other mechanism you need.

- If you're using Microsoft Windows and Microsoft SQL Server, you can turn on **"Use Windows Authentication (Single Sign-on)"**. This option lets FileMaker automatically connect to the SQL database using the Windows user name and password. Your database administrator has to configure the Windows accounts properly for this setup to work (you can find details in the FileMaker help by searching for "ODBC Single Sign-on"). Also, you have to get the Service Principal Name (SPN) from your database administrator.

Note: You may be wondering why you have to enter a user name and password here at all, since you already typed them in when you created the ODBC data source. It turns out the ODBC system just really wants that information so it can test your data source and ease configuration. It doesn't actually *use* that login info when you open the database.

In this case, turn on "Specify user name and password (applies to all users)," and type the user name and password for your SQL database. Click OK to tell FileMaker you're done. Click OK again in the Manage External Data Sources window to get back to your main database window.

Adding SQL Tables to a FileMaker Database

Your database now has a pipeline to the tables in a SQL data source. But you haven't told it what to do with those tables yet. Your next stop is the Relationships tab of the Manage Database window, where you can fold the SQL database tables into your overall system.

Choose File→Manage→Database, and switch to the Relationships tab. Then click the Add Table button, just as though you were adding a normal FileMaker table occurrence. But this time, when the Specify Table window pops up (Figure 19-9), click the Data Source pop-up menu, and then choose the name of your SQL data source.

POWER USERS' CLINIC

Advanced ODBC Data Source Options

At the bottom of the Edit Data Source window, you see a section labeled "Filter tables" (Figure 19-8). These settings are entirely optional, but may prove very useful if you're connecting to a complex database system. These settings tell FileMaker which tables you consider important, and which ones it can safely ignore. Doing so means you don't have to look at very long lists as you build your database, and helps FileMaker keep things running as quickly as possible.

Database terminology is inconsistent from one system to another. The "Filter tables" section gives you three empty boxes to fill in, some with mysterious names. Here's how it shakes out:

- If you use Oracle, the Catalog box is irrelevant: leave it empty. In the Schema box, you can enter a user name. When you do, FileMaker will only look at tables owned by that user.

- If you use Microsoft SQL Server, you can put the name of a particular database in the Catalog box to limit FileMaker to only tables in that database. If you use schemas, or collections of tables and views, you can also restrict FileMaker to just one schema.

- If you use MySQL, the Catalog box has no bearing on things, so you can leave it empty. If you want to see only tables for a particular user, enter the user name in the Schema box.

- Whatever your database, if you care only about one particular table, enter its name in the Table name box. FileMaker will then show that table alone.

To the right of these three boxes, FileMaker offers three checkboxes. In the world of SQL databases, two or three *different* things act like tables.

- Tables are real honest-to-goodness tables, a lot like their FileMaker counterpart.

- Views are sort of like smart folders in iTunes or your mail program: They show portions of one or more tables based on criteria defined on the database server. If you're accessing a complex database, and you need read-only access to a specific portion, you might consider asking your database administrator to create a view that includes just the data you need. This will make things simpler for you down the road.

- System tables are tables the database system creates itself for various purposes. (MySQL doesn't have this kind of table, so don't fret about it if you're a MySQL user.)

Your job is to turn on the checkbox for each type you want FileMaker to show. You can also turn off all three checkboxes, and FileMaker will show everything it can.

If you don't know what any of this means, try leaving every box blank, and turning on Tables and Views. If FileMaker takes a long time showing tables to pick from, if the table you want isn't in the list, or if you feel like you're seeing loads of tables you don't want to see, consult your database administrator for help.

The list below the pop-up menu changes to show all the available tables in the SQL database. Choose the table you're interested in, adjust the table name as necessary (in the Name box at the bottom of the window), and then click OK.

Creating relationships

When you're viewing a record from the Web Leads table, you might want FileMaker to show you if that person is already in your Customers table. To make this possible, you need some kind of connection between Customers and Web Leads. When you add a table from an external data source, FileMaker puts a table occurrence right on the relationship graph, so making the connection is easy. The table occurrence looks, smells, and functions just like a FileMaker table. For example, it would make sense to connect it to the Customers table by Email Address, since they both have that information in common. Just drag the email_address field from the Web Leads table to the Email Address field in the Customers table. FileMaker now knows how they relate.

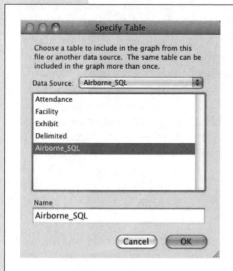

Figure 19-9:
Once you've worked through the complexity of ODBC configuration, adding a table from a SQL database to your FileMaker relationships graph works exactly the way you'd expect: simple.

You're free to relate tables in any combination you want: Connect a FileMaker table to a SQL table, or connect two SQL tables together. Connect a SQL table to a File-Maker table, which then connects to another SQL table. You can even connect tables from two *different* SQL databases.

Shadow tables

If you switch to the Tables tab in the Manage Database window, you may see something unexpected. FileMaker includes every SQL table you've added to your graph in the Tables list (in stark contrast to tables from other FileMaker databases, which never show in the Tables tab).

Note: No matter how many *table occurrences* you create for a particular SQL table, the underlying table is listed only once. Also, SQL tables are always shown in italics so they're easy to spot.

The italicized entry in the Tables tab is called a *shadow table*. In other words, it isn't the table. Rather, it's a representation of the real table. It reflects information about the real table, and even lets you add a little FileMaker magic to an otherwise bare bit of computer science.

If you double-click the table (or switch to the Fields tab, and then select the table from the Table pop-up menu), you'll see the fields (sometimes called *columns* by non-FileMaker database folks) from the SQL table listed in italics as well. You can do certain things to these italicized fields:

- You can't rename a field or change its type. That sort of thing is controlled on the SQL database side of things.

- You can add a field comment if you want.

- You can click Options and set auto-enter and validation options for the field. Remember, though, that the rules you set here apply only when you add or edit records *in FileMaker*. Other systems that interact with the database are restricted only by settings in the SQL database.

- You can delete a field. You're not actually deleting the field from the SQL table. Rather, deleting a field tells FileMaker you simply don't want to see that field in FileMaker anymore. (You can always get it back later by clicking the Sync button, as explained below.)

SQL databases tend to be more restrictive about acceptable values than FileMaker itself. For instance, a text field in a SQL database usually has a maximum size that's relatively small, compared to FileMaker's 2 GB field limit. If you select a field, click the Options button, and then visit the Validation tab, here you might see that the "Maximum number of characters" option is turned on, and you can't turn it off. Right by the checkbox, FileMaker also shows how many characters the field can hold.

Perhaps most important, you can *add new fields* to the shadow table. Specifically, you can add unstored or global calculation fields and summary fields. Neither of these field types work with SQL databases, but both are super important to FileMaker developers. By adding them to the shadow table, you can treat the SQL tables a little more like normal FileMaker tables. For example, you can add summary fields so you can do complex reporting on the SQL data, or add a calculation field to show a subtotal on a FileMaker layout.

Tip: Remember, the fields you add to the shadow table aren't in the real table. They live only in FileMaker.

Finally, if the underlying SQL table changes in some way (perhaps the database administrator added a new column you're particularly interested in seeing), click Sync at the top of the window. This button tells FileMaker to go back to the SQL database and find out if any columns have been added, removed, or adjusted.

Syncing has nothing to do with the *data* in the database, though. FileMaker always interacts with the SQL database directly to show up-to-the-moment data as you perform searches or make changes. The Sync button synchronizes only the field definitions from the SQL table.

Using SQL Tables

There's no secret to using a SQL table—it works just like any other FileMaker table. You can create a new layout to show records from the SQL table. You can view those records in List view, Form view, or Table view. You can write scripts that loop through SQL records, or use the "Go to Related Record" script step to find the records associated with a particular customer.

Everything you know about FileMaker still applies. But keep a few points in mind as you develop your database around SQL tables:

- You can configure access to a SQL table using privilege sets just like any other FileMaker table. But a privilege set can't overrule the underlying SQL database. If the user name and password you're using to connect to the SQL database don't provide permission to delete records, FileMaker can't delete them, no matter how hard you try. FileMaker does its best to give meaningful error messages in such situations.

- Speaking of error messages, since SQL databases are more restrictive than FileMaker, you may see error messages in places you wouldn't normally expect. For example, a Name field might be limited to 30 characters. If you try to enter more than that, FileMaker lets you, but you can't then commit the record. It would be nice if FileMaker simply stopped you from typing too many letters, but it doesn't. It's up to you to go back and delete enough to make it happy.

- FileMaker does some powerful computing magic to make these SQL tables work. So if you have a large amount of data in your SQL table, FileMaker can take a long time to show you data. Be patient and grateful for FileMaker's efforts.

- FileMaker may have trouble performing some finds efficiently. If you include only fields from one table in your find request, then it should move quickly. But if you search in related fields, and there are thousands of matches in the related table, FileMaker can take a very long time to sort things out. If you find that SQL tables aren't performing well, and you can't simplify your find requests, consider enlisting the help of a SQL expert (or learning it yourself). You may be able to offload some of the heavy lifting to the SQL database server, where ready access to the data makes things faster. For example, a complex find in FileMaker could be converted to a SQL view that's super-snappy. This same advice applies to large summary reports. If you're dealing with lots of records, it may be faster to let the SQL database server calculate the subtotals and averages for FileMaker.

You can use ESS to get direct access to enterprise data, interact with the back end of your website, or even replace chunks of FileMaker data with a set of tables that's more open to other programs. This powerful feature may need a little setup and some new expertise, but if you have big needs, it can be an incredibly powerful option.

Exporting Data

The "Save/Send Records As" options (page 800) make good sense when you just want to send FileMaker data to an associate. But sometimes your recipient is a computer. You may send your customer information to a mailing house to be printed on postcards, or load it into QuickBooks. In cases like this, you *export* the data.

When you export data, FileMaker needs to know *what* data to export. You tell it with the Export dialog box (Figure 19-10). The Table pop-up menu shows you what File-Maker considers the *current layout*—in this case, People Detail. Below it, the field list shows every field in that current layout. But click the pop-up menu, and you can choose Current Table, which shows you all the fields in the current table, instead of just the fields on the layout. You're also welcome to pick other tables from the pop-up menu and see their fields. When you choose fields from other tables, you're still exporting Customer records. If you include fields from other tables, FileMaker gets the values from the first record related to each customer record.

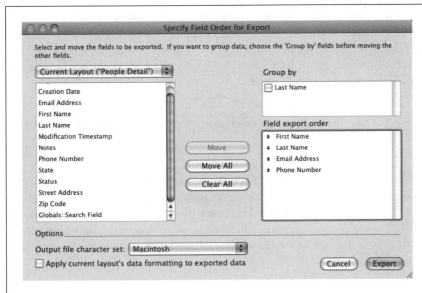

Figure 19-10:
When FileMaker exports the data, it includes each field in right-hand list in the export file. The order of the fields in this list determines their order in the export file, and you can change it by dragging fields up or down in the list. To add every field in the field list to the export order list, click Move All. Likewise, to remove all fields from the export order, click Clear All.

To choose a field for export, select it, and then click Move, or just double-click it. FileMaker adds the field to the "Field export order" list, but doesn't actually move it there. Rather, the field stays in the list because you may want to export the same field *twice* in the same export file. Imagine, for example, you're creating an export file that needs the billing address info in the first four fields and the shipping address info in the next four fields. Since your database has only one set of address fields, you can export them twice so the resulting file has the right number of fields. (Unfortunately, you can't ask FileMaker to export a blank field. If you often export to a format that needs fields you don't have, and leaving them blank is OK, just export an empty global field in each one's place.)

Note: If a field isn't on the current layout, it doesn't show up in the list of available fields on the left side, so if you're wasting time scrolling through fields that you don't need, you can Cancel, and then switch to a simpler layout from the same table. But if you can't find a field that you *know* is in the table, use the pop-up menu to choose Current Table. That way, you'll get a list of all the fields in the table, regardless of which ones are on the current layout.

At the bottom of the window, the "Output file character set" pop-up menu lets you tell FileMaker how to *encode* characters in the export file so the receiving computer can read them properly. For instance, if you're using Mac OS X and you know the person receiving the export file is using Windows, it probably makes sense to choose the Windows (ANSI) choice. Unfortunately, the conversion from Macintosh to Windows or Windows to Mac is imperfect, so some less common characters may be switched out for others in the output file. Unicode is the best choice, assuming your recipient can accept it, because it can handle *all* the characters you may have in your database (even foreign language characters like Chinese and Korean).

Finally, the checkbox called "Apply current layout's data formatting to exported data" is a little misleading. It has nothing to do with font, size, style, or color. Rather, when you turn this option on, FileMaker formats numbers, dates, times, and timestamps according to the formatting options for each field on the layout: number of decimal places, date formats, and so forth. If you leave this option off, FileMaker exports the data exactly as it was originally entered.

Note: The "Group by" list lets you summarize data as you export it. You'll learn how this feature works on the next page.

The following steps take you through a typical database export. You've hired a printing company to print, address, and mail personalized cards to all your customers at holiday time. To do the job, the card company needs a list of names and addresses. Instead of typing all your customer info by hand, you can produce the list by exporting it from your database in the appropriate format. Often, plain text is fine, so that's what this example uses.

1. **Switch to the Customers layout.**

   Like many FileMaker features, the Export command is layout-based—that is, it decides which table to export (and from which table occurrence to find related data) by looking at the current layout. To export customer records, you need to be on a layout associated with the Customers table.

2. **Choose Records→Show All Records.**

   If this command is grayed out, then all records are already showing. Otherwise, take this step to ensure that you export *every* customer.

3. **Choose File→Export Records. If the command isn't available, you're probably in Find mode, so switch to Browse mode.**

   You can also export from Layout and Preview modes, too, should the need arise. The "Export Records to File" dialog box appears. It looks a lot like a normal Save dialog box, except that it has a pop-up menu at the bottom called Type.

4. **Name the file *Holiday Card List.txt*, and then choose any location you want.**

   When FileMaker exports data, it creates a new file and puts the data in it. You use this window to tell FileMaker what to call the file and where to put it.

5. **From the Type pop-up menu, choose Comma-Separated Text, and then click Save.**

   You'll learn what each of these types means in the next section. The "Specify Field Order for Export" window appears (Figure 19-10).

6. **While pressing Ctrl (⌘), select these fields in the field list: First Name, Last Name, Company Name, Street Address, City, State, and Zip Code. Then click Move.**

   FileMaker adds the highlighted fields to the Field export order list.

Tip: If you want to export most of your fields, but not quite all of them, it may be faster to click the Move All button, and then clear the few you don't want from the Field export order list.

---

7. **Click Export.**

   FileMaker creates the file and returns you to your database.

So what just happened? If you open the Holiday Card List file you just created, you see names, company names, and addresses from your customers file. Dig a little deeper and you notice:

- Each *record* is on its own line. If the program you're viewing the file in wraps lines, it might look like a record goes across two or more lines, but there's a return character at the *end* of each record, and nowhere else.

- Each field value is in quotes, and there are commas between them.

These factors are important because this file conforms to a standard. Other programs—including the program used by the card printing company—that recognize the Comma-Separated Text format can read this file and grab the data.

Grouped Exports

You may have noticed the "Group by" list in the "Specify Field Order for Export" dialog box. Under normal circumstances, you see "(Unsorted)" in this list. But if you sort the records in the found set *before* choosing the Export Records command, you see instead a list of the fields in your sort order, each with a checkbox by its name. You can see this in action in Figure 19-11.

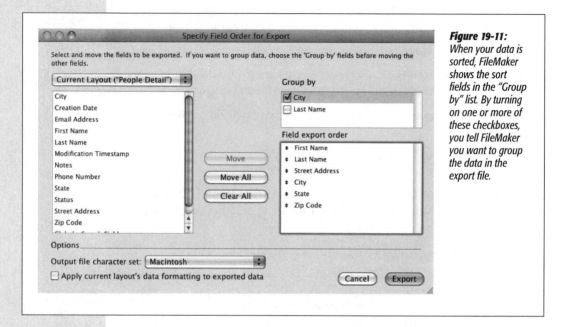

Figure 19-11:
When your data is sorted, FileMaker shows the sort fields in the "Group by" list. By turning on one or more of these checkboxes, you tell FileMaker you want to group the data in the export file.

If you opt to group the data, you get just one record in the export file for each *unique* value in the "group by" field. For example, if you export 300 people records, grouped by state, you get one record for each state. If you include *summary* fields in your Export order list, FileMaker summarizes all the records represented by each group. You can see, for example, how many people you have in each state.

You're free to select as many fields as you want in the "group by" list. If you select more than one, you get a hierarchical list of records, similar to a Sub-summary report (Chapter 14). For example, if you sort first by state, then by city, and turn on the checkbox next to both fields in the "group by" list, you get a list of states, and below each state, you see one record for each city in that state. Again, summary fields included in your export show proper totals for both the state as a whole, and each city.

Export formats

When exporting data, you always create a file, but you get to decide what *format* the file should be in. In the previous example, you exported your data to a Comma-Separated Text file. This example is one of the many file formats FileMaker can produce when it exports. Most formats exist simply because computer software has put forth a lot of standards in the last 50 years, and FileMaker wants to be as flexible as possible. Some formats do have unique advantages, though.

UP TO SPEED

Where's My Style?

Most of FileMaker's export formats are *text based*. In other words, what gets produced is just a normal, plain text file. The structure of this file determines which format it is, but you can open them all in Notepad or TextEdit and read them directly. A side effect of this reality is that none of them support *styles*. In other words, if you go to great lengths to change the first names in all your records so the font matches the customer's personality, you can kiss your hard work goodbye when you export.

In addition to the font, you lose the size, style, and color of the text. The notable exception to this rule is the FileMaker Pro format. Since this export format creates another File-Maker Pro database, all the formatting you painstakingly put in place is preserved.

If you *must* have text styles in your exported data, there is an option, but it ain't pretty. FileMaker has two calculation functions designed to aid this process: *GetAsCSS()* and *GetAsSVG()*.

Each function takes a single text parameter and returns a snippet of ordinary text with style information embedded using special *tags*. *GetAsCSS()* produces text that can be put on a web page. When viewed in a web browser, the text takes on its original fonts, sizes, styles, and colors. *GetAsSVG()* works the same way, but uses a different tagging scheme: the one used in the SVG, or Scalable Vector Graphics format.

To take advantage of these functions, you need to create a calculation field with a formula something like this:

```
GetAsCSS ( First Name )
```

You then export *this* field instead of the First Name field. If you do this with the HTML Table export format, you get properly formatted text on your web page. More realistically, you'd use these along with the XML format and a special XSLT style sheet that produces a web page or an SVG image. You'll learn more about this option at the end of this chapter.

The first question you need to ask is, "Where's the data going?" Your export format choice almost always depends on what the person you're sending it to needs. Each is explained below:

- **Tab-Separated Text** and **Comma-Separated Text** are very common formats for database data. They put each record on its own line. With tab-separated text, you get a tab between each field value, while comma-separated text has quotes around field values, and commas between them. Almost every program in the world that can import data supports one of these formats. If you're not sure, try Tab-Separated Text first—it's the most common.

Note: Sometimes the Comma-Separated Text format is called *Comma-Separated Values* in other programs. They're the same thing.

- The **Merge** format is just like Comma-Separated Text format, with one difference: The first line of the file shows individual field names. The advantage is that when you import this file in another program, you can see what each field is called, making it easier to get the right data. Unfortunately, most programs don't expect this extra line, and treat it as another record. People most often use this format for mail merge in word processing programs.

- If you want to put the data on a web page, use **HTML Table**. The resulting file isn't suitable for importing into another program, but it can be displayed nicely in a web browser. You can also open the file, copy the HTML table from inside it, and then paste it into another web page.

- The **FileMaker Pro** format is your best choice if your data is destined to go back into FileMaker some day, or if you just want to view and work with the exported data directly. When you choose this format, FileMaker creates a brand new database with just one table and only the fields you choose to export. This format is the only one that preserves font, style, size, and color in field data (see the box on page 823) and one of the few that supports repeating fields (see page 255).

Note: Usually, if you just want to export records from one FileMaker file to another, you don't have to export them first. Just go to the database where you want the data to end up, and then import them directly (page 826). Of course, if one database is in South Africa and the other is in Tibet, then by all means export them first.

- For the ultimate in flexibility, choose **XML**—the un-format. When you export XML, you get to apply something called an XSLT style sheet. An XSLT style sheet is a document written in a programming language all its own that tells FileMaker exactly how the exported data looks. If you need to produce an export format that FileMaker doesn't support directly, XSLT is the way to do it. But be forewarned: XSLT is *not* in the same league as FileMaker itself, ease-of-use-wise. You may need some hired help. (XSLT is introduced briefly on page 841.)

Note: Although it applies to one *field value* and not a set of records, don't forget about the Edit Export Field Contents command. This command lets you export the data in the current field to a file. It exports text, number, date, time, and timestamp fields to a plain text file. Container fields create a file whose type is appropriate for the data in the field.

- Last but not least, you can choose one of the **Excel** options to create a bona fide spreadsheet. To ensure that most people can use the spreadsheet, choose "Excel 95–2004 Workbook," which creates an .xls file that works in just about any version of Excel. If you know your recipients have the most recent Excel version, use the new .xslx format, otherwise choose "Excel Workbook". When you choose either format, FileMaker opens an extra dialog box, which lets you put FileMaker's field names in the first row of your new spreadsheet. You can even give your Excel file a worksheet Name, document Title, Subject, and Author if you so desire.

Regardless of which format you choose, the "Export Records to File" dialog box has two options that let you determine what happens to the file after FileMaker creates it. Choose "Automatically open file" to avoid hunting down the file on your hard drive, and then launching it yourself. And "Create email with file as attachment" does just what it promises: opens your email program and creates a new message with your fresh new document attached. To share your data, you just need to supply the email address, add a subject line, and then click Send.

Making It Fit

A lot of FileMaker's Export formats use special characters for important things. For instance, the Tab-Separated Text format uses a return character to separate records. What happens if I have a return character in my field?

Good question! Special characters are one of those problems with no ideal solution. But FileMaker does the best it can within the limitations of each export file type. For a file to be called Tab-Separated Text, for example, you simply can't have return characters inside records. It's just against the rules. In this particular case, FileMaker turns the return character into something else, called a *vertical tab*, which is a standard but rarely-used character left over from when computers had green screens. Presumably, you don't have any of these in your fields (you can't type them, so it's a pretty safe bet you don't), so it's easy enough to turn vertical tab characters back into return characters when you open the file in another program. In fact, that's exactly what happens when you *import* a Tab-Separated Text file into FileMaker.

Another character of concern is the quote mark. If you have these in your fields, and you export a Comma-Separated Text file, FileMaker has to do something with them so they don't interfere with the quotes around field values. In this case, FileMaker turns your quote mark into two quote marks together.

That doesn't sound like a solution, but it is. If you assume any quote mark that's immediately followed by a second

one is really just data, and not the end quote mark for a field value, you can figure out which is which in the export file. Most programs that support Comma-Separated Text understand this convention. (You might think commas would also be a problem with Comma-Separated Text, but they're not. Since every field value is in quotes, commas are OK. Only the commas between quoted values are considered field separators.)

The HTML and XML formats have all kinds of special characters, but each has a special *entity* form that's used if they're supposed to be treated as ordinary data. FileMaker converts any such characters appropriately, and every program that processes these formats understands the conventions.

Finally, FileMaker has a data-structure concept that most formats simply don't understand: repeating fields. The idea that one field could hold several values is foreign to most database programs. When you export repeating fields, FileMaker pulls another freaky character out of its hat: the Group Separator, which is used to separate each value. Thankfully, this action is almost never a problem because you generally don't export repeating field data to a file that needs to be read by a program that doesn't understand repeating fields. One last note: The FileMaker Pro export format *does* directly support repeating fields.

Importing Data

Sometimes, the data you need is already somewhere else, and you need to get it into FileMaker. Before you start lamenting your lackluster words-per-minute typing skills, consider doing an *import*. Chances are FileMaker can load the data directly into its tables with just a little help from you to tell it where things go.

FileMaker can handle the most common data types—and quite a few lesser-known ones—by a straightforward process. You tell FileMaker which file contains your incoming data, and then show it how you want to match the incoming data (the source) with the fields in your file (the target). This procedure is called *field mapping*, and it's the only time-consuming part of any import. See Figure 19-12 for a preview of the Import Field Mapping dialog box.

This window lists all the fields in the source file on the left, and the fields in your table on the right. FileMaker will transfer the data, field by field and record by record, into your database. The first field in the Source Fields list goes into the first field in the Target Fields list.

Unfortunately, FileMaker can't always tell which fields match. You might be importing records from a system that uses different field names, for example. How is FileMaker supposed to know that *t_fname* is the First Name field in your old contact manager software? Worse still, many data formats have no field names, so all you have to work with is the data itself.

Using the Import Field Mapping dialog box, your job is to tell FileMaker which source fields match with each of the target fields. The concept is simple, but the procedure can be a real drag. First of all, you can't rearrange the fields in the Source Fields list at all. They match the order in which they appear in the file you're importing and that's that. So instead, you move the target fields up or down so they line up next to the appropriate source fields. (You move them just like you do fields and tables in the Manage Database window—by dragging the little arrows.)

If you don't have many fields, this process is quick and painless. If you have lots of fields, it can be tough for a few reasons:

- Since the whole point of this operation is to put the target field list in a very particular order, you can't simply sort the list by name whenever you're having trouble finding a field. If you're looking for First Name in a long list, there's no way to find it short of looking through the list field by field. If this process proves overwhelming, here's a trick: Click Manage Database, and in the familiar Manage Database window it summons, rename the field with a whole lot of X's at the end of its name. When you close the Manage Database window, the field in question will stand out from the list.

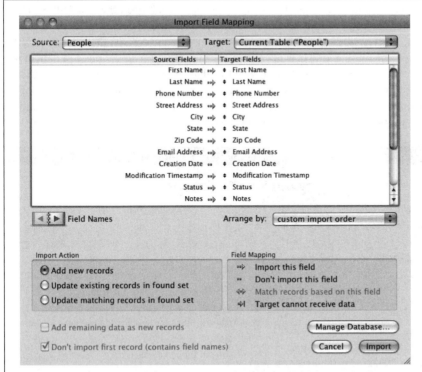

Figure 19-12:
Use this dialog box to tell FileMaker what data to import and where to put it. In the top-left corner of the window, FileMaker tells you where this data is coming from. To the right, you see where the data's going. The arrows down the middle show you what data will go where. Creation Date, for instance, has no arrow, so FileMaker won't import it.

- As you drag fields up and down, if you have to drag beyond the visible list (because your destination has scrolled past the top or bottom), FileMaker sometimes scrolls the list by so quickly while you drag that you easily overshoot your destination, repeatedly. To avoid this runaround, don't drag. Instead, click the field you want to move to select it. Then hold down the Control (⌘) key, and use the up or down arrow keys to move the field. As long as you hold the appropriate modified key down, you can move the field up or down as far as you want by repeatedly pressing the arrow keys. This more controlled method may go a little slower, but it makes it easy to hit the right spot.

- Finally, if you accidentally drop a field in the wrong spot, the field you're moving changes places with the one you dropped it on top of. If the one you replaced was already in the right spot, it's now far away, and you have to reposition it once you correctly place the first field. In other words, an accidental drop leaves *two* fields in the wrong place. The only solution to this problem is to be careful (and use the keyboard trick from the previous paragraph to minimize mistakes).

Sometimes you don't care about some of the fields in your source file (maybe it in-cludes a Fax Number for each customer, and you don't need that particular value). Between each source and destination field, you see one of two symbols: an arrow or a line. The arrow means FileMaker plans to import the data on the left side into the field on the right. A line tells FileMaker to ignore this particular piece of data in the import file. Click an arrow to change it to a line, or vice versa. Just make sure there's a line next to the field or fields you don't want to import. (You sometimes see *other* symbols between fields, but they show up only when you change the Import Action setting. You'll learn about that on page 834.)

UP TO SPEED

Mapping Out Your Options

FileMaker's smart, but when it comes to something as picayune as deciding which field to put where, there's no substitute for human input. As you can see in Figure 19-12, the Import Field Mapping dialog box looks a trifle crowded, but every tool, button, and gizmo has saved a life (or a career, anyway).

For example, your input data source may or may not in-clude field names. If it doesn't, the Source Fields list shows you the first record in the import file instead. Or, even if your data already has named fields, you may *want* to see some of the data being imported so you can see what's really in that field called Q1GPFnw. Either way, FileMaker lets you check as many records as you wish before you im-port by providing arrow buttons below the list. As you click, FileMaker replaces items in the source field list with data from the next (right) or previous (left) record. When field names are included, you see them as the *first* record. Oc-casionally, the format you're importing doesn't accommo-date field names, but the import file has them anyway, as the first record. When this happens, turn on "Don't import first record" so FileMaker doesn't treat that record as data.

The "Arrange by" pop-up menu lets you bulk-reorder the target fields in the list. Most choices are obvious (alpha-betical by field name, and by field type), but others aren't

so clear. If you choose "matching names," FileMaker tries to match fields up by matching their names. If your input file has the same field names as your database, this option sets the right order for you. The "last order" choice restores the field order you used the last time you imported data. Choose "creation order" to see the fields in the order in which you created them. Finally, if you manually drag the fields in the list, FileMaker switches to the "custom import order" choice. If you decide to try one of the other arrange-ments, you can get back to the order you were working on by choosing "custom import order" yourself.

Finally, just like the export dialog box, this window lets you specify a character set (page 820). This time, though, you don't decide what you *want* it to be. Rather, you need to tell FileMaker what it *is*. If you're lucky, this pop-up menu is grayed out, meaning FileMaker was able to figure out the encoding itself. Otherwise, you need to make sure you make the right choice so special characters in the import file come through intact. You'll choose either Windows (ANSI) or Macintosh 99 percent of the time. And for typical data (letters, numbers, and basic punctuation), the choice is largely irrelevant.

Note: If you forget what the importing icons mean, never fear. The Import Field Mapping window has a legend at the bottom right.

For the sake of illustration, here's the simple rundown on how importing works:

1. **Choose File→Import Records→File.**

   FileMaker can import data from all kinds of sources. In this case, you're telling it you want to import records from a *file*. When you choose this command, the standard Open File dialog box appears.

2. **Choose the file you want to import, and then click Open.**

   The Import Field Mapping dialog box pops up.

3. **Drag the fields in the target field list on the right so they line up properly with the input data on the left.**

   As you drag, you can ignore the field mapping arrows completely. You can fix them once you've got the fields in the right order.

Tip: If your data source has a field that doesn't match any existing field in your target table, and you decide you want to import that field anyway, just click the Manage Database button to create a new field, and then return to your field mapping. See page 836 for how to handle an entire *table* that's missing.

---

4. **Click the arrows or lines between fields until each matching field has an arrow, and each remaining field has a line.**

   This part is the most time-consuming. Just take it slow and be glad you don't have to type all this data.

5. **Make sure the "Add new records" radio button (in the Import Action area) is turned on.**

   This action tells FileMaker you want a new record created in the Customers table for each record in the import file. (The Import Field Mapping dialog box has more features, but you don't need them right now. See page 834 for the full details.)

6. **Click Import. When the Import Options dialog box appears (Figure 19-13), turn on "Perform auto-enter options while importing".**

   You want to make sure the new customers have valid customer IDs, and those come from auto-enter serial numbers.

   Click Import one last time.

   After a very short delay, the Import Summary dialog box appears (Figure 19-14). Click OK to make it go away.

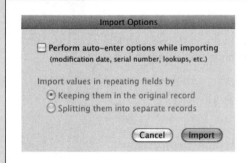

Figure 19-13:
If you have any auto-enter fields, or you're importing repeating fields, you see this window after clicking Import. Turn off "Perform auto-enter options while importing" if you don't want FileMaker to auto-enter data in your records as they're created. When importing repeating fields, you usually want to choose "Keeping them in the original record." If you don't, FileMaker makes a new record for each repetition that has data in it.

Note: If you import into a field that has auto-enter options set, and you tell FileMaker to perform auto-enter options when importing, you might wonder *which* value will wind up in the field: the auto-entered data or the imported data. In almost every case, the imported data wins. The one exception: If a field is set to auto-enter a looked-up value, FileMaker performs the lookup and thus overrides the imported value.

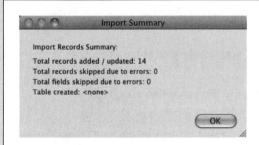

Figure 19-14:
This window appears after FileMaker completes the import operation. It tells you important information about your import, including how many records were imported. Sometimes problems can happen during import (for instance, some data in the import file may violate your field validation settings). When this happens, FileMaker may skip certain fields or whole records. This window also tells you when that happens (although it doesn't tell you which fields or records were skipped).

After the import is complete, FileMaker shows you a found set of just the records it imported. But don't reach for the Show All Records command yet: The fact that it's a found set is your safety net. If something goes wrong with your import (the wrong records came through, field mapping doesn't look right, or whatever), just delete the found set, and then start over. You can scan through the data and make sure you got what you wanted and that the data went into the fields you intended. You can also take this opportunity to perform other actions (like use the Replace Field Contents command) on every imported record.

Recurring Import

When you import records into FileMaker (File→Import Records→File), the Open File dialog box has an inconspicuous little checkbox labeled "Set up as automatic recurring import" (Figure 19-15). Recurring import is a new FileMaker Pro 11 feature that can spare you some tedium. If you find yourself importing updated versions of the same spreadsheet over and over again, a Recurring Import can make that process almost automatic.

The Recurring Import Setup dialog box asks you questions about what you want FileMaker to do with the imported data. The result is a new table with the data you imported, a new layout to display it, a new script to rerun the import, and a script trigger that updates the data each time you switch to the new layout. These are all things you can program for yourself, but not in the two seconds it takes FileMaker to pull it off.

Here's how to get your own recurring import:

1. **Choose File→Import Records→File, and then select a file to import.**

   Make sure the "Set up as automatic recurring import" checkbox is turned on, of course. The Recurring Import Setup dialog box opens. As shown in Figure 19-16, it displays the path of the file you just chose.

Note: You can't do recurring imports with FileMaker files. Within FileMaker, related tables are the way to keep all information in a database updated.

Figure 19-15:
If you're about to do an import that you expect to do again and again, turn on the "Set up as automatic recurring import" check box before you click Open.

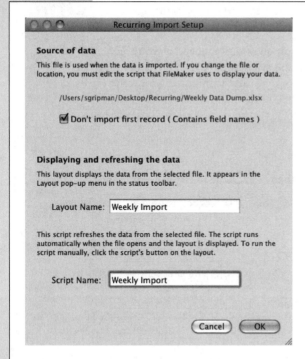

Figure 19-16:
The Recurring Import Setup dialog box has only three settings to configure. "Don't import first record" is the only one of the three that affects the execution of a recurring import. Layout Name and Script Name can be anything you like.

2. **Answer the dialog box's three questions:**

— Does the first row of your import file contain field/column names?

If it does, turn on the checkbox, and FileMaker uses the contents of that row to name the fields. If you leave the box unchecked, FileMaker names the fields of your new table f1, f2, f3, and so on.

— What do you want the name the new layout?

— What do you want to name the script?

For simplicity, FileMaker suggests using the same name as the file you selected. You can name it something different, but there's no compelling reason to.

3. **Click OK.**

Moments later you have it: a new table, a new field for every column in the source file, a new script to rerun the import and a set of freshly imported records on a new layout (Figure 19-17).

And now, here's the big payoff: Any time you need to refresh that data, just switch to the new layout or, if you're already there, click the button furnished up in the header. FileMaker goes back to the source file, grabs the new information, and updates the database according the choices you made in the Recurring Import Setup dialog box.

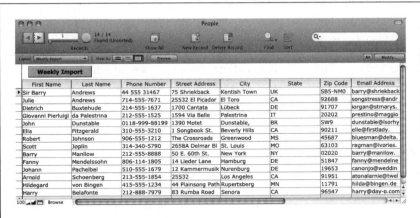

Figure 19-17:
Your new table full of data is presented to you in Table view. You certainly don't have to leave it that way. You can switch among Form, List, and Table views with impunity.

GEM IN THE ROUGH

What a Recurring Import Is Not

Now that you know what a Recurring Import is, be sure you understand what it is *not*.

1. **It's not synchronization.** Once it's in FileMaker, the data loses all association with the source file. It's strictly one way.

2. **It's not a merge.** When you switch to a Recurring Import layout, or push its button, the import script *deletes every record* in the table and imports them all over again. It doesn't update existing records or merge the current source file with the changes you made. It just obliterates the data and brings it in again.

3. **It's not your mom.** Every time you trigger a Recurring Import, FileMaker looks for the source file in the exact same place with the exact same name. If you rename it, move it, or even change the name of the folder that it was in, FileMaker won't look all over your hard drive to find it for you.

4. **It's not a mind reader.** FileMaker expects the same file, with the same columns in the same order every time. If you're presented with a new version of the source file with, say, a few new and reordered columns, FileMaker doesn't have a way to sense that and adjust. It merrily imports the records again, without displaying an error, even if phone numbers are going into the email address field. And those new columns you added? Ignored. If the structure of the source file changes, scrap your old Recurring Import, and then set up a new one.

Importing over Existing Data

When you import data into a file that already has some records in it, the Import Action section of the Import Field Mapping dialog box (Figure 19-12) gives you three ways to specify how you want to deal with that existing data. Normally, it starts out with the "Add new records" setting turned on, meaning that FileMaker simply adds imported records to your database. Sometimes, though, you want to update existing records instead. For example, suppose your database holds shipping rates for every state you ship to. When your freight company updates its rates, it sends you a new file with one record for each state, and the new rates in a Rate field. If you add these records to your database, you end up with *two* records for each state, which is probably not what you want. So FileMaker gives you two other choices that let you update records as you import.

Update existing records in found set

To avoid creating duplicate records as in the shipping rates example, you can turn on "Update existing records in found set", and then map just the Rate field to the appropriate field in your table. When you import, FileMaker takes the rate from the first record in the import file and puts it in the first record in the found set. It then copies the second rate into the second record. This process continues until it has imported every rate.

If your import file has more records than the found set, FileMaker simply skips the extra records. If you'd rather import *all* the records (adding new records once all those in the found set have been updated), turn on "Add remaining data as new records."

Warning: This import action is useful only if you're certain the records in the import file are in the *same order* as those in the export file. If they're not, FileMaker updates the wrong records, leaving you with incorrect data. If you aren't positive the records are in the right order, use "Update matching records in found set" instead.

Update matching records in found set

"Update matching records in found set" works much the same way. When you import with this action, FileMaker updates data in existing records by copying it from the import file. This time, though, you get to tell FileMaker how to figure out which records in the import file match each record in the found set. You tell FileMaker this by specifying one or more *matching fields*, as described in Figure 19-18.

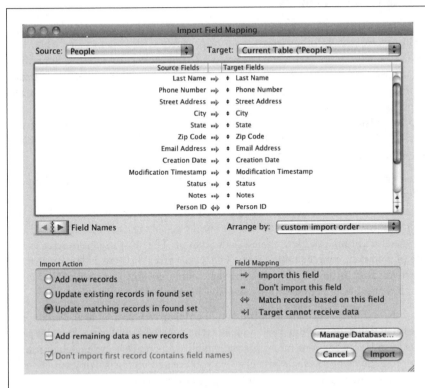

Figure 19-18:
When you turn on "Update matching records in found set" FileMaker lets you use a new symbol between source and target fields. Person ID at the bottom of the list has a "<->" symbol beside it. This symbol tells FileMaker to match records based on ID. In other words, when it imports the first record, it finds a record in the found set with the same ID. FileMaker then updates that record's data based on the import file. If FileMaker doesn't find a match, it skips the import record. It's safest to use a key field for import matching.

Warning: Pay special attention to this command's name: "Update matching records in *found set*." FileMaker notes your found set when it starts the import. When looking for matches, it looks only at the records in the found set. If you have a customer with a matching first and last name, but that customer isn't in the found set, FileMaker will either skip that record, or add a new duplicate. In most cases, you want to do a Records→Show All Records operation before starting this kind of import.

To get the new symbol in the field mapping list, just click the spot between fields. FileMaker now toggles between the three possible symbols: Import, Don't import, and Match. (If you forget what each symbol means, the Field Mapping area in the window reminds you.) Again, if you'd rather have FileMaker import every record in the import file, adding new records when no match is found, turn on "Add remaining data as new records."

Creating Tables on Import

All the importing you've learned about so far assumes that your tables and fields are already created. In other words, your target table is already in place when you choose your source file. But when you're doing a big conversion job (say, upgrading from 15 over-extended Excel spreadsheets to a smooth-running FileMaker dream system), it'll take you quite some time to create all those tables and fields. And even though you have access to the Manage Database dialog box while you're importing, this process isn't quick or easy when you've got hundreds of fields coming in from dozens of files. FileMaker's already thought of that, and offers to handle the tedious work of table and field creation for you.

Choose Import→File, and then select a data source. In the Import Field Mapping window, there's a handy pop-up menu called Target. Click it, and you see the current table (remember that's based on the layout that was active when you chose the Import command), all your other tables (grayed out, so you can't choose them), and a very useful command, New Table (Data Source). The stuff in parentheses is the name of your data source and the name FileMaker gives the new table it creates for you. (If you already have a table with the same name as your data source, FileMaker appends a number to the end of the new table's name.)

Choose New Table, and then click Import. FileMaker creates a table and an appropriate set of fields for you, and then populates the new fields with data. You also get a simple form layout for your new table and a table occurrence on your Relationships graph. You can treat this table just like one you created yourself. For example, you can start creating relationships to hook it up to other table occurrences.

Tip: See page 510 to see how FileMaker Pro Advanced lets you import tables and fields *without* the data that normally comes with them.

When you let FileMaker create fields for you, it does its best to create the field types you want. For instance, if the data source is a FileMaker file, your new fields match the old file's field names and field types. But if the source is a plain text file with no formatting information to go by, FileMaker doesn't have any names to go by, so the new fields become text fields and get the prosaic names of f1, f2, f3, and so on. In either case, check the fields in your new table to make sure you get the names and field types you want. You have to manually create any calculations you need.

Creating a New Database from an Import File

If you have a file full of data, and you want to build a brand new database around it, FileMaker has an even simpler option than creating a database, and then importing the data. Just choose File→Open, and then select the file you want to convert. You can also use drag and drop: On Windows, drag it to the open FileMaker Pro window. FileMaker promptly converts the file to a database for you. On the Mac, drag a file onto the FileMaker icon.

Note: If you can't see the file you want in the Open dialog box, or it's grayed out, change the option in the "Files of Type" (Windows) or "Show" (Mac) pop-up menu. If your file is one of the formats FileMaker supports, you can select it once you identify its type.

If FileMaker finds data with a first row that looks like field names, it asks whether you want to use those when FileMaker creates fields. If it can't find anything that looks like field names, you get those old standbys, f1, f2, f3. In addition to a single table and the appropriate number of fields (complete with data, of course), you get two very plain layouts. One is a generic form layout, showing one record at a time, and the other is a simple columnar list.

Converting Older FileMaker Files

Use this same process (the Open file command) if you're converting files from very old versions of FileMaker (FileMaker 3, 4, 5, 5.5, or 6) to the more capable format used by FileMaker 7, 8, 8.5, and 9. FileMaker does its best to carry all the data, scripts, layouts, and so forth from the old file into the modern era. But if the original file was complex, you'll almost certainly have some work to do to get things up to snuff. Converting old files is a huge topic, and most people find that conversion requires a certain amount of retrofitting, either to make scripts and other things that break during conversion whole again, or to take full advantage of the .fp7 multiple-table-per-file power. (FileMaker offers an excellent document on this subject. Go to *www.filemaker.com* and search for Migration Foundations and Methodologies.)

Import Data Sources

You've learned about the most common importing task—when your data's coming in from a single file. But you have other needs and FileMaker's got other choices. File→Import is an entire submenu, with commands to suit even the most demanding database manager. From there, you get to pick where the data should come from (the data source), and you get several choices.

File

The File→Import→File command shows an Open File dialog box. Select any file that matches one of the export formats explained earlier in this chapter. You see your old friend, the Import Field Mapping dialog box (Figure 19-12). Match your source to your target, and away you go.

You can also use a similar command when you have to move data from one table to another within the same file. Go to your target layout and choose File→Import Records→File. In the dialog box, choose the database you're in, and you see the Import Field Mapping dialog box. Select the table that's your data source from the Source pop-up menu and you're ready to go.

Folder

Using this command, you can pick any folder, and FileMaker imports the contents of each appropriate file in that folder. It creates *one* record for each file it imports, and puts the file into the field you specify. In other words, if you have a folder full of letters you've written, you can import them into a Letters database using this command. The complete text of each letter would go in a field, with one record per letter. (Remember, though, that FileMaker only supports pictures, movies, and plain text files when importing. If your letters are in Microsoft Word format, for example, you're out of luck.)

Choosing File→Import→Folder summons the "Folder of Files Import Options" dialog box shown in Figure 19-19.

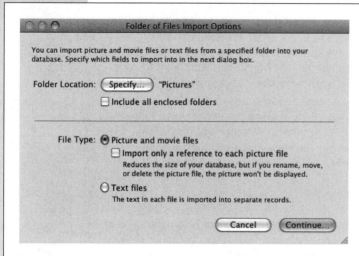

Figure 19-19:
This window is what you see when you choose the File→Import→Folder command. In the top part of the "Folder of Files Import Options" window, you get to choose which folder to import (click Specify). In the bottom half, you decide what kind of files you're interested in.

Normally, FileMaker finds only files directly inside the folder you pick; it ignores any other folders contained inside. You have to turn on "Include all enclosed folders" to make FileMaker look inside those folders, too. With this option turned on, it digs as deep as necessary to find every file.

Once you've picked a folder, you get to decide what kind of files to import. You have only two choices: "Picture and movie files" and "Text files." In the first case, FileMaker ignores every file that isn't a supported picture or movie type. You choose whether the files themselves are inserted in the container field or just references to them. If you choose the "Text files" option instead, it seeks out only plain text files.

Importing a folder of pictures or movies

When you choose the "Pictures and movie files" option, and then click Continue, you may be in for a bit of a wait. Depending on the number of files FileMaker has to look through, you may see a progress dialog box for as long as several minutes.

When the import is complete, you see the now-familiar Import Field Mapping dialog box. But the list of source fields looks entirely unfamiliar—in a good way.

As outlined in Figure 19-20, FileMaker translates the file information into logical field types, perfect for database use.

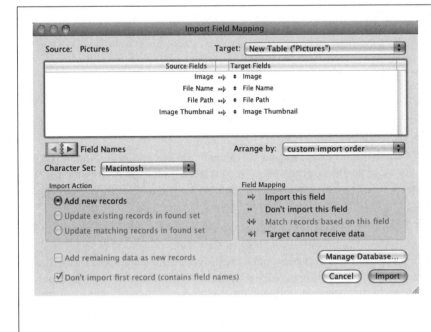

Figure 19-20:
When you import a folder full of pictures, FileMaker practically reads your mind. It not only lets you dump the picture into a container field, but it also offers you the chance to put the file name and full path into text fields. Best of all, FileMaker can shrink the picture down to a thumbnail and put that into a container field, too, which saves space by reducing size and resolution. The thumbnails appear even when the original images aren't available (if a network drive is unavailable, for instance).

Importing a folder of text files

When you choose to import text files, you still get an Import Field Mapping dialog box. This time, the source field list includes Text Content, File Name, and File Path. Each expects to be imported into a text field.

Digital Camera

If you're using Mac OS X, the File→Import Records menu has a Digital Camera option. Unfortunately, this option relies on a feature unique to Mac OS X, so you can't import directly from a camera on Windows. You have to download the images to your computer first, and then import them. (There's a workaround if you can set up your camera to show up as a USB disk on Windows. In that case, use the Import→Folder command to import images directly from the camera.)

When you first plug your camera into your Mac, chances are iPhoto launches and prepares to import the images. To avoid any potential confusion, quit iPhoto first (or be careful not to click iPhoto's Import button while FileMaker's working with the camera).

Note: If you import from your camera to FileMaker a lot, you can tell iPhoto to get out of the way: Just launch Image Capture (in your Applications folders) and then, in its Preferences→Camera tab, select FileMaker. If you use iPhoto sometimes and FileMaker others, choose No Application in the pop-up menu instead. That way, you get to decide what program each time.

With the camera connected, choose File→Import Records→Digital Camera. The verbosely titled "FileMaker Pro Photo Import Options" dialog box appears (Figure 19-21).

If you want to import *everything* on the camera, turn on "All images." But if you just want, for example, the last five shots you took, turn on the last radio button—"The last [blank] images"—and put the right number in its box. Finally, you can choose "Some images," and then click Specify to see a list of image thumbnails to choose from.

Even if you want to import all the images, the "Some images" choice can come in handy. It's the only place you can *rotate* the images before you import them. There's no direct way to rotate an image once it's in the container field. You have to export it, rotate it in another program, and then insert it again.

Even if you're importing the images directly into FileMaker (rather than just a reference), it still puts them in the folder you specify in the "Download to" pop-up menu. If you want to, you can simply delete them when you're done. (If you're storing references, though, the folder you pick becomes very important. If you import the pictures, and then move them to a different folder, the references are wrong, and the pictures don't display in FileMaker.)

When you're through making choices, click Continue. The Import Field Mapping window that appears next is loaded with source fields this time. FileMaker lets you import loads of image data along with the pictures, including dimensions, resolution, shot date and time, and all that photographer-speak stuff you see when you accidentally put your camera in advanced mode.

At this point, you're in familiar territory. Just match up the fields, and then click Import. Be prepared for a wait as it takes FileMaker longer to import full-color digital pictures than, say, Zip codes.

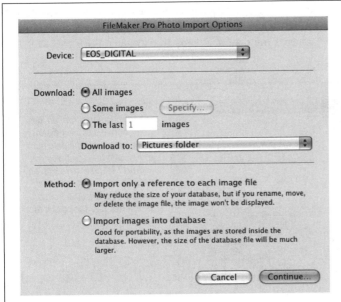

Figure 19-21:
This dialog box appears when you import from a digital camera in Mac OS X. The device pop-up menu lets you pick which camera to import from (on the off chance you have several connected). You also get to decide which images to import, where to put them (more on these options in a moment), and whether or not you want to store just references to the pictures.

XML Data Source

Because so many programs and data formats exist out there, the World Wide Web Consortium (W3C) created the XML format to make data exchange more predictable. FileMaker uses a special subset of XML's code, called FMPXMLRESULT, to facilitate import. If your data source was created by another FileMaker Pro database, it already uses FMPXMLRESULT, and you can import that data straight up, no chaser. But if the XML document doesn't use FileMaker's Document Type Definition (DTD), you'll need an Extensible Stylesheet Language (XSLT) document to tell FileMaker how to make the XML file work with FileMaker. In fact, with the help of XSLT style sheets, FileMaker can import *any* XML file in any form. An XSLT style sheet converts the XML you're importing into FMPXMLRESULT.

Note: You can learn to write your own XSLT style sheets, and thereby turn FileMaker's XML into just about anything, from specialized XML your accounting software uses, to an HTML web page, to a standard RSS news feed. XML and XSLT are complex languages and this book can't cover them in full. If you're ready for a challenge, check out the book *Learning XSLT* by Michael Fitzgerald (O'Reilly). You can also find dozens of premade style sheets on FileMaker's website at *www.filemaker.com/*.

To import XML data, choose File→Import Records→XML Data Source. When you do, you'll see the window in Figure 19-22. Here, you tell FileMaker where to get the XML data, and optionally what XSLT style sheet to apply. (If you don't apply a style sheet, FileMaker assumes the data is already in its special FMPXMLRESULT format.)

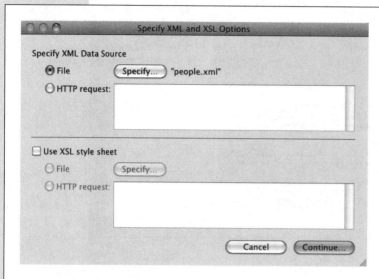

Figure 19-22:
When you import from an XML data source, FileMaker first asks you where to get the data from, and how to process it. You can instruct FileMaker to look in any XML file on your computer, or to fetch the XML data from a web server (see the box on the next page).

Unlike the typical import command, when you import XML data, you don't actually have to have a *file* to import from. This window also lets you specify a "HTTP request," which is just a fancy way of saying "web page." Type the URL of a web page here, and FileMaker goes out over the Internet, grabs the page, and pulls it down for you. Believe it or not, a lot of XML data is available hot off the Web like this. Likewise, you can choose to fetch the XSLT template from the Web as well.

When you're finished choosing XML and XSL options, click Continue. FileMaker processes the XML and XSLT (which may take a few minutes), and then shows you the Import Field Mapping dialog box. From there, you can proceed like any import, as described earlier in this chapter.

XML export

When you export to XML, FileMaker exports the data in the FMPXMLRESULT format, and then applies the style sheet. You create the style sheet to translate this XML into the appropriate format for your intended recipient. You have slightly more flexibility when exporting than when importing: XSLT can translate only XML documents, but it can *produce* any text-based format. So although you can import only XML files, you can export just about anything.

Bento Data Source

If you use Mac OS X and have Bento (see the box on page 5), you can import data directly from your Bento libraries into a FileMaker database. Just choose File→Import Records→Bento Data Source. When you do, the window in Figure 19-23 appears.

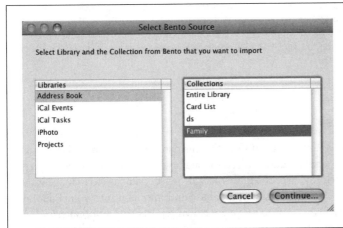

Figure 19-23:
The Bento Data Source import option lets you take information from any of your Bento libraries. Just choose the library you want from the left-hand list. If that library has collections, they appear in the list on the right. There's also an Entire Library option.

POWER USERS' CLINIC

XML and HTTP

Sometimes the XML data you want to import is in a file on your computer. But a big part of the XML data source feature's power is that FileMaker can also get XML data from other computers using *HTTP*, or Hypertext Transport Protocol. You probably recognize this acronym because it usually sits in front of web addresses (as in *http://www. missingmanuals.com/*). HTTP is the way web browsers talk to websites, but it's used for a lot more than that. Often, companies make important information available on HTTP servers in XML format. It's this kind of information that File-Maker wants to let you tap into:

Many news-oriented websites make headlines and article excerpts available in XML formats called RSS or Atom. Using the XML Data Source feature in FileMaker, you could import news directly into your FileMaker database.

You can grab current or historical exchange rates from various sources to perform accurate currency conversions in FileMaker.

Some shippers let you track packages by downloading XML data. You can build package tracking right into FileMaker Pro.

FileMaker's XML import does have two significant limitations. First, it can't access data that's available only over a secure connection (in other words, it doesn't support HTTP over SSL, or HTTPS). If the data you need to access is available only in this form, you need to find another way.

Second, some XML data sources need information passed to them as *post arguments*—the equivalent of form fields on some web pages. FileMaker can't send post arguments with the URL. Luckily, most data sources let you pass this information as part of the URL instead. Refer to the documentation for your data source for details.

Once you select the appropriate library (and optionally a collection), click Continue to see the standard FileMaker Import Records window. From here, you can match up fields and configure options, just like any other data source.

Note: Bento automatically turns your Mac OS X Address Book, Calendars, and To Do lists into libraries in which you can link up to your own data in various ways. While this tool doesn't have nearly the power of FileMaker Pro, its ability to seamlessly integrate with your existing data is compelling. And since you can easily import from Bento to FileMaker, you can use it as a conduit to get address, calendar, and to-do info into your FileMaker databases too. For $49, it's the easiest and least expensive way to import this info into FileMaker.

ODBC Data Sources

The last import data source is called ODBC. This data source is a popular standard to let programs access information stored in database systems. For instance, if your company has an Oracle, Sybase, or Microsoft SQL Server database to manage orders, you can extract data directly from that database and import it into your FileMaker Pro database (perhaps you want to make your own reports with FileMaker).

Note: Although you can *import* data from other big database systems, FileMaker also offers a much more powerful means to interact with some of them: External SQL Sources, or ESS (page 806), which lets you work directly with data from Oracle, Microsoft SQL Server, and MySQL in FileMaker. ESS is often a simpler and more powerful choice unless you're just after a one-shot copy of the data.

ODBC is the most complex import data source to set up. It's a two-step process:

- First, you need to install an ODBC driver for the kind of database you're connecting to. For example, if your corporate database is in Oracle, you need an ODBC driver for Oracle. These drivers are platform specific, and most vendors supply only drivers for Microsoft Windows. If you're using Mac OS X, you can buy high-quality FileMaker-compatible drivers from Actual Technologies at *www.actualtechnologies.com/filemaker.php/*. (When you visit their site, make sure you get the version that's appropriate for the number of simultaneous users you'll have.)

- Next, you need to set up an ODBC data source. FileMaker doesn't connect to the database directly. Rather, it uses a data source that's been specified in the ODBC system on your computer. So you have to set up that data source first. In Microsoft Windows, you do this setting up in the ODBC control panel. In Mac OS X, you use the ODBC Administrator program in your Utilities folder.

Once you have a driver installed and a data source set up, you can use the File→Import Records→ODBC Data Source command. When you do, you see the Select ODBC Data Source window (Figure 19-24).

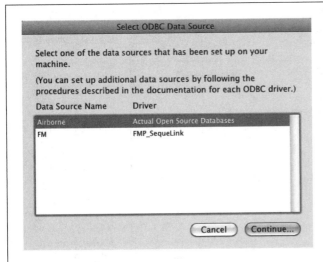

When you click Continue in this window, you probably need to enter a user name and password for the database you're connecting to. You need to get this information from the database administrator, unless you created it in the ODBC software yourself.

Next, FileMaker shows the SQL Query Builder dialog box (Figure 19-25).

When you extract data from *most* databases (FileMaker being the notable exception), you have to use a special programming language called Structured Query Language, or SQL (often pronounced *sequel*). Writing an SQL *query* (or program) is a complicated affair. Luckily, in most cases, FileMaker can do it for you—you just make the right choices. (For more detail, see the box on page 847.)

When you're all finished building your query, click Execute. FileMaker performs the query, gathers the data from the data source, and shows the same Import Field Mapping dialog box you always see when importing data. If you find yourself doing a lot of ODBC imports, you may be well served by a good book on SQL.

Although the query builder supports only a little SQL, you can use any SQL commands supported by your database server if you type the query directly. And SQL can do *a lot*.

Importing and Exporting in a Script

Like almost everything else in FileMaker, you can completely control the import and export process from a script. You use the Import Records and Export Records scripts, which you can find in the Records section of the script steps list. You also find script steps for "Save Records as Excel" and "Save Records as PDF", with similar options.

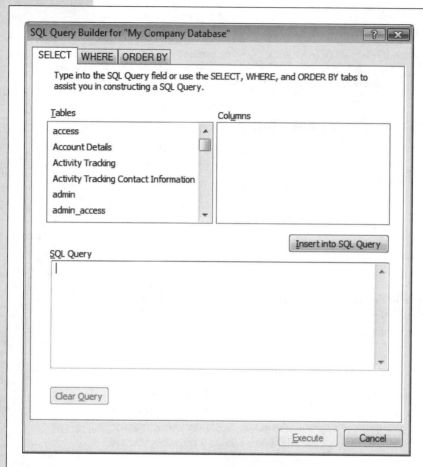

Figure 19-25:
In the SQL Query Builder dialog box's SELECT tab, the Tables list shows every table available from the database you're connecting to. When you select a table, FileMaker lists all its fields (called columns in most database systems) in the Columns list. Select a field, and then click "Insert into SQL Query" to include that field in the data you're importing. If you're a SQL pro, you can simply type in the SQL Query box instead.

Save Records Script Steps

To automate the creation of Excel spreadsheets, use the "Save Records as Excel" script step. Not surprisingly, there's a "Save Records as PDF" script step as well. Each of these lets you specify all the options the standard menu commands offer, so you can completely automate the process.

As an added bonus, the "Save Records as PDF" script step includes one option you don't get when you run the command manually: an "Append to existing PDF" checkbox. When you turn this option on, if the file you're saving already exists, FileMaker adds the new pages to the end of the existing file. This scheme makes it possible to lump together several reports, or data from several different layouts into one complete PDF package for printing or distribution.

SQL Queries

To make use of FileMaker's query builder, you need to know just a little bit about SQL. A SQL query is made up of *clauses*, each of which influences the results you receive from the database server. Although SQL understands several clauses, the query builder window supports just three of them: SELECT, WHERE, and ORDER BY. The window has a tab for each of these.

The SELECT clause is where you tell the database what *fields* you want to import. You can include fields from more than one table if necessary. A SELECT clause alone imports every record in the table. If you include fields from more than one table, you get a result that may surprise you: Every record from each file is mixed in every possible combination. In other words, you import lots of records (multiply the record counts from each table to figure out how many).

The WHERE clause's job is to control which *records* get imported and how the tables are related. To specify certain records, you build find criteria into the WHERE clause. First, select a table and column from the pop-up menus. Then select something from the Operator pop-up menu. You can match this field with a value you type yourself (turn on the Value radio button) or with another field (turn on the Column radio button). Either way, enter or select the correct value. Finally, select either the And radio button or the Or radio button, and then turn on Not if you want to *omit* the matching records. When you're finished defining the criteria, click "Insert into SQL Query."

Relationships in SQL are probably the most confusing. SQL databases don't have a Relationship graph like FileMaker, so the database doesn't know how things relate to one another at all. Each time you build a query, it's your job to tell it how to relate records from one table to those in another. You do this job by matching field values in each table in the WHERE clause.

For instance, you might pick the Customer ID field from the Customers table, the "=" operator, and the Customer ID field from the Orders table. When you add criteria like this to your WHERE clause, you've told the database how Order and Customer records relate. You can add as many criteria in this way as you need.

The last tab is called ORDER BY. This clause lets you specify a sort order for your data. It works just like FileMaker's normal Sort dialog box: Just add the fields to the Order By list, selecting Ascending or Descending as appropriate. When you've given it the order you want, click "Insert into SQL Query" again.

As you do these things, FileMaker builds the actual query in the SQL Query box at the bottom of the window so you can see how it comes together. If you feel adventurous, you can manually change this query at any time.

The Import Records Script Step

This script step has three options. First, you get to specify the data source to import from. Your choices match those in the File→Import Records menu: File, Folder, Digital Camera (Mac OS X only), XML Data, and ODBC Data. Whichever option you choose, FileMaker asks you for more information (*which* file to import, or *which* ODBC data source to use, for instance). When specifying a file, you get the standard path list dialog box. In other words, you can specify several paths if you want; FileMaker imports the first one it finds. (If you don't specify a source, your users have to do it as they run the script, in a potentially confusing series of dialog boxes. Since you're presumably providing a script to make things easier for people, it's best to store source files in a safe place and have the script escort your users to them.)

Once you've specified the source, you can turn on "Specify import order" to record the import field mapping, and other import options. Finally, you can turn on "Perform without dialog" if you want FileMaker to import the data directly, with no input from your users. If you leave this option off, FileMaker displays the Import Field Mapping dialog box when the script runs, so folks can make changes to any field mapping you specified.

The Export Records Script Step

The Export Records script step offers similar options. You can specify the output file and export order, and you can choose "Perform without dialog" if you don't want your users to see the export dialog box.

When you specify the output file, you may be surprised to see an Output File Path list. In other words, FileMaker lets you specify *more than one file*. This choice doesn't mean FileMaker exports more than one file, though. Instead, it exports to the first file path that's *valid*. If the first path in the list includes a folder name that doesn't exist, for example, FileMaker skips it, and then tries the next one.

Part Six: Appendixes

VI

Appendix A: Getting Help

Appendix B: FileMaker Error Codes

Getting Help

This book provides a solid foundation in FileMaker and takes you well into power user territory, but it doesn't cover everything there is to know about this vastly versatile program. (You wouldn't be able to lift it if it did.) This appendix is a guide to the many resources available to help you plumb the depths of FileMaker database design and development.

Some of the resources in this appendix are available a variety of ways. For example, you can get to FileMaker's online Knowledge Base by going to *www.filemaker.com*, clicking the Support menu, and then choosing Knowledge Base. But there's also a quick link in the help files so you don't have to remember the links to click. Read on to see some of the ways to get to the bountiful resources provided by FileMaker and from third parties.

Getting Help from FileMaker Pro

Like most commercial software packages, FileMaker has a Help menu. Choose Help→FileMaker Pro Help to launch the Help file. The main screen (Figure A-1) lets you choose from a variety of ways to find help on the topic you're interested in. Major topics are listed on the left side of the screen, and some featured topics are listed on the top right.

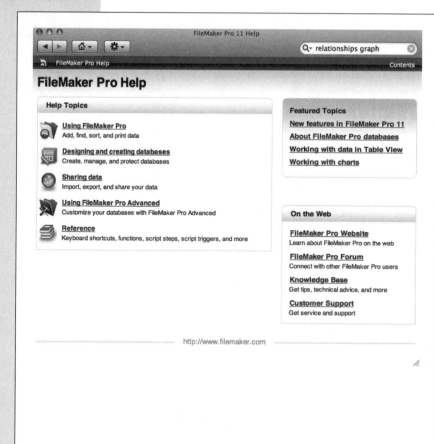

Figure A-1:
The Mac Help Screen lets you click links to find the topic you want, but it's usually faster to type a question in the search box in the upper right (where you see the words "relationships graph" in this illustration). Just type a few words that'll identify your subject, and then press the Return key. The main screen changes to show a list of topics that relate to your search terms. Double-click the item that sounds closest to your issue. If it's not quite right, scroll to the bottom of the page, where there are links to related topics. You can usually find what you need in a few clicks. (Windows fans, your search works a little differently. See Figure A-2 for your help window.)

The Help file is organized by main topics, as listed on the main screen. Click a topic and you'll get a list of clickable subtopics. Use this method if you're searching for general information, or aren't in a particular hurry. For example, to find information on creating a calculation field, you have to click through five lists to get to the Defining calculation fields detail page. Sometimes that's very helpful because the information goes from general to more specific and you're bound to learn something on the way. Sometimes you see an interesting related topic on your journey. But when you're in a hurry, just use the search box.

FileMaker gives context sensitive help, but the methods vary by OS. On Windows 7, most FileMaker windows have a question mark button in the upper right, near the close box. Click the question mark button, and then click the window, and Help will launch directly to the topic that addresses that window (Figure A-2).

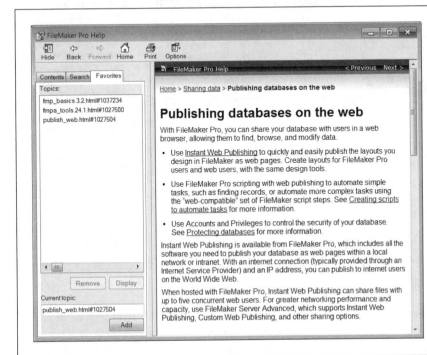

Figure A-2:
Windows Help has an extra pane at the left of the Help files with three tabs: Contents, Search and Favorite. The Contents tab is a repeat of the Home page, which is useful when you're eight clicks deep into Help and just want to get back to the main screen. The search tab lets you search, and re-search previous results. Plus you can mark favorite topics using the Add button at the bottom of the Favorites tab. The pages you mark appear in a list.

On the Mac (Snow Leopard), the Help menu itself contains a search box. Type your term, and then FileMaker gives you two lists of results. One lists menu commands that pertain to your search term and the second lists Help topic pages (Figure A-3), one above the other in the menu. If your Help menu doesn't contain the normal Help commands, delete the search term in the box and the menu returns to normal display.

Hot Tip: If you type a layout name (like "Customers Refund Form") into the search box (Mac only), one of the Menu Items will be Go to Layout→Customers Refund Form. That's incredibly helpful when you have hundreds of layouts and can't remember which folder you placed the one you need in or if it's near the bottom of your lengthy list and takes too long to scroll all the way down there.

Figure A-3:
The Mac Help menu gives you help two ways. If it can find a menu command or commands that matches your search terms, it puts those results at the top of the Help menu in a section called "Menu Items." Then if you select one of those items, the menu will be pulled down for you, and a big blue, dancing arrow (yes, it moves to make sure you see it) points to the command you selected. That's very helpful when you know there's a command that does what you need, but you can't find it.

A comprehensive list of FileMaker's functions is one of the Help file's most useful parts. As in the Specify Calculation window, the functions are listed two ways: by type, and alphabetically. The detail page for each function gives you the function name, parameter(s), data type returned, and a description of what the function does. Use these pages to help you when you're using a function for the first time.

The bottom right of the Help file's main screen also provides links so you can venture beyond the Help files:

- The FileMaker Pro website links goes to FileMaker's home page, from which you can navigate or do a search to get more information. You'll find the usual set of marketing materials, but lots of great technical information too.

- The FileMaker Pro Forum link goes to a forum created by FileMaker, Inc. to help you get in contact with other FileMaker Pro users and developers. Questions range from basic topics to detailed discussions on the use and care of specific functions. Follow normal forum etiquette when you first visit. That is, you should scan or search the topics list to see if your question has been addressed. If it hasn't been covered, or if the thread you find doesn't answer your particular situation, then post a new question. You have to register to post a question or answer somebody else's post, but registration is free and quick. The forum is moderated by FileMaker staff. It has an English language section (the busiest), and also French, German, and Japanese areas.

- The Knowledge Base link takes you to a section of the FileMaker website where technical issues are addressed. New issues or alerts are posted on this page. You can search the knowledge base with keywords or skim through a list of recent documents to see what's new. If you're logged in (the same account you set up to use the forum), you can mark pertinent documents and get email sent to you if the document is updated.

- The Customer Support link goes to a page with links for common topics, like finding the right product, software registration, and paid tech support options.

All these outside links, plus links to Downloads, Training and Consultants are also found in the Support menu on FileMaker's website. This and other help available from FileMaker, Inc. is detailed later on in this appendix.

FileMaker's Installed Extras

The installation package for FileMaker Pro and FileMaker Pro Advanced includes a suite of ways to get extra help for FileMaker:

- Electronic Documentation. This folder includes several PDF user guides that cover various topics :

- Installation and New Features Guide for FileMaker Pro 11 and FileMaker Pro 11 Advanced

- FileMaker Pro 11 User's Guide

- FileMaker Pro 11 Advanced Development Guide (FMPA only)

- FileMaker Pro 11 Instant Web Publishing Guide

- FileMaker Pro 11 ODBC and JDBC Guide

    — Examples including XML Documentaion and XML Examples

    — Starter Solutions are more than 40 template files you can customize

The installer program *always* installs online help, but the other items are optional. Choose Custom Install in the Install panel of the installation wizard to pick and choose which of the optional files you want installed. When you choose the Easy Install option, you get *everything* installed. On Windows, you can find these helpers at Program Files→FileMaker→FileMaker Pro 11→English Extras. And on the Mac, look in Applications→FileMaker Pro→English Extras.

And if FileMaker's already installed on your computer, but the helpers listed above are missing, then you can perform a Custom Install and choose the helper files you need without having to uninstall and reinstall FileMaker itself. They're also available in the Downloads section of FileMaker's website.

Starter Solutions

You got a glimpse of these starter solutions in the box on page 104. The Quick Start window has a link to those solution files. When you click the link, Mac users see a window that shows thumbnails of each solution (Figure A-4). Pick the one you want, and FileMaker creates a new copy of the file for you. You can add data, create and edit scripts, or delete objects you don't need without affecting the original template.

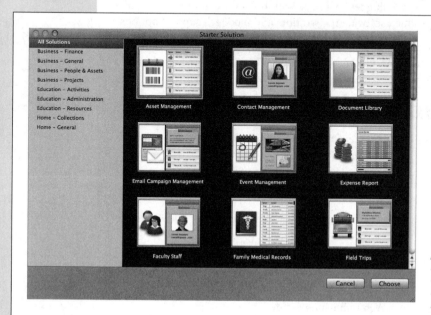

Figure A-4:
The Mac version of the Starter Solution window shows groups of solutions in the same window. The Windows version shows a single thumbnail when you click a solution from the list. Either way, use the thumbnails to help you decide which one you want. Then, click the Choose button to create a template. By popular request FileMaker Pro 11 added an Invoice solution to the mix. You can find it listed under Business-General.

Note: If you prefer, you can navigate to the Templates folder, and then launch the solution you want just like any other file. When you launch a solution file directly, though, you're opening the original template file, and any changes you make to the template are reflected in any new copies you make when you choose File→New Database.

Starter Solutions can help you get up and running with basic data management tasks if you don't have time to figure out how things work in FileMaker's universe. But these templates also serve another purpose—as an introduction to onscreen-display design. They have a clean, uncluttered look you can adapt for your own purposes. Feel free to copy the design as is or use it as a jumping-off point for your new database.

Each template stores different kinds of data, so it's helpful to explore several templates to get ideas for arranging and grouping your data effectively. In general, you usually see an easy-to-read name at the top of the layout, which serves to orient people to the task at hand. Underneath the name, you find a couple of rows of navigation tools and buttons grouped together by function. The largest portion of the layout is dedicated to a logical arrangement of data fields.

Finally, FileMaker's templates contain ideas you can use for creating relationships, buttons, and scripts to make your own databases more powerful. For instance, the Contact Management template contains a script that lets you swap a contact's main address data with the secondary address data. You might not ever need to swap address in two sets of fields, but the script is a good study guide on moving data.

Hands-On Tutorial

The tutorial is a 94-page PDF and sample files that walk you through the basics of using and creating a database. It's meant to be worked through from start to finish and assumes that you're coming to FileMaker as a beginner. Nothing is covered in detail, so you can breeze through the work. You'll get exposure to a variety of topics by the time you're done.

XML Examples

You get example files, including a database and sample XML and XSLT files, in the English Extras folder, in a folder called Examples. These simple files serve as a primer for working with FileMaker and XML. To get started, open the database file (*xml example.fp7*), and then run each script to see how XML import and export work. Then take a look at the steps that make up each script, paying particular attention to the options set for the Import Records and Export Records steps. Finally, take a look at the files that are imported and the files that are created by the export scripts. You see how your XML pages should be structured.

The Quick Start Screen

The Quick Start Screen (Figure A-5) provides a quick link to open Starter Solutions so you don't have to navigate through your OS to find them. But it also gives access to some free online help, like the Resource Center, which has its own section below. The Quick Start Screen opens when you first launch FileMaker, and then hides when you open a database. When you close all open databases, the Quick Start Screen reappears, unless you deselect the "Show this screen when FileMaker Pro opens" option. To get the Quick Start Screen back, choose it from the Help menu.

Getting Help from FileMaker, Inc.

FileMaker's website has the usual marketing materials you'd expect from a great software company. But there's lots of substance there, too. In its main navigation menu, Look for "Support", where you find free and fee-based help.

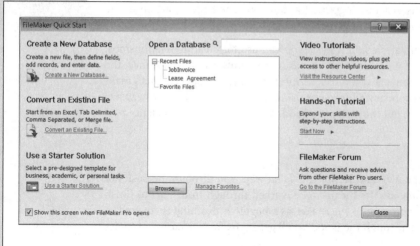

Figure A-5:
The Quick Start Screen is warehouse central for FileMaker help. At the bottom of the left column, you can open Starter Solutions. The right column links to a spot on FileMaker, Inc.'s website where videos and other training resources are available for free. The hands-on tutorial takes you through setting up a basic database and the FileMaker Forum link lets you ask (and answer) questions from other FileMaker developers.

The Resource Center

After the Help files, your next best stop for FileMaker assistance is the FileMaker Resource Center. Just choose Help→Resource Center. FileMaker takes you to a special website covering many FileMaker topics. When you click a general topic, you see several related links. Not all these links are alike, though. Some are similar to the help topics FileMaker installs on your computer, but the Resource Center also has downloadable PDFs and short video demonstrations with tutorial databases. The Resource Center doesn't have everything there is to know about FileMaker, but the topics it covers are covered in depth.

Updaters and Downloads

Like most programs, FileMaker's latest software versions are those on the software company's website. You find software updates and support files, like localized language packs at *www.filemaker.com/support/downloads*. Updaters for the most recent versions of FileMaker and Bento products are listed at the top of the page. A link to a page for previous versions appears just below the current updaters.

The Downloadable Resources section includes the documentation that comes with each FileMaker product, technical resources, trial software, training materials, and some free solution files. There's a link for PHP libraries and some open-source tools, Development tools, including an XLST library and a list of recently released plug-ins, are also available on the Downloads page.

If your installation is missing some (or all) of its templates, click the Kits, Solutions, Examples and References link to show the Starter Solutions link, where you can download new copies. You can also download a free, readymade solution called the Business Productivity Kit. It lets you manage contacts, organize products and inventory, process sales orders, track projects and send emails. Plus, it's customizable.

Even if the Productivity Kit doesn't meet your exact need, it's useful for study purposes. There's some pretty heady stuff under the hood, but the files are full of developer tricks of the trade you can analyze. Even if you don't use the exact techniques you see, you can develop your analytical skills by picking the file apart. You'll also learn different ways to approach and solve particular database problems—maybe ways you hadn't thought of!

Web Seminars

FileMaker periodically presents live, web-based seminars. Invitations are usually sent by email to members of the TechNet (page 860), but you can view the webinars even if you're not a member. Recordings are posted at *www.filemaker.com/support/webinars* a few days after the live event. Webinars are conducted by FileMaker staff or by recognized FileMaker trainers/developers. Topics are grouped by New, Current and Advanced users and range from getting started with FileMaker to beginning scripting and from virtualizing a server to using external SQL data sources.

FileMaker Training Series

This series is the official training curriculum from FileMaker, Inc. It's 12 training modules that cover the essentials of FileMaker solution development and is targeted at intermediate to advanced developers. FileMaker, Inc. recommends the training series as a preparation for taking the FileMaker Certification Exam. The training series materials (book and CD) cost $99.

Technical Support

FileMaker supports the current version of its software and one version prior. In addition to the resources listed above, you can speak with a human being to get help with specific issues. The phone number for free and fee-based tech support, plus customer service to help you decide which products you need is 1-800-325-2747 or 408-727-8227. Phone tech support is available 7:00 a.m. to 5:00 p.m. Pacific Time weekdays (except holidays).

Technical Support deals with technical problems, like when a feature isn't working as advertised, and you need help figuring out why. Teaching you how to create databases, or writing your calculations and scripts for you aren't considered technical support.

Note: If your question isn't tech support, or your files are in an older version for which FileMaker, Inc. no longer offers support, then you need to get help from a third party, usually a consultant, trainer or a user group. See the next page to find out how to find those animals.

Free support

You can't start making databases until FileMaker's installed, so everybody who purchases FileMaker gets unlimited tech support phone calls regarding installation or activation. Plus, you get one free troubleshooting call for each product you buy, which is helpful when you have a bunch of staffers on FileMaker Pro, a copy or two of FileMaker Server, and your very own copy of FileMaker Pro Advanced.

Paid support

Get out your credit card when you call, and then decide how you want to pay:

- You can choose a $45 flat fee and they'll solve a single issue for you, or you can roll the dice (and get multiple problems solved at once) by choosing the $3 per minute rate, with a $75 maximum.

- An Annual Support Contract costs $899 per year. You nominate one person from your company who can call a special toll-free number as many times as needed for 12 months. Add $699 for each additional person who needs the same access. If you have a Volume License Agreement (VLA), the rate goes down to $719 for the primary member and $599 for each additional member. Download the order form at *www.filemaker.com/downloads/pdf/prof_support_form.pdf.*

Tip: A VLA gives you special incentives when you buy multiple copies of FileMaker. One license code works for all your seats and discounts start at five copies. You can add seats whenever you need them and all new VLAs include 1 year of maintenance (which entitles you to a free upgrade if a new version is released during the maintenance period).

File corruption isn't common with FileMaker, but it's devastating when it happens. FileMaker offers file recovery services at $500 per file. Go to *www.filemaker.com/downloads/pdf/filerecovery.pdf* for more information.

Developer Programs

FileMaker runs two programs to help developers keep in touch with each other, and with FileMaker, Inc. itself.

TechNet

The FileMaker Technical Network (*www.filemaker.com/technet*) gets you access to an email discussion forum (called Tech Talk) crawling with FileMaker experts swapping ideas and helping one another. You also get access to exclusive technical white papers and how-to articles on important FileMaker topics. Finally, TechNet subscribers get free FileMaker add-on software and a special developer version of FileMaker Server Advanced for testing purposes. To call yourself a member, you just pay the dues: $99 per year.

FileMaker Business Alliance

If you're a professional FileMaker developer (meaning you build FileMaker databases for other companies for pay), you may qualify to join the FileMaker Business Alliance (FBA) as well. In addition to online discussions, technical info, and free software, FBA members get outstanding software perks. You can purchase FileMaker products for your own use (or your company's use) for deep discounts. You can also get discount pricing on FileMaker products, which you can then resell to your customers. FBA members (along with their products and services) are listed on FileMaker's website, and in the Resource Guide. Membership requires approval, and costs $499 per year. Find out more at *www.filemaker.com/fba*.

DevCon

If total FileMaker immersion is what you seek, the annual Developer's Conference (DevCon) is the way to go. Each day you can attend as many as seven sessions on about 30 different topics, ranging from running a FileMaker consulting firm to web publishing, so you're sure to come away from the 3-day conference with a brain-pan full of new ideas. For details, see *www.filemaker.com/developers/devcon/index.html*.

Getting Help from the Community

Even outside the members-only programs, the FileMaker developer community is a congenial bunch. You'll find lots of resources on the Internet, including free newsgroups and websites. Many independent consultants' sites have free or low-cost resources, too, like lists of custom functions free for the taking or sample files that show specific techniques.

Local User Groups

The most hands-on way to stay abreast of what's new with FileMaker is to join a local user group. There you'll meet other power users and developers. Meetings usually consist of a presentation and Q&A session. Presenters can be FileMaker staff or out-of-town developers. Some groups also sponsor day-long programming camps. Check out *www.fmpug.com/filemaker_data.php* to get the current list of local groups.

Mail Lists and Newsgroups

A listing of email lists is available at *www.filemaker.com/support/mailinglists.html*, but new sites are cropping up all the time, and URLs change even on established sites. So use the link above, or check your favorite search engine, to get the latest links for these groups. To get your feet wet, try general lists, like the one run by Dartmouth University or FileMaker Today. Fmpug.com is a membership-based, online user group with forums, reviews, and resources, including podcast interviews with subject-matter experts. For more specialized topics, have a look at FileMaker XML Talk, FileMaker Pro CGI Talk, and Troi FileMaker Plug-in Talk.

Training/Consultants

FileMaker's website lists trainers and consultants who are members of the FBA. And the FileMaker Resource Guide also lists the FBA group, plus it takes paid advertisements. Your favorite search engine will yield hundreds of results. FileMaker has a certification program, so look for the FileMaker Certified Developer logo or ask the consultant if she's been certified, as part of your selection process.

FileMaker Error Codes

The following table lists the error codes that may pop up when FileMaker detects something out of whack in your database, especially when you're writing or running a script. Like any things written by and for computer programmers, these official descriptions may not make much sense in English, but they may provide a little more guidance than the error number alone.

Error codes marked with an asterisk (*) pertain only to web-published databases.

Error number	Description
–1	Unknown error
0	No error
1	User canceled action
2	Memory error
3	Command is unavailable (for example, wrong operating system, wrong mode, etc.)
4	Command is unknown
5	Command is invalid (for example, a Set Field script step does not have a calculation specified)
6	File is read-only
7	Running out of memory
8	Empty result
9	Insufficient privileges

10	Requested data is missing
11	Name is not valid
12	Name already exists
13	File or object is in use
14	Out of range
15	Can't divide by zero
16	Operation failed, request retry (for example, a user query)
17	Attempt to convert foreign character set to UTF-16 failed
18	Client must provide account information to proceed
19	String contains characters other than A–Z, a–z, 0–9 (ASCII)
20	Command/operation canceled by triggered script
100	File is missing
101	Record is missing
102	Field is missing
103	Relationship is missing
104	Script is missing
105	Layout is missing
106	Table is missing
107	Index is missing
108	Value list is missing
109	Privilege set is missing
110	Related tables are missing
111	Field repetition is invalid
112	Window is missing
113	Function is missing
114	File reference is missing
115	Specified menu set is not present
116	Specified layout object is not present
117	Specified data source is not present
130	Files are damaged or missing and must be reinstalled
131	Language pack files are missing (such as template files)
200	Record access is denied
201	Field cannot be modified
202	Field access is denied
203	No records in file to print, or password doesn't allow print access
204	No access to field(s) in sort order

205	User does not have access privileges to create new records; import will overwrite existing data
206	User does not have password change privileges, or file is not modifiable
207	User does not have sufficient privileges to change database schema, or file is not modifiable
208	Password does not contain enough characters
209	New password must be different from existing one
210	User account is inactive
211	Password has expired
212	Invalid user account and/or password; please try again
213	User account and/or password does not exist
214	Too many login attempts
215	Administrator privileges cannot be duplicated
216	Guest account cannot be duplicated
217	User does not have sufficient privileges to modify administrator account
300	File is locked or in use
301	Record is in use by another user
302	Table is in use by another user
303	Database schema is in use by another user
304	Layout is in use by another user
306	Record modification ID does not match
400	Find criteria are empty
401	No records match the request
402	Selected field is not a match field for a lookup
403	Exceeding maximum record limit for trial version of FileMaker Pro
404	Sort order is invalid
405	Number of records specified exceeds number of records that can be omitted
406	Replace/Reserialize criteria are invalid
407	One or both match fields are missing (invalid relationship)
408	Specified field has inappropriate data type for this operation
409	Import order is invalid
410	Export order is invalid
412	Wrong version of FileMaker Pro used to recover file
413	Specified field has inappropriate field type
414	Layout cannot display the result
415	One or more required related records are not available
416	Primary key required from data source table

417	Database is not supported for ODBC operations
500	Date value does not meet validation entry options
501	Time value does not meet validation entry options
502	Number value does not meet validation entry options
503	Value in field is not within the range specified in validation entry options
504	Value in field is not unique as required in validation entry options
505	Value in field is not an existing value in the database file as required in validation entry options
506	Value in field is not listed on the value list specified in validation entry option
507	Value in field failed calculation test of validation entry option
508	Invalid value entered in Find mode
509	Field requires a valid value
510	Related value is empty or unavailable
511	Value in field exceeds maximum number of allowed characters
512	Record was already modified by another user
513	Record must have a value in some field to be created
600	Print error has occurred
601	Combined header and footer exceed one page
602	Body doesn't fit on a page for current column setup
603	Print connection lost
700	File is of the wrong file type for import
706	EPSF file has no preview image
707	Graphic translator cannot be found
708	Can't import the file or need color monitor support to import file
709	QuickTime movie import failed
710	Unable to update QuickTime reference because the database file is read-only
711	Import translator cannot be found
714	Password privileges do not allow the operation
715	Specified Excel worksheet or named range is missing
716	A SQL query using DELETE, INSERT, or UPDATE is not allowed for ODBC import
717	There is not enough XML/XSL information to proceed with the import or export
718	Error in parsing XML file (from Xerces)
719	Error in transforming XML using XSL (from Xalan)
720	Error when exporting; intended format does not support repeating fields
721	Unknown error occurred in the parser or the transformer
722	Cannot import data into a file that has no fields
723	You do not have permission to add records to or modify records in the target table

724	You do not have permission to add records to the target table
725	You do not have permission to modify records in the target table
726	There are more records in the import file than in the target table; not all records were imported
727	There are more records in the target table than in the import file; not all records were updated
729	Errors occurred during import; records could not be imported
730	Unsupported Excel version (convert file to Excel 7.0 [Excel 95], 97, 2000, XP, or 2007 format and try again)
731	The file you are importing from contains no data
732	This file cannot be inserted because it contains other files
733	A table cannot be imported into itself
734	This file type cannot be displayed as a picture
735	This file type cannot be displayed as a picture; it will be inserted and displayed as a file
736	Too much data to export to this format; it will be truncated
737	Bento collection or library is missing; data cannot be imported
800	Unable to create file on disk
801	Unable to create temporary file on System disk
802	Unable to open file
803	File is single user or host cannot be found
804	File cannot be opened as read-only in its current state
805	File is damaged; use Recover command
806	File cannot be opened with this version of FileMaker Pro
807	File is not a FileMaker Pro file or is severely damaged
808	Cannot open file because access privileges are damaged
809	Disk/volume is full
810	Disk/volume is locked
811	Temporary file cannot be opened as FileMaker Pro file
813	Record Synchronization error on network
814	File(s) cannot be opened because maximum number is open
815	Couldn't open lookup file
816	Unable to convert file
817	Unable to open file because it does not belong to this solution
819	Cannot save a local copy of a remote file
820	File is in the process of being closed
821	Host forced a disconnect
822	FMI files not found; reinstall missing files

823	Cannot set file to single-user, guests are connected
824	File is damaged or not a FileMaker file
900	General spelling engine error
901	Main spelling dictionary not installed
902	Could not launch the Help system
903	Command cannot be used in a shared file
905	No active field selected; command can only be used if there is an active field
906	Current file must be shared in order to use this command
920	Can't initialize the spelling engine
921	User dictionary cannot be loaded for editing
922	User dictionary cannot be found
923	User dictionary is read-only
951	An unexpected error occurred (*)
954	Unsupported XML grammar (*)
955	No database name (*)
956	Maximum number of database sessions exceeded (*)
957	Conflicting commands (*)
958	Parameter missing (*)
1200	Generic calculation error
1201	Too few parameters in the function
1202	Too many parameters in the function
1203	Unexpected end of calculation
1204	Number, text constant, field name or "(" expected
1205	Comment is not terminated with "*/"
1206	Text constant must end with a quotation mark
1207	Unbalanced parenthesis
1208	Operator missing, function not found or "(" not expected
1209	Name (such as field name or layout name) is missing
1210	Plug-in function has already been registered
1211	List usage is not allowed in this function
1212	An operator (for example, +, –, *) is expected here
1213	This variable has already been defined in the Let function
1214	AVERAGE, COUNT, EXTEND, GETREPETITION, MAX, MIN, NPV, STDEV, SUM and GETSUMMARY: expression found where a field alone is needed
1215	This parameter is an invalid Get function parameter
1216	Only Summary fields allowed as first argument in GETSUMMARY
1217	Break field is invalid

1218	Cannot evaluate the number
1219	A field cannot be used in its own formula
1220	Field type must be normal or calculated
1221	Data type must be number, date, time, or timestamp
1222	Calculation cannot be stored
1223	The function is not implemented
1224	The function is not defined
1225	The function is not supported in this context
1300	The specified name can't be used
1400	ODBC driver initialization failed; make sure the ODBC drivers are properly installed
1401	Failed to allocate environment (ODBC)
1402	Failed to free environment (ODBC)
1403	Failed to disconnect (ODBC)
1404	Failed to allocate connection (ODBC)
1405	Failed to free connection (ODBC)
1406	Failed check for SQL API (ODBC)
1407	Failed to allocate statement (ODBC)
1408	Extended error (ODBC)
1409	Error (ODBC)
1413	Failed communication link (ODBC)
1450	Action requires PHP privilege extension (*)
1451	Action requires that current file be remote
1501	SMTP authentication failed
1502	Connection refused by SMTP server
1503	Error with SSL
1504	SMTP server requires the connection to be encrypted
1505	Specified authentication is not supported by SMTP server
1506	Email(s) could not be sent successfully
1507	Unable to log in to the SMTP server

Index

THE MISSING MANUALS
The books that should have been in the box

Answers found here!

Most how-to books bury the good stuff beneath bad writing, lame jokes, and fuzzy explanations. Not the Missing Manuals. Written in a unique, witty style that helps you learn quickly, our books help you get things done. Whether you're looking for guidance on software, gadgets, or how to live a healthy life, you'll find the answers in a Missing Manual.

Personal Investing: The Missing Manual
By Bonnie Biafore, Amy E. Buttell & Carol Fabbri
ISBN 9781449381783
$21.99 US, 27.99 CAN

Access 2010:
The Missing Manual
By Matthew MacDonald
ISBN 9781449382377
$39.99 US, 49.99 CAN

QuickBooks 2010:
The Missing Manual
By Bonnie Biafore
ISBN 9780596804022
$29.99 US, 37.99 CAN

Excel 2010:
The Missing Manual
By Matthew MacDonald
ISBN 9781449382353
$ 39.99 US, 49.99 CAN

Your Money:
The Missing Manual
By J. D. Roth
ISBN 9780596809409
$21.99 US, 27.99 CAN

Look for these and other Missing Manuals at your favorite bookstore or online.

www.missingmanuals.com

©2010 O'Reilly Media, Inc. O'Reilly logo is a registered trademark of O'Reilly Media, Inc.
All other trademarks are the property of their respective owners.

Get even more for your money.

Join the O'Reilly Community, and register the O'Reilly books you own.It's free, and you'll get:

- 40% upgrade offer on O'Reilly books
- Membership discounts on books and events
- Free lifetime updates to electronic formats of books
- Multiple ebook formats, DRM FREE
- Participation in the O'Reilly community
- Newsletters
- Account management
- 100% Satisfaction Guarantee

Signing up is easy:

1. **Go to: oreilly.com/go/register**
2. **Create an O'Reilly login.**
3. **Provide your address.**
4. **Register your books.**

Note: English-language books only

To order books online:

oreilly.com/order_new

For questions about products or an order:

orders@oreilly.com

To sign up to get topic-specific email announcements and/or news about upcoming books, conferences, special offers, and new technologies:

elists@oreilly.com

For technical questions about book content:

booktech@oreilly.com

To submit new book proposals to our editors:

proposals@oreilly.com

Many O'Reilly books are available in PDF and several ebook formats. For more information:

oreilly.com/ebooks

O'REILLY®

Spreading the knowledge of innovators   www.oreilly.com

©2009 O'Reilly Media, Inc. O'Reilly logo is a registered trademark of O'Reilly Media, Inc.

Buy this book and get access to the online edition for 45 days—for free!

FileMaker Pro 11: The Missing Manual

By Susan Prosser & Stuart Gripman
May 2010, $39.99
ISBN 9781449382599

With Safari Books Online, you can:

Access the contents of thousands of technology and business books

- Quickly search over 7000 books and certification guides
- Download whole books or chapters in PDF format, at no extra cost, to print or read on the go
- Copy and paste code
- Save up to 35% on O'Reilly print books
- **New!** Access mobile-friendly books directly from cell phones and mobile devices

Stay up-to-date on emerging topics before the books are published

- Get on-demand access to evolving manuscripts.
- Interact directly with authors of upcoming books

Explore thousands of hours of video on technology and design topics

- Learn from expert video tutorials
- Watch and replay recorded conference sessions

To try out Safari and the online edition of this book FREE for 45 days,
go to **www.oreilly.com/go/safarienabled** and enter the coupon code OZCIPXA.
To see the complete Safari Library, visit safari.oreilly.com.

Spreading the knowledge of innovators

safari.oreilly.com

©2009 O'Reilly Media, Inc. O'Reilly logo is a registered trademark of O'Reilly Media, Inc.